Further praise for *Go Down Together*

'A real strength of this book is that you get a strong sense of the historical landscape against which their story took place – a historical moment that enabled both their criminal career to proceed in the way it did and their myth to grow' Book of the Week, *Daily Mail*

'Jeff Guinn's terrific biography of Depression-era gangsters Clyde Barrow and Bonnie Parker couldn't be more timely . . . This is the clearest view yet of a pair of mythologised hoodlums whose career illuminates the short, brutal period that marked the last days of the Wild West' *Time Out*

'This is a gripping account of the grim lives of Bonnie and Clyde, and the spell they cast over Depression America' *Sunday Times*

'An exhaustively researched, crisply written biography of one of the most notorious criminal duos in U.S. history' *Bloomberg.com*

'A book pulsing with a narrative rhythm that has all the shock and excitement of a tommy gun's rat-a-tat-tat' *Barnes & Noble Review*

Jeff Guinn

GO DOWN TOGETHER

The True, Untold Story of BONNIE and CLYDE

POCKET BOOKS

LONDON • SYDNEY • NEW YORK • TORONTO

First published in Great Britain in 2009 by Simon & Schuster UK Ltd
This edition first published by Pocket Books, 2010
An imprint of Simon & Schuster UK Ltd
A CBS COMPANY

3 5 7 9 10 8 6 4 2

Simon & Schuster UK Ltd
1st Floor
222 Gray's Inn Road
London
WC1X 8HB

www.simonandschuster.co.uk

Simon & Schuster Australia
Sydney

A CIP catalogue copy for this book
is available from the British Library.

ISBN: 978-1-47113-402-9

Designed by C. Linda Dingler
Printed and bound by CPI Group (UK) Ltd, Croydon, CR0 4YY

In memory of Max Lale,
an historian who inspired me,
and in honor of Cissy Stewart Lale,
a mentor and friend who still does.

Contents

GO DOWN TOGETHER

Prologue

If it had been raining twenty miles west of Dallas on April 1, 1934, H. D. Murphy probably wouldn't have become the most famous dead motorcycle cop in America. Officers of the Texas Highway Patrol usually didn't take their two-wheelers out in inclement weather. But on this sunny Easter Sunday Murphy and two partners, Polk Ivy and E. B. Wheeler, were on holiday duty, cruising on their motorcycles along two-lane Texas Highway 114 near the town of Grapevine. It was considered onerous to be working on Easter, but not particularly hazardous. On a day like this the trio might nab a few speeders, or perhaps help motorists stranded by car trouble. It was the twenty-four-year-old Murphy's first day on motorcycle patrol. He was tagging along with veteran officers Ivy and Wheeler. Ivy rode a few yards ahead of the other two.

Up to the moment he was gunned down, this was a particularly good time in H. D. Murphy's young life. In twelve days he was to marry Marie Tullis, his twenty-year-old girlfriend. They'd just found an inexpensive furnished apartment to rent. Until the nuptials, Murphy was living at the YMCA. Marie had purchased her wedding gown. In spite of the current terrible times—Americans were still reeling through the Great Depression—Murphy seemed destined for a happy life. He had a secure job with a steady income and a loving fiancée who was about to become his wife. For most twenty-four-year-old men in 1934 America, that was as good as it got.

At about 3:30 in the afternoon, Murphy and Wheeler were still lagging behind Ivy when Wheeler spied a flashy black Ford V-8 with yellow wire rim wheels parked off Highway 114 on a narrow side road. The car could have been there because it had broken down, in which case whoever was in it might need assistance. Wheeler gestured for Murphy to follow him as he turned off to make a routine check. Polk Ivy, apparently oblivious, kept riding ahead. Wheeler and Murphy clearly didn't expect trouble. They both had shotguns, but neither pulled his weapon from the harnesses by the seats of their motorcycles. Murphy's shotgun wasn't even loaded. He had the shells in his pocket. The patrolmen rolled up to the Ford; two men in nice suits stood beside the car, and there was a woman sitting inside it. Wheeler and Murphy had no idea they were in the presence of the country's most notorious criminals.

Twenty-four-year-old Clyde Barrow and twenty-three-year-old Bonnie Parker had come to the area for a holiday get-together with their families, who lived in the slum known as West Dallas. Clyde and Bonnie realized the local police would be on the lookout for them—it was well known that they frequently ran the risk of visiting loved ones on special occasions—so they had decided to meet the other Barrows and Parkers out in the isolated countryside. Earlier in the day, Clyde had dispatched henchman Joe Palmer to hitchhike into West Dallas and tell the families to rendezvous off Highway 114 outside Grapevine as soon as possible. Meanwhile, he and Bonnie took long naps in their parked car and enjoyed a pleasant break from their normally frantic lives on the run. Bonnie also spent some time sitting on the grass and playing with the Easter gift she intended to give her mother that day—a live white rabbit that Bonnie had named Sonny Boy.

Thanks to newsreels at movie theaters and photos transmitted to newspapers through the recent magic of wire services, most Americans believed they knew exactly what Clyde Barrow and Bonnie Parker looked like. The young couple loved to strike dramatic poses for the cameras that they carried along with their guns, and some of these pictures had fallen into the hands of lawmen who made them available to the media. So the nation became familiar with nattily dressed Clyde brandishing a menacing Browning Automatic Rifle, and with Bonnie assuming unladylike postures on the bumpers of stolen cars. The most famous photo showed Bonnie with a cigar dangling from the corner of her mouth, a particularly eye-catching image in a time when most respectable women would discreetly puff cigarettes in private. Thanks to the media, Clyde and Bonnie had quickly come to be considered the epitome of scandalous glamour. But in person Clyde was short and scrawny, and Bonnie's looks were ordinary. They were both crippled, Clyde from cutting off two of his own toes in prison and Bonnie as the result of a car wreck nine months earlier in which her right leg was burned so badly that bone was visible in several places. She hopped now rather than walked. Clyde often had to carry her. They had little in common with the glittering images of themselves that mesmerized the public. So as the two patrolmen approached the Ford, Wheeler and Murphy were relaxed rather than on guard. There seemed to be nothing threatening about these two strangers or the stocky young fellow who was with them.

But people had a way of dying around the Barrow Gang, and that Easter Sunday proved to be no exception. Clyde Barrow had never intended to kill so many people. Of the seven men who'd died directly by his hand to date—he'd been erroneously blamed for two other murders—only two killings had been premeditated. The first was in 1931, when Clyde used a lead pipe to crush the skull of a fellow inmate who'd repeatedly raped him on a Texas prison farm. The second came six weeks before H. D. Murphy died outside Grapevine, when Clyde helped Joe Palmer murder a guard who'd abused Palmer in prison. Otherwise Clyde always preferred to run rather than fight. Previously he'd even taken lawmen as temporary hostages rather than engaging in unnecessary shootouts, and he always released them unharmed. That was his intention when Wheeler and Murphy rode up. While Bonnie remained in the Ford with Sonny Boy, Clyde turned to twenty-two-year-old Henry Methvin, the third Barrow Gang member present, and muttered, "Let's take them."

But Henry, an escaped con who'd joined the gang ten weeks earlier, misinterpreted his boss's instructions. Henry was always prone to violence, all the more so when he had been drinking. On this Easter afternoon he and Bonnie, a borderline alcoholic, had indulged themselves with whiskey. As usual when he was out in public, Clyde had abstained. Tipsy and mean to begin with, Henry leveled a rifle he'd been concealing behind his back and shot E. B. Wheeler at point-blank range. The veteran patrolman died instantly. Murphy fumbled for his shotgun and the shells in his pocket. Clyde, furious with Henry but resigned to finishing what his partner had foolishly started, shot Murphy.

The rookie fell to the ground, badly wounded but not dead. Once again, Henry Methvin overreacted. He stood over the fallen Murphy and fired several more shots into his body. Then he jumped into the Ford with Clyde and Bonnie, and the trio fled. Clyde, at the wheel as usual, cursed Henry while he drove away at breakneck speed, heading northeast toward the Oklahoma state line. This was one of Clyde's regular tricks—lawmen from one state in pursuit of criminals had no jurisdiction in any other.

Back outside Grapevine, officers gathered at the site of the shooting. Wheeler was dead on the scene, and Murphy died soon afterward. One particularly gregarious witness, who claimed to have watched the whole thing from his farmhouse porch several hundred yards away, swore that two men shot down the patrolmen, and then the woman with them fired more shots into the fallen Murphy while her victim's head bounced off the ground like a rubber ball. His false statement, combined with less colorful testimony from a couple who'd been driving by on the highway and several other bits of evidence, convinced the authorities that Wheeler and Murphy had become the Barrow Gang's latest victims. They said as much to the reporters who swarmed to the scene, and these journalists gladly printed every shocking allegation.

Depression-era readers were desperate for entertainment, and stories about the Barrow Gang invariably boosted newspaper and magazine circulation. Many Americans considered cops and bankers to be their enemies. Although Clyde and Bonnie were never criminal masterminds or even particularly competent crooks—their two-year crime spree was as much a reign of error as terror—the media made them seem like they were, and that was enough to turn them into icons. Celebrities reflect their times and cultures: from the spring of 1932, when the newly formed Barrow Gang pulled its first holdups, through May 23, 1934, when a posse led by the only lawman in America who was as famous as they were led the ambush that killed them, Clyde and Bonnie came to epitomize the edgy daydreams of the economically and socially downtrodden. Resentful of their own powerlessness and poverty, Barrow Gang fans liked the idea of colorful young rebels sticking it to bankers and cops. Clyde and Bonnie were even better than actors like Jimmy Cagney who committed crimes onscreen, because they were doing it for real.

But as historian Iris Chang noted in an interview a generation later, "Celebrities are really distractions for the general public, first created, then most often destroyed, consumed, for our amusement." Up to April 1, 1934, Clyde Barrow and Bonnie Parker provided distraction for most Americans. Their victims in robberies and shootouts were generally perceived as part of a faceless Them who in some sense deserved what they got. But the stories following the shootings in Grapevine emphasized the death of H. D. Murphy—his partner E. B. Wheeler got at most fleeting mention. There were articles about brokenhearted Marie Tullis, who wore her wedding gown to her fiancé's funeral, and descriptions of the apartment she and Murphy had been about to share. Bonnie Parker had been regarded as the sexy companion of a criminal kingpin. Overnight, she was newly perceived as a kill-crazy floozy who laughed as she finished off an innocent rookie patrolman and simultaneously ruined the life of the sweet young girl who'd been about to marry him. The vicarious love affair between Americans and the Barrow Gang was over. Having been entertained by Clyde and Bonnie for many months, the public now turned on them. It was time for the couple to get its comeuppance. Clyde Barrow and Bonnie Parker still had seven weeks to live, but during those weeks they would be more reviled than celebrated. Their destruction, their consuming, had begun.

BEFORE

"Americans have fought one war to win their independence and another to preserve the Union. Now they face a new war, between the men who possess more than they have earned and the men who have earned more than they possess."

—Former president Theodore Roosevelt in 1910, the year of Clyde Barrow's birth

CHAPTER 1

Henry and Cumie

Clyde Barrow's father, Henry, never had much luck in life, and the hard times started for him right out of the womb. There is some question about his birthplace and date—it seems most likely he was born to shoemaker Jim Barrow and his wife, Marie, in Pensacola, Florida, on January 10, 1873—but there is no doubt Henry was sickly from birth. The chills and fever he suffered regularly as an infant continued to plague him as an adult. No record exists of a doctor diagnosing the illness—which might have been recurrent malaria—and prescribing treatment. Sick babies lived or died in those days and Henry lived, barely. A tall, skinny boy, he staggered through early childhood. The first day Henry attended school he collapsed before noon, was taken home in a buggy, and never went back again. Throughout his life, he was completely illiterate.

Henry's mother apparently died in 1884. Afterward, Jim Barrow decided to make a fresh start in a new location with an equally new vocation. With sons Henry and Frank in tow, he moved from Pensacola to Grimes County in East Texas, where he set himself up as a farmer by renting a small plot of land and cultivating cotton. Tenant farming, in those years, had several attractions. Crop prices were decent, and landowners with extensive acreage were usually glad to have some of it tilled by renters who would pay a portion of their annual harvest or profits in return for a place for their families to work and live. The most fortunate tenant farmers would string together several good years and eventually save sufficient money to buy land of their own. And as long as weather and economic conditions were favorable, the renters had the satisfaction of being their own bosses, beholden to no one but themselves, their independence baptized with their own sweat.

Jim apparently remarried in Texas—Henry would eventually claim two half-brothers, Ed and Jim, as well as Frank—and expected, as farming fathers did in that age, that his children would pitch in as unpaid laborers. Henry did, though his continuing health problems made him a sporadic contributor. East Texas was less swampy than the Florida Panhandle, so the episodes of illness weren't as frequent. He found he liked farming just fine, but there was something else he soon came to love better.

Horse racing was a popular recreation in the East Texas backwoods. A man with a fast horse and a willingness to wager could make tidy sums. Henry had the willingness but not the fast horse, and as the son of a tenant farmer it wasn't likely he would ever have one. The only horses on Jim Barrow's place were bred to pull a plow. Henry still dreamed of someday owning his own racehorse rather than placing wagers on someone else's. He spent his limited leisure time at the races, watching and dreaming, and making small bets the few times he had any money. He was pulled in once by the local law on some unspecified racing-related charge. Nothing came of it—Henry was never convicted of anything in his life—but the brief brush with alleged crime alarmed devout Baptist Jim Barrow enough that he decided it was time to take his teenaged boy in hand.

Jim, by the standards of the day, would never have been considered a particularly strict parent. All country children expected to receive occasional whippings, usually some stinging lashes on the calves or hands or rear with thin switches cut and trimmed specifically for that purpose. Corporal punishment was as much a part of a farm childhood as chores. Henry would say later that his father "seldom if ever" whipped him, and even in this moment when Jim felt Henry was teetering on the abyss of unredeemable sin he still talked to his son rather than hit him. From that moment on, Jim decreed, Henry would attend church and Sunday School regularly, so that he would be constantly reminded of the difference between right and wrong. Gambling or anything else to do with horse racing was the first major step toward total dereliction. Henry, a dutiful son, did as he was told. He stopped going to the races and started going to church.

Soon afterward, Henry followed his father's example in another way. Denied his goal of owning a fast horse, Henry now set his sights on at least owning his own land. Starting from scratch, he couldn't afford the tools necessary for tenant farming, so when Henry was about sixteen he moved to nearby Nacogdoches and took a job in a sawmill to earn enough money for a grubstake. He didn't intend to spend the rest of his days turning out lumber and obeying somebody else's orders about what work to do and when to do it. The sawmill was just a jumping-off point.

Nacogdoches wasn't a particularly big town, and sometime in late 1890 Henry made the acquaintance there of teenager Cumie Walker. Like Henry, Cumie was the child of a farming father, and the two also shared similar beliefs in the value of hard, honest work. But in almost every other way, they were different.

Cumie had lived in Nacogdoches all her life, and was part of a family that adhered to the most conservative of Christian faiths. A tiny girl just under five feet tall, she was a churchgoing Baptist of the "hard shell" variety, raised in the belief that she needed to be good because that was what Jesus expected, and reminded of it by her parents, W. W. and Mahaly Walker, with frequent beatings for the slightest transgression. When she met Henry, she had just endured what she later recalled as "one of the worst whippings I ever got" for some perceived misstep with a previous beau. Cumie was not allowed to apply the profane face paint known as "make-up," which was just starting to sneak its Satan-inspired way into the Texas countryside. She was so swayed by her parents' lectures on the subject that, for the rest of her life, Cumie assumed that any woman using cosmetics was at least someone of low morals and most likely a prostitute.

Rigorous discipline didn't mean Cumie's childhood was unhappy. She loved animals, cats especially, and had many pets. Though some conservative Christian homes banned all but religious music, secular tunes were allowed in Cumie's. She had a knack for playing instruments, and was especially talented on the Jew's harp. And, very much unlike Henry, she went to school regularly.

On December 5, 1891, Henry and Cumie were married in her parents' house. The bride was sixteen, ten months younger than her new husband. Cumie immediately embraced Henry's dream of owning his own farm. It was a fine Christian ambition, one she could understand and wholeheartedly support. Newlywed Henry quit his job at the sawmill and rented a few acres near town. It was risky. The sawmill paid regular wages, and people always needed lumber. But there was no reason for Henry to doubt he could someday evolve from tenant to landowner. Many young men shared similar ambitions. Forty percent of all Americans lived on farms. Of the 4.6 million farms operating in 1891, more than one-fourth were at least partially worked by tenants. In Texas, it was closer to one-third. During good years, even a smallish tenant farm of five or six acres could produce three thousand pounds, or about five bales, of cotton, enough after sale to pay the landlord, provide at least a subsistence living for the tenant's family, and, perhaps, leave a few dollars over for savings. The work was arduous, but Henry was mostly past his bouts with illness. Cumie recalled in her unpublished memoir that the first half-decade of her marriage was "bright and rosey then, for we were young and saw things with the eyes of youth. . . . But we soon awoke to a realization that life was indeed earnest."

The fortunes of Nacogdoches farmers fluctuated more than Henry and Cumie liked. It was a given that farm couples produced children as well as crops, since every offspring who survived infancy, as all Henry and Cumie's babies did, eventually meant an additional pair of hands in the field. But the arrivals of son Elvin in 1894 and daughter Artie in 1899 initially added just two more mouths to feed, and their parents decided a move to Milam County, also in East Texas, might provide better opportunity. They did not consider giving up farming.

The Barrows rented another small acreage in Jones Prairie, where they continued to grow cotton and produce babies. A second son, Ivan, was born in 1903, and another daughter, Nell, came in 1905. Later there would be considerable dispute over whether Ivan's year of birth was 1903 or 1905; in the terrible times to come, Cumie sometimes mixed up the dates and order of her children's births. But she entered 1903 as Ivan's birth year in her family Bible, Cumie's most sacred possession. She would never have recorded inaccurate information there.

Milam County didn't prove any more profitable for Henry than Nacogdoches. Cumie would recall "it got pretty rough." When Henry's few acres couldn't financially support the family, they all—mother and older children as well as father—had to begin "hiring out" to help pick the cotton on other farmers' property. It now seemed obvious that Henry Barrow was never going to be in a position to buy a farm of his own, but still he wouldn't give up the dream.

Once again, Henry packed his family and few possessions into his wagon and moved on, this time a little to the north near the tiny hamlet of Telico in Ellis County, Texas. The familiar pattern immediately began to repeat itself: Henry struggled to break even, and more babies came. The first was Clyde in 1910, and his date of birth, like Ivan's, was destined to be incorrectly reported. Cumie, in the subsequent time of confusion, told some authorities that her third son was born in 1909, but she entered the date as March 24, 1910, in the family Bible, which would seem more authoritative. Farm women like Cumie usually gave birth in their shacks, often with the help of local midwives (Clyde's was Annie Curtis of Telico), and public birth records were kept haphazardly. None for Clyde Chestnut Barrow apparently exist. L.C. (the initials were his full name) came in 1913, then Marie in 1918, and the family was complete with seven children.

All four Barrow sons were addressed in the family by nicknames rather than their given ones. Elvin became "Jack." No one seems to recall why. Ivan was nicknamed "Buck" by an aunt. Clyde was "Bud" because he was such buddies with his little brother, and L.C. was "Flop" thanks to an unfortunate pair of ears. Jack was serious and industrious like his father, Buck and Bud were high-spirited, and Flop was a good-natured tagalong.

Looking back on life in Telico, Nell Barrow later said, "I suppose we weren't a very happy family." Being happy took energy her parents didn't have. Henry came home to their three-room shack every day from his rented fields feeling exhausted. Cumie spent some of each day out working with him while the older children minded the younger ones. Then she had to come in, fix dinner, haul water, wash clothes, nurse anyone who was sick, and do whatever else needed to be done. Clothing and food were equally hard to come by. Running water and electricity were unimaginable for most rich rural Texans, let alone any poor ones. After dark, children sleeping on pallets took up much of the floor. A few family photographs were taken at the Telico farm, no one knows by whom. Certainly the Barrows didn't have the money to hire a photographer to come out to their rented property. The original prints and negatives have long since disappeared—sold to or stolen by collectors—but L.C.'s stepson Buddy still has a few grainy copies. In them, Cumie Barrow's mouth is striking. Her lips are pursed in a thin, pinched line. Families of the time liked to pose formally, but there is not even the slightest hint of warmth or contentment in Cumie's face, and the expressions of her husband and children are equally joyless. "We had no time, then, for day dreaming," Cumie would write. "Life was very much of a struggle."

Cumie divided that struggle into two parts: for earthly survival, and for heavenly glory. None of her children demonstrated interest in emulating their father as farmers. Accordingly, they, unlike him, needed educations. Although they had to go to country school "by the littles," attending in between working their own family harvests and hiring out as field workers to other, more well-to-do neighbors, Cumie saw to it that they were in class whenever possible. She tolerated no debate, telling them, "If you don't go to school, you'll grow up to be idiots."

Even more important to Cumie than her children's ongoing education was the state of their faith. Jesus constantly watched and judged all; life on earth was an eyeblink of eternity, and Cumie wanted her offspring weighing that into every decision they made. The Jesus worshipped by Cumie Barrow and her fellow backcountry fundamentalists saved through fear rather than forgiveness. You did what the Bible said because Jesus would send your soul straight to hell if you didn't. At home, the Barrow children were reminded of this daily. It would have also been pointed out to them in church as well as by their mother that, in fact, their poverty was a plus in their relationship with Christ. The Bible was replete with reminders that Jesus loved poor people a lot more than he did rich ones. Wearing patched clothes and sometimes not having enough to eat were, in effect, evidence of personal godliness. The implication was obvious, if not declared outright: poor people were good, rich people were bad.

The Bible as well as her own experience guided Cumie's approach to discipline. She did not want to spoil her children, so she never spared the rod. The legs of all seven kids were constant targets. Youngest child Marie would later recall how her mother made them "dance." Cumie never doubted her stern methods. She was hitting those kids to save them.

Cumie was the Barrow parent who did the hitting, not Henry. He was a typical man of his time and background. The father's job was to provide for his family, and Henry took this seriously. It was the mother's responsibility to discipline the children. Taciturn to the point of muteness, Henry would mutter, "Cumie, make that child mind," and expect it to be done.

It speaks well of Cumie that none of the Barrow children grew up hating or even resenting their grimly determined mother. All seven had close relationships with her throughout their lives. She loved them, and in spite of her sternness and whippings, they realized it. Whatever problems any of the Barrows ever had with the outside world, within their family they were devoted to each other.

Most of the Barrow kids didn't give Cumie cause for concern. They were fairly typical East Texas country youngsters who did their chores, played when they had time, loved going to the picture show as a special treat—the theater in Telico was a three-mile walk from the family farm, but they happily made the six-mile round-trip—and went to church and school as mandated by their mother. Their worst offenses were simple ones, like smoking primitive cigarettes packed with grapevine. But then Buck and Bud began straying from the straight and narrow, and Cumie's preaching and whipping didn't seem to help.

Buck started out attending school, and he did well when he was there. But he loved the outdoors better and aggravated his mother by frequently playing hooky. Buck quit school for good after the third grade, and was almost as illiterate as his father. For a while, Cumie still had hopes for him because he kept attending church, but even there he eventually defied her.

It wasn't that Buck was in any way mean-spirited. He'd always been as happy-go-lucky as his family's hardscrabble lifestyle allowed. When, as a little boy, he had no toy horses to play with, he pretended to be a horse himself. Hunting and fishing, critical to keeping food on the Barrow table, were pastimes Buck considered fun rather than a chore. He had a quick temper, but would cool down just as fast. And though he flouted Cumie's edicts about school and church, he never was insolent. Instead, he was just—*Buck*.

But as a teenager, Buck began getting involved in cockfighting. Much as his father had once yearned for a horse so he could compete rather than bet, Buck wanted his own pugnacious rooster, and it was easier for a country kid to acquire one of those than a racehorse. Cumie noted in her memoir that Buck "had some game roosters that he got hold of." It wouldn't be the last time Cumie chose not to know what one of her sons had really been up to. Nell Barrow was more specific: her brother, she said, wasn't above "lifting" a bird. And Buck developed a personal philosophy, one he shared with his younger siblings. "A good run," he would lecture them, "is better than a poor stand."

There appeared to be little chance of reforming Buck, but Bud was seven years younger. He didn't like school any more than Buck did, but he stuck with it, and to Cumie's pleasure he very much enjoyed attending church. Later, at age fourteen, Bud would even be "saved" and baptized at the Eureka Baptist Church, a necessary step in the life of any fundamentalist believer who hoped to gain a place in heaven. It involved admitting before the congregation that he was a helpless sinner who wanted to accept Jesus and His teachings into his own life, for fear of being damned for eternity. Cumie didn't doubt Bud meant it.

But there were still those bothersome traits, like hero-worshipping Buck and bossing even his older sister Nell around. When she and Bud and Flop played, Bud had to be the one in charge, saying who would pretend to be who, and no backtalk. He had a forceful enough personality to make them go along with it. And the roles Bud inevitably chose for himself were outlaws. He was Jesse James or Billy the Kid. Nell and Flop were variously members of his gang, outfoxed lawmen, or victims. Sometimes Bud had a toy gun; usually, just pointed sticks. All the kids around Telico played games mimicking frontier violence, at least in part because that was a regular theme of the picture shows there. Flashy, gun-wielding William S. Hart was Bud's favorite actor, and Jesse and Billy had been poor people's folk heroes for years, defiant rebels who stood up to for themselves and died doing it, each betrayed by someone he trusted but never wavering in his disdain for powerful oppressors.

Bud liked and was handy with real guns, too. Every country family had a rifle or two, which were necessary for hunting and also for doing away with farm animals too sick or decrepit to be of further use. Cumie recalled that Bud "could shoot good," adding the caveat that "he hardly ever carried a gun much." Bud liked handling the guns far more than he liked shooting animals. Unlike Buck, he hunted out of duty rather than for pleasure, and avoided it as much as possible. Target practice was more to his taste.

Bud's temper was different, too, from his older brother's. Bud remembered every slight, every insult. His anger would smolder long-term. Forgiveness was not part of his character.

Cumie fretted most about Bud's behavior in fights. All country boys had their share of scraps. Bud usually tried to avoid them, preferring to talk rather than punch his way out of disagreements. But when fighting was inevitable, when Bud believed he had no other option, then he completely lost control and exploded into violence. He'd use fists, sticks, rocks, or any other handy weapon, and never showed mercy to opponents. If Bud lost a fight, he brooded and waited for the opportunity to attack again.

Perhaps Bud's greatest pleasure was music. He took after his mother that way, and it was a special bond between them. (Cumie would later brag that "all during his life his mother seems to have been first in his thoughts.") There was a guitar in the Barrow shack, and Bud taught himself to play. Cumie's religious strictures were also flexible regarding dancing. Bud excelled at this among the Barrow kids, to the extent that his mother pronounced him "an extra good dancer." He had some thoughts of making music his livelihood. His first announced professional ambition was "to be in some kind of band with other boys."

Bud spent part of each year living with his uncle. Frank Barrow had set himself up farming in Corsicana, Texas, about twenty-seven miles from Henry's place in Telico, and Nellie and Bud, and later Flop and Marie, would be sent there for weeks at a time. Frank was a little more successful than Henry, and it's probable the younger kids among the Ellis County Barrows were sent to him so they could still have something to eat when the cupboard was mostly bare in Telico. But the sojourns at Uncle Frank's weren't vacations. Visiting nieces and nephews were expected to go to school, and, outside the classroom, to pitch in and work just like at home, picking cotton or hoeing corn. Bud's cousins, Pete and Dood, enjoyed his company, but they did have one complaint. The guy never wanted to hunt. Instead, he wanted to play Billy the Kid or Jesse James.

So, despite his love of religion and music, Cumie continued to fret about Bud, and she agonized over Buck. In her later years, as with many parents who regret tragedy in their children's lives, Cumie decided she and Henry were at least partially to blame. "We have both learned since that each child born is a challenge, and a duty and responsibility we should all try to fully and squarely meet," Cumie reflected. "Perhaps had my husband [and I] understood that then and taken more time to really be with our children, played with them more and watched over their growing up as we should have, things might have been far different from what they were."

At least Buck and Bud were out in the country, where their potential for mischief was mostly confined to stealing roosters, cutting school, or pretending to be famous outlaws. There wasn't that much trouble available for them to get into, until a war's aftermath and the ambitions of their older siblings conspired to end their isolation from more substantial temptation.

When World War I ended on November 11, 1918, American farmers went down to defeat along with the Germans. The term "global economics" would have meant nothing to Henry and Cumie, but it was deadly to the tattered remnants of their dreams.

During the war, farm production in Europe came to a standstill. American grain and cotton were suddenly in worldwide demand. There wasn't enough to go around, and, because of scarcity, prices skyrocketed accordingly. From the halls of Congress in Washington, D.C., to the tenant farms of East Texas, no one apparently anticipated that the price boom would ever end. Cotton had been selling for about ten to twelve cents a pound in the years prior to the war, but just before Armistice Day it was forty cents, and rumored to soon be shooting up to fifty or even sixty. Between 1910 and 1918, the average value of Texas farms had doubled. Big landowners took out loans to acquire even more property and additional seed to plant on it. Banks were glad to cooperate. Tenants like Henry didn't have money to invest, but they did hope the effects of the boom would eventually trickle down to them. Instead, soon after hostilities ceased, European farmers once again had their own crops to sell, international supply was great enough to meet or even exceed overseas demand, and cotton prices in America plummeted to eight cents a pound. Wealthy U.S. landowners who'd borrowed to take advantage of the high prices were hard-pressed to meet their loan payments. They were no longer in position to extend credit to tenants who needed extra time to pay their rent. In East Texas, the price of cotton seed was more than what the resulting crop could be sold for after harvest. Devastated tenant farmers began giving up their land and moving their families to the cities, where there was the promise of jobs in factories. American industry, unlike agriculture, was still booming.

Henry wouldn't quit. He kept working the land and supplemented his evaporating income with a part-time job at a brickyard in Telico. This might have made the most marginal survival possible, but it caused another problem.

Although Henry had to be away from his fields when he was baking bricks in town, the Barrows' rented land still required just as much labor—constant planting and weeding and picking. Ideally, Cumie could have taken up the slack with the assistance of her entire brood, with the greatest responsibility falling on the oldest. But those children had already begun leaving the farm for the city.

These weren't unexpected desertions. Jack and Artie and Nell had seen the never-ending pressure and poverty their parents endured. For young people like them, farming now seemed like a near-suicidal choice. Cities promised a better living, and, better still with their bijous and nightclubs and shops and restaurants, *fun*, something that seemed permanently absent now from impoverished country life.

Jack left first, marrying a girl named Drusilla. They moved north to Dallas, where Jack set up a small mechanic's shop in the back of their house. He had a knack for repairing any kind of machinery or motor. All the Barrow boys did. Drusilla used another part of the house to operate a small beauty parlor. More and more lah-de-dah city women wanted stylish hairdos and manicured nails. Drusilla was smart enough to take advantage of that, and soon afterward Artie and Nell decided they would do the same. They moved to the city, too, and trained as beauticians. Nell settled in Dallas like Jack and found work in a hotel beauty shop. Artie lived in Dallas awhile—Nell would brag that her sister was Dallas's first woman barber—then moved north to the Texas town of Denison, where she married a newspaperman and opened her own beautician's shop. And when Jack got his mechanic's business going, Buck left home, too. He promised he would go to work for his brother and learn the trade. Cumie probably had her suspicions, but she couldn't stop him. It was arranged for Buck to temporarily move in with Cumie's sister, a widow named Belle, who had a place in Dallas. Beyond that, all his mother could do was pray.

She and Henry were left with rented acres that couldn't provide a living and three remaining children—Bud, Flop, and Marie—who still had to be fed and clothed. It may have seemed things couldn't get worse, but another unpleasant surprise followed. In 1920, just as cotton prices fell to their lowest, some Ellis County farmers discovered boll weevils devastating their already nearly unsellable crops. There were also reports of cotton root rot, a soil-generated disease.

Henry and Cumie Barrow were not quitters. In three decades of marriage they'd labored hard and honestly, doing their best to live as good Christians and never expecting or asking for help from anyone but themselves. When things hadn't worked out in one place, they'd moved on to another. But the many years of honorable effort only emphasized one more reason why their farming dreams were about to end.

Cumie and Henry were in their forties. Four of their seven children had already left the farm for the city, and there was no reason to doubt the remaining three would go as soon as they were old enough. In their declining years, which usually came upon undernourished, overworked country folk sooner rather than later, Henry and Cumie would be physically unable to tend land all by themselves, even if through some miracle cotton prices shot up again and the boll weevils took their devastating presence elsewhere. A means had to be found to support themselves in their old age, and it couldn't be discovered out in the country. It wasn't the fate Henry and Cumie had wanted, but they had no other options left. Just as they'd done several times before, they would load the wagon, hitch up the old white horse, and move along. This time, though, they'd go to the city, where a hardworking man like Henry had a better chance, maybe his only remaining chance, to provide for his family. Their goal now was survival. They had to last long enough in the city for Henry to get himself started in some small business.

They weren't sure what kind of business that might be, but there was never any doubt which city they'd go to. It wasn't far away, and Jack, Artie, Nell, and Buck were already there. In desperate times like these, the comfort of being near their children meant more to Henry and Cumie than ever. So in 1922 they took twelve-year-old Bud, nine-year-old Flop, and four-year-old Marie and moved thirty miles north to Dallas.

CHAPTER 2

The Devil's Back Porch

Dallas was a fine place to live in 1922, and not by accident. From its founding in 1841 on the east bank of the Trinity River, civic leaders planned for orderly, controlled growth. Each of its rivals for supremacy among major Texas cities—Houston with its haphazard sprawl, Austin with its rowdy state legislature and university, San Antonio with its messy cultural and architectural ties to Mexico—exhibited the flaws of spontaneity. There was nothing spontaneous about Dallas. Its economic heart was progressive industry, evolving from sawmills to cotton gins to manufacturing. Major rail lines intersected in Dallas, making it the state hub of travel and trade. Downtown Dallas had its first skyscraper in 1907, and was the home of one of the nation's twelve Federal Reserve Banks. Banking was Dallas's religion, and capitalism was its creed.

Problems were solved cooperatively by the wealthy leaders who knew best, always with a constant view to the future. A series of floods plagued the city, and in 1908 the Trinity swelled until five residents died, four thousand were left homeless, and property damage reached $2.5 million. Dallas businessmen banded together, raised money, and hired renowned St. Louis landscape architect George Kessler, who proposed grassy levees to divert the river and hold back floodwater, and bridges to safely and attractively link the city to the outside world. The levees and bridges were promptly built, and Kessler was summoned back a few years later to upgrade his original plan to include parks and playgrounds, and better, wider streets.

Dallas leaders' vision encompassed more than economic prosperity. They wanted a vibrant, sophisticated city as well as a rich one. Those with the price of admission could attend performances by the Dallas opera or symphony. A dozen different theaters presented the hit films of the day. On Dallas's south side, Fair Park spread over more than a hundred acres, with movie theaters, some of the first rental cars in the country available for pleasant drives along the park's shady lanes, and even a skating rink. Every fall, the State Fair of Texas took over the park and treated Dallas residents to carnival rides, livestock exhibits, and the latest entertainments. Buffalo Bill Cody and Annie Oakley performed there. Once on "Colored People's Day," Booker T. Washington took the stage and gave a rousing speech.

Dallas had immense pride in its plethora of downtown shops and hotels, in Southern Methodist University with its graceful campus, and, perhaps most of all, in the quality of people choosing to live within its carefully controlled boundaries. The goal of its leaders, many believed, was to build a city that rivaled San Francisco or even Athens or Paris as a cultural mecca. They did not want Dallas thought of as just another "Texas" town. It must reflect modern, forward-looking attitudes. Cowboy imagery in any form was anathema to them.

Population growth had, for decades, been much on the minds of Dallas power brokers. To remain a truly dynamic city, recognized as such across the nation, Dallas needed a constant influx of new residents—investors to keep its economy stimulated, taxpayers to fund its ongoing civic improvements, philanthropists to underwrite artistic endeavors, and affluent consumers to keep afloat the sort of high-end shops, nightclubs, and restaurants that Dallas wanted to boast. In 1905, businessmen formed the 150,000 Club, with the goal of doubling the city's population to that figure by 1910. They missed by about fifty thousand, and began incorporating a few of the more acceptable suburbs. The chamber of commerce stepped up its efforts to publicize Dallas's charms to the right sort of potential residents. One chamber publication claimed that the Dallas businessman "conducts his large enterprise in impressive, modern office buildings, goes home to his attractive residence, with a landscaped lawn that enhances the beauty of a wide, tree lined street; takes his exercise on the sweeping, sporty golf courses, the hard, smooth tennis courts, or the sandy beaches that his own public spirit has created; pays his homage to God and educates his children in magnificent churches and schools that are second to none in beauty and facilities."

And, gradually, it worked. By 1910 Dallas had doubled in area to about eighteen square miles. It built a magnificent zoo, downtown municipal buildings, new railroad terminals, and the Houston Street Viaduct, described as "the longest concrete bridge in the world." The city acquired expansive White Rock Lake Park, and the "sandy beaches" described in chamber of commerce puffery became reality. Dallas's population topped 150,000 in 1920, and kept climbing. There was opportunity for young arrivals like Jack, Artie, and Nell Barrow, whose skills in mechanics and hairdressing were needed. They were welcome in Dallas because they could, in their very minor, supporting-role ways, help move things forward by making life a little easier, a little more comfortable, for the people who really counted.

But Henry Barrow had no such potential. Arriving by archaic horse and wagon in 1922, broke and desperate with a wife and small children, illiterate and without any discernible skills that might contribute to the community, Henry was the sort of interloper Dallas leaders didn't want cluttering up the civic path to further progress. He and his farm-fleeing ilk were seen as comprising another flood spilling into town, this one consisting of destitute families rather than overspill from the Trinity River. But its effects, they feared, would be every bit as devastating.

It was understood that Dallas, like every major city, needed poorly educated laborers to work for low pay in menial jobs, from sweeping streets to working on the line in factories. But there were only so many of those jobs, and it was important that the less-desirables applying to fill them didn't too far exceed the number of low-end jobs available. Refugees of the East Texas farm crisis didn't care whether they were welcome or not. The slightest chance for employment in Dallas was better than the even more minuscule odds of survival back in the country. It took Dallas eighty years to reach its population goal of 150,000 in 1920. The next 100,000 arrived within five or six, and most of them weren't the kind of residents that Dallas wanted.

At first, civic leaders tried to stem the tide by indirect means. As early as July 1920, there were meetings about "stemming the tide of immigration from farm to city." It was suggested that tenant farmers be taught how to make their rented acres more productive, but that missed the point. The tenants couldn't sell the crops they were already raising. Forums were held to allow disgruntled farmers the opportunity of explaining what they would need to stay in the country and not invade Dallas. "Better crop prices" was something city leaders couldn't deliver. Then came meetings to identify empty buildings that could be used to provide temporary shelter to the unwelcome influx, but these raggedy bumpkins showed no intention of passing through and inflicting themselves on less elite communities. They wanted to stay in Dallas.

And there Dallas differed again from other Texas cities. Like all the rest—Houston, Austin, San Antonio, El Paso, Fort Worth just thirty-five miles to the west—Dallas was soon overrun. But unlike the others, Dallas did not gradually assimilate the newcomers. It had a special place for them instead.

The bridges and levees of Dallas had been built to protect and beautify the area east of the Trinity. The west side of the river, the floodplain there, was unincorporated semimarsh where impoverished newcomers could squat for as long as they liked, out of sight and mind of nice people. Two adjacent communities sprang up: Cement City, named for the plants whose manufacturing operations supplied jobs, albeit low-paying, backbreaking ones, along with pollution; and West Dallas, associated with no industry at all, an appalling collection of ramshackle shanties and tent camps set up along the west bank of the Trinity. Every city had its slums, but in all of Texas, West Dallas was recognized as the worst. Its fetid air and swarming bugs, open sewers and garbage-strewn blocks bisected by narrow dirt streets contributed to dozens of deaths annually from tuberculosis and pneumonia. Even a few drops of rain turned those dirt streets to mud: West Dallas was known as "The Bog" because it often was. In 1922, nobody knew exactly how many people were there, or cared, so long as they weren't across the river in Dallas ruining its carefully crafted image. In 1948, when a social service agency in the city finally got around to the first formal survey of West Dallas, its estimated population was 24,150.

Dallas had tough vagrancy laws in place to keep out the riffraff. Jack, Artie, and Nell had no extra room for their parents and three young children, let alone an old horse and older wagon. Henry and Cumie couldn't find a pleasant spot inside the city limits to set up camp without inviting arrest. So they went to West Dallas, and joined hundreds of other impoverished families in a campground a few dozen yards from the river and near the railroad tracks. It was the most primitive of places. There was one well, where everyone drew marginally potable water, and a few outhouses. Many families lived in tents. Henry and Cumie Barrow had no tent. They slept with the kids under their wagon, the horse tethered alongside them.

They were very hungry, with little money for food. When there was something to fix, Cumie cooked out in the open on an old-fashioned camp stove. The older children undoubtedly tried to help, but mostly the Barrows had to depend on the Salvation Army. Every day, its wagon would appear at the camp, and representatives would distribute sandwiches of "West Dallas Round Steak"—thin discs of bologna between slices of stale bread. Sometimes even bologna was scarce, and plain bread had to do. On holidays, children were given oranges. The oranges were the only Christmas gifts the Barrow kids received.

During the week, many of the adults in camp would go out looking for work, usually in Dallas's factories-cum-sweatshops, or else in manufacturing plants in Cement City or on the other side of the river. They walked to these places; the Dallas factories were five or six miles away, but West Dallas job seekers couldn't afford the bus. Downtown Dallas itself was less than a mile away across the viaduct. Its skyscrapers gleamed in vivid contrast to Cement City's smokestacks, which spewed thick, foul smoke. The lucky few from the wrong side of the river who found jobs invariably didn't make enough to escape West Dallas for the inviting environs of the so-near city. Once you arrived in West Dallas, you usually stayed.

Henry Barrow didn't have the luxury of thinking long-term. His family needed income, fast. Other fathers living in the campground made the rounds of the factories and begged for jobs, but Henry's preference for working in the open air and answering to no boss other than himself remained. Besides his own work ethic, he had two other assets. So each morning he hitched up the horse and took his wagon over the bridge into Dallas, where he spent the day picking up scrap metal of any kind and hauling it to nearby foundries, which for pennies on the hundred pounds bought the scrap to be melted down. It was a hard way to make a meager living. Dallas city streets were now intended for cars, not horses. The Texas summer sun was scorching, and in winter Dallas endured "northers" blowing unimpeded all the way down from Canada. Nice Dallas businesses didn't like a ragamuffin junk man picking through their trash, and every time Henry did hit a big haul, he had to load everything into the wagon and unload it at the foundries all by himself. On slow days, he guided the old white horse up and down residential streets, looking for discarded cast iron skillets and similar bits of metal household effluvia. Other people's trash had become the Barrow family's livelihood.

But almost every day Henry came back to the camp with a little money. The growing children needed clothes, and the family diet couldn't consist entirely of Salvation Army sandwiches. The Barrows acquired a tent, which made for slightly more comfortable sleeping quarters than underneath their wagon. Cumie spent only what she absolutely had to. Anything left over, even if only a few pennies, went for wood, shingles, and nails. In the few daylight hours when he wasn't "rag picking," the pounding of Henry's hammer reverberated through the camp. He was building a house, really just a cramped shed, but at least something to offer more protection from the rain and wind. It took a long time, but gradually the frame of a structure appeared, then walls and a roof added on literally inch by inch. At some point, no one recalls exactly when, the Barrows moved into their boxy house right there on the campground, sheltered by a roof when almost everyone else had only tent canvas above their heads.

While Henry sold scrap metal and bought wood, Cumie spent her days watching over Flop and Marie. Bud was splitting time between the camp and Uncle Frank's farm in Corsicana. Mostly, he was in the country. It was a better place for him than West Dallas. The campground was congenial. Everyone there was in the same desperate straits, and Cumie even made a new best friend named Tookie Jones, a widow who had three sons almost exactly the same ages as her own three youngest. But there was no denying that West Dallas was essentially a lawless place. Many families, some thought most, supplemented the little they could earn honestly with shadier income. People in the camp generally didn't steal from each other—they had so little, what was the point? But across the river, other families' chickens, knickknacks, and even cars were considered fair game. Victims on the east side of the Trinity gave West Dallas another nickname: "The Devil's Back Porch." Because it was outside the official city limits, West Dallas was supposedly beyond the jurisdiction of the Dallas police department, but the city cops prowled the campground anyway, accusing and arresting whomever they pleased. "Suspicion," in those days, was sufficient in the eyes of the courts for the police to take in anyone for questioning. The Dallas County sheriff's department, which did have the technical authority to act in West Dallas, also made its share of arrests. Its deputies seemed to assume, not without cause, that almost every West Dallas family included thieves.

Cumie didn't want that to be the case with the Barrows. For the time being, Bud was safer, better off, on the farm in Corsicana, where he couldn't fall into the cesspool of big-city sin.

Buck, unfortunately, was already swimming in it. Every troublesome trait he'd exhibited in the country found full flower in West Dallas.

When he arrived in the city, Buck didn't go to work for Jack as promised. Instead, he began making a living from vague pursuits that didn't bear close inspection. Cumie said he "bought and sold poultry," a sugarcoated description of chicken theft that even she certainly didn't believe. He got married, too, to Margaret Heneger, and the couple somehow had the money to rent an apartment. The chicken business, illicit or not, didn't provide the income Buck and Margaret required, so Buck moved into the same scrap metal business as his father, but on a more sophisticated scale. He and some partners only described by Cumie as "other boys" got their hands on a car and began driving the Dallas streets in search of booty. One day they filled up the car with a load of brass, valuable metal that attracted the attention of the police. Buck swore he'd been told it was scrap; the cops said it was stolen. Buck held up well enough during questioning that "the laws" let him go after they'd confiscated his haul. But now he had come to the attention of the police, and they'd noted him as a likely suspect in future theft investigations.

Things went poorly between Buck and Margaret. They became the parents of twin boys, but one died after only five months. They divorced, and Buck temporarily rejoined his parents, Flop, and Marie at the West Dallas camp. He brought with him a new means of income: a vicious pit bull he was entering in dog fights. The pit bull hated everyone but its master. After it ripped little Marie's dress right off her, Cumie insisted the dog or Buck had to go. The dog went and Buck stayed, but not for long. He fell in love again, and married Pearl

Churchley, a name Pearl's new mother-in-law undoubtedly admired. But Buck's second marriage ended much the same way as his first. Pearl gave birth to a daughter, and then the couple divorced. As with the surviving twin boy, after the divorce the child lived with her mother. Buck took up with other West Dallas undesirables, and it seemed inevitable that great trouble loomed in his future.

Then Henry had another of his spells, but this time he wasn't alone. Bud was spending some time in West Dallas when he, his father, and little sister all became so ill they had to be admitted to a local hospital as charity patients. Marie said later that they suffered from either malaria or yellow fever, common enough diseases among residents of the musty West Dallas camp. She also swore that Bud was so cheerful, all the nurses considered him their favorite patient. The three Barrows were still shaky when they were allowed to go home—no records apparently still exist of how long they were hospitalized, or what treatment they received. Without Henry out picking up scrap metal every day, family finances must have been especially abysmal. But Cumie insisted that the invalids gulp down huge daily doses of foul-tasting Grove's Chill Tonic, a questionable elixir in which she had considerable faith. Each bottle cost fifty cents, an enormous expenditure. Though the elder Barrows were determined to be self-sufficient, Cumie probably had to turn to Jack, Artie, and Nell for help until Henry recovered enough to resume working.

Bud went back to Corsicana for a while, but he didn't stay. His parents' time in the West Dallas campground began to stretch out—one year, two, then three. Uncle Frank's farm undoubtedly seemed backward compared to the city wonders Bud glimpsed on his visits to Henry and Cumie. Buck, Bud's hero, was up to all kinds of interesting things. Pit bull fights, one romance after another, and even close calls with the law over contraband might have horrified Cumie, but to Bud they must have seemed exciting compared to his own dull country life of school and farm chores. On his visits to the campground, he would stand staring raptly over the river at the towering skyscrapers. No wonder, then, as he turned fifteen, that Bud decided he'd henceforth spend most of his time in Dallas. Country Bud would become City Clyde.

CHAPTER 3

Clyde

Everything about Dallas excited fifteen-year-old Clyde Barrow.

The city dazzled him with its endless stream of possibilities. Unlike tiny Telico, if you wanted to go to the picture show, you could choose between dozens of films instead of just one. Some Dallas theaters changed features four times a week, and not long after Clyde arrived for good in 1925, silent movies began gradually giving way to talkies. Fair Park had its carnival rides, exhibit buildings, picture-taking booths, and a skating rink with real ice. Skyscrapers beat farm silos any day, and in downtown Dallas every store window displayed the kinds of treasures Clyde knew he had to have, clothes and musical instruments especially. Clyde still wanted to make his living as a musician. He spent hours gazing through plate glass at the guitars.

Campground life in West Dallas didn't dismay the short, skinny teenager—Clyde's height topped out at just under five feet, six inches, and he weighed 125 pounds. The Barrows hadn't exactly existed in luxury on their tenant farms, so living rough was natural for the teenager. Some nights, Clyde would go over to one of the many campfires and play his guitar and sing. He was a social sort of boy, so he made new friends easily among West Dallas kids. Two of the closest were Clarence Clay and Tookie Jones's oldest son, who shared both Clyde's age and first name.

It was great fun for Clyde to be reunited with Buck, who had clearly found ways to live an exciting city life. Clyde's sister Nell had just married a man named Leon, who supplemented his factory wages by leading a band at night and on weekends. The couple lived fairly close to the campground, on Pear Street in South Dallas. Clyde went over to see them all the time, and slept there as often as in his parents' tent. Leon played the saxophone, and he was happy to give lessons to his new brother-in-law. It wasn't long before Clyde's sister Artie was telling everyone how she loved hearing her little brother tootling "Melancholy Baby" on the sax.

Cumie Barrow still had her rules about school, and Clyde obeyed—sort of. His country schooling had reached approximately sixth-grade level, but he attended Sidney Lanier High in Dallas. It was a long walk from the campground, and he was expected to chaperone L.C. and Marie part of the way to Cedar Valley Elementary. Often Clyde and L.C. never made it to school. In nice weather, Dallas's parks beckoned, or else window shopping downtown proved irresistible. Marie profited by their poor example. Young as she was, she developed a knack for blackmail. In return for not tattling to Cumie, Marie demanded use of L.C.'s bicycle, the only bike in the family. L.C. would always give in for the privilege of spending time with his brother. He hero-worshipped Clyde.

And there was the other thing about Dallas that thrilled Clyde. Girls were everywhere, too many pretty ones to count, often dressed in the very latest fashions and fixed up fine with lipstick and rouge like the glamorous ladies in the movies. Cumie warned him about these "wayward women" in their sinful makeup, but it was the look modern girls wanted. Admiring swains like Clyde couldn't agree more, and his obsession with fashion extended to his own wardrobe. He wanted to dress stylishly, too.

That desire wasn't unique to Clyde. Poor kids in West Dallas fixated on nice clothes above all else. How a person dressed was crucial to his or her public image. Everyone, even those in flat-broke families like the Barrows, had "Sunday clothes," something nicer than overalls to wear to church. Males might have one dress shirt and a pair of cheap department store slacks. Women would have a single frock made of material that was store-bought rather than homespun.

The unmistakable sign of success, the proof of being someone to respect, came when you wore your Sunday clothes all through the week. The vast majority of Texas men didn't. The most desirable girls often sized up a prospective boyfriend by what he was wearing, and Clyde Barrow meant to impress them. That required decking himself out daily in a nice suit with a vest, and also a snowy dress shirt with a fashionably wide tie. Then he would clearly be someone special. His pride demanded it.

To do that—to have the money for clothes, and dates, and the guitars and saxophones in shop windows—he needed a job. Country school hadn't appealed to Clyde at all, and city school was worse. His new teachers, stuck in bad neighborhoods and with classes full of unruly poor kids, tolerated their students at best. If they had to teach in that part of Dallas, it was either their first job or, more likely, they weren't very good teachers and these were the only jobs they could get. It wasn't as though getting a high school diploma was going to make much difference in Clyde's life. He was willing to work hard to get all the things he wanted. Sticking around school was just delaying his chance to get a job and start generating disposable income.

So when Clyde was around sixteen he quit school forever, and Cumie really couldn't object. For West Dallas kids, the object of going to school was to learn to read and write decently. They were expected to leave school in their midteens and then go to work to help support their families until they married, moved out, and started the cycle again with their own offspring. Across the country, only about 40 percent of all students during Clyde's lifetime ever went beyond the eighth grade.

There were jobs in Dallas factories for dropout boys like Clyde. His ability to read and write made no difference at all. But he was good with his hands. The same fingers that could race along guitar frets or saxophone keys were nimble enough for the most intricate shop piecework. Clyde didn't like the idea of having bosses—he always wanted to be the one giving orders—but he needed a paycheck.

So Clyde took a job at the Brown Cracker & Candy Company for a dollar a day. Some biographers would later claim he worked at Western Union as a messenger boy instead, but L.C. had the only bike among the Barrows, and the Western Union messengers had to supply their own. Clyde was glad to have the job at Brown, right up to the time he got his first few pay envelopes and realized that most of what he wanted, he still couldn't have.

Clyde Barrow might love all the fine things in Dallas, but Dallas didn't love him back. As a useful worker bee he was tolerated, but that was the extent of it. In Dallas and all across America, the mid-1920s was a time when social and economic standing was rigid: you stayed where you were born. That was certainly true in Clyde's new job. Almost as soon as he figured out a dollar a day didn't go all that far, he also realized he had nearly reached the peak of his earning potential. The rich men he worked for were glad to have him as a line employee, but he would never be a manager. That was for his social superiors. People from Dallas owned and ran the factories. People from West Dallas worked in them, and were expected to be grateful for the opportunity. Unlike the East, where postwar industry was often affected by strikes called to win workers higher pay, in Dallas labor unions were virtually nonexistent. Those holding factory jobs there averaged less than $7 a week. Would-be union organizers claimed prostitution was common among female workers because they earned so little in Dallas's factories, dime stores, and restaurants.

During his leisure hours, no one could keep Clyde from visiting downtown Dallas. But it became frustrating to go there. The nice suits on display in store windows cost $20 or more. A saxophone was twice as much. When Clyde went to the movies—he could at least afford the dime admission for that—he saw actors wearing the latest fashions, dining in swanky restaurants, driving flashy cars, living the kind of life he wanted for himself. Around downtown, or in the leafy expanse of Fair Park with all its exhibits and attractions, if he happened to meet teenagers from the nicer parts of town, he was snubbed. Jim Wright, who spent some of his teenage years in Dallas and grew up to become speaker of the U.S. House of Representatives, recalled that even among Dallas middle-class youth, "I would not say West Dallas residents were considered subhuman, but they certainly were thought to be less than everybody else in every way. You wouldn't want to be friends with, let alone date, a kid from West Dallas."

It was bad enough on the east side of the Trinity, but to Clyde's dismay he found he was also at the bottom of the West Dallas social pecking order. Families there didn't have much, but some still had more than others, and it mattered. The Barrows lived in the campgrounds and showed no signs of ever being able to leave. Henry Barrow was a junk man. Clyde was the son of the lowest of the low. Many West Dallas fathers would not allow their daughters to go out with him. Decades later, Louise Barrett's family would tease her about a "double date" with Clyde. Louise's grandfather, who sold milk and vegetables, was several West Dallas social rungs higher than Henry Barrow, and he would not have permitted Clyde to court Louise. The kids got around that by going out as part of a group to Fair Park. It was one of the most popular destinations for West Dallas teenagers. Walking in the park was free, as was admission to many of the car and animal exhibits. But the main attraction, when they could afford it, was posing for silly pictures in the photo booths. The girls donned huge hats and flourished frilly parasols. The boys decked themselves out in goofy cowboy gear. They pointed fake guns at each other, brandished "cigarettes" in long holders, and struck exaggerated poses behind rubber prison bars. The photos came in strips of three for a nickel. The girl would take one, the boy another, and the third might be given to a parent or friend. The daily lives of West Dallas kids were hard and essentially hopeless. They savored these few moments of make-believe.

Clyde Barrow wouldn't settle for make-believe. The teenager who always had to be in charge wouldn't accept that in Dallas he had no control over his own destiny. He was willing to work hard to have a better life in the city. He'd grown up in the country, where there was minimal social stratification. In rural farm communities, everybody wore the same clothes, went to the same dances, interacted on a more even basis. Now he was locked into a system intended to permanently separate the haves and have-nots. There was no doubt which category he belonged to, and Clyde's frustration gradually festered into anger.

He tried the most traditional means of legitimately earning more money by changing jobs, upgrading from Brown's dollar a day to Procter & Gamble's thirty cents an hour. One of his pay packets, signed for in a rounded schoolboy hand, held $18 for a sixty-hour workweek. Then Clyde moved on to the United Glass Company, where he worked as a glazier. Long afterward, his family would insist with pride that during this time he was never fired. Every job change came through Clyde's own choice. He was trying to make something of himself. At one point he even tried to enlist in the navy. He was turned down because of lingering effects from the illness that hospitalized him soon after the Barrows had arrived in West Dallas. It was a major disappointment—in anticipation of military service, Clyde had adorned his left arm with a "USN" tattoo.

Back in the West Dallas campground that was always soggy with river dampness and noisy from the rumble of freight trains passing nearby, Clyde looked at his father and saw his own socially mandated future. Every day Henry Barrow returned exhausted from picking up junk metal, and after a skimpy supper spent his last few waking hours tacking together a pathetic shack. His life would continue to be hard until he was released by death.

But there were other potential role models for Clyde in the West Dallas slums, young men who hadn't surrendered themselves to lives of impoverished drudgery. Their career choices usually didn't involve working in factories like Clyde did. Instead, they took control of their own lives by breaking the law.

Many West Dallas teenagers engaged in petty theft across the river, mostly small crimes of opportunity—a shop clerk being distracted by another customer, a rich woman momentarily leaving her purse unattended in a park. These weren't instances of shoplifting or purse snatching for the thrill of it. The juvenile perpetrators were trying to acquire self-respect as well as loot. A take of even a few dollars meant multiple trips to the movies, bus rides instead of miles-long hikes to Fair Park, or a nice shirt to wear all during the week and not just on Sunday—the chance, for a few precious moments, to not be poor.

Clyde didn't give up his day job, but he did decide to illegally supplement his factory earnings. He started dipping his toe in the criminal waters. Stealing chickens that pecked and scratched their way around innumerable Dallas backyards was one of the most common types of minor local crime. Snatching a chicken was relatively easy, and if you somehow couldn't sell it, the evidence could be disposed of with a satisfying family meal. Dallas County deputy Bob Alcorn told a reporter that his first encounter with Clyde Barrow came sometime around 1926, when he picked up the sixteen-year-old for poultry theft. In keeping with Dallas legal custom, Clyde wasn't jailed. There weren't enough cells in the county to hold all the poor boys caught heisting a hen or two. Instead, Clyde got a bawling out, and Henry and Cumie were probably summoned to pick up their wayward son. Whatever the light punishment, it wasn't enough to discourage Clyde. He wasn't just stealing for himself anymore. There was a girlfriend involved.

Eleanor Bee Williams was a pretty high school student from the east side of the Trinity, and Clyde was completely smitten. Being with a classy girl like Eleanor gave him instant status. Amazingly, her parents didn't forbid the teenagers to date. Clyde added an "EBW" tattoo to his arm, gave Eleanor a hand mirror he made at work with her initials engraved on the back, and according to his mother "in some way" always had money to buy the girl gifts. Soon, Clyde was telling friends they were engaged.

Then Eleanor and Clyde quarreled in late 1926, and she left Dallas to stay for a while with relatives in the East Texas community of Broaddus. Clyde was distraught and decided to follow Eleanor and win her back. His plan involved renting a car—no train or bus for a sophisticated boyfriend like Clyde Barrow—and driving there. He not only came up with money for the car rental, he invited Eleanor's mother to make the drive with him. A few days after they arrived in Broaddus, Eleanor and Clyde reconciled, but their rekindled romance was interrupted when the local sheriff arrived looking for Clyde. To save a few dollars on the fee, he hadn't told the rental agency he was taking the car out of town. When he didn't return the car on time, agency employees came looking for Clyde in West Dallas. His parents told them where he was supposed to be staying in Broaddus, and the agency contacted the sheriff there.

If Clyde had faced the Broaddus cops and explained the mix-up, things might have been worked out, but when they arrived he hid in the attic. After the lawmen collected the car and left, Clyde hitchhiked back to Dallas, leaving Eleanor and her mother to find their own way home. The rental agency filed an official complaint. On December 3, Clyde was arrested by the Dallas police for car theft. There was no bawling out and immediate release this time. The mug shot of Prisoner 6048 shows a tight-lipped teenager with slicked-down hair parted neatly down the center and prominent, pointy ears. He looks resigned rather than scared. Since the agency had its car back, the company eventually decided not to press charges and Clyde was released. But he now had an official arrest record.

Despite the Broaddus debacle, Eleanor soon took Clyde back. Still just sixteen, he persuaded her to elope, and they left town with another couple. As Cumie dryly noted, "they were away several days, when the girl got suspicious that Clyde really didn't intend to marry her, and she came home, and Clyde showed up a few days later." Soon afterward, Eleanor was permanently out of Clyde's life. She was not the type of girl who held a grudge. Decades later, asked about long-standing rumors suggesting that her infamous former beau was either gay or impotent, she assured the interviewer that Clyde "didn't have any problems at all," and left no doubt that she spoke as an authority on the subject.

Clyde had been out of jail for only about three weeks when he was arrested again, this time with Buck. The elder Barrow brother asked Clyde to help him pick up a truckload of turkeys to be sold for the holidays. Buck kept the details vague about how he'd acquired the turkeys, but Clyde wasn't missing the dual opportunity for extra money and time with his big brother. The police received a complaint that the turkeys were stolen and arrested the Barrow boys before they could dispose of their haul. Both claimed they had no idea they were in possession of stolen property, but Buck offered to take full responsibility if Clyde was released. Buck spent a week in jail; Clyde avoided any prison time, but two arrests in one month encouraged the Dallas police to consider him a likely suspect in future robbery investigations. Dallas County deputy Ted Hinton wrote that the police began referring to Buck and Clyde as "the Barrow Boys . . . a term that signified no-accounts."

Sometime in late 1927 or early 1928 Clyde left United Glass for the Bama Pie Company, where he worked with Nell's husband, Leon. Then he switched jobs again, to A&K Top and Paint Shop. Besides the continuing curse of low wages, there was a new complication. Clyde would frequently be picked up at work by Dallas police officers on "suspicion" and taken downtown for questioning. He was never formally charged with any crimes. But when he was released after questioning, the officers never offered to drive him back to work. So he had to walk, often distances of several miles in the sweltering summer heat or biting winter cold. He was not paid by his employers for the hours he missed.

Clyde resented what he considered unfair, ongoing harassment, and his family felt he was turning harder. Cumie wrote that her son "just came to form a kind of contempt or hatred for the law, and figured it didn't do much, if any, good to try to do right . . . he became somewhat discouraged at trying to get by honestly, which to him seemed to be the hardest way after all." Henry made a rare attempt at parental counseling, but to no avail. "A working man just don't have time to sit on his kids," he later told Hinton. "And he's really not all bad."

Clyde still cared very much about dressing nicely and impressing women. Eleanor was followed by other girlfriends—the names "Anne" and "Grace" joined "EBW" and "USN" as tattoos on his arms. One girl named Gladys made a particular impression on the rest of the Barrows. Nell described her as "a likeable person, very slim and pretty," adding, "She wanted a lot of clothes, a watch, money for good times, and a car. When these things were not all forthcoming, she was very disagreeable." Gladys soon moved along, but she stayed agreeable long enough to join Clyde on a vacation in Mexico. A postcard he sent home was proof to Cumie that her child was being corrupted by a hussy: "Drunk as hell. Having fun with Gladys." The postcard became one of Marie's favorite mementos of her brother.

Clyde financed that vacation and other expenditures, such as a shiny new saxophone, by involving himself in higher-revenue crime. Car theft was an obvious, relatively new option for poverty-stricken young men like him who wanted to make lots of money in a hurry, and who didn't care if they broke the law in the process. There were suddenly so many cars, and they were so easy to steal.

There had been automobiles on America's roads since the mid-1890s, when hundreds of manufacturers turned out limited numbers of prohibitively expensive models, mostly purchased by wealthy hobbyists who could afford chauffeurs. Around the beginning of the twentieth century, automobile manufacturers' attention turned to the potential middle-class market, and Henry Ford made automotive history in 1908 by declaring he'd "build a motor car for the great multitude. . . . It will be so low in price that no man making a good salary will be unable to own one." The 1909 Model T Ford was the first market smash, with almost 11,000 sold that year for $825 each. By 1915 there were 2.5 million cars on the road, and many of these were almost impervious to thieves because of their primitive technology. Starting them involved squatting in front of the vehicle and turning a hand crank, which whipsawed back when the engine caught. Would-be thieves had to engage in this noisy, prolonged procedure, which eliminated the element of surprise, and, with it, the potential for theft. But by 1912, inventors had perfected electric starting systems, and within a few years they became standard on all car models. Many car owners fell into the habit of leaving their keys in the ignition, and, even if the keys weren't handy, now it was easy for thieves to hot-wire the cars.

Ford in particular stepped up production and kept lowering prices. In 1927, as Clyde Barrow began actively pilfering whatever vehicles he could, a basic Model T cost $260. General Motors introduced "hire-purchase," allowing customers to put down one-third of a car's price and then pay the rest in installments, and the process was quickly adopted by the company's competitors. Henry Ford's prediction had come true: anyone making a good salary could afford to own a car. In the late 1920s, Dallas County registered more than seventy thousand. Dallas police began regularly bringing in Clyde on suspicion of stealing some of them. None of the charges stuck, but even his family was aware of what he was up to. Nell caught Clyde filing the serial number off the engine of a car he was hiding in a garage and confronted him. Instead of denying her accusations, he accused his sister of being disloyal.

There was considerable profit in stealing a car and then disposing of it. Cars stolen in North Texas were usually driven across the border to Oklahoma and sold to fences there, who'd repaint the vehicles and sell them as slightly used. A stolen car in good condition could bring Clyde $100 or more. That made the risk well worth it. He began dressing much better.

The attention paid to him by the Dallas police convinced Clyde to conduct his car thefts out of town. Denton to the north and Waco to the south were prime locations. On February 22, 1928, he was held for "investigation" thirty-five miles west of Dallas in Fort Worth, a general charge that allowed the police to hold him while they tried to find evidence he'd committed a specific crime. To Clyde's immense satisfaction, they couldn't and he was released again. It would have been impossible for Clyde not to begin developing a sense of invulnerability. The law seemingly couldn't touch him.

But then it touched Buck, who had also started making out-of-town trips to steal cars. He was arrested on August 13 in San Antonio when police caught him trying door handles on a series of vehicles. He'd just hopped into one when the arrest was made. Buck was given a court date and released on bond, but he didn't appear for his hearing. The San Antonio police had Buck picked up, and they deposited him in the city jail to await trial. Since he'd been caught in the act, it was likely Buck would do serious prison time.

Cumie and Henry didn't approve of stealing, but they were loyal to their son. When Buck's trial was set for late January 1929, his parents decided they would go to San Antonio to lend whatever moral support they could, and possibly by their presence influence the judge to show leniency. It was 275 miles from West Dallas to San Antonio, and the Barrows couldn't afford train or even bus fare. Henry hitched up the horse and loaded Cumie, L.C., and Marie in the wagon. Tookie Jones, Cumie's best friend in the campground, came along, too, bringing her youngest sons, W.D. and Leroy. They left without even enough money to buy meals. The trip took almost three weeks. Every few days along the way they would stop and hire out at roadside farms where cotton was being picked or some other field work needed to be done. Marie recalled how, during the trip, her father's fingernails were literally ripped off by prickly plants. All seven of them got down on their knees in the dirt and worked, though ten-year-old Marie was excused after the first day when her cotton sack contained as many twigs and leaves as fluffy bolls. When they were paid for their labor, they used the money to buy inexpensive food for themselves and feed for the horse. At night, Cumie cooked potatoes and pots of beans over a campfire. They slept under and around the wagon.

Perhaps swayed by the presence of the accused man's family, the judge in San Antonio dismissed the charges against Buck. After all, no car had actually been stolen. But it was increasingly clear to everyone except Buck and Clyde that such good luck couldn't last much longer.

Soon after they returned to West Dallas, Cumie and Henry were dismayed to discover that Clyde had a new, clearly undesirable friend. Frank Clause was about Clyde's age, and he had grown up on the east side of the Trinity in Dallas proper. Clyde said they met at work, but the Barrows believed they became acquainted while both were in custody at the county jail. Frank was a "second-story man," someone who broke into houses and businesses. With his encouragement, Clyde's immersion in crime escalated. Nell Barrow wrote later that if she had realized just how bad an influence Frank would be, she would have shot Clyde dead before she allowed them to become friends. Soon after Frank and Clyde teamed up, they came by Nell's apartment late one night with armloads of ice cream bars, pocketknives, and hot water bottles. They swore everything had been tossed out on the street for anyone to claim by employees trying to put out a fire at a drugstore. When she called them liars, Clyde shouted at her and left.

Sometime in the fall of 1929, Frank Clause, Clyde, and Buck were arrested on suspicion of planning to burglarize a lumber company. They were released the next day, and had just returned to see Cumie in West Dallas when the police came for them again, telling Cumie and Nell, who was also there, that they were being taken back in for questioning about a different crime. Nell followed her brothers and their friend downtown and confronted the chief of police, accusing him and his officers of picking on the Barrows, Clyde in particular. The chief asked Nell about the canary yellow Buick roadster she was driving, a car she often loaned to Clyde. Was she aware that the car had been spotted in the towns of Lufkin and Hillsboro just before recent safecrackings? Even though they hadn't been able to prove anything yet, Nell was told, the police had no doubt her brother Clyde was guilty of those robberies and several more. "I could figure back," she wrote. The alleged crimes had all occurred since Clyde became friends with Frank Clause. Clyde and Buck were released again, but the rest of the Barrows took little comfort from it. "It wasn't a happy day," Nell concluded.

There was at least one happy day for Henry Barrow in the fall of 1929, though it wasn't as pleasant for his horse. Henry was following his usual scrap metal route along the Houston Street Viaduct when a car careened out of control and hit the horse. The mortally injured animal bolted all the way back to the campground before it died. Henry—or, more likely, his older children—threatened a lawsuit, and the driver settled for "either $600 or $800," according to Marie. Henry used some of the money to buy a Model T Ford, probably a truck rather than a coupé. The Ford was the only car Henry ever owned. Using it to search out and haul scrap metal increased the amount of ground he could cover every working day. It was a rare bright spot in the life of a man who needed them desperately.

Then things turned desperate for the entire nation. In late October, the stock market crashed and America was instantly plunged into the economic depths later known as the Great Depression. The worst effect was initially in the Northeast, where businesses shut down in droves and many previously well-to-do citizens found themselves penniless in a matter of days. There was far less immediate impact in Texas, where the state economy was already in ruins due to the ongoing farm crisis. Many Texas families never even realized that a national economic depression had begun. There was certainly trepidation among Dallas business leaders—the city's banks were the backbone of its economy—but for many families like the Barrows in West Dallas, their lives didn't change a bit. They didn't own stocks and bonds, or have money in a bank.

In fact, early November 1929 brought the Barrows reason to feel hopeful. Buck had a new girlfriend, one his parents and sisters believed might be able to coax him back to honest work. Pretty, petite Blanche Caldwell Callaway was eighteen, the daughter of an Oklahoma preacher. Her parents, Matthew and Lillian Caldwell, were divorced, and Blanche had lived with her father until at her mother's insistence she reluctantly married a much older man named John Callaway. The marriage was disastrous, and Blanche fled to West Dallas, where she stayed with a friend named Emma Lou Renfro. Emma Lou's house wasn't far from the campground where the Barrows still lived, and on November 11, Blanche met Buck somewhere in the neighborhood. Though she was still legally married to John Callaway, Blanche was instantly attracted to Buck, whom she nicknamed "Daddy." Buck called her "Baby." He'd been dating another woman, but gave her up for Blanche. Cumie was ecstatic—the daughter of a preacher, even one who was married and hiding out from her husband, was exactly the kind of good influence she felt her wayward son needed. Marie wrote that Blanche struck the Barrows as "a good, nice, sweet gentle person . . . as proper and respectable as a preacher's daughter could be expected to be."

Buck told Blanche about his two previous marriages, and the two surviving children from them. He didn't mention being involved in car thefts and robberies, but Blanche hadn't known her charming new boyfriend for three weeks before she was presented with irrefutable evidence of his darker side.

The cocky Barrow brothers had bragged to their little brother, L.C., that "you never break the law until you're caught." On November 29 they did, and Buck was. He, Clyde, and an accomplice named Sidney Moore drove north in a stolen Buick. In the small town of Henrietta, they abandoned the Buick in favor of a Ford. They spied a house that appeared to be empty and broke into it. The haul was disappointing—some bits of jewelry and very little cash. They split the proceeds in thirds and turned back for West Dallas, passing through the medium-sized town of Denton on the way. It was one in the morning, and they weren't returning home with much to show for the trip. Motor Mark Garage looked promising, so they broke in and found a small safe that defied their efforts to crack. Unwilling to give up, they lugged the safe outside and loaded it into the Ford. They were spotted by a patrol car, and Clyde, who was driving, decided to run for it. The chase didn't last long. Clyde took a turn too fast and smashed the Ford's front axle on the curb. He, Buck, and Moore took off on foot, and the Denton police began shooting. Buck was hit, suffering flesh wounds in both legs. The cops arrested him where he fell screaming in pain, and Moore surrendered. Clyde kept going. He hid under a house until the police gave up hunting for him, then he hitchhiked back to Dallas. The owner of the garage told the cops he had only $30 in the safe. Buck's freedom had been squandered for a pittance. Searching him and Moore after their arrests, the lawmen also found jewelry from the Henrietta break-in. This time, there was plenty of evidence to convict Buck Barrow.

There was no cockiness left in Clyde when he arrived back in the campground. He'd spent his hours in flight thinking Buck had been killed, so there was some relief in learning he'd just been wounded, and not too badly. Denton's wheel of justice spun fast, and on December 6, Buck and Moore were indicted for burglary, then tried on December 17. A jury took only a few minutes to pronounce them guilty. Buck was sentenced to four years in the main state prison at Huntsville. Blanche promised she'd wait for him.

In early January 1930, just before he was transferred from the Denton jail to Huntsville, Buck sent a letter to his parents. Because he was illiterate, he had to dictate it to another prisoner, but the message was what Cumie had been praying for. Buck promised that "if God gives me one more chance I shall try to the best that is in me to lead a life worth while in the future and be a man that the people will respect and my relatives will honor. I know the heart aches and sorrow that my crookedness has did to you and Father."

Cumie found it "a terrible disgrace" to have a son in prison, but she "felt some better" when Buck's first letter from Huntsville arrived a few days later. He said he was in the prison hospital because his legs were hurting, and that "it sure looks hard but I am going to take it." He urged Cumie to get him a "furlow" or parole; she soon was in contact with the governor's office in Austin. It was typical for prisoners' families to request paroles. With Texas prisons plagued by overcrowding, pardons were the most convenient means of reducing the number of inmates. They were granted on a regular basis.

The rest of the Barrows knew Clyde had nearly been captured with Buck in Denton. They hoped that close call would make Clyde reconsider his criminal ways before he otherwise inevitably joined Buck in prison. He was nineteen, between jobs, and frequently hauled in for questioning by the Dallas police. Clyde also knew what the rest of his family didn't—he was being sought in several other towns for crimes ranging from car theft to burglary. This contributed to a crushing sense of being powerless. Clyde wanted to be the one in charge, but now he couldn't even walk out on the street without being afraid the cops would pick him up. Marie thought he was "thoroughly shaken and unnerved."

Unlike Buck, Clyde didn't promise his parents he'd give up crime, but he did start spending time again with old West Dallas friends who were better influences than sinister Frank Clause. One of Clyde's rediscovered pals was Clarence Clay, who on January 5, 1930, invited Clyde to a party. With his spirits at their all-time low, Clyde went with Clarence to 105 Herbert Street, a boxy little residence a few blocks away from the campground, and that was where he met her.

CHAPTER 4

Bonnie

On the day she met Clyde Barrow, nineteen-year-old Bonnie Parker's life was also in complete shambles. Everything that could be wrong in it, was. She'd lost her job and couldn't find another. The handsome young husband she'd expected to make all her romantic dreams come true was gone for good. After years of predicting she'd be a famous star on Broadway, or perhaps a renowned poet, she was still a nobody in the Dallas slums. It was enough to make her cry, and she frequently did. But after each temporary surrender to the blues, she came back strong. A bone-deep belief that great things were in her future kept Bonnie going. The worse her circumstances were in life, the grander her fantasies became. Something amazing was going to happen because she was Bonnie Parker. She just had to be ready when it did.

Bonnie learned unshakable self-esteem from her mother. All Bonnie's life, Emma Krause Parker believed—and acted like—her family was better than everyone else's. It began in the little West Texas town of Rowena where Bonnie was born. Most of the men who lived there were farmers, but Bonnie's father, Charles Parker, was a brick mason. As far as her mother, Emma, was concerned, that placed the Parkers at the top of the social ladder. Charles had a trade, unlike the sodbusters whose yearly fortunes depended on enough rain to coax cotton out of the dry West Texas soil. Emma had an equally high opinion of her two-year-old son, Hubert, nicknamed Buster, and the baby daughter she delivered on October 1, 1910. In *Fugitives*, a family memoir published a quarter-century later, Emma approvingly described Buster as "sober," an appropriate personality for a boy who was destined to go far, and infant Bonnie inspired her mother to descriptive heights. Bonnie, Emma gushed, "was a beautiful baby, with cotton colored curls, the bluest eyes you ever saw, and an impudent little red mouth."

Rowena's community life revolved around its First Baptist Church, and Emma made certain the Parkers were in the middle of it—"socials, box suppers and the like." She took every opportunity to show off her children, and from the time she could toddle, Bonnie thrived as the center of attention. Sunday School provided an early example. Three-year-old Bonnie was one of several children selected to stand on a platform and take solo turns singing favorite hymns to the congregation. Emma thought her daughter looked "resplendent in starched bows and ruffles," but when precocious Bonnie took the stage she shocked the crowd by belting out the honky-tonk tune "He's a Devil in His Own Home Town." Afterward, Bonnie was thrilled. She'd wanted extra attention, and she got it.

In 1913 Emma gave birth to her third child, a daughter named Billie Jean. Bonnie enjoyed her new sister, but she found special pleasure in expanding her own vocabulary. One of Charles Parker's brothers came to Rowena for a visit, and he delighted his feisty little niece by teaching her to swear. Bonnie immediately addressed her father in salty language. Charles spanked Buster for even the slightest use of questionable slang—"darn" was forbidden—but he couldn't bring himself to paddle Bonnie. She was just too cute.

Then, in December 1914, Charles Parker died. There is no record of the cause, but it seems to have been unexpected. Emma described herself as "left with three small children and the problem of providing for them." There were no jobs for young widows in Rowena, so Emma packed up her three kids and moved 240 miles east. Her parents, Frank and Mary Krause, lived in Cement City across the Trinity River from Dallas. Frank had been a farmer, and now he worked in a mill. Like everyone else in Cement City, the Krauses were barely getting by, but they didn't hesitate to take in their daughter and grandchildren. Many Cement City and West Dallas households included two or even three generations. Family loyalty was strengthened by poverty. When relatives had nothing else, they had each other.

It was a difficult adjustment for Emma. Back in Rowena she had been a lady of considerable substance, but in Cement City she was just one more flat-broke woman scrambling to support her children. Staying home to care for them wasn't an option—Frank Krause didn't make enough to feed four more dependents. So Emma looked for work, and eventually found it as a seamstress in a factory manufacturing overalls. The work was hard and tedious. Based on average salaries in the area for "garment workers," Emma probably earned about nine and a half dollars a week.

Like West Dallas, Cement City was a dirty, boisterous place. It was slightly farther away from the Trinity River and downtown Dallas, and most of the adults living there worked at menial jobs in the various factories and foundries that lined the dirt streets. Chalk Hill Road separated the white and black neighborhoods. The smokestacks of the Trinity-Portland Cement Company and other manufacturers towered over everything. Air pollution made it hard to breathe. The stink of industrial fumes clung to skin and hair.

Yet Emma Parker did not surrender her opinion of herself and her family as high-class. Circumstances might have forced her to move to a slum and work sewing overalls, but she still carried herself like a queen. Every Sunday morning, she and the children walked several miles to church, ignoring the dust that swirled up when the weather was dry or the mud coating their shoes if there had been recent rain. Cumie Barrow made family church attendance mandatory because that was what Jesus wanted. Emma Parker marched her brood to church on Sunday because that was what the best people did.

While Emma was at work, her mother cared for the Parker kids, as well as for Bonnie's cousin Bess, who was three years older than Bonnie. Mary Krause did her best, and Buster and Billie Jean usually behaved. But Bonnie was an adorable terror. Emma wrote that Bonnie kept the household "generally in a stew from morning to night," often in tandem with Bess. There was nothing mean-spirited about the little girl. From setting small fires because she liked the pretty flames to raiding her grandfather's stash of wine—she passed out—Bonnie did what she wanted without regard to consequences. No punishments could deter her.

That trait carried over when six-year-old Bonnie began attending Cement City School. She was cute, and undeniably bright. School pageants included Bonnie Parker in featured roles. But on any public occasion, Bonnie was liable to do something outrageous to make herself stand out from everyone else. One of the most memorable moments came during an elementary school program. Blackface performers were the rage in vaudeville, so Bonnie and her classmates had their faces darkened with powder and were sent on stage to play "pickaninnies." Bonnie had a stocking cap covering her blond hair. During the show, one of her classmates pulled the cap off Bonnie's head, revealing her light curls. The audience laughed, and the little girl felt humiliated. She began to cry, the dark makeup on her face streaked, and there was more laughter. According to Emma, "it gave her a new idea." Tears still dripping down her cheeks, Bonnie started doing somersaults and cartwheels. The laughter turned to cheers, "and the program broke up in a riot."

Bonnie had a hot temper. Even genteel Emma admitted her daughter "fought her way" through school. She was willing to slug it out with boys as well as other girls over stolen pencils or perceived snubs. But many of the little boys in Cement City School developed crushes on her, which she encouraged. Even at an early age, Bonnie always liked to be someone's girlfriend. Gifts of candy and gum were expected from her prepubescent beaus.

She expected special consideration from her family, too. On weekends, the Parker girls would often be sent out to fish. Anything they caught was a welcome addition to their dinner table. Billie Jean loved fishing, but Bonnie found it boring. While Billie Jean waited silently for a bite, Bonnie sang at the top of her lungs. Billie Jean recalled that when she tried to hush her sister, Bonnie's usual reply was, "When I'm on Broadway and I have my name in lights, you'll be sorry you talked to me like this." Besides Broadway tunes, Bonnie liked to serenade the fish or anyone else who'd listen with popular hits of the day. Her absolute favorite performer was Jimmie Rodgers, the "Singing Brakeman." Bonnie loved Rodgers songs like "My Old Pal," "T for Texas" (also known as "Blue Yodel") and, prophetically, "In the Jailhouse Now."

Puberty brought with it an obsession with clothes and makeup. The teenaged girls in Cement City yearned to look like the glamorous movie stars they saw in the picture shows. Thanks to films and magazines, the "flapper look" that dominated East Coast fashion extended its influence to Texas. Even in the Dallas slums, girls wanted to wear cloche hats over short permed hair, and slenderizing long skirts with jersey tops. Makeup was essential, too—lots of eyeliner, rouge, and lipstick. Bonnie and her friends all undoubtedly acquired the latest cosmetic must-have, a newfangled rouge holder known as a "compact." When they felt properly attired and made up, many of the girls rushed to Fair Park to capture their magnificence in the three-for-a-nickel photo strips. That wasn't good enough for Bonnie Parker. When she was about fifteen, she scraped together the money to pose for a studio "glamour shot." In it, the heavily made-up girl tilts her head alluringly, eyes gazing up and off-camera toward dreams she's certain will someday come true.

And that was the problem for Bonnie. Most of her dreams had to remain fantasies. The grandest of them—singing in Broadway musicals, acting in Hollywood movies, writing best-selling volumes of poetry—were virtually impossible, even if she refused to accept it. Broadway and Hollywood producers didn't scout for talent in Cement City. Publishers didn't seek out the next Emily Dickinson there. Perhaps, with her dedication to endless self-promotion and a degree of talent, she might have become a star if she went to California or New York, but Bonnie wasn't going anywhere. She had no money to make such a trip, let alone to live on while she made the rounds of auditions.

There wasn't even a realistic chance for her to become somebody special in Cement City. Bonnie was one of the best students in her high school, where she won a spelling bee. That was a source of considerable pride to Emma. But it made no difference. Smart slum girls still had limited career opportunities. Staying in school, getting a high school diploma, wouldn't have improved Bonnie's prospects. College was out of the question. Emma Parker barely made enough to feed her children, let alone pay tuition. Whether Bonnie left high school as a graduate or a dropout, if she worked for a living she would still have to choose between becoming a factory line worker, a maid, a waitress, or a clerk in a shop. Those were the professional options for Cement City girls.

But there was another kind of option with the possibility of at least temporary joy. A vivacious teenaged girl like Bonnie could do more than dream about meeting and marrying a wonderful man. She could actively go out and try to find one. Marriage itself didn't promise much. Cement City girls usually married young, were soon pregnant, and ended up like their mothers, raising children in poverty with no chance for anything better. But between puberty and marriage there was the potential for at least a few brief years of coquetry and romance before a poor girl's life became as hard and hopeless as her mother's. Bonnie, who never let evidence to the contrary spoil a good fantasy, believed she would be the exception to the rule. Her romance would equal or surpass the happily-ever-after love stories that mesmerized her at the movies. All that was necessary was the right man, and when she was fifteen she decided she'd found him.

Bonnie met Roy Thornton in high school. He was big, good-looking, and well dressed—appearance always mattered to her. And Roy was fun. He had money for dates, and it didn't matter to Bonnie where he got it. The timing was just right in her life. There was no sense staying in school, she didn't want to work in a factory like her mother, and Roy seemed like he could support a girl in style. So Bonnie fell in love, going overboard as she did in everything else. Roy was perfect. No criticism of him was permitted. She ran out and got a tattoo high up on the inside of her right thigh. It had two red hearts connected by arrows, and the hearts were labeled "Bonnie" and "Roy." She insisted she had to marry him right away—true love couldn't wait. Emma Parker wasn't in favor of the marriage, but Bonnie was headstrong and wore her mother down. She became Mrs. Roy Thornton on September 25, 1926, just a few weeks before her sixteenth birthday.

The young couple found a place to live near Emma's house, and their problems began almost immediately. Roy had mysterious ways of making money to pay the bills, and didn't confide in his new wife. Bonnie suddenly couldn't stand being apart from her mother. Every night she made Roy take her over for a visit, or else she'd insist that Emma spend the night with the newlyweds at their place. Emma couldn't help feeling sorry for the new son-in-law who "was having a lot of difficulty with his honeymoon." Finally, she told Roy they might as well move in with her.

Bonnie loved children and wanted a baby. Emma Parker and Marie Barrow hinted later that there were unspecified gynecological problems, and that some medical procedure left Bonnie unable to conceive.

But the result was no children then or ever. Never mind that motherhood might have interfered with her dreams of stardom—Bonnie mourned. She had a talent for that.

In August 1927, Roy disappeared for ten days. He didn't tell Bonnie he was leaving, wasn't in touch while he was gone, and offered no explanation after he got back. He started drinking heavily, and when Bonnie rebuked him for it he hit her. Things like that didn't happen in the movies. Then in October he left again and stayed away nineteen days. Even a dreamer like Bonnie couldn't avoid facing the facts: her grand romance wasn't so grand after all. Emma counseled divorce, but Bonnie wasn't ready for such a drastic step. When Roy vanished for the third time in December, she suspected he'd left her for another girl named Reba Griffin.

Bonnie briefly began keeping a diary. Its entries alternated between righteous anger at Roy's actions, moony declarations of endless love for him, and general frustration: when was something great going to happen in her life?

In her first entry, dated January 1, 1928, seventeen-year-old Bonnie wrote, "I wish to tell you that I have a roaming husband with a roaming mind. We are separated again for the third and last time . . . I love him very much and miss him terribly. But I intend doing my duty. I am not going to take him back." She added that she and her friend Rosa Mary "have resolved this New Year's to take no men or nothing seriously. Let all men go to hell! But we are not going to sit back and let the world sweep by us."

In a second New Year's entry, she noted she'd gone to see Ken Maynard in *The Overland Stage* that night and then "I got drunk. Trying to forget. Drowning my sorrows in bottled hell!" Prohibition was the law of the land, but a flirtatious girl like Bonnie could always get a drink.

On January 2, she and Rosa Mary saw another movie, Ronald Colman and Vilma Bánky in *The Night of Love*. A boy she knew named Scottie came on to her, but she "gave him the air. He's a pain in the neck to me." The next day, believing Roy was gone for good, she went looking for work: "Searched this damn town over for a job . . . I guess luck is against me." She hunted down Reba Griffin. Roy wasn't with her, but Bonnie thought "she has taken my place in his heart."

Over the next ten days Bonnie had casual dates with boys named Lewis and Raymond, brushed off advances by a few other would-be suitors, frequently went to the movies, and confided that "Oh, God, how I wish I could see Roy! But I try my best to brush all thought of him aside and have a good time. If I knew for sure he didn't care for me, I'd cut my throat and say here goes nothing! Maybe he does though. I still have hopes."

By January 11 Bonnie hadn't found a job and asked her diary plaintively, "Why don't something happen?" She repeated the question two days later. On January 16 she made her final entry: "Sure am blue tonight. Have been crying. I wish I could see Roy."

Bonnie probably abandoned her diary because she found a job waitressing at Hargrave's Café on Swiss Avenue in Dallas. It was several miles from Cement City in a neighborhood split between residences, small businesses, and the Baylor Medical College. Her outgoing personality was an immediate plus, since waitresses in 1928 received very small weekly salaries—no more than $3 or $4 a week—and had to rely on tips. Most of those tips were meager, a penny or two. Big spenders trying to impress their servers might leave a dime.

She became special friends with the women who worked at a laundry behind the café. When it was time for their lunch break, they'd whistle and Bonnie would run around the building to take their orders. Sometimes, if business in the café was slow, she'd visit the laundry just to chat. The employees there thought she always seemed especially fresh and clean.

She also dressed well, even though she made very little money at the café. Her wardrobe might have reflected income from occasional prostitution. If so, she wasn't doing anything out of the ordinary for working-class girls from the Dallas slums. If they were cute—and Bonnie was—they had to at least consider the option. Hargrave's was in a much more affluent neighborhood than the greasy spoons of Cement City and West Dallas. As a waitress there, Bonnie would have been in position to judge prospects among the Hargrave's patrons. If they were friendly and tipped generously, why not? Because of her infertility, there was no danger of pregnancy. Bonnie hadn't given up on any of her big dreams, but until they came true a girl still had to eat and find a way to pay for her clothes. Circumstances forced her to have a practical streak.

Roy finally came back a year later, in January 1929. Bonnie told him they were through, and meant it. She had her own income now, and Emma Parker believed "she was seeing Roy through new eyes." A few months later, Roy was picked up for robbery and sentenced to five years in prison. He hadn't just been courting Reba Griffin during his long absences. Bonnie never saw Roy again, and didn't try to communicate with him in prison. But she didn't divorce him, either. That, she said, "just wouldn't be right," kicking a man while he was down. She continued wearing Roy's wedding ring.

Early in 1929, Bonnie changed jobs. She began working at Marco's, a restaurant in downtown Dallas near the courthouse and post office. The tips were undoubtedly better, since Marco's customers included lawyers, judges, and bankers. One of Bonnie's regulars was Ted Hinton, a postal worker who later became a Dallas County deputy. Hinton enjoyed bantering with her. She told Hinton she wanted to be "a singer, or maybe a poet." Many of Bonnie's male customers flirted with her, and Hinton noticed she "could turn off the advances or lead a customer on with her easy conversation." If she was still turning occasional tricks, the move from Hargrave's to Marco's meant a more well-to-do clientele.

Emma, ever alert for evidence her family was morally superior, was proud rather than dismayed when the manager at Marco's told her that Bonnie's job was in jeopardy. Bonnie, he complained, had such a soft heart that she gave food away to indigents who couldn't afford to pay for their meals. Despite several warnings, she continued to do it, and if she didn't stop he was going to "can her." Emma agreed to speak to her daughter, and as she recalled later Bonnie "promised to do better but she didn't . . . as long as she worked at Marco's, she fed people, and she never got fired for it, either."

In November 1929, the effects of the previous month's stock market crash hit downtown Dallas. Many small businesses closed, and Marco's was among them. Bonnie was out of work, and suddenly there were no jobs to be found. Working-class girls in cities all over Texas were left without income and no prospects of employment. Things were so desperate that convents throughout the state faced a sudden deluge of applicants, most of whom weren't even Catholic. Emma didn't lose her job, but money in the Parker household was scarce. Frank Krause had died in 1919. Buster was grown and self-supporting, but Billie Jean had married Fred Mace, and the young couple lived with Emma. Bonnie had to find some way to contribute income. Unable to find anything permanent, she began hiring out as a temporary housekeeper or babysitter.

Bonnie was miserable. She still believed in the fairy-tale lives of the characters she saw in movies, with their gorgeous clothes and grand love affairs and exciting adventures. Daily reality was the exact opposite: she was broke, unemployed, and didn't have a husband anymore. The farm crisis had already crippled the Texas economy for almost a decade. The Depression was taken as just one more sign the bad times were permanent. Hanging on to dreams of fame and hopes for true love got tougher every day, yet Bonnie still wondered, as she'd written twice in her diary, "Why don't something happen?"

When it finally did, she knew right away. Bonnie's brother, Buster, married Clarence Clay's sister, and in early January 1930, Bonnie went over to their house for a party. There were enough people living in Cement City and West Dallas that they didn't all know each other, and Clarence brought along a stranger who caught Bonnie's eye. At the moment they met, Clyde Chestnut Barrow and Bonnie Elizabeth Parker exactly filled the needs in each other's lives. He wasn't as tall or as good-looking as Roy, but he liked making all the decisions. Bonnie always responded to a man who acted like he was in charge, just like Ronald Colman in *The Night of Love* or Milton Stills in *Framed*, two movies she had recently seen and enjoyed. Clyde had nice clothes and drove a fancy car. She might have suspected he stole it, but so what? Being with him promised some fun, of which there had recently been precious little in her life. So she fell instantly in love.

For Clyde, the attraction was mutual. Bonnie was tiny as well as cute, a plus for a short man so sensitive about his height that he had stood on curbs to appear taller when posing for photos with previous girlfriends. Well-dressed Bonnie was clingy, always hanging adoringly on his arm. This bolstered Clyde's self-image, which was probably still shaken from his narrow escape in Denton. Best of all, Bonnie's fanatic determination to rise up out of poverty, to not meekly accept second-class status, matched his own.

They were immediately inseparable. Clyde didn't take Bonnie over to the campground right away to be introduced to his family—Cumie was unlikely to be impressed by a girl so fond of cosmetics—but Bonnie was eager for him to meet her mother. Emma's first impression was that Clyde "was a likable boy . . . with his dark wavy hair, dancing brown eyes and a dimple that popped out every now and then when he smiled." As crazy as Bonnie had once been about Roy, Emma thought, "she never worshipped him as she did Clyde."

Clyde found it very pleasant to be worshipped. It helped get his mind off Buck being in prison and his own ongoing risk of arrest. It's not clear whether he told Bonnie about his problems with "the laws." If not, she found out soon enough.

In early February, Clyde made an evening visit to Bonnie's home to tell her he'd be leaving town the next day. He'd undoubtedly planned a car theft or robbery. Squiring his new lady friend in style required cash. Bonnie made it obvious how much she would miss him until he returned, and their parting dragged on and on until Emma finally suggested he just go ahead and spend the night. It wasn't an invitation to share Bonnie's bed. Emma was much too starchy for that. Because the Parkers' house was crowded—besides Emma, Bonnie, and Grandma Mary, Billie Jean and her husband still lived there, along with their newborn baby—Clyde had to sleep on the living room couch. That made it convenient for him to answer the front door the next morning when the Dallas police came to arrest him.

CHAPTER 5

Dumbbells

Clyde went quietly. He hoped this arrest wasn't any different from all the previous ones—that he was being picked up on the generic charge of "suspicion," and that after routine questioning, he'd be out of the Dallas County jail in a matter of hours. There was, of course, the embarrassment of being hauled off by the police in front of his new girlfriend and her family, but that could be smoothed over once he was released and things calmed down.

There was nothing calm about Bonnie's reaction as her boyfriend was taken into custody. She flew into hysterics, pounding her hands on the walls and begging the officers not to arrest him. Clyde tried to soothe her. As he did, Emma asked the cops why Clyde was being arrested. They told her he was wanted in other cities; they were just making the initial arrest, and he'd be held in the county jail until the outside jurisdictions arranged for his transfer. If Clyde had heard this he might have attempted an escape, but Bonnie was making a considerable racket.

As the police drove off with Clyde in custody, Bonnie collapsed in a sobbing heap. Emma tried to console her while suggesting to her older daughter that it might be a good idea to stop falling in love with felons. But Bonnie found the potential for drama, even glamour, in her new heartbreak. True, Roy was in prison and she was done with him, but Roy had shut her out of his life entirely. Clyde was different. He was a good man who'd perhaps made a few piddling mistakes and needed her now as no one had ever needed her before. She would support him in his time of trouble and save him with her love. She told Emma as much, then immersed herself in what promised to be the most satisfying role of her life.

Bonnie began with visits to Clyde in the Dallas County jail. He would have been informed that police in Denton and Waco wanted him transferred to their jurisdictions, so seeing Bonnie was a welcome distraction. When she wasn't visiting Clyde, she wrote him long, rambling letters pledging eternal love and predicting a long, happy future together. One, dated February 14, 1930, and snarkily addressed to "Mr. Clyde Barrow Care The Bar Hotel," was full of inconsequential chat about feeling blue and spraining her wrist. Some hopeful boy had brought her a box of Valentine's candy, and "I didn't appreciate the old candy at all, and I thought about my darling in that mean old jail, and started to bring the candy to you. Then I knew that you wouldn't want the candy that that old fool brought to me."

Bonnie mentioned Clyde's former partner Frank Clause—Clause was up to his old criminal tricks, and in a Dallas County cell on some charge or other—and finished with a plea: "I'm so lonesome for you, dearest. Don't you wish we could be together? Sugar, I never knew I really cared for you until you got in jail. And honey, if you get out o.k. please don't ever do anything to get locked up again."

The mention of a prospective, candy-bearing suitor couldn't have pleased Clyde, and he certainly must have wondered why it took his arrest to convince Bonnie she really cared for him. But there was one more line in the letter that probably made his blood run cold: "I went out to your mother's today."

Clyde had deliberately kept Cumie and his new girlfriend apart, but Bonnie felt that in such a terrible time she should bond with the rest of the Barrows. She liked them immediately—Nell especially, she wrote Clyde, was "so sweet"—but the feeling wasn't entirely mutual. Cumie took in Bonnie's heavily mascaraed eyes and fashionable clothes and sized her up as a pleasure-obsessed vixen. "Bonnie," Cumie declared in her unpublished memoir, "just cared for a good time and believed in spending money as [she] went."

Eleven-year-old Marie, grown enough to be tantalized by makeup herself, had a more generous first impression. "She was just a cute little old girl," Marie recalled decades later, adding that "Bonnie could have been characterized as cute, even pretty when she fixed herself up." Cumie, Marie thought, couldn't help comparing Bonnie to Buck's girlfriend, Blanche, who was a preacher's daughter. That meant Bonnie would always pale in comparison.

Ever the opportunist, Marie saw an immediate advantage in Bonnie's determination to become a quasi-member of Clyde's family. The Parker home was considerably more comfortable than the campground, so Marie requested frequent sleepovers at her new pal Bonnie's.

About a week later, Bonnie borrowed a car and drove to downtown Dallas to visit Clyde. She was told he'd just been transferred to the Denton jail, where he would face charges on the attempted robbery of the previous November 29. Bonnie's letter to him there described her reaction on hearing the news: "I was so blue and mad and discouraged, I just had to cry. I had maybelline on my eyes and it began to stream down my face and I had to stop on Lamar street. I laid my head down on the steering wheel and sure did boohoo. A couple of city policemen came up and wanted to know my trouble. I imagine I sure looked funny with maybelline streaming down my face."

Then she returned to her familiar theme—after this, Clyde was going to go straight, and she was going to inspire him to do it.

"They only think you are mean," Bonnie wrote. "I know you are not, and I'm going to be the very one to show you that this outside world is a swell place, and we are young and should be happy like other boys and girls instead of being like we are."

Clyde got lucky in Denton. The grand jury ruled there wasn't enough evidence to indict him for the attempted November robbery. That was the extent of the good news. McLennan County lawmen were waiting to take him to Waco, where he was wanted on seven different charges ranging from car theft to possession of stolen goods.

Bonnie followed Clyde south. She and Cumie made the trip together on the "interurban" train. Any conversation during the journey was undoubtedly one-sided. Cumie would have to leave as soon as the

McLennan County grand jury finished its deliberations, but Bonnie had a married female cousin in town. She could stay indefinitely.

Unlike Denton, the Waco jurists had a substantial amount of testimony to consider. Clyde had previously been picked up there on suspicion, giving his name as Elvin Williams. It was revealed during testimony that Clyde hadn't been quite as reformed after Buck's capture as the rest of the Barrow family hoped. Prosecutors offered evidence that in January alone, Clyde stole two different cars in Waco. On March 3, 1930, the grand jury returned seven counts against Clyde Barrow, aka Elvin Williams, Eldin Williams, Jack Hale, and Roy Bailey. Clyde had given the additional pseudonyms to authorities when picked up on suspicion in other cities.

Clyde was held in the county jail with William Turner of Waco, who may have been Clyde's partner in some of the robberies there. On the same day Clyde was indicted on seven counts, the grand jury charged Turner with twenty-five. It was clear that prison sentences were inevitable for both. Perhaps encouraged by a note from Bonnie swearing "if you do have to go down I'll be good while you're gone and be waiting—waiting—waiting for you," Clyde joined Turner before Judge Richard Munroe on March 5 to plead guilty on all counts. It was a smart move. Clyde was technically a first-time offender, and Turner's family was from Waco. Since they made statements declaring they'd learned their lessons, their sentences were relatively light. Turner got twenty-five four-year terms to be served concurrently, which meant just four years in prison. Clyde was assessed seven concurrent two-year terms. Saddened by the sentence but relieved by its relative leniency, Cumie returned to West Dallas. Bonnie stayed on, determined to stand by her man right up to the moment he was transferred ninety miles southeast from Waco to Huntsville in the state's infamous "One Way Wagon."

Cumie left Waco thinking she now had two sons in jail. She'd scarcely arrived home when the number was reduced by half. On March 8, Buck escaped from Huntsville. It wasn't hard. He'd been working as a trusty in the main prison's kitchen, where supervision was minimal. Buck and another prisoner jumped into a car belonging to a guard and drove back to Dallas. Cumie recalled that he came to the campground, walked up to the shack, "stuck his head in and laughed." He was still wearing his white prison overalls. He changed clothes, tracked down Blanche, and headed to Oklahoma to hide out with her.

Cumie was appalled—Buck's last letter from Huntsville, dated February 24, had assured her "the guards and the Captain down here treat me awfully good . . . so I see no reason why I should not get along." As she'd promised Buck, Cumie had been pleading with the governor's office for a pardon. But he'd gotten impatient and decided not to wait. Henry shook his head at his son's impulsiveness and declared, "That's Buck."

Back in Waco, Clyde had no idea of his brother's escape. He was preoccupied with his own situation. A two-year sentence sounded easy to endure, but in practice it would be the opposite. Clyde hated relinquishing control under any circumstances, and now he faced twenty-four months of obeying orders nonstop. He'd eat, sleep, work, and even relieve himself only after someone else gave permission. As a first-time convict, he could hope for an easy assignment. In the main prison at Huntsville, known as "the Walls," prisoners usually worked indoors with little direct supervision. But surrounding the central facility were a series of work farms, where convicts who were judged to be escape risks or potentially violent provided slave labor cultivating crops, mostly cotton, in all kinds of weather. They labored under the direction of guards who could discipline their charges as frequently—and, often, as sadistically—as they liked. He might end up on one of those farms. The more Clyde thought about it, the more determined he became not to serve his time after all. Because of overcrowding, the state prison board had recently forbidden additional prisoners to be sent to Huntsville. Individual counties had been instructed to hold newly sentenced convicts in their own jails until room opened up. That might happen any day. Clyde had to break out of the McLennan County jail before the One Way Wagon arrived to cart him off. To make that escape, he'd need an accomplice on the outside. There was an obvious candidate.

On Tuesday, March 11, Bonnie made her usual morning visit to Clyde on the second floor of the county jail. She'd become a familiar figure there and thought the Waco jailors were nicer than the ones in Dallas and Denton. When she met with Clyde, he whispered details of a getaway plan. William Turner had lived with his parents in a house in East Waco. The parents were gone during the day. In the house, Turner had hidden a revolver. Clyde wanted Bonnie to go to the house, get the gun, and smuggle it back to him later in the evening. It had to be done that day—who knew when the One Way Wagon would begin making pickups again? Once Clyde had the gun and Bonnie was safely away, he'd break out, get clear, and come back for her as soon as he could.

It was a watershed moment for Bonnie. She'd been reveling in her new real-life role as a convicted criminal's supportive lover, but there was nothing illegal about that. She could walk away from Clyde Barrow anytime she liked, innocent of the slightest wrongdoing. Maybe times were tough back in Cement City and West Dallas, but there were still lots of other boys who wanted to be with her. If she did what Clyde wanted and was caught in the act, she might go to prison, too, a horrifying possibility. He was asking Bonnie to risk everything for him.

And that was so romantic. No movie heroine would turn down such a perfect opportunity to prove her love. If she wasn't caught, if Clyde got away, they would live an exciting life on the run where every day would be a new adventure. They might even assume false identities and settle down together somewhere far away from the Dallas slums. Without Clyde, Bonnie's future involved slinging hash and perhaps turning tricks until her looks were gone, something that happened to poor girls relatively early. Life on the run had to be better than that.

So Bonnie said she'd do it. For Clyde, it was proof she was completely loyal. He was the boss. She would do whatever he told her to do, and that was what he always wanted in any relationship. For Bonnie, it was the ultimate commitment she could make to Clyde. She was putting her life in his hands.

As Bonnie was leaving, Clyde passed her a note scratched out on rough tablet paper. It included a helpful map of the Turner house, with the hiding place of the revolver clearly noted. Underneath the chart, he had scribbled, "You are the sweetest baby in the world to me. I love you." Bonnie cherished those scrawled words. Four years later, Cumie Barrow found the note tucked carefully in the pocket of a purse Bonnie had left at the Barrows' shack.

Bonnie went to the Turners' house. As Clyde had promised, Turner's parents weren't home. She went inside and looked for the gun, but Clyde had gotten the map wrong and the weapon wasn't where she thought it would be. Nervously, she poked under bureaus and beds until she found it.

Then came the problem of how, exactly, she could smuggle it into the county jail. Her purse would be routinely searched. The revolver was too bulky to be stuck in her boot, and it was too heavy to conceal under a hat. She finally buckled an extra belt under her dress to hold the gun. Unless she was subjected to a thorough body search—and the county jailors hadn't subjected her to one on her previous visits—she could smuggle it in to Clyde. If the guards weren't watching closely, once they were together she could reach inside her dress, loosen the concealed belt, and pull out the gun. From there, she had no idea what would happen besides Clyde's instructions that she should leave quickly. Sometime after the escape he would find a way to come back for her.

When she returned to the jail that evening, Bonnie had a scary moment when the guard on duty didn't want to let her back in. She'd already had her daily visit, he said, so she should come back tomorrow. But Bonnie persuaded him, and it was easy after that. There was very little supervision—having been assessed a relatively light sentence for minor crimes, Clyde wasn't considered much of a flight risk. Bonnie passed him the gun and hurried back to her cousin's house to wait, though she wasn't sure for what.

Clyde and William Turner involved a third prisoner in their plan. Emery Abernathy was being held in the county jail on charges of burglary and bank robbery. The trio were locked in adjacent second-floor cells. About 7:30 in the evening, assistant county jailor Irving Stanford and turnkey Huse Jones were on duty. Turner called down that he was sick. Stanford went to check. Turner said he was nauseated, and asked for some milk to settle his stomach. It wasn't an unusual request. The guards and prisoners at the jail were on reasonably good terms. Bringing Turner some milk was less trouble and a lot more pleasant than mopping up vomit. When Stanford returned with a small bottle and opened Turner's cell door to hand it to him, Abernathy brandished the gun and ordered the jailor to hand over his keys. They undoubtedly warned Stanford that if he made a sound before they were out of the building they'd come back upstairs and kill him. Then they locked the jailor in one of the cells and hurried down the staircase. Jones was doing paperwork at his desk, and they took him by surprise. Barrow, Turner, and Abernathy again chose not to use their gun. Instead of shooting Jones, they told him to stay silently at his desk for five minutes, and disappeared through the jail door that opened onto Waco's adjacent Sixth Street.

The moment they were gone, Jones jumped up and ran after them. They hadn't been smart enough to take his sidearm, and when Jones spotted the trio running down the street he drew his pistol and began shooting at them. Downtown Waco at night was not jammed with pedestrians. The fugitives were pulling away from their pursuer, and all Jones's shots missed. Abernathy turned and snapped off a shot of his own despite being well out of range. Someone heard Abernathy's shot and telephoned the police. Within minutes, they were on the scene, but the escapees weren't.

Clyde's auto-stealing skills worked to their advantage. Within blocks of the jail, he hot-wired a car and the three hopped in. They drove a short distance to the north end of town and swapped the first stolen vehicle for a better one. The choice of the second car was fortuitous. It had been loaned to Dr. William Souther by a friend, and when Souther went outside about 8 P.M. and found it missing, he assumed the friend must have come by and picked it up. Accordingly, Waco police thought the fugitives were still driving the first car, and their initial emergency bulletins to authorities in the counties surrounding Waco gave the wrong information. It was eight the next morning before Souther finally contacted the Waco cops.

Clyde, Turner, and Abernathy used that twelve-hour head start to drive west. It appears their only initial plan was to get as far away from Waco as they could. As they traveled, they kept switching cars. Vehicles presumably stolen by them were reported all the next day in a westbound pattern—Lampasas, Goldthwaite, Brownwood.

Clyde was too busy running to send any word to Bonnie. She fretted at her cousin's house from Tuesday night until Thursday morning, when the *Waco Times-Herald* plastered its front page with articles, photos, and editorials about the jail break. By then the police had connected enough dots for the main headline to read, "Trio Leaves Trail of Stolen Cars," with sub-headlines noting the fugitives were heading west. The newspaper made it clear that the breakout hadn't been engineered by criminal masterminds. Because of his youth, Clyde in particular was singled out for ridicule. An editorial sneered, "Schoolboy Barrow, Willie Turner and Emery Abernathy are at large this morning. But they'll be back. They haven't the brains to stay free. It's the dumbbell in them that brings them back."

Bonnie may have been offended on her boyfriend's behalf, but her reaction to the stories was mostly relief. The paper mentioned that the fugitives had somehow gotten a gun smuggled into their cells, but there was nothing that even remotely linked Clyde's female visitor to it. She had, apparently, pulled it off, and now Clyde was going to promptly send for her or even come back to fetch her. Then their exciting new lives would begin.

Except Clyde didn't come that day, and there was no word from him. On Wednesday night Bonnie decided to wait for Clyde back in Dallas. She and her Waco cousin had become frightened when two strange men came up the sidewalk and pounded on the front door. Bonnie thought it was the police coming to arrest her after all. The young women huddled in a back room and didn't answer the door. The men finally went away. Later, Bonnie wondered if they might have been sent by Clyde to bring her to him. But for the moment she was convinced that the cops were watching her every move and might be planning to pick her up. So at four on Thursday morning, fearful of showing her face on the bus or train, she had her cousin drop her off by the highway. Bonnie hitchhiked back home.

When she got there, Bonnie didn't tell Emma about the jailbreak. She ran out the next morning to get the early editions of the Dallas newspapers just in case there was a story about Clyde. As another day passed with no word from him, Bonnie's jumpiness evolved into near-hysteria. Maybe Clyde wasn't ever going to come back for her. Had she been cruelly used and discarded? Finally, four or five days after the breakout, a telegram arrived from Nokomis, Illinois. Clyde's message was brief. He was all right. He'd be in touch. Bonnie was thrilled. Then the bad news came.

From West Texas, Clyde, Turner, and Abernathy had driven north out of the state, stealing cars as they went. It was a sensible ploy. By the time local police had bulletins out about one missing automobile, the fugitives had swapped it for another. They ended up in the southwest corner of Ohio, just above Cincinnati and south of Dayton in the small village of Middletown. They needed money, and the local train depot seemed like a good target. On the afternoon of March 17, Clyde wandered into the station and asked for a train schedule. He was new to this sort of banditry, and his clumsy attempts to case the joint caught the attention of a ticket agent, who took down the license number of the latest car the trio was using. It didn't allay the agent's suspicions when they parked nearby for the rest of the afternoon.

After dark, Clyde and his partners first broke into a dry cleaner's and then into the office of the Baltimore & Ohio Railroad at the depot. Their take was around $60. Anxious to get out of town, they followed unpaved roads into the countryside. They got lost and soon had no idea where they were and which direction to drive in. They gave up for the night and slept in the car.

The next morning the robberies were reported and the station agent gave the license number of the suspicious vehicle to the police. Harry Richardson and George Woody, two members of the Middletown force, had just recorded the plate when they saw a car with that license coming past the depot. It was the Texas fugitives, who'd become completely turned around and inadvertently returned to the scene of the crime. The cops jumped in their patrol car and pursued them. Woody started shooting, and the three escapees abandoned their vehicle to flee on foot. Richardson cornered Turner in an alley and arrested him. Abernathy was picked up an hour later.

Clyde almost got away. As he had in Denton, he hid under a house for hours. In the early afternoon he emerged and stole another car. Middletown patrolman Tom Carmody spotted him and gave chase. Clyde was winning his desperate race when he turned down a dead-end street. He left the car and started running, but was hemmed in. Just before Carmody took him into custody, Clyde pitched the gun from Waco into a nearby canal.

Clyde told the Middletown police his name was Robert Thomas. He claimed he was seventeen and from Indianapolis. He then launched into a preemptive confession to petty crimes around Cincinnati, obviously hoping to be slapped on the wrist as a youthful offender and not held until word could reach Middletown from Waco about the three McLennan County fugitives. Unfortunately for Clyde, Turner and Abernathy had already admitted they were escaped Texas felons—in an effort to protect Clyde, they claimed he was a hitchhiker they'd recently picked up—and the Middletown cops were in the process of contacting the McLennan County sheriff's office. A wire soon arrived from Waco with descriptions of all three escapees, and Clyde was sunk.

On Friday, March 21, McLennan County sheriff Leslie Stegall arrived in Middletown to take custody of the three escaped prisoners. The *Waco Times-Herald* was jubilant. "Baby Thugs Captured" was the banner headline, and an accompanying editorial noted that the "baby dumbbells" had proven they deserved the derogatory nickname. Getting turned around and driving right past the very cops who were looking for them? How stupid could crooks be? Clyde, at least, got a little grudging praise. A sub-headline noted, "Barrow, the Youngest of the Trio, Makes Most Spectacular Attempt to Escape Capture." A Waco reporter even made the trip up to West Dallas to interview Cumie. Marie, eavesdropping, recalled that her mother "had quite a bit to say on the matter." Cumie blamed Clyde's old criminal running buddy Frank Clause for everything—she swore his bad example had lured her innocent young son into sin. Cumie added that she was afraid the escape would prejudice the Waco court against Clyde and result in a longer sentence.

When Clyde, Turner, and Abernathy arrived back in Waco, they were marched in chains from the train station to the county jail. The three escapees were confined to new maximum security cells on the third floor. Clyde wouldn't be able to persuade Bonnie to help him in another escape attempt.

Even if jailhouse security hadn't been tightened, Bonnie wouldn't have been there to try again. After learning about Clyde's recapture from the Dallas papers, Bonnie decided not to travel south to Waco. She'd found another job as a waitress and, besides, the whole jailbreak experience had upset her. Some degree of disillusionment was inevitable. Bonnie had imagined herself as the glamorous companion of a dashing young fugitive. Instead, she was the humiliated girlfriend of a bumbling baby dumbbell. She didn't break up with Clyde, but she didn't rush to be at his side before his new trial, either.

Criticism in the local paper had left Judge Richard Munroe wrathful when Clyde and Turner appeared before him for the second time. Abernathy, who had yet to stand trial, was with them. The *Times-Herald* noted that Munroe had become "hard-boiled," and in the process of sentencing Clyde to serve his full fourteen years in prison, and Turner to serve forty, the judge tongue-lashed the trio.

"I think it would be a good thing to save you boys from the [electric] chair, eventually, to send you up for long terms," Munroe lectured them. "You are liable to go around here shooting a peace officer—if you can shoot straight. You keep breaking into houses, and some of these days you're going to either get shot or shoot somebody else. With the records you've got, you'd probably get the chair when you were tried."

Turner was gone the next day, shipped off to Kansas to serve a three-year term for robbery there before being returned to Texas to begin his forty-year sentence in that state. Clyde stayed in the county jail until the moratorium on sending new prisoners to Huntsville was lifted several weeks after his sentencing.

On the morning of April 21 the One Way Wagon showed up in Waco to transport Clyde to the state prison. Prison records indicate that when he arrived and was processed in Huntsville, his height was five feet, five and one-half inches, and he weighed 127 pounds. Clyde gave his date of birth as March 24, 1912, making him eighteen rather than twenty. It was a calculated lie. The younger he claimed to be, the more likely prison officials might be to grant him some kind of easy work assignment. Clyde listed his middle name as "Champion" rather than "Chestnut"—even on such a nerve-wracking occasion, his sense of humor remained intact—and he claimed that Bonnie Parker was his wife. That would allow him to exchange mail with her. Prisoners could only communicate through letters with immediate family members. Despite her mother's ongoing pressure to dump Clyde for someone else, Bonnie was still being faithful. She had finally gone to Waco to see him shortly before he was taken away to state prison. They apparently argued during the visit, because on April 19 Clyde sent her a letter apologizing for being jealous, claiming he couldn't help it. "Just be a good little girl and always love me," he pleaded.

Clyde was initially an occasional boarder in Huntsville rather than a full-time inmate. During the rest of the spring and all of the summer of 1930 he was shipped back and forth across the state to face various charges. One, in Houston, was for the July 1929 murder of a twenty-year-old named Buster Gouge. Frank Clause was also suspected in the killing. The charge was specious—until he used William Turner's revolver in his Waco jailbreak, Clyde never committed an armed criminal act. Clyde was quickly returned to Huntsville after the Houston grand jury found insufficient evidence against him. But the hearing did inspire future generations of Houston historians to erroneously claim that Clyde Barrow began his infamous killing spree in their hometown.

In the late summer of 1930, Clyde was sent back to Waco to face additional robbery charges. None stuck, but while he was back in the McLennan County jail he learned what his work assignment in state prison would be.

In Huntsville, prisoners were officially segregated only by race. A petty thief could be thrown into a work detail with a pack of convicted killers. But usually common sense prevailed. Youthful, first-time offenders were often kept inside the Walls, the main prison unit. Work there usually trained prisoners in job skills like printing or animal husbandry that might lead to post-incarceration employment. Repeat offenders mostly drew assignments to one of the several working farms located in or around Huntsville. The most callous, dangerous cons found themselves on the prison's Eastham cotton farm thirty-five miles northeast of the main buildings. Here, on 13,000 acres of swampy bottomland adjacent to the Trinity River, they performed backbreaking labor under the supervision of guards hired for their ability to maintain order at any cost.

Short, scrawny Clyde Barrow had just turned twenty. His Middletown misadventures were evidence that he was anything but a cool, calculating criminal. Before his conviction, Clyde had been a commendable employee for several Dallas companies. He was an obvious candidate for a job inside the Walls where he could put his previously demonstrated work skills to good use, serving his time productively and in relative safety.

But some anonymous prison official decided otherwise. It was almost certainly a capricious decision. Despite the press he'd received in Waco as one of the baby dumbbells, Clyde hadn't built up any sort of adversarial reputation with lawmen on a state level. Over the past several years, crop production on the prison farms had taken a nosedive. Possibly more new inmates than usual were being assigned to work on them as a result.

No matter why it happened, around the middle of September 1930, Clyde got news that would have terrified even the most hardened Texas con. He was assigned to Eastham Prison Farm, the filthiest hellhole in the entire corrupt Texas criminal justice system.

CHAPTER 6

The Bloody 'Ham

On the night of September 17, 1930, Bud Russell parked the One Way Wagon outside the McLennan County jail. In Texas, the vehicle and its driver were equally notorious. Russell was a tall, taciturn man who made his living transporting prisoners from rural and city lockups to state prison facilities. Escape from his custody was considered practically impossible. Any prisoner who talked back, let alone seemed to be considering a run for it, was calmly informed by Russell that he would be wrong to "think you're tougher than me." The words were uttered with such calm certainty that few dared cross him. The .44 on Russell's hip and his double-barreled shotgun reinforced the message. But his reputation among convicts was notable for fairness as well as fearsomeness. Everyone who cooperated with him—and almost all the prisoners being transported did—was treated with stern courtesy. In Russell's thirty years of service to Texas, he drove an estimated 3.9 million miles through forty-five states and Mexico and Canada, transporting 115,000 convicts. Only one escaped.

The One Way Wagon was as intimidating as the man who drove it. Essentially, it was a massive cage mounted on the long bed of a truck.

The cage was constructed of black boiler plate and steel mesh. Prisoners loaded in it were chained to each other by the neck. There was just enough length in the chain between them to allow everyone to sit down along two hard, flat benches. In Waco the next morning, there was an audience as the prisoners to be transported were brought under guard from the county jail. Wherever Russell made his jail pickups, townspeople would gather around to enjoy the spectacle. Convicts were brought out, collars and chains were adjusted around their necks, they were shackled together, and then, caterpillar-like, they climbed up into the cage. It made for some free entertainment.

Russell had stopped the day before in Dallas, so there were already several convicts in his charge when he began loading the Waco prisoners on the morning of the 18th. Clyde Barrow didn't give him any trouble. Even if he had planned to, there was no opportunity. Russell knew his business. Clyde was efficiently shackled by the neck and loaded onboard. The cage was padlocked and Russell threw the truck into gear. Waco spectators didn't see anything out of the ordinary that morning.

As soon as the One Way Wagon started rolling southeast toward Huntsville, Clyde began asking if anyone had been on the Eastham farm. Nineteen-year-old Ralph Fults, sitting on the bench directly across from Clyde, said he had. In fact, he'd escaped from there six months earlier. He'd just been recaptured, and was on his way back to Eastham. Clyde wanted details about their mutual destination, and couldn't have liked what Fults told him. The Eastham guards, Fults said, killed their charges for two reasons—not working, and running. Unsuccessful first escapes only merited beatings, but second failed attempts earned a bullet to the back of the head. Fults knew an unpleasant welcome back to prison would be waiting for him, painful but hopefully not lethal.

"They can do any damned thing they want to," Fults told his anxious new acquaintance, adding that there was an Eastham farm graveyard "full of guys who thought otherwise." Fults's first impression of Clyde wasn't positive. He wondered how long the skinny little kid could survive at Eastham. Even the toughest cons there were in constant fear for their lives.

That was, in fact, the intention. The philosophy of the Texas prison system in 1930 was not based on the concept of rehabilitation. The value of an individual inmate's life was negligible. If conditions were horrible enough, any scarred, emaciated inmate who survived his sentence would provide a useful object lesson to potential lawbreakers he met after his release.

For decades there had been sporadic public outcry and legislative investigations concerning inhumane prison conditions. Just nine months before Clyde Barrow was hauled off to Eastham, Texas governor Dan Moody and a group of elected state officials toured the main Huntsville prison and most of the adjacent work farms. Their primary concern was overcrowding—at just over five thousand prisoners, the system had about one-third more inmates than it was designed to handle. Governor Moody hoped additional furloughs and paroles might alleviate some of the problem. But there were also criticisms of overcrowded hospital units, merciless punishments bordering on torture, inadequate food, and, ominously, growing concern that prisoners might have too much idle time in which to concoct escape plans or other mischief. Additionally, the prison system farm units, like farms everywhere in Texas, had begun operating at deficits. The state prison board was instructed to make immediate changes.

In March 1930, board member Lee Simmons agreed to become general manager of the prison system. His concept of reform involved squelching the complaints of the reformers, particularly in the area he referred to as "discipline." Simmons proclaimed himself a proud proponent of "corporal punishment in the home, in the schoolroom, in the reformatory, in the penitentiary," adding, "in most cases, firm discipline, fair treatment and plenty of work to keep everybody busy will keep the riotously inclined out of mischief." He especially endorsed frequent use of "the bat," a leather strap anywhere from eighteen inches to three feet long and three to five inches wide with a long handle. Greased for maximum velocity and striking power, it would be used to lacerate the bare back, buttocks, and thighs of recalcitrant prisoners spread-eagled face down on the ground. Fellow inmates would be assigned to hold the victim's arms and legs; other convicts would be ordered to form a circle and watch. Every blow from the three-ply leather bat tore skin, ripped into muscle, and drew copious amounts of blood. Sometimes the whippings were interrupted so sand could be poured into the victim's open wounds. The limit was twenty lashes, but inmates swore the guards administering the beatings never bothered to count and routinely went far beyond the proscribed number. The prisoner being beaten almost invariably screamed, lost control of his bowels and bladder, and finally passed out. Most inmates witnessing the beatings, Simmons believed, would remember them and comply with any orders rather than suffer one themselves. After the beatings, convict witnesses were required to line up and closely inspect the bloody bat as an added means of intimidation. There were even claims from some surviving inmates that they were ordered to lick it.

When the One Way Wagon arrived at the main prison facility in Huntsville, Clyde and Fults spent a few days locked up there before being sent over to Eastham. In the interim, Simmons welcomed Fults back by ordering him to "ride the barrel," another form of punishment popular among the guards. After being handcuffed, Fults was made to straddle a pickle barrel. This was, as designed, impossible to do for very long. Fults's legs soon went numb, and attempts to shift his weight from one foot to another resulted in a fall off the barrel. He was hauled up by the guards and stood back up on the barrel. The punishment continued all of one night and well into the next day. Simmons believed any prisoner escapes reflected badly upon him, and punished recaptured cons accordingly.

From there, Fults and Clyde were transported to Eastham Prison Farm about thirty-five miles away. They were assigned to Camp 2, which differed from Camp 1 only in that it was more lightly wooded, offering additional room for fields of cotton and corn. Together, the two camps usually had between four and five hundred convicts available to work the land. Its operation was a direct legacy of the antiquated Texas "convict lease" system. An 1871 law passed by the state legislature decreed that any convicted felon was considered "a slave of the state," human property to be disposed of as prison administrators deemed appropriate. That resulted in prisoners being leased to railroads, sawmills, coal mines, and wealthy farmers, who gained workers for a dollar a day each without any inconvenient rules about how to feed, shelter, and punish them. Families of prisoners and social reformers gradually raised a storm of protest, and in 1912 all convict leases were terminated. But by then, the prison system had acquired over seventy thousand acres of farmland, and the prisoners were simply transferred over to perform the same slave labor, under the same cruel circumstances, for the state.

Eastham Prison Farm was named for the family that originally owned the property. The sumpy river bottomland was perfect for raising cotton and corn. The property was isolated enough to make it difficult for prisoners to escape on foot. There was a river to cross, and the farm bloodhounds were renowned for their relentless tracking ability. Those who did run were almost inevitably caught and sent back. In 1929, the year before Clyde arrived, there had been 302 escape attempts from Eastham and the other prison system facilities. Two hundred and ninety-eight of the escapees, including Fults, were immediately or eventually recaptured.

At Eastham, the guard-to-prisoner ratio was one to eight. The farm's manager, B. B. Monzingo, had been fired for mistreatment of inmates by the pre-Simmons administration. Simmons, though, hired him back and placed him in charge of Eastham, where checks and balances on treatment of prisoners were nonexistent.

Clyde learned this as soon as he arrived on the farm. Monzingo walked up to the new batch of inmates, picked out one at random, and smashed him in the face with a stick. As his victim fell to the ground, the manager ordered the rest of the startled arrivals to run, not walk, out to the fields and start working. All inmates were required to run to and from their work stations each day. Some of the fields were as much as two miles away, but distance didn't matter. Obeying orders to run did. The farm's heavily armed guards were mounted. They had no trouble keeping up, and were quick to strike stragglers.

As Clyde and Fults sprinted ahead of the guards, Clyde wanted to know why Monzingo had administered the beating. Fults told him it was psychological, a way to cow new prisoners into complete submission. It didn't work on Clyde. He muttered to Fults that nobody better try that crap on him.

Field work at Eastham was exhausting. The crops had to be constantly weeded and picked. Workdays lasted ten hours. On Saturdays, prisoners could knock off a half-hour early to bathe. Sundays were supposedly days of rest, but during harvest months they were spent in the fields. Fults and Clyde found themselves assigned to woodpile duty. They spent their workdays swinging double-bladed axes under the supervision of guards with shotguns. Before each day's near-endless labor exhausted them completely, they talked as they chopped, and learned more about each other. Both came from large, close families. They had mutual admiration for Jesse James and Billy the Kid. Clyde told Fults about a girl he loved named Bonnie.

Mealtimes were a disappointment to Clyde. The noon break out in the fields lasted only five or ten minutes, just enough to gulp down a crust of dry corn bread and a cup of water. Food on the prison farms was notoriously bad. Breads and cereals made from the same dried corn fed to farm livestock were common fare. Sometimes there would be vegetables—peas, turnip greens, or potatoes. Any scant helping of meat for supper was boiled into a leathery state. Near-raw, rancid bacon was frequently on the menu. There were no overweight convicts on Eastham Prison Farm.

Nor were many inmates well rested. At night they were marched back to a concrete dormitory; there were small administrative offices in the front, along with a dining area and kitchen. The dormitory itself was blocked off by a line of steel bars sunk into the concrete floor. Behind the bars, bunk beds were stacked close together. Farther to the back were the toilets and showers, which were not cleaned on any regular basis. While the inmates shouldered each other for the smallest bit of space, the guards relaxed upstairs in larger second-story rooms. The two floors were connected by a spiral staircase. If there was a disturbance downstairs, the off-duty guards descended with rifles in hand. If shouted warnings failed to be effective, they started shooting through the bars, high over the prisoners' heads at first, then progressively lower until the commotion stopped. The far walls inside the cage were pocked with bullet holes.

The guards rarely had to step in. Every prison dormitory area was supervised by a team of building tenders, usually the biggest and strongest convicts in the facility who were most feared by the other inmates. Building tenders received a few special privileges, including extra rations and the right to carry clubs or even knives, but the real attraction of the job was being able to manhandle anyone they wanted. What they did to keep order in their barred fiefdoms was of little interest to the guards, farm managers, and prison administrators.

On Clyde's first night in the Camp 2 dorm, he listened while other cons whispered to Fults that he had more punishment coming for his escape. The guards had drawn straws, Fults was told, with the winners getting the privilege of beating him up. The next morning, a half-dozen of them clubbed Fults with gun barrels and kicked him with their sharp-toed boots. Throughout the assault, Clyde stood glaring at his friend's assailants, and made a point of helping Fults to his feet after the guards had enough of their bloody fun. Fults was impressed. By openly sticking with him, Clyde had caught the guards' attention—one of them asked if he wanted any of it, too. But loyalty clearly meant more to the kid than personal safety. Clyde not only tended to Fults's bruises, he immediately began planning revenge. Someday he and Fults would be released from prison, he swore, and after that they would put together a gang, raid the farm, and free all the convicts there. Fults found himself caught up in Clyde's enthusiasm. At the very least, it gave them something to occupy their minds while they slaved away on the woodpile.

But Fults soon began to wonder if Clyde would even live to leave Eastham. Ten hours a day of hard labor clearly pushed him to his physical limits. Constant harassment and inadequate nourishment drained even the toughest convicts on the farm, and short, scrawny Clyde wasn't very strong to begin with. Worse, in Fults's opinion, was Clyde's attitude toward the guards and their harsh, condescending ways. Prisoners successfully served out their sentences on the farm by learning to quietly accept whatever poor treatment they received. The idea was to blend in, to be so passive that the guards and building tenders hardly noticed you. Clyde did the opposite. He'd scowl when given orders, and talk back when silence was by far the more practical response. Beatings resulted. Nell Barrow recalled that on one visit to see her brother, both Clyde's eyes were blackened. Everything about prison galled him. Clyde, who craved control, was under the complete domination of others.

That even extended to his friendship with Fults. Simmons and Monzingo feared that Fults would attempt another escape, and had the guards constantly monitor him. Other inmates understood it was dangerous to be seen socializing with Fults. Anyone talking to him even briefly was suspected of planning a breakout. Within days of his return to Eastham, fellow convicts avoided Fults whenever possible. Only Clyde was constantly at his side. Simmons and Monzingo assumed the duo were plotting together. Late in 1930 when a Camp 2 inmate suspected of being an informer suffered a near-fatal accident—a freshly chopped tree fell on him—they were certain Clyde and Fults had cut it down with just that intent. And, years later, Fults admitted that they had.

A week after the informer was injured, guards came up to where Fults and Clyde were working on the woodpile and led Clyde away. When Fults returned to the Camp 2 dormitory that night, all Clyde's possessions were gone from beside his bunk. Anxious to separate Fults from his only remaining friend among the inmates, Simmons and Monzingo had transferred Clyde to Camp 1. A new enemy was waiting for him there.

Ed Crowder was a monster, a hulking brute who was even more likely than other Eastham building tenders to enforce his will with his fists. Crowder had been named a building tender for precisely that reason. His own prison record was far from exemplary. Sentenced in 1926 to fifteen years in prison for robbery and illegally transporting bootleg liquor with his brother Sid, Crowder escaped from the Walls a year later and was recaptured after just a few days of freedom. In 1929, he made another brief escape from one of Huntsville's less oppressive working farms. That got him assigned to Eastham's Camp 1, where among even the most hardened, violent criminals in the entire state prison system he stood out as especially fearsome. That led to his appointment as a building tender. Standing over six feet tall and weighing two hundred pounds, he was physically imposing, and so long as the inmates under his nightly supervision didn't cause trouble in the dormitory, the Camp 1 guards didn't care about Crowder's penchant for preying on the smallest and weakest of his charges.

In late 1930, Crowder was twenty-nine. His escape attempts had expanded his original sentence to ninety-nine years, and even in the current overcrowded conditions there wasn't going to be any furlough or parole for him. He was on Eastham Prison Farm for life, so he had no incentive to rein in his brutal appetites. When skinny little Clyde Barrow was placed in his section of the dorm, Crowder pounced.

Then as now, sodomy was not uncommon among prisoners. Huntsville records show a few inmates were occasionally punished for homosexual acts, but for the most part it was accepted. Those who did it might be ridiculed by other prisoners—there was complete lack of privacy on the prison farms. Everyone knew what everyone else was doing, and with whom. Gossip about couplings offered some diversion for work-weary farm inmates. But those relationships were by mutual consent. When Ed Crowder got his huge hands on Clyde Barrow, Clyde didn't consent to anything. It didn't matter to Crowder. He terrorized Clyde, frequently beating him into submission and then raping him, certainly in the hearing and probably in view of the other prisoners in the Camp 1 dorm. If Clyde screamed or cried out for help, no one responded. The guards couldn't be bothered, and the rest of the inmates were undoubtedly glad Crowder was raping Clyde instead of them.

The pain must have been awful for Clyde, but the humiliation was worse. Proud Clyde Barrow, the cocky clotheshorse from West Dallas who'd stolen cars and robbed safes at will, the happy highwayman who laughed in the faces of "the laws" when they tried to catch him, the smooth-talking Romeo who'd wooed and won a pocket-sized blond Juliet named Bonnie Parker, was reduced to being Ed Crowder's prison bitch. Other Camp 1 prisoners, desperately needing someone to feel superior to, made certain he heard whispers about how he was probably enjoying it. Then there was Crowder himself, violating his victim at will and gloating about it.

This was the ultimate degradation, and it went on for almost a full year. Clyde couldn't stand it. It wasn't his nature to meekly submit. Aubrey Scalley, another building tender in the Camp 1 dormitory, hated Crowder almost as much as Clyde did. The reason for the Scalley-Crowder feud is unknown, but over time Scalley encouraged Clyde when the twenty-year-old muttered promises to murder Crowder. Scalley was serving a life term as a habitual criminal and promised Clyde that if he killed Crowder, Scalley would claim responsibility. But the risk would be entirely Clyde's. If he failed to finish off his rapist, Crowder would undoubtedly tear him apart. Scalley wouldn't interfere on Clyde's behalf if that happened.

But Clyde didn't intend to fail. He had no compunction about killing Crowder. All alone, with the odds terribly against him, he put together a rudimentary but lethal plan. On October 29, 1931, he concealed a length of lead pipe in his pants leg as he came in from the fields. That night in the dormitory, after the other prisoners had gone to their bunks, Clyde walked to the toilet and shower area in the back of the room. Crowder, seizing the apparently easy opportunity, followed. When his rapist was within reach, Clyde brought the pipe down on Crowder's head in a savage blow, fracturing his skull and killing him. Scalley had been lurking nearby. He rushed up and, after giving himself a superficial cut on the ribs, began stabbing a homemade shiv into Crowder's corpse. The guards heard shouting and rushed into the dormitory cage. It seemed clear that Ed Crowder had lost a knife fight to Aubrey Scalley. Scalley confessed to the killing. The subsequent investigation was cursory. Scalley's only weapon was the shiv, and no one seemed to wonder if another convict might have been involved even when Crowder's death certificate, signed by Monzingo and the prison doctor, listed his cause of death as "knife wounds and fracture of the skull." If Scalley wanted to take full responsibility for the killing, that just made everybody's job simpler.

On November 20, a grand jury no-billed Scalley for Crowder's murder, ruling that he must have acted in self-defense. Crowder's reputation had worked against him. He was buried and forgotten. Clyde never expressed remorse for the murder. He had proven for the first time that he would kill without hesitation if he felt cornered.

Even with Crowder dead, Clyde's troubles weren't over. Though Cumie was continuing to petition the governor for a parole or pardon, Clyde worried that he'd have to serve his entire fourteen-year sentence. The prospect of suffering on the prison farm that long was daunting enough, but Clyde had to deal with another concern. He wasn't going to have a girl waiting for him when he finally got out.

During the last few months of 1930, Bonnie's letters to Clyde arrived less frequently until finally around Thanksgiving they nearly stopped altogether. Possibly she'd heard rumors in West Dallas that he'd said something uncomplimentary about her. A letter dated December 11, 1930, from Clyde to Bonnie mentioned that "you know I didn't say anything like that about my little blue-eyed girl." He was writing in response to the first letter he'd received from Bonnie in weeks, and Clyde admitted "it really gave me a great surprise to hear from you." When Bonnie surprised him further by writing again, Clyde thanked her in a December 21 missive for the "most sweet and welcome letter." He promised to ask his brother L.C. to bring her down for a visit, and swore that "some day I will be out there with you and then we can be happy again."

But there were no visits, or any more letters, from Bonnie. "Some day" wasn't good enough. She had just turned twenty. It had been four years since she married Roy Thornton, and almost a year since she became the girlfriend of Clyde Barrow. Those two romances hadn't turned out well for her. There was nothing glamorous or exciting about being the estranged wife of one convict and the lonely girlfriend of another. Just as she'd finally cut her losses with Roy, it seemed time to do the same with Clyde. Bonnie was bored with her nunlike existence. Other girls had boyfriends to take them out for some fun. Not unreasonably, she began dating someone new.

Bonnie's mother, Emma, later wrote, "I was more relieved than I would have admitted to anyone" when her daughter stopped talking about Clyde Barrow all the time. She hoped Bonnie's new boyfriend, whose name has been lost to history, would be a better influence than Clyde Barrow and Roy Thornton.

Clyde knew what no more letters from Bonnie meant. He didn't intend to give up his girl without a fight. If Bonnie wouldn't correspond with him anymore, he'd have to wait until he got out of prison to win her back. It might happen soon. Cumie was continuing to inveigle the governor's office into granting a pardon. Meanwhile, a major change in his family's circumstances gave Clyde an idea about what he might eventually do for a living after his release.

In 1931, Jack, Artie, and Nell Barrow helped their father, Henry, acquire two small adjacent lots along Eagle Ford Road in West Dallas. The lots were less than half a mile from the campground and the railroad track. Though Eagle Ford Road was the main West Dallas thoroughfare, it was still hard-packed dirt and pebbles rather than asphalt. Henry moved the house he'd built on the campground to the new property. It was so small it could be loaded onto a wagon bed and hauled there. Henry made an agreement with an oil company and converted the shack into a Star service station with two gas pumps out in front. He built an extra "oil room" onto the shack to use as a business office and storage space. The Barrows' living conditions remained primitive. During winter, icy winds whipped right through the thin walls. They had no running water. There was just one bedroom. Henry and Cumie slept in it. L.C. and Marie had pallets in the other small front room that served as a living room during the day. Henry built on another small enclosed area that Cumie used as a kitchen, cooking on her old wood-burning stove. The family's greatest new luxury was a private outhouse in the back. Marie bragged to friends that it was a two-holer.

Gas sales—the premium Star brand was twelve cents a gallon—didn't bring in enough income to support the family. Henry had anticipated that. The station was really intended to serve as a general trading post. Henry dug a well on the property, and sold water to his West Dallas neighbors. He charged a quarter per barrel. The Barrows later put in a telephone and charged for its use. Money was not part of many transactions. A phone call or a gallon of water might be swapped for a secondhand pair of pants for L.C., or some lightly used shoes for Marie.

Bootleg hooch was another product for sale at the Barrow service station. Prohibition was in full force, and West Dallas residents were thirsty. Henry quietly brewed beer and white lightning in his office/storage room. L.C. manned the moonshine stand. Word got around, and L.C. never lacked customers. Alcohol proved to be a more sought-after trade item than water or phone use. Sometimes, Henry could talk a really desperate drinker into exchanging a pig for a few jars of pick-me-up. Then the Barrows would slaughter the hog and trade some of the pork for other things they needed. Cumie certainly knew what her husband was up to, but times were hard and the kids had to be fed and clothed.

The only automobile service Henry was set up to provide was selling gas. Down on Eastham Prison Farm, Clyde thought he might persuade his father to expand the business. "I sure wish I was there to help you," he wrote to Cumie on December 3, 1931. "After you get everything going ok, Papa should build him a little place and handle used auto parts. You can buy them for a song." Like his father and brothers, Clyde had a knack for auto repair. It seemed like a decent way to make a living, and if he worked for his father he would finally be free of despotic bosses and prison guards.

In the same letter, Clyde asked if his family had "heard anything from Blanche or not?" He was really asking for news of Buck. After fleeing to Oklahoma with her fugitive boyfriend, Blanche had divorced her first husband and married Buck in July of 1931. But being on the lam was not to Blanche's liking. She pleaded with Buck to turn himself in and complete his four-year sentence so they could lead open, law-abiding lives. Cumie agreed. Soon Buck was being constantly badgered by both his wife and his mother. After months of hectoring, he finally agreed to give himself up, so long as he didn't have to do it before Christmas, which he wanted to spend with his family.

On December 27, 1931, the Huntsville warden was shocked when Buck Barrow drove up to the main building and announced he was back after twenty-one months on the run to complete his sentence. Cumie later claimed her son's voluntary return was unprecedented in Texas prison history. At the very least, it was rare. Buck did have a request—he wanted a safe assignment inside the Walls, not on a prison farm like his unfortunate brother Clyde. His legs, wounded in the 1929 Denton robbery, still bothered him. He didn't think he could physically hold up doing farm labor. Prison administrators were so impressed with his actions that Buck got the placement he suggested, and no additional time for the escape was added to his original sentence. Cumie grandly invited Blanche to live with her and Henry until Buck completed his prison term sometime in 1933.

The Barrow brothers didn't see each other after Buck arrived back in Huntsville. Clyde was still isolated with the most hardened cons on Eastham farm. In the two months since he'd killed Ed Crowder, Clyde wore down even more from endless field work. He still faced nearly twelve more years of the same unforgiving toil if Cumie couldn't get his sentence reduced. In January 1932, he decided he couldn't take any more of it. Clyde's appalling solution was common to Eastham inmates who wanted reassignment at any cost to less murderous jobs inside the main prison compound.

Eastham Prison Farm was nicknamed "The Bloody 'Ham" because of the high incidence of self-mutilation among its convict laborers. Barring parole, the best chance an Eastham inmate had of getting away from its deadly fields was to cut off his own toes, fingers, or even hands or feet. If the convict couldn't bring himself to perform the deed, he would ask a fellow prisoner to swing the hoe or axe. Amputations had to be complete. Cons with partially severed digits were bandaged and sent back to the fields as object lessons. Grossly mutilated prisoners were transferred to the prison hospital in the main Huntsville facility, and after healing were sometimes judged to be incapable of further field labor. These lucky amputees would be reassigned to jobs inside the Walls. That was Clyde's goal—to have easier work, and, as a bonus, to be reunited with Buck. He believed that if he didn't do something drastic, he very well might drop dead of exhaustion in the Camp 1 cotton fields.

Though prison general manager Lee Simmons swore convict self-mutilation was relatively rare—he told one newspaper that there had been no more than twenty cases in the entire Texas prison system during his first four years on the job—it was so common as to represent an ongoing epidemic. No specific records of convict self-maiming were kept, but Clyde's friend Ralph Fults said they witnessed fourteen separate incidents at Eastham farm in a single week.

It's not clear whether Clyde wielded the axe himself, but on January 27, 1932, he was admitted to the main Huntsville prison hospital after cutting off his entire left big toe and part of a second toe. The loss of the big toe affected Clyde's balance. He never walked normally again. He was that desperate to get away from Eastham.

Ironically, the painful ploy was unnecessary. Clyde's timing couldn't have been worse. On February 2, he was still learning to walk on what remained of his left foot when the news arrived. Thanks to Cumie's incessant pleading, Texas governor Ross Sterling had finally paroled him.

Clyde hobbled home on crutches. In slightly less than a year and a half on Eastham farm he'd been half-starved, beaten, and raped. He'd killed Ed Crowder, worked to the point of physical collapse, and cut off two of his own toes. He might be returning to the noxious West Dallas slums where an uncertain future awaited him, but the intent of the Texas prison system's brutal hospitality had, in Clyde's case, been fulfilled. The twenty-one-year-old told his family that prison had been "a burning hell." Clyde swore to them that he'd die before he let "the laws" send him back there again. There was no doubt that he meant it.

CHAPTER 7

Decision

During the seventeen months Clyde served on Eastham Prison Farm, Bonnie found a new job and a new boyfriend. There are no specifics about the employment or the romance. Apparently, there was nothing special enough about either to merit recording. So when Clyde limped up to her front door as soon as he got back home in early February 1932, Bonnie yelped "Darling!" and ran to him, even though her current beau was right there in the living room with her.

Without Clyde, Bonnie's existence had become humdrum. She had some low-paying job. She hadn't divorced Roy, so she couldn't remarry even if she wanted to, and, besides, her boyfriend of the moment was an ordinary guy who clearly wasn't fantasy material even in Bonnie's rich imagination. Far from fulfilling her ambition to be famous, she was depressingly ordinary. On her next birthday she would be twenty-two—her life was dwindling away in spirit-crushing tedium. And then, just like it might have happened in the movies, her tragically crippled former lover unexpectedly arrived to reclaim her. Clyde and Bonnie fell into a passionate embrace while her suddenly ex-boyfriend slunk out of the house.

Emma tried to talk her daughter out of rekindling the romance with Clyde, but Bonnie was having none of it. When her mother's carping made her uncomfortable, Bonnie began staying every possible minute with Clyde at the Barrow family's service station on Eagle Ford Road. Clyde spent his first week at home helping Henry with small chores. His real challenge was learning to walk without crutches. He eventually managed to move around reasonably well, though there continued to be a slight lurch in his step. Bonnie was constantly at his side, which didn't please Cumie. She wrote in her memoir that "Bonnie came here and you might say stayed here at the house until Clyde got off his crutches, then they started running around together." Clyde wanted badly to run around, to act carefree again. When his sisters offered to buy him a nice wardrobe as a welcome-home gift, he insisted that all his new shirts be made of silk. Nell Barrow told her brother that only bootleggers and gangsters wore silk shirts. That pleased Clyde rather than changing his mind. He got the silk shirts, and a pair of fancy dress gloves to wear with them.

Clyde did impress his family by offering to join and expand the Barrow business. As he'd suggested in his letter to Cumie from prison, he wanted to open an automotive parts and repair shop on the small lot the family owned adjacent to the service station. It was a sensible idea, but one that would require capital. Henry and Cumie didn't have money to spare for building materials and an initial inventory. Clyde had to go out and find a full-time job so he could save up his salary.

But he began job hunting at a time when the state and local economies were at their lowest point yet. Particularly in the South and Southwest, 1931 had been financially devastating. Cotton prices dropped to four cents a pound. The year's wheat crop set a record of 250 million bushels, but the twenty-five-cent sales price of each bushel was half of what it cost the farmer to grow it. Banks had no choice but to foreclose on farms, and then the government began its own stream of farm foreclosures for failure to pay taxes. An average of twenty thousand farms across America failed each month. Destitute families abandoned the country for cities that had no jobs or shelter to offer them. Like every major city in the region, Dallas was inundated with new, desperate residents. City leaders conferred, trying to find some solution, and in February 1932 made an announcement: All "negro unemployed" in Dallas were strongly advised to move back to the country, since their swelling numbers took up space in breadlines intended for white indigents. Negroes who did so would have plenty to eat, the "Committee for the Relief of Unemployment" promised, because farm surpluses meant "farmers have made their houses storehouses." Apparently, cotton and raw wheat made for satisfying meals. There was however no Negro exodus from Dallas, and breadlines there remained impossibly long. Then nature commenced its own ferocious attack on the city.

For more than a year, West Texas and parts of adjacent states had been raked by corrosive dust storms. These were the result of modern farming technology wreaking havoc on the natural order. The grassy plains several hundred miles to the south and west of Dallas were camouflage. The grasses sealed off grainy soil, and when farmers first brought plows, then tractors, to tear up the grass and clear land for crops, there was no longer a protective covering to hold the dust at bay. Within a few years, journalist Timothy Egan notes, "the tractors had done what no hailstorm, no blizzard, no tornado, no drought, no epic siege of frost, no prairie fire, nothing in the natural history of the southern plains had ever done. They had removed the native prairie grass . . . so completely that by the end of 1931 it was a different land—thirty-three million acres stripped bare in the southern plains."

The first resulting massive dust storm hammered southwest Kansas, Oklahoma, and the Texas Panhandle in September 1930. It was disastrous for people living in those regions, but far enough removed so Dallas residents could consider the storm a news item rather than a threat. But the storms kept coming, and gradually they advanced eastward. In late January 1932, about the same time Clyde cut off two of his toes, a ten-thousand-foot-high black cloud enveloped Amarillo and moved east. Witnesses described it as "a black blizzard . . . with an edge like steel wool." Almost immediately, there began to be days in Dallas and all of East Texas when the sky was dingy brown instead of blue. Until the Dust Bowl blew out its filthy heart some seven years later, it was impossible to draw a secure breath. The storms occasionally raged all the way to the East Coast. Even New York City residents endured several panic-stricken days of grit-filled lungs.

In West Dallas, the effects of the dust storms were especially dire. The slatted sides of the Barrow shack on Eagle Ford Road, unequal to holding out cold winter winds, yielded easily to suffocating dirt. During dust storms, government agencies counseled, wet sheets should be hung on windows to keep out as much dirt as possible. But Cumie would have had to wallpaper her entire shack with wet sheets, and she couldn't. The dirt whistled through loose seams, and Cumie's floors disappeared under inches of grime.

If it was bad sheltering from the storms inside, it was worse to be caught in them on the outside. The land around Dallas was mostly flat, so it was possible to see the storms coming from the west. But they hurtled in, sometimes arriving mere minutes after their first sightings, and Clyde's little sister, Marie, out riding L.C.'s bike or Bonnie walking home from work would sometimes be caught in them. Then came the sensation of being encased in a dirt coffin, with clots of dust clogging mouths and nostrils and other flying granules stinging any additional exposed skin. It was terrifying. Nature had become a murderous adversary. Gradually, because the storms just kept coming, people adjusted to the latest crisis. They didn't expect the storms to ever end. The black cloud assaults became one more thing to endure in already hard lives.

During the last few weeks of February 1932, Clyde went into Dallas whatever the weather to look for work. He was hired, then fired, in several places. The cause for dismissal was always the same. The Dallas police were well aware he was back, and they didn't want him around. As soon as he returned home, the old pattern of being regularly picked up for questioning resumed. Clyde swore he intended to go straight. The cops didn't believe him. Clyde and the rest of the Barrows were convinced the police wouldn't stop harassing Clyde until he gave up and left Dallas for good. His employers, deluged with applicants for the most menial jobs, didn't have any patience for an employee who was regularly yanked away from work by the law. So Clyde was fired. He never lasted more than a few days in any job.

In late February, Nell Barrow had a suggestion. She'd met a man who ran a construction crew in Framingham, Massachusetts. He said he'd hire her brother if Clyde moved there. Clyde was reluctant to go. Bonnie hadn't remained faithful the last time he was away from West Dallas. But he needed steady income to get start-up money for his auto parts business. Emma Parker claimed she told Clyde it would be fine with her if, once he'd gotten himself established up in Framingham, Bonnie moved there, too. If she did tell him that, she didn't mean it. Bonnie sister, Billie Jean, swore that her mother was unstinting in her appeals for Bonnie to drop Clyde the minute he left town.

Clyde went, and he hated Framingham. At first, he meant to stick it out until he'd raised enough money to come home and open his shop.

Right after he arrived in Massachusetts, he sent Cumie a letter claiming "I like it up here and I guess I will go to work Monday . . . I am lonesome all ready." He added that Nell's friend Jim "is sure a good fellow. . . . Well Mother I dont know any thing mutch right now but will write more when I here from you so answer real soon and let me know how ever thing is in Dallas. Tell every one hello for me and send my mail to FRAMINGHAM, MASS. General Delivery. Send it to Jack Stuwart. Jack Stuwart that is my name here."

Clyde probably adopted an alias because he was afraid Dallas police would warn their Massachusetts counterparts about a newly arrived ex-con. There was really no reason for him to worry. The Dallas cops would just have been glad that he was somebody else's problem.

But he wasn't gone from Texas for long. Nell's friend Jim, whose last name went unrecorded, wrote her that Clyde seemed restless and wasn't able to settle down to work. About two weeks after he'd left, Clyde was back at Eagle Ford Road. He told an angry Nell that he'd nearly died from loneliness in Massachusetts.

More out of habit than hope, Clyde resumed job hunting in Dallas. Bonnie was thrilled to have him back, but the rest of the Barrow family anticipated disaster. To them, Clyde's aborted employment in New England had been what Marie later described as "a last resort sort of action." As soon as Clyde found work, the Dallas police began rousting him for suspicion again, and the hired/fired cycle repeated itself.

Further temptation for Clyde to give up on going straight arrived in the person of his Eastham pal Ralph Fults. Fults had been released from the prison farm before Clyde on August 26, 1931. He'd gone home to the northeast Texas town of McKinney to wait for Clyde's release. Then, Fults figured, the duo would organize the dramatic Eastham prison break they'd talked about while swinging axes on the farm woodpile. He knew Cumie Barrow was working hard to secure a parole for Clyde, and with prison overcrowding it would be just a matter of time before he, too, was set free.

Fults was more pragmatic than Clyde about post-prison employment. He didn't look for a job while waiting for his friend to get out. Instead, Fults supported himself by gambling. It was a lot more fun than slaving away in some sweatshop. Though Fults himself managed to avoid being arrested, he couldn't resist aiding in a January 1932 breakout from the McKinney jail. An eighteen-year-old named Raymond Hamilton was awaiting arraignment there on several charges of auto theft. Raymond, from West Dallas, claimed he was an old friend of Clyde's. That was an exaggeration. The two might have known each other casually. But it was enough for Fults to smuggle in some hacksaw blades he concealed in the spines of several magazines. Hamilton used the blades to cut his way out of his cell on January 27, 1932. He ended up back in West Dallas, grateful to Fults and hoping to hear from him again.

Fults eventually saw a small article in the newspaper listing Clyde Barrow as one of several prisoners recently paroled by the governor. Around the middle of March, he hopped a train to Dallas. This trip came soon after Clyde had returned to Texas from Massachusetts. After arriving at the main Dallas station, Fults stole a car and drove out to the Barrow service station. When he introduced himself to Henry, he was told that Clyde was at work and would be home soon. That surprised Fults, who hadn't thought Clyde would attempt to make an honest living.

It was a cold day. Henry and Cumie invited their visitor to wait inside, where L.C., Marie, and Buck's wife, Blanche, were huddled around a wood-burning stove. Fults thought Blanche was exceptionally attractive. In a memoir published sixty-four years later he still remembered and praised her high cheekbones and dark eyes. Blanche said Clyde had told his family all about Fults. While they chatted, Fults took in the rest of the shack. It was tiny and cramped. Almost every inch of limited floor space was taken up with pallets.

When Clyde got home, he announced that he'd just been fired again. A man named McCrary, his latest boss, let him go after the cops showed up to take Clyde in for questioning. Enough was enough: Clyde informed his parents and Fults that he was never going to work again. Fults knew what that meant—Clyde had decided to make crime his occupation. Previously, car theft and small-business safe crackings had been intended to supplement his honestly earned income. Now he'd devote his full attention to lawbreaking. One of his first acts, Fults expected, would be to attempt the long-discussed prison break at Eastham farm.

A few days later, Bonnie told her mother, Emma, that she'd been offered a wonderful job selling cosmetics in Houston, 240 miles south of Dallas. Sometime very soon she'd be moving there. Emma was delighted, less for the employment opportunity than for the fact that her daughter would get away from the malign influence of Clyde Barrow.

But Bonnie was lying. Clyde and Fults had formed a gang with Raymond Hamilton, and at Clyde's invitation Bonnie planned to leave home and travel with them. Whatever the hardships in her new life might prove to be, Bonnie was betting that they'd still be preferable to toiling at low-paying, menial jobs and dating dull men who courted her in the Parkers' living room under the watchful eye of her prissy mother.

Clyde was no innocent unwillingly forced back into crime. No one deserved the inhuman conditions he'd had to endure on Eastham Prison Farm, including physical abuse from the guards and rape by Ed Crowder. The Dallas cops were clearly making it impossible for him to go straight in his hometown. But he'd brought the prison sentence and local police harassment on himself—Clyde had stolen a lot of cars before being caught and sent to Eastham. After his release, he was still reasonably healthy and possessed good job skills. If at age twenty-two he'd tried to rebuild his life anywhere else but Dallas, the city where his criminal past had stained his reputation with police beyond repair, Clyde might eventually have parlayed his strong work ethic into a decent, law-abiding existence. Though it wouldn't have been easy, it was certainly possible. But as he'd proven in Massachusetts, he was unwilling to make that effort. Being a criminal simply suited the strong-willed Clyde better. The world, in his opinion, had treated him unfairly, especially the guards and administrators of Eastham Prison Farm. He was more interested in getting even than in getting ahead.

Bonnie also had other options. She could have turned down Clyde's offer to join him in a life of full-time lawbreaking. She'd had bad luck, too, marrying a crook and then being abandoned by him. But it was Bonnie's decision not to divorce Roy Thornton, leaving her unable to marry someone else who would treat her better. Her dreams of finding fame as an actress or a poet hadn't come true, but she had that in common with thousands of other girls who still didn't turn to crime. Bonnie wanted adventures in her life like the ones she saw in the movies, and at age twenty-one she was willing to risk arrest to have them. She'd already proven that once, when she helped Clyde break out of jail in Waco.

Clyde and Bonnie both saw lives devoted to crime as offering possibilities that going straight couldn't. They had no long-term plan beyond Clyde's initial intention to free as many convicts from Eastham Prison Farm as he could. Otherwise, Clyde wanted control. Bonnie wanted excitement. They weren't fools. They realized there would be inevitable consequences—as Bonnie later noted in a poem, "the laws" always won in the end. But they'd had enough of hoping their lives would change for the better. In her diary four years earlier, Bonnie had plaintively asked, "Why don't something happen?" Now, they would make something happen. Clyde Barrow and Bonnie Parker were insignificant because of who they were, but they would force the world to acknowledge them because of what they did.

THE BARROW GANG

"A good run is better than a poor stand."

—Buck Barrow's self-professed philosophy of life

CHAPTER 8

A Stumbling Start

The first three weeks of Clyde Barrow's and Bonnie Parker's new lives as career criminals were notable mostly for bad decisions and worse luck. At times, their misadventures would have constituted slapstick comedy if lives hadn't been at stake.

After dark on March 25, 1932, the trio of Clyde, Ralph Fults, and Raymond Hamilton set out to commit its first robbery. They didn't have to go far. The Simms Oil Refinery was just a few blocks down Eagle Ford Road from the Barrow family garage in West Dallas. Clyde picked the fume-spewing target. He swore to his cohorts that a Simms employee had told him the company would have a large amount of payroll cash in its safe on the night of the 25th. It would be simple to sneak there under cover of darkness, cut through the chain-link fence surrounding the refinery, overpower a guard if one happened to be there, crack the safe, stuff their pockets with loot, and roar out of Dallas with their haul. Clyde anticipated a large take, perhaps as much as several thousand dollars.

As Clyde had promised his partners, cutting through the fence was easy. He hadn't known that four employees were still going to be in the building, but they were quickly subdued and tied up. The refinery safe was located and its door cracked open with a hammer and chisel. But then Clyde's foolproof plan imploded—the safe was empty.

The would-be thieves bolted. Clyde's initial attempt to lead his newly formed criminal gang had been an abject failure, and Raymond Hamilton let him know it. Though he was still only eighteen, Hamilton had been supporting himself through petty crime for several years. He'd begun by stealing and reselling bicycles, then graduated to stealing cars. After the Simms fiasco, Hamilton wanted the gang to focus on automobile theft. The individual takes would be much smaller than they might be from robbing banks or businesses, he argued, but at least you didn't have to wonder whether there was money in a safe.

Fults and Clyde had a different plan. Their immediate goal was conducting the long-planned Eastham Prison Farm break, and for that they'd require a lot more money than they could earn by fencing stolen cars. To successfully pull off the Eastham raid, they knew, the gang would need additional members and a lot more firepower than the cheap weapons they'd used in the Simms break-in. Fults had some specific acquaintances in mind as recruits. He knew several crooks living in and around Denton who he believed would make enthusiastic, competent partners. But there was no sense asking them to join up without enough powerful assault weapons to overwhelm the prison guards.

The gang's current arsenal consisted of the cheap Saturday Night Special handguns that were readily available anywhere, plus a couple of shotguns. In the 1930s, almost every Texas family had a gun or two—it was considered strange to be weaponless. Small-caliber pistols and shotguns were available on street corners for a few dollars. These, however, were notoriously inaccurate even at close range. More upscale weaponry could be purchased in hardware stores. Every town of any size had one. There were no background checks involved when guns were purchased. Even Thompson submachine guns—"tommy guns"—were on sale for a few hundred dollars each. Those who didn't have nearby stores selling guns could send away for them by enclosing a check with the mail-order forms routinely found in popular magazines. For the Eastham raid, Clyde and Fults also wanted bulletproof vests and a large supply of ammunition. So Hamilton was overruled; the gang would try to make its Eastham budget in one grand haul. Fults preferred banks to small businesses. Even though Clyde had never tried to rob a bank, after the Simms blunder he was in no position to disagree.

While Bonnie waited at home with her mother, Emma, the trio of Clyde, Fults, and Hamilton staged a series of small stickups in and around Dallas to gather some traveling money. They couldn't stay in the area long. After the Simms break-in, the West Dallas cops were on the lookout for their old target Clyde Barrow. The decision was made to drive north and find a bank to rob somewhere far away from the local heat. Long-distance travel for business, recreation—and crime—had become much easier. The post–World War I Federal Highway Act added 300,000 miles of hard-topped interstate highways. In 1924, Rand McNally published its first national road map, making it relatively simple to plan out routes, and including many smaller state and farm roads as well as the major thoroughfares. Clyde loved the newfangled maps. Throughout his criminal career, they would be found in virtually every stolen car he abandoned along the way.

Clyde, Fults, and Hamilton drove through Oklahoma, Kansas, and Iowa before finally picking out a bank almost nine hundred miles from Dallas in Okabena, Minnesota. It seemed like a perfect target. The bank was set in the middle of a town square. There were roads leading away in several directions. But at the last minute, Clyde called the robbery attempt off. There was too much snow and ice on the local roads, he told Fults and Hamilton. Their car might skid out of control during the escape. It would be better, he insisted, to turn back south and find another bank to rob in a less frigid region. According to Fults's memoir, they'd seen one, the First National Bank in Lawrence, Kansas, that might do.

They had driven almost nonstop from Texas to Minnesota, pausing only for meals and gas. All three were exhausted, and when they took turns driving on the four-hundred-mile trip back to Lawrence, each fell asleep at the wheel and let the car veer off the road into adjacent fields.

In Lawrence, Fults claimed in his memoir, they had enough money to check into a local hotel, the Eldridge. The next two days were spent casing the bank and the town. After the Simms fiasco, they wanted to be absolutely certain of success. They learned that the First National Bank's president usually arrived at 8:45 in the morning, with the rest of the bank staff showing up some ten minutes later. There seemed to be only one guard, but as soon as the bank opened for business there was a steady stream of customers.

On the third day, the bank president arrived at the bank at his usual time. Clyde and Fults, brandishing shotguns, rushed into the building after him while Hamilton waited outside at the wheel of the getaway car. Clyde forced the bank president to open the vault, while Fults guarded two employees who arrived while the robbery was in progress. The Lawrence bank's vault wasn't empty. Clyde was given two bags of currency. Then he and Fults locked their prisoners in the vault and ran out to join Hamilton. A few miles out of town they stole another car. It all seemed ridiculously easy. The bank guard hadn't even arrived for work by the time the gang grabbed the money and fled. If the town cops made any attempt to pursue them, they never got within sight or sound of the thieves.

According to Fults, the trio fled 290 miles to East St. Louis, Illinois, where they paused to count their loot and discovered their take was an astounding $33,000. No old Lawrence newspaper accounts exist to verify or disprove Fults's claim, but $33,000 would have been enough to recruit and supply an army to assault Eastham Prison Farm. Fults might have been wrong about the location of the robbery as well as grossly exaggerating the take from it. But whatever the amount and whichever bank the gang robbed to get it, the haul was substantial enough to impress Raymond Hamilton. He wanted to hit more banks right away. Clyde and Fults refused. They wanted money to finance their Eastham plan, and now that they had some in hand they intended to buy guns and head back to Texas.

Fults knew of a pawn shopowner in Dupo, Illinois, who fenced high-caliber weaponry. It seemed more logical to make their purchases through him than at a hardware store where the shopkeeper might mention a substantial purchase of guns to the police. Fults and Clyde spent their shares of the Lawrence take on .45-caliber pistols, tommy guns, and bulletproof vests. Raymond Hamilton wanted nothing further to do with them or their Eastham plans. He took his cut of the money and left for Bay City, Michigan, where his father lived. Clyde and Hamilton had disliked each other from the beginning, and Clyde told Fults he hoped Hamilton "chokes on that wad of money."

Clyde and Fults drove back to Texas in early April, making a quick stop in West Dallas so Clyde could visit his family and spend a few hours with Bonnie. The cops there were still looking for him. Clyde's father, Henry, kept his radio on during the day, listening for police bulletins that might indicate his son's pursuers were nearby. When Clyde sneaked over to see Bonnie, he brought Fults with him. Fults had never met Bonnie before, but they liked each other immediately. Her mother was less friendly. Emma Parker refused to let "the cons" enter her house.

After the brief visit Clyde and Fults drove forty miles north to Denton, where they met with four local crooks—Johnny Russell, Jack Hammett, Ralph Allsup (called "Fuzz" because of his burr haircut), and Ted Rogers, who eerily resembled Raymond Hamilton. The quartet was enthusiastic about the proposed Eastham raid, probably because they'd all done at least some local jail time. The new group called itself "the Lake Dallas Gang" after the area waterway. Clyde thought six assailants would be enough to pull off the raid. At night there were four picket guards outside Eastham's Camp 1 dormitory. If the Lake Dallas Gang could get the drop on them, they could then break the prisoners out of the dorm before the other guards sleeping on the second floor could wake up and stop them. While many inmates had tried to escape from Eastham, nobody had ever attempted to orchestrate a break from the outside. Eastham was considered too remote and forbidding. That meant the gang should have the advantage of complete surprise. What would happen to most of the escaped prisoners afterward apparently was not discussed, beyond helping as many as possible get clear of Eastham and arming them with the guards' captured weapons. They would then have to be responsible for maintaining their own freedom. But Clyde was especially concerned that Aubrey Scalley would be broken out. He was grateful to Scalley for taking the rap in the Ed Crowder killing.

In preparation for the raid, Clyde, Fults, and their new partners found an isolated spot by Lake Dallas to test the guns and vests they'd bought in Illinois. They were joined by another recruit known only as Red, who was an acquaintance of Jack Hammett's. The tests near the lake were less enjoyable. The vests, probably propped against trees, were perforated by every bullet striking them, and many of the guns wouldn't fire at all. The pawnbroker in Dupo had bilked Fults and Clyde.

To get money to buy a replacement arsenal, the gang members planned a simultaneous April 11 stickup of two banks located in

Denton's main square, only to be scared off that morning when they saw two Texas Rangers sitting in a car parked on the square. It was odd that the Rangers would be hanging around in town. They usually arrived to investigate after a crime had been committed. Clyde suspected someone in his new gang might be an informer, but he had no proof and decided to go ahead with plans for the Eastham raid.

Besides its recurring need for better weapons, the Lake Dallas Gang was also having second thoughts about whether it had enough members to successfully carry out the Eastham attack. Clyde and Fults knew two brothers in Amarillo who might agree to join them, so they drove 365 miles northwest to the Texas Panhandle to track them down. Red had asked to come along. He brandished his .44 revolver and bragged that he'd "part the hair" of any cop that got in their way.

They arrived in Amarillo on April 13, but the brothers, never identified in any existing Barrow Gang lore, were nowhere to be found. Clyde, Fults, and Red turned back toward Dallas, but their car broke down in the small town of Electra about two hundred miles east of Amarillo. Normally, that wouldn't have presented a problem. Clyde could have easily hot-wired another car. But an Electra city employee named A. F. McCormick found it suspicious that a trio of strangers had apparently parked in front of a warehouse, and he called Electra sheriff James T. Taylor to investigate. Taylor hurried over with J. C. Harris, another city employee. They arrived in Harris's vehicle just as Clyde, Fults, and Red left their stalled car and began walking into town, undoubtedly planning to steal another automobile. Taylor leaned out and asked the trio if they had a problem. Fults explained their car had died, adding they were from Wichita Falls. Small-town Texas sheriffs often made the assumption that young male drifters were up to no good. Taylor said he would have to take them into custody and check out their story. Instead of surrendering, Clyde pulled a .45 and told the sheriff and Harris to put up their hands. As they did, McCormick drove up in a Chevrolet. Fults, who had just relieved Taylor of his revolver, pointed the gun at McCormick and made him a captive, too. Then Clyde and Fults jammed into McCormick's car with the three prisoners. There was no need to make room for Red—he'd run away as soon as the confrontation commenced. Clyde later decided that Red was the traitor who had tipped the Texas Rangers to the aborted April 11 bank robberies in Denton.

Clyde and Fults hadn't anticipated having three hostages on their hands, one a sheriff. As Clyde drove south out of town he and Fults began apologizing to Taylor, McCormick, and Harris for causing them any inconvenience. About eight miles out of Electra, they pulled the car to the side of the road and let the trio go. Fults kept Taylor's gun, joking "We'll take good care of this." There was a clear risk in releasing three witnesses who'd gotten good looks at them. Kidnapping was considered a much more serious crime than car theft or bank robbery. But whatever mayhem Clyde and Fults were hoping to commit on Eastham prison guards, they intended no physical harm toward anyone else.

To elude potential pursuit, Clyde drove back north toward Oklahoma. Once past the state line, he planned to drive east for a while, then south back to Denton, where he and Fults could rejoin the rest of the Lake Dallas Gang. But they were barely underway again when McCormick's Chevrolet ran out of gas. Clyde wasn't necessarily negligent in checking—car gas gauges in the early 1930s were notorious for inaccurate readings.

Rural mail carrier Bill Owens, slowing down as he passed the stalled Chevy, was astonished when the two men standing beside the car leaped up onto his running board and forced him to pull over at gunpoint. Clyde got behind the wheel of the Ford; Owens was ordered into the front passenger's seat while Fults sat in the back. Owens expected to be shot. Clyde assured Owens that as long as he cooperated he wouldn't be harmed, but they had a scary moment on a toll bridge across the Red River and the Texas-Oklahoma border. Instead of stopping to pay the toll and call as little attention to the stolen Ford as possible—Owens was certainly cowed enough to sit quietly and not yell for help—Clyde crashed through a chain barrier and barreled into Oklahoma as a pair of bridge guards fired at the car. Though their shots missed, the guards called in a report and soon there was an all-points bulletin issued for Owens's vehicle. Clyde had the car radio tuned to a local station, and as they neared the town of Fletcher there was an announcement that state police were setting up roadblocks on major roads in the area. Clyde immediately swerved off onto a small farm-to-market road and told Owens to get out. The postman asked the outlaws to leave him his mailbag, and they handed it over. Then Owens asked what Clyde intended to do with his car. Clyde promised that he and Fults would eventually abandon the Ford "in plain sight" where the vehicle could be easily found. Owens requested a favor: Would Clyde and Fults please burn his car rather than just abandoning it? If the Ford was destroyed, the government would be obligated to buy Owens a new one. Clyde was glad to oblige; he thought it was funny. A day later, the smoldering remains of Owens's Ford were discovered nearby. Clyde and Fults had stolen another car to complete their much interrupted trip back to Denton.

Nothing was going right. Clyde and Fults still didn't have high-caliber guns to blast their way past the Eastham guards, and they had lost Red instead of returning from Amarillo with two additional members for the Lake Dallas Gang. But Clyde and Fults remained determined to go ahead with the Eastham raid. The rest of the gang was agreeable. Jack Hammett offered to hit a hardware store in the nearby town of Celina and filch a new arsenal. Clyde and Fults said they'd travel east to Tyler and steal two cars large enough to haul escaped prisoners away from Eastham and fast enough to outrun any lawmen in pursuit. They'd meet back by Lake Dallas afterward and make their final plans for the attack. Clyde also wanted to get a message about the impending raid to Aubrey Scalley, and he wanted his girlfriend to deliver it.

Bonnie's involvement with the Lake Dallas Gang until then was strictly ornamental. She was Clyde's lover, available between jobs to offer moral support and physical comfort. But now she had a chance to get in on the action, albeit in a relatively risk-free way. Female friends and relatives visited Eastham inmates all the time. On April 17, Clyde and Fults drove Bonnie southeast toward the prison farm, hopping out of the car about a mile away from the main gate and letting her drive in alone while they hid in the woods. Bonnie played her role perfectly, telling the guards she was Scalley's cousin. Nobody was suspicious. This tiny girl obviously wasn't a threat. As a building tender, Scalley was able to enjoy a private conversation with Bonnie; ordinary cons were supervised while meeting with visitors. When she returned to pick up Clyde and Fults, Bonnie told them Scalley liked the plan and would be ready whenever his rescuers arrived.

It certainly meant a lot to Bonnie that Clyde trusted her enough to use her as a go-between. Unlike her estranged convict husband, Roy Thornton, Clyde clearly wanted to include her in, rather than exclude her from, every crucial aspect of his life. The Scalley visit had gone so smoothly, and she had enjoyed being involved so much, that it seemed natural for her to ride along with Clyde and Fults when they went to

Tyler to steal big, fast cars for the Eastham raid. Fults didn't mind her tagging along. They'd had several good conversations; he found Bonnie to be "articulate, thoughtful and witty." Bonnie, in turn, felt the Eastham and Tyler trips gave her new status as a full-time member of Clyde's gang. Before leaving for Tyler, she told her mother she was finally moving to Houston to take the made-up job selling cosmetics there.

No one expected trouble when they set out for Tyler on the night of April 18. Clyde had a lot of experience driving away in stolen cars before anyone noticed. Still, Fults asked to stop on the way when they drove through the small town of Kaufman. There was a hardware store there, and he wanted to buy some ammunition. When he rejoined Clyde and Bonnie in the car, he told them the store had a fine selection of guns. The other Lake Dallas Gang boys were supposed to be stealing a new batch of weapons in Celina, but what would it hurt to swing back through Kaufman on the return trip from Tyler and swipe some there, too? It made sense to Clyde, and Bonnie was agreeable. It would just add to the evening's adventure.

Things went as planned in Tyler. There were many cars to choose from, and Clyde picked out and hot-wired a Chrysler. Fults stole a Buick. Both cars were big enough to transport several Eastham escapees as well as Lake Dallas Gang members, and they were fast, too. On the gravel road between Tyler and Kaufman, Clyde and Fults raced their new rides at speeds approaching 90 miles per hour. They were impressed with the massive vehicles, which rolled into downtown Kaufman around midnight, well after its townspeople had turned in for the night. While Bonnie waited in the Chrysler, Clyde and Fults began breaking the padlock on the door of the hardware store.

Unfortunately for the would-be gun thieves, Kaufman employed a night watchman downtown. He noticed the two huge cars and the men in front of the hardware store. He approached them with his gun drawn, Clyde spotted him, and the two exchanged wild shots. Clyde told his family later that he deliberately fired high. Then the watchman ran for help as Clyde and Fults jumped back into their cars and sped out of town, with Clyde's Chrysler ahead of Fults's Buick. Behind them, a bell began ringing loudly—the watchman's cries had been heard and someone was sounding the alarm.

The townspeople of Kaufman might have gone to bed early, but they awakened ready for action. In the few minutes it took Clyde and

Fults to figure out an escape route to the main road back toward Dallas—there was no time to consult a road map now—the highway was blocked, probably with a pair of giant road graders. The fleeing criminals had no choice; they yanked their cars into U-turns and drove back through town again, whizzing past a growing crowd of alarmed citizens and finally blundering east onto a narrow country road of packed dirt. There was no roadblock there. Clyde and Fults had cars that were undoubtedly much faster than any vehicles the country bumpkins they'd just left behind could use to pursue them. They hadn't gotten the guns, but they'd clearly gotten away. And then it began to rain.

In spring 1932, almost all the back farm roads in Texas were still dirt, and Clyde and Fults were driving down one of them. It had been raining recently in and around Kaufman County, and as the Lake Dallas crooks tried to make their getaway a heavy new storm struck. The already saturated farm road quickly deteriorated into thick, goopy mud, and the weight of the massive Buick and Chrysler sank the tires of the cars so deep in the sludge that the vehicles stuck fast. Try as Clyde, Fults, and Bonnie might to get them up and out, they wouldn't budge. The fugitives were drenched. The lighter, slower vehicles of their Kaufman pursuers would probably be able to skim over the worst of the mud. The trio had to abandon their immobilized cars and slog off on foot. They knew pursuit was coming. Everyone gathering in downtown Kaufman had seen the two cars racing away on the farm road.

The rain hammered down hard in the pitch-black darkness as Clyde, Bonnie, and Fults stumbled through sodden pastureland. When they came upon a farmhouse at about 1 A.M. they pounded on the door to wake up whoever was inside. The bleary-eyed farmer who emerged had no car for them to steal, but he offered the use of his two mules. There wasn't much choice. Clyde and Bonnie clambered up on one mule, and Fults got on another, though not before it pitched him into the mud. The town of Kemp was a few miles away, and they guided their balky mounts in that general direction. Bonnie's splendid adventure had degenerated into complete misery. She was soaked to the skin, petrified at the prospect of imminent capture, and perched on the uncomfortable, bony spine of a mule. They had to ride bareback because the farmer had no saddles.

It was almost dawn before they finally reached the outskirts of Kemp. There was some relief in spotting a car parked in a driveway; it belonged to a local doctor named Scarsdale. They hot-wired the car and drove away, leaving the mules behind, but only got a mile out of town before Scarsdale's car ran out of gas.

Now they were really in trouble. The sun was up. The posse of angry Kaufman citizens had surely found the abandoned Buick and Chrysler by now, and learned from the farmer about the trio's escape by mule. The car theft in Kemp would arouse additional pursuit, from that town and the nearby community of Mabank. Clyde, Bonnie, and Fults were miles from anywhere else, with no way to get word to other Lake Dallas Gang members to come and rescue them. Shivering, scared, the trio had no option other than trying to hide in the brush.

Soon pursuers appeared. Led by the city marshal of Kemp and Mabank's chief of police, a motley pack of farmers and small-town citizens was painstakingly picking its way through the countryside, checking every gulley, grove of trees, and clump of underbrush. They knew the backcountry well, and their quarry realized it was only a matter of time before they were discovered. Clyde and Fults still had their handguns, but they were far too outnumbered to win a shootout.

They went undiscovered until about 5 P.M. when, in desperation, they ran across a road to a small store on the other side. A car was parked there, but before Clyde could get it hot-wired they were spotted and the posse was on them. The fugitives stumbled to the banks of nearby Cedar Creek. Clyde and Fults tried shooting over their pursuers' heads, but that only caused the posse members to start shooting, too, and they weren't trying to miss. Fults was hit in the left arm. It would be only a matter of moments before Clyde and Bonnie went down, too.

Clyde made a quick decision. He didn't want Bonnie to be caught or shot. But if they made another attempt to flee, she would be a liability. Bonnie would never be able to outrun the men chasing them. If Clyde slowed his own pace to match hers, they'd both be captured. But Clyde didn't consider surrendering. He'd sworn he'd never go back to prison, and meant it. His only remaining option was to try to get away alone, then see what could be done later about rescuing Bonnie and Fults.

There is no way to be certain what Bonnie thought as her boyfriend, Clyde, blurted out that he was abandoning her in a muddy creek bottom where she was being shot at by lots of angry men. If she begged him to not leave her, Clyde wasn't persuaded. Perhaps she summoned up a movie heroine moment and agreed that her lover should save himself if he could. Probably she was too panic-stricken to understand what he was saying. In any event, Clyde vaulted up out of the creek bed and ran straight toward the men firing at them. For once, he was in luck. The two closest posse members he charged were both reloading their guns. There was so much confusion that Clyde was able to run free while the posse descended on Bonnie and Fults. Clyde made his way back to Kemp, where he stole one car, drove a little way and stole another, and finally reached his family in West Dallas.

Back on the banks of Cedar Creek, as soon as Clyde had sprinted away Fults told Bonnie to give herself up. In his memoir, he said he suggested she tell the posse that she'd been kidnapped and forced to come along on the failed hardware store robbery with him and Clyde. Bonnie emerged and was immediately taken prisoner. Fults, still bleeding in the creek bed, was captured a moment later. Someone guessed he might be the notorious Oklahoma bandit Pretty Boy Floyd. The posse dragged Bonnie and Fults back into Kemp, where they were locked together for the night in the town's minuscule, one-cell jail.

Bonnie was calm enough to ask that someone examine Fults's injured arm. The local physician was summoned—Dr. Scarsdale, who was so put out by the theft of his car that he refused to treat Fults.

Fults was in agony. Bonnie, peering outside through a barred window, could see dozens of armed men ringing the jail, forming a guard to prevent anyone from rescuing the prisoners. On the night of April 19, 1932, just three weeks after they'd begun, it seemed that her glamorous criminal partnership with Clyde had come to a sudden, ignominious end.

CHAPTER 9

Bonnie in Jail

Clyde meant what he promised Bonnie at Cedar Creek: he only ran so he could come back and rescue her and Fults. He briefly stopped in West Dallas on the morning of April 20. Clyde told his family what had happened, and asked his little brother, L.C., and his sister-in-law Blanche to go down to Kaufman right away. They were to find out where Bonnie and Fults were being held, so Clyde could return with the rest of the Lake Dallas Gang and set the prisoners free. Though he and Fults had failed to rob the hardware store in Kaufman, Clyde believed the gang would still have plenty of firepower because Jack Hammett had promised to steal guns from another store in Celina.

But when he rejoined his partners later in the day in Denton, Clyde learned Hammett hadn't followed through, and Ted Rogers and Johnny Russell had no idea where he and Ralph Allsup were. Clyde couldn't wait until Hammett and Allsup reappeared. That night, Clyde, Rogers, and Russell hit the hardware store in Celina that Hammett had been supposed to rob. They got away with some rifles and shotguns, but not before mistakenly breaking into a nearby drugstore and having to lock three prisoners, including the Celina mayor, in an empty railroad boxcar. They also took $14 from the mayor. The pair of other captives had only $2 between them.

The next afternoon, Clyde, Russell, and Rogers found another spot on the banks of Lake Dallas to test-fire their new guns. Clyde wanted to be certain there would be no misfires when they tried to free Bonnie and Fults. Unlike the flawed weapons purchased from the pawnbroker in Illinois, these guns worked well—too well. A farmer working in a nearby field was alarmed at what sounded like an endless barrage of shots. He called Denton County sheriff G. C. Cockrell, who loaded several deputies into a car and hurried out to investigate. Clyde's senses were always keen. He heard rustlings in the brush and correctly assumed "the laws" were approaching. Though they had to abandon the Celina arsenal, Clyde, Russell, and Rogers were able to sneak away on foot before Cockrell and his men could catch them. But even as those three members of the Lake Dallas Gang escaped, the missing duo of Jack Hammett and Ralph Allsup drove up looking for their partners. Cockrell arrested them, and also took possession of the Ford V-8 Clyde had stolen and driven back to Denton during his escape two days earlier.

Over the next few days, everything the Lake Dallas Gang had planned fell apart as various county and town law enforcement agencies sent out and responded to bulletins. In Texas during the early 1930s immediate communication was always a problem between regional police departments, especially those in isolated rural areas. Phone service was intermittent; telegrams were most often used to report crimes and disseminate descriptions of fugitives. Often, telegram delivery wasn't prompt. But when prisoners and apparently stolen property were in custody, laws officers in far-flung, smaller communities had time to compare notes. In this instance, the Denton County sheriff sent out word about his haul of captives, weapons, and a car, and there were multiple responses. The owner of the Celina hardware store confirmed the guns had been stolen from his shop on the night of the 20th. The stolen Ford was linked to the escape of the so far unidentified "third man" who'd participated in the aborted Kaufman robbery on the night of April 19. A pistol found among the Lake Dallas arsenal was claimed by Electra sheriff James T. Taylor, who explained how it had been taken from him ten days earlier. Taylor was then taken to see the man captured by the Kemp posse. He identified Fults as one of his two kidnappers. So did mail carrier Bill Owens. Finally, one of Clyde's Kaufman County pursuers erroneously identified Jack Hammett as the third fugitive who'd managed to escape from Cedar Creek. The crimes in Electra, Kaufman, and Celina were now linked. That meant Hammett, Allsup, and Fults faced lengthy prison terms. (Bonnie was being held only for the attempted robbery in Kaufman.) After just a few days in Kaufman County custody, Fults was sent to Wichita Falls to be tried on kidnapping charges. That was considered the more serious crime, and its prosecution took precedence.

Though he remained at large, Clyde was still in desperate straits. He, Rogers, and Russell had nothing but the clothes they wore and the weapons they carried when they raced away on foot to escape Denton County sheriff Cockrell and his men. There's no record of where Rogers and Russell hid themselves immediately after April 21, but within a few days Clyde made his way back to West Dallas. He soon learned that Fults had been moved to Wichita Falls while Bonnie had been transferred from the tiny one-room Kemp jail to the larger jail in Kaufman. Hammett and Allsup were in custody somewhere, too, but Clyde apparently wasn't worried about them.

For one of the few times in his life, Clyde tried to reason things through rather than act impulsively. The Eastham raid was clearly a lost cause. The three participants left—Clyde, Russell, and Rogers—didn't comprise a large enough assault force to pull it off, and, besides, they no longer had the guns and big, fast cars that were necessary. Clyde himself was still wanted by the West Dallas police for the botched Simms Refinery job. He probably assumed, correctly, that he hadn't yet been identified as a participant in the Electra, Kaufman, or Celina crimes, so at least there was only local rather than regional heat for him to avoid. But Fults was in terrible trouble. A conviction for kidnapping, along with additional sentences for burglary attempts, would send him straight back to Huntsville and possibly Eastham Prison Farm. Bonnie was in less danger. True, she was stuck in jail at least until June when the Kaufman County grand jury would next convene and decide whether to charge her with anything. The odds were that they wouldn't. She had taken Fults's advice, and told her captors that she'd been kidnapped and forced to accompany him and Clyde. When L.C. and Blanche met with Bonnie in the Kaufman jail after her capture and transfer from Kemp, they reinforced that suggestion. Bonnie had never been previously arrested, let alone charged with any crimes.

Texas juries were notorious for leniency toward women. If Bonnie behaved herself in jail and didn't say anything to incriminate herself, she would probably walk away as a free woman in June. Any attempt by Clyde to break her out before that would put him at risk; even if he did set Bonnie free, her cooperation in an escape attempt would indicate she'd been a willing participant on the night of April 19, and then she'd be a fugitive on the run, too.

No matter what Clyde decided to do about Bonnie and Fults, he knew he needed money for traveling expenses and to buy better guns for potential shootouts with the law. Attempts to steal guns in Kaufman and Celina had gone awry. It seemed smarter to rob a small business somewhere and then purchase whatever weapons were needed. At least he still had Johnny Russell and Ted Rogers to help him.

So Clyde decided that acquiring a new bankroll was his first priority. From there, he'd find a way to free Fults before his friend was shipped back to Huntsville. Bonnie would have to cool her heels in Kaufman for another six weeks or so. If the grand jury did indict her in June, he could plot a breakout scheme then. This was pragmatic rather than romantic reasoning, and because Clyde couldn't go himself, he sent L.C. and Blanche back to Kaufman to inform Bonnie, who never would have placed pragmatism ahead of love.

Decades later in an unpublished memoir, Marie, Clyde's little sister, recalled that Bonnie wasn't upset by Clyde's decision. Various members of the Barrow family regularly visited her in the Kaufman jail, bearing gifts of clothing and snacks and constantly assuring her that Clyde would be waiting when she was released in June. "She was glad to see us and didn't seem to have the slightest bit of bitterness against Clyde or our family," Marie wrote. In her memoir, Clyde's mother, Cumie, added that her son gave her money to buy Bonnie shoes and underwear. He also brought home a dress he wanted his mother to take to Kaufman, but Cumie "didn't know where the dress came from"—obviously, she thought it was stolen—and took Bonnie one of Marie's dresses instead. Bonnie and Marie were about the same size, both very short and slender.

But it would have been very unlike Bonnie not to have at least occasional panic attacks. She couldn't be certain that Clyde meant his promise to be waiting when she was released. Her husband, Roy Thornton, had deserted her—maybe all men were like that. When

Emma Parker heard about Bonnie's incarceration and rushed to Kaufman, her daughter had plenty to say about Clyde Barrow. As Emma later recalled, none of it was good. Bonnie swore she was through with Clyde forever. Stressed, scared, and lonely, she probably wasn't really certain how she felt about him.

Though Clyde was willing to let Bonnie remain in jail until her grand jury hearing, Emma considered bailing her out. There was, Emma wrote, "a crazy negro woman" in the cell next to Bonnie, and she didn't want her daughter exposed to that sort of person. But Emma talked with the wife of the Kaufman jailor, who persuaded her that a short jail stint might be just what Bonnie needed to cure her attraction to the criminal element. According to Emma, the jailor's wife, identified only as Mrs. Adams, counseled that "they really haven't a thing against her . . . she's not suffering, and time to think matters over may mean all the difference in the world to the child in the future."

So Bonnie Thornton—the authorities called her by her married name—languished in a jail cell, though on nice days jailor Adams permitted her to sit outside on the lawn. If it was less than an idyllic existence, it wasn't especially unpleasant, either. Bonnie whiled away the hours writing poetry. Mrs. Adams gave her some old bank forms to use as stationery. Between April 20, when she was caught, and June 17, when the Kaufman grand jury convened, Bonnie composed a collection of verse she whimsically titled *Poetry From Life's Other Side*. All ten poems reflect outstanding penmanship, a credible vocabulary, pedestrian rhyming skills, and an inordinate fondness for quotation marks. A few are quite maudlin—in verse as well as in life, Bonnie enjoyed a good cry. Her choice of subject matter, and how Bonnie viewed the fictional participants in these imaginary adventures, are certainly indicative of her mixed emotions about her current plight. "I'll Stay" promises an absent lover that "I'll stay with you forever/Whether you are wrong or right," but "The Fate of Tiger Rose" relates that its protagonist "looks old and bent/And her years are spent/Walking this 'prison yards'/But once she was fair/With golden hair/Tho her eyes were somewhat hard."

At 105 lines, the longest poem by far is "The Story of 'Suicide Sal,' " about a naive country girl from Wyoming who falls for the slick patter of Jack, a "heat man" from "Chi." The innocent Sal is lured into crime by her lover, admitting "Jack was just like a 'god' to me." During a robbery attempt, Jack flees while Sal is captured and sentenced to a "5 to 50" year sentence. Jack sends word that he'll break Sal out, but as time passes she wonders if he's really coming:

I took the "rap" like a "sportsman,"
Not even one "squawk" did I make,
Jack "dropped himself" on the "promise"
We'd make a "sensational break."
Well to shorten a lengthy sad story,
Five years have gone over my head,
Without even as much as a letter,
At first I thought he was dead.
A short while ago I "discovered"
From a gal in the "joint" named "Kate,"
That Jack and his "moll" had "got [married]"
And was planning on "going straight."
Now if he had returned to me some time,
Tho he hadn't a penny to give,
I'd forget all this "hell" he has caused me,
And love him as long as I live.
But theres no chance of his ever coming
For he and his "moll" have no fears,
But that I will die in this "prison,"
Or else "flatten" this fifty years.

Sal is released after serving five years, but since "State's prison" would "poison" a "goddess's mind," the "jilted gangster's gal"—Bonnie's alter ego—is gunned down by someone's tommy gun two days later.

Emma Parker read the poem during a jail visit and was horrified. "It was clear from the numerous quotations used in the poem that Bonnie was learning the jargon of gangdom, and striving desperately to fit into it and become part of it," she wrote in *Fugitives*. "I realize that I am not learned in such matters, but to my inner consciousness there seemed to be a strange and terrifying change taking place in the mind of my child." Emma could be forgiven for near-hysteria; her younger daughter, Billie Jean's, husband, Fred Mace, was arrested for burglary just two weeks after Bonnie landed in jail. Her proud opinion of the Parker family was shaken, but it would have been worse had Emma seen two other poems Bonnie wrote in the Kaufman jail. "The Girl with the Blue Velvet Band" is an account of "a Hop Fiend" and her drug addiction. " 'The Prostitutes' Convention' " (Bonnie used quotation marks to set off the title) is nothing less than a roll call of Dallas hookers and a listing of the street corners where they worked. Some of "the broads" indulge themselves in a "pop" of "Sweet Morphine" before "the laws" come to break up the fun. Even if Bonnie never dabbled in drugs or turned a trick herself, she'd been around such scenes enough to describe them in detail. Emma Parker believed her sweet daughter was corrupted by Clyde—she said as much all the rest of her life, including to members of the Barrow family, who didn't appreciate it—but these poems lend credence to the strong possibility that Bonnie was at least a part-time prostitute, and perhaps even an abuser of drugs, before she ever began her relationship with Clyde Barrow.

While Bonnie stewed, writing verse and fluctuating between devotion to and disdain for her boyfriend, Clyde was formulating a plan for a quick-hit robbery, after which he'd break Ralph Fults out of the Wichita Falls jail. He thought of a likely target. According to the memoir of Marie Barrow, during the time three years earlier when Clyde had been running with Frank Clause, he'd met another young man named Bucher whose parents ran a combination jewelry store/general store/optician's practice/garage in the town of Hillsboro sixty miles south of Dallas. Sometime during the last few days of April 1932, Clyde, Ted Rogers, and Johnny Russell stole a car and drove down to check the place out as a potential target. It looked promising. With such a variety of goods sold there—everything from tools to musical instruments—there had to constantly be money in the till, and the jewelry operation almost guaranteed there would be bracelets, necklaces, watches, and other valuable items kept in a safe. Sixty-year-old John N. Bucher, the owner, was also well known in Hillsboro for owning one of the first automobiles in town. He lived with his wife in an apartment above the store. Bucher was proud of the shop—an old photo shows that almost half of its front window was obscured by a huge sign proclaiming "J. N. BUCHER JEWELER GRADUATE OPTICIAN."

Rogers, Russell, and Clyde explored the store, pretending to examine guitars and hammers and watch fobs. They noted a heavy safe directly across the aisle from the main counter. True, it was too big to attempt to crack by hand. They'd have to make Bucher open it, perhaps at gunpoint. But in general everything seemed in place for a quick, clean job until Clyde noticed Bucher's wife, Madora, staring at him. Mrs. Bucher had briefly met Clyde through her son. She didn't speak to Clyde, but he felt certain she'd recognized him.

Clyde wanted to call off the robbery, but Rogers and Russell wouldn't pass up such a potentially lucrative heist. They suggested that they return to Hillsboro well after dark so there would be few pedestrians. They would park in front of the shop, and Clyde could stay in the car while the other two knocked on the door and asked Bucher to open up, using the pretext that they needed to buy some small item or other. Proprietors of small-town Texas general stores would routinely do business with after-hours customers. Bucher would let them in, they'd offer to pay using a large denomination bill, and Bucher would have to open the safe to make change. When he did, they'd pull their guns, clean out the safe, and be gone before anyone could stop them. There would be no opportunity for Madora Bucher to see Clyde again, and she certainly wouldn't recognize Rogers and Russell.

Marie Barrow wrote later in her unpublished memoir that Clyde "felt the job was jinxed." But he needed his share of the take; Fults was scheduled to be tried in Wichita Falls around May 10 and had to be broken out before then. So about 10 P.M. on April 30, Clyde drove up in front of the Bucher store. Russell and Rogers banged on the door, and when Bucher finally got downstairs to let them in they said they wanted to buy guitar strings. These cost a quarter. Russell and Rogers offered a ten-dollar bill in payment. Though surviving accounts of what happened next differ in many respects, it's certain that Madora Bucher came downstairs and the two Denton County crooks pulled out their pistols. Either Mrs. Bucher or her husband opened the safe, which held a gun besides some jewelry and a small stack of currency. Bucher went for the gun, and Ted Rogers fired. Bucher died shortly afterward.

Waiting in the car out on the street, Clyde heard a shot. Rogers and Russell rushed out of the store, jumped in, and told him to get going. When they finally stopped to look, their take amounted to about $40 in cash, plus jewelry worth perhaps $1,500. The incident marked the end of what remained of the Lake Dallas Gang. Clyde, Rogers, and Russell each took a third of the loot and went their separate ways. Clyde hadn't gone inside, hadn't drawn a gun, hadn't fired a shot—but under Texas law, if he was ever identified as a participant, he would be just as guilty of Bucher's murder as his partner who pulled the trigger.

Clyde certainly hoped Madora Bucher wouldn't identify him. Maybe he'd been wrong about being recognized by her on the afternoon before the killing. But the Hillsboro cops asked the Dallas police for help in investigating the murder, and the Dallas lawmen brought mug shots of potential suspects for Mrs. Bucher to look at. The photos included one of Clyde, and she immediately picked him out. That led the officers from Dallas to show her a mug shot of Raymond Hamilton. Since the failed Simms robbery on March 25, the Dallas police—who knew Raymond well as a bicycle and car thief—assumed he was still running with Clyde. Ted Rogers, the Lake Dallas Gang member who shot her husband, looked very much like Hamilton, and Madora Bucher picked Raymond's photo out, too. Now the Dallas cops believed they'd identified Clyde and Raymond as two of the three robbers, and even though Mrs. Bucher couldn't be certain since she hadn't seen the driver of the getaway car, they felt sure they knew the identity of the third. Because of their frequent arrests together in the late 1920s, Dallas police thought Frank Clause remained Clyde's constant partner in crime. And so, police departments throughout Texas received bulletins that Clyde Barrow, Raymond Hamilton, and Frank Clause were wanted for the murder of John N. Bucher in Hillsboro.

Because Madora Bucher had unequivocally identified Clyde and Raymond, their guilt was considered a fact rather than a strong possibility. Texas governor Ross Sterling, who'd previously paroled Clyde from prison, authorized a $250 reward for the capture and conviction of each, astronomical at the time when $25 or $50 rewards for aiding in the apprehension of murder suspects were the norm, and the subsequent wanted posters noted "Take no chances on them as they are desperate men."

Two years earlier at Clyde's sentencing in Waco, Judge Richard Munroe had warned him that if he kept attempting robberies, someone would be shot and killed. Now that prediction had come true, and Clyde Barrow was no longer running from the West Dallas, Denton, and Kaufman police on charges of petty theft. He was being hunted as a killer, and cops all over Texas were on the lookout for him.

CHAPTER 10

Murder in Stringtown

Though the local newspapers didn't identify the leading suspects in the Bucher shooting by name, everybody in West Dallas was soon aware that Clyde Barrow was now wanted for murder. Clyde expected the police to stake out the family service station on Eagle Ford Road, so he made only a quick visit after the killing, swearing to his family that it had all been a terrible accident. In fact, Clyde could have hung around home longer. Cumie Barrow wrote in her memoir that in the next few weeks after Bucher was shot, the Dallas police came by the Barrow place only once to see if Clyde was there. It wasn't a matter of the local cops losing interest in him. But it was one thing for officers with a free hour or two to haul Clyde in for questioning about local burglaries and car thefts. There was little risk he'd violently resist arrest. Now he was on the run in a murder investigation, believed to be armed and ready to pull the trigger, at least according to the testimony of Bucher's widow. A full-scale, around-the-clock stakeout required manpower the Dallas police didn't have.

Clyde still wanted to break Ralph Fults out of the Wichita Falls jail, and Bonnie remained locked up in Kaufman. Then in early May,

Fults got word to Clyde, probably via a mutual acquaintance, that a rescue attempt wouldn't be necessary. He had his own escape plan.

In Wichita Falls, Fults shared a cell with Hilton Bybee, a serial murderer recently sentenced to be transferred south and die in the Huntsville prison's electric chair. Bybee had gotten his hands on some hacksaw blades and invited Fults to break out with him whenever there was an opportunity to cut through the rusty cell bars. On the night of May 10, they made their move. Bybee and Fults managed to get out of their cell, overpower a deputy, and grab his gun. When another officer appeared, Bybee tried to shoot him, but the gun he'd taken misfired. Fults and Bybee were recaptured before they had even gotten out of the building.

Bybee was moved to the fortresslike Tarrant County Jail in Fort Worth to await transfer to Huntsville. Fults was tried in Wichita Falls. On May 11, the day after he'd made his escape attempt, Fults was sentenced to ten years for armed robbery. It was a lenient sentence, and Fults was further relieved to be assigned to the Walls main prison unit instead of to another stint at Eastham farm. There he would strike up a friendship with Clyde's older brother Buck.

For the rest of May 1932 and the first few weeks of June, Clyde contented himself with a series of small holdups in and around Dallas. His family believed he pulled these jobs in partnership with Frank Clause, who along with Raymond Hamilton had been wrongly accused of complicity with Clyde in the Bucher murder. If Clyde and Clause did team up, their efforts weren't profitable. Marie Barrow later estimated that the total take from her brother's robberies of several service stations and a liquor store "didn't even add up to $100." Clyde was clearly marking time until the Kaufman County grand jury met to decide Bonnie's fate.

On June 17, Bonnie was called before the grand jury. No transcripts are known to survive, but the gist of her testimony was simple: Bonnie swore she'd been kidnapped by two men who forced her to come along as they unsuccessfully attempted to rob a Kaufman County hardware store and then fled. She must have been convincing—the grand jury ordered her released, and Emma Parker took Bonnie home. Before she left, Bonnie gave her collection of handwritten poems to Mrs. Adams, the wife of the Kaufman jailor. There is little doubt which of the poems meant the most to its creator. Bonnie kept a copy of "Suicide Sal," and in the months ahead she constantly tinkered with it, substituting various words and phrases but never abandoning the basic theme of a trusting girl betrayed by her crooked lover.

Emma felt her daughter "was soberer, more quiet and a great deal older than the Bonnie who had left home three months before. . . . We talked the situation over and I pointed out to her the trouble she had caused herself by following her heart instead of her head." According to Emma, Bonnie replied, "I'm through with [Clyde]. I'm never going to have anything more to do with him."

The Barrow family knew better. As soon as Bonnie was released, they carried messages back and forth between her and Clyde. Marie Barrow believed "Bonnie was only trying to keep her mother happy. . . . There was no way she would've ever have stayed away from Clyde." Yet it would have been understandable if Bonnie had meant every word she said to her mother about Clyde. She'd known him for two and a half years. He'd been in jail for nearly half that time, and on the run for most of the rest. Thanks to Clyde, Bonnie had been shot at in Kaufman, bounced on the back of a mule while being chased by a posse, shot at again on the banks of Cedar Creek, arrested and hauled off to jail, and finally interrogated by a grand jury that could have charged her with attempted robbery and sent her to prison. Now Clyde was wanted for murder. If the trends in her boyfriend's life were any indication, things for Clyde were only going to get worse, and that also went for anyone foolish enough to throw in with him. Logic dictated that Bonnie heed her mother's advice and stay away from Clyde Barrow forever.

But logic held little attraction for Bonnie Parker. Being logical meant waiting tables again, or, if she couldn't find an honest job, maybe even working one of the street corners she'd described so vividly in " 'The Prostitutes' Convention.' " The Depression economy, the swirling dust storms, the tedium and hopelessness of ordinary life—how much worse could life on the run with an accused murderer turn out to be? Maybe her time with Clyde so far hadn't been the best, and it was bound to end badly, but at least it would never be boring. So, logic be damned. Bonnie sent word to Clyde, probably through the Barrows, that she was ready to rejoin him.

She wasn't the only one. Raymond Hamilton had been working on a construction crew in Bay City, Michigan. Sometime in June 1932 Raymond was laid off, and since his mother, brother, and sisters lived in West Dallas it was natural for him to head back to Texas. Raymond arrived concerned that there might be some lingering heat from the failed Simms Refinery robbery, and was shocked to learn he was wanted for the Bucher murder. Though Clyde and Raymond had parted with hard feelings on both sides, Marie Barrow had become best friends with Raymond's little sister Audrey. Clyde soon knew that Raymond was back in town, and at some point the two fugitives met. They apparently settled their differences, because by mid-July, Clyde and Raymond had rented a small house or apartment in Wichita Falls. They used it as a base while committing a series of armed robberies.

Bonnie lived there with them. She told her mother that she'd found a job in a Wichita Falls café. "Something whispered to me that she'd gone to Clyde," Emma recounted two years later in *Fugitives*. "[But] in a few days I had a letter from Bonnie telling me all about the new job, where she was staying, and what hours she was working. I heaved a sigh of relief." Bonnie still hadn't turned twenty-two, and she remained enough of a child to not want her mother disappointed in her.

The re-formed Barrow-Hamilton team had no more initial luck as thieves than it did back in March. After a holdup at the Grand Prairie "Interurban" train station netted just $12, they decided to hit another small business in Dallas. The Neuhoff Packing Company was a few miles away from the Barrow place on Eagle Ford Road, and on August 1, Clyde dropped Bonnie off at his parents' service station before driving away with Raymond and Ross Dyer, a new partner recruited for the job because someone was needed to handle the getaway car. It was about 4 P.M., and Cumie Barrow had no doubt what her son and his cohorts were up to. While Bonnie nervously listened to the radio for any news reports, Cumie "asked her why she didn't try to get [Clyde] not to do it." Bonnie replied that Clyde "often told her that if she asked him not to do anything like that, he started thinking about it and couldn't keep his mind on the job." This conversation seems to mark the beginning of an understanding, if not a friendship, between Cumie and Bonnie. Though she'd previously had plenty of unflattering things to say about her son's girlfriend, for the remainder of her unpublished memoir Cumie never again wrote negatively about Bonnie.

Soon, Clyde, Raymond, and Ross Dyer returned, picked up Bonnie, and drove away. For a change, things had gone as planned. While Dyer had waited outside at the wheel of the getaway car, Clyde and Raymond went into the building, held three employees at gunpoint, and escaped with $440. That night the gang celebrated in an abandoned farmhouse in nearby Grand Prairie. They stayed there until the afternoon of August 5, when Clyde dropped Bonnie off again at the Barrow service station. From there, she took a taxi to her mother's house. Bonnie still didn't want Emma to know she'd gone back to Clyde.

Clyde realized he was persona non grata at Emma Parker's house, and he also understood Bonnie was very attached to her mother. But letting her enjoy an overnight visit with Emma also gave him, Raymond, and Ross Dyer an opportunity to blow off a little steam. By the beginning of August, Clyde had been wanted for murder for three months. Any initial panic had worn off. There didn't seem to be much difference between his life as a fugitive now and when he was wanted just for robbery. The successful Neuhoff robbery probably bolstered his confidence, too. So, after telling his mother he'd meet her the next morning "at seven or eight" at a cousin's house near the Barrow family service station, Clyde was in a party mood as he, Raymond, and Dyer drove their stolen car north from West Dallas. They apparently had no particular destination in mind. They just wanted to get out of town and have some fun.

At about 9 P.M. the trio reached Stringtown, Oklahoma, and saw that many of its nine hundred residents were gathered for a dance at an open pavilion some fifty yards off to the left of the highway. It was a small-scale event in a backwater town. The band consisted of two musicians, one playing guitar and the other the fiddle. Some couples swayed together on a raised wooden dance platform. Everyone else milled about, chatting and laughing. Despite Prohibition, flasks of bootleg liquor, known locally as "wildcat whiskey," were passed around. No one was charged admission to the dance. The musicians were to be paid by passing the hat. Because it was a neighborly affair where everyone was dressed comfortably in overalls or homespun frocks, it was impossible not to notice the flashy Ford V-8 that rolled into the gravel parking lot and the three strangers in suits who hopped out to join the festivities.

Far from worrying about sticking out in such a country crowd, Clyde, Raymond, and Dyer called further attention to themselves by taking turns ambling over to the raised platform and asking girls to dance. Their poor judgment had the predictable result. Some of the local men, their irritation fueled by alcohol, began grumbling. The outsiders started drinking, too, slugging down whiskey from their flasks just as openly as the Stringtown revelers. Trouble seemed imminent, and two local lawmen decided to do something about it.

During the Depression, many small-town men struggling to support their families were glad to take jobs in law enforcement. Pay was minimal. In some isolated communities, there was no salary at all. Cops received remuneration only when they caught crooks whose crimes were sufficient to merit rewards from the state—$10 to $25 was the usual range. Other county sheriffs made their livings by charging the state a few dollars for each night their jails housed prisoners. Most rural lawmen received no formal training at all in securing prisoners or handling weapons. They were resposible for furnishing their own guns and vehicles. Since they were probably poor if they were applying for these jobs to begin with, the sidearms they carried were mostly small-caliber and cheap, and they usually drove battered old cars or pickups kept in operating condition by baling wire and crossed fingers.

Still, Atoka County undersheriff Eugene Moore was thrilled when he was hired part-time by Sheriff Charlie Maxwell. Moore, thirty-one, had been making a comfortable living as a farmer and investor until he was wiped out by the Depression. He still had a wife and three children to support. No record exists of what Maxwell paid Moore, but it surely wasn't much. Fifteen dollars a week was about the norm for a full-time deputy. Still, the job in Atoka County wasn't supposed to be dangerous. Arresting drunks and breaking up fistfights was about as risky as it ever got way out in the country, which was why Maxwell and Moore were on hand at the dance in Stringtown. They didn't expect trouble, but the combination of young men with girls to impress and whiskey to drink always had the potential for some.

So long as things remained peaceful, Sheriff Maxwell had no intention of rousting his Stringtown constituents for a little illegal boozing. They were just having fun. But the pushy behavior of the three strangers in the fancy suits was bothersome, and when the two-man band took a break Maxwell mentioned to Duke Ellis, the guitar player, that he was going to arrest the trio for drinking before the local boys got riled enough to beat them up. As the band began to play its next set of songs, Maxwell strolled over to where Clyde and Raymond sat in their Ford. Dyer was a dozen yards away on the dance platform. Almost seventy years later Ellis recalled that he'd just hit the first chords of "Way Down Yonder" "when hell broke loose, and I mean hell."

Later, Clyde swore to his family that everything that happened was really Raymond Hamilton's fault. It was Raymond, Clyde said, who had insisted that they stop when they spotted the pavilion and heard the music. It was Raymond and Dyer who were foolish enough to try to dance with the local girls. Clyde said he stayed in the car the whole time, not even drinking when Raymond and Dyer did—a direct contradiction of Duke Ellis, who recalled seeing Clyde tipping a flask. Sheriff Maxwell, according to Clyde, approached him in the Ford not for illicit possession of alcohol but because one of the Stringtown boys had reported seeing a gun in the back seat. That is unlikely—according to Ellis, the sheriff "went over real casual" to the car without even drawing his own pistol. He would have been more cautious if he'd been warned about a gun. Probably Clyde just didn't want to admit to ultra-religious Cumie that he'd been drinking. Like Bonnie with Emma, he didn't want to disappoint his mother.

Maxwell leaned forward with one foot on the Ford's running board and told Clyde and Raymond they were under arrest. With the Bucher murder charges hanging over their heads, they weren't about to meekly surrender. Instead, they pulled their guns and fired at Maxwell. Ellis recalled that the sheriff's body "went flying back off that running board." An onlooker named Harry Bryant snatched up Maxwell's gun and started shooting at Clyde and Raymond. Moore ran up firing his pistol as Clyde yanked the Ford into gear and tried to speed off. But almost immediately he rammed a front tire into the edge of a culvert, and the car overturned. Clyde and Raymond scrambled out, spraying pistol shots back at Bryant and Moore as the crowd screamed and raced for cover. Moore fell down dead. Clyde and Raymond ran into the brush. Tentatively, people emerged from whatever cover they'd found. Ellis and a couple of other strapping young men carried the severely wounded Sheriff Maxwell to the nearest house and laid him on a bed. Within moments, the covers were soaked with blood. According to Ellis, the local bootlegger saved Maxwell's life by "pouring whiskey down him. He had six bullet holes in him—I counted them."

Within hours, a massive manhunt was underway, with posses from surrounding towns and counties joining in the chase. Clyde and Raymond managed to stay ahead of their pursuers by stealing a series of cars, the last of which they abandoned in Grandview just outside Dallas. Ross Dyer initially had it a little easier. He mingled with the panicked crowd during the gunplay, and afterward walked to a nearby bus stop and caught a ride back to Texas. There, his luck ran out. Dyer, who was using the name "Everett Milligan," was picked up almost immediately in McKinney and taken back to Atoka for questioning. Apparently an all-points bulletin from Oklahoma had reached Texas cops. After being positively identified as one of the three strangers who'd barged in on the Stringtown dance, Dyer was held for further interrogation in the Oklahoma town of McAlester. The Barrow family always assumed he fingered Clyde and Raymond as the shooters. They were undoubtedly right—just two days after Dyer's arrest, an Oklahoma newspaper identified "Clyde Barrow, wanted for murder of J. Bucher, a merchant of Hill county, Texas" as the main suspect in the killing of Undersheriff Moore. "Raymond Hamilton, pal of Barrow" was named as the second suspect.

At 7 A.M. on August 6, Cumie Barrow went out to meet Clyde in West Dallas. As promised, he and Raymond were waiting at his cousin's house, sprawled across a bed and keeping watch on the street through a window. Cumie didn't think Clyde seemed upset in any way. She asked where Ross Dyer was. Clyde replied "We lost him," and asked his mother if she'd seen the morning papers. Cumie mentioned a story about a lawman being killed in Oklahoma; Clyde and Raymond "looked kind of funny, and I became scared." When his mother asked if he killed Moore, Clyde denied it. When he finally admitted to her a few days later that he'd been involved in the shooting, he placed most of the blame on Raymond Hamilton.

It was clear to Clyde and his family that a criminal line had been irrevocably crossed. Prior to Stringtown Clyde was already wanted for murder, but he might have been able to wangle a life sentence rather than death in the Huntsville electric chair by convincing a judge and jury that he'd been waiting outside in the getaway car when John Bucher was shot. Texas governors were then still granting frequent paroles to relieve prison overcrowding. If the Bucher murder had been the only killing on his criminal record, Clyde might very well have become a free man again after five or ten more years in Huntsville. But the cold-blooded murder of a lawman ended any chance that he might have had for leniency. In the eyes of the law he was now a serial killer, and police everywhere were renowned for never abandoning the pursuit of a criminal who'd murdered one of their own. There were dozens of Stringtown witnesses to testify that Clyde had shot Eugene

Moore. If he was ever captured, Clyde believed he'd receive an automatic conviction and a date with the electric chair.

Clyde had crossed a moral line, too. He might claim that in Stringtown as in Hillsboro, murder occurred because other people made mistakes. According to Clyde, Raymond Hamilton was the one who insisted on stopping at the dance, just as Ted Rogers had fired the fatal shot in the Buchers' store while Clyde waited peacefully outside. But at least in Hillsboro he'd been separate from the bloody action. In Stringtown, Clyde's finger pulled a trigger. Counting Ed Crowder at Eastham Prison Farm in October 1931, Clyde had now been involved in three murders within the last eleven months. Yet Cumie noted in her memoir that the morning after he'd gunned down Eugene Moore, her son didn't seem particularly concerned. Perhaps he had already grown too comfortable with killing.

The rest of the Barrows didn't minimize the consequences to others from Clyde's actions in Stringtown. Marie Barrow wrote in her unpublished memoir that "we felt extremely bad for those who were injured due to the things in which Clyde became involved . . . [Eugene] Moore left a young wife and a couple of small children, a fact that hit my mother extremely hard." The family also knew that with the Stringtown killing, Clyde's eventual fate was sealed: "All my brother could do now was to try to stay ahead of the pursuing forces of the law until the chase reached its inevitable conclusion."

Clyde, too, may have understood his demise was inevitable, but he had no intention of allowing it to be immediate. He and Raymond needed to get far away from West Dallas and Oklahoma, where the search for them would be intense. He didn't make the chivalrous gesture of leaving his girlfriend behind so she wouldn't share the danger with him. Bonnie had sworn to stay with Clyde for better or worse, and he took her at her word. As soon as he'd had his meeting with Cumie, Clyde sent Raymond to collect Bonnie from her mother's house.

Bonnie had spent the previous evening promising Emma that she really was through with Clyde, insisting that she'd learned her lesson in Kaufman. Bonnie laid the lies on thick, tossing in fictitious descriptions of the Wichita Falls café where she supposedly worked. Emma thought Bonnie looked worn out, and decided it was because of long hours on the job coupled with the stifling Texas summer heat. When Raymond came to pick her up about 8 A.M. on August 6, Bonnie met him outside so Emma wouldn't realize she was getting a ride with Clyde's criminal sidekick. It would be several months before Bonnie saw her mother again, and almost a year before they had the opportunity for another long, private conversation.

The death of Eugene Moore was the direct result of Clyde's and Raymond's terrible judgment in stopping at the Stringtown dance at all, let alone calling additional attention to themselves after they did. But loyalty was one of Bonnie's most distinguishing characteristics. Even when Clyde made mistakes, in her mind it really wasn't his fault. She constantly told family and friends that unrelenting persecution by "the laws" pressured Clyde into becoming a career criminal and multiple murderer: "They made him what he is today. He used to be a nice boy. . . . Folks like us haven't got a chance." Modern-day psychologists would call Bonnie an enabler.

Beginning on August 6, 1932, Bonnie Parker's life became entwined completely with Clyde Barrow's. After the tragic events in Stringtown, she was the one who suggested where they ought to go next to throw off pursuit. It marked the moment Bonnie began to evolve from mostly ornamental girlfriend into Clyde's full-fledged partner in crime.

CHAPTER 11

Clyde and Bonnie on the Run

Millie Stamps, Emma Parker's sister, lived just outside Carlsbad, New Mexico. On Saturday, August 13, she was surprised when a new Ford V-8 drove up and her niece Bonnie hopped out. Bonnie announced she'd come for a visit with her new husband, James White, and their friend, Jack Smith. Aunt Millie had been out of touch with her Dallas relations for years. For all she knew, Bonnie really was a newlywed out on a driving trip honeymoon, though it seemed odd that she and James would be bringing a friend along. Family hospitality dictated that she couldn't turn them away, so Aunt Millie invited them to stay as long as they liked. It was working out just the way Bonnie planned.

She, Clyde, and Raymond had dithered for several days after reuniting on the morning of August 6. They knew they had to get far away from Dallas, where Clyde and Raymond were all too familiar to the police. They couldn't follow the usual roads north and east—Oklahoma was swarming with posses searching for them. While they tried to come up with a plan, Clyde and Bonnie hid out again in the abandoned Grand Prairie farmhouse. Raymond had a separate hiding place—even in such a desperate time, he and Clyde weren't getting along well enough to want to spend every hour in each other's company.

During this nervous interim, Clyde and Bonnie managed a late-night meeting with Clyde's family near the Houston Street Viaduct. Clyde's sister Nell was surprised by her brother's appearance. Clyde's hair had been dyed a bright, unnatural shade of red by Bonnie, who Nell thought looked "very tired and worn" and "without her usual sparkle." They talked a little about Stringtown. Clyde said he wasn't certain whether he or Raymond fired the shot that killed Eugene Moore. He joked a little about needing a blond wig to disguise himself. Bonnie snuggled against Clyde's shoulder. The late-night visit was a short one. Clyde was worried about being spotted by the cops.

When Bonnie suggested making a surprise visit to her aunt in New Mexico, Clyde liked the idea. There was no reason for the New Mexico police to be on the lookout for him and Raymond. They'd never committed any crimes in New Mexico, and communications between police in Texas and its neighboring state to the west were notoriously poor. Even better, road maps indicated that the highway from Dallas to Carlsbad ran mostly through deserted countryside. They would pass through very few towns, meaning there was little chance of getting spotted by suspicious local police.

It was 475 miles from Dallas to Carlsbad, and the road was packed dirt rather than paved asphalt. In Texas, the speed limit was 45 miles per hour, but Clyde routinely ignored speed limits. He drove, as always, in his stocking feet. The mutilation to his left foot may have prevented him from being able to properly feel the pedals while wearing a shoe. Even though Raymond and Bonnie were available to spell him behind the wheel, Clyde drove all the way to Carlsbad himself. He never liked to let anyone else drive. It was one more sign of his determination to be in control of everything.

Soon after her guests settled in, Aunt Millie became suspicious. Bonnie and her new husband were driving such a nice new car. How could they afford that kind of luxury vehicle? James White and Jack Smith seemed to have a lot of money between them, several hundred dollars at least—probably the remaining proceeds of the Neuhoff robbery, though Aunt Millie wouldn't have known that. Plus, they had all these guns, and the two men took them outside to do some very loud, annoying target shooting. Clearly, Clyde hadn't learned anything in

Stringtown about unnecessarily calling attention to himself. Family loyalty was one thing, but Millie Stamps was a woman who prided herself on possessing the very highest moral character. Surreptitiously, she contacted Eddy County deputy Joe Johns and asked him to drop by.

There had been a recent rash of car thefts in and around Carlsbad and Roswell. Johns thought Millie Stamps's niece and the two men with her might be involved. About 9 A.M. on August 14 he drove over and spotted the new Ford V-8 parked outside. That was enough for Johns to knock on the Stamps's front door. His intention was to quiz the visitors about where they got the car. If their story didn't check out, he would lock them up.

Bonnie answered the door. Johns asked to speak about the Ford with the two men who'd come to Carlsbad with her. Bonnie replied that the car was their property. Both men were getting dressed—she'd send them right out. Johns went over to inspect the V-8. He obviously didn't believe the suspected car thieves presented any danger to him. Johns paid for that careless mistake. While he poked around the Ford instead of remaining on his guard, Raymond and Clyde exited the Stamps house through the back door. They circled around the house and got the drop on the deputy, threatening him with a shotgun they'd found in a closet. They couldn't use their own guns because they had locked them in the trunk of the Ford. Whichever one was holding the shotgun fired a warning shot. Johns surrendered without a fight.

Once again, Clyde had taken a lawman hostage and had to do something with him. He chose not to kill the deputy, but he couldn't just let him go to spread the alarm. So Clyde, Bonnie, and Raymond forced Johns into the Ford at gunpoint, and Clyde drove east toward Texas. It was a habit Clyde was never able to break. No matter who was hunting him, no matter how close pursuit might be, Clyde always gravitated back to the state he knew best. That pattern, probably subconscious, would become even more pronounced, and thus more obvious to the law, in the months ahead. Now, with Johns as his hostage, he headed for the South Texas city of San Antonio.

In the early 1930s, three hundred miles even on paved highways was considered a full day's driving. It was about 450 miles on rough, mostly unpaved roads from Carlsbad to San Antonio, and Clyde didn't drive there directly. To throw off potential pursuit, he took several side roads, often relying on a road map so he wouldn't become lost. He still reached San Antonio sometime on the night of the 14th.

A frenzied search was underway for them, and not only in New Mexico. Several people had heard the warning shot that Clyde or Raymond fired at Joe Johns outside Carlsbad. A few hours later, two truck drivers discovered a headless corpse ninety miles outside El Paso. Authorities immediately assumed it was Johns—the two fugitives from Carlsbad must have blown his head off. Often, New Mexico and Texas authorities had difficulty communicating, but in this case the word went east fast and clear: Millie Stamps of Carlsbad had identified her niece, Bonnie Parker of Dallas, in the company of two men who'd apparently murdered a New Mexico county deputy and driven away in a Ford V-8 with Texas plates. From the descriptions provided, Texas lawmen were able to fill in the blanks: the men were probably Clyde Barrow and Raymond Hamilton, and now they'd killed another officer. Every cop in Clyde's home state was on the alert for him.

In San Antonio, Clyde drove endlessly in the dark, trying to find another car to steal. The V-8 he was driving now looked battered rather than flashy. In the course of racing along rock-strewn dirt highways all day and night at speeds up to 70 or 80 miles an hour Clyde had torn loose both bumpers, and cementlike dried mud coated the windshield and door panels. At least his hostage had been cooperative. Johns even suggested alternate routes to avoid major cities like Odessa. Though the New Mexico lawman had no idea who his captors were—the names Clyde Barrow, Bonnie Parker, and Raymond Hamilton weren't well known yet beyond the Texas border—he still took Clyde's threats to kill him seriously. At one point Bonnie asked Johns how he liked being on the run. "You've had just twenty-four hours of it," Bonnie told him. "We get 365 days of it every year." All four passengers in the Ford were tired and hungry. Clyde had been willing to stop for gas, but not food.

About 5 A.M. on August 15, Clyde gave up looking for a car to steal. He wanted another of the new V-8 "flatheads" that had just been introduced by Ford. These beauties could outrun anything else on American roads. But there weren't any to steal in San Antonio, at least not in the neighborhoods where Clyde was looking. So he steered the battered V-8 he was driving about fifteen miles out of the city. Then he ordered Deputy Johns out of the car, remarking, "You sure have caused us a lot of trouble." He asked Johns not to raise any alarm for another hour—a naive request. Still, the deputy had to hike almost a mile to the nearest houses, and it took several tries before he found someone with a phone who could call the San Antonio police. One newspaper reported the next day that Johns "was mystified" when informed that his headless body had been discovered back in West Texas.

Police immediately set up roadblocks on the main highway between San Antonio and Dallas, figuring Clyde might be heading home by the most direct route. But he drove southeast instead, and during the afternoon he and Raymond found a suitable Ford V-8 to steal in Victoria, 120 miles from San Antonio. They didn't abandon the mud-splattered, bumperless car they'd been driving since they originally left West Dallas for Carlsbad. Probably Clyde thought it would be a good idea to have two cars. There weren't a lot of big cities between Victoria and Houston, where they were heading next. If they only had one vehicle and it broke down miles away from civilization, they'd be left on foot. Clyde and Bonnie certainly remembered trying to get away from the Kaufman County posse on mules. So Raymond drove the newly stolen Ford, following Clyde and Bonnie in their battered car. The two-vehicle caravan proceeded toward Houston, some 125 miles away.

But they hadn't made a clean getaway while stealing the Ford in Victoria. The owners spotted them driving off, and a neighbor briefly gave chase. The police were called, and the description of the thieves matched that of the fugitives who'd kidnapped Deputy Joe Johns. When last seen in Victoria, they were speeding down Rio Grande Street, the most common route to Houston. It seemed likely that was where the trio was heading next. As fast as Clyde and Raymond might have been driving, telephone and telegraph messages still preceded them, warning police in towns along the way to be on the lookout for the newly stolen Ford. Besides descriptions of the occupants, its license plate number was provided.

The town of Wharton was sixty miles northeast of Victoria, about two-thirds of the way to Houston. Two Wharton policemen, identified in newspapers later as "Deputy Seibrecht and City Marshal Pitman," decided to set a trap in case the car thieves–kidnappers came driving through. The Colorado River ran just west of town, and the highway crossed the river on a narrow bridge. Seibrecht pulled his car into a ditch on the west side of the bridge. Pitman parked on the east side. If Seibrecht saw the stolen car pass, he'd signal Pitman, who'd pull his car onto the road on the far side of the bridge. Seibrecht would swing his vehicle across the road on the other side, effectively trapping the stolen car and its occupants. It was a plan that almost worked.

Soon two Ford V-8s came roaring along the road; the second was the stolen car from Victoria. Seibrecht jumped up from the ditch and signaled to Pitman across the river. But in the lead car, the muddy, bumperless Ford, Clyde spotted Seibrecht and suspected a trap had been set. For the last two days, Clyde had demonstrated his ability to drive improbably long distances without rest. Now he proved he could turn on a dime at high speed. Slamming on the brakes, he came to a skidding stop just before the bridge, swung the Ford around and roared back in the opposite direction. Raymond Hamilton, following in the second Ford, wasn't able to duplicate Clyde's nifty U-turn. It took him several more seconds to stop, swing around, and drive away, enough time for Seibrecht to get off several shots. Raymond wasn't hit. Since the Ford V-8s were far more powerful than the cars being driven by the Wharton cops, there was no chance of overtaking the three fugitives. The mud-coated Ford with no bumpers was found abandoned by the side of the road a few miles from the bridge. Police from New Mexico and Oklahoma soon arrived on the scene, and the next day's paper specified that besides kidnapping and car theft, the Wharton escapees were wanted for murder in Stringtown and Hillsboro, for the robbery of the Neuhoff Packing Company in Dallas, "and for numerous other crimes." Bonnie had always wanted to be famous. Now she, Clyde, and Raymond were—at least in Texas, Oklahoma, and New Mexico. Their names and descriptions were printed in newspapers throughout the region and mentioned frequently on the radio. That's how Emma Parker learned that Bonnie wasn't working at a café in Wichita Falls.

Using back roads instead of main highways, Clyde, Bonnie, and Raymond drove back to Dallas. They hid out at the same abandoned farmhouse, and made at least one trip thirty-five miles west to Fort Worth, where they broke into the state guard armory and stole several powerful Browning Automatic Rifles. Clyde had been able to outdrive pursuit in Carlsbad and Wharton. He wanted to be certain he could outshoot the law, too, if it became necessary. This was the first, but far from the last, time Clyde broke into a state guard armory. Most Texas towns of any size had armories for storing state-owned weapons intended to arm citizen militias in the event of widespread emergency. Legislative red tape kept the high-caliber weapons from being available on loan to outgunned local police. Clyde had easy access to them by breaking a few locks.

The new guns weren't enough to convince Raymond to stick

around with Clyde in Texas. He didn't like Clyde to begin with, and his association with him had only resulted in being wanted for kidnapping and two murders, one of which occurred while Raymond was thousands of miles away. Raymond considered himself a gentleman bank robber, not a mistake-prone crook who stumbled from one bloody mishap to the next. About September 1 he told Clyde and Bonnie he was going back to Michigan for a while, and they drove Raymond almost a thousand miles north to Bay City. It was less a friendly gesture than an opportunity to get a break from local pursuit. After dropping Raymond off, they were in no hurry to go back to Texas. Clyde's sister Marie noted in her memoir that "they lived off of small robberies that Clyde committed," probably quick heists at small country stores and service stations. They stole several cars, too, driving them across state lines. When police searched one car stolen in Illinois and abandoned in Oklahoma, they found a medicine bottle in it that was traced back to Clyde. Even though Clyde had stolen cars and driven them across state lines before, he'd never been sloppy enough to leave behind evidence that irrefutably linked him to the crimes. It was a critical error, and one that would come back to haunt him. This car theft was the first federal crime charged to Clyde—bank robbery and murder, by law, were still the concerns of the individual states in which they took place. The authority of nonfederal lawmen was limited to their specific jurisdictions. Even the Texas Rangers had to cut off pursuit at the state line. Now Clyde could legally be pursued anywhere by agents for the U.S. Justice Department's Division of Investigation headed by J. Edgar Hoover. It didn't make an immediate difference—in September 1932, when the car stolen in Illinois was found in Oklahoma, Clyde was still a tiny criminal fish compared to whoppers like Pretty Boy Floyd and Alvin Karpis as far as Hoover and his feds were concerned. But the basis for unrestricted pursuit of him by federal agents was established. Clyde had passed one more criminal point of no return.

A series of postcards kept the rest of the Barrow family generally apprised of Clyde and Bonnie's Midwest wanderings. They didn't sign the postcards or indicate where they were headed next, just in case the Dallas police were intercepting and reading Cumie and Henry's mail. Most of Clyde's previous trips outside his normal Texas-Oklahoma stomping grounds had been hectic—to Middletown, Ohio, after escaping from the Waco jail; driving north to Minnesota with Ralph Fults and Raymond Hamilton, looking for a bank to rob; the recent debacle in Carlsbad, New Mexico. Now his leisurely tour with Bonnie took on aspects of a vacation. The postcards they sent back to West Dallas told about drives along the Great Lakes, and described the skyscrapers in Chicago. For a change, they were having fun.

Fun didn't preclude practical considerations. Clyde and Bonnie needed places to stay, food to eat, clothes to wear, gas for their stolen cars, and money to pay for it all. They didn't consider robbing a bank to be a good option. Any bank with money still left in its vaults would have a guard or two, a staff of tellers, and probably customers lined up in its lobby. Bonnie wasn't taking an active role in holdups yet, and Clyde couldn't simultaneously hold people at gunpoint, crack a safe, and handle a getaway car. He could rob shops in small rural communities without needing help. Besides, any robbery attempt on a big city bank or major business would draw much more attention from the local law than the relatively insignificant holdup of mom-and-pop grocery stores or service stations out in the country. The downside of small-time stickups was that they needed to be repeated every few days. Takes of $5 or $10 didn't finance road expenses long, even in the Depression.

Beginning with this trip, Clyde and Bonnie liked to stay at motor courts, a recent innovation in travel lodging. Since the end of the First World War, more Americans were taking advantage of cheaper cars and improved roads to drive themselves on trips for business and recreation, and they needed convenient, inexpensive places to stay along the way. First in the less-populated Southwest, then all over the country, roadside "auto camps" began to spring up—cleared areas where, for a few cents, travelers could park their cars for the night. Often they would pitch tents beside their vehicles and cook dinner over a campfire. By the late 1920s, these had evolved into "cabin camps," offering rudimentary shacks and communal restrooms. Within a few years, coinciding almost exactly with the time Clyde and Bonnie began their brief era of roaming banditry, cabin camps morphed into "motor courts." These featured stand-alone cottages with bathrooms and carports. Besides beds, the cottages had other homelike amenities—rugs, bureaus, tables, and sometimes even kitchens. With rental fees of about a dollar a day, they were pricey enough to keep out completely impoverished riffraff, but still affordable to rank-and-file travelers. It was pleasant for Clyde and Bonnie to check into a motor court under assumed names and enjoy indoor plumbing and beds with clean sheets.

There was one more advantage—because the motor courts were always beside major roads and usually some distance from downtown traffic congestion, if the need arose they offered better options for quick getaways than hotels in the middle of bustling cities.

But often when Clyde and Bonnie found themselves on an isolated back road at the end of the day there wasn't the option of sleeping in a comfortable motor court. In these instances, they looked for farmhouses and asked whoever lived there for permission to spend the night. Particularly in rural areas during the Depression, it was considered almost mandatory for those lucky enough to have roofs over their heads to share their food and homes with passing strangers. There was a pervading sense that, except for the rich, everyone else was caught up in a common struggle to survive. In their flashy cars, dressed in Sunday clothes, Clyde and Bonnie clearly weren't run-of-the-mill hobos angling for a handout. But the farm families they approached didn't ask for any more personal information than whatever made-up story their visitors chose to share. Clyde and Bonnie always paid for their overnight room and board, sometimes with a dollar or two, more often with a box of food purchased from a nearby store or another present of some kind. Clyde occasionally reimbursed rural hosts with the gift of a shotgun or pistol. Certainly even the least observant among them had suspicions, but it didn't matter. Most of these families were so poor themselves that money or food was a godsend. And, though Clyde and Bonnie were clearly on the run, farmers struggling to protect their property from foreclosure generally had a low opinion of the government and the law. By the middle of 1932, one out of every eight farms in the United States had been foreclosed because of mortgage or tax delinquencies. It was unlikely any of Clyde and Bonnie's farmer hosts would turn them in. But just to be certain, they rarely stayed with any family for more than a day.

Bonnie enjoyed these overnight visits. She was always sociable, and with her natural vivaciousness and knack for lively conversation she made friends easily with everyone she met. Clyde was moodier. Sometimes he didn't feel like talking and failed to make a good impression on his host families. Bonnie always did. She particularly made a fuss over children. Often, she'd coax Clyde into giving kids rides on the running board and bumpers of their gleaming stolen cars. For many youngsters living on isolated farms, it was the first time they'd seen such a fancy automobile, let alone had a chance to ride in or on one.

But there were also times when no motor courts or farmhouses were available, and then Clyde and Bonnie had to camp out in their car. They'd pull off the road, often driving through thick brush until they felt safely out of sight. Whenever possible, Clyde tried to park by a creek so there would be water for bathing. Even though the nice seats in the big cars he stole were more comfortable to sleep on than the hard ground, they still weren't as good as a bed. Bugs were a constant irritant, and Bonnie was petrified of snakes. If she thought there was even a remote possibility of one nearby, she wouldn't get out of the car. She was also afraid of thunder and lightning. Because a fire might draw unwanted attention, their camp meals were usually cold—crackers, Vienna sausages, sardines, cans of beans in gluey tomato sauce. Bonnie hated the primitiveness of it—relieving herself behind bushes was hardly the glamour she craved—and annoyed Clyde by complaining and occasionally consoling herself with bootleg whiskey. Clyde liked to drink himself, but whenever they camped out he tried to remain as alert as possible. Even in states such as Michigan, Illinois, and Kansas where they weren't as notorious, there was always the possibility that some passing lawman might spot their camp and try to run them in as vagrants. When Bonnie whined and drank, it got on Clyde's nerves. They had arguments that occasionally escalated into hitting. Bonnie swung at Clyde as often as he did at her.

Mostly, he did his best to keep her happy. Clyde even stole a typewriter for Bonnie; sometimes while he drove she'd sit with it in the back seat, tapping out new poetry and fresh versions of "Suicide Sal." Bonnie and Clyde both liked to dress in clean, fancy clothes, and on this and all their subsequent trips they anchored their otherwise nomadic lifestyle around towns with dry cleaners. They would drop off several suits and dresses, spend a few days in the surrounding countryside, then come back to pick up the freshly laundered clothes. Whenever their wardrobes needed replacing, Clyde would give his brother L.C. and sister Marie money at family meetings, then send them to shops in downtown Dallas. L.C. especially loved buying suits for Clyde in stores near public bulletin boards displaying his wanted posters.

In October, Clyde and Bonnie began a gradual return to Texas. They both wanted to see their families again, and it had been several months since the shooting of Eugene Moore in Stringtown. Maybe the heat among the cops back home had abated. They lingered awhile in Kansas. The reason was never recorded, but Clyde probably liked the long, straight stretches of highway. They finally arrived in West Dallas on Halloween. As Clyde drove past the Barrow service station on Eagle Ford Road, he tossed out an empty Coke bottle with a note inside. It gave a time and place outside town where he wanted the family to meet him that night. As soon as it was dark, Clyde and Bonnie made a quick stop at Emma Parker's house. Bonnie took just a few minutes to tell her mother she was fine, hurrying away before Emma could launch into a lecture on the foolishness of being with Clyde. Emma and Bonnie's sister, Billie, weren't invited along to the Barrow gathering—the two families weren't in constant touch yet, as they would be later on. Then Clyde whisked Bonnie off to the isolated spot outside town that he'd selected as a meeting place. Henry, Cumie, Nell, and Marie were there. They had news for Clyde and Bonnie, none of it good: Clyde's younger brother, L.C., was in jail on suspicion of car theft, and Clyde was wanted for another murder.

CHAPTER 12

The Price of Fame

In 1932, most Texas journalists were not about to let facts get in the way of a good story. Newspaper circulation throughout the state was down, in some smaller cities by as much as half—people hard-pressed to feed their families often weren't willing to spend a nickel during the week or a dime on Sunday for a newspaper. Advertising revenues had dropped almost as precipitously. Fewer stores bought newspaper ads touting sales because there weren't enough potential customers to buy the featured products. What even the most impoverished were tempted by instead was entertainment, anything that could even briefly take their minds off their considerable, ongoing troubles. Texas newspapers weren't going to survive featuring stories about more farm foreclosures and the damage done by the latest dust storms. They needed to entice readers with tales of high adventure and preferably the exploits of colorful criminals, the same themes that kept Depression-impoverished audiences packing movie theaters. The silver screen had Jimmy Cagney. Now, many Texas newspapers hitched their fortunes to Clyde Barrow.

Two murders—in Hillsboro on April 30 and in Stringtown on August 5—plus the kidnapping of a New Mexico deputy and a subsequent high-speed, long-distance drive that included escaping the bridge trap in Wharton gave reporters plenty of colorful material to embellish further. Clyde became "the Southwest's will-o'-the-wisp bandit." He was always willing "to shoot it out when capture threatens." One newspaper would print something outrageous and others would reprint the story, until by repetition it became accepted as part of the ever-expanding library of entertaining Barrow lore. Readers of Texas newspapers were treated to colorful accounts of John Bucher's last moments. As he fell with Clyde's bullet in his heart, "Mrs. Bucher ran toward her husband," only to be warned "get back, or I'll give you some of the same." In Stringtown, Sheriff Maxwell supposedly admonished Clyde for drinking by calling out, "Here, you can't do that." Clyde's reply, according to the papers, was "We can't, can't we?" followed by "a blast of gunfire." Readers might have wondered why such quotes and descriptions weren't attributed to specific witnesses, but, just like the reporters who wrote the stories, most of them valued entertainment more than truth.

Playing fast and loose with facts about Clyde wasn't confined to journalists. Police reports got lots of things wrong, too, either through careless distribution of erroneous information—one federal wanted poster for Clyde listed his female companion as "Mrs. Roy Harding"—or else the urge to make their own fleeting encounters with Clyde seem more heroically life-or-death than they actually were. In Wharton on August 15, 1932, two deputies fired shots at cars driven by Clyde and Raymond Hamilton as they approached the bridge over the Colorado River. The fugitives never fired back. They had all they could do to get their vehicles turned around while bullets fired by the lawmen buzzed past them. But that wasn't the story told in an August 30 bulletin issued by Wharton County sheriff J. C. Willis to "All Peace Officers in the United States" warning them to be on the lookout for Clyde and Raymond. According to Willis, the bloodthirsty duo wheeled into Wharton and "tried to kill one of my deputies. . . . They abandoned a V8 Ford coupe which they had stolen at Grand Prairie, Texas after shooting at our deputy sheriff." Willis concluded his inaccurate message by pleading, "Wire all information to me collect and please make every effort to arrest these parties and stop their running over the country shooting officers wherever they go."

Such reports were the basis for additional inaccurate newspaper articles. Stories about the Wharton escape dutifully reported that Clyde and Raymond fired the first shots there, more proof for readers that they were trigger-happy in the extreme. Coupled with the reports that Clyde drove incredible distances at high speeds in his stolen cars—that much, at least, was true—people all over Texas had plenty of cause to believe that Clyde might pop up anywhere, anytime, probably robbing and definitely shooting as he went.

When Raymond Hamilton was included in the newspaper stories about Clyde, he inevitably received second billing. He was the "pal of Barrow." Clyde had already served a term in Huntsville, while Raymond had just been in a county jail for car theft. It was Clyde's mug shot that Dallas police always passed around first. Bonnie was often mentioned in the articles, but almost always as "a Dallas girl" or Clyde's "frequent companion" rather than by name. It wasn't because the cops didn't know who she was—her aunt, Millie Stamps, had seen to that. Rather, it was another example of Texas chauvinism. A woman wasn't considered strong-minded enough to be a part of criminal activities through her own choice. If Bonnie wasn't being forced to ride along with Clyde, then she was just a silly, love-addled girl who couldn't be expected to know better.

So everywhere in Texas, and in parts of Oklahoma and New Mexico because of their well-publicized crimes there, Clyde and Raymond and Bonnie were often what people talked about in barbershops and on porches after evening meals. It didn't stop when Raymond went back to Michigan and Clyde and Bonnie took their two-month Midwest working vacation. Innumerable holdups and several shootings back in Texas were still blamed on them. When two service stations were robbed in Lufkin, when a Piggly-Wiggly grocery was knocked off in Abilene, Clyde and Raymond were immediately identified as the prime suspects. When Sheriff John C. Moseley was shot in Tulia a few months later, it seemed to witnesses that three persons were involved, and "officers investigating the affray suspected that one of the three fugitives might be a woman." Nobody realized that Raymond had split off from Clyde and Bonnie. Even if they had, they probably wouldn't have cared. Clyde was short and scrawny with light brown hair, average-looking enough so that anyone fresh from the shock of witnessing a violent crime might make an honest mistake in picking him out from mug shots. And in such cases, eyewitnesses were usually the sole means of identifying and convicting perpetrators. Fingerprinting had been a tool in crime investigation since the 1920s, and the fingerprints of Clyde, Raymond, and Bonnie were all on file from their previous arrests. But few small towns had the capacity to dust store door handles and service station cash boxes for prints. Guesswork was far more common than even the most basic forensics. So on October 11, 1932, when a butcher in Sherman, Texas, was brutally murdered during a robbery at the store where he worked, police and reporters were quick to assume it was the bloody work of Clyde Barrow.

At around 6:30 P.M., a young man entered Little's Grocery. He asked Homer Glaze, the store's clerk, and Howard Hall, the shop butcher, for a few items before pulling a gun and demanding that they hand over the money in the cash register. There wasn't much—$60 was the amount later reported. If the bandit had arrived just a few minutes earlier, he might have intercepted the store owner taking most of the day's receipts over to the bank. Instead, he scooped up the money that remained and ordered Glaze and Hall outside. According to Glaze, Hall began arguing out on the sidewalk and was shot several times at close range. He died an hour later. The gunman tried to shoot Glaze, too, but his gun jammed. He ran down the street and drove away with another man in a large black sedan.

When police arrived, Glaze described the killer as about five feet, six inches tall and twenty to twenty-five years old. The Sherman cops circulated the description, and the Dallas police came sixty miles north with mug shots of Clyde. Glaze identified him from these as the assailant who'd shot and killed Howard Hall. Clyde was further implicated when Walter Enloe, a Grayson County deputy sheriff, said he'd just seen Clyde in Sherman, too. L.C. Barrow was in the county jail there, awaiting a grand jury hearing on a charge of car theft. According to Enloe, on the afternoon of October 11, Clyde came to the jail to visit his kid brother. Apparently, Enloe didn't ask to see any identification and let the renowned killer come right in. He identified Clyde afterward from the Dallas police's mug shots. The Grayson County grand jury added charges for a third murder to the rapidly expanding list of alleged crimes on Clyde's wanted posters, and the sheriff's office offered a new $200 reward for information leading to his capture.

Clyde certainly might have tried to rob a small-town grocery store—it would have been typical of him. Shooting an unarmed man when he was in no immediate danger himself would not. Neither was visiting L.C. in the Grayson County lockup. Clyde had already demonstrated when Bonnie was in the Kaufman County jail that he was too wary to visit incarcerated loved ones himself. (Soon after the Hall murder, L.C. was no-billed for lack of evidence by the Grayson County grand jury.) Glaze and Enloe might have picked out his mug shot, but misidentification by eyewitnesses was common. Back in Hillsboro, Madora Bucher had mistaken Ted Rogers for Raymond Hamilton. Enloe's testimony becomes even more suspect because it's unclear from surviving state and local records whether, on October 11, L.C. Barrow had even been transferred yet to Grayson County from Dallas, where he'd originally been arrested.

Then there's the most mitigating factor of all—on October 11, Clyde hadn't yet returned to Texas. In *Fugitives*, Clyde's sister Nell insists he and Bonnie only arrived on Halloween, when he learned from his family that he had been charged with Hall's murder and that L.C. was in jail. It's possible, but not probable, that Clyde misled them. He and Bonnie could have been back in Texas weeks earlier, and learned about L.C.'s incarceration from someone else. But from John Bucher in Hillsboro through his final victim two years later in Oklahoma, Clyde never lied to his family about the murders he committed. He often tried to place most of the blame on someone else, suggesting to the other Barrows that he was almost as much a victim of circumstance as whoever died, but he never denied being involved. If he'd killed Hall, he would have admitted it during the family gathering on Halloween night. Marie wrote that Clyde "vehemently denied" having anything to do with the Sherman murder. In her opinion, the Dallas police told Glaze and Enloe to say it was Clyde they'd seen. Nell Barrow wrote that her brother was philosophic about the news, saying, "They've got to hang it on somebody, you know."

It would be a continuing source of frustration to the rest of the Barrows that Clyde was repeatedly blamed by police and journalists for crimes he didn't commit. But Clyde usually liked it. He and Bonnie began saving the newspaper articles, which they'd reread and savor. Police would find the clippings in abandoned stolen cars, the newsprint creased and smeared from frequent handling. To Clyde and Bonnie, every story whether true or not was further proof they were important now, people to be reckoned with by the laws and the public. If some of the newspaper descriptions of Clyde tended toward the demonic ("Barrow, his mean little eyes snapping, was pointing a revolver at Hall and Homer Glaze. . . . Barrow stood over the old butcher and fired three shots into Hall's body"), it just reinforced his opinion of himself as someone other men ought to fear. Smart people had been scared of Jesse James and Billy the Kid, too. Bonnie wanted everyone to like her. Clyde wanted to be intimidating.

Of course, criminal celebrity had its drawbacks. Just as the newspaper articles extended Clyde's reputation in Texas, they also reminded lawmen all over the state of what to be on the lookout for. There weren't that many twenty-two-year-olds in suits barreling down the roads in flashy Ford V-8s with blond girls perched by their sides. Clyde had no intention of completely abandoning his home state—no cops were going to keep Clyde Barrow from seeing his family and pulling holdups wherever he pleased—but he did realize he ought to exercise more caution. He and Bonnie wouldn't camp any longer in abandoned farmhouses outside Dallas for weeks at a time. They'd need to be on the move almost every day, and sometimes expand their criminal hunting grounds beyond Texas and Oklahoma, the states where they were most familiar to police. And that was fine—Clyde loved to drive. The trip to Michigan and drive back through Illinois and Kansas whetted Clyde's and Bonnie's appetites for travel. After getting the news about the Hall murder from Clyde's family on Halloween night, they decided to try their luck in Missouri for a while. But before they left, there was one more bit of business Clyde had to attend to.

From his first forays into crime as a West Dallas teenager, Clyde rarely worked alone. He'd teamed at various times with his brother Buck, Frank Clause, William Turner, Ralph Fults, the Lake Dallas boys, and Raymond Hamilton. It made sense to have partners. Robberies were easier with one man pointing the gun, another emptying the safe or looting the cash drawer, and still another accomplice outside revving the engine of the getaway car. In that respect, Bonnie didn't count. Clyde was still keeping her away from the action. Having male sidekicks was an advantage Clyde always wanted and appreciated.

But, as his reputation grew, there was another reason he wanted partners. Being the leader of a gang would give even more heft to his burgeoning fame. The legendary outlaws Clyde idolized didn't work alone. Jesse James had the fearsome James Gang. Billy the Kid terrorized New Mexico with a pack of henchmen. The most famous criminals of Clyde's own general era—John Dillinger, Pretty Boy Floyd, Al Capone—all led gangs. There was extra cachet in being boss. Clyde always wanted to be the one giving orders. Until now in his criminal career, it wasn't possible. Buck was Clyde's big brother. Frank Clause took the inexperienced Clyde under his wing. Ralph Fults was Clyde's equal. Raymond Hamilton considered himself that, too—it was probably the main reason Clyde didn't like him.

Now, anointed by the Texas press as a criminal mastermind, Clyde had the opportunity to establish a Barrow Gang in which there was no doubt as to who was in charge. So before he and Bonnie left West Dallas after their Halloween visit, Clyde recruited two new partners to go north to Missouri with them. Frank Hardy and Hollis Hale were eager to join up. They believed that in working with Clyde Barrow, they were breaking into the criminal big time. Clyde, Bonnie, and their two new partners headed north into southern Missouri, where they eventually holed up in a motor court in Carthage, a few miles northeast of Joplin.

Uncharacteristically, Clyde now took his time choosing the newly formed gang's first target. Even more uncharacteristically, he decided to rob a bank. He might have wanted to impress Hardy and Hale. There was one false start—Marie Barrow Scoma mentions in her unpublished memoir that Clyde and his new cohorts broke into an unnamed Missouri bank, only to be informed by the lone clerk on duty that the institution had failed a few days earlier. He had no money left for them to steal. So Clyde next selected the Farmer and Miners Bank of Oronogo. Time had become of the essence—the Barrow Gang was down to its last few dollars. Still, Clyde planned the robbery far more carefully than usual. On November 29, Bonnie was sent to reconnoiter, which might have been a mistake. Very few women went into banks, and those who did were expected to be properly dressed—hat and gloves were socially mandatory—and in the company of their husbands or, at least, a male companion to do the talking for them. The Barrow family never had a bank account back in West Dallas, and Clyde almost certainly had no idea of proper bank etiquette for females. Bonnie probably dressed appropriately, but she may never have been in a bank before. Coming in alone, uncertain of how to behave and with no business to transact, she was bound to seem suspicious. Perhaps as a result of Bonnie's visit, when Clyde, Hardy, and Hale arrived to stage their holdup at 11:30 A.M. on November 30, it didn't go as they'd anticipated. Hale waited outside in the getaway car while Clyde and Hardy went in. Clyde probably carried one of the BARs he'd stolen from the armory in Fort Worth. A story the next day in the *Carthage Evening*

Press noted that it was the first "sub-machine gun" ever used in a local robbery.

There was only one customer in the bank, but the teller had a pistol handy. Ducking down behind the counter—which was lead-lined as a precaution against holdups, something Bonnie would have had no way of learning during her previous day's scouting expedition—the teller started blasting away. Fortunately for the robbers, his gun jammed after a few shots. Clyde fired back, but his bullets couldn't penetrate the thick shielding and the teller wasn't hit. Hardy grabbed for the cash lying within reach on a table in the cubicle, in the process cutting his hand on glass smashed by Clyde's shots. Then he and Clyde ran for the car outside. But somebody had sounded an alarm, and several armed Oronogo citizens were waiting. They opened fire as Clyde and Hardy jumped in the car and Hale drove away. They weren't hit, and nobody bothered chasing them. Their take, according to the Carthage paper, was "less than $500." It was actually a lot less—$110.

For Clyde, it was just one more job that hadn't been especially lucrative. But the gang had gotten some money, and nobody had been hurt aside from Frank Hardy's cut hand. As far as Clyde was concerned, they'd pack up, drive on, and try it again somewhere else.

Frank Hardy and Hollis Hale reacted differently. They'd signed on with big-shot Clyde Barrow to commit spectacular robberies of banks with piles of money in their vaults. They'd read about the Barker Gang's recent raid on a bank in Concordia, Kansas, where the reported take was $240,000. Neither had realized that kind of job was far beyond Clyde's capabilities. Almost all the major bank thefts by Dillinger, Floyd, or the Barker boys were pulled off because the perpetrators either secretly colluded with bank officers or else paid off local police. Sometimes they did both. It was never a matter of them randomly picking out a bank, driving up to it, going in with guns, and emptying the vault. Clyde didn't have the resources or contacts necessary to plan and carry out sophisticated schemes. No matter what exaggerated descriptions of his criminal prowess the Texas newspapers might print, where robbery was concerned he was strictly a small-timer.

But Hardy and Hale had expected six-figure takes, and in their two bank robberies as members of the Barrow Gang they'd come up first with nothing, then with a measly $110 that would have to be split three ways. Their disillusionment was complete. Back at the motor court in Carthage, they lied and told Clyde they'd only gotten $80. Then, after splitting that reduced amount, Hardy and Hale said they needed to go into town to buy ammunition. They never came back. Clyde and Bonnie were left with about $25.

Within a few weeks the couple was back in Texas, hoping to rescue two old friends from the McKinney jail. Ralph Fults had been sent there from the state prison in Huntsville to be tried on an old charge of car theft. Though there is some doubt that Fults was guilty of that particular crime, he still had an additional five years tacked onto his current sentence. Ted Rogers was also in the McKinney lockup, held on charges unrelated to his brief partnership with Clyde. Somehow, word reached Clyde and Bonnie. On December 19, while Fults and Rogers were waiting to be transferred back to Huntsville by Bud Russell and the One Way Wagon, Fults was told he had a visitor. Bonnie Parker gave Fults a pack of cigarettes and whispered that Clyde was outside ready to break him and Rogers out. Fults hissed that the jailor kept the cell keys at another location, and wouldn't have them again until breakfast the next day. Clyde and Bonnie prepared for a morning rescue, but were thwarted when Bud Russell arrived at 4 A.M. to take Fults and Rogers away.

A few days before Christmas, Clyde and Bonnie made plans for another quick visit to West Dallas. They wanted to bring presents to their families, whom they hadn't seen since Halloween. Nineteen thirty-two had been a tumultuous year, beginning with Clyde cutting off two of his toes and being paroled by the governor just days later. Bonnie had spent several months in jail. Clyde was involved in two murders and blamed for three, in the process becoming the most famous outlaw in Texas. He and Bonnie were more certain than ever that they would die in the end, gunned down by lawmen in some desperate shootout. There was clearly no going back to their old lives even if they wanted to—and they didn't. Whatever they suffered, whatever anyone else suffered, was worth it to them. Even if their lives were the eventual price, they'd broken free from insignificance and tedium. They mattered. People were paying attention to them.

CHAPTER 13

Raymond and W.D.

Raymond Hamilton had never intended to stay in Michigan after Clyde and Bonnie dropped him off there in early September 1932. He hung around in Bay City for about a month, then went back to Texas during the first week of October. Like Clyde and Bonnie, Raymond had family in West Dallas—his mother, an older brother, and several sisters. Using West Dallas as a base, staying with friends rather than family in case the police were watching his mother's house, Raymond made his return to crime on October 8 when he single-handedly held up the First State Bank of Cedar Hill, a small Dallas suburb. The job went amazingly well. Raymond caught two bank staffers and two customers off-guard, snatched up $1,401, and locked his prisoners in the vault while he made a getaway. For a few days following the robbery, Raymond lay low in Houston, where he bought an expensive new suit. Who needed Clyde Barrow?

But, like Clyde, Raymond realized the advantages of having partners. From Houston he went west to Wichita Falls, where he teamed up with small-time hood Gene O'Dare. Raymond probably had met O'Dare earlier in the year when he lived in Wichita Falls with Clyde and Bonnie. On November 9, Raymond and O'Dare drove several hundred miles to the central Texas town of La Grange, where they robbed the Carmen State Bank and got away with $1,061. O'Dare took his half of the money back to Wichita Falls. Raymond returned to West Dallas, where he recruited a new partner named Les Stewart. On November 25, Raymond and Stewart hit Cedar Hill's first state bank again. The teller there remembered Raymond, who told him he wanted this stickup to be quicker than the first one. It was, and Raymond and Stewart escaped with $1,802.

Raymond had never had so much money, and he was ready to blow it on good times. Since cops all over Texas were on the lookout for him, it made sense to give the heat time to die down by taking another vacation in Michigan. Raymond didn't go north alone. He convinced Gene O'Dare to come along with him. O'Dare's wife, Mary, was left back in Wichita Falls. Fidelity apparently wasn't one of O'Dare's priorities. As soon as he and Raymond arrived in Bay City, they began pursuing local girls, taking their dates to a skating rink and spending lots of money to impress them. Still nineteen, Raymond had just demonstrated adult acumen as a bank robber, but now he proved he wasn't mature enough to know when to keep his mouth shut. When one girl wasn't sufficiently awed by his personal charms and bankroll, Raymond bragged that he was among the most famous criminals in Texas. Instead of being swept off her feet, she went to the local police. On December 6, Michigan state police surrounded the rink and took Raymond and O'Dare prisoner. Raymond had no chance to run—he had ice skates strapped to his feet. The Michigan authorities contacted lawmen in Texas, who were disappointed to learn they were about to gain custody of Raymond but not Clyde. A week later, Raymond and O'Dare were extradited to Texas. They arrived in Dallas on December 14. Raymond was held in the county jail on several charges of burglary. O'Dare was shipped on to La Grange to face charges for the bank robbery there.

The Cedar Hill bank staffers were brought to Dallas, where they picked Raymond out of a lineup as the man who'd robbed them twice. A few days later, Madora Bucher was driven up from Hillsboro. The first time she saw Raymond, she said he wasn't one of the men who murdered her husband, John. Mrs. Bucher was asked to take a second look. This time, she identified Raymond as one of the killers.

Raymond was also identified as a participant in the Neuhoff Packing Company and La Grange bank robberies. No one came down to

Dallas from Stringtown to confirm Raymond's part in Eugene Moore's murder, but it wasn't necessary. Clearly, Raymond was going to eventually be convicted of the Bucher murder, even though he'd been in Bay City, Michigan, when the killing occurred. His word would count less to a jury than that of a grieving widow. Shortly after Christmas, Raymond was transferred to the Hillsboro jail so he could stand trial there in the spring.

Predictably, Texas newspapers couldn't get enough of the story. Raymond's picture was printed everywhere, and every article linked him with Clyde. But Raymond continued to get short shrift: the headline in a *Dallas Morning News* story lauded "Quick-Shooting Clyde Barrow," while mocking "Boastful Raymond Hamilton."

Because of all the articles, Clyde soon learned that Raymond was in custody. In some ways, he wouldn't have been sorry. He disliked Raymond intensely, and it must have galled him that Raymond had pulled off three highly successful bank robberies in Texas while Clyde was lucky to escape with his life during the Oronogo holdup. Raymond was back in a Texas jail now because of his own big mouth. He deserved it.

But Raymond didn't deserve the death penalty or a life sentence in prison for the murder of John Bucher, and Clyde knew it. Throughout Clyde's life he demonstrated a strong commitment to fairness, or at least fairness as he defined it. Raymond hadn't been there when Bucher was killed, so even though Clyde didn't like his ex-partner, he was obligated to rescue him. Nothing could be done while Raymond was held in the downtown Dallas jail. Clyde's face was familiar to every cop in the city, and Bonnie was too well known to them to pose as one of Raymond's relatives. Clyde had to wait until Raymond was transferred to the smaller, less secure Hillsboro jail before attempting to break him out. He was determined to try.

Meanwhile, it was almost Christmas. Clyde and Bonnie had presents for their families, so they planned another quick trip to West Dallas. Some of the gifts were purchased in stores, but others were contraband. Clyde's sister Marie recalled many years later how thrilled she was when Clyde presented her with a bicycle, and always added that they both laughed when she asked him where he stole it.

Clyde and Bonnie arrived in West Dallas on December 24. It was after dark when they drove in on Eagle Ford Road. They hadn't reached the Barrow service station when they spotted Henry Barrow's truck coming in the opposite direction. Clyde's nineteen-year-old brother, L.C., fresh from his release by the Grayson County jury, was at the wheel, joyriding with his friend W. D. Jones. Clyde had L.C. take a message to their mother, designating a time and place to meet later that night. Cumie then relayed the information to Emma Parker. W.D., sixteen, also came along to the very brief holiday gathering, and had a request for Clyde and Bonnie. He wanted to join them.

The Jones and Barrow families had been close friends since 1922, when Cumie Barrow met Tookie Jones in the West Dallas campgrounds. Three of Tookie's sons were almost the same ages as Clyde, L.C., and Marie. When Cumie, Henry, L.C., and Marie went to San Antonio in January 1929 to attend Buck's trial there, Tookie and her brood went along to provide moral support. W.D.—William Daniel—hero-worshipped Clyde just like L.C. did. As Clyde's criminal reputation grew, so did W.D.'s admiration. He tried to make himself useful to his idol in small, important ways, like stockpiling license plates for Clyde to switch on stolen cars. By late 1932, he was talking about becoming a full-fledged member of Clyde's gang, which amused the rest of the Barrow family. Surely Clyde wouldn't consider letting the kid tag along with him and Bonnie.

But when W.D. made his plea on Christmas Eve, Clyde decided it might not be a bad idea. If nothing else, he'd make a useful lookout. W.D.'s age was a consideration, but he wasn't that much younger. Clyde and Bonnie were both still just twenty-two. A few days on the road would probably convince W.D. that he didn't want to be a criminal after all. And if he did demonstrate an aptitude for crime, Clyde might finally have a loyal henchman who would never desert him after a botched bank robbery or question his absolute authority. So W.D. joined Clyde and Bonnie as they said goodbye to their families that night and drove 130 miles south to just outside the central Texas town of Temple, where they checked into a motor court. They took a single room. Clyde and Bonnie got the bed. W.D. had to sleep on the floor.

The newest member of the Barrow Gang needed an initiation, and Clyde didn't put it off until after the holiday. Late Christmas morning, he picked out a grocery store in Temple and told W.D. that the two of them were going to rob it. Bonnie waited in the car while Clyde and W.D. got out. Clyde had either a shotgun or a handgun—W.D.'s description of the weapons involved changed every time he told the story later on—and he handed W.D. a battered old .45. But when they got inside the store, W.D. froze. He shook his head to indicate to Clyde that he couldn't do it. They went back to the car, where Clyde proceeded to ream out his new recruit. He called W.D. a coward, and Bonnie compounded the insult with peals of mocking laughter.

Still fuming, Clyde began driving around town, looking for another target and informing W.D. he was going to do what he was told. W.D. whined that he wanted to go home. Then Clyde spotted a Ford Model A roadster parked beside a house on the curb of a residential street. The keys were in the ignition, which wasn't unusual. Clyde told W.D. that if he wanted to go home, he'd have to steal the Model A first.

It was foolish for Clyde to pick that particular car. Model As were notoriously difficult to start—besides turning the ignition key, it was necessary to pull out the choke while simultaneously pressing down with both feet on the clutch and accelerator pedals. Clyde himself would never have stooped to stealing one. He probably picked the vehicle to humiliate W.D.—anyone who didn't have the guts to rob a grocery store wasn't worthy of stealing a *good* car like the Ford V-8s Clyde favored. But whatever Clyde's motive, he shoved W.D. out to the sidewalk and told him to get on with it.

W.D. dutifully climbed into the Model A. Though it wasn't his first attempt to steal a car—the Dallas police had previously hauled him in on suspicion of auto theft, but couldn't make charges stick—he'd certainly never tried with Clyde Barrow only a few yards away glaring at him. Predictably, the nervous kid couldn't get the Model A started. It would have made sense for Clyde to let W.D. hop out and get back in the V-8 with him and Bonnie and drive away before anyone noticed them, but Clyde was too aggravated to be sensible. Instead, he got out of his car and joined W.D. in the front seat of the Model A, apparently intent on shaming the kid further by starting the car himself.

The Model A belonged to twenty-seven-year-old Doyle Johnson, who was spending Christmas with his wife, baby daughter, and other family members. Johnson was taking a nap when his father-in-law, Henry Krauser, happened to look outside and saw Clyde and W.D. fumbling at the controls of the Johnsons' car. Krauser, his son Clarence, and Johnson's wife, Tillie, all spilled out into the front yard. Clyde jumped from the Model A, pulled out a pistol, and warned them to stay back. He leaped back into the car and finally got it started just as Doyle Johnson emerged from the house and bolted straight for his car. He reached through the open driver's side window, grabbing at Clyde, who yelled, "Get back, man, or I'll kill you." Johnson didn't get back. He managed to get a grip on Clyde's neck. Bonnie, watching from the Ford V-8, screamed for Clyde to let Johnson go, and for Clyde and W.D. to come back to their car. She started the engine, ready for a quick getaway. But it wasn't a matter of Clyde releasing Johnson. Johnson wouldn't give up his stranglehold on Clyde.

W. D. Jones always swore that Clyde Barrow shot Doyle Johnson, ramming his pistol into Johnson's body and pulling the trigger several times when Johnson wouldn't let go of his throat. Clyde's sister Nell, who heard her brother's and Bonnie's versions of the incident, insisted that W.D. still had a pistol from the aborted grocery store robbery, and he shot at Johnson, too. No matter whose gun fired it, the fatal bullet snapped Johnson's spinal cord, and he died soon afterward.

Clyde and W.D. barreled off in the Model A, with Bonnie right behind them in the V-8. After a few blocks, the Model A was abandoned and all three drove away in the newer, faster Ford. They hid out in East Texas motor courts for a few days before heading back to West Dallas. Clyde told W.D. that whether he liked it or not, he was now a permanent member of the gang. He'd participated in a murder, there were plenty of witnesses, and the cops were after him for sure. That wasn't true. It took almost seven months for the police to charge someone with Johnson's murder, and it wasn't W. D. Jones. But as far as Jones knew on Christmas Day 1932, Clyde was right—the law was hot on his trail and he no longer had the option of going home to his mother, Tookie.

If Clyde Barrow and Bonnie Parker regretted Doyle Johnson's death, there is no record of them expressing it to their families or anyone else. Marie Barrow Scoma's sole comment in her unpublished memoir was that, to Clyde, it was a matter of choosing between squeezing the trigger and going to the electric chair.

Remorseful or not, Clyde turned his attention to a lingering obligation. Raymond Hamilton was still in jail, about to be unfairly tried for the murder of John Bucher. Clyde had a plan to help break him out and needed to return to West Dallas so it could be implemented. Then his penchant for bad timing reasserted itself.

A complex chain of events that culminated in another killing began on December 29, when West Dallas crooks Les Stewart and Odell

Chambless robbed the Home Bank of Grapevine, in a Fort Worth suburb. Stewart had been Raymond Hamilton's partner for the second holdup of the First State Bank of Cedar Hill. Chambless was friendly with Raymond, too. Chambless's sister Mary was married to Gene O'Dare, currently in the La Grange jail after being arrested with Raymond in Michigan. The criminal world of West Dallas was a small one.

Stewart, captured shortly after the Grapevine robbery, sold out his partner in hopes of a lenient sentence. Odell Chambless, he said, regularly visited the West Dallas home of Lillian McBride, Raymond Hamilton's sister. If the cops staked out Lillian's house, Stewart said, there was a good chance Chambless would eventually walk right into their trap. Previously, such an ambush would have been considered beyond the scope of the Dallas County sheriff's office, but there was a new incumbent. Richard "Smoot" Schmid took office on January 1, 1933, after being elected on a campaign theme of more aggressive law enforcement. A tall, shambling man who wore a white ten-gallon hat and size 14 cowboy boots, Schmid had previously run a Dallas bicycle shop, where he wasn't a stickler for honesty. Raymond Hamilton later swore that as a kid he sold hot bikes to Schmid, who knew they were stolen and didn't care. But as sheriff, Schmid was eager to make good on his promise to voters that he'd crack down on criminals. The Grapevine robbery had occurred in nearby Tarrant County, and when its district attorney contacted Schmid to suggest a joint effort to nab Chambless, the Dallas County sheriff was all for it. They decided to lie in wait for Chambless in West Dallas on the night of January 6.

Sometime around the first of the year, Clyde visited Lillian McBride, whose house was only a few blocks away from the Barrow service station. Her brother Raymond had just been moved from the Dallas County jail to the lockup in Hillsboro. Clyde couldn't risk going there—his face was too well known in the town where John Bucher died. But it was the most natural thing in the world for Lillian to go down and see her brother. Clyde suggested that Lillian bring a radio to Raymond as a gift. Hacksaw blades would be concealed inside the radio. Then Raymond could cut his way out of his cell. Clyde apparently supplied the radio and blades.

During the afternoon of January 6, a Dallas County deputy came to the McBride house in Dallas. He asked Lillian McBride a few questions, probably about her brother Raymond since he would not have wanted to alert her to the plan to catch Odell Chambless. The real purpose of the visit was undoubtedly to get an idea of the layout of the place. Like almost every other residence in West Dallas, it was a tiny, poorly constructed shack. Lillian left the house soon afterward. Around sundown, Clyde, Bonnie, and W.D. drove up. Clyde wanted to find out if the radio and hacksaw blades had been successfully smuggled in to Raymond. Maggie Fairris, Raymond and Lillian's younger sister, answered the door. When she told him that Lillian wasn't there, Clyde said he'd come back later. He, Bonnie, and W.D. spent the next several hours visiting first with Bonnie's mother, Emma, then with the Barrows and probably Tookie Jones. Bonnie had been drinking, which upset Emma.

About 11 P.M., a five-man posse arrived at the McBride house. It consisted of Tarrant County assistant district attorney W. T. Evans, Special Ranger J. F. Van Noy, Dallas County deputy sheriff Fred Bradberry, and two Fort Worth deputies, Dusty Rhodes and Malcolm Davis. Lillian McBride still wasn't home. Maggie Fairris told the cops she had just put her small children to bed. They set up the ambush for Odell Chambless anyway. Bradberry, Evans, and Van Noy settled themselves in the front room of the small house. Rhodes and Davis waited outside by the back porch. Bradberry ordered Fairris to turn off all the lights inside the house. She asked for permission to leave on one red bulb in the window of her children's bedroom. She explained it was a night-light. Actually, it was a time-honored West Dallas signal that the law was lurking nearby, something the officers lying in wait clearly didn't know.

An hour later, Bradberry and the other two officers watching from the front of the house saw a Ford V-8 coupé drive slowly down the street with its headlights switched off. The car rolled past the house and turned the corner. The lawmen thought it might be Chambless checking out the house to make certain the coast was clear. Bradberry made Fairris turn off the red light in the children's room. A few minutes later, the car was back. This time, it stopped—its occupants had apparently not noticed the red light. Holding a shotgun against his side, Clyde got out and walked toward the porch. He carried a shotgun. As Clyde approached, Maggie Fairris swung open the door and screamed, "Don't shoot! Think of my babies!"

Clyde reacted instantly. He swung up his shotgun and fired through the front window of the house. The three lawmen inside threw themselves on the floor. Clyde tried to fire again, but the shotgun jammed.

He backed away from the porch, trying to claw the spent cartridge out of the breech. Behind the house, Fort Worth deputies Malcolm Davis and Dusty Rhodes heard the shotgun blast. They drew their guns and ran around to the front, with Davis just ahead of Rhodes.

The newspapers noted later that the fifty-one-year-old Davis "was known to friends and fellow-officers as a quiet-mannered, curly-headed bachelor who liked to catch big catfish at Lake Worth and to invite his friends to help him eat them. The Davis fish dinners were famous in Fort Worth." But Clyde Barrow wasn't encountering Malcolm Davis at a friendly fish fry. Clyde cleared the spent cartridge that was jamming his shotgun, chambered a fresh shell, and blew a hole in Davis's chest at point-blank range. Later, he told his family he'd just fired a quick shot into the dark as "four other guns began going off right in my face," but the only one shooting up to that point was Clyde. Rhodes managed to drop to the ground quickly enough so that Clyde missed a second shot at him.

Then the three officers inside the McBride house started shooting, and W. D. Jones began firing wildly from the car in their general direction. People in other houses on both sides of the street ran outside. Frightened women screamed. In the confusion, Clyde slipped away, running between houses toward Eagle Ford Road.

Bonnie thought fast. She ordered W.D. to stop shooting, saying sensibly that he was just as likely to hit Clyde or some innocent bystander as he was the cops. She started the car and drove around the block, catching up to Clyde. He jumped in the front seat, taking over for Bonnie behind the wheel, and raced west down Eagle Ford Road heading out of town. He passed his fourteen-year-old sister, Marie, who was pedaling the other way on the bicycle Clyde had just given her for Christmas. Telling the story decades later, Marie never suggested it was odd for a child her age to be out riding a bike in the middle of the night.

The scene back at the McBride house was chaotic. Rain began pouring down. It was hard to see. One of the lawmen snapped off a shot at several men who ran into the yard. Luckily, it missed. They were bystanders trying to get the mortally wounded Malcolm Davis into a car so they could rush him to the hospital. When Lillian McBride and her friend Lucille Hilburn finally showed up around 3 A.M., they were arrested as accessories and held while Schmid and his deputies tried to figure out what had happened.

Clyde's effort to help Raymond Hamilton was futile. On January 8, Raymond was caught trying to use the hacksaw blades from Clyde to saw through the bars of his cell in the Hillsboro jail. He was immediately transferred back to the more secure Dallas County jail, where he remained in custody until his trial. For the second time in two weeks, Clyde had committed a murder that served absolutely no purpose, though killing Malcolm Davis did earn him a new, implacable enemy.

Dallas County sheriff Smoot Schmid was extremely sensitive to criticism, and the bungled ambush resulting in the death of a Fort Worth deputy got his new administration off to a terrible start with the press. The earliest news reports were positive. Stories blamed Fairris and McBride for tipping off Davis's killer—the red light was prominently mentioned. Odell Chambless was identified by Schmid as the leading suspect. But there was also the matter of who had been in the V-8 coupé firing at the lawmen, and a day after the incident the *Dallas Morning News* reported that it was "Clyde Champion Barrow, 22, sought by police for a score of holdups and killings in Texas, Oklahoma and New Mexico." The story added that Schmid was directing a statewide search for the fugitives.

For the next several days, stories chronicled Schmid's efforts to follow up on tips from the public. Rumored sightings of Chambless and Clyde resulted in the sheriff sending "heavily armed Deputy Sheriffs and city detectives speeding in squad cars to various parts of Dallas and Dallas County." Schmid made a point of leading several of these searches himself—when Chambless and Clyde went down, he wanted to be there to get the credit. On January 13, an unidentified officer, undoubtedly Schmid, told a reporter that "a tough, two-gun girl" was "riding with the hunted slayers . . . she is as tough as the back end of a shooting gallery and she has been missing from these parts for some time." It was the first suggestion by a lawman in the press that Bonnie might be a functioning member of the gang instead of a giddy, lovestruck girl tagging along with the wrong men.

But Schmid's efforts to be lionized in print were thwarted on January 18, when Odell Chambless voluntarily surrendered to police in the Texas Panhandle town of Pampa. Chambless told lawmen there that he left Texas on January 4 and hitchhiked to California. He was arrested in Los Angeles on the 6th on suspicion of robbery, held while his fingerprints were checked against those at the crime scene, and only released on the 12th. Heading back to Texas, he learned he was wanted for Davis's murder. On the advice of his father, who lived in Pampa, Chambless decided to turn himself in. Los Angeles police corroborated Chambless's alibi. Smoot Schmid had done his best to pin a murder on the wrong man.

Schmid tried to backtrack, claiming that "According to the information we had, it was possible for him to have been involved in the shooting." It didn't help his cause with reporters, who were undoubtedly embarrassed for lending so much credence to Schmid with their earlier stories. The sheriff in Tarrant County suggested that the shooter might have been notorious Oklahoma outlaw Pretty Boy Floyd, who was vaguely rumored to be in the general vicinity of West Dallas on January 6. Inspired by that straw grasping as well as Schmid's ineptitude, on January 20 a front-page headline in the *Dallas Morning News* sarcastically wondered, "Pretty Boy Is New Suspect in Killing; Jesse James Next?" The accompanying story reminded readers that because James was dead he was "therefore practically eliminated from the search for the slayer of Deputy Sheriff Malcolm Davis of Fort Worth." Schmid, asked to comment, "extended a deprecating hand."

For the thin-skinned Schmid, it was humiliation of the most public sort. But there was one certain way to restore his reputation. Maybe Odell Chambless hadn't shot Malcolm Davis, but multiple murderer Clyde Barrow was still prominent in the investigation. It was common knowledge that Barrow and his girlfriend made frequent trips to West Dallas to visit their families. Dallas County didn't have the resources to keep an around-the-clock watch on the Barrow service station, but Schmid did have a new deputy who knew Clyde's family well, and Bonnie, too—Ted Hinton, who'd quit a job at the post office to come to work for the sheriff. Veteran deputy Bob Alcorn also had past dealings with the Barrows. From now on all Schmid's officers, but especially these two, would be on heightened alert for clues that Clyde and Bonnie were coming to town. Perhaps an inside source could be found. It wouldn't be easy—people in West Dallas hated the cops. But an ambush that bagged Clyde Barrow would surely erase the memory of the Chambless-Davis debacle from media and public memory. Whatever it took, Smoot Schmid was willing to do.

CHAPTER 14

"It Gets Mixed Up"

After escaping the ambush in West Dallas on the rainy night of January 6, Clyde raced his Ford V-8 coupé only a few miles north before he missed a turn in the dark. The car veered off the road into a muddy field, where it sank up to its axles. Clyde, Bonnie, and W.D. couldn't budge it. Soon, they knew, the police would be combing the area for them—they had to keep moving. Clyde found a house, pounded on the door, and paid the farmer he woke up $3 to pull the car back onto the road with a team of mules. Once it was free, Clyde drove northeast while Bonnie and W.D. slept. When they woke up they were in the eastern hills of Oklahoma.

During the next few months from January through March they drove in aimless, meandering patterns through parts of Oklahoma, Arkansas, and Missouri. Travel money was acquired in stickups of grocery stores and service stations well away from major cities. The jobs weren't big enough to merit much attention from the law or any coverage from the area newspapers. For Clyde and Bonnie, this was the time that came closest to the carefree criminal life they'd hoped to enjoy. There was no organized pursuit on their trail. Any small-town cops they encountered could be outrun, or, if necessary, outgunned, but suddenly no shooting seemed necessary. It was as though there had been a bad period when bullets flew everywhere, but now it was past. They carried a tool kit with them, and years later Clyde's sister Marie would muse that during these months they wielded a screwdriver far more often than they did guns.

The screwdriver was used to change license plates on the cars they stole, and they changed plates far more often than they did cars. Though Clyde could hot-wire almost any model automobile in seconds, it was still a chore to switch from one vehicle to another because they had so much baggage. There were suitcases packed with their suits, shirts, and fashionable dresses. Bonnie had her typewriter, and Clyde had a guitar. He still loved to play and sing. They had their arsenal of handguns, shotguns, BARs, and boxes of ammunition. Moving everything from one car to the next took a while, so Clyde extended the road life of each stolen vehicle by frequently changing its license plates. They kept a wide variety of license plates on hand, pilfering some in every state they passed through. Clyde always drove. They'd keep going until Clyde announced he was tired and ready to stop. Bonnie handled the road maps.

W.D. was often called on to act as photographer. Clyde and Bonnie enjoyed posing for pictures. Sometimes they'd strike the same sort of silly poses they had assumed at the photo booths in Fair Park, though now they were waving real guns. Clyde and Bonnie smoked cigarettes but sixteen-year-old W.D. puffed on cigars, probably trying to look and act more grown-up than he was. Once they stopped along the highway and W.D. snapped a photo of Bonnie posing with a gun dangling from her hand and one of his cigars clenched in her teeth. She was just fooling around a little.

Most nights they stayed in motor courts. In Arkansas and Missouri, the Barrow Gang was still relatively anonymous, so they didn't have to worry about being recognized. They would rent only one cabin. It was cheaper, and W. D. Jones was afraid of the dark and always wanted to sleep in the same room as Clyde and Bonnie. Later, lawmen in Texas would spread rumors that Bonnie was promiscuous and slept with other members of the Barrow Gang besides Clyde. They had no idea that, at least in the case of W.D., they were telling the literal truth. Having the kid in the room with them certainly imposed on the couple's privacy, but Clyde had grown up sleeping in tiny rooms with his brothers and sisters. He wasn't accustomed to privacy anyway. W.D. was often sent out on errands. That was probably when the lovers were intimate. A big surprise for W.D. was discovering that Clyde and Bonnie both prayed frequently. The religious faith ingrained in them by their mothers hadn't been entirely abandoned.

Meals were usually taken in their rooms at motor courts or by the side of the road. If they didn't have much money, the entire menu sometimes comprised bologna-and-cheese sandwiches. For a treat, they'd have buttermilk. Clyde and Bonnie drank whiskey, too, but Clyde was more circumspect. He thought he needed to be constantly alert. Bonnie agreed. If she felt he'd had too much, she'd warn, "The laws might be right on us."

There was time, most days, for the kind of personal grooming that remained important to Bonnie. She carefully applied makeup and fussed to make her hair look just right. Bonnie set off her freshly laundered dresses with high-heeled shoes, feeling safe enough during such a relatively stress-free interlude to choose fashion over flat heels and a greater ability to run. Sometimes she colored her hair, going from golden blond to streaky auburn to full-blown red and back again. Clyde liked all the different looks. She dyed his hair a few times, too. Bonnie called Clyde "Daddy," and his name for her was "Honey." W.D.'s nickname was "Boy." He referred to Bonnie as "Sis" and to Clyde by his old childhood nickname of "Bud." They were especially careful not to call each other by their real names whenever they were out in public because, W.D. told *Playboy* years later, "somebody at a filling station or a tourist court might pick up on [it] and call the law." Previously they'd been careless about drawing attention to themselves and they soon would be again, but during this short, idyllic time they exhibited more common sense than usual.

That was most evident on the evening of January 26, 1933, in Springfield, Missouri. Twenty-four-year-old Thomas Persell had eked out a living selling adding machines before joining the Springfield police force in 1932. He was good at his new job, nabbing two car thieves soon after being hired. That earned him a promotion to motorcycle patrol. About 6 P.M. on January 26 as he cruised through the downtown area, Persell noticed three persons in a V-8 Ford studying parked cars in a suspicious manner. There had been a car theft in town earlier that day. Persell decided to follow the Ford and its occupants as they drove away, and just before an elevated bridge over a railroad track he rode up behind the car and waved the driver over. Clyde, always wary and thinking about potential escape routes, kept going until he was over the bridge. But there was no use trying to outrun a cop on a motorcycle in the middle of town, so he pulled to the side of the road. When Persell got off his motorcycle and walked up, Clyde and W.D. greeted him with drawn guns. But instead of blasting away, Clyde ordered Persell to get in the car. Wisely, he obeyed. W.D. took Persell's pistol. The patrolman sat between Clyde and W.D. in front. Bonnie was in back.

Persell said later that Clyde was "quite profane" as he quizzed his prisoner about the fastest way out of town. They drove northeast in the direction of St. Louis for a while, then turned south toward Joplin. Bonnie consulted a road map in the back seat. When they stopped for gas, Clyde made Persell climb into the back with her. Bonnie threw a blanket over Persell and then covered him with a pistol while they were at the service station. When they drove away, Clyde told Persell to clamber back into the front seat. As the patrolman did, he kicked open a suitcase and saw, in his words, "a veritable arsenal bigger than the one at the police station. . . . They had a couple of sawed-off shotguns, a couple of rifles, I don't know how many pistols and this Thompson sub-machine gun. They were damn proud of it—like kids with their first toy." Somehow, conversation in the car turned to the November shootout in Oronogo. Clyde told Persell that "some monkey from the bank" shot at them there. Persell asked if they had been involved in the car theft in Springfield earlier in the day. Clyde said they'd stolen the vehicle, another Ford V-8, but decided they didn't like its tan color. Helpfully, Clyde told Persell where they'd abandoned the car.

About five hours after Persell was abducted, the battery in Clyde's stolen V-8 died—coincidentally, just as they reached the outskirts of Oronogo. Clyde ordered W.D. to walk the rest of the way into town and steal a battery from another car. Further, he had to take Persell with him. It was obviously another test for W.D. The sixteen-year-old led his captive into Oronogo. The town was dark so late at night. W.D. and Persell pried a battery out of a car parked on a residential street and lugged it back to where Clyde and Bonnie were waiting. The battery was heavy, and W.D. told Clyde that Persell had helped him carry it.

When the Ford was running again, Clyde drove a few miles south into Joplin. A little after midnight, he stopped in the suburb of Poundstone's Corner and told Persell to get out of the car. As a reward for helping W.D. with the battery, Clyde was releasing his prisoner in a town rather than out in the country where he'd have a long walk back to civilization. Persell asked them to return his handgun—it was fitted with custom grips and cost a lot of money. Clyde turned him down and drove away. He'd kept calm throughout the night, even when the car battery died outside Oronogo. Shooting Persell, a lawman, would have made Clyde one of the most widely hunted criminals in all of Missouri. But he let the patrolman go, unharmed. So, besides his indiscreet admission about being part of the Oronogo bank robbery, the kidnapping only earned Clyde a little more notoriety in the southern part of the state.

During their time in the Missouri section of the Ozarks, Clyde and Bonnie sent a steady stream of postcards to their families back in Texas. Clyde signed the cards "Bud," Bonnie was "Sis," and W.D. was "Jack." Besides the postcards, they sneaked three or four hundred miles into West Dallas for quick visits, at least one a month. Dallas County sheriff Smoot Schmid might have hoped to trap them, but he didn't have informers in place yet, nor the personnel to constantly monitor the Barrow service station on Eagle Ford Road. To schedule family gatherings, Clyde and Bonnie would simply drive past and toss out Coke bottles containing messages telling where and when to meet outside of town. As soon as she read Clyde's instructions, Cumie would phone her daughter Nell and Bonnie's mother, Emma, using the family code "I'm fixing red beans" to let them know Clyde and Bonnie were in town and ready for a reunion. The Barrows thought Dallas police might be tapping their phone, but they weren't—yet. Cumie, Nell, L.C., and Marie always went out to see Clyde and Bonnie. Henry sometimes stayed home to keep an eye on the service station. Clyde's oldest siblings, Jack and Artie, rarely saw their brother. Jack and his wife were raising four daughters and thought it was wise to keep clear of Clyde, who understood. Artie and her husband lived in Denison, seventy-five miles away. Because of the distance involved, Artie usually wasn't able to see her brother during his brief Dallas visits.

Bonnie's mother, Emma, and sister, Billie Jean, always came. Smoot Schmid's deputies were always on the lookout, and if Clyde and Bonnie had to make two stops for family visits they would be doubling the danger of being caught. Emma Parker and Cumie Barrow even forged a grudging friendship. They had little in common other than loving their outlaw children very much. But that was enough. They spoke regularly on the telephone, sharing their concerns about what would eventually happen to Clyde and Bonnie.

During their visits, Clyde and Bonnie gave their families money, sometimes as much as $100 or more if they had it. But even a few dollars made a difference. Marie Barrow told friends later, probably exaggerating only a little, that Clyde's gifts often kept the rest of the West Dallas Barrows from going hungry. The service station didn't always provide Henry with sufficient income. The Depression and the Dust Bowl still throttled the Texas economy. Even proud Emma Parker took handouts from Bonnie, knowing full well she was accepting stolen money. W. D. Jones rarely had anything to give his mother, Tookie. Clyde and Bonnie kept all the money from their robberies. Clyde occasionally gave W.D. a dollar, like a father doling out an allowance.

On one visit, Nell had a question for her brother Clyde. How did it feel, she asked, to know that he'd killed someone? According to *Fugitives* (written by journalist Jan I. Fortune with the help of Nell Barrow and Emma Parker), Clyde gave a rambling, philosophic answer, with Hamlet-like digressions about why "God should bother with the whole mess." Almost every word of it seems phony. Clyde was never given to orations. In common with much of the other dialogue in *Fugitives*, it sounds like something Fortune conjured up. But Clyde's actual response may be buried in the verbiage: "It gets mixed up." In less than a year since being paroled from prison, he'd killed three men—Eugene Moore, Doyle Johnson, and Malcolm Davis—and been blamed for murdering two more. For all the excuses he offered his family—about not wanting to stop at the Stringtown dance in the first place, or wildly shooting his gun in the dark during the West Dallas ambush only because others were shooting at him first—the deaths had to hang heavy on the conscience of a twenty-two-year-old who was still devout enough to say his nightly prayers. Driving around the Ozarks, hundreds of miles from the scenes of his fatal crimes, Clyde might have been able to put the murders out of his mind for a while. But they were ultimately inescapable. Things were badly mixed up for Clyde Barrow, and not even God could make it all go away.

The visits to West Dallas helped. They were proof that despite the things Clyde had done, there were still people who cared about him. Family ties meant everything to Clyde, which is why he never mocked Bonnie's strong attachment to her mother and her sister, Billie Jean. A few times, he even allowed Billie Jean Parker to come with them. Billie

Jean had endured some tough luck of her own. Her husband, Fred Mace, was in prison for burglary and she was back living with her mother. Every once in a while Bonnie would tell Billie Jean, "I get so lonesome to talk about home," and ask her sister to ride with them for a few days. Billie Jean and Fred Mace had two small children; apparently they were looked after by their grandmother Emma when their mother went out on the road with the Barrow Gang. Billie Jean shared their car and single room at the motor courts, but she was still just an occasional companion for Bonnie.

For three months, beginning on Christmas Eve in 1932, the full-time members of the gang were Clyde, Bonnie, and W. D. Jones. But in late March 1933, they added two more, by accident rather than design. One was Clyde's big brother Buck. The other was Buck's wife, Blanche, who didn't want anything to do with criminals and crime. She believed that being around Clyde and Bonnie would lead to disaster for her and her husband. She was right.

CHAPTER 15

The Shootout in Joplin

Buck Barrow still had four years left to serve on his robbery sentence when he voluntarily had returned to the Texas state prison in Huntsville on December 27, 1931. As soon as he was back in custody, his mother, Cumie, and wife, Blanche, began petitioning the governor's office to parole him. Meanwhile, Clyde was paroled just a few weeks after Buck gave himself up. While Buck readjusted to life as an inmate, his little brother embarked on the crime spree that soon, with the enthusiastic support of the Texas press, made him the most notorious outlaw in the state.

Whenever Blanche, Cumie, and Buck's sisters Nell and Marie came to visit him in Huntsville, Buck wanted to talk about Clyde. He felt responsible for Clyde's predicament—after all, he was the one who had inspired his kid brother to get started in crime by stealing cars. Buck was seven years older, and Clyde had always looked up to him. If he talked to Clyde, Buck believed, he could convince him to either give himself up or else leave the country for good. There were all sorts of places where an American on the run could hide in Mexico. And if Clyde did choose to turn himself in, plenty of Texas murderers were being sentenced to long prison terms instead of the electric chair. By surrendering instead of being captured, Clyde might incline a jury toward leniency.

Buck swore that he himself would never turn to crime again. All he wanted was to get out of Huntsville, talk some sense into Clyde, and then build a new, law-abiding life with Blanche. She was living in Denison and working at the Cinderella Beauty Shoppe, which was owned by Buck's sister Artie. The original plan when Buck gave himself up was for Blanche to live at the West Dallas service station with Buck's parents, plus his brother L.C. and sister Marie. It didn't work out. Cumie never liked having women other than her daughters around the house. Blanche thought Cumie resented Buck's devotion to his wife. Within a few months Artie suggested that Blanche move to Denison and learn how to dye hair and give permanent waves. It was a relief to everyone when she did.

So on March 23, 1933, after Buck was set free in Huntsville he stopped in West Dallas only to change clothes before hurrying up to Denison. He had great news for Blanche. Miriam "Ma" Ferguson, the new Texas governor, had granted him a full pardon instead of a simple parole. That meant all Buck's previous crimes were completely wiped from the legal record as though he had never committed them. He and Blanche could truly make a fresh start. Buck was thirty, and Blanche just twenty-two. They had plenty of time to build a wonderful life together—but first, even though Blanche begged him not to, Buck wanted to find Clyde and talk to him.

It didn't take long. The day after Buck returned, he and Blanche went to visit her mother and stepfather, who owned a small dairy farm in Wilmer, about fifteen miles outside Dallas. Blanche was probably less excited about seeing her mother, with whom she'd always had a tense relationship, than she was to be reunited with her dog, a tiny white mongrel named Snow Ball. Cumie Barrow disliked the dog, and hadn't let Blanche keep Snow Ball while she lived at the service station in West Dallas. Blanche took it as just one more indication of Cumie's meanness, and asked her mother to board the animal.

Buck and Blanche decided to spend the night on the farm. About midnight, there was a knock on the door. Blanche's stepfather opened it, and found Clyde, Bonnie, and W. D. Jones outside. They'd gone to West Dallas for a quick visit and learned from Clyde's family that Buck had been pardoned, and that he and Blanche were probably at her mother's place in Wilmer. The house on the dairy farm was two-storied, and the bedroom where Buck and Blanche were sleeping was on the second floor. Buck recognized Clyde's voice and hurried downstairs. Blanche stayed in bed. Her husband led all three visitors up to see her—Blanche wasn't charmed. Clyde and W.D. both carried shotguns. Bonnie was drunk, and Blanche thought she looked like she hadn't slept for a week.

Bonnie crawled into bed with Blanche, and W.D. kept a lookout through the bedroom window while Clyde talked about a new plan he had to raid Eastham prison. He wanted his brother and sister-in-law to help, though he swore they wouldn't be asked to do anything dangerous. Blanche refused to get involved and said Buck wouldn't, either. After a while, Clyde, Buck, and W.D. went outside. At 4 A.M. they trooped back up the stairs. Clyde had a new proposal. He wanted Buck and Blanche to join them for a few weeks in Missouri. They'd rent an apartment in Joplin and just relax together. It would be like a family holiday. Bonnie chimed in. She told Blanche she was tired of sleeping in cars, and she wanted another girl to talk to. Clyde promised Blanche that he wouldn't include Buck in any burglaries—they had enough money to last for a while. He'd even keep most of the guns locked in the trunk of the car so Blanche wouldn't have to be around them. She and Bonnie could have fun fixing up the apartment. Blanche was adamant: she and Buck weren't interested. But at dawn, just after Clyde, Bonnie, and W.D. left, Buck told her he'd promised Clyde they'd go to Joplin. It would give Buck a chance to talk some sense into his kid brother. He was trying to save Clyde's life. If Blanche still wouldn't agree, then he'd go without her. She gave in. Buck said she could bring her dog.

Clyde and Buck had worked out a plan to rendezvous a few days later at a motor court in Checotah, Oklahoma. Buck and Blanche, with Snow Ball in tow, made the trip in a 1929 Marmon sedan Buck bought from a Dallas acquaintance named Carl Beaty. They met Clyde, Bonnie, and W.D. in Oklahoma as planned and formed a two-car caravan to Joplin. Bonnie rode part of the way with Buck and Blanche, chattering about how uncomfortable she felt any time she, Clyde, and W.D. drove through a town and there were cops around. When they got to Joplin, they rented cabins in another motor court to live in for a few days while Buck and Blanche looked around Joplin for a suitable apartment. Buck, Blanche, and Snow Ball took one cabin, while W.D.

bunked in as usual with Clyde and Bonnie. At night they fixed supper in one of their kitchenettes. Blanche discovered that Bonnie was anything but a homebody. She disliked fixing meals and hated washing dishes. Blanche and Clyde did the cooking. Because they were settling in for a few days, they bought a greater variety of groceries than usual. In her memoir, Blanche described the fare: Buck and Bonnie liked pickled pig's feet and olives. Clyde wanted french fries, and especially "English peas cooked with a lot of cream and pepper." It was the sort of dish Clyde couldn't enjoy while camping out in a car or sheltering with isolated farm families who barely had enough food for themselves, let alone guests. So he took the opportunity to gorge himself on the fancy pea recipe. Blanche recalled that "he ate [it] at almost every meal except breakfast." At night after supper was over, Clyde, Buck, and W.D. would clean their guns and play poker. Bonnie didn't mind having guns around. She just didn't want to shoot them. Blanche hated guns and claimed she couldn't figure out how poker was played, despite Buck's coaching. She wasn't the kind of person who tried very hard to fit in.

On April 1, Buck and Blanche, using the pseudonym of Callahan, rented an apartment near the intersection of 34th Street and Oak Ridge Drive in Joplin. The exact, odd address was 3347½ 34th Street. It had two bedrooms, a small living room, a kitchenette, and a bathroom. The apartment was in a fashionable part of town, and they paid a hefty $50 for a month's lease on the place. For Clyde, Bonnie, W.D., and Buck, who'd lived so long in the squalor of West Dallas, these relatively extravagant digs must have seemed like paradise. The apartment was built over a two-door garage. Stairs inside the garage led up to the apartment. Harold Hill, who lived in an adjacent house, parked his car in the right side of the garage. Clyde parked his stolen Ford V-8 of the moment on the other side. There was no room for Buck's Marmon, so he rented garage space in one of the adjacent houses. The neighborhood was exclusive enough for residents to employ a night watchman. Soon after they arrived, the Texas transients agreed to pay him a dollar a night to guard their apartment and garages, too. Clyde and Bonnie thought that was hilarious.

The apartment was only minimally furnished, so the renters bought linens, blankets, pillows, and utensils. Playing house was a new experience and they enjoyed it, though Blanche believed she had to do more than her fair share of cooking, cleaning, and picking up. They stayed up late at night playing cards, then slept through the mornings. Because Blanche couldn't or wouldn't learn how to play poker, she amused herself with puzzles purchased from a nearby Kress's five-and-ten-cent store. Soon she had Clyde hooked on them, too. On April 7, new legislation allowed beer sales for the first time since Prohibition became the law of the land thirteen years earlier. Clyde, Bonnie, W.D., and Buck celebrated by buying and drinking a case each night. Blanche didn't have any beer. She wanted to go home to Texas before something bad happened and Buck got caught up again in a life of crime.

Buck wasn't ready to leave. He still believed he could talk Clyde into giving himself up. The brothers discussed it over and over. Clyde insisted he had no chance for clemency. If "the laws" caught him, he'd go to the electric chair. Buck argued that wasn't necessarily the case. Raymond Hamilton had been convicted by a Hillsboro jury of John Bucher's murder just a few days before Buck was pardoned. The jury was still undecided over the appropriate sentence for Raymond—a long prison sentence or the death penalty. If Raymond did end up being sent to a Huntsville prison farm instead of the electric chair, Buck said, Clyde could hope for the same kind of verdict. Clyde wasn't buying it. After his awful experience at Eastham, he wasn't willing to endure life as an inmate again. Buck kept trying. He wouldn't accept what was clear to everyone else. Clyde preferred death to prison.

While Buck pursued his fruitless debate, all five of them continued to live in the kind of comfort they'd never experienced before. They had indoor plumbing. Food was delivered right to the apartment. A laundry service came by each day to pick up soiled clothes and deliver freshly laundered ones. Clyde insisted that none of the deliverymen be allowed to enter the apartment. Bonnie or Blanche had to meet them on the staircase. Clyde also wanted the window blinds pulled shut at all times. Blanche kept the blinds up in the bedroom she shared with Buck. Some afternoons, she and Bonnie treated themselves to the movies or shopping trips to Kress's. Blanche recalled in her memoir that the two women would return to the apartment "with our arms loaded with ashtrays, glassware, small picture frames, and anything else we saw that was pretty or that we wanted or needed, plus a lot of things we didn't need." Once they bought some costume jewelry, rings and earrings whose cut-glass settings vaguely resembled real diamonds. It was the kind of mindless, minor-league consumerism that a poor girl like Bonnie could never have enjoyed back in West Dallas.

But those department store sprees along with grocery deliveries, laundry service, and cases of beer cost money, and despite what he'd told Blanche back on the Wilmer dairy farm, Clyde didn't have an endless supply. So on several nights he and W.D. or he and Buck disappeared for a few hours. They were later connected to a series of robberies in the area. Buck's pledge to go straight didn't last three weeks beyond his release from prison. One night, he and Clyde even returned with several Browning Automatic Rifles, which they had pilfered from a National Guard armory. Blanche was appalled.

On April 12, W. D. Jones stole a Ford V-8 roadster in Miami, an Oklahoma town about thirty miles west of Joplin. Clyde wanted a new car to replace the Ford V-8 he'd been driving. It wasn't smart to stay in the same stolen car too long. They made a deal with their neighbor Harold Hill to park both the V-8 roadster and the V-8 sedan in the double garage under their apartment. Probably they promised Hill they'd be leaving soon, so he would only have to park his vehicle along the curb for a day or two. They didn't realize it was too late. They were already under police surveillance.

In the two weeks since they'd moved in, the Texans had kept mostly to themselves—a little girl named Beth, whom Bonnie befriended, was the exception. Their neighbors noticed that they often seemed to come and go late at night, which was unusual in that upper-middle-class section of Joplin. One afternoon, Clyde was in the garage cleaning a rifle, probably one of the BARs stolen from the armory, when he accidentally fired a quick burst of shots and the concussion reverberated beyond the garage walls. No one came to ask what had happened, but people in nearby houses heard it. A neighbor went to the police to complain. Officers began to keep an eye on the apartment. When the new V-8 roadster appeared, it was another warning sign. Joplin had been a hotbed for bootleggers, and the police knew their city was also home to several fencing operations specializing in stolen cars and guns. It seemed likely that the five strangers in the apartment on 34th Street were involved in something shady.

On the night of April 12, after W.D. returned with the newly stolen roadster and negotiations with Hill to park it in the garage were complete, Clyde and Bonnie had a terrible fight. Bonnie thought it was stupid to bring another stolen car to the apartment when they were trying to keep a low profile, and Clyde didn't like having his decisions questioned. Partly from stress, partly because they both had feisty streaks, they routinely argued, but this was one of the times when things turned violent. Blanche wrote that "he knocked her across [their] bedroom a couple of times but she got up and went back for more." Eventually they made up as they always did, and Bonnie went to bed. Clyde sat up awhile longer talking with Buck. He finally convinced his big brother that he had no intention of surrendering to the cops. Clyde added that their holiday was over. They'd stayed in the apartment long enough. He was worried the laws might be on to them. Buck said he and Blanche would go back to Texas, but he wanted another day to get ready for the trip. Clyde suggested some motor courts where they might stop on the way home to Dallas.

April 13 was a Thursday. Buck spent the morning getting his Marmon ready for the trip. He changed the oil and took it to a service station to fill up with gas. Around 4 P.M. Clyde and W.D. went out in the roadster, presumably to pull one more robbery for traveling money before they left Joplin. They left the V-8 sedan behind in the garage. Blanche packed, and Buck took a nap. Bonnie had just gotten out of bed—earlier, she'd said she didn't feel well. Now she sat on the living room floor, idly rewriting a few verses of "Suicide Sal." She was still wearing her nightgown and slippers. Bonnie asked if Blanche would boil an egg for her. Then they heard the Ford roadster out on the street, a surprise since Clyde and W.D. had been gone only a few minutes. But the car had developed engine trouble, and Clyde and W.D. decided to return to the apartment. Clyde pulled the roadster into the garage. They were just tugging the door down when another car suddenly veered into the driveway.

Earlier that day, officers in the Joplin police force and the Missouri State Highway Patrol had decided to raid the apartment. Their best guess was that the five suspicious characters living there were selling bootleg liquor. Prohibition repeal had so far only reinstated beer as a legal alcoholic beverage in Missouri. A five-man squad was assembled, and the men drove to the apartment in two cars. Highway patrolmen G. B. Kahler and W. E. Grammer were in the lead auto. Joplin policemen Tom DeGraff and Harry McGinnis were in the second car. McGinnis, fifty-three, was a career cop who'd recently been named acting chief of Joplin detectives because his boss, Ed Portley, had been sick. Otherwise, Portley would have gone on the raid instead of McGinnis. Riding with McGinnis and DeGraff was Wes Harryman, a county constable. Harryman, forty-one, went along because the other lawmen needed an official with the authority to issue a warrant to search the premises. Harryman owned and operated a small farm outside town, and, like most Depression farmers lucky enough to hang on to their land, he still had to supplement his income. As a constable, he didn't earn a salary. Instead, he was paid a few dollars for each warrant he served. Being invited to issue a warrant and come on a raid was an opportunity for Harryman. The officers were armed with only small-caliber handguns. None of the lawmen expected trouble.

Arriving as Clyde and W.D. began lowering the garage door, Kahler swung his car along the curb just past the apartment while DeGraff pulled up right in the driveway, effectively blocking both Fords inside the garage. DeGraff yelled at Harryman to get inside the garage before the door was closed.

Harryman drew his gun, leaped from the car, and tried to duck inside. He was met with blasts from a shotgun, probably Clyde's. Harryman managed to fire one shot as he fell beside the driveway. The shotgun pellets had struck him in the shoulder and the neck, severing arteries. He bled to death as the fight raged on.

McGinnis hopped out and fired three shots through the garage door's glass window. W.D. was struck in the side by one of those shots or the single bullet fired by Harryman. Clyde fired back with his shotgun, and McGinnis was hit in the face, left side, and right arm, which was almost severed from his body. As McGinnis dropped in the driveway, DeGraff got out of the car. He snapped off a few shots, picked up McGinnis's revolver, and ducked around the side of the garage. Kahler took cover behind his car and Grammer ran around the building, where he met DeGraff. DeGraff told him to go find a phone and call for backup.

While Kahler and Clyde traded shots, W. D. Jones lurched upstairs as Buck ran down to help his brother. Bonnie and Blanche were bewildered, and only became more confused when W.D. appeared with blood soaking through his shirt. It was clear they'd have to run for it, and that fleeing on foot wasn't an option. There was no way to know how many cops were outside. The apartment might be surrounded. But they had to get moving as quickly as possible. There was no time to gather their belongings. Driving out was the best bet, and they had the Ford V-8 sedan in the garage. But when Clyde and Buck opened the garage door in front of it, they realized the driveway was blocked by DeGraff's car and McGinnis's body. The women were ordered to get in the sedan. Blanche's dress was spattered with W.D.'s blood. Bonnie was still in her nightgown. W.D. was bleeding heavily, but he tried to help Clyde push DeGraff's car out of the way. Buck dragged McGinnis off to one side. Across the street, Kahler fired again. One shot hit Clyde in the chest. The bullet struck a button on his shirt. Luckily for Clyde, the lawman was firing a small-caliber pistol rather than a high-powered rifle, and the button absorbed much of the impact. The slug barely penetrated Clyde's skin, and afterward Bonnie was able to tug it out with her fingers and a hairpin. Buck was slightly wounded, too—a spent slug bruised his chest. He grabbed a shotgun and joined Clyde in returning Kahler's fire.

In the middle of the gunfight, Blanche's dog, Snow Ball, ran out of the garage and into the street. Blanche ran right after it, calling for the frightened mongrel to come back. Clyde ordered everyone else into the V-8 sedan. He revved the engine and rammed DeGraff's car, shoving it out of the driveway. Their escape route was finally clear, and Clyde drove into the street. Someone, probably Buck, yanked Blanche into the car. Snow Ball kept running. No one knows what became of the dog.

The battered Barrows didn't flee under a hail of bullets. Kahler stopped shooting, probably realizing that bullets from his handgun couldn't dent the panels of the sedan. DeGraff fired only four shots before ducking behind the house. Harryman was dead and McGinnis was dying. Grammer never fired his pistol at all. By the time reinforcements arrived, the gang was long gone.

As soon as he felt they were clear of immediate pursuit, Clyde checked W.D.'s wound. The teenager was in tremendous pain and thought the bullet might still be inside him. They had no medical supplies, and couldn't risk trying to have W.D. examined by a doctor. So Clyde trimmed a thin tree branch, wrapped cloth around it—possibly from Bonnie's nightgown or Blanche's dress—and poked the stick directly into the hole where the bullet had entered W.D.'s abdomen. When the stick protruded through another hole in W.D.'s back, they figured the slug had gone through his body. When they came to a service station, they stopped to buy gas and a packet of aspirin. The pills were the only immediate treatment W.D. received.

Clyde, Bonnie, Buck, Blanche, and W.D. were in terrible straits. They had a few guns, the ones they'd used in the Joplin shootout and some others Clyde had locked in the sedan. Besides the weapons, they had only the clothes they were wearing. Everything else, from their fancy suits and dresses to their cameras and Clyde's guitar, had been abandoned back at the apartment. Two cops had gone down, both undoubtedly dead or dying. The Joplin police had surely sent out an all-points bulletin describing the shooters. Their relative anonymity in Missouri was over. The state was no longer a safe haven.

Clyde headed back to Texas, probably more out of habit than anything else. He avoided Dallas, and at dawn the fugitives found themselves in Shamrock, a town about 95 miles east of Amarillo. Exhausted, wounded himself, Clyde had driven almost six hundred miles since the late afternoon firefight in Joplin. They found a dingy motor court to rest in. Bonnie and Blanche washed and dressed W.D.'s, Clyde's, and Buck's wounds. Blanche, hiding the spots of blood on her dress as best she could, walked to a nearby grocery store and bought some food. They ate and talked about what had happened. Blanche cried because now Buck was on the run again. After a few hours Clyde decided some cars parked nearby looked suspicious. They got back in the sedan and drove through the outskirts of Amarillo until after dark. Then the others waited while Clyde and Buck went into the city and robbed a store or service station that was never identified. Blanche wrote in her memoir that "the next day we got some clothes. . . . We drove so much and so fast, most of the day and night, sleeping only a few hours at a time. One of us always kept watch while the others slept. We traveled through New Mexico, Kansas, Nebraska, Iowa, and Illinois, back through Missouri, Arkansas, Oklahoma, and Louisiana. When the money gave out, something was robbed. I don't remember sleeping in a bed more than three or four times in the next two weeks."

They were wise to keep moving. Before, they only had to worry about being spotted by lawmen in Texas and parts of Oklahoma and New Mexico. Now, cops all over the country were on the lookout for them. Thanks to a plethora of damning evidence they left behind in Joplin, the Barrow Gang wouldn't be limited to a regional reputation anymore.

In the aftermath of the Joplin shootout, city police swarmed into the apartment at 3347½ 34th Street. Wes Harryman was pronounced dead on the scene, and Harry McGinnis was rushed to the hospital, where he would die of his wounds six hours later. The mood of the investigating officers was grim, and it only got grimmer as they made their first discovery—a cache of guns in the garage. The arsenal included four rifles, a shotgun, a pistol, and "an automatic rifle similar to a submachine gun." It was a BAR, a weapon so unfamiliar to rank-and-file city policemen that the Joplin cops didn't know what it was. Clearly, the gunmen who shot Harryman and McGinnis weren't run-of-the-mill bootleggers.

In one bedroom of the apartment was a purse, and its contents provided the first proof of the identity of the fugitives. There was a marriage license for Buck and Blanche, the title to a 1929 Marmon purchased from Carl Beaty, and a criminal pardon issued to Buck by Texas governor Miriam Ferguson. The Joplin police immediately contacted their counterparts in Dallas County, where Smoot Schmid ordered deputies Bob Alcorn and Ted Hinton to rush to Missouri and offer whatever assistance they could. The Texas cops brought mug shots of Buck Barrow and his brother Clyde, whom they believed must have been in Joplin, too.

There were nice clothes left in the apartment, lots of them, most packed in suitcases, which indicated the felons had been getting ready to leave. Several glittering rings and sets of earrings were assumed to be diamond jewelry stolen recently in nearby Neosho. Somebody had abandoned a guitar, and on a living room table the officers found several scribbled sheets of poetry. The subject matter appalled them. The *Joplin Globe* reported the next morning that "the poem entitled *Suicide Sal*" was "morbid and gangster." There were also cameras and rolls of undeveloped film. The film was sent to a laboratory for immediate processing.

Meanwhile, the Joplin police sent out bulletins urging lawmen in neighboring counties and states to be on the lookout for Buck and Clyde Barrow. Also identified were Blanche Caldwell, whose name appeared with Buck's on the marriage license, and "the woman with Clyde Barrow [who] has tentatively been identified as Bonnie Parker." None of the police reports or newspaper articles mentioned W. D. Jones at all.

In its edition published on April 14, the day after the shootout, the *Joplin Globe* reported that "Buck Barrow did virtually all the shooting from the garage," and that the fugitives had escaped because their car "was too fast for the pursuing equipment of officers, who were quickly outdistanced." The Joplin police obviously didn't want the public to know that there hadn't been any immediate pursuit. Buck, according to the story, was the ringleader of a particularly vicious Texas gang that included his younger brother. A day later, after Alcorn and Hinton arrived to brief their Joplin counterparts on the real hierarchy on the Barrow Gang, a "Wanted for Murder" poster was printed and distributed by the Joplin police. It offered $600 for information leading to the capture and conviction of the Barrow boys. Clyde's mug shots were prominent, placed above Buck's. He was described as "very dangerous, his record shows that he has killed at least three or four men," while Buck, demoted to supporting status, merited only "this man was pardoned from the Texas Penitentiary on March 23, 1933."

That same day the police got back processed prints from the undeveloped roles of film, and these were revelatory. Previously, the only photos of the fugitives anyone had seen were mug shots of Clyde and Buck from Texas. Now, they had dozens of pictures, candid ones not only of the Barrow boys, but also of the women and one still unidentified man with them—W. D. Jones. In the photos the male desperadoes struck all sorts of poses, often leaning against their car and always dressed in snappy suits. Shots of the car were quite helpful—they clearly showed the Texas license plate of a Ford V-8 sedan. That made it easy to trace the car as one stolen several weeks earlier in Marshall, Texas.

The best photos—the ones certain to attract public attention and therefore make it easier to get tips on the gang's whereabouts—featured one of the women. Dallas County deputy Ted Hinton said it was Bonnie Parker. In one snapshot she held a grinning Clyde Barrow at mock gunpoint. In another, she propped one foot on the fender of the V-8 sedan—a very unladylike posture—and then compounded the shock value by waving a handgun that she also brandished or wore in several other pictures. It was quickly identified as the one stolen back in late January from Springfield motorcycle patrolman Thomas Persell. Dallas, Marshall, Joplin, Springfield—the police began to get an idea of just how wide-ranging the Barrow Gang was. Then there was the most noxious detail of all about this particular photo. Bonnie Parker had a cigar between her lips. Decent women puffed decorously on cigarettes, taking care to never actually inhale. Bonnie Parker, companion of multiple murderer Clyde Barrow, not only dangled a cigar insolently from the corner of her mouth, she was brazen enough to be photographed doing it.

The photographs were made public on Friday, April 15, in the *Jop-*

lin Globe and on a new wanted poster that featured a photo of Clyde with Bonnie and didn't mention Buck at all. But Bonnie's name was on it, right next to Clyde's. Maybe Clyde's nondescript mug shots resembled those of innumerable other scrawny, Depression-era bandits, but his pictures with Bonnie were unique. The *Joplin Globe* printed three of the photos on its front page—Clyde with Bonnie, Clyde himself, and Clyde with Buck.

These and other captured pictures of the gang weren't printed exclusively in the Joplin press. Many Depression-era newspapers subscribed to newfangled "wire services," which could electronically transmit stories and photographs. The *Joplin Globe* sent its Barrow Gang photos out on the wire, and they triggered a widespread sensation. Plunging circulation was a concern common to newspapers across the nation—publishers in Texas weren't the only ones mandating more stories pandering to the public's preference for entertainment over endless economic bad news. Movie stars, sports heroes, and colorful criminals were preferred subjects. Possibilities in the latter category were limited. Few real-life villains had the same roguish charisma that Jimmy Cagney and Edward G. Robinson brought to movie screens. Al Capone was clearly a barbaric thug. Ma Barker was a dumpy middle-aged woman. John Dillinger had matinee-idol good looks and Pretty Boy Floyd had the best possible nickname, but the Joplin photos introduced new criminal superstars with the most titillating trademark of all—illicit sex. Clyde Barrow and Bonnie Parker were young and unmarried. They undoubtedly slept together—after all, the girl smoked cigars. Whether they'd even heard of the term or not, the Freudian implications did not escape journalists or their readers. That made it easy, when writers exaggerated Clyde's and Bonnie's exploits, for readers to buy into far-fetched stories about these young criminal lovers.

And such stories weren't published only in newspapers. In the early 1930s, magazines devoted to garish, fictionalized descriptions of criminals and crimes hit newsstands and became immensely popular. They served the same purpose as the dime novels of the previous generation, only with bigger type and more photographs. Many of these magazines promoted veracity in their titles—*True Detective, True Crime*—and delivered the opposite. Their contents were generally overwrought and with little if any basis in fact, but millions of readers didn't mind. As soon as they saw the photos of Clyde and Bonnie, editors of the crime magazines didn't hesitate. They wanted to cram as many Barrow Gang stories into their publications as possible before the cops inevitably caught the kids and ruined a good story line. The Joplin shootout took place on April 13, 1933. The photos went out on the national news wires on April 15. Just weeks later, Clyde Barrow was featured in *True Detective Mysteries.* It was only a short profile with his Dallas mug shot in "The Line-Up," a monthly listing of eight fugitives selected by the magazine for special attention, but longer, more garish stories with accompanying graphics and photos took longer to produce. Eventually, multi-page features on Clyde's and Bonnie's supposed exploits would be ubiquitous in the crime publications. But that still didn't complete the flood of Barrow Gang–related publicity.

Bonnie Parker had always wanted to be in the movies, and suddenly she was. Unlike her lifelong fantasy, however, she didn't appear onscreen as the star of a drama or musical. Instead, Bonnie and Clyde were featured in newsreels, short presentations about real individuals and current events that played in theaters prior to feature films. Camera crews went to Joplin and recorded footage of the apartment and interviews with neighbors and police. In the months ahead, there would be newsreel coverage in the wake of almost every shooting or holdup involving the Barrow Gang. Bonnie and Clyde were always the focus. Other members of the gang were considered inconsequential. Audiences settling in to watch Cagney or Robinson pretend to be villains in their latest feature films were treated beforehand to glimpses of what actual outlaws supposedly looked and acted like. The newsreels helped sell tickets and popcorn, and in the minds of many Americans they elevated Clyde and Bonnie into celebrities on a par with the most popular movie stars.

With their celebrity came controversy. The combined newspaper, crime magazine, and newsreel coverage of Clyde and Bonnie managed to simultaneously demonize and deify them. Some perceived the couple as despicable hoodlums with no respect for human life and property. But to many others, they were heroes. True, they robbed banks and shot it out with lawmen, killing some in the process. But in 1933 bankers and law enforcement officials, widely perceived to have no sympathy for decent people impoverished through no fault of their own, were considered the enemy by many Americans. For them, Clyde and Bonnie's criminal acts offered a vicarious sense of revenge. Somebody was sticking it to the rich and powerful.

Without Bonnie, the media outside Texas might have dismissed

Clyde as a gun-toting punk, if it ever considered him at all. With her sassy photographs, Bonnie supplied the sex appeal, the oomph, that allowed the two of them to transcend the small-scale thefts and needless killings that actually comprised their criminal careers. It didn't happen overnight, but over the course of the next several months most people who read newspapers, bought crime magazines, or went to the movies learned all about Clyde Barrow and Bonnie Parker, or at least thought they did. In the weeks immediately following Joplin, Clyde and Bonnie along with Buck, Blanche, and W.D. lived like animals—sleeping in their car in the woods, bathing in creeks, letting bullet wounds heal themselves, and fearing attack or capture every time a twig snapped or a passing car slowed. But Americans began to imagine them in entirely different circumstances.

"Their whole image was one of glamour," recalls former speaker of the U.S. House of Representatives Jim Wright, who grew up in Texas and Oklahoma and was eleven when he first saw the photos of Bonnie and newsreels featuring the Barrow Gang, and read stories about them in *True Detective.* "You rather imagined them holed up in some upscale hotel. They always dressed perfectly, wielding guns in a deadly manner, coolly evading capture against all odds. It was a very romantic existence we felt they must enjoy. And even if you did not approve of them, you still would have to envy them a little, to be so good-looking and rich and happy."

CHAPTER 16

Shooting Stars

In 1933, Miss Sophia Stone of Ruston, Louisiana, was employed as her parish's "home demonstration agent," a fancy term for a job teaching local residents basic household money-saving techniques like how to preserve and can fruit. She was featured on local radio broadcasts, which made her something of a celebrity. On April 27, exactly two weeks after the Barrow Gang's narrow escape in Joplin, she and Dillard Darby, the local undertaker, were relaxing on the porch of their boardinghouse after lunch. Stone, a very proper single lady concerned about her reputation, emphasized later to reporters that the two were not engaged in any inappropriate behavior—Darby was married, and she was being courted by a man named Cook. They were just casual friends enjoying a postprandial chat. Both Stone's Ford and Darby's Chevrolet were parked along the curb. Suddenly another Ford roared down the street and screeched to a stop by Darby's car. A young man hopped out, got into the Chevy and sped away, followed by the first car. It all happened in a matter of seconds. It wasn't necessary for the thief to waste any time hot-wiring the car. Darby had left his keys in the ignition. The undertaker rushed from the porch and managed to get a foot on the running board, but the thief stepped on the gas and Darby couldn't hang on. Stone told Darby to get into her Ford, and they tore out after the stolen Chevy.

Clyde, Bonnie, Buck, and Blanche thought W. D. Jones would be right in front of them as they raced north, but somehow they lost sight of him. Clyde was irritated—they needed a second car, and this was supposed to be a quick, simple job preparatory to a bigger one. Once the Chevy was secured, Clyde intended to rob the Ruston bank. Now W.D. and the Chevrolet had vanished on the web of backcountry roads and they'd have to drive around looking for him. The Ruston police had enough time now to be on full alert—so much for robbing the bank there. Clyde didn't find W.D., but he did spot the Ford coupé that had followed the Chevy out of Ruston. Stone and Darby lost W.D. around the small town of Hico, and they'd decided to head back home when Clyde roared up behind them. After ordering them out of Stone's coupé, he asked why they had been following the Chevrolet. Darby snapped, "Because it's my car." Clyde lost his temper and hit the undertaker on the head with the butt of his pistol. When Darby staggered back to his feet, Clyde ordered him into the front seat of the Barrow Gang's Ford. Buck and Blanche were in the back seat. Bonnie, in a bad mood herself, cursed at Stone and instructed her to climb into the front, too. It was crowded up there with four people. Darby's head was bleeding from a superficial wound, and ammunition clips kept spilling out of the glove compartment onto their laps. That made Clyde even angrier, and he told Stone to hold the clips. There was no room for someone to move to the back seat. Besides Buck and Blanche, it was crammed with rifles. After Joplin, one of Clyde's first priorities had been to restock the gang's arsenal.

They looked a while longer for W.D. and the stolen Chevrolet, but eventually gave up. Clyde drove north over the state line and into Arkansas. Sophia Stone wasn't impressed with her captors. She said later that they were dressed shabbily and smelled bad, clearly the result of living in their car for the previous two weeks. Bonnie in particular always prided herself on looking nice—her bad mood might have been aggravated by embarrassment at Stone and Darby seeing her looking so slovenly. The ride was tense for everyone. Clyde drove at breakneck speed. Stone later estimated it at 90 miles an hour, unheard of on rough country roads. A few times Clyde wondered out loud about killing his prisoners, and Buck goaded him by asking, "What are you waiting for?"

Stone thought Buck might be drunk. Finally Clyde told Stone and Darby that he'd release them unharmed if they didn't try anything. Blanche wrote in her memoir that Clyde informed the two exactly who their captors were. Like everywhere else, the newspapers in Louisiana had been full of stories about the Barrow Gang. The hostages were suitably intimidated.

Even in a bad mood, Bonnie was too social to let an opportunity for conversation pass. She asked Stone and Darby what they did for a living. When Darby said he was a mortician, Bonnie laughed and asked him to promise to be the gang's embalmer. Stone told reporters later that when she mentioned she gave cooking lessons, Bonnie asked her to describe some of the recipes. By the time Clyde stopped outside the Arkansas town of Waldo in the late afternoon, everyone was on reasonably friendly terms. Clyde ordered Stone and Darby to get out, drove a few yards, backed up, and asked if they had enough money to get home. When Darby said he only had a quarter, Clyde, perhaps feeling remorseful about cracking him on the skull, handed the undertaker a five-dollar bill. As the gang drove away, Blanche thought she saw Darby copy down the license number of their Ford.

From there, Clyde decided to take a roundabout route back to Louisiana that passed through Hope, Arkansas. On their way through Hope they were spotted and followed by a police car, possibly because Darby had already reported their license number, more likely because small-town lawmen all over the region were on the lookout for a Ford V-8 and the now infamous Barrow Gang. Many local lawmen earned most of their income by claiming rewards for capturing criminals, and the rewards for Clyde in Texas, Oklahoma, and Missouri were widely known to cumulatively total around $1,000. One of the Hope cops stuck a rifle out of his car window. The police car was close to the Ford, and Buck raised a BAR. With such superior firepower he could easily have blown the pursuers right off the road. Instead, Buck held his fire. Clyde gunned the car's powerful V-8 engine and outran the cops. Despite what many newspaper stories and police reports claimed, the Barrow Gang always preferred flight to shootouts whenever both options were available.

Nobody wrote about Buck's and Clyde's act of mercy toward the Hope cops until it was mentioned in Blanche's memoirs decades later, but there were plenty of stories about the kidnapping of Sophia Stone and Dillard Darby. For one thing, it was the first confirmed sighting of

Clyde and Bonnie since the highly publicized Joplin shootout. For another, Stone was eager to supply reporters with colorful accounts of the terrible abuse she had suffered during her five- or six-hour ordeal. Interviewing Stone the day after she'd been taken hostage, the *Ruston Daily Leader* reported that Bonnie Parker "cursed her and slugged her in the back of the neck with her pistol butt. . . . Miss Stone sustained no severe injuries from the blow inflicted by Bonnie's gun as the weapon struck her on the back of the neck where a heavy braid of hair was entwined." This happened, Stone testified, after Clyde used his gun to strike Darby. It made for colorful copy. Three days later, Darby's Chevrolet was found abandoned in eastern Arkansas a hundred miles from Ruston, but there was no sign of the fifth gang member who had stolen it. For Clyde and Bonnie—as well as the police—it was as though W. D. Jones had vanished.

That worried them. The gunshot wound W.D. had sufferred in Joplin still wasn't completely healed. He might have been picked up by some Arkansas or Louisiana small-town cops. If the kid was still free, he'd have no idea where the rest of the gang was. In that event, it seemed likely W.D. would make his way back to West Dallas, since he knew Clyde and Bonnie would continue making periodic trips there to see their families. So for the first time since Joplin, the Barrow Gang headed home.

Their visit was kept short. The Ruston kidnapping had generated a new wave of stories, meaning that Sheriff Smoot Schmid and his deputies had fresh incentive for setting a West Dallas trap. To Schmid and other lawmen, almost everything about the Barrow Gang—where they traveled, what places they chose to rob, how they at times seemed determined not to hurt anyone and at others showed no compunction about killing—was frustratingly random. The only constant was their visits to their families. This time, Clyde didn't bother driving by the family service station and tossing out a Coke bottle with a note about a late-night meeting. He just parked in the driveway for five minutes while his mother, father, and sister Marie came out to stand by the car. Clyde told them that if and when W.D. showed up, he was to sit tight. They'd come back for him when they could. But Cumie was less interested in her friend Tookie's youngest child than in one of her own sons. She pleaded with Buck to stay in West Dallas and give himself up. In the immediate aftermath of Joplin, Cumie had told Dallas reporters that both her boys must have been framed, but of course she knew better. Now she didn't bother suggesting that Clyde surrender, too. With the deaths of two more lawmen on his record, he was beyond any possibility of mercy. Buck gently informed his mother that "there isn't a chance in the world for me to get by the chair." He'd been at Joplin, he'd fired a shotgun in a gunfight where two lawmen died, and now the cops had his picture and name plastered on every post office bulletin board. All he could do was remain part of the Barrow Gang until the moment came when they finally didn't escape. Clyde interrupted to say he would write and sign a statement swearing that Buck and Blanche had only been visiting him and Bonnie in Joplin—they weren't part of the gang and had found themselves in the middle of the shootout by accident. Marie thought "Clyde was now talking to Buck like Buck had talked to Clyde before the Joplin fight." Buck didn't think that would work, either. So they said goodbye, and Clyde sped away down Eagle Ford Road. Every moment they weren't moving was dangerous.

They headed north out of Texas again. Clyde apparently liked driving on Highway 69, which rolled smoothly all the way through Kansas and into Minnesota. They spent several days in Indiana, and probably circled back through Oklahoma, Arkansas, and Louisiana. Blanche Barrow wrote that "when we needed money, which was often, some filling station, grocery store or drug store was robbed." They weren't staging these robberies to fund a lavish lifestyle. They were just trying to get away with enough money for gas, food, and clothing. While the gang was always eager to break into armories and hardware stores to grab guns, there is no record of them sneaking into a department store to stock up on suits, dresses, and shoes. On visits to West Dallas, they'd hand money over to L.C. and Marie, who'd make Clyde's and Bonnie's clothing purchases at nice downtown Dallas stores, adding a few items for themselves in the process. Apparently for Clyde and Bonnie, it was a point of pride to have money for wardrobe purchases in hometown establishments where, in their old lives, they could never have afforded to shop. L.C. purchased many of Clyde's snappy suits and hats at Harry the Haberdasher's, a swanky store across the street from the downtown courthouse where local lawmen met to plot the capture of the Barrow Gang. It was another way of putting one over on the Dallas establishment.

• • •

Everyone was sick of camping in the car. Besides the obvious inconveniences, the Dust Bowl was still raging. Getting caught in even the slightest of the swirling storms meant picking dirt from between their teeth for days afterward. But checking into a motor court was no longer a daily option. Thanks to the media, the Barrow Gang, Clyde and Bonnie especially, were now familiar names and faces. The woman checking them into a cabin, the man parking his car next to theirs in the motor court lot, might recognize them and contact the police. Though the motor courts were becoming more ubiquitous, they were still usually found on the outskirts of midsized to major cities. "The laws" were never more than a few minutes away from any of them. So the gang risked a layover at a motor court only when they were either convinced it was isolated enough to be safe, or else they were so worn out they were willing to accept the additional risk. Other famous criminals like Dillinger and Pretty Boy didn't have to stoop to grimy motor court cabins. Whenever they wanted a break from the pressures of evading the law, they could spend a few days in a safe house in places like St. Paul or Kansas City. These were usually quiet, nicely decorated lodgings—hotel rooms or apartments—and payoffs to local cops ensured uninterrupted privacy. But staying in such places cost amounts far beyond the Barrow Gang's means. Clyde also lacked the underworld connections to know where these safe houses were, and how to arrange for their use.

But if fame deprived them of much opportunity to stay in motor courts, it proved quite helpful when the Barrow Gang wanted to spend a night in beds rather than a car. If "laws" and potential stool pigeons all over the country were aware of them now, so were hardworking people anxious to help out the newest American folk heroes. Before, when Clyde and Bonnie appeared and asked to stay the night at some farm family's isolated house, they were welcomed for whatever small sum they might pay or the gift they'd leave for the privilege. Nobody knew who they were, and no one wanted to. Now such families might very well recognize the gang from newspaper stories or crime magazines or newsreels, and they'd be invited in because people thought it was exciting to harbor criminal celebrities. Clyde didn't disregard the potential for betrayal. He had huge rewards on his head. So he, Bonnie, Buck, and Blanche would stay in most homes no longer than one night.

Clyde and Bonnie liked it when their new acquaintances recognized them. Bonnie had always wanted to be famous. Now that she was, she didn't want to be well known for the wrong reason. Bonnie told everyone that she absolutely, positively did not smoke cigars. She did other things to protect her newfound celebrity. Bonnie still drank, often quite a lot. But she began to carry lemons with her. Whenever she took a drink, afterward Bonnie chewed on pieces of lemon peel, partly to cut the burn of the liquor and also to have the smell of lemon rather than liquor on her breath. This wasn't unique to Bonnie—lots of Texas girls did it. But because she was so well known it became a sort of trademark for her, noticed and commented upon enough so that lawmen became aware of it.

If starstruck fans hosting or otherwise spending time with the gang felt disappointed with Bonnie, it was usually in another regard. They'd seen her posed pictures, they'd read descriptions of her in newspapers and crime magazines, and they expected to meet a young woman of exceptional beauty and sexual allure. Bonnie was supposed to be a vamp, a real-life femme fatale. In person she was nice-looking enough, even cute, but they often had anticipated something more. Buck's wife, Blanche, just a year younger than Bonnie, was much more striking, a fact Bonnie undoubtedly realized and didn't appreciate. But if Bonnie couldn't win the hearts of everyone with her looks, she could still use her personality to charm them. Joking, telling stories about her adventures with Clyde, flirting just enough, Bonnie knew how to make people believe she thought they were special, and they responded accordingly. Because she talked much more than Clyde and because she was clearly smart, some people believed that Bonnie Parker was really the brains of the Barrow Gang. The suggestion became widespread enough that Marie Barrow, in both her unpublished and published memoirs, repeatedly emphasized that her brother Clyde was the boss of the gang, period. W. D. Jones felt compelled to tell *Playboy* decades later that "Bonnie was the only one Clyde trusted all the way. But not even Bonnie had a voice in the decisions. His leadership was undisputed."

Under Clyde's leadership, on May 11 the gang tried to rob another bank. This one was the Lucerne State Bank in Lucerne, Indiana. Clyde had a new strategy—he was trying to learn from past mistakes. On the 11th, a Thursday, he and Buck cased the place, and then late that night Bonnie and Blanche dropped them off and drove their latest stolen

Ford V-8 out of sight. Clyde and Buck broke into the bank, hid themselves, and waited until morning. The idea was to get the drop on the bank clerks when they arrived at work, before the bank officially opened for business. Then there wouldn't be any customers to get in the way.

In theory, it made sense. In practice, it was a fiasco. Bank staffers Everett Gregg and Lawson Selders arrived at 7:30 on Friday morning. As soon as the men were inside, Clyde and Buck popped out of their hiding places and ordered them to put up their hands. But officials at the Lucerne State Bank also had a plan in place in case of attempted robbery. Gregg had a rifle hidden somewhere, probably behind his cashier's desk. It hadn't occurred to Clyde and Buck to search the place for guns. Gregg and the would-be thieves exchanged wild shots. No one was hit.

At that moment, Bonnie and Blanche roared up in the Ford. Bonnie was driving. They'd expected to see Clyde and Buck running from the bank with bags of money. Instead, the men were fleeing empty-handed from a man with a rifle. They leaped into the car, and Clyde took over at the wheel. Getting out of town wasn't easy. Early risers were strolling along the street. One of them, hearing the gunshots and guessing that a robbery attempt was in progress, chunked a thick piece of wood in front of the Ford. Clyde had to swerve into someone's yard to get around it. Another man leaped onto the hood of the Ford. Clyde screamed at Bonnie to shoot him. She grabbed a gun and fired a few wild shots. The man got off the hood, scared enough to desist even though Bonnie had missed him. She later told her family that she'd missed deliberately—he had white hair, and she didn't want to hurt an old man.

But the disaster wasn't finished yet. More townspeople were swarming toward the scene. People shot at the Ford, and its panicky occupants fired back. Two women, Doris Minor and Ethel Jones, were slightly wounded. They were luckier than some pigs being herded across the road in the Ford's path. Clyde plowed his car right through them. Two hogs were killed—the only fatalities in Lucerne that morning.

Afterward, Clyde was undeterred. He decided to try the same strategy at another bank. Over a year earlier in March 1932, out on the road with Raymond Hamilton and Ralph Fults, he'd spotted a likely target in Okabena, Minnesota, only to call off the job when the streets there were too treacherous with late-winter ice and snow. But more than a year later, in spring, the First State Bank of Okabena would do very well. Ever since Joplin, Clyde had shown a renewed interest in bank robbery. Though the gang had been supporting itself since the April 13 shootout in Missouri with the usual Barrow run of smaller grocery store and service station holdups, Clyde may have decided that such small-scale stuff was really beneath the dignity of America's most newly famous criminals. At least every once in a while they should attempt something grander. Besides, he had Buck with him now, and Bonnie had proven she could drive the getaway car. Blanche refused to take any active role, but she seemed resigned to life on the run. She could have gone back to her father in Oklahoma or her mother in Texas anytime she wanted. No one was making her stay.

On the night of May 18, Bonnie and Blanche dropped Clyde and Buck off behind the bank building in Okabena. They broke in, hid there overnight, and in the morning caught two arriving employees by surprise. Unlike Everett Gregg of the Lucerne State Bank, these two didn't have guns handy. When a pair of customers arrived, Buck and Clyde took them prisoner, too. They snatched up all the money they could—about $1,600, $700 of which was in gleaming silver dollars. One of the prisoners managed to trigger an alarm as the Barrow brothers ran into the street with their lumpy sacks of loot and jumped into the waiting Ford V-8 with Bonnie and Blanche. Some alert Okabena citizens shot at them as they drove away, and the gang returned fire. No one was hit. For a change, the Barrow Gang wasn't even initially blamed for the robbery. Two local cons, Floyd and Anthony Strain, along with Anthony's wife, Mildred, were arrested and convicted of the crime. But Barrow family members later admitted that Clyde and Buck pulled off the theft—Cumie and Marie even wrote in their unpublished memoirs about seeing all the silver dollars.

They saw them because Clyde and Bonnie's immediate goal after the Okabena job was to get back home as soon as possible to share the take with their struggling families. Conflicting dates have been given as to when this meeting east of Dallas took place. In her memoir Blanche Barrow remembers she was sent ahead by bus on Mother's Day to arrange the get-together, but Mother's Day in 1933 fell on May 14, four days before the Okabena heist. Probably the gang made its brief visit home a week later. It wasn't the easiest trip. At one point, jammed into their car with guns and suitcases, Clyde and Buck lost their tempers and got into a fistfight. Blanche, sitting between them, recalled later that she got hit more than they did. She also embellished her husband's heroic conduct in the scrap. According to Blanche, Buck told Clyde they could get out of the car and continue swinging, while Clyde reached for a shotgun before backing down. To Blanche, it seemed like the brothers were no longer able to get along—in her mind, it was all Clyde's fault because he was so bossy. Some tension between the two was inevitable. Buck was used to telling his kid brother what to do. Clyde believed he was the undisputed leader of the Barrow Gang. But by the time they arrived back in Texas for the family reunion, the brothers were pals again.

Blanche's recollection of the fight may have been colored by her equally poor opinion of the rest of the Barrow family's behavior when she arrived in West Dallas to set up the meeting. Clyde had sent her ahead because, of the four on the run, Blanche was by far the least well known to Sheriff Smoot Schmid and his crew. She was given $400 of the bank's money along with instructions about where and when everyone would meet, then dropped off at a bus stop. Blanche recalled that she arrived at the Dallas bus station at 5:30 on a Monday morning, meaning the date was probably May 22. She splurged on a cab to take her to Jack Barrow's house, a curious choice of destination since Jack always tried to keep his distance from the family's criminal element. He reluctantly let her in, and Blanche called Cumie. When her mother-in-law arrived, Blanche swore to Cumie that she and Buck had no part in shooting the lawmen in Joplin, leaving out the small detail of Buck firing a shotgun during the gun battle. Then she asked Cumie to go tell Emma Parker about the meeting that afternoon. Blanche also asked about W. D. Jones. Cumie said he'd been seen back in West Dallas, but she didn't know where he was at the moment.

Blanche next called Nell and Artie Barrow. Her sisters-in-law came by, but only to say they were too busy to attend a family gathering that day. Blanche was indignant that they wouldn't even take her out to buy some boots beforehand. This is undoubtedly more of Blanche's embellishing. Nell Barrow remembered that she and Artie "got the clan together" while Blanche ran out to go shopping. Blanche returned not only with impractical riding boots for herself but also skintight "breeches, and very nice and trim she looked in them, too." Nell wrote that she and Artie did go to the gathering, along with L.C., Marie, and Cumie. Emma Parker went, too, with Bonnie's sister, Billie Jean. They rendezvoused with Clyde, Bonnie, and Buck on a country road east of Dallas. Blanche thought those three had taken advantage of her absence to do some drinking. Buck, her beloved husband, only took a couple of drinks "because he had promised me he wouldn't get drunk." Clyde and Bonnie, according to Blanche, drank too much. The Barrow family accounts of the meeting don't mention anyone being in bad shape from alcohol.

But everyone agreed it was an odd gathering, festive and fretful at the same time. Cumie brought red beans, corn bread, and fried chicken, so things began with a picnic. Photos were snapped—having learned a hard lesson with the film left behind in Joplin, Clyde and Bonnie were careful from then on to cover the license plates with strategically placed coats or hats before posing by their stolen cars. Clyde and Buck gave the other Barrows several hundred silver dollars from the Okabena robbery. Bonnie gave Emma and Billie Jean $112, and Blanche gave Cumie $30 to pass on to her mother. As a birthday gift Clyde gave his sister Marie, who was about to turn fifteen, extra money to buy some nice bedroom furniture.

Everyone teased Blanche about her tight new pants, and L.C. dared her to race him in her fancy boots. She accepted, and was quickly out of breath. The way the Barrow family would remember it, Blanche was the life of the party. She told funny stories about Bonnie panicking during thunderstorms, and described an argument between Clyde and Bonnie that ended with Bonnie stomping off through a corn field and Clyde dashing down the rows after her, trying to get her to make up. Marie had something more serious to discuss. A teacher at her high school had been harassing her, greeting her "every morning as I entered the school building with the cheery question, 'Well, have they caught your brothers yet?' " Marie planned to come back to the school after she graduated and "whup her up one side and down the other."

Clyde asked about W.D. He really wanted the boy back in the gang. Then he asked his mother to contact the Joplin police and request that they send his guitar back to West Dallas. (She did, but was turned down.) The four fugitives gave their version of the Stone-Darby kidnapping—they just wanted "a lark"—and told about the bank robberies in Lucerne and Okabena. Bonnie explained that she hadn't shot the man who jumped on the hood of their car in Lucerne because he had white hair. Then she said she liked the nice blue outfit Marie was wearing. They were the same size, and Marie was feeling generous. So

Bonnie and the younger girl retired to "a discreet place out of sight" and swapped clothes.

Then Emma Parker asked Bonnie to walk down the road with her so they could talk privately. The Barrows knew Emma was trying to convince her daughter to leave Clyde and surrender to the police. Emma's argument to her daughter was that all Bonnie would face was a prison sentence, if there was any jail time at all—the Kaufman County jury had already let her go, and maybe another jury would do the same. Bonnie refused. She told her mother that it was inevitable that Clyde would die and, when he did, she wanted to die with him. For a change, she was matter-of-fact instead of dramatic.

While Emma was failing to persuade Bonnie to surrender, Cumie had no better luck with Buck. He told his mother that he and Blanche would stay with Clyde and Bonnie, "the four of us together 'til they get us, I guess." Then there were extended goodbyes, and promises from the fugitives that they'd be back in touch soon.

With money in their pockets, the Barrow Gang felt ready for another vacation, this one in Florida, Georgia, and Alabama. As soon as they could after crossing the Texas state line, they stole a second car so Buck and Clyde wouldn't have to ride together all the time. Bonnie's younger sister, Billie Jean, apparently came along part of the way and later talked about Clyde and Buck joking together, so the additional space had its intended effect.

For about ten days they made their leisurely way along the Gulf of Mexico and the Atlantic coast, taking time to stop and swim and sun themselves on the beach. Blanche posed for one provocative picture modeling racy swimwear and another lounging pinup style on the sand. There were a few close calls with cops, but nothing that involved shooting. At some point they received interesting news. On June 2, a jury finally passed sentence on Raymond Hamilton for the murder of J. N. Bucher in Hillsboro. Raymond avoided the death penalty but was given ninety-nine years in prison. Tacked onto other sentences he'd received for various car thefts and bank robberies, his cumulative sentence totaled 263 years. Oklahoma officials demonstrated no interest in extraditing Raymond so he could be tried for the murder of Eugene Moore in Stringtown. So Raymond was immediately hauled off to Eastham Prison Farm by Bud Russell and the One Way Wagon. Since Raymond wasn't facing an imminent date with the electric chair, Clyde probably felt no immediate obligation to free him. He was only going to make a rescue attempt out of duty rather than friendship. If Raymond had to spend some months or even years sweating out in Eastham's cotton fields before Clyde got around to breaking him out, so what? Besides, it would take more Barrow Gang members than the current lineup to pull off a raid on Eastham, and right now they were on vacation with no time for recruitment. (Hearing that Raymond received a ninety-nine-year sentence rather than the death penalty must have been a real relief to Clyde's former partner, Lake Dallas Gang member Ted Rogers, who'd actually shot John Bucher. Already in prison in Huntsville on an unrelated conviction, Rogers had promised other inmates to come forward and admit he was Bucher's killer if Raymond was sentenced to death. But since Raymond had avoided the electric chair, there was no reason for Rogers to do so. Even without the additional ninety-nine years assessed by the Hillsboro jury, Raymond's other convictions still were the equivalent of a life sentence.)

During their coastal trip, Clyde and Buck apparently had only one disagreement—Clyde wanted W.D. back in the gang, and Buck thought the teenager would either do something stupid and get himself killed, or else get picked up by the cops and tell them enough to get the rest of the gang caught, too. Clyde was adamant, and contacted Cumie. She was instructed to find W.D. and tell him Clyde and Bonnie would come to West Dallas shortly to pick him up. While they made that trip, Buck and Blanche could take the second car and go visit her father in Goodwater, Oklahoma. Then late on the night of June 10, they'd reunite with Clyde, Bonnie, and W.D. on a bridge between the southwest Oklahoma towns of Erick and Sayre.

Blanche hadn't seen her father for some time. Their reunion was tearful on both sides. Matt Caldwell said he'd read stories about what had happened in Joplin and couldn't believe his baby girl was involved in such a terrible thing. Blanche cried and told him that she and Buck were completely innocent of any wrongdoing. Blanche may have believed it herself, even though she was wearing spiffy riding boots she'd paid for with stolen money.

Meanwhile, Clyde and Bonnie drove back to West Dallas, where they picked up W.D. and headed out into West Texas on a roundabout route to the rendezvous point in Oklahoma. They probably spent the night of June 8 at a motor court in Vernon, Texas, and June 9 found them in the small West Texas town of Wellington. The cotton-farming community had been hit hard by the Depression, and the arrival of three well-dressed strangers in a flashy Ford V-8 caused a stir. Clyde and Bonnie surely didn't mind. It didn't seem as though anyone recognized them and, if necessary, they always felt certain they could outrun or outfight any backcountry cops. There was no reason not to stay a little while. They had time to kill before meeting Buck and Blanche late on the 10th. Soon after Clyde, Bonnie, and W.D. arrived in town and checked into its small hotel—this far from any big city, it was the equivalent of a convenient motor court—several employees at a nearby garage wandered over to inspect the V-8 Ford the strangers had parked in the street. They were impressed.

The V-8 wasn't as impressive the next morning when the garage mechanics saw it again. The Ford was now a battered wreck resting on its side in the Salt Fork branch of the Red River just outside of town. Clyde's reckless driving had finally cost the gang dearly, and Bonnie most of all.

CHAPTER 17

Disaster in Wellington, Murder in Arkansas

The terrain around the small West Texas town of Wellington is so flat that it defies the concept of distance. There aren't many hills or, except for a few wooded areas, trees. Brush is low-slung, prickly, and just a slightly darker shade of brown than the dirt stretching to the horizon. Whenever there has been enough rain to produce standing water, sluggish rivers and streams trickle in wide cuts often ten or twelve feet deep, evidence of some prehistoric underground upheaval that left cracks on the earth's barren crust above. Because it's cotton country, during the hot months when bolls bloom and are picked, clouds of dirty cotton fluff float free and get tangled on brush and the shoulders of roads. This gives the unsettling impression of recent light snowfall on days when temperatures routinely reach 100 degrees or more. Sometimes depth perception is difficult even in broad daylight. At night, it's practically nonexistent. Locals understand the necessity of driving with care.

On the night of June 10, 1933, Sam and Sallie Pritchard had their extended family over for a visit. The Pritchard house was a few miles north of Wellington and about one hundred yards from the Salt Fork branch of the Red River and two parallel roads running north–south. One road was new and freshly paved. The other was older and consisted of packed dirt. The county was building a bridge over the river on the new road, so there was a detour sign on both sides ordering motorists to switch over to the old road and its bridge. The Salt Fork actually had very little water in it, but the cut of the river was deep, probably twelve feet. Some later estimates by reporters made it closer to thirty. The Pritchards' guests at their house by the Salt Fork that night included their son Jack, daughter Gladys, daughter-in-law Irene, son-in-law Alonzo Cartwright, and Alonzo and Gladys's baby, whose name and gender no one seems to remember now. Jack wanted to talk about the possibility of everybody moving to Arkansas—he thought things were pretty well played out around Wellington. Jack and his wife were especially poor. They couldn't afford a car and had to ride horses to the house that evening. After a while the family made ice cream, and around 10 P.M. Sam and Jack took their bowls outside and sat on the porch, eating and talking. Suddenly they heard the thrum of a powerful car engine clearly roaring north at high speed. Jack told his father that the driver must be a darn fool.

The darn fool was Clyde, driving 70 miles an hour on a pitch-black night when it was hard to see much of what was coming up on the road. Bonnie sat in the front seat with him. W.D. was in back. Clyde raced right past the detour sign and, seconds later, the road ended and the Ford V-8 blasted through a wooden barricade and flew into the air. It spun on the way down, made metal-rending contact with the hard rock of the riverbed and rolled over several times before coming to a stop on its side, facing back south the way it had come. Sam, Jack, and Alonzo sprinted over, and Jack recalled forty-seven years later that the V-8 had its "doors jammed and the glasses [windows] broked out." A pair of arms was reaching up through where the windshield used to be. Alonzo grabbed them, and Jack helped him pull Clyde from the wreck. Then they hauled out W.D., and Alonzo yelled to Jack that he thought there was "a kid or something down here in the bottom" of the Ford.

Though some later accounts claimed the V-8 burst into flames, causing Bonnie's terrible injuries, that didn't happen. Her right leg was coated with acid spurting from the car's smashed battery. The scalding was instant and ferocious—W. D. Jones said later that "the hide on her right leg was gone, from her hip down to the ankle. I could see the bone at places." As Jack and Alonzo lifted her out, they thought she was having trouble breathing. Clyde and W.D. were dazed, so Jack carried Bonnie to the Pritchard house, recalling later that even though she was so tiny she was still "all limber and kinda hard to carry," meaning she probably had passed out from the pain. Bonnie was laid down carefully on a bed, and Sallie Pritchard and her daughter Gladys began swabbing her wounds with baking soda and yellow Cloverine Salve. Putting baking soda on burns was a popular country home remedy—in this case, it kept the battery acid from eating into Bonnie's leg any further. With that done, Sallie Pritchard told Clyde it was time to get a doctor. According to Jack Pritchard, Clyde refused, adding, "If she dies, she will just have to die." During the next few days, Clyde demonstrated that the last thing he wanted Bonnie to do was die. He took extraordinary personal risks to save her life. If, in those first terrible moments in the Pritchards' house, he did say something so callous, it was probably because he'd also been battered around in the wreck. Jack Pritchard said Clyde was "skinned up a little," too. He was still trying to gather his wits about him.

Clyde's immediate instinct was to prepare to fight. He told W.D. to stay at the house while he went back to the wreck to salvage some of the gang's guns. The family saw what he was doing and became suspicious. When Bonnie regained consciousness and distracted W.D. by calling out to him, Alonzo Cartwright sneaked away in his father-in-law's old Dodge. He drove into Wellington and alerted Collingsworth County sheriff George Corry and town chief of police Paul Hardy. After requesting an ambulance, they jumped into a Chevrolet and drove off to the Pritchard place. Alonzo had trouble getting the Dodge started again and lagged behind.

Corry and Hardy certainly had no idea they were about to confront the notorious Clyde Barrow. Based on Alonzo Cartwright's description, they figured the accident victims were local kids who'd been out drinking, and who maybe "carried a gun or two for a thrill." When they arrived at the Pritchard house and went in, they had trouble seeing much. The only illumination was from a kerosene lamp. Then Clyde emerged from the shadows, brandishing a BAR. He took Corry and Hardy prisoner, and Bonnie managed to stagger off her bed and grab the lawmen's guns. W. D. Jones, toting a shotgun, came inside and told Hardy, "You boys are just in time. We want to borrow your car."

Amid all the confusion, Gladys Pritchard Cartwright worried that her baby, who'd begun crawling, might get out the back door in the kitchen. Picking up the child, she went into the kitchen and reached to close the door latch. W.D. thought she was reaching for a weapon and fired a blast from his shotgun. Subsequent Barrow Gang lore frequently described the woman's fingers or even hand being blown completely off, but Gladys actually was much more fortunate. W.D. was still reeling from the crash, and his aim was off. A few stray pellets nicked one of Gladys's fingers, inflicting the most superficial of wounds. The baby's scalp was slightly scratched from bits of window screen from the door absorbing most of W.D.'s blast. But the near-miss unsettled everyone, and Clyde decided it was time to clear out and meet Buck and Blanche in Oklahoma. He had no intention of leaving the lawmen behind to organize pursuit. For the moment, they undoubtedly made useful hostages, bargaining chips if the gang was cornered. So Corry and Hardy were prodded into the back seat of their Chevrolet. Clyde got behind the wheel, Bonnie was settled in beside him, and W.D. climbed in the front seat, too, twisting around so he could hold the prisoners at gunpoint.

After driving only a few miles, Clyde pulled over and placed Bonnie in the back seat with Corry and Hardy. She lay across their laps, and they tried to cradle her as the car bumped along the rough country road. Hardy was impressed with Clyde's driving. He'd stopped racing along at foolhardy speeds, dropping back to what the Wellington police chief estimated at 50 to 60 miles an hour. Whenever Clyde passed a car coming the other way, he steered slightly toward the center of the road, forcing the other driver to inch close to the ditch and concentrate on not running off the road. That, Hardy believed, was Clyde's clever way of preventing the other motorist from getting a good look at the stolen Chevrolet.

At some point, Clyde had a terrible lapse in judgment. Still shaken from the crash, worried about Bonnie, he couldn't resist asking his prisoners if they'd heard of the Barrow brothers. Hardy and Corry both had, but they played dumb "to string them along." Finally Hardy said he thought he'd heard of Buck Barrow, but not anybody named Clyde. At that point, Clyde knew he'd been fooled, and couldn't help laughing. What he didn't realize was that now Corry and Hardy not only knew that they were prisoners of the Barrow Gang, they also realized the notorious Bonnie Parker was seriously hurt. Somewhere, somehow, Clyde might try to get her medical attention, and that clue could help pursuers track him down.

It was well after midnight when Clyde finally guided the Chevrolet over the bridge at the designated meeting place in Oklahoma between Erick and Sayre. Buck and Blanche were asleep in their car—Clyde had to honk the Chevrolet's horn to wake them. Clyde told them there had been a wreck, Bonnie might be dying, and there were two lawmen to get rid of. When Bonnie was carried over to Buck's car, Blanche, taking in her terribly burned leg along with a profusion of cuts on her face and arms, thought "she would die before daybreak." Clyde's nose appeared broken, and W.D. had a few burns, too.

Once Bonnie was settled on a pile of clothes in the back seat of his brother's car, Clyde had to decide what to do with Corry and Hardy. Buck asked if he planned "to bump them off." Clyde asked the prisoners what they'd do if he set them free. Hardy promised they'd just try to get back home, and Clyde replied that they'd probably run to the nearest phone. But he was touched by how gentle they had been with Bonnie after she'd been placed across their laps in the back seat. He remarked to Buck that "I've been with them so long, I'm beginning to like them," then told his brother and W.D. to tie the lawmen to trees by the side of the road. They didn't have any rope, so they used Corry's and Hardy's own handcuffs, plus lengths of barbed wire they pulled from a fence. Afterward when they told Clyde about using the barbed wire, he was angry with them. Because of the lawmen's kindness to Bonnie, he hadn't wanted them to suffer in any way.

After a half-hour, Corry was able to work his way free. The lawmen found their Chevrolet abandoned not far down the road, and drove back to Wellington in it. They told their story and bulletins went out—the Barrow Gang was traveling with a badly wounded member, Bonnie Parker. Lawmen should be alert for strangers seeking medical attention for a young woman with a horribly burned leg.

Wellington residents trooped out to the crash site, hunting for souvenirs. Today, visitors to the Collingsworth County Museum can still see two ammunition clips for Clyde's BAR and a pair of Bonnie's gloves. She had very tiny hands. The Ford V-8 was pulled out of the creek bed and hauled back to the town garage. The mechanics there rebuilt and sold it. The *Wellington Leader* proved itself just as capable of Barrow-related exaggeration as any big-city newspaper, noting in a front-page story that Gladys Cartwright's barely nicked thumb "might have to be amputated." Some of the men in town got a posse together and set out roadblocks, but by then the battered Barrow Gang was long gone—though not as long gone as usual.

For the next three days, Clyde worked his way through Oklahoma and Kansas. With Bonnie in such terrible condition, he couldn't embark on one of his thousand-miles-at-a-time driving marathons. Her wounds needed frequent treatment, and Clyde didn't dare consult a doctor until enough time had passed for talk about the Wellington crash to die down a little. So the gang made its relatively painstaking way east. They'd quickly abandoned the Chevrolet belonging to Corry and Hardy, knowing that cops everywhere would be on the lookout for it. Clyde stole a new Ford V-8 in Hutchinson, Kansas, so the gang had two cars now, including the Ford coupé Buck was driving. Each day when they stopped, Blanche was dispatched to some small-town drugstore to buy Unguentine salve and bandages, and they'd treat Bonnie's burned leg. The pain prevented her from sleeping. She'd start to doze and then wake up "groaning with pain." The first nights they pulled off the road and slept in their cars. In Pratt, Kansas, they risked staying overnight in a tourist court, taking only one cabin so the owners wouldn't suspect there were five of them. Money was running out, and Buck and W.D. went out to pull a few quick robberies. Clyde wouldn't leave Bonnie's side.

On Thursday, June 15, the gang reached Fort Smith, Arkansas, and Clyde decided they had gone far enough. They rented two cabins at the Twin Cities Tourist Camp, a relatively plush place. These cabins had indoor plumbing, showers, good mattresses, hot plates, and enclosed garages, which meant their stolen cars could be kept out of sight. Clyde told the camp owners that his wife had been burned when a stove exploded. Then he went to the office of Dr. Walter Eberle and asked him to come inspect his "wife's" injuries. Clyde was risking his freedom and probably his life by doing this. If Eberle had read the stories about the wreck in Wellington, he might become suspicious and call the local police. Yet Clyde still brought him over to the cabin. After examining Bonnie, Eberle said she had to go to a hospital. When Clyde didn't agree, the doctor recommended that a nurse at least be hired. A few days later, he made a second visit and the same recommendation.

Besides the murders and thefts he committed, Clyde Barrow routinely exhibited several glaring personality flaws. He became irritated easily and held grudges. He often couldn't resist calling attention to himself in situations where it endangered not only him but innocent bystanders as well. If he was one of the best drivers anyone had ever seen, he was also one of the most needlessly reckless. Bonnie's life hung in the balance because Clyde had been driving too fast to notice a detour sign.

But now Clyde demonstrated one of his undeniably good qualities. If someone was loyal to him, Clyde was always loyal in return. Through gun battles, bank robberies, and even a stint in the Kaufman County jail, Bonnie had proven her commitment to him. Only weeks earlier, she'd turned down a plea from her mother to put her own best interests ahead of Clyde's and leave him. As her condition worsened in Fort Smith, he wanted her to at least have the comfort of another loved one. Around noon on Sunday, June 18, he left Bonnie in the care of Buck, W.D., and Blanche and drove eight hours nonstop to West Dallas. This risk was huge. Sheriff Smoot Schmid and his deputies knew all about the events at Wellington, and realized that if Bonnie really was badly hurt the odds were reasonably good that the Barrow Gang might eventually seek refuge with their families. Dallas County deputy Ted Hinton even visited the Barrows and Emma Parker after hearing the news, mostly as a friendly gesture but undoubtedly to see if there was any sign of Clyde and Bonnie. When he visited Emma Parker, Hinton said later, some of her meaner neighbors had just been assuring her that Clyde would shoot Bonnie and leave her by the side of the road rather than risk his own capture by keeping her with him. Though there wasn't a stakeout on the Barrow service station or the Parker home, when Clyde arrived in West Dallas around 8 P.M. on June 18, all the Dallas County lawmen were on heightened alert for him.

There's no record of where, but Clyde, his family, and Emma and Billie Jean Parker met almost immediately. Cumie and Marie Barrow both volunteered to accompany Clyde back to Arkansas, and Emma insisted that she should be the one to go. But Clyde wanted Billie Jean. Bonnie and her sister were close, and Billie Jean had been on the road with them before. He promised Cumie that he'd let her spend a week with them when Bonnie was better.

Around midnight, Ted Hinton drove into West Dallas and passed a car going the other way. He recognized Clyde behind the wheel, and a young woman Hinton didn't immediately recognize. Clyde had the V-8 gas pedal all the way to the floor, and though Hinton wheeled his own car into a U-turn and attempted pursuit, the deputy couldn't keep up, even though he claimed later to have prodded his own car up to 80 miles an hour. Hinton stopped and made a call reporting what he'd seen, hoping roadblocks might be set up in time to catch Clyde, but it was too late.

Things hadn't gone well in Fort Smith while Clyde made his dash to West Dallas for Billie Jean. With Bonnie an invalid, Blanche had to shoulder even more responsibilities, going out daily to get Bonnie's medicine as well as doing all the cooking and cleaning in the cabin at the Twin Cities Tourist Camp. She took loads of laundry to the cleaners and went shopping for food. All these chores exacerbated her already pronounced tendency to consider herself a martyr. And, clearly, Bonnie felt and acted at her absolute worst. Dr. Eberle apparently wrote a prescription for the narcotic Amytal to dull the pain from her burns and Bonnie quickly developed a dependency on the drug. Whenever it wore off and the pain returned, her temper flared. While Clyde was gone, Bonnie apparently came out of her latest Amytal haze and began quarreling with Buck and Blanche. Buck snapped back at her, which wasn't like him. The pressure had to be terrible for the happy-go-lucky fellow who only three months earlier had left prison with the intention of never breaking the law again. Besides the constant stress of wondering when the next gun battle might erupt, Buck was also saddled with a wife who liked to complain. Certainly, Blanche had plenty to complain about. If Buck had listened to her, if he hadn't insisted they go to Joplin to join Clyde and Bonnie for a vacation, they wouldn't be on the run. Blanche didn't have to keep reminding her husband of it—Buck often said so himself. He couldn't help but feel guilty about the mess he'd created for the wife he loved so much. Now, in Fort Smith, when a pain-wracked Bonnie began bickering with Blanche, Buck lost his temper. He told Bonnie that he and Blanche weren't "practically crazy like you and Clyde." Bonnie jumped out of bed and screamed that she only wanted W.D. to stay with her until Clyde got back. The sudden movement broke open the scabs on her legs, and her wounds started bleeding again. Clyde and Billie Jean arrived to find Buck and Blanche temporarily estranged from Bonnie, though Blanche was quick to note in her memoir that she kept on cooking meals for everyone and couldn't understand why Bonnie was being mean: "I had tried to be so good to her."

Within a few days, the gang needed money again. Bonnie began to show a few signs of improvement—the Unguentine salve had kept the scabs on her legs too soft to heal properly, so Clyde began using another disinfectant. With a lot of encouragement and occasional threats he weaned Bonnie off the Amytal. But he still didn't want to leave her alone with Billie Jean at the tourist court. He probably feared that the minute he was gone, Bonnie would bully her little sister into giving her Amytal again. So when Clyde decided that more robberies were necessary, he told Buck and W.D. to go out and commit them while he stayed behind with Bonnie, Billie Jean, and Blanche. Because he desperately didn't want to put Bonnie through the additional stress of a frenzied escape from Fort Smith, Clyde insisted that his brother and W.D. choose only targets well away from the town. He also told them not to try to rob any major businesses like banks. Sticking up a couple of small service stations or grocery stores might keep the gang's presence in Fort Smith a secret. The last thing they needed were squadrons of Arkansas cops swarming the streets and conducting dragnet searches of the state's motor courts. Buck had an additional plan. He wanted to steal a big Ford sedan to replace the smaller roadster he had been driving. Then the gang would have two cars with lots of room. After all, counting Billie Jean, there were six of them now. That was fine with Clyde. If there was one criminal act at which the Barrow Gang seemed to excel, it was car theft.

Buck and W.D. left the Twin Cities Tourist Camp around noon on Friday, June 23, driving the Ford V-8 Clyde had stolen in Kansas. Following Clyde's instructions, they headed north from Fort Smith on Arkansas Highway 71, a two-lane road famous for its steep hills and blind hairpin turns. Their plan was to find stores to rob in Fayetteville, which was sixty miles away. When they arrived in Fayetteville, Buck and W.D. promptly made the amateurish mistake of being too obvious as they strolled around looking for the best prospective store to rob. The owner of one shop even wrote down their physical descriptions and car license number. About 5:30 P.M. they finally picked their target, Brown's Grocery. Buck parked the Ford V-8 a block away and waited while W.D. stuck a pistol in his pocket and went inside. There were only two people there—Mrs. Brown, the owner, and Ewell Trammell, a youngster who bagged the customers' purchases in hopes of tips. W.D. brandished his gun, ordered both to stay quiet, and rummaged in the cash drawer. He took about $20 he found there. W.D. somehow missed the two diamond rings being worn by Mrs. Brown, but he did relieve Ewell of thirty-five cents the youngster had in his pocket. Then, looking outside, W.D. spotted the store's Model A delivery truck and informed Mrs. Brown that he was going to take it. This made absolutely no sense. The truck would easily be spotted by any pursuing cops, and it couldn't be driven fast enough to outrun them. But W.D. wanted it, and Mrs. Brown informed him the keys were in the ignition. She chose to let W.D. find out for himself that the battery was dead.

W.D. hustled outside, knocking over a small girl as he went to the truck. It wouldn't start, and instead of giving up, W.D. kept trying, finally getting the engine started by pushing the truck down a hill, jumping back inside and popping the clutch. Having finally succeeded, he apparently decided he didn't want the truck after all. He drove it back up the hill, parked it, hopped out, and finally rejoined Buck in the Ford. Buck sped off, going south now on Highway 71. But W.D.'s clumsy attempt to steal the Model A truck had left Mrs. Brown time to call the police before he and Buck were clear of Fayetteville. When the cops arrived minutes later, the store owner who'd written down Buck and W.D.'s descriptions and their license plate number was eager to share the information. Phone calls went out to every area police officer, including Marshal Henry Humphrey of Alma, a small town in Crawford County ten miles north of Fort Smith on Highway 71. As it happened, the fifty-one-year-old Humphrey was in the mood to capture some bandits.

Henry Humphrey was popular in his hometown, a hardworking fellow who made his living doing custodial jobs at the high school and farming a small plot with a team of mules because he couldn't afford horses. Just six weeks earlier, in May 1933, he'd been elected town marshal. The job was essentially that of a night watchman. With only eight hundred residents, Alma couldn't afford a full-time law officer. Humphrey's salary for his new position was $15 a month, not enough even in the Depression to let him give up his handyman and farming chores. Not that the extra money didn't help—though their three children were grown, Humphrey still had a wife to support.

At least the marshal's job wasn't supposed to be dangerous, but just the day before Humphrey fielded the call about Buck and W.D. from Fayetteville he had his first run-in with armed bandits. It didn't go well for the newly elected marshal. While making his rounds about 2 A.M. on June 22, Humphrey was captured by two gunmen who'd taken his pistol and flashlight, tied him up with baling wire, and left him lying helplessly on the floor of the town's bank while they hauled away its safe. Whoever the thieves might have been, they weren't members of the Barrow Gang, though it would soon be assumed by local lawmen and citizens that Clyde must have been involved. The safe was eventually discovered in a nearby lake. The crooks had tossed it into the water after they failed to break it open. There was $3,600 still inside when it was retrieved by police. The Barrows weren't the only incompetent safecrackers around.

So the next afternoon, freshly humiliated by his capture and the theft of his gun, Marshal Humphrey received the call from Fayetteville warning him that two armed thieves apparently were heading south on the road that ran by Alma. Humphrey was given their descriptions and the license number of their car. It was clearly an opportunity for redemption, particularly if these two turned out to be the same ones who'd robbed the Alma bank. Red Salyers, an electrician who doubled as Crawford County deputy sheriff, volunteered to drive Humphrey out to the highway in his maroon Ford. Like most small-town Depression-era lawmen, they brought along their own weapons because no guns were issued to them by their respective departments. Salyers had a seven-shot Winchester rifle that he liked to use for squirrel hunting, and Humphrey carried a .38 revolver he'd borrowed that day from his brother-in-law.

They drove onto Highway 71 and turned north toward Fayetteville, keeping the car windows open because the twilight heat was still over 100 degrees. Some two miles out of Alma they began to descend a steep hill. This was when they passed a blue Chevrolet going the other way. Humphrey and Salyers waved—they both knew Weber Wilson, who worked at a service station run by Humphrey's son Vernon. There was another car coming up the hill right behind Wilson's. It was a Ford V-8 sedan with two men in it. Humphrey and Salyers failed to look closely, and so they didn't see that its license number matched the one they'd been given by the Fayetteville police. Through incredible luck, Buck and W.D. had escaped detection—right until, just over the crest of the very steep hill and driving way too fast like his brother Clyde, Buck crashed the Ford into the back of Wilson's slower-moving Chevrolet. Fifty yards down the road, Humphrey and Salyers heard the collision and whipped into a U-turn. As they approached the wreck, they saw that Wilson's car had been knocked upside down in a ditch. The other car involved, the Ford, had its front end bashed in. It was only then that Humphrey noticed that its license number matched the one on the car he'd been warned to watch for. He and Salyers grabbed their weapons and prepared to make an arrest.

Buck and W.D. didn't wait for Humphrey and Salyers to reach their car. They jumped out, Buck holding a shotgun and W.D. aiming a BAR. With such obviously superior firepower, they could have attempted to take the lawmen hostage. Perhaps they were so badly stunned in the crash that they weren't thinking straight. But Buck and W.D. had been making terrible decisions all day, and now they made a lethal one. Unlike his younger brother Clyde, Buck Barrow had always been more of a rascal than a rebel. All he ever really wanted out of life were good times and the love of his wife and family. He'd never wanted to be part of a notorious outlaw gang, eternally on the run. Somehow it had just happened. And now it happened that as hardworking, popular Henry Humphrey ran toward him, Buck Barrow pulled the trigger of his shotgun and blew the Alma marshal into the ditch. W.D. was shooting, too. Salyers ducked back behind his car and returned fire. But the Crawford County electrician-deputy was using a rifle whose magazine held just seven relatively low-caliber shots. W.D. had a twenty-round clip in his BAR, and its rounds could punch right through the sides of the car Salyers was using as cover. Salyers was fortunate that W.D. was a terrible marksman—all of his shots missed. While W.D. paused to reload, Salyers sprinted toward a farmhouse about one hundred yards away. Buck didn't try to bring him down—his shotgun had jammed. When W.D. had another magazine loaded into the BAR, he fired several more times at Salyers. He still didn't hit him, but the barrage kept Salyers pinned down. That gave W.D. and Buck the opportunity to make a run for the only car on the scene that was still drivable—Salyers's four-door maroon Ford. As they passed the fallen Humphrey, one of them reached down and took the .38 that the marshal had borrowed from his brother-in-law. Seeing that the gunmen were trying to escape, Salyers fired several shots. He was more accurate than W.D. One of his bullets smashed the horn button on the Ford's steering wheel. Another clipped off two of W.D.'s fingertips. As Salyers watched, and as Wilson cautiously emerged from the ditch where he'd wisely ducked when all the shooting started, Buck wheeled the Ford a few hundred yards back north on Highway 71, then steered west on a smaller road. As he did, someone in the car—probably W.D. if his wounded hand allowed it, since Buck was driving—fired at B. C. Ames, a motorist who was driving by. Ames wasn't hit, and volunteered to drive the gravely wounded Marshal Humphrey to the nearest hospital in the town of Van Buren while Salyers found a phone to report the gunfight to area lawmen. Humphrey lived through the weekend, but died of his wounds on Monday.

By then, Crawford County sheriff Albert Maxey had another charge besides murder and theft to add against the two fugitives he'd erroneously identified as both of the notorious Barrow brothers. A Mrs. Rogers, who lived in the hills above Highway 71, claimed that Clyde and Buck appeared at her door and raped her shortly after the Alma gunfight. They hadn't. Clyde was back in Fort Smith with Bonnie, Blanche, and Billie Jean. Buck, fleeing with W.D., was far too preoccupied with flight to have time or interest in rape, and anyway sexual assault was never a crime committed by any members of the Barrow Gang. Two other men raped Mrs. Rogers, but that fact wouldn't be confirmed by police until weeks later when it became obvious that Clyde and Buck couldn't have been anywhere near her home at the time she was attacked. But by then the story of the supposed assault had been widely disseminated, taken as fact in newspaper stories and emblazoned on post office bulletin boards and telephone poles in the form of prominent *WANTED for Murder and Rape* posters pinned up by the Crawford County Sheriff's Department.

Rather than stalking sexual prey, immediately after the shootout Buck and W.D. careened down backcountry roads in Deputy Salyers's stolen Ford, well aware that every lawman in the region would soon be on the lookout for them. W.D. sniveled at the slightest provocation, so it's reasonable to imagine him in hysterics at the sight of his two mangled fingers. Buck believed he'd just killed someone—other members of the Barrow family would later claim W.D. told them he shot Humphrey, but from the moment he pulled the trigger of his shotgun Buck had no doubt that he was the one who murdered the marshal. So, undoubtedly panic-stricken, the two outlaws drove west while Deputy Salyers made his calls and a massive regional manhunt began to be organized.

Buck and W.D. wanted desperately to get back to the motor court in Alma. Three miles east of Van Buren they spotted a married couple, later identified as the Loftons, driving by in a car whose make apparently was never noted. Eager to ditch Salyers's telltale maroon Ford, Buck and W.D. stopped the Loftons at gunpoint and commandeered their vehicle. The fugitives got within a few miles of the motor court, but word about them had spread and a bridge they had to drive across to get there was blocked. So Buck and W.D. abandoned the Loftons' car and sneaked back into Fort Smith on foot. It was just after 10 P.M. when they staggered into the cabin and poured out their awful story to Clyde, Bonnie, Blanche, and Billie Jean.

There was no time for recriminations. Clyde quickly organized the gang's escape. The only car left to them, the relatively tiny Ford coupé, couldn't carry all six at once along with their suitcases and guns. Clyde told Buck and W.D. to start packing up. He'd take the women in the car, drop them off at a safe camping spot out in the country, and then come back for the other two and the luggage. Buck was in a terrible emotional state. He clung to Blanche and cried that now he had murder on his soul. Billie Jean Parker pointed out that her sister would need to lie down in the woods, so they had to bring bedding. Clyde stripped the blankets and sheets off a bed in the cabin. The owners of the camp had been kind to them—their daughter volunteered a few times to nurse Bonnie—and he didn't want to steal their property, so he left $10 on a chest of drawers in payment. Then he drove Bonnie, Billie Jean, and Blanche out of town and into a wooded area where he thought they would be safe until morning.

When Clyde drove away, Blanche and Billie Jean used the blankets and sheets to fix up a place for Bonnie. After they got her settled, they sat beside her to wait until the men returned. It was very dark, but they didn't dare light even a match. Blanche was terrified for Buck. Billie Jean had just begun a convenient romance with W.D., so she was concerned about his injured fingers. They tried to brush away mosquitoes and other bugs until Clyde, Buck, and W.D. finally drove up, still in the Ford coupé. They hadn't been able to find a bigger car to steal, and they wanted to be gone before daylight. The manhunt would certainly reach Fort Smith then. All six of them crammed into the car, and Clyde drove into the Ozark Mountains.

Once again someone was dead, and the Barrow Gang was on the run with no plan beyond trying to survive for another day.

CHAPTER 18

The Last Interlude

On Monday, June 26, Dr. Julian Fields of Enid, Oklahoma, made the mistake of leaving his medical bag in the Ford V-8 he had parked in a hospital lot. When he returned, the car was gone. It turned up the next day outside the north-central Oklahoma town, but the medical bag was missing. The bag was packed with syringes, morphine, and various sulfates, just what was needed to treat the wounds of a badly burned woman. Clearly, Clyde's main priority on fleeing Arkansas was to ensure that Bonnie at least had the medication she needed. They could no longer hope to rely on the discretion of a doctor. Thanks to the wanted posters widely circulated by Crawford County sheriff Albert Maxey, lawmen in all of Arkansas's neighboring states soon knew that Bonnie Parker of the Barrow Gang was badly injured. Maxey's wanted poster urged his fellow lawmen to "inquire of your doctors if they have been called to treat a woman that has been burned in a car wreck." Bonnie needed long-term bed rest, not daily jouncing as Clyde drove hundreds of miles over rough roads, but the gang had to stay on the move. At least morphine to dull the pain and sulfates to treat her burns could make her marginally comfortable.

And Bonnie's health was only one of several pressing problems. Buck and W.D. had abandoned most of the gang's arsenal during their flight from Alma to the motor court in Fort Smith. If they were going to be in a position to outfight pursuers, they needed guns again, preferably BARs, and those were only to be had from a National Guard armory. Then there was Billie Jean Parker: clearly, they had to get her back to West Dallas. They had never intended for her to become a permanent part of the gang. But Clyde couldn't risk driving her home himself. After Alma, every lawman in Texas was on heightened alert for the Barrow boys. There was a lot of money in it for them. In Crawford County, Sheriff Maxey was offering an especially generous reward—$250 each—and Maxey wasn't even basing payment on their eventual conviction for the murder of Marshal Henry Humphrey. All anyone had to do to get the money was capture and hold Clyde and Buck until Maxey came for them. The danger of arrest was especially great in West Dallas, where Ted Hinton had been regularly dropping by the Barrow family service station. Clyde and Buck, he believed, would inevitably show up soon. Cumie made Hinton her occasional confidant. She didn't betray Clyde and Buck in any way, but she was resigned enough to tell Sheriff Smoot Schmid's deputy that her sons, along with Bonnie and Blanche, were living on borrowed time. On another occasion, Cumie, who surely considered self-pity to be an egregious sin, couldn't help complaining to Hinton about "the troubles I've seen."

But Clyde was grateful to Billie Jean for risking her own safety to help nurse her sister. He was determined that she get home. After stealing a bigger car, he took Billie Jean just over the Texas state line into the town of Sherman, where he bought her a new dress and put her on a train back to Dallas. Then Clyde, Bonnie, Buck, Blanche, and W.D. drove, traveling long stretches of isolated country, trying not to attract police attention. Blanche wrote later that they ranged as far west as Pueblo, Colorado, where they spent the Fourth of July. On the night of July 7, they were back in Oklahoma, staying at a tourist camp thirty-five miles from Enid. Not long after they checked in, Clyde and Buck left W.D. in a cabin with Bonnie and Blanche. The Barrow brothers returned about 4 A.M. with what Blanche recalled as "more guns and ammunition than I had ever seen at one time in my whole life." They'd hit the National Guard armory on the campus of Phillips University in Enid, and the haul of BARs and pistols was so grand that

Clyde later told his mother that there were "so many guns [he] didn't know what to do with them." They tried to stack the new arsenal in the cabin's bathtub, but there were too many weapons for all of them to fit. The take also included ammunition and a pair of powerful binoculars. Once again properly armed, the gang camped out in the country for the next few days. The three men spent part of each day target shooting. At night, Clyde was concerned enough about pursuit to insist that someone stand watch until dawn. Blanche wrote that she usually drew guard duty. She'd perch all night on the roof of their car to get better sight angles, and use the binoculars stolen from the Enid armory to scan roads and the surrounding countryside. Blanche had trouble staying awake, so she would periodically wash her face with rubbing alcohol. She never saw anything alarming.

Around the second week in July, the gang moved on to remote areas of Kansas and Iowa. In a series of postcards to West Dallas, they assured the Barrows and Parkers that "Sis" was getting better. She was, but not enough. Though Bonnie's burns were healing, the battery acid had permanently damaged her right leg. In the clumsy but descriptive words of her sister Billie Jean, Bonnie "never walked any more straight." Perhaps if she'd been admitted to a hospital and under a doctor's care, that wouldn't have been the case. But because the tendons and ligaments in her injured knee and ankle tightened as they mended without benefit of daily therapy, the damaged leg "was drawn up" and Bonnie could not straighten it for any extended length of time, or even put much weight on it. For the rest of her life, whenever she had to move on her own, she usually hopped rather than walked. Clyde often carried her. Sometimes, W. D. Jones said later, either he or Clyde "had to carry her to the toilet and take her off when she was finished." For a lifelong flirt like Bonnie who always wanted to appear alluring, that must have been the ultimate degradation.

And yet Bonnie stayed with Clyde. There has never been any suggestion that she wanted to leave him after becoming crippled. If ever Bonnie had the opportunity to go home and avoid prison, this was it. Particularly in Texas, most juries would surely have believed she'd been punished enough. Bonnie probably didn't realize just how seriously she'd been hurt. Perhaps she thought her leg would heal to the point where she would eventually walk normally again. That never happened.

Still, if Bonnie wasn't all the way back to normal, at least Clyde and the others no longer feared she might die from her original injuries or subsequent infection. They had good guns again. It was time to get back in the game, to rob a few grocery stores or service stations, put together traveling money, and perhaps make a quick trip back to West Dallas. Except for Clyde's emergency visit to fetch Billie Jean shortly after the Wellington wreck, they hadn't seen their families since late May. So on July 18, the five of them showed up in Fort Dodge, Iowa, with Clyde behind the wheel of a 1929 Chevrolet. Apparently they hadn't come across any new, unattended Ford V-8s recently. In rapid succession they robbed three service stations. It all took about ten minutes. At the last station, they took the attendant's car keys so he couldn't follow them. He asked if they'd at least toss the keys out on the road after a few blocks—he didn't want to have to get another set. They obliged. Local newspapers later estimated the gang's take at between $125 and $150.

From Fort Dodge, Clyde drove south. At some point he found a Ford V-8 to steal and abandoned the Chevrolet. By 6 P.M. they had covered 250 miles and were approaching Kansas City. Buck didn't want to stop for the night near such a major town. He warned Clyde that the big-city cops might be on the lookout for other crooks and "we would run right into their heat without knowing it." But Clyde wasn't in the mood to listen. He and Buck had spent some of the ride arguing, and he probably didn't want the others to think his big brother could tell him what to do. Besides, long rides still bothered Bonnie. She'd be better off if they spent the night at a decent motor court. They had money from the three service station robberies in Fort Dodge—he'd find a nice place and they'd stop, even if Buck didn't like it.

About twenty miles out of Kansas City they reached the suburb of Platte City, Missouri, at the intersection of Highways 71 and 59. There was an interesting conglomeration of buildings there—a combination service station/café/grocery store called Slim's Castle, a restaurant/ballroom named the Red Crown Tavern, and a stand-alone, two-cabin motor court with the cabins attached to opposite sides of a closed garage. Slim's Castle was across the street from the Red Crown Tavern and the cabins. In all, it was rather upscale, and exactly the kind of place the gang usually avoided. For one thing, it was much too close to Kansas City and its legions of cops. Police in Kansas City had been on high alert since June 17. That was when a gang of mobsters supposedly led by Pretty Boy Floyd brazenly stormed Kansas City's downtown

Union Station to rescue bandit Frank Nash from police and federal agents as they attempted to take him to Leavenworth prison by train. Three local policemen, a federal agent, and Nash died, but the gunmen escaped. "The Kansas City Massacre" had quickly become one of the most famous shootouts in modern crime annals, and local cops did not plan to be caught off-guard again.

Another problem with the Barrow Gang staying at the Red Crown was that they would be occupying the only two tourist cabins there. That meant they wouldn't be able to blend in with other guests and their cars. But Clyde, still stinging from his squabble with Buck, was more interested in proving who was boss than in exercising caution. He pulled up at Slim's Castle and asked the gas pump attendant who he had to talk to in order to rent the cabins across the street. After learning they were operated by the Red Crown Tavern, Clyde drove a short distance down a side road, then parked. Buck and W.D. curled up on the floor of the Ford and were covered with blankets. Just in case anyone in Platte City was on the lookout for the five-member Barrow Gang, Clyde intended to present himself at the Red Crown as a man traveling with his wife and mother-in-law, the latter undoubtedly a dig at Blanche. So W.D. and Buck were concealed and Blanche moved into the front seat with Clyde and Bonnie.

They didn't know it, but these would be their last moments of relative good luck. Polled on the spot, all of them might have sworn they were barely surviving the most terrible of times. Clyde and Buck were wanted for murder. Bonnie was newly crippled. Blanche hated being on the run, and W.D. had been shot twice, in Joplin and outside of Alma. They often slept out in the open, they rarely had much money, and they were in constant danger of being arrested or gunned down.

But they were also feared, which pleased Clyde, and famous, which was something Bonnie had always wanted. They were their own bosses. They wore nice clothes and drove only the best cars. Despite Bonnie's terrible burns and W.D.'s injuries, they still must have felt a certain sense of invulnerability. In every showdown with "the laws," they had won the fight. Other people died, not them. The Barrow Gang always escaped. For all the times they told their families they accepted the inevitability of a terrible end someday, Clyde was still only twenty-three and Bonnie twenty-two, ages when even under the direst circumstances "someday" seems very far away. Their fatalism was tempered by their youth.

So was their perspective about why they were still alive and at large. They didn't realize that they'd been lucky in two critical ways. First, though the Barrow Gang had committed dozens of well-publicized crimes since March 1932, they had never been the target of any organized pursuit. Authorities in individual jurisdictions hoped to nab Clyde, Bonnie, and their companions if they showed up in their town or county or state. But a travel/crime pattern was starting to emerge: Texas to Oklahoma to Missouri to Arkansas, though not always in the same order and sometimes with other states like Iowa, Kansas, and Louisiana thrown in.. Lawmen were beginning to notice.

On July 18, the same day that the Barrow Gang robbed three service stations in Fort Dodge, Iowa, and made its way to Platte City, Missouri, Joplin chief of detectives Ed Portley sent a letter to his counterparts in Van Buren, Hillsboro, Atoka, Sherman, Lufkin, Wellington, Waco, Abilene, and Dallas. Though coordinated pursuit of criminals was practically unheard of on an interstate basis between county and city lawmen, Portley proposed an alliance "among those who are most interested in [the] arrest and conviction" of the Barrows. His letter asked each sheriff or police chief to share information about "any associates or hang outs that [the Barrow Gang] may have . . . we believe that something special should be done to secure the capture of these murderers." Portley's proposal came to nothing, but it was the first attempt to hunt Clyde and Bonnie in a pragmatic, cooperative way. There would soon be others.

The second way in which the gang had been lucky was that they had always been opposed by local lawmen who had no idea they were taking on the Barrows. The poorly armed cops expected to confront small-timers whose firepower was equally limited. That gave Clyde and his cronies a tremendous advantage. The gang had yet to experience a coordinated assault by well-prepared, well-armed officers aware of exactly who they were up against.

Then after dark on July 18, 1933, Clyde drove back to the Red Crown Tavern in Platte City, and all that changed.

CHAPTER 19

The Platte City Shootout

N. D. Houser, the owner-operator of the Red Crown Tavern and its adjoining two-cabin motor court, was suspicious from the moment Blanche Barrow walked into his office on July 18 and asked to rent the cabins overnight for a party of three. For one thing, Blanche was wearing her beloved "riding breeches"—*jodhpurs* was the correct fashion term—that were skintight across the rear and flared out from the hip to the knee. Pants like that were seldom seen in Platte City, Missouri, and several people who saw Blanche there were still remarking about them decades later. Then she paid the $4 rent in loose change, undoubtedly looted earlier in the day from the cash registers and gum machines at the three service stations in Fort Dodge. Houser took the money and watched as the fellow driving the Ford V-8 pulled up to the cabins, opened the door of the garage between them, and backed his car in. Criminals were notorious for doing that so they could make fast getaways.

Clyde got Bonnie settled in the right-hand cabin. W. D. Jones joined them there as usual. Buck and Blanche took the cabin on the left. Almost as soon as everyone was inside, Clyde sent for Blanche. He gave her more loose change and told her to go over to the tavern and buy five dinners and beer. She was to bring the food back so they could eat in the cabins. Blanche reminded Clyde that they'd just checked in as a party of three. Buying five meals would be a tip-off that there were more of them than that. But Clyde said he didn't care—she was to get five dinners, period, and he wanted chicken if they had it. Blanche did as she was told, and as she poured more coins into his palm Houser said he'd have to go back to the cabins with her. He'd forgotten to take down the license number of their car, and it was required information from all their guests. Feeling helpless, Blanche led him back to the right-hand cabin and called for Clyde to come out. He opened the garage door so Houser could jot down the V-8 sedan's license number: Oklahoma 75-782. Clyde didn't think it was an immediate problem as he routinely switched plates on stolen cars. But it should have served as a warning sign that the staff at the Red Crown was especially vigilant. Clyde apparently didn't care. He told his family later that he liked the Red Crown cabins. They had stone and brick walls, which made him feel secure. If they needed to get to their car in a hurry, there was an interior door in Clyde's cabin that opened directly into the garage. Buck and Blanche's cabin didn't have one. They could only go in and out through the front door.

After dinner, everyone went to bed. They slept late on the morning of July 19. When Buck woke up, he told Blanche to go over to the other cabin and see when Clyde, Bonnie, and W.D. would be ready to leave. Clyde said he'd decided they would stay another day. He wanted Blanche to fetch some more food and beer. Clyde felt relaxed about their situation. The cabins were nice. Bonnie needed rest. So Clyde gave Blanche yet another pile of change. After she brought the food, he sent her out to pay Houser $4 for a second night's stay. Blanche wasn't exaggerating in her memoir when she complained about having to run all the gang's errands. Houser took the money and told Blanche she could have a refund if her group decided to leave before nightfall. She thought it was an odd remark, and told Clyde that Houser "was the type that might tell the law we were there if he had the slightest suspicion about us." He was, and he didn't have to go far to do it.

The Barrow Gang had no idea that the Red Crown Tavern served as a gathering place for local cops and the state highway patrol. Two-way radios were still nonexistent for most lawmen in the region, so officers and supervisors would often meet somewhere at mealtimes to exchange messages and receive orders. The Red Crown was a favorite spot because the food was so good. On July 19, Missouri Highway Patrol captain William Baxter and some of his men met there for lunch. Either Houser or one of his employees mentioned to Baxter that the people in the two tourist cabins were acting awfully strange. The woman checking them in said they were a party of three, but she was buying meals for five. Besides paying for everything in loose change and parking backward in the garage the way crooks often did, whoever was in the right-hand cabin had taped paper across the windows to block anybody looking in. Houser described them to Baxter, and also gave him the Ford's license number. Baxter made a note to check the plate, and meanwhile put the cabins under surveillance.

Someone also passed the word about suspicious characters at the Red Crown cabins to Platte County sheriff Holt Coffey. Coffey and Baxter got along well. When they conferred early in the afternoon of the 19th, they concluded it was possible that the four or five people (they weren't entirely sure whether it was three men and two women, or two and two) might be the notorious Barrow Gang. Bonnie Parker was known to be badly injured, and a farmer in Iowa had recently reported finding used bandages at a campsite in the country. That meant the Barrows were probably somewhere in the region—why not Platte City?

The Barrows packed BARs, and Coffey worried that his own officers and the members of Baxter's highway patrol only had handguns and a few low-caliber rifles to return fire if it really was the gang and they tried to arrest them. Determined not to be outgunned, he went to see Sheriff Tom Bash, whose Jackson County department had jurisdiction for Kansas City and whose available armaments included machine guns, steel bulletproof shields, tear gas launchers, and armored cars. When Coffey drove over to ask for Bash's help, he didn't get the hoped-for offer of cooperation. As Coffey recalled it later, Bash snarled that he was "getting pretty damn tired of every hick sheriff in the country coming in here telling me they have a bunch of desperadoes holed up and wanting help." When Coffey insisted that they might be able to corner the infamous Barrow Gang, Bash finally agreed to send along a few officers and one armored car. This was an ordinary sedan whose sides had been reinforced with extra metal.

While Coffey pleaded with Bash, Lieutenant Baxter of the highway patrol got a report back on his license check. The number matched the plate on a Ford V-8 stolen on June 26 from a Dr. Fields in Enid, Oklahoma. Clyde, of course, had long since left that vehicle behind, but he foolishly kept the plate and screwed it on the bumper of the V-8 he stole outside Fort Dodge on July 18. The Barrow Gang was suspected of the car theft in Enid, so Baxter felt he had more proof that Clyde and his cohorts were holed up in the Red Crown cabins.

By midafternoon, Baxter and Coffey began planning their raid. They knew Blanche had paid for the gang to stay a second night, so they decided to attack well after dark. The lawmen did their best to keep a low profile, but customers at the service station, grocery, and tavern all noticed highway patrolmen and county cops gathering and watching the tourist cabins. Word spread, and it soon seemed as though everyone but the Barrow Gang knew a confrontation was imminent. The newspaper Clyde had taped to his cabin windows to keep people from looking inside also prevented him from seeing what was going on outside.

At some point, either Clyde or Blanche walked to a local drugstore to buy bandages and over-the-counter medical supplies for Bonnie. Witnesses subsequently disagreed about who it was. Apparently, the lawmen let him or her come and go freely, not wanting to alert the rest of the gang and risk letting them escape. The druggist, who'd heard the rumors about criminals being in town, contacted Coffey to tell him about the purchases. The sheriff now felt certain that Bonnie Parker was in one of the Red Crown cabins.

That night in the left-hand cabin, Buck and Blanche talked about what they wanted to do next. Both were ready to leave Clyde, Bonnie, and W.D. They were tired of being bossed around. While Buck shined Blanche's boots, he suggested that they go north to Canada and find an isolated cabin to hide in. Buck thought they could make a living as trappers. Blanche said it would be fine with her—anything to get away from the others. Then Blanche walked over to the grocery across the road to buy some soap. When she went inside, she noticed there were quite a few people there, and all of them stopped talking as soon as she entered. While Blanche waited for her purchases, she stepped on a scale and discovered she weighed ninety-one pounds, almost twenty less than she had back in March when Buck was released from prison.

Back in the cabin, Blanche told Buck the people in the store had acted strangely. He suggested that she go tell Clyde about it. Buck added that he thought they'd be fine if they didn't leave until the morning. Clyde told her the same thing. He sent Blanche back to the left-hand cabin, and a few minutes later W.D. followed to say Clyde wanted her to return to the grocery for sandwiches and beer. She refused, so W.D. went. After he got back—apparently, W.D. didn't notice anything suspicious going on—everyone had some food and then went to bed.

Around 1 A.M. on July 20, Baxter and Coffey gathered their men together. Counting themselves, the highway patrolmen, county cops, and two officers sent by Sheriff Bash of Jackson County in the armored car, the posse numbered thirteen. Coffey's nineteen-year-old son, Clarence, was one of the highway patrolmen, along with Leonard Ellis and Thomas Whitecotton. Whitecotton had rushed from the department office to be there. He was still wearing the fancy seersucker suit and Panama hat he favored for days spent behind a desk instead of out on patrol. Baxter and Coffey had machine guns. They also had thick metal shields that they carried in front of them like medieval knights. The shields were supposed to protect them from even high-caliber bullets.

Coffey and Baxter were in the lead as the posse closed around the cabins. Jackson County officer George Highfill steered the armored car in front of the door of the garage connecting the cabins, effectively blocking the Ford V-8 inside. Then he shone the car's lights directly on the left-hand cabin door. Crouching behind their shields, Coffey and Baxter moved forward. Coffey knocked on the door. Blanche jumped out of bed and began pulling on her jodhpurs and boots. Stalling for time, she asked who it was. Coffey yelled, "The sheriff—open up!" From the right-hand cabin a man's voice replied, "Just a minute," and then the Barrow Gang started shooting, Clyde and W.D. from the right side and Buck from the left, blasting their bullets at the lawmen right through the cabin doors and windows.

Watching from behind, Clarence Coffey told reporters later that he saw his father "pushed him back like he was hit by a high-pressure hose" as the bullets from the BARs smashed into his metal shield. Baxter was knocked back, too. The high-caliber slugs couldn't penetrate the shields, but their impact was still staggering.

Except for the headlights of the armored car shining on the door of the left-hand cabin, the light in the area in front of the cabins was patchy. All highway patrolmen Whitecotton and Ellis could see were two shadowy figures lurching in front of the cabins while gunfire exploded everywhere. Whitecotton mistakenly thought Sheriff Coffey must be one of the Barrows and yelled to Ellis, "There's one of 'em!

Get him!" Ellis, armed with a shotgun, raised his weapon and fired. A bit of buckshot scratched Holt Coffey's neck. Afterward, when Coffey bragged about being shot by the Barrow Gang and living to tell about it, Whitecotton and Ellis decided not to ruin the Platte County sheriff's story by revealing that he'd been hit by friendly fire.

Inside the cabins, Clyde yelled for W.D. to go into the garage through the interior door and start the Ford. Bonnie fished the keys out of Clyde's pocket and tossed them to the teenager. When W.D. had the engine engaged, Clyde yelled for him to pull the garage door open, but the posse was pouring tremendous fire into the cabins and W.D. was too scared to do it. Holding his BAR in one hand, Clyde ran into the garage through the interior door and began pulling the door open himself. W.D. tried to help. As the door rose, they saw the armored car about fifteen feet in front of them blocking the way out. Clyde opened up on the car with his BAR. The car's side armor was supposed to repel any bullets, but Clyde's slammed through, wounding driver George Highfill in both legs. Another bullet smashed the horn button on the steering wheel, and the shrill howl of the horn blended with the gunfire. If Highfill had held his ground, the rest of the posse could have tightened their circle around the cabins and eventually captured the whole gang, but the injured officer astounded both his fellow lawmen and Clyde by easing the much perforated armored car several dozen yards to the right, opening a way for Clyde to drive the V-8 straight through the surrounding cops. Both sides realized what was about to happen, and for a few seconds there was no more shooting.

Using the interior door in the right-hand cabin that opened directly into the garage, Bonnie hobbled into the V-8. Clyde and W.D. climbed in. But Buck and Blanche had to leave their cabin through the front door to get to the car, and as they slammed the door open and began running for the garage, the posse laid down a high-caliber fusillade. A bullet from Baxter's machine gun struck Buck in the left temple and exited out his forehead, taking away part of his skull and exposing his brain. He dropped between the cabin door and the car.

Ever since she unwillingly joined the gang back in late March, Blanche Barrow repeatedly engaged in whining and other petty behavior. But now she proved she had courage. With bullets flying all around her, Blanche stopped to loop her arm under Buck's waist. Skinny and scared as she was, Blanche still helped Clyde drag Buck into the car while W.D. provided covering fire.

Somewhere behind the cabins, one of the lawmen fired a tear gas rocket that overshot the Ford, sailed across the highway, and exploded next to the service station. Clouds of stinking smoke added to the chaos. Clyde floored the gas pedal of the V-8 and drove straight out of the Crown Tavern lot, past Holt Coffey with his metal shield and onto Highway 71. Everyone in the posse was shooting and their bullets smashed into the Ford. In the back seat Blanche was bent over Buck, trying to shield him from further harm. Her face was turned toward the right, and that was the side where most of the posse were standing and firing. One of their bullets struck the car's back window. It exploded. Though her body protected her mortally wounded husband, glass splinters drove straight into both of Blanche's eyes. She screamed, "I can't see," but Clyde had to concentrate on getting them out of there and kept on going, around a sharp corner and then off into the night.

The posse didn't immediately pursue them. The armored car was a sieve. Besides Highfill's wounded legs and Holt Coffey's nicks, several other officers had been injured, though none seriously. The Barrow Gang hadn't added to their body count of lawmen this time. Baxter got to a phone and called in a description of the gang's Ford, which like the Jackson County armored car was riddled with bullet holes. He emphasized that his posse "had a shooting scrape with the Barrow brothers." The lawmen found some pistols and a BAR in one of the cabins, along with syringes and morphine. The latter discoveries sparked rumors that the Barrow Gang were junkies, but the needles and dope were just the last remnants of booty from the doctor's bag Clyde had stolen back in Enid.

While the posse poked about the Red Crown cabins, Clyde was finding it tough to get away from Platte City. He spent several hours lost on backcountry roads. At one point a tire went flat, and the V-8 had to bounce along on the rim until Clyde found a suitable place to stop and change it. They encountered several locals but no police. Clyde assured Blanche that despite the glass slivers driven into them, her eyeballs weren't "busted." The right eye was less damaged than the left—she could discern light and movement through it, but very little else.

Buck faded in and out of consciousness. Blanche tried to keep her fingers pressed tightly against the hole in his head. The floor by the back seat was soaked with Buck's blood. He asked for water—they had none to give him—and even in his dire condition Buck tried to comfort Blanche by telling her his head only hurt a little.

At dawn they stopped for gas at a service station north of Kansas City. Clyde told Blanche to cover Buck with a blanket, hoping the attendant wouldn't notice anything was wrong. Apparently he didn't think the man would see dozens of bullet holes in the car. But as soon as the attendant walked over, Buck began vomiting loudly, and the fellow looked in and saw the blood and carnage. Shaken by his brother's condition, Clyde simply drove away, telling Blanche he was sure the attendant would call the Kansas City cops to report seeing them. There was still enough fuel in the tank so that they could keep driving for a while.

Clyde headed north into Iowa with no particular destination in mind. He just wanted to find a place where the gang could rest and get a better idea of everyone's physical condition. Buck was clearly doomed—you could look right inside his head—but it was hard to tell how much damage had been done to Blanche's eyes. W.D. had suffered some minor wounds in the shootout, and Bonnie was still in terrible shape. They stopped for gas again, and Clyde bought bandages, Mercurochrome, hydrogen peroxide, and aspirin. That was all they had to treat their injuries. They poured the hydrogen peroxide directly into the hole in Buck's skull, and then did their best to wrap his head. A pair of sunglasses helped protect Blanche's eyes. They drove toward Des Moines, pausing occasionally to change the bandages on Buck's head and Bonnie's leg, tossing the soiled ones to the side of the road and not realizing they were leaving a clear trail for pursuers. All day other motorists reported finding used bandages to the police. These Iowa lawmen knew about the shootout the night before—Platte City police had issued regional bulletins—so they were already on the lookout for the Barrow Gang, with injured Bonnie Parker and now at least one other member badly hurt and bleeding hard.

Late on July 20, just west of Des Moines, Clyde decided they had to stop. They needed rest, food, and to give Buck the chance to die a little more comfortably than he could in the back seat of a car. Staying at a motor court was out—there was no way they could check in without someone noticing their pitiful, bloody condition. That meant camping in the country, someplace off the main road where no one would see them. Then, like a miracle, off to the right of the road not far past the town of Dexter there appeared what seemed to be a perfect spot, lush rolling woods bisected by a wide river. Dexfield Park—named for its location between the towns of Dexter and Redfield, and ringed by local farms—had once been a popular gathering place, opened in 1915 and featuring carnival rides, softball diamonds, a dance hall, a massive swimming pool, and lots of wooded areas for picnicking and camping. But the Depression had left few who could afford admission, and the park closed in early 1933. By the time the Barrow Gang arrived six months later, the abandoned park's green acres still attracted lovers, local berry pickers, and occasional indigent campers. Clyde pulled off the road and drove back into a grove of trees. He used seat cushions from the car to make a bed of sorts for Buck. Clyde, Bonnie, W.D., and a weeping Blanche expected Buck to die any minute. He was suffering greatly. They waited, hoping they were far enough away from cities and prying eyes to be safe, but they weren't.

CHAPTER 20

The Battle of Dexfield Park

Sometime soon after they stopped in the park Clyde and W.D. dug a grave for Buck, but the night of July 20 passed and Buck was still living. No one had any hope that he might survive his head wound, Buck most of all. Sometimes he was alert enough to talk. His main concern was Blanche. She kept telling him she wanted to go with him, clearly hinting at suicide. Buck urged her to eat and get some rest, but no one really rested much during the night.

On the morning of the 21st, Clyde took stock of their situation. They needed food, and most of their belongings had been abandoned back in Platte City. Whenever Buck died and the rest of them left Dexfield Park, they'd need new, clean clothes and another car so they wouldn't attract attention. The basic medical supplies they'd bought on the two-hundred-mile flight from Platte City to Iowa were already gone. Buck and Bonnie both needed fresh bandages—during the night, they'd been reduced to using strips torn from shirts as dressings—and Bonnie's burns required frequent applications of salve. So Clyde decided he had to risk driving into Dexter. He made a clumsy attempt to disguise the damage to the V-8, plugging more than a dozen bullet holes with mud. He drove off to Dexter with Bonnie, leaving W.D. behind to guard Buck and Blanche.

Buck was awake, and he and Blanche listened as W.D. confessed he was ready to give up the outlaw life for good. They encouraged him, pointing out that he was still relatively anonymous. There was a chance he could blend back into the general population. If he stayed with Clyde, Blanche predicted, he'd either end up in prison for life or else die in the electric chair. Recently, Clyde had even been threatening to turn W.D. over to the law himself. A month earlier back in Texas, Clyde's former partner Frank Hardy had been charged with the Christmas 1932 murder of Doyle Johnson in Temple. After Hardy was arrested on an unrelated charge, Johnson's widow mistakenly identified him from mug shots as the man with Clyde Barrow when her husband was killed. It was an eerie parallel to Raymond Hamilton being wrongly accused of murdering J. N. Bucher in Hillsboro. Clyde told W.D. that if Hardy was sentenced to the electric chair for Johnson's murder, W.D. would have to come forward and admit he was the killer. That was the last thing W.D. wanted to do. Still just seventeen, his goal now was to get back home to his mother, Tookie, who'd recently moved from West Dallas to Houston.

While W.D. poured out his heart to Buck and Blanche, Clyde and Bonnie drove into Dexter. Later, it would become town lore that Clyde had been there lots of times before, either as a participant in local rodeos or else on trips with his father, Henry. Neither scenario is true. Clyde was the furthest thing from being a cowboy. Over a year earlier he'd had trouble staying on the back of a mule after the aborted hardware store robbery in Kaufman. Henry Barrow rarely ventured outside West Dallas, let alone all the way to Iowa. Clyde might have driven by Dexter as he and the rest of the gang crisscrossed Iowa, but if they'd stopped there at all it would have been only briefly to buy gas or get a quick meal.

Now on Friday, July 21, he went into the Myron Williams Clothing Shop while Bonnie waited in the V-8, undoubtedly acting as a lookout. Clyde bought several shirts from clerk John Love, not noticing until he paid for his purchases that a gold badge gleamed inside Love's shirt pocket. Love served as Dexter's night marshal. Clyde got out of the store fast. Love didn't notice much about his customer besides that the fellow was short and walked with a slight limp. From there, Clyde went to Blohm's Restaurant, where he ordered five dinners to go and a block of ice, the latter to chip and apply to Buck's head wound in an effort to reduce the swelling of his brain. While the food was being prepared, he visited Pohle's Pharmacy and purchased bandages, burn salve, and hydrogen peroxide. The purchases weren't unusual. Lots of people couldn't afford doctor's fees and tried to treat even severe injuries themselves. Back at the restaurant, Clyde asked for plates as well as the food. He promised he'd bring the plates back the next day. Again, the request wasn't out of the ordinary. Dexter was a small, friendly town. If some stranger politely asked for dinnerware and said he'd return it, there was no reason not to believe him.

Clyde made another food run to Dexter on Saturday, returning the used plates to the restaurant and taking back new ones along with fried chicken dinners. Buck, somehow still hanging on, had mentioned he thought he would like fried chicken. They didn't kid themselves—Buck was surely going to die. But Clyde thought that if Buck was going to take so much time doing it, he might be able to fulfill a promise he and Buck had made to Cumie. They'd told her that if one of them was badly wounded, the other would try to bring his brother back to West Dallas so he could die surrounded by family. Maybe now they could make a run home from Iowa to Texas, and Buck could be left with Cumie and Henry. Blanche could stay there, too. Her eyes were seriously hurt. The left one in particular still had a large piece of glass stuck in it—they'd tried to pluck it out with tweezers but failed. Clearly Blanche needed medical attention if her eyesight was to be saved. The bullet-riddled V-8 they'd been driving would never make the trip—even if it did hold up for 750-plus miles, it would attract too much attention. So on the afternoon of Sunday, July 23, Clyde and W.D. drove into the neighboring town of Perry and stole another Ford V-8 sedan. They drove both cars back to the campsite. Then Clyde and Bonnie went into Dexter for a final food run. They had decided to start back to Texas in the morning.

But the Barrow Gang weren't the only ones in their part of Dexfield Park that Sunday. Henry Nye, a hired hand for one of the local farmers, had wandered through the woods near the Barrow camp in search of blackberries. He may not have seen the gang's camp, and, even if he did, there wouldn't have been anything odd about some temporary squatters. But in the nearby timber, Nye discovered the ashes of a fire where someone had tried, mostly unsuccessfully, to burn bloody bandages and car seat cushions. That was unusual enough for

Nye to head to Dexter, where he told store clerk and night marshal John Love about what he'd found. Love went out to the park himself, found a vantage point and used binoculars to study the camp and the people in it. Nobody now is sure if he saw all five gang members, or if he did his spying while Clyde and W.D. were away stealing the Ford V-8 in Perry. But whatever Love saw, it was enough. He hurried back to Dexter and called the sheriff's office in the county seat of Adel. When Sheriff Clint Knee heard the various descriptions—the bloody, partially burned bandages, a badly hurt man lying on a makeshift bed, two women, a short, limping stranger in Dexter who was driving a car full of bullet holes—he told Love that Dexfield Park was apparently occupied by the Barrow Gang. Love asked him to bring his "heavy artillery" and get right on over. Knee put in calls to the state's Bureau of Investigation, the Des Moines police department, the Polk County sheriff, and the National Guard. Everybody wanted a piece of the capture of the Barrows.

Even as the law began to converge on the town, Clyde and Bonnie drove into Dexter. They returned all the plates to Blohm's Restaurant and bought hot dogs to cook for breakfast the next day. It's possible word had already gotten around about who they were—decades later, lots of Dexter old-timers would claim to have seen them that evening. If so, Clyde and Bonnie apparently didn't notice anything unusual. They made their purchases and went back to the camp in Dexfield Park.

That night, Buck slept in the back seat of the freshly stolen V-8 sedan. Blanche, still mostly blind and exhausted from sitting up with him, prepared for another long dark-to-dawn vigil. Bonnie, wracked with pain herself, generously offered to sit up with Buck instead. She told Blanche to lie down in the front seat and get some sleep. Blanche tried, but sleep wouldn't come. She wrote later about how everyone felt jittery, especially when a screech owl kept sailing by the car and "hollering."

Back in Dexter, the lawmen convened to plan a dawn attack on the camp. Besides Clint Knee and John Love, there were Polk County officers Rags Riley and L. E. Forbes and two police detectives plus six other officers from Des Moines. That was a strong contingent, but the townspeople of Dexfield wanted to get in on the action, too. Knee and Love didn't mind. It made sense to attack the fearsome Barrow Gang with as many armed men as possible. Herschel Keller, an area dentist who served in the National Guard, helpfully brought his own Thompson submachine gun. The rest of the locals carried an array of weaponry that ranged from small-caliber rifles to handguns. The Des Moines newspaper sent a photographer. A few teenaged boys added themselves to a mob that eventually totaled about fifty. Before they left for the park, many in the unruly posse fortified themselves with liquor. John Love thought too many of them acted "like it was a hayride or something. We had to take guns off three of them who weren't safe to have them." Still, Knee and Love managed to get their crew out to the park under cover of night. Several of them used cars to block the bridge and road leading out of the park. As the sun came up just past 5 A.M. on Monday, July 24, the rest of the posse advanced on their quarry.

Clyde, Bonnie, Buck, and Blanche began to stir in the two cars. Bonnie wore only a thin nightgown. July nights were hot in Iowa. W.D. was up ahead of everyone else. He started a fire and began roasting hot dogs for everyone's breakfast. Then someone in the posse stepped on brittle brush or a branch, and the crackling sound alerted Clyde. He screamed out a warning, and the posse started shooting. Clyde and W.D. grabbed BARs and returned fire, but both were quickly wounded. W.D. had superficial wounds to his face. Clyde was hit in the left arm, which was either broken or at least badly injured. Another shotgun pellet dug a bloody groove across his left cheekbone. He and W.D. joined Bonnie, Buck, and Blanche in the V-8 sedan—Buck was stretched across the back seat, and Blanche had thrown herself on top of him as a shield. Clyde tried to drive the car right through the posse, but the Ford got stuck on a tree stump. They got out, Clyde firing at the attackers, W.D. shooting and trying to help Bonnie, Blanche hauling Buck, who was trying to stumble forward, all of them scrambling toward their other car, but the posse saw what they were attempting and began firing at the vehicle and it rocked from the combined impact of their bullets. Taking only a handgun—the BARs were too heavy to carry on the run—Clyde turned and led his staggering companions north on foot, down a hill toward the South Raccoon River, which was fairly placid in the summer dawn but still waist-deep. Clyde tried to hold the posse at bay with pistol shots, but not even halfway down the hill Buck fainted.

Clyde faced a terrible decision. If he and the others kept going there was a chance they might be able to get across the river and escape the posse. But Buck was down and apparently done for. Bonnie was still crippled. To have even the slightest chance of saving her, he had to leave his doomed brother behind. There was no time to think everything through carefully. Clyde and W.D. dragged Bonnie down the hill toward the river. Blanche stayed with Buck where he had fallen.

The posse closed in cautiously. The BAR fire from Clyde and W.D. had convinced most of the amateurs that shootouts were more serious than hayrides, though only one of the attackers had been hurt so far—Polk County cop Rags Riley suffered a superficial head wound. Buck quickly regained consciousness and gasped to Blanche that she needed to run. He said he was too tired to go on. But she pulled him to his feet and they lurched toward some nearby trees before collapsing on the ground behind a log. Part of the posse continued pursuing Clyde, Bonnie, and W.D., but some of them, led by tommy gun–toting dentist Herschel Keller, split off after Blanche and Buck. When they spotted them behind the log they began firing. Buck had a pistol, and he fired back before he was hit several times in the body. Later, Keller claimed a shot from his tommy gun inflicted Buck Barrow's grievous head wound. He may have believed it. Blanche told Buck there was no more hope, and helped him stand up so they could surrender. The posse members pulled them apart, and Buck slumped back to the ground. The photographer from the Des Moines newspaper raised his camera to snap a photo and, as he did, Blanche shrieked. Because of her injured eyes, all she could see was a shadowy figure aiming something at her. She thought it was a gun, and that she and Buck were about to be summarily executed. Instead, they were placed in separate cars and driven into Dexter for emergency medical treatment.

Meanwhile, Clyde, Bonnie, and W.D. pushed into the thick brush at the bottom of the hill near the bank of the South Raccoon River. The undergrowth was so tangled that the posse couldn't spot them without plunging into it themselves. Their pursuers stood back, yelled for the fugitives to give themselves up, and fired some random shots into the brush. A few shotgun pellets hit Bonnie in the abdomen, not wounding her seriously but still cutting deep enough to soak the side of her nightgown with blood. Clearly, Clyde, Bonnie, and W.D. couldn't stay where they were. On the other side of the river, a board fence marked the boundary of a farm. Clyde told the other two to stay put until he called for them. Then, holding the .45 he'd emptied during their flight, he waded across the river. Apparently the posse didn't see him. Perhaps their attention was diverted by the capture of Buck and Blanche. As soon as Clyde was gone, Bonnie told W.D. she wished she had a gun. When he replied that she couldn't do any good with it, meaning she couldn't fight off the posse, Bonnie replied that she wanted to use it to kill herself, since Clyde was done for and she didn't want to live without him.

On the farm on the far side of the river, nineteen-year-old Marvelle Feller wondered why there was so much shooting going on at the old abandoned park. Marvelle and his family had no idea the Barrow Gang was cornered there. None of them had been to town the day before, and word hadn't reached them. As part of his usual morning routine, Marvelle was up at 5 A.M. to milk the family cows. His German shepherd, Rex, kept him company as he headed toward the barn. But the gunfire had him curious, so Marvelle climbed over the board fence, milk pail still in one hand, to see what was going on. Suddenly Clyde emerged dripping from the river. Rex barked, and Clyde pointed his pistol and told Marvelle to "pull your dog off, or I'll shoot him." The pistol was empty, but only Clyde knew that. He put his fingers to his mouth, whistled shrilly, and W.D. waded across the South Raccoon carrying Bonnie. She was nearly unconscious. The posse remained on the far shore of the river, apparently not yet realizing that their quarry had crossed it.

Marvelle's father, Vallie, and a hired hand came up just as W.D. and Bonnie reached the fence. Brandishing his empty .45, Clyde ordered Vallie Feller to help Bonnie over the fence. Vallie and Marvelle carried her toward their farmhouse. Scared as he was, Marvelle would recall almost seventy-five years later how nice he thought Bonnie looked in her thin nightgown, even though she was fainting and splattered with blood.

As they all came into the yard, Marguerite Feller and her nine-year-old daughter, Louise, emerged from the house, shouting out that someone from town had just called to say the Barrow Gang was across the river in the park. She stopped short at the sight of Clyde with his gun. Blood streaming down his face from the cut on his cheekbone, Clyde assured the Fellers that he didn't intend to hurt anyone: "The laws are shooting the hell out of us and all we want is a way out of here." In the Fellers' garage were two cars, a Model A roadster up on blocks and a 1929 Plymouth. When Clyde ordered him to back the Plymouth out of the garage, Vallie Feller replied that there was no gas it in. The family wasn't able to afford any. But he added that they had some kerosene, and if they used that the Plymouth would probably run for a while.

Clyde had no other option. The posse would figure out any minute that the fugitives had crossed the river. Bonnie was in terrible shape, and W.D. wasn't much better. Clyde's own wounds, especially the ones to his left arm, were also serious. Buck and Blanche were undoubtedly already in custody, if they were even still alive. It was the Plymouth and kerosene or nothing.

Vallie poured kerosene into the Plymouth's tank, got the engine started, and backed the car out of the garage. Clyde told Marvelle to pick up Bonnie and lay her in the back seat. The teenager didn't need much urging. He enjoyed carrying her, though the blood on the side of her nightgown shook him a little. After Bonnie was settled, Clyde got behind the wheel of the Plymouth and W. D. Jones clambered in beside him. Clyde yelled to Vallie, "Don't shoot at us," and drove out onto a narrow road in front of the farmhouse. The Fellers watched as their Plymouth went rattling off to the north, traveling at high speed for a car fueled by kerosene. Later that day it was found abandoned in Polk City, thirty-eight miles north of Dexter. The Plymouth's windshield was shattered—Clyde had rammed the car into a Polk City telephone pole—and its seat cushions were stained with blood. After some negotiations when the Polk City authorities wanted $15 to have the Plymouth towed to Dexter, the Fellers got their car back. But Marguerite Feller was traumatized by her family's brush with the Barrow Gang, and she refused to ever ride in the Plymouth again.

After the posse on the far side of the South Raccoon River finally crossed over to the Feller farm and learned of the gang's escape, officials of Iowa's State Bureau of Investigation launched a statewide search that included airplanes flying low along back roads trying to spot the three fugitives. They never did. In Polk City, Clyde replaced the Fellers' Plymouth with yet another stolen Ford V-8. Four days later, on July 28, that car was found abandoned in Broken Bow, Nebraska, its back seat littered with bloody bandages, medicine bottles, and copies of the Des Moines papers with stories about the shootout in Dexfield Park. But there was no sign of Clyde, Bonnie, and W.D. They'd gotten away again.

CHAPTER 21

Buck and Blanche

Doctors Keith Chapler and Robert Osborn were performing an early-morning tonsillectomy in Dexter on the 24th of July when the posse arrived at their office with Buck and Blanche. Surgery was interrupted while the physicians tended to their emergency patients. Buck was coherent enough to tell them that the only treatment he'd received was hydrogen peroxide poured directly into the hole in his head, plus some aspirin. Chapler and Osborn thought that primitive care had been surprisingly effective. The head wound was relatively clean. Buck was in more pain from several bullet wounds he'd received in Dexfield Park, particularly one from a .45 slug that struck him in the back, glanced off a rib, and lodged in his chest. The Dexter doctors recommended that he be transferred immediately to King's Daughters Hospital in nearby Perry.

Blanche's only injuries were from the glass in her eyes. Her main concern was for her husband. At first the lawmen tried to keep them separated, but finally Blanche was allowed to join Buck where he lay on a stretcher on the floor. He asked for a cigarette. Blanche lit it for him, then was taken to another room to have her eyes examined. She never saw Buck again.

Chapler and Osborn went with Buck to Perry, where they performed surgery the same day to remove the bullet from his chest. Afterward, their prognosis was grim—Buck would die either from his head wound or else from pneumonia resulting from the chest surgery. It was only a matter of days.

News of the ambush and Buck's capture and imminent death reached West Dallas that same day. Cumie immediately prepared to leave for Iowa. Though he was the archenemy of her sons, Dallas County sheriff Smoot Schmid showed considerable compassion toward the grieving mother, meeting with Cumie and providing a letter of introduction to the Iowa authorities. In it, Schmid asked that she be allowed to see Buck. L.C. accompanied Cumie, and so did Emma and Billie Jean Parker. May Turner, a friend of Blanche's, made the trip, too. Before they left early Tuesday morning, Cumie told a *Dallas Morning News* reporter that "I don't care what people say, they're my boys and I love them." In denial as always, she added, "I don't believe they've done all the things they're accused of." Schmid or one of his officers provided money for travel expenses, another generous gesture.

While they were on the way, riding in a Model T Ford driven by L.C.—the drive took thirty-six hours—two Arkansas lawmen came to Perry to question Buck before he died. Under heavy guard in his hospital bed, Buck was almost chatty as he greeted Crawford County sheriff Albert Maxey and Alma deputy Red Salyers. They arrived already convinced that Buck was the killer of Henry Humphrey—the pistol taken from Humphrey during the June 23 gunfight outside Alma was among the many weapons recovered by the posse at the gang's Dexfield Park campsite. Buck was quick to confess. When he entered Buck's hospital room on July 25, Salyers asked, "Do you remember me?" Buck replied, "I sure do. It was a good thing you got out of the way, or you might have got yours."

Buck was much less forthcoming about the identity of the man who'd been with him when Humphrey was killed. All he would tell Maxey and Salyers was that it wasn't Clyde. The as yet unidentified fifth member of the gang was of considerable interest to the authorities. Back in Dallas, Schmid was asked to question Henry Barrow about who it might be. Henry knew full well it was W. D. Jones—Clyde had invited the teenager to join his gang at the Barrow family gathering on Christmas Eve, 1932. But Henry played dumb and replied, "I just can't figure out who he is." The cops didn't give up. Unfortunately for W.D., his days of anonymity were numbered.

By the time Cumie, L.C., Emma, Billie Jean, and May Turner arrived on Wednesday, July 26, Buck had taken a turn for the worse. As the doctors predicted, pneumonia set in. Buck was delirious whenever he was conscious, and thought Billie Jean Parker was Blanche. He gripped her hand and begged her not to leave him. Emma tried to lend moral support to Cumie, but her main concern was Bonnie. Newspaper stories about the Dexfield Park shootout mentioned that Bonnie had been wounded, but doctors and lawmen in Perry had no additional information. Ever solicitous of her family's reputation, Emma lied to the Iowa reporters, telling them that Bonnie was Clyde's wife.

On Thursday, Buck fell into a coma. He never regained consciousness and died on Saturday, July 29, with his mother at his bedside. Buck was thirty. His body was sent back to Texas, and he was buried in West Dallas on the following Monday. About fifty family members and friends attended the funeral. The presiding minister read verses from the Bible and said nothing at all about Buck's life or crimes. Buck's ex-wife Margaret brought his eight-year-old son, Ivan Jr., and fainted as the casket was closed. Cumie wept silently throughout the service. Henry sat beside her with his head bowed, not speaking. Schmid and his deputies stood guard around the chapel, hoping Clyde might try to sneak into his brother's funeral. After the service was concluded and Buck was buried in the Western Heights Cemetery, rumors immediately began to circulate that Clyde had come after all, disguised as a woman in a dress and wig. Marie Barrow told friends later that it certainly was something her brother could have done, but hadn't. She said she knew because if Clyde had been at the service, he would have found some way to talk to his family.

Blanche didn't attend, either. By the time Buck was buried, she was in the Platte County jail awaiting trial. The authorities had only one surviving Barrow Gang member in custody, and they meant to make an example of her. After being captured with Buck in Dexfield Park and going with him to the doctors' office in Dexter, Blanche was transferred first to jail in Adel, then to a larger jail in Des Moines. Most of the time she was a passive prisoner, but occasionally she became hysterical and screamed for Buck. A Des Moines doctor extracted glass from her eyes, but she still had only limited vision in the right eye and practically none in her left. Someone weighed her—Blanche was down to eighty-one pounds, thirty-three less than when she became a reluctant Barrow Gang member in late March, and ten less than just one week earlier when she'd weighed herself in Platte City.

On Monday night and Tuesday morning in the Des Moines jail, Blanche was interrogated. She insisted she had nothing to tell. She'd been with the Barrow Gang because she didn't want to leave her husband. She hadn't been involved in any robberies and she'd never fired a gun at anyone. The cops were skeptical. "No one," Blanche wrote later, "would accept that I stayed with my husband simply because I loved him too much to allow him to go any place without me, even when it meant death or imprisonment for me." They harangued her about the fifth gang member—surely she knew who he was. Blanche said it was Jack Sherman, an alias W. D. Jones sometimes liked to use. Then she said the fellow's name was Hubert Bleigh, and bulletins went out alerting authorities in surrounding states to be on the lookout for either one. Nobody tracked down Jack Sherman, but two days later Hubert Bleigh was arrested near the Oklahoma town of Seminole. He was a small-time crook; Blanche must have met him at some point when his path crossed the Barrow Gang's. Bleigh was shipped to Arkansas to be tried for the murder of Alma marshal Henry Humphrey, but it soon became clear he wasn't the other gunman who'd been there with Buck. The unfortunate Bleigh was then sent back to Oklahoma, where he was arraigned on unrelated robbery charges.

Blanche thought the Iowa police treated her unkindly during questioning, but then she had to face another, and far more terrifying, interrogator. J. Edgar Hoover, director of the U.S. Department of Justice's Division of Investigation, personally came to Des Moines late Monday or early Tuesday morning to coerce Blanche into telling whatever she knew. Though he was only thirty-eight, Hoover's relentless ambition had already propelled him to national prominence. Following World War I, he'd risen in the Justice Department ranks by developing systems to gather and disseminate information about suspected domestic radicals. Within two years, Hoover and the U.S. government were keeping secret tabs on more than 450,000 citizens. By 1933, criminals had replaced suspected communist sympathizers as Hoover's main targets. Public obsession with political radicals had waned. Now

Americans were fixated on crime, so Hoover fully intended that his organization and agents would be prominent in bringing the most famous crooks to justice. Nabbing Clyde Barrow and Bonnie Parker would be a tremendous coup, one that would further establish Hoover's reputation with the general public and solidify his place in government power circles.

When Hoover confronted Blanche, she was wearing a patch over her left eye. Blanche claimed decades later that Hoover told her to talk or else he'd gouge out her good eye. No government records giving Hoover's side of the story appear to exist. Even if he did make the threat, Blanche didn't have anything more to tell him than she'd already told the other lawmen—she'd been with the Barrow Gang because she wanted to stay with her husband. She didn't know where Clyde Barrow, Bonnie Parker, and their unidentified partner might be. Apparently, Hoover believed her.

On Tuesday afternoon, July 25, Blanche was handed over to Platte County sheriff Holt Coffey, who took her back to Missouri. Because he'd been slightly wounded in the Red Crown shootout, Blanche expected Coffey to hate her. When she asked if he felt like killing her, Coffey replied that he didn't work that way. He said he tried to be kind to everyone, and he treated Blanche with courtesy.

Soon after Blanche arrived in Platte City, Dr. Silas Durham came to the jail to examine her eyes. He extracted more glass and told her he didn't think the vision in her left eye could be saved. He was correct. Dr. Durham liked Blanche and told his family that she was quiet and resigned, not terrifying or even slightly scary in any way. She liked him, too, and afterward was complimentary about the medical care he provided for her. After being in the shadow of Clyde and Bonnie for months, Blanche quickly became something of a folk hero in her own right to teenaged girls in the area. They thought it was very romantic that she hadn't abandoned her mortally wounded husband in Dexfield Park.

On Saturday, July 29, Blanche woke up in her Platte City cell after dreaming that Buck was calling to her. She took it as a sign that he had died, but no one would confirm it to her. It was Sunday afternoon before Blanche was officially notified that she was a widow. Holt Coffey and his wife did their best to comfort her. She remained in the Platte City jail for another six weeks. Then, on September 4, Blanche Caldwell Barrow pleaded guilty to a charge of assault with intent to kill Platte

County sheriff Holt Coffey. Highway patrolmen Thomas Whitecotton and Leonard Ellis weren't on hand to testify that Coffey's neck wound in the Red Crown shootout was the result of friendly fire. Blanche said later that she'd only agreed to plead guilty to spare herself the agony of a trial—no jury, she said, would ever have believed she was innocent, let alone that she'd never fired a gun during her whole time with the Barrow Gang. Blanche was remanded to the Missouri state prison for ten years and began serving her sentence the same night.

Bonnie Parker wasn't the only aspiring poet in the Barrow Gang. Following Blanche's death in Texas on December 24, 1988, long after she'd been released from prison in Missouri, friends went through her possessions in the trailer where she lived. In one box, stashed among bank receipts and canceled checks, they found a poem titled "Sometime" that Blanche apparently wrote during her months on the run:

Across the fields of yesterday
She sometimes comes to me
A little girl just back from play
the girl I used to be
And yet she smiles so wistfully
once she has crept within
I wonder if she hopes to see
the woman I might have been.
—Blanche Barrow, 1933

CHAPTER 22

Struggling to Survive

Clyde, Bonnie, and W.D. fled west from Iowa. They hoped to lie low for a while in Colorado, but when they arrived they read in a local paper that the state police were on the lookout for them. The three remaining members of the Barrow Gang wouldn't have been difficult for any alert lawmen to spot. Bonnie was crippled, Clyde's injured left arm dangled, and they were all wrapped in sheets found in the stolen Ford V-8 from Polk City. The clothes they'd worn during the July 24 attack were so bloodstained they had to be discarded. Their other belongings had been abandoned back in Dexfield Park, so there was nothing else but the sheets for them to wear. They cut holes in the middle and stuck their heads through. The most famous outlaws in America looked like children dressed up as ghosts for Halloween.

Since Colorado apparently wasn't safe, Clyde decided to throw off potential pursuit by following a zigzag route that took the trio as far north as Minnesota and Illinois before dipping back south through Nebraska and eventually into Mississippi. They got the money they needed through an ongoing series of small-town robberies. Their take was never very much, just enough for food and gas and some clothes. They tried to avoid even medium-sized towns where local police might be lurking. On August 20, Clyde and W.D. broke into an armory in Illinois, and came away with three BARs, a number of handguns, and lots of ammunition. Now they felt they were sufficiently armed again.

But W.D. told Clyde and Bonnie the same thing he'd told Buck and Blanche back in Dexfield Park. He wanted to go home to his mother. They understood, and Clyde coached W.D. about what to say if the law ever caught him. The smart thing, Clyde suggested, would be for W.D. to insist he'd been forced to participate in the various robberies and shootouts. The cops would probably believe anything that made Clyde Barrow sound evil, and a Kaufman grand jury had accepted the same story from Bonnie just a year earlier. W.D. agreed to stay with Clyde and Bonnie until they were healed enough to completely fend for themselves.

So it was the first week in September before the weary trio finally straggled back to West Dallas. Clyde and Bonnie hadn't seen their families for four months. It was not a joyous reunion. After dropping W.D. off on September 7—he immediately left for Houston, where his mother, Tookie, now lived—Clyde made contact with the other Barrows and Parkers and arranged a meeting outside of town. The Barrows and Parkers were shocked at Bonnie's appearance. Her body was skeletal, and she couldn't walk at all. Clyde carried her out of their car and placed her on a quilt that was spread on the ground. Then the fugitive couple described their lives on the run since Dexfield Park. Every night had been spent in their car, usually camped out in the country. Motor courts weren't safe for them anymore. The Red Crown in Platte City had proven that. But they'd learned a new trick—sometimes, late at night, they'd sneak into a town and park in someone's driveway. Any passing cops would think the car belonged to whoever lived in the house. They'd only been discovered by their unsuspecting hosts once, and managed to get away.

On most of their previous visits, Clyde and Bonnie had arrived with gifts and cash for their relatives. Now they had to ask for things instead. They wanted pillows so sleeping in the car would be more comfortable, and blankets because the early-fall nights were getting cooler. Bonnie needed bandages, burn salve, and crutches from a pharmacy. They had no money to buy these items for themselves. Roles were reversed—they'd become the poor relations. Clyde's sister Marie thought that for the first time her brother believed his family's lives in West Dallas looked good in comparison to his.

A pervading sense of doom clouded the September 7 gathering. Buck was dead and buried, but his grave had no headstone because Henry and Cumie were certain Clyde would die soon, too. They planned to bury him alongside Buck, and then save money by purchasing one headstone for both. Henry and Cumie were motivated by practicality, not callousness. Headstones were expensive. They told Clyde about it, and he liked the idea. He even had suggestions about the kind of stone to be used, and what he wanted inscribed on it.

After September 7, Clyde and Bonnie kept close enough to West Dallas to meet with their families frequently. Clyde in particular seemed unconcerned about the local police. The rest of the Barrows thought that Buck's death made Clyde value his remaining family members even more. He volunteered to drive his mother and sisters on visits to relatives living nearby, and spent several afternoons trying to learn to ride his brother L.C.'s motorcycle. He didn't have a knack for it, which amused L.C. much more than Clyde. At night, Clyde and Bonnie would usually sleep in deserted farmhouses. Thanks to the Depression and bank foreclosures, there were plenty of them to choose from.

Besides wanting to be near his family, Clyde had another reason for staying around West Dallas. As much as he loved Bonnie, in her current physical condition she was a liability rather than an asset during robberies. Her damaged leg prevented her from driving a getaway car, and she was too weak to hold service station operators or grocery store clerks at gunpoint while Clyde looted their cash registers. But now between her family and his there was always someone to take care of her back at one of the hideouts. That left Clyde free to recruit new gang members, then go out on the road with them to commit the sort of multiple-gunman holdups that would bring in better money.

Once again, it wasn't hard to find willing partners. Far from being damaged, Clyde's reputation was enhanced by the debacles in Platte City and Dexfield Park. Both times, he and the rest of his gang had been significantly outnumbered. Although Buck had died and Blanche had been captured, what mattered to the public was that Clyde managed to shoot his way clear and save Bonnie, too. If anything, he was a bigger celebrity than ever. Small-time Texas hoodlums Henry Massingale and Dock Potter, both escapees from Texas prisons, eagerly accepted his invitation to become the latest members of the Barrow Gang. Clyde apparently had some earlier dealings with them. Leaving Bonnie behind, Clyde, Massingale, and Potter drove north into Oklahoma with the intention of robbing some businesses around Enid. Clyde was familiar with the area, and it was only a day's drive from West Dallas. But once again, Clyde's timing was terrible. He and his new partners arrived just as a breakout from the Oklahoma state prison in McAlester had lawmen all over the area scrambling to recapture a trio of escaped convicts. The three Texas outlaws ended up being chased for hours by Oklahoma cops who were certain they were on the tail of the McAlester escapees. Trying to elude them, Clyde stole four different cars in the same day. When the fourth car got stuck in the mud in northern Oklahoma, Clyde, Massingale, and Potter hiked into a nearby town on foot. At one house, they saw some elderly women playing croquet in the front yard. Massingale ran up to them, waved a .45, and demanded the keys to one of the cars parked along the curb. Instead of giving him the keys, two of the ladies began whacking Massingale with their croquet mallets. Someone called the town police, and the battered crook was arrested. Massingale was eventually convicted of robbery with firearms and sent to prison for twenty years. Clyde and Potter managed to get back safely to West Dallas, but that ended their partnership. The Barrow Gang was back down to Clyde and Bonnie.

In mid-October, tragedy struck the Parker family. First Jackie, the two-year-old daughter of Bonnie's sister, Billie Jean, suddenly became ill and died. A few days later, Billie Jean's four-year-old son, Buddy, got sick and died, too. Their grandmother Emma later wrote that the children had been stricken with "a stomach disorder," but the real illness may have been pneumonia or typhoid. These diseases were common among poor children in Dallas. Bonnie was grief-stricken. She had doted on her niece and nephew. After they died, she began drinking heavily again, and this caused her appearance to deteriorate further. Just twenty-three, Bonnie no longer looked cute or even young. Emma intensified her efforts to talk Bonnie into leaving Clyde and surrendering to the authorities. She used Blanche Barrow as an example. Though Blanche had been in the middle of shootouts where policemen had died, Emma lectured her oldest daughter, she was still given only a ten-year prison sentence. Surely Bonnie realized a prison term was better than the miserable life she was living now, with death as its inevitable conclusion. Billie Jean Parker, mourning the loss of her children, sided with Emma. She didn't want her beloved sister, Bonnie, to die, too. Emma and Billie Jean made their pleas right in front of Clyde and the Barrows, who didn't blame them for what they were trying to do. But Bonnie was adamant. Yes, she knew she was going to die, but she wanted to die with Clyde. In fact, when they did die, she wanted them to be buried side by side, together for eternity. But Emma and Billie Jean kept trying to change her mind.

As October stretched into November and Clyde and Bonnie still stayed in the Dallas area, the rest of the Barrows and Parkers wondered why Smoot Schmid and his deputies hadn't tried to trap the fugitives. It was common knowledge in West Dallas that Clyde and Bonnie were often around. But the slum community's code of silence was holding fast. For many residents, lawmen were the enemy, and Clyde Barrow was a local boy who'd made good. Try as he might, Schmid hadn't been able to find a West Dallas informant who'd let him know when and where the next Barrow-Parker family gathering with Clyde and Bonnie was scheduled. Still, both families went to great lengths to conceal their comings and goings. Certain that their phones must be tapped by now—they weren't, yet—they used the code phrase "red beans" when they called to inform one another about a request from Clyde for a meeting. They also tried not to say Clyde's and Bonnie's names over the phone. Jesse James remained one of Clyde's heroes, and James had sometimes used the pseudonym of Mr. Howard. So, as an inside joke, the Barrows and Parkers referred to Clyde and Bonnie as "Mr. and Mrs. Howard" when they talked on the telephone.

But Smoot Schmid remained obsessed with capturing the couple. He confided to deputies Bob Alcorn and Ted Hinton that once he had Clyde and Bonnie in custody, he planned to "walk them down Main Street of Dallas to show the world what [I've] done." As the lawman who'd caught Clyde Barrow, Schmid predicted, he could be reelected sheriff of Dallas County for as long as he liked. There might even be a chance to run for higher office—governor was what Schmid had in mind. In November 1933, the opportunity he'd been waiting for finally arrived.

Cumie Barrow turned fifty-nine on Tuesday, November 21, and Clyde convened a family gathering to celebrate off Highway 15 in

Sowers, a tiny community a dozen miles northwest of Dallas. The Barrows and Parkers were together almost all day, but Clyde was upset because he hadn't brought his mother a birthday present. He told Cumie that he wanted to meet the next night in the same place—he'd have a gift for her then. His plan was highly unusual. Clyde never liked to hold family gatherings in the same place twice in a row. But the meeting place in Sowers was isolated, and there had never been any trouble when the Barrows and Parkers gathered there before. As the party on November 21 broke up, everyone agreed they'd reconvene in Sowers after dark the next day.

Dusk came early on November 22. About 6 P.M. a party of five left the Barrow family service station in West Dallas. Their car was driven by Joe Bill Francis, a teenager who was going steady with fifteen-year-old Marie Barrow. Joe Bill and Marie would marry in another six months. Cumie Barrow sat in the front seat with Joe Bill. Marie was in the back along with Emma and Billie Jean Parker. They drove out to Sowers and parked at the usual spot just off Highway 15. They didn't realize that another car was parked just to the south, concealed behind a fence. Smoot Schmid had finally found his informant. Years later, the Barrow family decided that either Joe Bill Francis or Billie Jean Parker sold Clyde out to the law. Joe Bill, they thought, would have done it for a reward. His marriage to Marie didn't last, and she came away from it with a bad opinion of him. If Billie Jean was the informant, the Barrows believed, she betrayed Clyde in return for a promise from Schmid that Bonnie either wouldn't be prosecuted or else would receive a very light sentence. The Dallas County cops never revealed the identity of the informant, but he or she must have come to them right after the meeting in Sowers on November 21, when Clyde asked for another get-together in the same place on the next evening.

So while Cumie, Marie, Emma, Billie Jean, and Joe Bill Francis waited by the roadside in Sowers for Clyde and Bonnie to arrive, Smoot Schmid was waiting there, too, along with Dallas County deputies Ted Hinton, Bob Alcorn, and Ed Caster. The lawmen were well armed. Alcorn had a BAR, Schmid and Hinton had Thompson submachine guns, and Caster carried a .351 repeating rifle. Schmid didn't expect much if any shooting. After Clyde and Bonnie showed up, the posse would emerge from hiding and arrest them. It was going to be simple, and afterward the newspapers would have to write glowing stories about the Dallas County sheriff for a change. Alcorn and Hinton argued that Clyde Barrow would never surrender no matter what circumstances he might find himself in, but Schmid ignored them.

At 6:45 P.M., Clyde and Bonnie approached the meeting place from the north. They were driving a black Ford V-8 sedan. Newspapers and true crime magazines constantly lauded Clyde's supposed "sixth sense," and now it may have come into play. According to his family, Clyde told them later that as he drove up to Joe Bill Francis's car he suddenly felt something was wrong. Perhaps he was just feeling nervous about meeting two nights in a row in the same place. For whatever reason, Clyde drove right past the car where his family was waiting, gaining speed, and the Dallas County deputies leaped to their feet. Schmid yelled "Halt!"—Hinton described it later as "the most futile gesture of the week"—and the lawmen started shooting, their bullets flying at Clyde and Bonnie in the V-8 and also past them directly at the car where Cumie, Marie, Emma, Billie Jean, and Joe Bill Francis were sitting. Everyone in it but Marie dropped to the floor. She sat up to watch what was happening. Cumie, curled under the dashboard, prayed out loud for her son to get away safely. Schmid's gun jammed, but Alcorn, Hinton, and Caster kept shooting. The windshield and the windows of Clyde's V-8 were smashed. The lawmen heard the glass breaking. Somebody in the V-8 fired back, probably Clyde, and Hinton's arm was grazed. Pocked with bullet holes, bumping on one side because of a tire flattened by a bullet, the V-8 veered off on a side road and disappeared into the night. By the time the Dallas County cops regrouped and got back to their own car, it was much too late for them to pursue Clyde and Bonnie. They had no portable radio equipment, so they had to drive into Sowers and find a telephone to alert area law officials that the Barrow Gang was on the run in a black, bullet-riddled Ford V-8. In the confusion, Joe Bill Francis drove Cumie, Marie, Emma, and Billie Jean back to West Dallas. None of them had been hurt, but they were all badly shaken.

Clyde and Bonnie were wounded. A slug from Bob Alcorn's BAR had penetrated the driver's side door of the V-8, then passed through their legs. They were bleeding badly, and when Clyde briefly stopped to get out and see how severely they were hurt, they had trouble standing. It was obvious they needed another car—the black V-8 couldn't go fast or far on its shredded tire—and medical attention. Driving west of downtown Dallas, Clyde spotted a 1931 four-cylinder Ford being driven by Thomas James, a lawyer from Fort Worth. That wasn't a powerful enough car to usually suit Clyde, but now he steered the V-8 in front of James, forcing the attorney to pull to the side of the road. When James and his passenger didn't move fast enough, Clyde fired a warning blast from a shotgun. After he and Bonnie transferred guns and some other belongings to the four-cylinder Ford they drove away, leaving their victims standing on the roadside. From there, Clyde and Bonnie headed north into Oklahoma. They contacted a doctor who had an underground reputation for treating wounds suffered by on-the-run criminals. Then they drove into eastern Oklahoma, seeking out another famous criminal.

Just as Clyde Barrow was always associated with West Dallas, Charles Arthur "Pretty Boy" Floyd was known to have his base in Sallisaw, near Oklahoma's Cookson Hills. Pretty Boy wasn't often there—he was eventually accused of ten murders and dozens of bank robberies all over the Midwest—but his wife and family usually were. Barrow family members and crime historians have disagreed for years where and when Clyde, Bonnie, and Pretty Boy might have met. J. Edgar Hoover's Bureau of Investigation was convinced the three infamous crooks at some point planned to work together. One thing seems certain: though Clyde and Bonnie admired Pretty Boy, he absolutely disdained them. His son told historian Rick Mattix years later that Pretty Boy thought the Barrow Gang was "too careless with the lives of civilians."

No matter how and when they may have become acquainted, after the Sowers ambush Clyde and Bonnie went to Sallisaw hoping that Pretty Boy would hide them for a while. He wasn't in town, but his sister-in-law Bessie Floyd greeted the fugitives. She didn't let them stay, but felt sorry enough for them—Bonnie in particular, who she thought "didn't look good"—to provide medical supplies, sheets, and canned food. Apparently the Floyd family kept a cache of such materials handy. When Pretty Boy came home and Bessie told him about the visitors and their plea for help, he told her never to assist Clyde and Bonnie again. Pretty Boy added that "if they don't like it, they can look me up." His attitude was typical of the era's other best-known outlaw toward the two. Master criminal John Dillinger dismissed Clyde and Bonnie as "a couple of kids stealing grocery money."

While Clyde and Bonnie hid out in Oklahoma nursing their

wounds, the Dallas County sheriff was suffering, too. The Dallas newspapers competed to ridicule Smoot Schmid after Clyde's latest escape from his clutches. Paperboys hawked extra editions about the failed Sowers ambush by piping, "Sheriff escapes from Clyde Barrow!" Reporters wanted to know why Schmid had laid his trap with only himself and three deputies. The clear suggestion was that the inept lawman had wanted all the credit for their capture for himself. Readers were reminded that this wasn't the first time Schmid had failed to catch Clyde. One story began, "Evading, as has become a habit of his recently, a trap laid for him by Sheriff Smoot Schmid, Clyde Barrow . . . fled in a machine gun bullet-riddled car." Schmid defensively announced Clyde and Bonnie had been seriously, maybe mortally, wounded. He and his men had found bloodstains all over the front seat cushions of the abandoned Ford V-8, along with "bed covers, pillows, medicines, lipstick, rouge, mirror, safety razor, knives and forks, a quantity of canned food, a sackful of pennies, and eleven different license plates." There were also copies of all the latest true crime magazines—Clyde and Bonnie still liked to read about themselves. When that didn't impress the reporters, Schmid defensively pointed out that he and his officers had at least done better than some of their counterparts, referring to the April shootout in Joplin. "[Sowers] wasn't a total failure," he argued. "At least we didn't get any of my men killed like they did up in Missouri." When the Dallas media failed to seem impressed, Schmid announced a bombshell. Maybe he hadn't caught Clyde Barrow and Bonnie Parker, but he had their partner in custody. W. D. Jones was a prisoner in the Dallas County jail, and he was singing like the proverbial canary.

Ted Hinton wrote later that the Dallas County cops had known that W.D. was with Clyde and Bonnie all along, but that couldn't be true. As late as in the aftermath of the shootout in Dexfield Park, when Iowa authorities asked Schmid for assistance in identifying the third male member of the Barrow Gang, he wasn't able to help them. It was the kind of vital information even an ambitious man like Schmid wouldn't have concealed. Withholding evidence would have been a criminal act on his part. Sometime between the first week in September 1933, when Clyde and Bonnie returned W.D. to West Dallas, and the night of November 16 when he was arrested in Houston, somebody tipped the law about his identity. W.D., who'd been supporting himself by picking cotton and selling vegetables, always thought it was "a boy in Houston . . . [who] knowed me and turned me in to the law."

W.D. was sent to the Dallas County jail. Schmid chose to not immediately announce his arrest and arrival, probably thinking that to do so might scare Clyde and Bonnie away from the area. As soon as Hinton and Bob Alcorn began questioning W.D., he fell back on the alibi suggested by Clyde. He'd been kidnapped and forced to participate in robberies and shootings, he swore in a statement recorded by sheriff's department stenographers. Every time someone had been robbed or shot, W.D. explained, he was either being held hostage by the rest of the Barrow Gang or else unconscious. At night, they either chained him to motor court cabin bedposts or forced him at gunpoint to sleep in cars. Once Clyde learned that he was cooperating with the law, W.D. whined, he'd come and try to kill him. He pleaded with the Dallas County cops not to turn him loose—he was only safe from Clyde in the fortresslike county jail.

When Schmid triumphantly presented W.D. to the Dallas media, their resulting stories were all the thin-skinned county sheriff could have hoped for. Headlines in the *Dallas Morning News* announced that the "Enforced Companion of Clyde and Bonnie Relates Weird Stories; Joined Them Voluntarily for a Time, Then Was Held Captive for Fear He'd Squeal." The accompanying story described the seventeen-year-old as "so frightened that he could not smile when asked to by a photographer." W.D. was mostly frightened by the possibility of being extradited to Arkansas for the murder of Alma marshal Henry Humphrey. Texas laws were more lenient than Arkansas's regarding criminal acts by children under eighteen. Part of W.D.'s deal with Schmid was that he'd be tried in Texas for the murder of Malcolm Davis instead. (Later, W.D. also cleared Clyde's former partner Frank Hardy for the murder of Doyle Johnson in Temple on Christmas Day, 1932.) On December 19, W.D. was indicted by a grand jury, and he eventually received a relatively lenient fifteen-year prison sentence.

Clyde wasn't bothered by W.D.'s imaginative testimony. He thought the kid had done the smart thing. The one Clyde immediately wanted to hunt down and kill after the Sowers ambush was Smoot Schmid. He believed the Dallas County sheriff had ignored an unspoken understanding not to place Clyde's family in danger. It was one thing for Schmid to try to gun down Clyde and Bonnie, who were armed and could shoot back. It was quite another to send bullets whizzing by the heads of Clyde's mother and sister. When he and Bonnie returned to the Dallas area a week after the incident in Sowers, Clyde parked outside the Dallas County jail for several hours hoping Schmid or deputy Bob Alcorn, whom he also blamed, would come out so he could shoot them. Eventually his sister Nell talked him out of murdering Schmid. She convinced Clyde that the murder might cause the Dallas County police to retaliate against other members of the Barrow family.

The close call in Sowers didn't discourage Clyde and Bonnie from staying around Dallas and frequently gathering together with their loved ones. Clyde did change part of his pattern for calling meetings—now, he confided where and when only to Cumie, and she would bring everyone else to the place. The bond between mother and son remained strong. Beginning on November 29, 1933, Cumie even recorded the dates of Clyde's visits, marking them on a wall in the Barrow family shack on Eagle Ford Road and later listing them in her unpublished memoir: "December 8th, 10th, 14th, 20th and 29th; January 4th, two times that day, 7th, 10th, 13th, 15th and 18th; February 13th, 18th, 22nd; March 3rd, 19th (12th?), 24th, 27th." Then she stopped keeping track. When Clyde and Bonnie came around on December 29, they brought baskets full of fruit, nuts, and candy as holiday gifts for their families. Bonnie reported that they'd had a nice Christmas dinner in a small-town Texas café. Apparently, their most recent robberies had been somewhat successful. Besides being able to buy their relatives Christmas presents, they also had enough money to get Clyde a new suit.

During the January 13 visit, Clyde's brother L.C. had a message for him from Raymond Hamilton's older brother Floyd. He wanted to see Clyde immediately about a plan to break Raymond out of Eastham Prison Farm.

CHAPTER 23

The Eastham Breakout

As soon as he arrived at Eastham Prison Farm on August 8, 1933, Raymond Hamilton began bragging that he wouldn't be there long. Clyde Barrow was going to break him out. It seemed to Ralph Fults, who'd been partners with him and Clyde during March 1932, that twenty-year-old Raymond loved attracting attention to himself with the boast. Prison officials didn't take it seriously. Clyde Barrow might scare the rest of the world, but Eastham was so isolated and well guarded that nobody would ever attempt an attack there.

Raymond spent the rest of 1933 picking cotton and chopping wood in the fields of Eastham's Camp 1. He renewed his friendship with Fults, and got to know some other cons. One was Joe Palmer, a thirty-one-year-old bank robber. Palmer suffered from various respiratory diseases, and the Camp 1 guards often abused him when he had trouble keeping up with the rest of his work detail. Palmer hated them for it, especially Major Crowson, a "high rider" or mounted overseer, and Wade McNabb, a building tender. Joe Palmer was a man who believed in revenge.

Another Huntsville acquaintance of Raymond's was James Mullen, who was released on January 10, 1934, after completing a sentence for burglary. Two days later he showed up on the West Dallas doorstep of Raymond's brother Floyd. Mullen claimed that Raymond had promised him $1,000 to contact Floyd and help arrange a breakout. Mullen wanted Floyd to get him together with Clyde Barrow right away. Floyd contacted Clyde's brother L.C., and a meeting with Clyde was arranged for the night of Saturday, January 13, in the countryside outside Dallas.

Raymond's plan as presented to Clyde by Mullen was relatively simple. Eastham Camp 1 work crews were currently cutting wood and brush near a back road on the edge of the prison farm property. Raymond wanted two loaded pistols left under a bridge there. Fred Yost, an old acquaintance of Raymond's who worked as an unarmed trusty at Eastham, had agreed to get the guns and bring them to him. Soon after they had the pistols, he, Joe Palmer, and Ralph Fults would go out in the early morning with the convict work crews, get the drop on their guards, and run to the road. That was where Clyde came in. Raymond may not have liked Clyde personally, but he knew that Clyde had considerable success driving his way out of tight situations. What Raymond wanted was for Clyde to park just past the bridge where the guns had been hidden, and drive him and the other escapees away before the guards could overtake them.

Clyde hated the plan. He told Mullen and Floyd that it was foolish to attempt an escape by car when there was only one escape road available. It would be too easy for the Eastham guards to follow them. He also didn't trust Raymond, who he thought might brag about the escape plan and alert the guards in advance, or Mullen, who he believed was a liar and probably a drug addict. Bonnie, whom Clyde brought with him to the meeting, was more enthusiastic. She thought that if Raymond rejoined them they would be able to rob banks again. Floyd Hamilton argued that Clyde was obligated to help. Part of Raymond's current 263-year sentence was based on the murder of John Bucher in Hillsboro, a killing by Clyde's gang when Raymond wasn't even in Texas. Decades later, Floyd still resented how long it took to talk Clyde into agreeing. When Clyde finally did consent, he said he wouldn't risk planting the guns under the bridge. Eastham Farm had too many guards and dogs. Mullen and Floyd would have to do it themselves. Clyde's sole role would be as driver of the getaway car.

Around 1:30 or 2:00 A.M. on Sunday, January 14, Mullen and Floyd managed to stash two .45 automatics in the designated spot under the bridge. They wrapped the guns in a rubber tire inner tube. Then later in the day Floyd visited Raymond and told him the guns were planted and Clyde had agreed to drive the getaway car. Raymond said the escape would take place between 6:30 and 7:00 on Tuesday morning, the typical time that the Eastham farm squads of prisoners began their day's work. Clyde should have the getaway car just out of sight down the road.

On Monday, Fred Yost retrieved the loaded .45s and brought them to Joe Palmer. Palmer pretended to suffer an asthma attack. The guards grudgingly allowed him to spend the remainder of the day in his bunk, and Palmer kept the guns hidden under the covers. There was a last-minute change in the escape plan. Ralph Fults was moved to another part of the Huntsville prison system. He asked Raymond to take Hilton Bybee, who'd previously shared a Wichita Falls cell with Fults, in his place.

Clyde was so concerned that Mullen might betray him that he insisted the fellow come with him and Bonnie when they drove south toward Eastham farm late on Monday night. No one knows why Bonnie came along. She wasn't involved in the breakout plot, but perhaps Clyde didn't feel he could safely leave her back in West Dallas, particularly if he was on the run for a while after the breakout. Clyde's current ride was another black Ford V-8 coupé, a smallish vehicle that could barely seat five adults. Fitting in six—Clyde, Bonnie, Mullen, Raymond, Palmer, and Bybee (instead of Fults; Clyde didn't know about the switch until afterward)—was going to be tough, but Clyde was less interested in comfort than security. They parked near a stream not far from the spot where Raymond planned to make the break.

Just after dawn, the camp's Plow Squads One and Two were led out to begin cutting and stacking wood and brush. There was heavy ground fog that morning, and it was hard to see. Squad One was closest to the road, and Raymond Hamilton found himself in Squad Two. He hurriedly switched places with another prisoner, hoping the guards wouldn't notice, but they did. As work commenced Olin Bozeman, standing watch over Squad One, called over high rider Major Crowson, who was toting a shotgun. "Major" was the thirty-three-year-old Crowson's given name, not a title. Bozeman told Crowson that Raymond Hamilton had switched squads. He might be up to something. But before Crowson and Bozeman could react, Joe Palmer walked up to them with a .45 in his hand and shot Crowson in the abdomen at point-blank range. Crowson tried to return fire, but his shotgun blast went high before he crumpled off his horse. Then Raymond Hamilton fired at Bozeman, hitting him in the hip. Bozeman dropped, too, and Raymond and Palmer ran for the road. Hilton Bybee fled with them, and so did two other prisoners—Henry Methvin, a young Louisiana thug serving a ten-year sentence for attempted murder and car theft, and J. B. French, a career criminal from Oklahoma. As they sprinted into the fog Joe Palmer yelled, "Give us something else," which Clyde, who'd heard the shots fired by Palmer and Raymond, interpreted as a request for covering fire. While Bonnie honked the V-8's horn to guide the escapees to the car, Clyde fired a burst from his BAR into the air. It was enough to send the remaining guards scrambling away.

Now there was an unexpected problem. Clyde had anticipated only three new passengers, which would mean excruciatingly tight quarters inside the V-8 coupé. Though French kept on running—he'd be recaptured a few days later—Raymond, Bybee, Palmer, and Methvin all wanted to be driven out. It seemed impossible to fit seven adults into the car, and they had to get moving before the panicked guards summoned help. Mullen said only Raymond and Palmer could come, but Clyde told him to shut up. He'd always imagined engineering an Eastham prison break, and now he wasn't going to leave anyone behind. All seven crammed in—at least two of the fugitives squeezed into the trunk—and Clyde raced away. By the time he stopped for gas in Hillsboro, news of the escape had already spread. The attendant at the service station said he just heard on the radio that Clyde Barrow and Bonnie Parker had sprung Raymond Hamilton from Eastham Prison Farm. The fog had surely kept the work squad guards from clearly seeing and recognizing Clyde. He was undoubtedly credited with masterminding the breakout because Raymond had bragged so often that his old partner would be coming soon to free him.

Clyde called the Barrow service station in West Dallas later on Tuesday afternoon. He instructed L.C. and Floyd Hamilton to bring some civilian clothes to the nearby small town of Rhome, where he and the others would meet them. Raymond, Palmer, Bybee, and Methvin were still in their prison overalls. The clothing delivery was made, and Mullen left with L.C. and Floyd. The four escapees from Eastham remained with Clyde and Bonnie—there was a new Barrow Gang.

Back in Huntsville, Major Crowson and Olin Bozeman were taken to the city hospital. Bozeman's wound wasn't life-threatening, but Crowson's was mortal. His intestine was perforated by the bullet from Joe Palmer's .45. Lee Simmons, the prison general manager, was fuming. Like everyone else, he assumed that the entire breakout was planned and carried out solely by Clyde Barrow. It was one thing for Simmons's former prisoner to drive around the country robbing small-town stores and shooting country cops. It was another for Clyde to have the audacity to raid what was supposedly Texas's most secure prison farm. Simmons, like Dallas County sheriff Smoot Schmid, was extremely sensitive to criticism in the media, and after the January 16 breakout it wasn't long in coming. An editorial in the *Dallas Morning News* speculated that if prison officials couldn't "offer capable resistance" against "the world of gangland," judges and juries should begin meting out more death sentences to reduce the number of desperate cons being held so ineptly in Huntsville. National publications chimed in. *Time* magazine, which had recently added a new page devoted entirely to coverage of crime, noted that "convicts left behind spotted the handiwork of Clyde Barrow, notorious outlaw-at-large," adding that he was joined by "his woman, gun-toting, cigar-smoking Bonnie Parker."

Major Crowson lingered until January 27, long enough for Simmons to call in a notary to take the fatally wounded man's final statement. Crowson swore he "never did shoot at Joe Palmer who shot me," and that the armed convicts "didn't give me a dog's chance." Before he expired, he begged Simmons to send Joe Palmer to the electric chair, and Simmons swore he would. At Crowson's funeral, the dead man's father reminded Simmons of his promise.

But Joe Palmer undoubtedly mattered less to Lee Simmons than Clyde Barrow. It was Clyde who had humiliated Simmons, Clyde who apparently devised the escape plot that made the prison system manager look like a fool in the eyes of the public. Only if he was integral in Clyde's capture or death would Simmons's own reputation be restored.

What was needed, the Texas prison general manager decided, was organized, ongoing pursuit. Even when several different law enforcement agencies had worked cooperatively in Platte City and Dexfield Park, they still made only one-time attempts to gun down the Barrow Gang. When Clyde got away, they didn't follow. The way to nail Clyde Barrow was to create a posse that tracked Clyde instead of waiting for him to come to them. Because Clyde ranged so widely, these pursuers would need the active support of authorities in several states besides Texas. That meant whoever led the Barrow Gang pursuit should command respect from lawmen everywhere.

Protracted pursuit wouldn't be cheap. Simmons had to convince Texas governor Ma Ferguson that running down the Barrow Gang was worth considerable expense. He believed he could. Simmons thought the tough part would be talking Governor Ferguson into letting him hire the man he wanted to head the posse, because she and former Texas Ranger Frank Hamer loathed each other.

But it had to be Frank Hamer. To catch Clyde Barrow and Bonnie Parker, Lee Simmons wanted the only lawman in Texas who was as famous—and as deadly—as America's most notorious criminal couple. In Austin, he persuaded Governor Ferguson to let him offer Hamer the newly minted post of "Special Escape Investigator for the Texas Prison System." But that was only half the battle. Now Simmons had to convince Hamer to take the job.

CHAPTER 24

Hamer

Thirty-one years before Texas prison general manager Lee Simmons asked him to hunt down Clyde Barrow and Bonnie Parker, Frank Hamer almost became an outlaw himself.

In 1903, the nineteen-year-old Hamer was working as a wrangler on a ranch outside the West Texas town of San Angelo. Hamer was a huge kid, six feet three inches and over two hundred pounds in an era when most grown men weren't even six feet tall. He was tough, too, having already survived a blood feud with a former friend. Three years earlier, Hamer and one of his brothers sharecropped a plot of land with Dan McSwain. McSwain, who knew Hamer was a dead shot with a rifle, shotgun, or pistol, offered the teenager $150 to ambush another rancher. Hamer refused, and promised to tell the intended victim about McSwain's plot. McSwain responded by stalking Hamer and leveling him with a shotgun blast. Badly wounded in the head and back, Hamer returned fire with a pistol and drove McSwain away. After he healed, Hamer tracked McSwain down and shot him dead. Mercy was not in his nature.

Neither was bank robbery, but in 1903 in San Angelo he was sorely tempted. An older wrangler convinced Hamer and several other younger ranch hands that if they robbed the town bank, they could use the money to buy and operate their own ranch in Mexico. But as they walked toward the bank to commit the crime, the ranch foreman rode up and told them it was time to get back to work. They did, and when he reflected on the close call with a criminal life decades later, Hamer told family and friends that it was the adventure of bank robbery that had appealed to him, not the money.

Though Hamer didn't join the ranks of lawbreakers himself in 1903, three years later he became their nemesis when he enlisted in the Texas Rangers. For the next three decades, he had all the adventure he wanted. Founded in 1835 as a small, elite force reporting directly to the state governor, the Rangers' reputation was controversial. Depending on the era and the enemy, they variously fought Indians, Mexicans, rustlers, bank robbers, and bootleggers. Their methods were routinely violent. Hamer, rising quickly to a captaincy, told his troops that "we're here to enforce the law, and the best way is a .45 slug in the gut." He meant every word. By the end of his Ranger career he was credited with killing fifty-three men and suffering seventeen wounds himself.

Everybody in Texas talked about the Rangers, and Hamer was the one talked about most. He established his reputation by restoring order in a series of lawless frontier towns—Mexia and Gander Slu and Borger. He was credited with accomplishing most of his great feats single-handedly. An early legend had him arriving alone in an unnamed town to quell a burgeoning race riot. A black man was accused of raping a white woman, and a mob had formed around the jail where the accused rapist was being held. Hamer arrived in town and walked directly toward the prospective lynchers, who turned and screamed at him to leave or be hanged, too. Hamer wore heavy Western boots with pointed toes. He warned everyone to clear the way, then began viciously kicking the shins of all those standing between him and the jail. They moved, and by the time Hamer reached the jail the mob was dispersing, many limping rather than walking. He had absolute confidence in his ability to control any situation.

Even celebrities were starstruck when encountering Hamer. When the Texas Ranger captain visited Hollywood in 1918, cowboy movie star Tom Mix was so impressed that he asked Hamer to quit the Rangers and become an actor in Western films. Hamer declined, but he did become a close friend of the actor, sometimes advising him how to play certain shoot-'em-up roles.

Hamer understood his reputation was just as intimidating to criminals as his favorite pistol—known in the press as "Old Lucky"—and did what he could to embellish it. He would rarely grant interviews, which encouraged journalists to add their own imaginative details. Hamer was taciturn in the extreme. Lee Simmons once joked that Hamer "was going to speak a long piece one day and the shock'll put him to bed." But when Hamer did talk to writers or friends, he wasn't shy about claiming near-superpowers, once telling historian Walter Prescott Webb that his eyesight was so superior he could actually see bullets in flight, and that he could hear far-off sounds as much as thirty seconds before anyone else.

His fame provided Hamer with job security. The legislature mandated the number of Rangers employed by the state, often reducing their ranks from three or four hundred to less than fifty if there seemed to be no immediate crises. The governor of Texas had the power to hire and fire individual Rangers. Several times, Hamer resigned and took other employment—city marshal of Navasota, special agent for the U.S. Prohibition Service—but he always returned to the Rangers. Sometimes he left for the opportunity to make money, but other times he resigned if he disagreed politically or personally with a governor. Whenever that happened, Hamer simply waited out that individual's two-year term and returned to Ranger duty when a governor more to his liking was elected. (Texas voters routinely voted out incumbents during Hamer's career in law enforcement.) Hamer could always rejoin whenever he wanted—no governor was going to spurn the services of the most famous Ranger of them all.

But for the first time that wasn't a given when Lee Simmons approached him in February 1934 to lead the hunt for Clyde and Bonnie. Hamer was a civilian again. He despised the politics of Ma Ferguson, who had been elected governor of Texas in late 1932, and had made the mistake of openly supporting her opponent in the campaign. This time, Frank Hamer really was in danger of being fired, and he left the Rangers before Ferguson took office and had the authority to terminate him. (As soon as she was sworn in, Ferguson immediately fired every Ranger and replaced them with political allies.) Ferguson had served as governor for an earlier two-year term, and Hamer guessed she probably wouldn't be in office beyond 1934. So he resigned his commission on February 1, 1933, placing himself on "inactive status" rather than retiring outright so he'd keep his future Ranger options open if and when Ferguson was ousted by Texas voters. Meanwhile, when his hopes to be named U.S. marshal for the Western District of Texas didn't work out—the U.S. senator making the appointment gave it to a longtime crony instead—Hamer stayed in Austin, working for an oil company as a "special investigator" (essentially, breaking strikes and identifying industrial spies), a job that paid a whopping monthly salary of $500, just over three times the monthly $150 that Hamer had been earning as a captain in the Rangers.

When Lee Simmons met with Hamer on Saturday, February 10, 1934, the former Ranger captain was a year into his self-imposed, well-compensated exile. Though he was aware of Clyde Barrow and Bonnie Parker, Hamer wasn't immediately interested in leading a posse to track them down. For one thing, he didn't believe Governor Ferguson and her husband, another former Texas governor who'd been impeached for corruption, would really support him unconditionally. Simmons swore they would; Ferguson, he promised, would even grant Hamer the authority to negotiate deals, including the right to offer pardons for crimes committed in Texas by criminals who would betray Clyde and Bonnie to the law. Then Hamer balked at the salary involved—Simmons admitted the "Special Escape Investigator for the Texas Prison System" would be paid only $180 a month. Approaching his fiftieth birthday, Hamer was concerned about providing for his wife and children after his death. Simmons had a solution for that concern, too. Besides any reward money he could collect, Hamer would be authorized to take whatever he wanted from among the Barrow Gang's personal possessions when he caught them. Even in 1934, collectors were glad to pay exorbitant amounts for authentic criminal memorabilia.

Hamer said that when he did corner Clyde and Bonnie, he was certain they wouldn't allow themselves to be taken alive. Simmons assured him that wouldn't be a problem: "I want you to put [them] on the spot and shoot everyone in sight."

That was fine with Hamer, but he had a final concern: catching up to the Barrow Gang might take a long time. He was always methodical rather than reckless. What if, after a few weeks or months, the governor and Simmons decided to call the operation off? Hamer wasn't willing to waste his time unless he had their complete commitment. Simmons promised that he would back Hamer to the limit "no matter how long it takes."

The most famous lawman in Texas replied, "Well, if that's the way you feel about it, I'll take the job."

THE HUNT

"I will be conquered; I will not capitulate."

—Samuel Johnson

"No man in the wrong can stand up against a fellow that's right and keeps on a-comin'."

—Captain Bill McDonald, explaining the philosophy of the Texas Rangers

CHAPTER 25

The New Barrow Gang

Shortly after 1 P.M. on Tuesday, January 23, 1934, two men entered the First National Bank of Rembrandt in northwest Iowa. One asked cashier Lloyd Haraldson, the only employee on duty, to change what was later described in newspaper accounts as "a large bill," probably $10 or $20. When Haraldson opened his cash drawer, the other stranger pulled out a gun and ordered him and customer J. F. McGrew to put up their hands. The thieves coolly rifled the drawer, took about $3,800, and walked out the bank's back door to an alley, where they climbed into a tan Ford V-8 and drove off. Witnesses reported seeing four men in the car. McGrew and Haraldson told county lawmen and local reporters that they were impressed with the professionalism of the crooks, who remained calm and polite throughout. The Barrow Gang had finally pulled off a quick, efficient bank robbery with a substantial take.

The credit belonged less to Clyde than to his cohorts. Raymond Hamilton and Hilton Bybee went into the bank and conducted the actual robbery. Clyde was left behind the wheel of the getaway car, with Henry Methvin beside him. A fifth gang member was along—Joe

Palmer spent the whole time curled in a fetal position and covered with blankets on the floor of the Ford's back seat. His always delicate health had broken down again, and he'd been too sick to participate. Bonnie apparently had been left nearby, and Clyde angered Raymond during the post-job divvy-up when he insisted that the loot be divided six ways, with Bonnie and Palmer receiving full shares. Raymond had an urgent need for cash—he owed James Mullen $1,000 for helping him escape from Eastham Prison Farm, and Mullen was the type who'd cause trouble if he didn't get paid. If Clyde had divided the money four ways rather than six, Raymond would have had almost enough to settle the debt.

Clyde was still the boss, which irritated Raymond but didn't bother Joe Palmer or Henry Methvin. Hilton Bybee didn't care one way or the other. As soon as he had his cut of the Rembrandt take, he left the gang for good. Bybee wasn't interested in running with Clyde, though he would have been better off staying with him. One week after striking out on his own, Bybee was recaptured near Amarillo and returned to prison.

On January 26, just three days after their successful robbery in Iowa, the gang hit another bank in the northeast Oklahoma town of Poteau. This heist went smoothly, too. Three men—probably Raymond, Henry, and Palmer—went into the Central National Bank, forced a cashier and some customers to sit on the floor, grabbed $1,500, and hustled out to a black Plymouth sedan waiting nearby. The Plymouth roared away on Highway 271, with Clyde at the wheel. It was a clean getaway.

With healthy finances for a change, the five-member gang could attend to matters other than robbery. Joe Palmer had business back in Texas, and Clyde drove everyone there. On the way, there was trouble between Palmer and Raymond. The two never liked each other—their partnership in the Eastham breakout had been based on convenience rather than friendship. Palmer, at thirty-one much older than the rest of the gang, thought twenty-year-old Raymond bragged too much, and suspected him of acting as an informant to the guards while he was on the prison farm. Raymond considered the constantly ill Palmer to be an unnecessary burden. He'd been too sick to participate in the Rembrandt robbery, and they even had to frequently pull over to the side of the road when Palmer became carsick. Why should Palmer be allowed to stay in the gang and get an equal share of all the stolen money? Raymond kept saying as much, and finally on the ride from Iowa to Texas Palmer had enough. He called Raymond a "punk blabbermouth braggart" in front of Clyde, Bonnie, and Henry Methvin, and accused him of being a prison snitch. Raymond was furious, but he was also afraid of Palmer. In Eastham, sick as he constantly was, Palmer still had a well-deserved reputation as a fighter. So Raymond waited until later in the ride, when Palmer fell asleep in the car. Raymond drew his pistol and pointed it at Palmer. Clyde, driving too fast as usual, took a hand off the wheel. He reached back, slapped Raymond and ordered him to put the gun away. It was a brave thing to do—Raymond didn't like Clyde either, and might have turned the gun on him instead. But Raymond complied, perhaps because in twisting to hit him Clyde lost control of the car and ran it into a ditch. Palmer woke up, discovered what had happened, and realized it wasn't safe for him to remain a full-time member of the gang. But before he left, Palmer wanted to go to San Antonio and then Houston. The San Antonio stop appealed to Clyde's sensitive side. After Palmer had been convicted of robbery and sent to prison, most of his family disowned him. But Palmer's sister Faye, who lived in San Antonio, remained loyal to him. Now Palmer wanted to see her. During his previous civilian days Palmer usually wore overalls and work shirts, but he arrived at Faye's home in a fancy new suit. He explained that Clyde insisted all the gang members dress up—they had a fashionable image to uphold. Brother and sister had a happy reunion in the San Antonio rock gardens. They posed for several pictures. Bonnie probably snapped them. She was often the gang's designated photographer.

Then Palmer wanted to go to Houston, and his sinister errand there also struck a chord with Clyde. While Palmer served his time on Eastham Prison Farm, he'd been abused by building tender Wade McNabb. McNabb frequently beat Palmer when he was too sick to take part in work details. Now Palmer wanted to get even, and Clyde empathized. He'd been repeatedly raped by Ed Crowder, whom he'd subsequently murdered in a prison dormitory shower area. No one knows the details, but apparently in Houston Joe Palmer contacted an attorney he knew and paid him to arrange for Wade McNabb to be offered a prison furlough. These were sometimes granted to convicts who cooperated with prison administrators. A furlough would allow a trusted prisoner to leave for thirty or sixty days, then return on his own recognizance. Whenever McNabb left Eastham, Joe Palmer planned to find and kill him.

After his meeting in Houston, Palmer was ready for a temporary break from the gang. About January 30, Clyde dropped him off in Joplin, Missouri. They agreed to rendezvous there in about a month. Clyde, Bonnie, Raymond and, Henry Methvin stayed together, and on Thursday, February 1, the Barrow Gang staged its third bank holdup in nine days. Things didn't go quite as smoothly at the State Savings Bank in Knierim, Iowa, about seventy miles southeast of Rembrandt. There was only $272 in the cash drawer, though Clyde and Raymond—both subsequently identified by witnesses from mug shots—also relieved customer Chris George of $35. As the thieves ran for their car, cashier Albert Arenson snatched up a pistol and fired at them. He missed.

Afterward the gang traveled to Bienville Parish in Louisiana so Henry Methvin could see his family. They stayed a few days, spending each night in their car out in the countryside, then left for Missouri. On February 12 they stole a car in Springfield. Local cops chased them out of town and Clyde got lost. Near the village of Reeds Spring the gang passed Joe Gunn, who was walking to a grocery store. They forced him at gunpoint to climb in the car, telling Gunn that they wanted him to guide them out of Missouri and into Arkansas. Apparently Clyde didn't have one of his beloved Rand McNally road maps handy. Gunn thought none of the four outlaws seemed nervous, and he was impressed that Bonnie cradled a rifle on her lap. Soon after the gang took Gunn prisoner they came upon a roadblock on the road south of Reeds Spring. Several lawmen had parked their cars across and along the highway. The Barrow Gang and the cops exchanged fire—Gunn told reporters later that the outlaws "showered the car[s] with bullets"—but no one on either side was hit. Then Clyde yanked his stolen vehicle into a sharp U-turn and drove away. Gunn, terrified now, suggested an alternate route to the Missouri-Arkansas border. Along the way they passed another carload of police parked on the side of the road, and the gang fired at them as Clyde drove by. Again, there were no injuries. Not long afterward they arrived in Berryville, Arkansas. Clyde ordered Gunn out of the car and gave him $10. In its story the next day, a local newspaper crowed that "Clyde Barrow and his gang of outlaws, including the cigar-smoking gun-girl Bonnie Parker, paid Stone County a visit on Monday of this week and created considerable excitement in the vicinity of Reeds Spring." Gunn said that Bonnie cursed a lot, but "they didn't harm me at all."

From Arkansas, the gang headed back to Texas. Raymond was dropped off in Amarillo, and the other three went east to Dallas. The Barrow-Parker family gathering on the night of February 13 was by far the happiest since Buck's death in Iowa the previous summer. Clyde and Bonnie had some of their sparkle back. The successful bank robberies in Rembrandt and Poteau had left them with money to distribute to their relatives again. Getting through the Reeds Spring shootout unscathed further restored Clyde's confidence. Despite what happened in Platte City and Dexfield Park, he could still outshoot and outdrive the law.

Everyone noticed how much Clyde seemed to like and trust his new sidekick Henry Methvin. The burly twenty-two-year-old—at about five feet nine inches and 170 pounds, he looked even taller and bulkier standing next to short, scrawny Clyde—had been serving a ten-year term at Eastham Prison Farm for assault with intent to murder and car theft. Nicknamed "Tush Hog" by other inmates as a tribute to his toughness, he seemed to be the antithesis of swaggering Raymond Hamilton. Henry didn't talk much, and was attached to his family back in northeastern Louisiana. Far from resenting Clyde's leadership, Henry appeared happy to take orders, exactly what Clyde valued in a partner. The rest of the Barrows and Parkers approved of him, too.

Clyde called another family meeting five nights later, and this time Raymond Hamilton attended. He didn't come alone. Raymond had stopped in Amarillo to pick up a woman. Clyde was always accompanied by Bonnie. Now Raymond would travel with a girlfriend, too. Nobody besides Raymond found anything to like about Mary O'Dare. She was the wife of Raymond's former partner Gene O'Dare, currently serving a ninety-nine-year prison term after being convicted for the November 1932 holdup of the Carmen State Bank in La Grange. Floyd Hamilton described his brother's new girlfriend as "a short girl with plenty of curves and a hard face covered by enough makeup to grow a crop." After her husband went to prison and before she took up with Raymond, Mary supported herself through prostitution, so the chance to run with the infamous Barrow Gang instead must have seemed like a huge step up. She immediately began complaining. The gang members still slept in cars in backcountry camps, but sometimes they treated themselves to nice meals ordered from, but not eaten in, restaurants.

Their routine was for one person to go inside and order several dinners to go. Then they'd drive around until the food was ready, pick it up and return to their camp, where they could eat without fear of being recognized. That wasn't good enough for Mary. She wanted to eat in the restaurants and afterward be taken to nightclubs for drinking and dancing, the kind of high life she expected as the newest member of one of America's most famous criminal gangs. Clyde and Bonnie refused and Raymond took Mary's side. Mary's carping ratcheted up the tension between Clyde and Raymond even more.

But Clyde didn't tell Raymond to take Mary and leave. Despite the problems caused by his demanding girlfriend, Raymond was clearly an asset to the gang. Bank robberies went smoothly when he took part in them, and the income from those jobs far exceeded what Clyde made hitting grocery stores and service stations. Because of her injuries, Bonnie would never be an active participant again, and although he was tough and willing to do whatever he was told, Henry Methvin was still green when it came to a full-time career in crime. So Clyde and Bonnie did their best to put up with Mary O'Dare. They called her "the Washerwoman" behind her back, and, because they believed she'd gladly sell out the gang to the law, Bonnie made it a nonnegotiable rule that Mary had to stay with her whenever the men were out on a job.

The next Barrow Gang theft involved ordnance rather than money. On February 20, they broke into the state armory in Ranger, Texas, and stole four BARs, thirteen Colt .45 handguns, and large quantities of ammunition. Well armed again, they prepared to rob their next bank.

On the morning of February 27, Bonnie and Mary O'Dare waited in a Ford V-8 sedan outside the Dallas suburb of Lancaster while Clyde, Raymond, and Henry drove into town in a Chevrolet. The three men walked into the R. P. Henry and Sons Bank and ordered the cashier and several customers to lie down on the floor. Laborer Ollie Worley, who'd just cashed his $27 paycheck, clutched his hard-earned currency as he followed the thieves' instructions. Worley had time to notice how well dressed all three were before one of them snatched the money from his hand. The other two took all the currency from the cash drawers and forced the cashier to open the vault. They stuffed the money stored there into a sack and turned to leave. Then the man who'd taken the $27 walked back to where Worley lay on the floor. Afterward, Worley identified him as Clyde Barrow after looking at mug shots provided by the Dallas police. Clyde asked, "You worked like hell for this, didn't you?," and Worley replied, "Yes sir, digging ditches." Clyde stuffed the money back into Worley's hand, saying, "We don't want your money, just the bank's." Then he, Raymond, and Henry hurried out to their car. They rejoined Bonnie and Mary O'Dare in the country, abandoned the Chevrolet, piled into the Ford V-8, and headed north. The take from the robbery was, by Barrow Gang standards, spectacular—$4,176, plenty to keep them going for a while.

Ready for another break, they drove to Terre Haute, Indiana, but there was trouble on the way. Clyde was at the wheel, and Bonnie and Henry Methvin sat in front with him. Raymond and Mary O'Dare were in the back seat. At some point, Raymond suggested that they divide the loot, which was fine with Clyde. The bag with the money was in the back with Raymond and Mary. Clyde told Raymond to divide the money equally, but there would be no share for Mary O'Dare.

Raymond didn't agree. If Bonnie, who hadn't done anything more than wait out in the country while the robbery took place, got a full share, then he thought Mary should, too. Clyde refused, and ordered Raymond to split the money as instructed. Raymond pretended to comply, but Clyde, using the rearview mirror to sneak glances into the back seat, saw Raymond surreptitiously stuffing some bills into his coat. Furious, Clyde stopped the car and ordered Raymond out. He found $600 that Raymond had hidden in one of his pockets, a shocking breach of gang etiquette as Clyde understood it. It was one thing to steal from rich people and their banks. But partners never stole from each other. Clyde took the $600 away from Raymond, and the money from the Lancaster bank was divided between Clyde, Bonnie, Henry, and Raymond after all. Clyde didn't immediately expel Raymond from the gang, but the protocol breach was significant. During the week that the gang spent in Terre Haute, they bought new clothes and felt safe enough to eat meals in restaurants, but then Raymond and Mary did something even more unforgivable than cheating on a divvy-up.

Clyde and Bonnie still had fights, screaming arguments where he was likely to swear he was taking her back to her mother and she would frequently threaten to shoot him. They always reconciled, usually within a few hours. The bond between Clyde and Bonnie was unbreakable. But when they had a blowup in Terre Haute, Raymond and Mary thought they saw an opportunity to get even with Clyde. Mary took Bonnie aside and told her that she shouldn't tolerate such terrible treatment. What Bonnie ought to do was to administer knockout drops to Clyde—Mary would be glad to help with that—take all his money, and then leave with Mary and Raymond. The three of them would form a new gang. Bonnie immediately told Clyde what Mary had suggested. It was the final straw. Clyde told Raymond he could only stay if he got rid of Mary, and Raymond refused.

On March 6, Raymond Hamilton and Mary O'Dare stole a car and drove back to Texas. The Barrow Gang was down to three members again. Henry Methvin's value to Clyde increased substantially with Raymond's departure. Clyde needed a partner to help with robberies, preferably someone who'd take orders rather than argue about them. Henry unquestioningly accepted Clyde as boss, and he got along well with Bonnie, too. It made sense for Clyde and Bonnie to do whatever they could to keep Henry happy, and there seemed to be one obvious way. Henry was always ready to visit his large family—parents, brothers, sisters-in-law, and innumerable Methvin cousins—in Louisiana. In early March, Clyde and Bonnie took Henry back to Bienville Parish for the second time, probably traveling there directly from Terre Haute. Henry was glad to go home for another visit, but not for the reason that his partners thought.

CHAPTER 26

Hamer on the Trail

Although Frank Hamer was initially reluctant to pursue Clyde and Bonnie, once he accepted the job from Texas prison general manager Lee Simons he began the hunt right away. On February 11 he drove to Dallas in a Ford V-8 chosen because it was the same type of car Clyde routinely stole and drove. Hamer wanted, as much as possible, to simulate the way Clyde and Bonnie traveled.

He started in Dallas, not adjacent West Dallas. The purpose of Hamer's first stop was to consult with Dallas County sheriff Smoot Schmid, who had the most experience trying to catch the Barrow Gang. Hamer didn't set foot in West Dallas, even to scout out the Barrow family service station and Clyde's favorite escape route along Eagle Ford Road. He knew that to do so would immediately result in Clyde learning that Hamer was on his trail. West Dallas denizens always kept a sharp eye out for the cops, and Hamer was the best-known lawman in Texas. It was extremely unlikely that any of the Barrows' neighbors would help him out with information. Try as he might for over a year, Schmid had been able to develop only one source, who tipped him to the Barrow-Parker family gathering in Sowers on November 22.

But Schmid was a cordial host in his office at the Dallas County jail. He welcomed Hamer and offered to cooperate however he could. The Dallas County sheriff and his deputies had plenty of stories to tell Hamer about their ongoing, frustrating attempts to corner Clyde and Bonnie. They'd seen them several times since Sowers—if anything, their family visits had become more frequent. Clyde's new strategy of only telling his mother in advance when and where he wanted to meet was working. The Dallas County lawmen were reduced to driving around the outskirts of town hoping they might get lucky and intercept the couple on the way to or from a gathering. Once Deputy Ted Hinton tried using a heavy truck to force Clyde off the road, but there was too much traffic and Clyde eluded him. Another time, the Dallas County lawmen borrowed a V-8 and tried to keep up with Clyde as he raced away in his own V-8. Clyde had plenty of experience driving such a powerful vehicle; Schmid's deputies didn't, and they burned out their car's engine as Clyde escaped again.

Hamer wanted to hear those stories and more. He quizzed Schmid and his men about even the smallest details concerning Clyde Barrow and Bonnie Parker. What kind of clothes did they wear? What brand of cigarettes did each smoke? He'd never seen the fugitives himself, and it wasn't enough to be shown mug shots. "An officer," Hamer told historian Walter Prescott Webb later, "must know the mental habits of the outlaw, how he thinks, and how he will react in different situations." Schmid and deputies Alcorn and Hinton told him what they knew, and when the meeting ended Schmid offered to send Alcorn out along with Hamer, since the Dallas County deputy had so much experience on the Barrow Gang's trail. Hamer turned down Alcorn's company for the time being. He was just beginning to gather information and could travel faster by himself.

From Dallas, Hamer went to the places where Clyde and Bonnie had recently been spotted. In Shreveport, Louisiana, he found stores where they had purchased pants, underwear, gloves, and an automatic shotgun. At a recently abandoned Barrow Gang camp outside Wichita Falls, discarded store receipts led Hamer back to a shop near Dallas, where the clerk helpfully told him about the sizes and colors of some dresses Bonnie bought. (After the Sowers ambush, Clyde and Bonnie were apparently reluctant to let Marie and L.C. risk doing their shopping for them.) Hamer visited with Joplin chief of detectives Ed Portley, who'd been trying for so long to organize a coordinated pursuit of the Barrow Gang. Naturally, Portley was glad to help, providing Hamer with details about the personal belongings the gang left behind after the April 13 shootout in Joplin the previous year.

Most of all, Hamer did his best to mimic Clyde's driving babits and the way the gang camped out in their car at night. He soon believed he'd discerned a pattern—after visiting with their families somewhere outside Dallas, Clyde and Bonnie would drive north into Oklahoma or northeast into Arkansas or Missouri, then swing south into Louisiana and finally west back to Texas. They'd occasionally extend their itinerary to states like Iowa, Kansas, and Minnesota, but the other five comprised their most regular haunts. Nonstop days behind the wheel convinced the ex-Ranger captain that Clyde could travel farther in a day than any fugitive Hamer had ever trailed. Sometimes when he camped in his V-8 at night, Hamer ate hot dogs and hamburgers purchased as takeout food from cafés, just like the Barrow Gang did.

In these early days of pursuit, Hamer made plans. He was certain he'd eventually corner Clyde and Bonnie. It was the manner in which he'd take down these two desperadoes that concerned him. Clearly, Clyde Barrow did not intend to be taken alive. He'd shot and driven his way out of apparently hopeless situations in Platte City, Dexfield Park, and Sowers. If possible, Hamer wanted to avoid a shootout. He didn't mind the idea of gunning down Clyde Barrow and any other male crooks that were with him. From newspaper accounts and police reports, Hamer learned about the post-Eastham robberies in Rembrandt, Poteau, and Knierim by the latest incarnation of the Barrow Gang. Hilton Bybee had been recaptured. Raymond Hamilton was clearly running with Clyde Barrow again, and apparently Joe Palmer was, too, along with young Henry Methvin, the punk from northeastern Louisiana. Hamer would have no problems shooting them, too, if it came to that. They were peripheral anyway. The two people he was after, the pair he'd been commissioned to put out of criminal commission, were Clyde and Bonnie. But the idea of killing a woman bothered him tremendously. Hamer had no respect for Bonnie Parker—he referred to her as "a female dog in heat," and, like many other lawmen, was convinced she must be a walking repository of venereal disease since any woman who voluntarily ran with outlaws was clearly promiscuous. Yet it seemed obvious to Hamer that Bonnie wouldn't allow herself to be separated from Clyde. If bullets flew at Clyde, they'd have to fly right at Bonnie, too. So Hamer decided he would try to trap the couple when they were "at home." Though they moved about a lot, it also seemed true that sometimes they would set up camp out in the country and stay in one place for several days. If Hamer could discover the location of such a relatively long-term camp and sneak up on Clyde and Bonnie while they slept, he believed he could "tap each one on the head, kick their weapons out of reach, and handcuff them before they knew what it was all about." If it worked out that way, not a single shot would be fired. If gunplay did occur, at least there wouldn't be any civilians around to be caught in the possible crossfire.

And so Hamer drove and stopped and questioned local authorities and moved on again. He kept detailed expense accounts, expecting reimbursement for job-related expenditures. These were turned in to Simmons every two weeks. One still exists, stuffed in a file folder in the archives of the Texas Ranger Hall of Fame in Waco. According to this document, during the two weeks of February 15–28, Hamer drove 1,397 miles and was reimbursed at the rate of three cents per mile. He spent a few nights in his car and ten in hotels, so he wasn't camping out most of the time during this particular stretch. From the 23rd through the 28th he spent the nights in a hotel in Sanger, a small town north of Dallas and just below the Texas-Oklahoma border. From there he probably ranged into Oklahoma and parts of Arkansas and Louisiana, returning to the hotel at night. Sanger was convenient to many of the places he needed to go.

Frank Hamer was a secretive man. He realized that the longer Clyde and Bonnie had no idea he was on their trail, the better chance he had of catching them off-guard or asleep in their camp. Lee Simmons had made no formal announcement of Hamer's hiring. As he drove, Hamer contacted county and town law officers, letting them know what he was trying to do and asking them to contact him (by mail via General Delivery in Dallas) or Lee Simmons in Huntsville if they had any leads. Word spread among law enforcement agencies. But where the general public was concerned, Hamer's policy was based on deception rather than honesty. He granted no interviews while the hunt was in its early stages, and after that Hamer gave journalists and historians details of his pursuit that weren't true. He undoubtedly did this to conceal the identities of those helping him—by Hamer's reckoning, the rest of the Barrow family or some of Clyde's criminal friends were apt to retaliate against whoever informed on him.

During the first four weeks of his pursuit, Hamer didn't have any informants to protect. Then around the second week in March, he was contacted by Henderson Jordan, sheriff of Bienville Parish in northwest Louisiana. Sheriff Jordan wanted Hamer to come meet with him and someone willing to help set a trap for Clyde and Bonnie—forty-nine-year-old Ivy Methvin, the father of the Eastham escapee who was still traveling with them as the third member of the Barrow Gang.

CHAPTER 27

The Methvins Make a Deal

Many of the people in Bienville Parish, Louisiana, who knew Ivy and Ava Methvin didn't like them. Ivy was a mean-tempered drunk and Ava was nasty, too. Along with other impoverished Methvins—their two sons and daughters-in-law, Ivy's brother, dozens of nieces and nephews—they lived in the parish's mazelike backwoods, but even among so many poor relations Ivy and Ava were probably the worst off of the lot. They made a habit of dropping in on other Methvins precisely at suppertime. Ava further annoyed everyone by routinely refusing to help wash the dishes afterward. For a while, Ivy and Ava may even have been reduced to living in a tent.

Ivy hadn't always been poor. Before the Depression, he had earned a decent living making chairs and hauling freight with a mule team. During Prohibition, local authorities were certain Ivy was involved in bootlegging, but he was never a big enough player to merit arrest. By 1934, he and Ava were just one more aging, hardscrabble couple trying desperately to hang on.

It helped that Terrell and Cecil, two of their three sons, lived in

Bienville Parish. They felt obligated to help their parents and did what they could for them. Their third son, Henry, the middle child, was another story. In 1930 at age eighteen he did the same thing as many other Depression-era poor boys, heading west in search of work. Henry found sporadic employment as an oilfield roughneck in New Mexico and Texas, but one night out on the West Texas plains an incident occurred that landed Henry on Eastham Prison Farm. His parents and cousins swore that while hitchhiking Henry accepted a ride with a man who made homosexual advances. In fighting the fellow off, Henry happened to pull out a small knife and slash him across the throat. Panicking, he tossed the would-be predator out of the car and drove away. The police saw it differently. According to them, Henry knifed a man who'd been kind enough to give him a lift, and stole the fellow's car besides. The victim survived, and Henry was arrested. A jury believed the victim, and Henry received a ten-year sentence on Eastham farm for assault with intent to murder and car theft.

Ivy and Ava Methvin became obsessed with getting Henry out of prison. Ivy made several trips to Texas, imploring state officials to grant his son a pardon or parole. Somehow Ava found $100 for lawyers, and by mid-January 1934 she believed they were close to bringing Henry back to Louisiana. But then Henry lost his head and ran off with Clyde Barrow during the January 16 break, when if he'd just sat tight at Eastham farm he could have walked out a free man shortly afterward. It grated on the older Methvins. They wanted their boy home where he belonged. As far as Ava and Ivy were concerned, Clyde and Bonnie weren't in any way Henry's saviors. Instead, they were messing up his life.

In February the Barrow Gang came to Bienville Parish, bringing Henry home for a brief visit. There was hardly time for his parents to talk to him, and Clyde and Bonnie were always nearby. Then the gang returned in early March. Ava remembered later that it was the first day of the month, but it was probably right after Clyde kicked Raymond out of the gang in Terre Haute on March 6. They hung around longer this time, several days, and Ivy volunteered to help them find a place to stay. The old Cole place near Cecil and Clemmie Methvin's home had been deserted ever since a couple of Coles died of tuberculosis a few years earlier. In 1934, TB was considered a mysterious, monstrous affliction, a deadly plague rather than an illness, and so the abandoned house remained exactly as it had been left, with beds and chairs and all the rest of its furnishings intact. Nobody would live there. Clyde and Bonnie weren't afraid of tuberculosis. They expected to die young, and not from disease. So when Ivy showed them the house they started using it as a day stop, though they still camped someplace else at night in their car. Clyde's reservation about the Cole place was that there was only one narrow dirt road leading to it—if the gang got ambushed there, they wouldn't have an alternative escape route.

To Clyde and Bonnie, Bienville Parish seemed a fine place to stay and rest awhile. Besides giving one of their gang members the opportunity to visit with his family—something they always encouraged—the location was perfect, too. An easy three- or four-hour drive on Highway 80 from West Dallas, the parish was also only forty miles or so east of Shreveport, meaning there was access to big-city restaurants and dry cleaners. The parish itself was in the heart of the northwest Louisiana woodlands. Before the Depression it had been relatively well-to-do cotton country. Now many of its residents eked out marginal livings cutting and hauling timber. The parish's two major towns, the county seat of Arcadia and, nine miles to the west, Gibsland, were linked by rail and also by Highway 80, the main east–west thoroughfare in the northern portion of the state. Itinerant salesmen making the upper Louisiana circuit between Shreveport and Monroe often stopped for the night in Bienville Parish, with Gibsland's Colbert Hotel a favorite lodging place. Gibsland also had a small college, an ice house, and two cotton gins. Residents and transients frequently took meals at Ma Canfield's Café on Main Street, though locals called it Rosa's because that was her first name. The rest of the parish sprawled away to the south, intersected by winding dirt and gravel roads and offering all sorts of hiding places among thick brush and timber. Smaller farming communities—Mount Lebanon, Sailes, Jamestown—dotted the area. Everyone knew everybody else's business. It was hard to keep secrets there.

Soon after Henry Methvin's visit home in early March 1934, a fellow named John Joyner requested a top-secret meeting with Bienville Parish sheriff Henderson Jordan. Joyner told Jordan that Ivy Methvin wanted to see him, but they'd have to meet somewhere out in the country so no one else would know. Jordan could guess what Old Man Methvin wanted to talk about. It was common knowledge that Henry

Methvin had been broken out of a Texas prison by Clyde Barrow and was now running with Clyde's gang. Along with Joyner and Bienville Parish deputy Prentiss Oakley, Jordan went out to meet Ivy Methvin on an isolated back road.

Ivy told Jordan that the Barrow Gang had twice come to Bienville Parish for visits, first in February and then just a few days earlier. During this second visit Henry had the chance to talk to his mother in private and told Ava he was prepared to put Clyde and Bonnie "on the spot" for lawmen in return for his own freedom. Henry believed Clyde and Bonnie were bound to be killed soon, and he thought that if he stayed with them he would probably die, too. So, to save his own life, he was willing to betray them. After the gang left, Ivy had asked Joyner to help him broker a deal for Henry with Sheriff Jordan.

Jordan, a country cop who had no background in the law before being elected sheriff, suggested to Ivy Methvin that his son simply turn himself in. Henry would undoubtedly have to serve out the time remaining in his Texas prison term, but at least he'd be alive. Methvin said his son wouldn't consider doing that. Clyde Barrow and Bonnie Parker were cold-blooded killers. If Henry turned himself in and went back to jail, they would think he might inform on them. So, even if Henry was in prison, they'd find a way to murder him. Besides, it was Clyde and Bonnie that the law really wanted, not his and Ava's boy. Henry would help bring them down, but he had to have a full pardon in return. Jordan explained to Methvin that he didn't have the authority to negotiate on behalf of the state of Texas. He asked for time to think about what to do next. Methvin begged him to keep their meeting a secret. He told Jordan that if Clyde and Bonnie found out what Henry wanted to do, they'd not only kill him but his entire family.

After Jordan got back to his office in Arcadia, he contacted Special Agent L. A. (Lester) Kindell, who ran the U.S. Justice Department's Division of Investigation office in New Orleans. Federal officers were after the Barrow Gang for car theft—murder charges were still state crimes. Kindell and Jordan talked several times. The federal agent certainly wanted to nab Clyde and Bonnie. His boss, J. Edgar Hoover, had made apprehending celebrity outlaws a top priority. Hoover's trip to Platte City, Missouri, to personally interrogate Blanche Barrow after her capture was evidence of that. But despite representing the federal government, Hoover and Kindell couldn't grant a pardon to Henry

Methvin for an assault with intent to murder conviction in Texas. For that, someone from Texas state government had to be involved. Jordan made inquiries, probably to Texas prison general manager Lee Simmons, and at an unspecified date in mid-March Jordan, Kindell, and Frank Hamer met in Shreveport. Dallas County deputy Bob Alcorn and John Joyner were also present. Jordan spelled out what Ivy Methvin wanted—a complete pardon for his son Henry. As part of his arrangement with Lee Simmons, Frank Hamer could negotiate such a deal. Hamer told Joyner that Henry would receive his pardon if the Methvins' help resulted in the capture or death of Clyde and Bonnie. Joyner replied that Ivy and Ava Methvin had to have the promise in writing. That was fine with Hamer. It took a few weeks, but he produced an agreement signed by Governor Ferguson and Simmons. The next time Clyde and Bonnie arrived in Bienville Parish with Henry for a visit, Ivy was to contact Sheriff Jordan and tell him when and where they could be found.

After negotiating the deal the Methvins wanted, Frank Hamer believed he would be contacted by Henderson Jordan as soon as the county sheriff learned that Clyde and Bonnie were back. Hamer said later that Jordan "agreed to assist me and pay no attention to other officers, state or federal." If Jordan did make such a promise to Hamer, he broke it. Though he didn't have the authority to cut the state deal required by the Methvins, Division of Investigation Special Agent Kindell still wanted the glory of catching the Barrow Gang to accrue to the Justice Department. Though murder and bank robbery were state rather than federal crimes, Kindell had the authority to pursue the Barrow Gang for car theft and kidnapping. On March 24, Kindell met with Jordan again at the Bienville Parish sheriff's office in Arcadia. Kindell's request was simple: if, at some point, Jordan found out where Clyde and Bonnie were hiding in the parish, he wanted the sheriff to call him before notifying Hamer. Maybe the couple could even be caught without a specific tip from the Methvin family. After all, Kindell wasn't bound by any agreement between the Methvins and the state of Texas. It made no difference to him whether Henry Methvin got pardoned or not. From that point, Jordan cooperated with Kindell as well as with Hamer, and Hamer didn't know it.

Hamer must have believed everything might work out perfectly. He conceivably would get the chance to take down Clyde and Bonnie less than two months after he'd been hired to hunt them. If he got the drop on the criminal couple in Louisiana, the Barrow Gang would be shut down, justice would be served, and at minimal time and expense. The deal agreed to with the Methvins was simplicity itself, with the state of Texas pardoning Henry Methvin for a single act of attempted murder. It wasn't like Henry had actually killed someone.

And then on April 1, Easter Sunday, that wasn't true anymore.

CHAPTER 28

Bloody Easter

After leaving Bienville Parish in early March, Clyde and Bonnie drove directly to West Dallas to see their families. Henry Methvin went with them. They trusted him completely, even though they had only known Henry since the Eastham breakout on January 16. Clyde always had at least some shared history with partners who remained on the road with him for more than a job or two: Ralph Fults was a friend in prison, Buck Barrow was his brother, and Raymond Hamilton and W. D. Jones were two fellow refugees from the West Dallas slums whose families had known the Barrows for years. But Henry's criminal credentials seemed impressive enough—he'd been serving time for attempted murder, and his participation in post–Eastham break robberies was enthusiastic and competent. He loved his family, another plus for Clyde and Bonnie. For all that the true crime magazines wrote about Clyde's near-mystical ability to sense potential danger, that instinct failed completely where Henry Methvin was concerned. While Henry's parents were betraying them to Henderson Jordan, L. A. Kindell, and Frank Hamer in Louisiana, Clyde and Bonnie were bringing Henry to a March 12 get-together with their parents and siblings out in the country near Dallas. None of the other Barrows or Parkers suspected Henry was up to anything, either—when Clyde's sister Nell accidentally ran her car into a ditch upon arrival, Henry yanked wire from a fence to help haul it out. Bonnie told everyone that Raymond Hamilton and Mary O'Dare had suggested that she turn on Clyde, and emphasized how Henry loyally stayed with them after the other two were gone.

Usually at these family gatherings, Emma Parker tried to talk Bonnie into leaving Clyde and giving herself up. This time, it was Clyde who made the suggestion. His devotion to Bonnie remained unwavering, and even though he accepted his own inevitable death at the hands of the law he didn't want her to share that fate. So in front of both their families, Clyde reminded Bonnie that it was still only a matter of time before they were caught. He said he would write a letter swearing that Bonnie had taken no active part in any murder or robbery. If she took it with her when she surrendered, Bonnie would probably go to prison for a while but at least avoid the death penalty. She still had public sympathy on her side. But Bonnie refused to consider giving herself up. She told Clyde and the others that whenever he went down, she wanted to be with him. They were together for life, however abbreviated that might be. Clyde didn't insist—he probably knew Bonnie wouldn't agree, but still made the suggestion to ease his own conscience.

Clyde, Bonnie, and Henry stayed around Dallas for the next few weeks, sleeping in their car or abandoned farmhouses at night. Though they didn't stage any robberies—the money from the bank job in Lancaster was certainly enough to keep them going for a while—the Barrow Gang was still blamed for a major theft thanks to Bonnie's colorful reputation. On March 12, the same day that Clyde and Bonnie were with their families in Texas, a bank in Atchison, Kansas, was robbed of $25,000. Local authorities decided it was a Barrow Gang job because witnesses reported seeing a woman smoking a cigar hours earlier in the lobby of an Atchison hotel.

Clyde, Bonnie, and Henry met with the Barrows and Parkers again on March 19, 24, and 27. On the 27th, a Tuesday, Clyde told everyone that he, Bonnie, and Henry were leaving for a while. But he promised they'd be back in five days. Sunday, April 1, would be Easter, and Bonnie wanted to give her mother Emma a holiday gift. That was typical—Clyde and Bonnie both loved giving presents to family members. But what they were leaving Dallas to do wasn't. For the first time since the Barrow Gang formed in March 1932, Clyde was about to participate in premeditated murder.

Clyde had kept in touch with Joe Palmer after dropping him off in Joplin at the end of January. Palmer's plot to arrange a furlough for Eastham building tender Wade McNabb had come to fruition. On February 24, 1934, McNabb left Eastham on a sixty-day pass. Apparently he didn't connect his unexpected temporary freedom to Joe Palmer. But Palmer was waiting to pounce, and Clyde came along to assist. It was the kind of blood vendetta Clyde respected, and by his own peculiar code he undoubtedly felt obligated to help. The sickly Palmer was too weak to take on McNabb by himself. Three years earlier, when smaller, weaker Clyde killed powerful Ed Crowder after the Eastham building tender repeatedly raped him, Aubrey Scalley helped carry out the murder plot. Now it was Clyde's turn to help an abused Eastham con kill a tormentor. It would take lawmen and historians years to link Palmer and Clyde to what happened to McNabb because, unlike most Barrow Gang criminal acts, they carried this one out with such lethal efficiency. Clyde's friend and former partner Ralph Fults eventually told people what happened.

Apparently, Palmer tracked McNabb after his release on furlough. On Thursday, March 29, McNabb disappeared from a domino parlor in the East Texas town of Gladewater. On Monday, April 2, an anonymous letter received by the *Houston Press* described abuse of prisoners at Eastham and included a crude map to where "one of Lee Simmons' chief rats" could be found near the Texas-Louisiana border. A *Press* reporter and the Shreveport sheriff went to the spot and found McNabb's body. The Eastham building tender's skull had been crushed by a powerful blow, and he'd also been shot several times. The subsequent newspaper story wasn't kind to the deceased. Apparently, he'd been making an illicit living while on furlough. The *Press* reported that McNabb had sixteen dollar bills in his pocket and "three pair of crooked dice."

Having gained his revenge with Clyde's help, Joe Palmer joined Clyde, Bonnie, and Henry Methvin as they returned to Dallas early on April 1. They weren't the only outlaws traveling there on Easter Sunday. About 240 miles to the south, Raymond Hamilton and Mary O'Dare were heading for Dallas, too.

Since leaving the Barrow Gang on March 6, Raymond had been

busy. He and Mary O'Dare returned to Texas, where Raymond soon put together a gang consisting of himself, his brother Floyd, and an unemployed truck driver named John Basden. The three men successfully robbed the Grand Prairie State Bank on March 19, splitting just over $1,500 afterward. A few days later, Raymond was spotted stealing a Ford V-8 in Lufkin. He'd been linked by then to the Grand Prairie bank heist, and because local lawmen didn't know that he'd split with Clyde they assumed it was the work of the Barrow Gang. Then on Saturday, March 31, the day before Easter, Raymond and Mary traveled eighty miles south of Dallas to the town of West, where Raymond single-handedly relieved the State National Bank of almost $1,900. Mary drove the getaway car, but after only a few miles she ran it into an embankment. Raymond's nose was broken. Mary was knocked out. Driving past with her four-year-old son, Mrs. Cam Gunter stopped to help. Raymond thanked her by pulling his gun. He forced Mrs. Gunter to put her child out of her car, then made her drive him and Mary away. Another witness called the sheriff, who had the little boy taken to safety and then issued an all-points bulletin for Raymond—the witness identified him from mug shots.

Mrs. Gunter took Raymond and Mary south to Houston. They arrived on Saturday night. Raymond rented a hotel room and promised his captive that he'd release her in the morning. Early on April 1 he let Mrs. Gunter go, first giving her a few dollars to cover travel expenses back home. Then Raymond stole a snappy black Ford V-8 sedan with yellow wire wheel rims and drove north to Dallas with Mary O'Dare.

Clyde, Bonnie, Henry Methvin, and Joe Palmer arrived back in the Dallas area late on Easter morning. They didn't stop at the Barrow family service station in West Dallas—Smoot Schmid and his deputies were all too aware of how Clyde and Bonnie liked to meet with their families on holidays. Instead, Clyde drove about twenty-five miles northwest and parked just off paved two-lane Highway 114 near the small town of Grapevine. The narrow dirt side road where he stopped was called Dove Road. At Clyde's request, Joe Palmer hitchhiked back into West Dallas and arrived on Eagle Ford Road about 1:30 in the afternoon. He found only Henry Barrow at home. Cumie was probably at church, and L.C. and Marie, according to Marie in her unpublished memoir, were off "celebrating Easter in their own way," which in the case of the hard-partying young Barrows probably meant sleeping off hangovers at the homes of friends. Palmer told Henry where Clyde wanted everyone to meet near Grapevine, and then went on to Emma Parker's house and passed along the same message to her. It took several hours for the various Barrows and Parkers to get home and organize themselves for the drive to Grapevine. Joe Palmer stayed in West Dallas, perhaps intending to catch a ride with some of them rather than have to hitchhike again.

Meanwhile Clyde, Bonnie, and Henry relaxed and waited on Dove Road in their latest stolen car, a flashy black Ford V-8 with yellow wire wheel rims. Their location was relatively isolated, though their car was visible to the sporadic holiday traffic about one hundred yards away on Highway 114. There was farmland on either side of Dove Road. The afternoon was sunny. Bonnie got out of the car to play for a while with the Easter present she'd brought for her mother—a live rabbit Bonnie had named Sonny Boy. It was the kind of silly, sentimental gesture she still liked to make. She thought it would be fun to surprise Emma on Easter with an Easter bunny. Despite all she'd been through, Bonnie never lost her sense of whimsy.

But she hadn't lost her taste for whiskey, either, and while she waited for Emma and the others to arrive Bonnie passed a bottle back and forth with Henry Methvin. Clyde didn't drink—it was his custom to abstain whenever they were out in public and might have to make a sudden run for it. On this Easter Sunday, Clyde felt relatively certain that the law wouldn't be a problem. He'd heard, perhaps on a service station radio while stopping for gas, that Raymond Hamilton had kidnapped a woman and left her in the Houston area. Cops would be on the lookout for Raymond, not the Barrow Gang. Clyde felt so secure that he stretched out in the back seat of the sedan and took a nap. Bonnie did the same in the front seat. She didn't want her mother to know she'd been drinking, so before she fell asleep Bonnie chewed on bits of lemon peel to mask the whiskey smell on her breath. Henry Methvin didn't nap at all. He was often jumpy and aggressive, and when he drank those traits became even more pronounced. Henry lurked near the car, his BAR within easy reach. Clyde and Bonnie dozed. The lazy afternoon wore on.

Around 3:30 P.M., three motorcycle officers from the Texas State Highway Patrol cruised along Highway 114 north of Grapevine. Senior officer Polk Ivy rode a little ahead of the other two. Twenty-six-year-old E. B. Wheeler had been a patrolman for four years. Easter Sunday was twenty-four-year-old H. D. Murphy's first day on two-wheel patrol.

Motorcycle cops for the highway patrol usually worked singly or in pairs. Murphy was undoubtedly riding with Ivy and Wheeler so the rookie could observe the veterans at work.

Ivy rode past the intersection of Highway 114 and Dove Road, but Wheeler noticed the flashy car parked a hundred yards away and gestured for Murphy to follow as he turned down Dove Road to conduct a routine check. Wheeler clearly didn't expect any trouble. He left his shotgun secured in its harness alongside the seat of his motorcycle. Murphy had a shotgun, too, but the rookie's wasn't even loaded. He had the shells in his pocket.

Clyde might have been alerted by the approaching rumble of two motorcycle engines, or else Henry Methvin may have warned him. Clyde sat up, saw the approaching lawmen, reached for his shotgun and prepared to reenact what had become almost a routine Barrow Gang scenario: kidnap some cops, drive them far away, and drop them off unharmed. Clyde swore to his family later that this was all he intended when he whispered to Henry Methvin, "Let's take them."

But Henry Methvin hadn't been with Clyde in Springfield, Missouri, on January 26, 1933, for the kidnapping of Officer Thomas Persell; or in Wellington, Texas, six months later when Clyde, Bonnie, and W. D. Jones took lawmen Paul Hardy and George Corry prisoner and released them later that night. Henry had been drinking, too, which further impaired his judgment. He interpreted Clyde's command as an order to take the two patrolmen on motorcycles down rather than prisoner. When Wheeler rolled to a halt and began to dismount, Henry raised his BAR and shot the officer in the chest, killing him instantly. Murphy tried to grab shells from his pocket and load his gun, but Clyde, realizing the opportunity to get away without bloodshed was lost, fired his shotgun and knocked the rookie patrolman off his motorcycle.

Back on Highway 114, Mr. and Mrs. Fred Giggal were out enjoying a leisurely Easter Sunday drive in the country. For some miles they had been tagging along behind three highway patrolmen on motorcyles, not getting in the officers' way at all, just following at a good distance, when they saw two of them turn off on a narrow dirt road and ride toward a parked black car. Then there were several explosions. The Giggals paused at the intersection of Highway 114 and Dove Road and watched the taller of two men with guns roll over the prone body of one of the motorcycle officers and shoot him several times. Then both armed men got into the black car, which had bright yellow wire wheel rims, and they raced east onto Highway 114 right past the Giggals. Later, Clyde told his family that Henry Methvin went over to where Murphy lay wounded and fired several more shots into his body. (Murphy would die shortly afterward as he was rushed to the hospital.)

Clyde's account jibed exactly with that of the Giggals. But it didn't match up at all with the testimony of the man who became the most quoted witness. William Schieffer lived on farmland adjacent to the scene of the murders. His house was several hundred yards away, and Clyde's sister Marie complained later in her memoir that it would have been impossible for Schieffer to see anything clearly from his porch. But Schieffer eagerly told Patrolman Ivy—who'd doubled back as soon as he realized Wheeler and Murphy were no longer riding just behind him—and then investigators and reporters a colorful tale.

Schieffer swore that a man and a woman killed the two motorcycle cops while a third man watched, and it was the woman who approached one of the downed officers and shot him repeatedly while his head bounced on the road "like a rubber ball." That was good enough for the media. Their stories the next day described the cold-blooded Easter execution of lawmen by the Barrow Gang, with Bonnie Parker pulling one of the triggers. The *Fort Worth Star-Telegram* informed readers that Clyde and Bonnie shot Wheeler and Murphy off their motorcycles and "then riddled their prostrate forms. . . . Fort Worth and Dallas authorities with other peace officers of Tarrant and Dallas counties branded the deed as the work of Barrow and his red-headed companion after hearing [William] Schieffer's description of the two." According to the article, Schieffer's story was corroborated by the discovery near the patrolmen's bodies of "a cigar butt bearing small teeth marks, such as might have been made by a woman . . . further evidence that a cigar-smoking woman took part in the shooting."

The cigar, if it even existed, would have had nothing to do with Bonnie, but when Dallas County deputy Bob Alcorn arrived on the scene he found other evidence that convinced him she'd been there. Bits of chewed lemon peel were scattered near an empty whiskey bottle. Alcorn was aware of Bonnie's habitual trick to hide her drinking. A man's fingerprint was on the bottle, and the press soon reported that it was Clyde Barrow's. In fact, it was Henry Methvin's.

Dallas radio stations interrupted their Easter Sunday afternoon broadcasts to announce that the Barrow Gang was fleeing from a local murder scene in a flashy black Ford V-8 sedan with yellow wire wheel rims. That news alarmed Floyd Hamilton in West Dallas. Just before the report came over the airwaves, he'd been visited by his brother Raymond's girlfriend. Mary O'Dare told Floyd that she and Raymond were in town, and that they'd arrived in style in a fancy black V-8 sedan whose wheel rims were bright yellow. Floyd raced out to find Raymond. The Hamilton brothers swapped Raymond's canary-colored wheel rims for something less noticeable, and Raymond and Mary left West Dallas in a hurry. They eventually drove to New Orleans. It seemed like a good place to hide while local police swarmed the area looking for Clyde and Bonnie, who were in the process of getting away from Dallas themselves.

Clyde drove away from the murder site at high speed, taking Highway 114 east. He cursed at Henry in the back seat. Bonnie was in shock. She still had the rabbit, and despite what had happened she hung on to it, hoping for another chance to give Sonny Boy to her mother. Not far from Grapevine, Clyde recognized a car coming the other way. His brother L.C. was at the wheel, with his sister Marie in the front seat beside him. The first members of the Barrow family were finally arriving for the Easter get-together. Clyde waved L.C. to a stop, leaned out the car window, and snarled, "You'll have to get out of here. Henry's just killed two cops back there." Then Clyde drove away, still heading east on the highway. L.C. turned his own car around and followed, but within moments Clyde's V-8 was lost from sight. "When Clyde meant business," Marie wrote later, "no one could keep up with him."

Clyde, Bonnie, and Henry drove on into Oklahoma, not risking a stop in West Dallas to pick up Joe Palmer. Back in Texas, media coverage of the Barrow Gang reached new heights. While the national press also reported the murders of the motorcycle cops, papers in Texas and particularly in the Dallas area printed numerous follow-up stories focusing on H. D. Murphy. The unfortunate highway patrol rookie had not only been murdered on his first day on the job, he'd been about to marry twenty-year-old Marie Tullis on April 13. She wore her wedding gown to his funeral, providing the grist for several articles. Another described the "cozy, furnished apartment" the young couple had just rented in anticipation of their marriage. Bonnie's coup de grâce shots into Murphy's body—always presented as fact rather than allegation—were emphasized.

These stories devastated Clyde's mother, Cumie. Marie Barrow said later that "what went on" in the wake of the Grapevine murders "drove Momma crazy . . . [it] acted as a sword through my mother's soul." After ignoring or explaining away all the other murders involving her beloved child Clyde, the thought of a young bride-to-be attending her fiancé's funeral in her wedding gown was what finally broke Cumie down. The woman who disdained sinful indulgence of any sort began drinking herself. She also stopped marking down the dates of Clyde's visits. Cumie never disavowed her son. She continued meeting with Clyde when he came home after the Grapevine slayings, and prayed for him constantly. But she was crumbling under the weight of his guilt.

Bonnie was also victimized by the fresh wave of inaccurate publicity. Before, she'd been the sexy, cigar-smoking companion of a colorful killer. Now she was apparently a killer herself, and the destroyer of a loving young couple's dreams at that. Besides the lawmen pursuing her, much of the public now believed Bonnie Parker had turned out to be every bit as vicious as Clyde Barrow. There was no chance now, even if she surrendered voluntarily, for Bonnie to get off with a light prison sentence. Previously, it had been her choice to stay with Clyde until death. After Grapevine, it was Bonnie's unavoidable fate.

CHAPTER 29

Hamer Forms a Posse

The Grapevine murders added a new sense of urgency to Frank Hamer's pursuit of the Barrow Gang. During the first seven weeks of his hunt, Clyde and Bonnie had been relatively quiet and the former Texas Rangers captain pursued them alone at his preferred methodical pace. But the outcry against Clyde and Bonnie after Grapevine was led by some of the same county and state officials whose support Hamer needed to successfully complete his assignment. L. G. Phares, superintendent of the highway patrol, immediately offered a $1,000 reward for "the dead bodies of the Grapevine slayers." In Austin, Governor Ma Ferguson added another $500 reward for each of the two alleged killers. That meant for the first time there was a specific price on Bonnie's head, since she was so widely believed to have shot H. D. Murphy. Clyde came in for special vituperation from Dallas County sheriff Smoot Schmid, who declared that Clyde was no longer a man but an animal. Perhaps most worrisome of all was a scathing editorial in the April edition of *The Texas Bankers Record*, a publication of the politically powerful Texas Bankers Association. The bankers of Texas were less concerned about murdered motorcycle cops than in protecting their deposits, but their hatred of the Barrow Gang was just as rabid. The April *Record* printed photos of Clyde, Bonnie, and Raymond Hamilton, listed twenty-three ways banks could protect their staff, customers, and, most of all, money from the murderous trio—suggestions included encasing safes in concrete "at least twelve inches thick" and not opening "too early in the morning"—and thundered that "depredations on Texas banks by bandits, highwaymen and thugs continue unabated. The peace officers seem helpless to prevent robberies, or even to catch the robbers after the damage is done." It was the type of criticism certain to be noted by Governor Ferguson, who wouldn't want the Bankers Association to believe she was lax regarding the pursuit of bank robbers and accordingly fund an opponent's campaign in the next gubernatorial election.

If Hamer had planned to lie low until a message from the Methvins via Henderson Jordan summoned him back to Louisiana, he now needed to change his strategy. Clearly, it was necessary to demonstrate that he was tracking Clyde and Bonnie diligently on a daily basis. To do that, Hamer gave up traveling alone and formed a posse. Its first member was an old friend. Thirty-eight-year-old Manny Gault, one of the Texas Rangers fired by Ferguson when she took office, had gone to work for the highway patrol. Superintendent Phares gladly assigned Gault to work with Hamer. Then Hamer approached Smoot Schmid. He'd already worked a little with Deputy Bob Alcorn on the case, and now Hamer wanted Alcorn along full-time. Schmid agreed, and also sent Deputy Ted Hinton to assist Hamer. Both Alcorn and Hinton had an advantage over Hamer and Gault—they knew Clyde and Bonnie personally. The two former Rangers had only seen their pictures.

The four-man posse traveled in two cars. Hamer and Gault rode in one and Alcorn and Hinton in the other. Members of Hamer's family suggested later that, though he liked Alcorn, Hamer didn't have much respect for Hinton. The newly formed quartet began working together on Tuesday, April 3. They drove north from Dallas into Oklahoma. Hamer believed it was Clyde's usual pattern to run there after committing crimes in Texas. It made sense—Clyde knew that Texas lawmen had no jurisdiction on the Oklahoma side of the state line. But the Hamer posse didn't operate under the usual regional restrictions. If they did corner the Barrow Gang in a state other than Texas, Governor Ferguson and Lee Simmons were ready to work out any temporary legal agreements necessary.

Almost immediately, the Texans discovered that they were on the right track. Stopping at various service stations along the highway from Sherman into Oklahoma, they learned from attendants that three people in a Ford V-8, including a man and woman matching the descriptions of Clyde and Bonnie, were driving ahead of them on the same road, buying gas and snacks along the way. The gang's trail meandered into the southeastern part of Oklahoma, and on Wednesday afternoon, April 4, the two-car posse arrived in the bustling town of Durant. Alcorn and Hinton were in the lead car, with Hinton behind the wheel. Hamer and Gault trailed a short distance behind. They drove along Main Street, which was busy with traffic moving steadily in both directions. Suddenly, Alcorn startled Hinton by blurting, "Here they come!" Driving in the opposite direction, first approaching and then passing Hinton and Alcorn's car, were Clyde and Bonnie. Henry Methvin was undoubtedly with them, riding in his customary spot in the back seat, but in describing the incident later Hinton didn't mention seeing him. The Dallas County lawmen quickly considered their options. Their quarry obviously hadn't noticed them—Clyde continued driving at the same steady pace, not in the pedal-to-the-metal fashion that was typical of him if he believed the law was nearby. Hinton could have swung into a quick U-turn, but traffic was heavy and there was too much possibility of a wreck. Trying to down Clyde with a lucky shot wasn't an option. Smoot Schmid had forbidden his deputies to shoot at the Barrow Gang "in any populated area." But if they let him go and followed at a safe, discreet distance, they might be able to take Clyde by surprise later on. So Hinton and Alcorn watched Clyde's V-8 disappear from view while they pulled off the road and waited for Hamer and Gault to catch up. Then they reported their Barrow Gang sighting, and the posse turned their cars around and followed. Try as they might, they didn't spot Clyde and Bonnie again, so the four pursuers resumed stopping at service stations and cafés along the highway, hoping to learn where the Barrow Gang was heading next.

On Thursday afternoon, April 5, rumors spread in portions of northeast Texas, southeast Oklahoma, and southwest Arkansas that the Barrow Gang had been spotted during the afternoon in the town of Texarkana, on the Texas-Arkansas border. According to an unidentified witness, Bonnie Parker walked into a Texarkana drugstore and ordered a sandwich. Two men waited outside for her in a car, and one of them came into the store and escorted Bonnie out before she'd finished eating. The witness identified Bonnie from her photo in a crime magazine prominently displayed on a rack in the drugstore. It probably wasn't her—Bonnie's crippled right leg prevented her from walking anywhere. Clyde usually carried her into cafés and other places where the gang bought meals. But the suggestion that Bonnie and Clyde might be around was plenty. In Oklahoma, radio stations began broadcasting bulletins warning listeners that the Barrow Gang might be lurking nearby. All over the state, nervous citizens fretted. Some kept their children home from school for the rest of the day.

Hamer and his posse may have heard the Texarkana rumors and driven in that direction to investigate. It wasn't easy traveling by car anywhere in Oklahoma on April 5. Heavy rains drenched the state. Even paved highways were bordered by dirt shoulders or ditches, and these were reduced to thick, sticky mud. Nowhere were conditions worse than in the very farthest northeast corner of Oklahoma, hundreds of miles away from Texarkana in the hilly mining country outside the town of Commerce. The Barrow Gang arrived there just after midnight on Friday, April 6. Clyde parked their latest stolen Ford V-8 on the muddy shoulder of State Road, stopping between the towers of the Lost Trail and Crab Apple mines. Probably he was worn out from driving for hours through thunderstorms. The bad weather meant the gang couldn't turn down some side road and set up camp in a more isolated spot. So Clyde, Henry Methvin, Bonnie, and Sonny Boy the rabbit slept in the car, certainly with the intention of driving on after daybreak when the skies would hopefully have cleared. But in the morning even Clyde Barrow had trouble driving in the muck around State Road, and that was why yet another lawman died.

CHAPTER 30

Another Murder

Just after 9 A.M. on Friday, April 6, Commerce chief of police Percy Boyd and town constable Cal Campbell drove to the Lost Trail and Crab Apple mines on State Road. A motorist had reported a Ford sedan parked along the highway there, with several people apparently sleeping inside. It sounded like some drunks had nodded off on the way home—a frequent occurrence around Commerce, where miners liked to play hard at night after swinging picks and shovels all day. Boyd often handled such calls himself, but since there were several possible drunks to deal with he brought along Campbell. Boyd, thirty-five, had been elected chief of police a year earlier. He considered law enforcement his chosen profession. Campbell didn't. Before the Depression, the sixty-year-old with the thick white mustache had made a decent living as a contractor. But his business cratered, and Campbell, a widower, had five children to feed. His Commerce neighbors sympathized, and voted him into the coveted $15-a-week constable's job. Campbell served warrants and assisted Boyd whenever he asked. On the morning of April 6, neither lawman expected any trouble. They each carried handguns, but these remained holstered as they neared the Ford parked on the muddy shoulder of State Road.

Clyde and Henry Methvin were taking turns sleeping and keeping watch. They'd lingered too long that morning. The storms were over and there was occasional traffic along the road, which connected downtown Commerce to the mining district. Clyde was awake when he spotted the police car driving toward them. He turned on the Ford's powerful V-8 engine, let it idle, and as soon as Boyd and Campbell stopped and prepared to get out Clyde threw the transmission into reverse and backed down the mucky shoulder of the road, undoubtedly planning to put enough distance between them to yank the Ford into a sharp U-turn and race away before the cops knew what was happening.

But the mud on the shoulder was too boggy, and Clyde hadn't backed the car up far when it skidded into a ditch and sank to its wheel rims, cementing the stolen Ford in place. Boyd and Campbell were probably amused. They got out of their car and walked toward the Ford. Boyd said later that Cal Campbell apparently thought he saw a gun in the hand of one of the occupants. Campbell, who had no experience in firefights, yanked out his pistol and fired. Boyd raised his own pistol, and then the doors of the Ford opened and two men in suits emerged, each firing a BAR.

It was an uneven gun battle. Sixteen-year-old Lee Phelps, working in the tower of the Lost Trail Mine, heard the first pops from Campbell's low-caliber pistol and looked down on State Road to see what was happening. Phelps watched as a small man leaned against the side of the Ford, aiming carefully as he fired a rifle at Chief Boyd and Constable Campbell. A bigger man who was also firing a rifle ran right at the lawmen, zigzagging to dodge the very few shots Boyd and Campbell managed to get off in reply. Campbell went down hard, his aorta severed by a slug. Then Boyd fell, too, hit on the left side of his head.

Clyde and Henry stood over the fallen town cops. Cal Campbell was dead or dying, but Percy Boyd's head wound was superficial. The bullet had only stunned him, and he was able to get to his feet as his assailants took him prisoner. After Grapevine, Clyde was taking no chances with Henry. He sternly ordered him to help Boyd back to their Ford sedan. Percy Boyd was going to be a hostage, not another corpse.

While Henry dragged Boyd toward the car, Clyde noticed several onlookers. They lived in nearby farmhouses, and had come outside when they heard the shooting. Clyde waved his BAR in the direction of several gawking men and yelled, "Boys, one good man has already been killed, and if you don't follow orders, others are liable to be." He commanded them to help push the Ford out of the muddy ditch. Bonnie got behind the wheel while Clyde, Henry, the onlookers, and even Percy Boyd, still bleeding from his head wound, tried to extricate the car from the mud. They heaved many times, but the sedan wouldn't budge. Clyde kept saying he would kill everyone if they didn't get his car out of the ditch. There was sporadic traffic on the road and when a few drivers stopped to see what was going on, Clyde pointed his BAR at them and made them get out and help, too. But the Ford stayed stuck until a local man named Charlie Dobson came by in a truck. He had a length of chain, and Clyde made him use it to tie the Ford to the truck. Then Dobson gunned his heavy vehicle and the Ford was hauled out of the ditch and back onto the road. The entire car was crusted with mud. Staring through the streaky windows, people saw that the woman in its front seat was wearing a red tam. She moved over to let Clyde drive. Henry Methvin motioned with his BAR for Percy Boyd to get in the back seat, then climbed in beside him. Clyde raced the Ford west down the road. It had been almost forty minutes since Boyd and Campbell arrived on the scene.

Clyde soon turned north, intending to cross the Oklahoma state line into Kansas. He hadn't gone three miles when he found the road blocked—not by police, but by the battered car of two local farmers who'd also gotten stuck in the mud. Clyde exaggerated slightly as he screamed, "We've just killed two men and we're in a hurry. The law is after us." The farmers were duly intimidated, but they still couldn't get their car unstuck. So Clyde and Henry got out of their car and helped pry the other vehicle free. Bonnie stayed in the Ford with their prisoner. She held a shotgun on her lap.

Percy Boyd expected to die. He'd heard all the bulletins the day before about the Barrow Gang being somewhere in Oklahoma, and since his three captors included a young woman it was easy to guess who they were. He asked Henry Methvin, "Is that Clyde Barrow?" and Henry nodded. Nervously, Boyd did his best to make friends with his captors. When Boyd promised he wouldn't try anything, Clyde snapped back, "I don't care what you do, we'll shoot you anyway." It was an attempt at intimidation rather than a promise. If Clyde planned to kill Boyd he would have done it back in Commerce. Boyd felt somewhat comforted when Bonnie made small talk. She examined the police chief's head wound and asked Clyde to stop when they passed a stream so she could wash out the cut. Bonnie even found some spare cloth for a makeshift bandage. After two years on the run with Clyde, she had plenty of experience in rudimentary treatment of gunshot wounds.

Clyde cruised west for a while after crossing into Kansas, then back east and north. Sometimes he'd stop and park a while. Boyd was never quite sure who Henry Methvin was, but since he was certain about the identities of Clyde and Bonnie he asked what happened in Grapevine. Clyde lied, saying they'd been nowhere near the murder site and only learned what happened to the two motorcycle cops when they read about it in the newspaper. Then, warming to his captive, Clyde talked about the previous April's shootout in Joplin. He told Boyd that if the cops there had just acted right, nothing would have happened to them. Clyde even complimented Boyd on his shooting, saying that during the morning gunfight he heard one of the police chief's bullets "zip close."

The day wore on. The only possible pursuit the fugitives noticed was a plane flying overhead. They stopped once for gas, and another time in the afternoon so Clyde could break into a gum machine and steal change. Boyd had $25 with him, but Clyde didn't want it. Using some of the change from the gum machine, Henry Methvin went into a diner in Fort Scott, Kansas, and bought food to bring back to the car. They parked on a road outside town and ate.

Clyde and Bonnie were concerned that Boyd's shirt was stained with blood from his head wound, so they rummaged in their luggage and found a new shirt to give him. Then they also gave the police chief a tie, and told Henry Methvin to hand over his suit coat when Clyde's was too small to fit Boyd. Fed and dressed in new finery, Boyd was released around midnight in the country southeast of Fort Scott.

During his daylong ordeal, Boyd had developed a special fondness for Bonnie. From their conversation he was convinced she and Clyde had never set out to deliberately kill any lawmen. True, they'd shot down Cal Campbell that morning, but Cal pulled his gun and fired first. Boyd thought that if his partner hadn't acted so foolishly, nobody would have been hurt. Bonnie had even asked Boyd for a favor: if they were caught or killed while Boyd was with them, would he please see that Sonny Boy the rabbit was delivered to her mother?

As soon as he showed up safe and relatively sound, Boyd knew, reporters would swarm in for interviews. So as Boyd got out of the Ford sedan he asked, "Bonnie, what do you want me to tell the press?"

It was a tremendous opportunity for the Barrow Gang to bolster their public image. In the five days since the Grapevine shootings, they'd been vilified in print and in newsreels as cold-blooded executioners of brave lawmen. Here was another cop, one who could testify to good treatment at their hands, asking what message they would like him to pass along to the public. Every newspaper in the country would print whatever Boyd had to say.

Bonnie wanted to contradict the part of her image that bothered her most. "Tell them I don't smoke cigars," she instructed the police chief. After he trudged back into Fort Scott, phoned for help, and was driven home to Commerce, Boyd dutifully gave Bonnie's message to reporters. Bonnie was thrilled when almost every story about the gang's latest cop killing mentioned it.

CHAPTER 31

The Letters of April

Raymond Hamilton had been unfairly linked in 1932 to the murder of John Bucher in Hillsboro, Texas. Two years later, he wasn't going to let the same thing happen again. As with the Bucher slaying, Raymond hadn't been anywhere near the scene when Clyde and his cohorts shot down H. D. Murphy and E. B. Wheeler in Grapevine and Cal Campbell in Commerce. But the media and most lawmen—the Hamer posse knew better—believed he was still part of the Barrow Gang when those murders occurred. On April 7, the day after Cal Campbell died, Raymond sat down in the New Orleans hotel where he was lying low with Mary O'Dare and wrote a letter to Dallas lawyer A. S. Basket, who'd represented him several times in court:

> Dear Mr. Basket,
>
> I am sending you a bill from a hotel I was staying at the time of that killing in Commerce, Oklahoma. I haven't been with Clyde Barrow since the Lancaster bank robbery. I'm sending you one hundred dollars and want this put before

public and proved right away. . . . I want you to let the public and the whole world know I am not with Clyde Barrow, and don't go his speed. I'm a lone man and intend to stay that way. . . . I was in Houston Wed. night April 4 and have been here [New Orleans] since then, even April fifth.

Yours Truly
Raymond Hamilton

The letter was written on stationery of the Lafayette Hotel in New Orleans. Raymond enclosed not only a hundred-dollar bill, but also a hotel receipt that he had decorated with an inky fingerprint.

Basket knew exactly what to do with it. Raymond's letter was published on April 9 in the *Dallas Morning News* and caused considerable speculation: if Raymond wasn't the other man with Clyde and Bonnie in Grapevine and Commerce, then who was? Even Percy Boyd had assumed his third captor was Raymond Hamilton. Boyd told reporters that Clyde and Bonnie never addressed the fellow by his given name—they called him "Boodles."

Clyde was predictably aggravated by Raymond's letter. He probably learned about it in Tulsa, Oklahoma, where he, Bonnie, and Henry Methvin were hiding out after releasing Percy Boyd. The Tulsa stopover was a break from Barrow Gang tradition. Instead of waiting out the post-Commerce heat in some backwoods camp, they holed up in a small house owned by Joe and Willis Newton, brothers who were notorious train robbers. Clyde had apparently met them sometime earlier. His mood following the Commerce gunfight was remarkably upbeat. For one thing, the events in Grapevine and Commerce had convinced Clyde that Henry Methvin would never betray him. After all, Henry had participated in the highly publicized murders of three lawmen. If the gang was captured, Henry's date with the electric chair would be just as certain as Clyde's.

It's possible that Clyde may have felt cocky enough to write one or two letters of his own that month. The first that has been widely attributed to him was addressed on April 3 to Amon Carter, publisher-editor of the *Fort Worth Star-Telegram.* In the wake of the Grapevine murders, the newspaper had crammed its pages with graphic, inaccurate stories about Bonnie's role in the killings, always citing the cigar clenched between her teeth as she blew the two motorcycle cops to pieces. The letter advised Carter to "think, decide and make up your mind and not let your Editor make another remark about Bonnie like you did the other day. They called her a cigar-smoking woman. Another remark about my underworld mate and I will end such men as you mighty quick. I know where you and your reporters live."

Clyde's objection to Bonnie's description as a cigar smoker rings true, but the rest of the letter doesn't. It uses a coarse obscenity in describing the couple's sex life and concludes that "men ought to abuse lots of women because they don't respect the men in the city or country either." Clyde wasn't given to graphic descriptions of his and Bonnie's lovemaking, and he was always respectful of, and chivalrous with, women. But Amon Carter, at least, believed Clyde wrote the letter, and also that the famous killer was ready to carry out his threat. Carter ordered his reporters not to refer to Bonnie in print as a cigar smoker, and only rescinded the edict after she and Clyde were dead.

The second letter reputed to have been written by Clyde in April 1934 has slightly better odds of authenticity. On the 13th, Henry Ford received a letter at his corporate office in Detroit. Its postmark indicated that it had been mailed on April 10 from Tulsa. The short missive read:

> Dear Sir:
>
> While I still have got breath in my lungs I will tell you what a dandy car you make. I have drove Fords exclusivly when I could get away with one. For sustained speed and freedom from trouble the Ford has got ever other car skinned, and even if my business hasen't been strickly legal it don't hurt anything to tell you what a fine car you got in the V-8.
>
> Yours truly
> Clyde Champion Barrow

The letter sounds like Clyde—writing a fan letter to Henry Ford would have appealed to his sense of humor. The spelling and grammatical errors are appropriate to Clyde's limited education, and the date of the mailing and the Tulsa postmark jibe with where Clyde was at the time. But after Ford made the letter public, Clyde's family swore it wasn't authentic because of its signature—"Clyde Champion Barrow." Clyde had entered "Champion" as his middle name on Huntsville records when he entered prison in 1930. His real middle name was "Chestnut." In any case, Ford had his secretary draft a thank-you note, which was mailed to Clyde via General Delivery in Tulsa. By the time it arrived, Clyde, Bonnie, and Henry Methvin had moved on.

They surfaced on Monday, April 16, when they robbed the First National Bank in the west Iowa town of Stuart, not far from Dexfield Park. Clyde and Henry walked into the bank lobby just after 9 A.M., told two cashiers and a customer to sit on the floor, and stuffed about $1,500 in bills and change into a bag. It was one of the few times that Clyde pulled off a relatively substantial bank job without Raymond Hamilton there to help him. Clyde and Henry ran outside to where witnesses reported a woman was waiting in a car. The gang's getaway wasn't quite clean—some Stuart residents chased after them in two cars, but lost the Barrow Gang after a few miles. From there, Clyde drove back to Texas. He and Bonnie hadn't seen their families since March 27, before the debacle in Grapevine. Henry Methvin was sent ahead by train to alert the Barrows and Parkers about meeting in the countryside outside Dallas, probably on the night of April 18.

As soon as the fugitives reunited with their families, Bonnie gave Sonny Boy the rabbit to Emma. "Keep him away from the cops," she cautioned her mother. "He's been in two gun battles and he'll land at Huntsville if the law finds it out." But Emma and the rest of the Barrows and Parkers weren't in the mood for jokes. Everyone thought Clyde and Bonnie looked terrible, drained and prematurely aged from constant stress. Food was passed around. Even though Cumie was still distraught over the stories about the bereaved fiancée of highway patrolman Murphy, she brought the food Clyde loved, including fried chicken. Clyde spent several minutes raging that Henry shouldn't have killed the two highway patrolmen at Grapevine. He called it "a damn fool stunt," and Emma Parker felt he was less upset that two men died than the fact that Henry Methvin had misinterpreted an order. Bonnie calmed Clyde down by saying that whatever was done, was done. He might as well let it go. Henry was apologetic—he made a point of assuring Emma that he, not Bonnie, fired the fatal shots.

Someone suggested that Clyde and Bonnie leave the United States for Mexico, where they might be able to avoid arrest and extradition to Texas. At first, Clyde didn't respond directly. Instead, he mentioned how he and Bonnie still said their prayers, especially whenever they approached "a place where there may be a trap." Then he said they would never flee the country because, besides their love for each other, seeing their families was all they had left. "We're staying close to home and we're coming in as long as we're alive," Clyde declared.

Then he brought up another subject, something he'd never mentioned before. Life in West Dallas was getting harder for the Barrows and Parkers, Clyde said. Harassment there by reporters and police had become commonplace. But he and Bonnie had found this wonderful community in Louisiana where Henry Methvin's family lived. Clyde said he planned to buy land there. The West Dallas Barrows and Parkers could use the property for long visits, and at night he and Bonnie would slip in to see them. The response he received was more polite than enthusiastic. No one asked where Clyde thought he could get the money to purchase property. He and Bonnie had trouble stealing enough just to cover their daily expenses. But it was nice to see Clyde and Bonnie excited about something even if it was so far-fetched, Emma said later, so "we let them plan."

By the time they met with their families in mid-April, Clyde's sister Marie wrote in her memoir, he and Bonnie were finally aware that they were being tracked by Frank Hamer. It would have been impossible for Hamer to keep his activities secret forever, but after Grapevine and the resulting pressure from various government agencies and business organizations, Hamer had been more open about his mission. The former Ranger captain gave interviews to Oklahoma newspapers after the murder of Cal Campbell and kidnapping of Percy Boyd. Apparently, he even began poking around West Dallas, not caring anymore who might alert Clyde or his family. Clyde wasn't especially worried. He and Bonnie already had a lot of people after them. As far as they were concerned one more, even a legendary figure like Hamer, hardly made much difference.

Clyde and Bonnie met several more times with their families over the next few weeks. They apparently also made a short visit to the Methvins in Bienville Parish. Texas prison general manager Lee Simmons told reporters later that it was April 22 when Henry learned from his father that a deal with Hamer and the state of Texas was in place. But the trip must have been too whirlwind for the Methvins to pass along word to Bienville Parish sheriff Henderson Jordan that Clyde and Bonnie were there. The Methvins' task was further complicated because the couple didn't still sleep in the Cole house as Henry's father, Ivy, had hoped. That would have allowed Ivy to tell Jordan exactly where the couple could be found. Instead, Clyde and Bonnie alternated spending the night between several different spots in the Louisiana backwoods, and some of these were as much as seventy-five miles or more from Bienville Parish. It was going to be more difficult than anticipated, if not impossible, for Henry's family to put Clyde and Bonnie "on the spot" in a convenient place so Hamer could sneak up on them while they slept.

In late April, Clyde, Bonnie, and Henry drove to Missouri and picked up Joe Palmer in Joplin. Palmer had traveled there after being left behind in West Dallas following the Grapevine murders. He wasn't upset with them for driving away without him. Palmer's connection to the gang was always sporadic. He and Clyde were pleased when news reached them of the arrest of another occasional Barrow Gang member. Raymond Hamilton was back in custody.

After more than three weeks of staying out of sight with Mary O'Dare, Raymond was broke again. He and his girlfriend wanted to move to California for a while. The obvious way for Raymond to bankroll their relocation was to knock off a bank, so around April 23 he and Mary came back to Texas. She stayed in Amarillo while Raymond and a new partner named Teddy Brooks went to Lewisville, a town about twenty-five miles north of Dallas. On the morning of April 25, Raymond robbed the First National Bank there while Brooks waited behind the wheel of their getaway car. They drove away with about $1,000, but Teddy Brooks couldn't handle a car nearly as well as Clyde Barrow. Area police erected a series of roadblocks, and Raymond and Brooks were cornered. They gave up without a fight. Raymond told his captors, "Don't shoot, boys. I'm fresh out of guns, ammo, whiskey and women." Then, almost preening, he asked, "Do you know who you've got?" They did. The next day, Raymond was back in a Dallas cell.

Clyde couldn't resist. Even the most otherwise skeptical members of his family later agreed that he wrote the letter delivered to Raymond at the jail. Bonnie undoubtedly helped—the lengthy message was typed, and lots of words were set off by the quotation marks she loved using in her poems:

> Raymond Hamilton
> 505 Main Street
> c/o Dallas County Jail
> Dallas, Texas
>
> Raymond:
> I'm very sorry to hear of your getting captured, but due to the fact you offered no resistance, sympathy is lacking. The most I can do is hope you miss the "chair." The purpose of this letter is to remind you of all the "dirty deals" you have pulled. When I came to the farm after you I thought maybe the "joint" had changed you from a boastful punk. However I learned too soon the mistake I had made.

Clyde made reference to Raymond's threat in January to shoot Joe Palmer while he slept in the car, to Raymond's "Prostitute Sweetheart," and noted that "I don't claim to be too smart. I know that some day they will get me but it won't be without resistance." The letter closed by assuring Raymond that "you can never expect the least of sympathy or assistance from me." It was signed "So long—Clyde Barrow."

The envelope was postmarked from Memphis, Tennessee, where Clyde, Bonnie, Henry Methvin, and Joe Palmer were treating themselves to a short vacation. While they were there, Bonnie bought Palmer a new suit. He probably wore it on May 3 when the gang robbed the Farmer's Trust and Savings Bank in Everly, Iowa. Clyde and Palmer went inside while Bonnie and Henry waited. They emerged with about $700, not a bad take but much less than the $2,000 initially reported in the press.

The gang escaped in a magnificent new Ford V-8 sedan stolen in Topeka, Kansas, on April 29 from the home of Ruth and Jesse Warren. The Ford was Cordoba gray, an odd tint that often reflected red or tan in different angles to the sun. It was the last car the Barrow Gang stole, just as Farmer's Trust and Savings was the last bank they ever robbed.

CHAPTER 32

The Noose Tightens

April was a hard month for the lawmen pursuing Clyde and Bonnie. In Dallas County, newspapers openly mocked Sheriff Smoot Schmid. Two cartoon punch lines read, "Clyde and Bonnie give Smoot Schmid twenty-four hours to get out of town" and "Clyde and Bonnie let Smoot Schmid get away again." Schmid was up for reelection in the fall. Defeat would completely crush his hopes of being elected to state office someday. He'd placed two of his deputies, Bob Alcorn and Ted Hinton, with Frank Hamer's posse, but Schmid couldn't afford to wait and see whether Hamer caught the Barrow Gang. Even if Hamer did, Schmid wouldn't get much, if any, credit. The Dallas County sheriff still hoped for the recognition, the glory, that would come to whoever finally brought down Clyde Barrow and Bonnie Parker.

So, in April, Schmid stepped up harassment of the Barrows living in West Dallas, and of their friends as well. Clyde loved his family—it was one of the few human traits for which the sheriff gave him credit. Maybe if Clyde's people complained to him, he'd be reckless enough to storm back home and leave himself open to capture.

So Clyde's brother L.C., his sister Marie's boyfriend Joe Bill Francis, and Steve Davis, husband of Raymond Hamilton's mother, Alice, were all repeatedly hauled off to the Dallas County jail and held for days at a time. Often, the charge against them was "investigation," which in 1934 Texas was not considered a violation of civil rights. Their families were not allowed to see or communicate with them while they were in custody. Once even Cumie Barrow was arrested. Nobody believed Clyde's fifty-nine-year-old mother had committed any offense beyond loving her wayward son. She was released after a few hours of questioning.

On April 18, Schmid finally tapped the phone at the Barrow family service station. The tap lasted only through April 30. Schmid didn't glean any crucial new information from it—the Barrows and Parkers had long assumed their phone conversations were being monitored, so they continued using the codes they'd invented. Whenever Cumie called her hairdresser daughter, Nell, or Emma Parker with an invitation to dinner that included beans, it meant Clyde had left one of his Coke bottle messages asking for a family meeting that night. Typical was a coded conversation on April 26 that a sheriff's department secretary transcribed in ungrammatical fashion:

> Mrs. B. called Nellie said what are you going to do tonite? She said I've got a down head of hair to curl at 6:00 p.m. and it will be too late to do anything when I get through with that. Mrs. B. said I wish you would come out I've got a big pot full of beans and some corn bread. Nellie said maybe I'll get through in time to come out a little while.

Sometimes, Cumie would pass along messages from "Mr. Howard"—that was Clyde, using his hero Jesse James's favorite alias. But mostly the phone tap picked up teenaged Marie chattering with girlfriends about going to the show or dancing, and Cumie and Emma Parker mournfully discussing their stress-filled lives. Bonnie's younger sister, Billie Jean, had just left Dallas to live and work anonymously in East Texas because she was sick of all the negative attention. Emma was heartbroken, but she understood. On April 30, Cumie called to commiserate:

> Mrs. P. said she had been writing Billie a letter Mrs. B said what did you do tell her to come home Mrs. P. said I sure would like to have her here but I am not going to tell her that I am lone some.

Mostly, the phone tap logs reveal two families succumbing to unrelenting tension. Even Marie interrupted gossiping with friends to complain that the police wouldn't allow her to see L.C. in the county jail. She described how, on a date with Joe Bill Francis, she was left to walk home alone after he was pulled in for investigation. There was also a great deal of drinking going on. Bonnie's brother, Buster, was one of the worst culprits, but even stoic Henry Barrow wasn't immune to seeking temporary oblivion through alcohol. On April 28, Nell lost her temper with her mother about it:

> Nellie called B. Buster ans. She asked to speak to mama. Mrs. B. ans. Nell said who was that ans? B. said it was Buster. Nell said well what was the matter with him? B. said he is drunk and your dady is too. Nell said he has got no business ans the phone why don't you run him off? B. said I can't afford to do that. . . . Nell said well I've been busy as the devil all day. I'll see you tomorrow.

Despite everything, Cumie hadn't entirely lost her trademark feistiness. On April 28, Mary O'Dare—who'd been picked up by police in Amarillo after Raymond Hamilton's arrest—arrived in Dallas while free on bond. Cumie and Emma Parker speculated in a long conversation that Mary must have betrayed Raymond to the cops. It was one of the few times the phone tap caught someone directly mentioning Clyde and Bonnie:

> [Cumie Barrow] said [Mary O'Dare] tried to get the kids caught when she was with them and finally got Raymond caught. Said she made the remark when she left C&B that she would get them caught before it was all over. [Mrs. P] said if you let her come in your house I'll never come to see you again. B. said I've got a big iron here if she starts in my house I am going to hit her over the head with it. Said I am not going to let that dam hussy sit her foot in (my) house.

On May 1 Schmid discontinued the phone tap. He'd learned about Marie's tastes in fashion, but not how he might get the jump on Clyde and Bonnie. It seemed that Schmid's best hope for even reflected glory would come if Hamer, with the assistance of Schmid's two Dallas County deputies, somehow managed to catch the Barrow Gang instead.

By the end of April, Hamer and his posse were frustrated, too. Ted Hinton wrote later that they'd trailed Clyde and Bonnie through "the swamps in the Louisiana back country and the smoky hills of Arkansas." They'd glimpsed them, then lost them, in Durant, Oklahoma. "If we were accomplishing anything—and most of the time it was difficult to convince ourselves that we were—it was that we were keeping them on the run," Hinton wrote in his memoir, *Ambush*. "But each time we seemed to have placed them in a definite area, reports would come of crimes committed at some distant point outside the area where they were last seen."

But Frank Hamer hadn't told the other posse members about his new plan. There were now two constants in the Barrow Gang's movements. They often came to see their families in West Dallas. It was clear they couldn't be taken quickly or cleanly there. And, since February, Clyde and Bonnie had kept returning to Bienville Parish. It was too bad they camped at night in a variety of locations rather than sleeping at the old Cole place, where they could have been easily trapped. But the logistics of the area, at least, gave Clyde no choice but to drive to get-togethers with the Methvin family on narrow roads far from any towns. In most places, these roads were lined with thick brush—it was impossible to see much on either side. If getting the drop on Clyde and Bonnie while they slept wasn't feasible, maybe an ambush was. The key was making the outlaw couple feel safe enough in Bienville Parish to let their guards down. Speaking several months later to *American Detective* magazine, Texas prison system manager Lee Simmons explained that Hamer deliberately made his posse's presence obvious in Oklahoma, Arkansas, Missouri, and Texas so that Bienville Parish "began to loom before [Clyde and Bonnie] as a haven, which was exactly what Hamer had planned."

Ted Hinton, Bob Alcorn, and perhaps even Manny Gault (among the posse members, Hamer had the closest relationship with the former Ranger) thought they were fruitlessly chasing the Barrow Gang around several states. Hamer knew better—but he was basing his strategy on someone who wasn't trustworthy. According to Hamer, Bienville Parish sheriff Henderson Jordan had promised to cooperate exclusively with him. Whenever Henry Methvin's father, Ivy, or Methvin family friend John Joyner tipped Jordan that the Barrow Gang might be taken by surprise in some spot or another, Hamer expected

Jordan to summon him and his posse immediately. Jordan did stay in touch with Hamer, frequently phoning him with updates. But he stayed in contact with Justice Department Division of Investigation Special Agent L. A. Kindell in New Orleans, too, and when, during the second week in April, John Joyner informed Jordan that Clyde and Bonnie were expected by the Methvins on April 13, Jordan invited Kindell instead of Hamer to come to Arcadia and help organize an ambush. Kindell showed up with an army of agents, but at the last minute Joyner arrived to say that the Barrow Gang's visit had been called off.

Sometime later in April, Hamer and Jordan's phone conversations began to focus on where in Bienville Parish an ambush could be set. Hamer expected Ivy Methvin to be actively involved. If the Methvin family invited Clyde and Bonnie to meet somewhere at a specific place and time, then Hamer could set up his ambush to surprise Clyde en route. But Ivy Methvin balked. Clyde was too smart to get surprised like that, he told Jordan. If the law tried a roadside ambush, Clyde would smell it out, somehow avoid it, and then kill everybody involved, including all the Methvins. The deal as the Methvins understood it was just to tip off Jordan when the Barrow Gang was staying in the area. Jordan told Ivy Methvin that "[you] had agreed to help us, and [you are] going to do that." Otherwise, there'd be no Texas pardon for Ivy's son Henry. Ivy Methvin accepted his new responsibility, though he made it clear he wasn't happy about it.

The logistics of Hamer's new roadside ambush plan were different from those for taking the couple by surprise in a camp. If Clyde was driving his usual Ford V-8 when Hamer's posse sprang its ambush, relatively low-caliber bullets from their current weapons would bounce right off the vehicle's doors. Heavier ordnance was needed. Hamer, Lee Simmons, or Smoot Schmid contacted Weldon Dowis, the commander of the Texas National Guard unit with jurisdiction over the state armory in Dallas, and asked that two BARs be loaned to the posse. It was always simple for Clyde to break into armories and steal all the BARs he wanted, but Dowis didn't make it easy for the lawmen to be similarly armed. He said the weapons in the armory's arsenal were for Guard, not civilian, use and turned down the request. But after Texas congressman Hatton Sumners intervened, Dowis reluctantly issued a pair of BARs to Hamer and his men. He said decades later that he had to teach the lawmen how to shoot them—the BARs were so powerful that they required a much stronger grip than ordinary rifles.

Hamer was confident that Clyde and Bonnie would come back to Bienville Parish in May. He had the firepower and the general location for staging his ambush. Now all he needed was a specific place and time.

CHAPTER 33

Final Meetings

After robbing the bank in Everly, Iowa, on May 3, Clyde, Bonnie, and Henry Methvin returned to Bienville Parish. Joe Palmer didn't go with them—he went north to Chicago because he wanted to attend the World's Fair there. When they arrived back in northwest Louisiana, Clyde and Bonnie resumed spending their days driving around the heavily wooded backcountry, often taking evening meals with various Methvins. They still camped out at night in a series of different spots. Only the two of them knew where or how many. Otherwise, Frank Hamer's strategy to lull them into a false sense of security obviously worked. The couple made no attempt to keep their presence a secret from parish residents. They offered local kids rides in their gleaming car, regularly patronized Ma Canfield's café in Gibsland—Clyde would carry Bonnie inside—and rewarded service station attendants with candy bars for filling the tank of the Ford V-8.

On Sunday, May 6, Clyde and Bonnie drove four hours west from Gibsland for another family gathering on the outskirts of Dallas. Henry Methvin apparently didn't come with them—recalling the get-together years later, none of the surviving Barrows or Parkers mentioned that he was present. Henry and his own parents undoubtedly had a lot to discuss while Clyde and Bonnie were away on their brief trip to Texas.

According to Emma Parker, Bonnie was in a contemplative mood while she and Clyde were with their loved ones that night. She pulled her mother aside, sat with Emma on the grass, and quietly asked that she be taken home rather than to a funeral parlor after she died. Emma was appalled and tried to shush her daughter, but Bonnie insisted on sharing a whole scenario she'd worked out. Her body must lie in state in the Parkers' front room, with her mother, brother, Buster, and sister, Billie Jean, sitting beside it—"A long, cool, peaceful night together before I leave you." There was no sense pretending it wouldn't happen soon, Bonnie added. Everyone knew what was coming. Realizing her mother's penchant for blaming Bonnie's troubles on the poor example set by Clyde, Bonnie also made Emma swear that in the future she'd never "say anything ugly" about him. It was a promise Emma wouldn't keep. Finally, Bonnie presented her mother with a poem she had recently written called "The End of the Line." In a matter of weeks, Emma would give a copy to a reporter, resulting in hundreds of newspapers reprinting the work that would become popularly known as "The Story of Bonnie and Clyde."

Bonnie Parker wasn't a gifted poet. She had a stuttering sense of rhythm and frequently indulged in overblown imagery. Some of those flaws are present in "The End of the Line," but this time she got almost everything right. Crafting the sixteen-stanza poem must have been cathartic for Bonnie. She tried to cram everything in—frustration with the Barrow Gang being blamed for crimes they didn't commit; scorn for the media; pride in the refusal of her hometown slum residents to cooperate with police; and the certainty that she and Clyde would pay for their crimes with their lives. The infamous Lindbergh kidnapping is also cited. "The End of the Line" sometimes smacks of self-pity; it reveals considerable self-awareness also. Even though the overall tone is resigned, Bonnie's sense of humor is also evident. "The End of the Line" includes Clyde suggesting that they find employment through the NRA. Bonnie was probably referring to the National Recovery Administration, which had received considerable recent publicity for enforcing collective bargaining rights for unions, setting maximum work hours, and mandating a minimum wage.

THE END OF THE LINE

You've read the story of Jesse James—
Of how he lived and died;
If you're still in need
Of something to read
Here's the story of Bonnie and Clyde.

Now Bonnie and Clyde are the Barrow gang.
I'm sure you all have read
How they rob and steal
And those who squeal
Are usually found dying or dead.

There's lots of untruths to those write-ups;
They're not so ruthless as that;
Their nature is raw;
They hate the law—
The stool pigeons, spotters, and rats.

They call them cold-blooded killers;
They say they are heartless and mean;
But I say this with pride,
That I once knew Clyde
When he was honest and upright and clean.

But the laws fooled around,
Kept taking him down
And locking him up in a cell,
Till he said to me,
"I'll never be free,
So I'll meet a few of them in hell."

The road was so dimly lighted;
There were no highway signs to guide;
But they made up their minds
If all roads were blind,
They wouldn't give up till they died.

The road gets dimmer and dimmer;
Sometimes you can hardly see;
But it's fight, man to man,
And do all you can,
For they know they can never be free.

From heart-break some people have suffered;
From weariness some people have died;
But take all in all,
Our troubles are small
Till we get like Bonnie and Clyde.

If a policeman is killed in Dallas,
And they have no clue or guide;
If they can't find a fiend,
They just wipe their slate clean
And hang it on Bonnie and Clyde.

There's two crimes committed in America,
Not accredited to the Barrow mob;
They had no hand
In the kidnap demand,
Nor the Kansas City Depot job.

A newsboy once said to his buddy:
"I wish old Clyde would get jumped;
In these awful hard times
We'd make a few dimes
If five or six cops would get bumped."

The police haven't got the report yet
But Clyde called me up today;
He said, "Don't start any fights—
We aren't working nights—
We're joining the NRA."

From Irving to the West Dallas viaduct
Is known as the Great Divide,
Where the women are kin,

And the men are men,
And they won't "stool" on Bonnie and Clyde.

If they try to act like citizens
And rent them a nice little flat,
About the third night
They're invited to fight
By a sub-gun's rat-tat-tat.

They don't think they're too smart or desperate,
They know the law always wins;
They've been shot at before,
But they do not ignore
That death is the wages of sin.

Some day they'll go down together;
And they'll bury them side by side,
To a few it'll be grief—
To the law a relief—
But it's death for Bonnie and Clyde.

After about two hours, Clyde and Bonnie said they had to leave. They promised they'd return in a few weeks. But the next night Clyde was back in West Dallas, arriving alone after dark at the Barrow family service station on Eagle Ford Road. This wasn't unprecedented. Clyde occasionally visited his parents without bringing Bonnie along. On Monday night, May 7, only Henry Barrow was home, and Clyde asked his father to meet him a block west from the busy road where a side street intersected with the Texas and Pacific railroad tracks. He drove ahead—just in case the police were waiting to pounce and he had to race away, Clyde didn't want Henry stuck in the car with him—and waited while Henry walked over. Then Clyde told his father he had some papers he wanted to sign and leave with him. He didn't say what kind of papers they were, and taciturn Henry didn't ask. Since Henry was illiterate, he couldn't read them anyway. The father held a flashlight as his son rummaged around the Ford's crowded back seat. No matter what car Clyde might be driving, there was always a lot piled there—suitcases, the latest true crime magazines and newspapers with stories about the Barrow Gang, Bonnie's typewriter, the saxophone

Clyde acquired after leaving his guitar behind in the April 1933 flight from Joplin—because there was never room for baggage in the trunk. That's where Clyde stored the gang's arsenal of BARs, handguns, ammunition, and loose license plates to switch onto the next cars he stole. Clyde pulled things out, balancing them on the car's running board, until he finally found the right suitcase. He rested it on the hood of the Ford, opened it, and removed two sheets of paper. After he signed them and added his thumbprint, he told Henry, they should be given to his mother, Cumie. She'd know what to do with them. But the pen Clyde took from his pocket was out of ink, and it was the only one he had brought with him. Henry didn't carry a pen—he never wrote anything, so he didn't need one. Clyde put the papers back in the suitcase and said that signing them could wait. He'd do it when he and Bonnie came back for their next visit. Then Clyde chatted with his father for a while until finally he decided they'd been out in the open long enough. Clyde said goodbye to Henry and drove away.

Henry told Cumie about the mysterious papers. She wrote in her unpublished memoir that he had "gained the impression it involved some land or money." Just a few weeks earlier at their family gathering in mid-April, Clyde had talked about buying property in Louisiana. The rest of the Barrows and Emma Parker privately considered that unlikely—where in the world could Clyde and Bonnie get enough money for something like that? But now they apparently had. When Clyde opened the suitcase, Henry said he saw it contained stacks of currency as well as the papers to be signed. As improbable as it seemed to his parents, after more than two years of eking out a scant illegal living, Clyde was suddenly flush with cash. Henry and Cumie wanted to ask their son where the money had come from, but they never got the chance.

CHAPTER 34

A New Line of Work

The Eastham Prison Farm breakout on January 16, 1934, that freed Raymond Hamilton, Joe Palmer, Henry Methvin, and Hilton Bybee had made front-page headlines for weeks. The remote, well-guarded farm property was believed by prison officials and the public to be invulnerable to attack. The relatively simple scheme Raymond Hamilton hatched with his brother Floyd—smuggle in two guns, have a getaway car parked nearby—proved otherwise, but nobody realized it was the Hamilton brothers' plan. Clyde was given complete if undeserved credit for masterminding a supposedly impossible feat. The media had proclaimed his genius for planning jail breaks, and a month later when someone organized a daring escape for several inmates in the Kansas state prison in Lansing, newspapers speculated that Clyde Barrow probably was behind that one, too. He wasn't—Clyde had spent February on the move with Bonnie, Raymond, Henry Methvin, and Joe Palmer—but the belief spread anyway: Clyde Barrow not only robbed banks, he could break anyone out of any prison. And that caught the attention of O. D. Stevens, who very much wanted to get out of jail in Fort Worth before a jury there could sentence him to the electric chair. The day after Clyde's death, U.S. Marshal J. R. "Red" Wright told the *Dallas Dispatch* that authorities had learned Clyde agreed sometime in early 1934 to break Stevens and two partners out of the Tarrant County jail for $18,000.

Stevens, thirty-eight, was a Fort Worth criminal kingpin, dealing hard drugs such as morphine, heroin, and cocaine and leading a well-organized, highly successful gang. On February 21, 1933, Stevens orchestrated the theft of $72,000 from Fort Worth's Texas & Pacific railroad station. Three masked men participated in the holdup itself, but they were only part of a wider plan. The loot had to be laundered elsewhere—Stevens handled that—and then he and partners W. D. May and M. T. Howard allegedly increased their shares of the take by murdering the original trio of bandits. Bloody clothing found floating in the Trinity River outside Fort Worth led police to the wife of one of the victims, whose testimony soon implicated Stevens, May, and Howard. They were arrested in July, and from the moment he was locked up, Stevens began financing attempts to help him and his two partners escape. He managed to have hacksaw blades smuggled in at least twice, but jailors discovered them before he could saw through the bars of his cell. The three men's murder trial was delayed while officials investigated some of Stevens's other alleged crimes, and April 1934 found him in isolation lockdown, secured to his cell wall by a neck collar and chain because he was so obviously determined to escape. Stevens's situation was dire. He was under constant guard, and already had been sentenced to twenty-six years in prison for the Texas & Pacific robbery. His conviction for murder seemed certain; the trial was set for mid-June. The Tarrant County jail in Fort Worth was fortresslike, and it seemed impossible for anyone to break him and his two partners out of it. But, according to what Stevens heard, Clyde Barrow had pulled off at least one miraculous breakout at Eastham Prison Farm, and maybe a second one in Lansing, Kansas, too. Perhaps Clyde would be willing to attempt another in Fort Worth.

Everybody in the Dallas–Fort Worth criminal underground knew how to get in touch with Clyde. His brother L.C. and sister Marie, who both saw Clyde frequently, could be found almost every night at the Fish Trap Dance Hall in West Dallas. It must have been relatively easy for Stevens to use one of his outside contacts to carry a message to them there, asking Clyde to rescue him and his partners. Breaking well-known criminals out of a heavily guarded Fort Worth jail would have appealed to Clyde's ego. Since his own incarceration on Eastham farm he'd always liked the idea of helping inmates escape. The fact that Stevens was a drug dealer and multiple murderer apparently didn't matter to Clyde. What did was the money Stevens offered—$6,000 each for himself, May, and Howard. That was plenty for Clyde and Bonnie to realize their dream of buying land for their families in Louisiana.

Though Marshal Wright didn't reveal to the *Dallas Dispatch* reporter when or how prison officials learned of the proposed breakout, he did explain how Clyde had planned to free Stevens, May, and Howard sometime before their mid-June trial: "Barrow was to appear at night with another man under the guise of an officer seeking lodging for a prisoner. . . . Once inside the jail, they were to take charge of [the] guards and free the prisoners."

Based on when Clyde and Bonnie first discussed acquiring property in Louisiana with their families, the deal between Stevens and Clyde was in place by mid-April. But Clyde would have had some concerns—what would happen, for instance, if he died while leading the breakout attempt? While the money involved was impressive, so was the risk. Bonnie was crippled, and without Clyde she probably couldn't fend for herself. Their families deserved some kind of guaranteed compensation for all they'd suffered. Desperate and well heeled, Stevens clearly would have been open to a demand from Clyde for payment in advance. Eighteen thousand dollars in cash would pay for land in Louisiana, provide a financial safety net for Bonnie, and bankroll several weeks of downtime for Clyde, Bonnie, and Henry in Bienville Parish while Clyde hatched a plan to free Stevens, May, and Howard from the Tarrant County jail. There's evidence Clyde tried to hire outside help for the job. Several months later, Henry Methvin told Justice Department Division of Investigation Special Agent L. A. Kindell that in late April Clyde made unsuccessful attempts to contact Pretty Boy Floyd in Oklahoma, once even driving there to look for him. Pretty Boy would never have agreed to work on a long-shot prison breakout with someone he disdained so much. But it would have made sense for Clyde to try to recruit him because Pretty Boy was involved in the June 17, 1933, assault at Union Station in Kansas City that attempted to free notorious criminal Frank Nash from federal custody. Floyd and his cohorts failed, but "the Kansas City Massacre," which left three local lawmen and a federal agent dead, was widely considered the most audacious rescue attempt in modern criminal history. This was "the Kansas City Depot job" to which Bonnie referred in her poem "The End of the Line."

By the time Clyde met with his father in West Dallas on the night of May 7, it is highly likely that he had some or all of Stevens's money in hand—Henry Barrow saw wads of cash filling Clyde's open suitcase. The $700 from the Everly bank robbery on May 3 wouldn't have taken up so much space.

Identifying the papers Clyde wanted to sign in West Dallas that night is more difficult. He seemed, when he spoke to his family about the matter in mid-April, to know exactly what property in Louisiana he wanted to buy—something near where the Methvin clan lived. Though his occasional presence with Bonnie in Bienville Parish wasn't much of a secret, Clyde couldn't walk into the parish courthouse in Arcadia and file documents for a land purchase. Perhaps he planned to use a middleman like Ivy Methvin, but in that case it wouldn't have been necessary for Clyde to sign anything. One possibility is that on May 7 Clyde wanted to sign and leave with his parents a will and testament bequeathing them all of his possessions, including the large amount of cash that could not be legally connected to any robberies by the Barrow Gang. Then if he died attempting to free O. D. Stevens from the Tarrant County jail, Henry and Cumie would still be able to buy the Louisiana property. If Clyde survived, he could negotiate the purchase himself.

So during the second and third weeks in May, Clyde, Bonnie, and Henry Methvin stayed in Bienville Parish. There were no Barrow Gang robberies during that time—for a change, they didn't need the money. Clyde and Bonnie weren't foolish enough to think the local "laws" were unaware of their presence, but it must have seemed as though the parish sheriff was willing to leave them alone as long as they didn't commit any crimes in his jurisdiction.

Sheriff Henderson Jordan was certainly avoiding the Barrow Gang, but not for the reason Clyde and Bonnie probably thought. Jordan and Frank Hamer were in constant contact. Hamer undoubtedly reminded Jordan to leave the couple alone so they'd feel safe in Bienville Parish and grow careless. The former Texas Ranger captain was waiting for just the right time to strike, a moment when Clyde and Bonnie were well away from civilians and in a spot where escape was impossible. Ivy Methvin was still expected to help arrange the ambush, even though he continued irritating Sheriff Jordan with his constant whining that Clyde and Bonnie were going to find out what was going on and kill them all.

On May 9, Hamer and his posse made a quick trip to Louisiana. They probably met Jordan in Shreveport so there was less chance of being spotted by the Barrow Gang. Jordan was confident enough to tell the four lawmen from Texas that they should get ready—something might break within the next three weeks. Until then, they should wait for his call.

CHAPTER 35

Haven

With the exception of Ivy, Ava, and Henry, the rest of the Methvin clan in Bienville Parish didn't know Clyde and Bonnie were being put "on the spot." The other Methvins treated the Texas couple as honored guests. During the first three weeks in May 1934, Henry's brother Terrell and sister-in-law Emma frequently invited Clyde and Bonnie to dinner. Henry would come, too, along with Ivy and Ava. Bonnie enjoyed playing with Van and Dean, Terrell and Emma's two young daughters. Sometimes they'd vary the routine with picnics at nearby Black Lake, cooking dinner on campfires near the shore. These were happy occasions. There was no sign of the law—Henderson Jordan was keeping his distance—and Clyde and Bonnie could relax with their hosts. They seemed to enjoy these tastes of normal family life. On their first visit to Terrell and Emma's home, they saw a beautiful handmade bed in Van and Dean's room. Ivy Methvin, a talented furniture maker, had crafted the bed for his granddaughters. Clyde and Bonnie couldn't resist lying down on it. Bonnie told Terrell and Emma it was the first time they'd been in a real bed "since they didn't know when."

Clyde undoubtedly repaid the hospitality with gifts, just as he had done for anyone offering hospitality since he and Bonnie left West Dallas for lives of roving crime. Clyde's sister Marie and other Barrow family members said later that his largesse toward the Methvins included buying Ivy Methvin land and a new truck. That was an exaggeration—there's no record of Ivy acquiring property during this time, and the truck he drove was well known in the parish as a rattletrap. Had Ivy suddenly begun tooling around the local roads in a gleaming new vehicle, his neighbors would have noticed. But certainly Clyde did give various Methvins at least small sums of money. He was always generous.

The only member of the extended Methvin clan who didn't immediately take to Clyde and Bonnie was Clemmie, the wife of Henry's brother Cecil. In May 1934, Clemmie, probably in her mid- to late teens, was newly pregnant and feeling queasy. Accordingly, she didn't go to the dinners or along on the picnics, and she pleaded with Emma Methvin not to let her daughters tag along with the famous criminals. "I told her them little old kids was innocent," Clemmie recalled later. The local "laws" would come after Clyde and Bonnie sometime, she was certain, "they'd start shooting in there and kill them little girls, and [Emma] wouldn't let me keep them and I wouldn't go [to the dinners and picnics]." Sometime around the middle of May, Clemmie was dismayed when Clyde, Bonnie, and Henry showed up at her house while she was fixing supper. It was apparently a spur-of-the-moment visit, and Clemmie felt obligated to invite them in. Bonnie was too drunk to get out of the car. Clyde left her there while he and Henry joined Clemmie and Cecil for a meal of ham and corn bread. Afterward, Clyde explained that Bonnie had a hard life and was in a lot of pain, so he let her have all the whiskey she wanted. He carried Bonnie in from the car, and she was alert enough to eat some corn bread herself, asking for more to take with her when she left. Then Bonnie and Clemmie had a private chat, the kind of girl talk Bonnie rarely had the opportunity to enjoy. When Clemmie mentioned she was pregnant, Bonnie replied that she was, too. Bonnie added that, like Clemmie's, her baby was due late in the year.

This was undoubtedly wishful thinking on Bonnie's part. Both her mother and Clyde's sister Marie made it clear in their memoirs that Bonnie had been unable to conceive from the time she'd married Roy Thornton, probably due to a botched gynecological procedure. Marie also insisted that Clyde was sterile because of the unspecified illness that had hospitalized him in Dallas a decade earlier. Drunk, probably feeling sad and sentimental, confiding to Clemmie Methvin that she was pregnant, too, may have been Bonnie's way of giving herself hope of motherhood. If she just said it with enough conviction, maybe it would come true. Clemmie believed her, and told some of the other younger Methvin women. They began to plan privately among themselves—clearly, Clyde and Bonnie couldn't raise the child, being on the constant run from the law and in danger of being killed at any moment. Perhaps one of the Methvin ladies could raise the baby, or at least they could find the child a good foster home. It would mean assuming considerable responsibility, but they were glad to do it. They cared about Bonnie. Crippled and frequently drunk, she could still turn on the charm. Henry's cousin Percy recalled that Bonnie "didn't weigh but about ninety pounds, and wasn't as big as a pound of soap after a hard day's washing, and she sure was pretty." Willie Methvin, another cousin, added that his whole family "loved Bonnie and Clyde. . . . They couldn't help themselves, you know."

Ivy Methvin didn't love them, and thanks to Clyde and Bonnie's unpredictable daily movements he must have been catching hell from Sheriff Jordan. It had been two months since Ivy cut his deal with Jordan and Frank Hamer for Henry to receive a pardon from Texas in return for assistance in apprehending the couple. The agreement had become more stringent in the interim. Originally, Ivy was just supposed to slip the word to Jordan whenever he knew Clyde and Bonnie were coming to Bienville Parish. Now he was supposed to provide specific information about where they would be and when so that "the laws" could set up an ambush. That was so much easier said than done. Sometimes Ivy knew when Clyde and Bonnie were coming to have dinner with various Methvins, or when they'd join some of the family for picnics at Black Lake. But those weren't the right times and places to tip off Jordan for an ambush. Ivy was betraying Clyde and Bonnie to save his son Henry, not to get more of his family in the line of any fire.

Hamer and his posse could still have jumped the couple on their way to Methvin family get-togethers, but that presented another problem. Most of the time, they had Henry with them, and because Clyde was obviously going to shoot rather than surrender, if Henry was present he might very well be gunned down, too. On one of the few occasions when Ivy and Ava got to talk to their boy without Clyde or Bonnie within hearing distance, they told him that he had to get away from the couple long enough for the Texas lawmen to carry out their ambush. They figured they had a way for Henry to do that. Prompted by his parents, Henry told Clyde that if they ever got unexpectedly separated, he'd find his way back to his parents' place. Clyde and Bonnie should look for him there.

That sounded fine to Clyde. He had other things to think about. There was the O. D. Stevens rescue attempt in Fort Worth to plan, and more. Prison breakouts were much on Clyde's mind. He'd already gotten five men (Raymond Hamilton, Henry Methvin, Joe Palmer, Hilton Bybee, and J. B. French) out of the Texas state prison—why not another old friend? In early May, former Barrow Gang partner and current Huntsville inmate Ralph Fults received an unsigned postcard with the message "Thinking of You. Hope to see you soon." Fults recognized Bonnie's handwriting, and knew he was being advised of a future attempt to break him out. Fults was especially touched by the final line Bonnie added: "Hope we all live to see the flowers bloom."

Despite letting down his guard as he enjoyed Methvin family hospitality in Bienville Parish, Clyde was still doing one thing to ensure that he and Bonnie lived to enjoy blooming flowers a while longer. Clyde continued setting up camp for the night in various spots, making it impossible for anyone to know in advance where he and Bonnie would sleep. Around mid-May, he did set up a semipermanent place in the backwoods outside the small Louisiana town of Mangham, about ninety miles east of Gibsland and a few miles past the big town of Monroe off Highway 80. It was isolated, yet an easy drive from Bienville Parish. Just off a nearly invisible dirt track, Clyde hacked out brush to form a clearing about twenty feet wide. He and Bonnie would park their gray Ford V-8 sedan there and still have room to spread out a blanket to sit on while they ate sandwiches or cleaned guns. Because they didn't bring Henry Methvin with them whenever they went to Mangham, Ivy Methvin had no idea they had a hideout there. But some of the Mangham locals realized somebody was staying out in the brush. They could occasionally hear gunshots—Clyde always believed in target practice. Once, some loungers at a Mangham country store stared at the shiny Ford when Clyde parked and went inside to buy Vienna sausage and crackers. No one asked the local sheriff to check out the stranger, or to investigate the shots back in the palmetto. In Mangham, practically everyone did some hunting in the backwoods. They were too busy trying to survive themselves to worry much about somebody else.

But Ivy Methvin was worrying, and so was Frank Hamer. It was one thing for Bienville Parish sheriff Henderson Jordan to say Hamer and his posse needed to sit tight in Texas until he summoned them. Sure, during their meeting on May 9 Jordan had suggested that something might happen within three weeks, but that was too long for Hamer and his men to wait around. He'd made his deal with Ivy Methvin back in March. Public outrage about the Grapevine killings on Easter Sunday hadn't abated. Lawmen in Tarrant County, Texas, assigned to the case were desperate to arrest somebody for the murders of motorcycle patrolmen Wheeler and Murphy. They summoned back farmer William Schieffer, who'd sworn he'd gotten a good look at the two men and the woman who'd allegedly done the shooting. Schieffer picked through mug shots and announced he'd spotted two of the three killers—Floyd Hamilton, Raymond's brother, and Billie Jean Parker, Bonnie's sister. That was enough for the Tarrant County police. Floyd Hamilton was already in custody, held on suspicion of helping Clyde Barrow with the Eastham farm prison break on January 16. Now Floyd was informed he was also being detained on charges of double homicide. Billie Jean had left Dallas to work as a waitress in East Texas. On Saturday, May 19, she was arrested there and extradited to the Tarrant County jail in Fort Worth. Twenty-year-old Billie Jean was in shock. She was thrown in a cell and kept under constant watch.

Also on May 19, fifteen-year-old Marie Barrow married Joe Bill Francis in West Dallas. Clyde was several hundred miles away in Bienville Parish or Mangham and didn't attend his sister's wedding. He may not have known about it—Marie was an impulsive girl who was not in the habit of planning very far ahead. Because they weren't in daily touch with their families Clyde and Bonnie didn't know about Billie Jean's arrest, either. They certainly had no idea that on this same fateful weekend of May 19–20 Frank Hamer decided he'd waited long enough for Henderson Jordan to arrange an ambush. Hamer, Manny Gault, Bob Alcorn, and Ted Hinton drove back to Louisiana. It was time to get their hunt for Clyde Barrow and Bonnie Parker over with.

CHAPTER 36

The Beginning of the End

On Sunday night, May 20, Clyde, Bonnie, and Henry Methvin visited Henry's parents. Henry managed to take Ivy and Ava aside to tell them that he, Clyde, and Bonnie were driving into Shreveport the next day. While they were there he'd try to get away. If he succeeded, he'd get word to Ivy and Ava, who could then contact Sheriff Jordan. The arrangement Henry had made with Clyde and Bonnie in the event of an unexpected separation was still in place: the couple would come to look for him at his parents' home about ten miles south of Gibsland off Louisiana Highway 154. Jordan and the Texas lawmen could set up their ambush somewhere along that narrow country byway.

On Monday, May 21, Clyde, Bonnie, and Henry went to Shreveport as planned. They had laundry to drop off, and afterward they stopped at the Majestic Café. Clyde and Bonnie waited in the car while Henry went inside and ordered three sandwiches and soft drinks to go. While he was in the café, a Shreveport police patrol car cruised past. Clyde threw the Ford V-8 into gear and drove away. He apparently had no sense that the cops had recognized him and Bonnie. It was just routine evasive action. He and Bonnie circled a few blocks, making certain the police car wasn't still on their tail, and then returned to pick up Henry. But the moment Clyde and Bonnie drove away, Henry bolted from the Majestic Café, leaving a bewildered waitress wondering what she was supposed to do with the sandwiches and soft drinks she'd been about to hand over to her customer. Then Henry stole a car and drove to his cousin Willie Methvin's house in Bienville Parish.

When Clyde and Bonnie got back to the Majestic Café and found Henry gone, they weren't surprised or upset. Henry might have seen the police car, too, and hidden himself somewhere. He would certainly find his way back to Bienville Parish. At some point, they could reunite with him at his parents' home. No one knows where Clyde and Bonnie spent the rest of the day. None of the Methvins mentioned seeing them again until Monday night.

The Hamer posse arrived in Shreveport sometime over the weekend and checked into the oddly named Inn Hotel. On Monday Hamer telephoned Shreveport chief of police Dennis Bazer. It was a courtesy call to inform Bazer that lawmen from another jurisdiction were in his city. Hamer had no intention of actively involving Bazer in the eventual ambush of Clyde and Bonnie. But Bazer mentioned an incident that occurred earlier—two of his officers had driven by the Majestic Café, and a Ford V-8 sedan parked in front sped away as they approached. The Shreveport cops tried to follow the Ford but whoever was at the V-8's wheel drove too well, and they soon lost sight of the car. When the officers went back to the Majestic, a waitress there told them a stocky young man had ordered three sandwiches and soft drinks to go, then rushed away without taking his food or even paying for it. Hamer recognized a familiar pattern.

The four Texas lawmen visited the Majestic and asked the waitress, whose name was not recorded, to look at several mug shots. She immediately identified Henry Methvin as the man who'd left without his sandwiches and soft drinks. She was absolutely certain—the man in the photo had the same eyes and pimply face. That was what the Texans had been hoping to hear. Clyde and Bonnie were in the area and perhaps separated from Henry Methvin. It was time for Henderson Jordan and Ivy Methvin to come through. Hamer, Gault, Alcorn, and Hinton hurried to their cars and drove fifty miles east on Highway 80 to Arcadia, where they met Jordan in his office. According to Hinton in *Ambush*, they told the Bienville Parish sheriff that they intended "to stake out the most likely road leading to [Ivy] Methvin's place," which was the Sailes–Jamestown road. There had been enough delays. With any luck, they could ambush Clyde and Bonnie the next day—Tuesday, May 22.

Hamer still had no idea that Jordan had also been cooperating with L. A. Kindell, special agent of the Justice Department's Division of Investigation. With the Texas lawmen on the scene and determined to carry out their ambush plans immediately, Jordan could no longer help Kindell beat them to Clyde and Bonnie. But he could at least invite Kindell to participate in the ambush—that way J. Edgar Hoover and his organization could share the credit for ridding the country of the criminal couple. Jordan told Hamer that it was first necessary to find Ivy Methvin. Maybe the old man could give them a definite time when Clyde and Bonnie would be coming to his home. If Hamer and the others would just go back to their hotel in Shreveport and wait, Jordan would locate Methvin, get the information, and then contact the Texans there. It must have seemed logical to Hamer. Arcadia was a gossipy country town. It wouldn't do for Hamer and his posse to spend the rest of the day hanging around in plain sight. People would begin talking, and someone might alert Clyde and Bonnie to their presence. Shreveport was less than an hour's drive from Gibsland and the Sailes–Jamestown road. When Jordan called—and the obvious implication was that it would probably be that evening, certainly no later than Tuesday—they'd be ready.

When the Texas lawmen were gone, Jordan tried to call Kindell at his New Orleans office. But the agent wasn't available—he was away on a field investigation. Jordan kept attempting to reach Kindell. If he was going to include the agent in setting the trap for Clyde and Bonnie, he had to do it soon. Hamer obviously wouldn't remain patient very long.

Meanwhile, Ivy, Ava, and Henry Methvin continued setting up what they clearly expected to be a Tuesday ambush. While Henry was separated from Clyde and Bonnie, he was not completely out of contact with them. How Henry arranged it has never been clear, but on Monday night, May 21, he and some of his relations met Clyde and Bonnie out at Black Lake. According to Henry's cousin Percy Methvin, the meeting took place after dark, and "the [half] moon was shining just as pretty as you ever saw." Percy, his father, Iris (some Methvin men had strange names), his brother Price, and Henry drove out to rendezvous with Clyde and Bonnie. They spent two hours chatting. Bonnie showed Percy how to load and shoot a BAR, though she refrained from actually firing any shots. She warned twenty-two-year-old Percy to "never go crooked," adding "it's for the love of a man that I'm gonna have to die . . . I don't know when, but I know it can't be long." Clyde voiced his usual complaint that the press kept blaming the Barrow Gang for bank robberies they hadn't committed. After a while Bonnie felt sleepy, and the group moved on to the old Cole place. At some point, it was apparently arranged for Clyde and Bonnie to pick up Henry at his parents' place the next day, Tuesday, sometime late in the afternoon. Then the Methvins said their goodbyes, and Percy assumed that Clyde and Bonnie would spend the rest of the night at the Cole place. They didn't. They drove to their camp in Mangham instead.

It was certainly simple for Henry to pass the word to his parents, and for Ivy to notify Henderson Jordan that Clyde and Bonnie could be ambushed the next afternoon on Highway 154. But that didn't work for Jordan. He still hadn't been able to contact Special Agent Kindell. He told Ivy that the Methvins would have to set up Clyde and Bonnie a second time, on Wednesday rather than Tuesday. That undoubtedly terrified Ivy Methvin—any delay would give the couple more opportunity to guess what was happening and wreak vengeance on his family. But Methvin certainly assumed Jordan was speaking for Hamer, and he wanted his son to receive the promised pardon from Texas. Thanks to Henderson Jordan, Clyde and Bonnie had an extra day to live.

CHAPTER 37

"Do You Know Any Bank Robbers?"

On the morning of Tuesday, May 22, Louis Brunson and his fifteen-year-old son, Robert, went hunting in the woods outside the northeast Louisiana town of Mangham. Louis had a small farm where he raised cotton and cattle, but the Depression had wiped him out financially. He and his wife had six children to feed, and their meals often consisted of whatever Louis and Robert could shoot and bring to the table. Squirrel was frequently on the Brunson family menu.

Louis and Robert spread out a little as they plodded through the thick brush. Black Boy, the family dog, trotted ahead of Robert. Black Boy disappeared from the teenager's sight, and then Robert heard the dog baying back in the palmetto. He hustled toward the sound, hoping Black Boy had cornered some kind of small game, and instead heard a man's voice saying, "Come on over here—here's your dog." Robert crossed a narrow dirt wagon track and found himself in a small man-made clearing. A shiny Ford sedan was parked by the side of the trail, and a man and woman sat near a blanket spread on the ground. There were guns and ammunition piled on the blanket, and also neat stacks of currency and mounds of gleaming coins. To the impoverished farm boy, it looked like these people had a million dollars out on display.

The man asked Robert his name and then added, "Do you know any bank robbers?" Nervously, Robert replied that he'd heard of John Dillinger, and a little about Pretty Boy Floyd. The fellow looked disappointed and asked, "No others? Well, I'm Clyde Barrow and this is Bonnie Parker, and we rob banks." That scared the kid. Bank robbers with guns weren't a promising combination. Bonnie apparently sensed he was frightened. She invited Robert to sit down next to her, and told Clyde to pick up a camera and take their picture together. Robert was still afraid of Clyde, but he thought Bonnie was sweet. After Clyde took a picture of the boy with Bonnie, she snapped a photo of Robert by himself. It occurred to Robert that he'd seen Clyde before—the youngster had been in the Mangham country store a week earlier when Clyde came in to buy Vienna sausage and crackers.

Clyde was still irked because Robert didn't know who they were. He handed the boy a newspaper—almost seventy-five years later, ninety-year-old Robert couldn't remember which one—and ordered the teenager to read a front-page story about how some Texas Ranger was looking for Clyde Barrow and Bonnie Parker. The article also mentioned huge rewards being offered for the couple's capture. Robert read the story and handed the newspaper back to Clyde. Now he was really shaken. Clyde, having finally made the impression he wanted, assumed the role of gracious host. Inviting Robert to join him and Bonnie beside the blanket, Clyde related how they'd been spending time "off and on" around Arcadia, mostly with one family. A member of that family, a young guy, had been working with them, but something happened and they'd gotten separated. Then Clyde joked with Robert a little. He asked the nervous teenager if he'd be interested in robbing banks, too. Robert, not sure whether he'd been offered a job, mumbled, "No, sir." Clyde, grinning, said, "I can tell you in a few minutes how to do it," and Robert replied that he didn't think he should.

Then they heard Robert's father, Louis, calling for the boy off in the brush. Robert told Clyde and Bonnie that he had to go. Clyde asked, "Is your family in bad shape? Do you need any money?" Robert admitted his family had fallen on hard times, and Clyde pulled some bills from his pocket. "Take any amount you want, or all of it," he told the fifteen-year-old. But Robert turned the money down. He thought that if it was from a bank, "the laws" might arrest him for having it even if he hadn't been one of the robbers who stole it. Robert told the couple goodbye, and Bonnie asked for his address. She wrote it down and promised to send him copies of the photos they'd just taken. Like many others who met Bonnie, Robert had fallen completely under her spell. He blurted, "Drop me a card, because I know I can't write to you." Bonnie, always pleased when a male was so obviously smitten, promised she would.

Clyde still wanted to give Robert a present. He offered a new shotgun, commenting that it was better than the one the teenager was carrying. Robert politely declined. The last thing Clyde said to the boy was that he and Bonnie would be leaving that afternoon to drive back to Arcadia.

The way Clyde and Bonnie behaved with Robert on the last full day of their lives suggests that despite all they'd been through, they never really changed much. Both of them still wanted to feel important, even if it just involved awing a bashful farm boy. Once Robert was properly impressed by Clyde and charmed by Bonnie, they demonstrated characteristic generosity by trying to press money and then a shotgun on the teenager.

And they still believed in keeping commitments to friends. There was no question on Tuesday afternoon whether Clyde and Bonnie would drive to Ivy and Ava Methvin's place to pick up Henry. At Black Lake on Monday night they had promised to be there.

Clyde and Bonnie took the winding Highway 154 through Bienville Parish that afternoon. It was the only direct route to the Methvins' from Gibsland off Highway 80. This unpaved backcountry byway was what locals termed "a three-rut," meaning that over the years car and wagon wheels had carved three deep grooves into the packed dirt. If vehicles passed going in opposite directions, one had to pull off to the side. That wasn't a problem—drivers in Bienville Parish were courteous. Because the road was so narrow and curvy, people didn't drive very fast on it. There was really only one long, straight stretch—that came about eight miles south of Gibsland and two miles north of the Cole place where Ivy and Ava Methvin lived. Just after the road passed through the small rural community of Mount Lebanon, the track swooped downhill and then up a low rise. At the top of the rise, the sides of the road were effectively barricaded by brush and trees. On the east side a steep hill reared a dozen feet above the road. From the top of the hill it was possible to look north and see a car coming from about a quarter-mile away, but because of the angles the occupants of the car couldn't possibly see anyone in the thick brush on top of the hill. It was the only such vantage point on the whole road between Highway 80 and the Methvin place. Clyde and Bonnie certainly drove right by it on their way to pick up Henry at his parents' house on Tuesday afternoon. They arrived unmolested—thanks to Henderson Jordan's ongoing, futile attempts to contact L. A. Kindell, Hamer and his posse were still waiting at the Inn Hotel in Shreveport instead of hiding on the hill ready to shoot. But Henry wasn't at Ivy and Ava's like he'd promised. He was staying with his cousin Willie.

Ivy Methvin came outside when Clyde and Bonnie drove up. As instructed by Henderson Jordan, Ivy told them that Henry wasn't there but would be the next morning. They should come back then around 9 A.M. Beyond being mildly aggravated by Henry's no-show, Clyde and Bonnie had no reason to be suspicious. Ivy probably told them that Henry was off somewhere with his cousins, which was true. Clyde said they'd be back in the morning, and he and Bonnie left. No one knows where they went immediately afterward or where they spent Tuesday night, but as soon as they were out of sight Ivy got in his truck and drove to Henderson Jordan's office in Arcadia. He told the Bienville County sheriff that Clyde and Bonnie would be coming down Highway 154 on Wednesday morning around nine o'clock. "The laws" should jump them then, and immediately afterward the Methvins wanted Henry's pardon from Texas just like they'd been promised.

Sheriff Jordan finally gave up trying to contact L. A. Kindell, whose field investigation was apparently keeping him away from telephones. He'd done his best, and the Division of Investigation agent would just have to understand. Jordan called Frank Hamer at the Inn Hotel in Shreveport and told him it was time. Hamer, Gault, Alcorn, and Hinton gathered their guns and drove to Arcadia. Jordan and his deputy Prentiss Oakley said they'd selected an ambush site "on the road south of Mount Lebanon." Ivy Methvin had promised that Clyde and Bonnie would drive past about nine on Wednesday morning. They'd go out to the spot and set up well ahead of time.

The six lawmen discussed whether they should offer the couple a chance to surrender. Hamer didn't believe Clyde would ever give up, but he felt obligated to try. Everyone expressed concern about shooting a woman. They worked out the ambush strategy—most people didn't drive very fast on the backcountry highway, but Clyde Barrow was going to be an exception. Even if they had the perfect shooting angles, it would be hard to hit a man and a woman speeding by at sixty or seventy miles an hour. But if Clyde slowed appreciably at the ambush site, or even came to a complete stop—what would make him do that? Clearly, Clyde and Bonnie felt some attachment to the Methvins. If Ivy was standing by the road alongside his jacked-up truck, surely Clyde would stop to see if he needed help. Sheriff Jordan had already informed a reluctant Ivy that he was to join the lawmen at the ambush site well before Clyde and Bonnie arrived. Jordan insisted that the elder Methvin be there because he didn't trust him. Unless he was right where Jordan could watch him, the sheriff suspected Old Man Methvin might very well panic and somehow alert Clyde to the impending trap. So Ivy and his truck became integral parts of the ambush plan. Hamer was so confident of its success that before he and the rest of the lawmen left to set up the ambush on Tuesday night he called his family back in Texas. Hamer promised his son Frank Jr. that "the chickens are coming home to roost tomorrow about nine o'clock."

CHAPTER 38

The Setup

The six-man posse reached the hilltop ambush site around two on Wednesday morning. They parked their cars on a little trail behind the hill and lugged their arsenal up. It was a drawn-out, clumsy affair. They had trouble seeing what they were doing—the half-moon didn't provide much light—and their weapons were heavy. The two BARs from the Dallas state guard armory weighed seventeen pounds each. Once they had all their ordnance on top of the hill, the lawmen began piling branches in front of themselves like hunters setting up a duck blind. They knew logically that Clyde wouldn't be able to see them as he approached from the north in his stolen V-8 sedan, but logic was already giving way to nerves. All six were well aware of Clyde's near-mystical ability to drive and shoot his way out of seemingly inescapable situations. The posses in Platte City and Dexfield Park had been certain they had him surrounded. The failed trap six months earlier in Sowers taught Bob Alcorn and Ted Hinton from personal experience that Clyde was quite capable of surviving a roadside ambush. The current issue of *Startling Detective Adventures* declared, "Barrow's uncanny ability to murder and then vanish as though the earth had swallowed him has never been explained. . . . A score of times he has been surrounded, a dozen traps have been laid for him, time after time all highways have been guarded after he committed some atrocious crime—and each time he has vanished." The media was always prone to gross exaggeration where Clyde was concerned, but that particular description was as much fact as hyperbole, and the posse knew it.

Worrying about what would happen in the morning was unsettling enough, but there were physical discomforts on the hilltop, too. Bob Alcorn thought he'd detected a snake slithering in the brush by their feet. Mosquitoes buzzed in their ears and bit their exposed faces and hands. The six men squatted about ten feet apart. Bienville Parish deputy Oakley was farthest on the right, or north, with Texas Highway Patrol officer Gault to his immediate left, then Sheriff Jordan, Dallas County deputy Hinton, Dallas County deputy Alcorn, and finally Hamer, who anchored the line on the south as the final gun-wielding barrier between Barrow and escape. They each hefted weapons selected especially for the ambush. Alcorn and Hinton had the BARs. Henderson Jordan brought a Winchester lever-action rifle. Its caliber was relatively light, but the gun was accurate. Manny Gault had a Remington Model 8 .35-caliber rifle loaned to him by Hamer. Prentiss Oakley also carried a Remington Model 8. The Remingtons were designed to bring down big game. Hamer was laden with the heaviest arsenal of all. If necessary, it would be Hamer's last-ditch responsibility to step directly in front of the Ford sedan and prevent Clyde's escape, a task that required especially lethal close-range weapons as well as nerve. So Hamer brought to the hilltop a Remington Model 11 shotgun and a Colt Monitor Machine Rifle with a twenty-shot magazine. The high-powered shotgun blasted a wide load of lead projectiles that, whistling over short distances, could reduce human flesh to pulp. The Colt Monitor was the ultimate "kill shot" weapon, powerful enough to drive its slugs straight through, rather than deflecting off, bone or the thick windshield of a car. All of the lawmen carried sidearms. Ted Hinton had an extra shotgun, and also a 16-millimeter movie camera to record the aftermath of whatever happened.

Someone, probably the Louisiana officers, had brought along sandwiches and a thermos of ice water, so they ate and talked quietly. The six-man posse was clearly split into buddy teams of two—Hinton and Alcorn, the Dallas County deputies; Jordan and Oakley from Bienville Parish; and former Rangers Gault and Hamer. No pair particularly liked or trusted the other four, but these animosities didn't surface until afterward. As they waited for the sun to rise, everyone was still cooperative, working out the final details of the ambush. Only Jordan and Oakley had the authority to arrest, let alone shoot down, Clyde Barrow and Bonnie Parker in Louisiana. Hamer's powers granted by Texas governor Ma Ferguson meant nothing across state lines. To satisfy legalities, it's likely that Jordan temporarily deputized Hamer, Gault, Alcorn, and Hinton while they waited on the hilltop. The six men also agreed that it would be Alcorn's responsibility to confirm that Clyde and Bonnie were in the car when the V-8 sedan was finally spotted. He and Hinton were still the only posse members who had seen them in person. Alcorn was probably assigned the extra duty because Hamer liked and trusted him more than he did Hinton.

The predawn hours passed slowly, and the sun brought no relief. The humid morning heat soon caused everyone to become drenched in sweat. Mosquitoes swarmed even more furiously around the posse, but they weren't the most aggravating pests as far as the lawmen were concerned. Sometime around sunrise, they were joined on the hill by Ivy Methvin. According to subsequent Oklahoma court testimony by his wife, Ava, Ivy "left pretty early" on Wednesday morning to participate in the ambush. She wasn't certain of the time but knew it was after Ivy had breakfast, which country folk in Bienville Parish usually took just before dawn. Ivy arrived as ordered, but made it clear that he wasn't happy about being there. As soon as there was light enough to see, the posse helped Ivy position his truck on the southbound side of the road, partially on the shoulder with the nose of the truck's hood sticking out onto the road itself. Then they jacked up the front end of the vehicle and pulled off its right front tire to suggest a blowout caused by the flinty rocks speckling the dirt road. It would be impossible for anyone coming south on narrow, three-rut Highway 154 to drive straight past. At the very least, southbound drivers would have to slow and maneuver their cars around Methvin's truck. Methvin was told that when Clyde and Bonnie appeared around nine, he was to hurry down the hill so they would see him standing beside his presumably disabled vehicle. That really set Ivy off. Now that his son's deal was in place and Henry was well away from Clyde and Bonnie and the ambush site, the father was worried about his own hide. Clyde and Bonnie were killers, he kept repeating, monsters with no concern for human life. If they did show up, if shooting did start, it was the lawmen and poor Ivy Methvin who'd be killed. Finally Jordan snarled that if Ivy didn't shut up, Clyde and Bonnie wouldn't get the chance to kill him because Jordan would.

With the morning came another complication. Working people in Bienville Parish were early risers, and cars began moving past the ambush site—not many, because the spot was sufficiently far from town, but the farmers in their old clunkers and the loggers in their long-bedded vehicles conformed to standard 1934 road etiquette and stopped beside Methvin's jacked-up truck to offer help or a ride. Each time, Methvin had to stumble down the hill and explain that things were fine, he was about to get the wheel back on the truck, so thanks and go ahead on your way. If Clyde drove up while another motorist was already stopped by the truck, the posse members believed, he might very well keep on going, and even if Clyde did pause, how could they unleash a fusillade with innocent bystanders right beside their prey? They apparently had less concern about Ivy's ability to dodge their bullets when the time came.

An hour passed, then two. At nine o'clock there was no sign of Clyde and Bonnie, but the posse stayed in place. Hamer had no doubt he was coming—he knew from months of careful study that Clyde always kept his word about appointments. Finally at 9:15 they heard a car approaching from the north several seconds before it even came into sight. The throaty purr of the engine indicated the automobile was more powerful than most other vehicles on Bienville Parish roads. Then the gray Ford V-8 sedan roared into view a quarter-mile to the lawmen's right. Clyde as usual had a heavy foot on the gas pedal, and in contrast to the lumbering trucks that had passed earlier, the Ford was moving fast, possibly at 60 miles per hour or more on this long, straight stretch. Hinton and Alcorn squinted at the vehicle.

"This is him," Hinton whispered to Alcorn. "This is it, it's Clyde." Alcorn agreed, and passed the word to the rest of the posse. Ivy Methvin hustled down the hill. The Ford approached where he stood beside the jacked-up truck and slowed. The posse on the hill could clearly see Clyde behind the wheel and Bonnie in the front seat beside him. The lawmen raised their guns. The waiting was over.

CHAPTER 39

The Ambush

A little before nine on Wednesday morning, Clyde and Bonnie drove into Gibsland and parked in front of Ma Canfield's café. Clyde probably went inside by himself to order their breakfast sandwiches to go. They were expected at the Methvins' place, which was about a twenty-minute drive from Gibsland, and carrying Bonnie in would have taken extra time. The locals eating breakfast at Ma Canfield's watched Clyde warily. By now, they were used to having him and Bonnie around, but propinquity never entirely erased trepidation. Afterward, the people in the café would disagree about whether the sandwiches Clyde ordered were fried bologna or bacon, lettuce, and tomato. Ivy Methvin, who got an uncomfortably close look on the Sailes–Jamestown road a few minutes later, told his family afterward that Clyde and Bonnie's takeout breakfast consisted of hamburgers. Whatever he ordered, Clyde took the food out to the car and the couple drove away, heading south out of town. He saved his sandwich for later, but Bonnie began eating hers. After a few bites she wrapped the rest of the sandwich in a napkin and held it on her lap along with a road map. Bonnie was wearing a red dress. Clyde had on a suit and blue

Western dress shirt. He also wore a hat. Bonnie had a tam, but she'd tossed it into the back seat. They kept several guns handy, but these were also on the back seat because there was no room for them in front.

It was a warm, muggy morning and Clyde rolled down the two driver's side windows in the V-8 sedan so fresh air could circulate in the car. About a mile and a half out of town the highway took a ninety-degree turn to the west, then gradually curved south again. By the time Clyde reached the long, downhill straightaway two miles from the Methvin place, he had the Ford barreling down the rutted dirt road at 60 or 65 miles an hour. They weren't going to make their scheduled 9 A.M rendezvous with Henry exactly on time, but they'd only be fifteen or twenty minutes late.

Then looking ahead down the road Clyde must have seen a jacked-up truck and probably a familiar figure standing beside it. There was also a massive logging truck coming in the other direction, heading north toward Mount Lebanon and Gibsland. There was no way the logging truck, Ivy Methvin's truck, and the V-8 sedan were all going to fit on the same section of the narrow road. Then the driver of the logging truck slowed and pulled over to the side, giving Clyde right-of-way. Clyde didn't take it. He slowed, then put the Ford into first gear and came to a complete stop beside Ivy Methvin and his apparently disabled truck. The V-8's engine was still idling. Though he didn't think it would do any good, this was the moment when Frank Hamer had agreed to call out for Clyde and Bonnie to surrender. The grizzled former Ranger probably prepared to stand up and shout.

On the hilltop, fifty feet to Hamer's right, twenty-nine-year-old Bienville Parish deputy Prentiss Oakley was amazed to find himself no more than thirty feet away from two of the most famous criminals in America. Oakley had come to the ambush site prepared to kill. He had the right weapon for it, a Remington Model 8 with a special five-shot clip that he'd borrowed from an Arcadia dentist. The owner considered the Remington to be so lethal that he kept it locked in the vault of Arcadia's bank when he wasn't using it. He apparently didn't want to risk having the rifle fall into the wrong hands.

But now it was in Prentiss Oakley's hands, and the young deputy couldn't control himself. Before Hamer could stand and offer Clyde and Bonnie a chance to surrender peacefully, Oakley jumped to his feet and aimed the Remington down the hill at Clyde. Later, trying to give the impression that they began firing out of self-defense, the posse members claimed that Clyde sensed Oakley's movement on his left and reached for either a shotgun or a BAR. If Clyde did, he had barely begun to move when Oakley squeezed the Remington's trigger and fired a burst at about a forty-five-degree angle. Several of the bullets deflected off the post between the Ford's windshield and the driver's door, but one flew straight and true through the open driver's side window and hit Clyde in the temple just in front of his left ear, plowing through his head and exiting out the right side of his skull. Clyde died instantly. He had been driving as usual in his stocking feet, and now his left foot slipped off the clutch and the Ford began rolling forward slowly and at an angle, heading for the shallow ditch on the other side of the road.

Because of the thickness of the brush on the hill and their distance from each other, none of the other five posse members could see Oakley. But they'd heard the shots, and now they saw the Ford moving ahead. There was a very brief interval, no more than two or three seconds, and then Manny Gault, Henderson Jordan, Ted Hinton, and Bob Alcorn began blazing away.

In those few seconds Bonnie screamed, a high shrill wail that haunted the men about to kill her for the rest of their lives. It had been one thing for Bonnie to tell her family and to believe herself that she and Clyde were doomed to violent deaths. Even after so many close calls, death had always been an abstraction, something in the future, and suddenly it was happening. As the Ford rolled forward toward the ditch Bonnie had just enough time to realize that Clyde was dead and she was about to die too and then she did. There is no way to be certain whose bullet killed Bonnie. She was riddled by the barrage laid down by the lawmen on the hilltop. Any number of her wounds would have been fatal. Hinton wrote later that he and his partners fired "about 150 shots." Many deflected off the Ford, or were trapped in between its double door panels. But some punched through the metal, and others flew unimpeded through the open driver's side windows. As the Ford passed their vantage points on the hill, Oakley, Gault, Jordan, Hinton, and Alcorn kept firing, and the slugs from their rifles smashed into the sedan's trunk and through its rear window. Some of the bullets that penetrated the car's interior passed through Clyde and then hit Bonnie.

Throughout his 102-day pursuit, Frank Hamer had often declared that he was reluctant to kill a woman. But once the shooting started, Hamer's lethal instincts kicked in. He'd always told his Ranger troops that the best way to enforce the law was a .45 slug in the gut, and that philosophy remained intact. As the Ford gradually rolled to a stop in the ditch beside the road, Hamer hustled down the hill, brandishing his powerful Colt Monitor Machine Rifle. He was taking no chances. First, he fired a burst into Bonnie through the rear passenger window. Then, when the car had completely stopped, the six-foot, three-inch Hamer walked forward, leaned his towering frame over the front seat where Bonnie was slumped, and fired a final series of shots down through the window and windshield directly into her.

A mile away in the pine forest, Olen Walter Jackson was cutting and hauling trees for the railroad. Jackson and the rest of his crew had been ordered to cut the trees by hand and not use the easier but noisy alternative of placing dynamite at the roots and blasting the trees down. Hearing explosions off to the west, Jackson decided that somebody was dynamiting trees after all. The noise was surely too extended, too concussive, to be gunshots.

In fact, just sixteen seconds elapsed between the first shots from Prentiss Oakley and the last ones fired by Frank Hamer. Though no one could have survived the ambush, the six lawmen were still cautious as they surrounded the well-perforated Ford. But Clyde and Bonnie were clearly dead. Clyde's shattered head had fallen through the spokes of the steering wheel. Bonnie slumped forward in the passenger seat. The napkin-wrapped sandwich from Ma Canfield's was still clutched in her hand. Blood and bits of flesh were splattered all around the interior of the car.

In the end, it had been surprisingly quick and easy. Clyde and Bonnie were killed without firing even a single shot in reply. Ted Hinton told people that "when all was said and done, they weren't nothing but a bunch of wet rags." On Tuesday night, Frank Hamer had promised his son that the chickens would come home to roost at about nine the next morning. He was only off by fifteen minutes.

CHAPTER 40

"Well, We Got Them"

As the posse surrounded the bullet-riddled Ford, Ivy Methvin emerged from wherever he'd sheltered during the ambush, probably under his truck. Now he wanted someone to help him get the right front wheel back on his vehicle so he could go home, but the lawmen paid no attention to him. The driver of the logging truck and two passengers who'd been riding with him tiptoed nervously from the woods. When the shooting had started, they'd jumped out and scurried into the trees. Now they milled about, too—between Clyde's Ford and Ivy Methvin's still disabled truck, narrow Highway 154 was effectively blocked.

Dallas County deputy Ted Hinton produced his 16-millimeter movie camera and filmed the other officers examining the Ford. The first moments in Hinton's film seemed to show fog partially enveloping the ambush site. In fact, the wispy clouds were lingering gunsmoke. When the lawmen opened the passenger side front door, Bonnie's limp body almost fell out. They saw the half-eaten sandwich in her hand, and the now blood-smeared road map still on her lap. Henderson Jordan reached into the back seat and pulled off a blanket concealing a lumpy heap of guns and suitcases. The posse members talked back and forth but had trouble hearing each other. The gunfire temporarily deafened them.

Frank Hamer conducted a quick inventory of the Ford's contents—Texas prison general manager Lee Simmons had promised Hamer that he could have anything Clyde and Bonnie had in their possession at the time of their killing or capture. In their car on the morning of May 23 the lawmen found three BARs, two sawed-off shotguns, almost a dozen handguns, thousands of rounds of ammunition, fifteen sets of stolen license plates, several suitcases full of clothes, a makeup case, a box of fishing tackle, several true crime magazines, road maps, and Clyde's saxophone. There was also a book, *The Saga of Billy the Kid* by Walter Noble Burns. Hamer took the guns and the tackle box. The other posse members contented themselves with lesser souvenirs. Dallas County deputy Bob Alcorn grabbed Clyde's saxophone. Later his conscience bothered him and he returned the instrument to the Barrow family. The suitcase full of cash disappeared. The Barrows always believed that it was taken by Henderson Jordan, who soon after the ambush purchased an auction barn and land in Arcadia.

Once the booty was distributed and locked in the cars behind the hill, it was time for the lawmen to contact their bosses. Alcorn and Manny Gault stayed behind to guard the car and bodies while Hamer, Hinton, Jordan, and Oakley drove back into Gibsland. They took turns using the telephone at the service station there. Jordan called the Bienville Parish coroner in Arcadia, asking him to come to the ambush site and bring a tow truck for the Ford. Hinton called Smoot Schmid, and the Dallas County sheriff gleefully notified the local press before racing to Louisiana to share the inevitable spotlight. Hamer telephoned Lee Simmons and said simply, "Well, we got them." Then, already trying to spin the story into self-defense rather than slaughter, Hamer added, "They died with guns in their hands."

Jordan, Hinton, and Hamer didn't realize their conversations were overheard by some locals lounging around the service station. Word spread quickly in Gibsland that Bonnie and Clyde were dead, and within minutes a procession of cars, trucks, and people on foot began heading south on Highway 154. As they returned to the ambush site, the four lawmen were annoyed by the throng tagging along after them, but when they arrived they were taken even more aback to discover that a crowd had already formed there. The cacophony of gunfire attracted farmers and logging crews eager to see what was going on. Observing the carnage wasn't enough for many of them—the side of the road opposite the hilltop teemed with souvenir hunters trying frantically to dig bullets out of tree trunks with pocketknives. Others wanted even more significant memorabilia and rushed to the Ford itself. Alcorn and Gault did their best to keep everyone away, but some people managed to reach inside the car where Clyde and Bonnie's bodies still slumped in the front seat. One man tried to cut off Clyde's ear. Another attempted to sever his trigger finger. The lawmen prevented those mutilations, but somebody with scissors managed to snip off locks of Bonnie's hair and bits of her gory dress before being pulled away.

The wrecker arrived and the Ford was chained to it. Bienville Parish coroner J. L. Wade made a cursory examination of the bodies inside the vehicle and offered the preliminary, obvious finding that Clyde and Bonnie died of gunshot wounds. The next legally required step was for their remains to be taken to Arcadia so Wade could conduct a more thorough examination. With the two corpses still in its front seat, the Ford was towed back north. Jordan and Oakley's car led the way, followed by Hamer and Gault. Then came the wrecker, Hinton and Alcorn in their car, and a line of vehicles driven by locals. Hinton guessed there were at least two hundred cars following the wrecker by the time it reached Gibsland.

And then, still nine miles away from Arcadia, the wrecker broke down in the worst possible place. The macabre procession passed Gibsland's public school just as many students were sent outside for recess. After the wrecker hauling the battered Ford stalled directly in front of the building, screeching children swarmed around the car. Someone, probably Coroner Wade, had covered Clyde and Bonnie with a sheet, but one of the students reached in and pulled the sheet off them. Hundreds of pairs of juvenile eyes took in the ghastly sight of the two mutilated corpses. Polly Palmer, then twelve years old, said more than sixty years later that she remembered how Bonnie's lip was almost severed from the rest of her mouth. Teachers tried to shoo the kids away until another wrecker arrived, and finally the ever-lengthening line of cars continued on to the parish seat.

But the fuss in Gibsland paled in comparison to the chaos that erupted when the motley parade finally reached Arcadia, where the usual population hovered around three thousand. It was later estimated that 16,000 people milled about the town hoping for a glimpse of Clyde's and Bonnie's bodies. Grasping hands snatched at the corpses as staff from the funeral parlor tried to remove the bodies from the car and roll them inside on gurneys. Many were shocked by how small the famous criminals had been. One onlooker, disappointed by Clyde's scrawny frame, announced, "He was nothing but a little bitty fart!" When members of the swelling mob wouldn't stop trying to climb inside the Ford, Jordan had the vehicle moved to a fenced impound lot.

The two bodies were taken into the funeral parlor, which occupied a back room in Conger's Furniture Store. Coroner Wade convened a six-member panel to monitor a hasty inquest. His investigation that morning was minimal. Wade examined the bodies, listed distinguishing characteristics including the heart tattoos on the inside of Bonnie's right thigh, catalogued their many potentially fatal wounds, and concluded by asking Bob Alcorn to formally identify the deceased. Then he stepped aside so an embalmer could begin his work.

Outside, hysteria evolved into festival-like glee. Radio stations were broadcasting the news, and newspaper reporters began arriving into town. According to one article describing the scene, "it was impossible to purchase a cold drink in the town, and storekeepers and stand operators were calling frantically upon neighboring towns to send supplies to meet the unprecedented demand . . . beer which sells for fifteen cents a bottle during normal times was sold for twenty-five cents. Cigarettes went up to twenty cents a package and it was almost impossible to get a sandwich, two slices of bread and a small piece of ham, at any price."

The journalists wanted a statement from Hamer, who explained that he'd "hated to bust a cap on a woman." Hamer didn't mention the last series of shots he fired into Bonnie to make certain that she was dead. He did expand on what he'd told Lee Simmons, saying "both Clyde and Bonnie reached for their guns and had them halfway up before we started shooting."

Rumors were flying that the posse had been tipped off by a local informant, and some reporters guessed it must have been Henry Methvin or a member of his family. Hamer refused to comment, saying that there were some things the public had no right to know. The attempted subterfuge failed. Headlines in the next day's *Dallas Morning News* proclaimed, "Clyde Barrow and Bonnie Parker Trapped and Killed When Underworld Associates Give Tips to Officers."

Henderson Jordan offered an alternative version of events to a reporter from the Associated Press. According to Jordan, he'd personally broken the Barrow Gang case after working on it for about six weeks. Jordan said he "got in touch" with Hamer and the Dallas County lawmen because he wanted someone involved "who knew Barrow and Parker personally in order not to make a mistake in shooting them if we found them."

Earlier, news photographers had snapped pictures of Clyde's and Bonnie's still clothed remains. Coroner Wade removed the clothing from the corpses to conduct his abbreviated inquest, and somehow another cameraman got in the room and took photos of the bodies as they lay naked on embalming tables. Some newspapers and magazines subsequently printed his pictures, treating readers to the sight of dead Bonnie's breasts. Hamer didn't care about the pictures, but he liked the idea of giving the crowd outside a good look at how Clyde and Bonnie had paid the ultimate price for their crimes. At his direction, once the bodies were decently covered again people were allowed to line up, come in, and view them. When the line failed to maintain a respectful distance from the corpses, one of the funeral parlor staff sprayed the gawkers with embalming fluid.

Dallas County sheriff Smoot Schmid arrived in Arcadia by early afternoon. He pulled Alcorn and Hinton aside and told his two deputies that he knew of at least $26,000 in reward money to be divided among the six participants in the ambush. Schmid anticipated a flood of positive publicity for his previously maligned department. He must have been sorely disappointed the following day, when a *Dallas Morning News* editorial lauding the ambush mentioned only Bienville Parish sheriff Henderson Jordan by name.

Clyde's father, Henry, and brother Jack reached Arcadia soon after Schmid. Bonnie's brother, Buster, didn't arrive until almost 10 P.M. He'd gotten lost on the way. Both families learned the bad news earlier in the morning when they were called by journalists asking for comments. Emma Parker fainted. Cumie Barrow told an Associated Press reporter that "I prayed only last night that I might see [Clyde] alive just once more." Henry was sorrowful but resigned as he waited in Arcadia to claim Clyde's body. He assured the media there that the Barrow family felt no animosity toward the lawmen who killed Clyde—they were simply doing their jobs. Ted Hinton noticed that the Barrows and Parkers had contacted separate Dallas funeral homes to arrange transportation of the bodies back to Texas. He assumed that meant Clyde and Bonnie would not be buried together, and he was right. Emma Parker told family and friends that Clyde might have had Bonnie in life, but she wouldn't let him have her in death, too. With Bonnie gone, Emma felt no further obligation to pretend that she had liked Clyde.

After presenting their relatives with boxes containing the clothes Clyde and Bonnie had been wearing during the ambush, funeral parlor staff released the bodies for transport by hearse back to Texas. Late that night, Clyde's remains arrived at Sparkman-Holtz-Brand Funeral Home in Dallas. Bonnie's corpse was delivered to McKamy-Campbell Funeral Home. The surviving Barrows and Parkers tried to rest as best they could, and woke up Thursday morning to find that the public was every bit as interested in Clyde's and Bonnie's funerals as it had been with their crimes.

The *Dallas Morning News* anticipated the furor that would envelop both services. In its editorial praising authorities for "tracking down the criminals, cornering and finishing them," the newspaper added, "the community owes a debt to itself and to posterity to see to it, by injunction if need be, that no show is made of the interment of the brutal pair who have met a fate that they deserved." But what the community wanted was one final show from Clyde and Bonnie. On Thursday the bodies were available for visitation at their respective funeral homes, a mistake both the Barrow and Parker families immediately regretted. Ten thousand people overran Sparkman-Holtz-Brand Funeral Home to get a glimpse of Clyde's corpse. Clyde's brother L.C. tried to block the most boisterous pseudomourners from approaching the coffin. Some of them were drunk. One man offered Henry Barrow $10,000 for his son's body. Finally, Dallas police were summoned to move the crowd outside. Things went a little better for the Parkers at the McKamy-Campbell Funeral Home. Emma Parker guessed later that twenty thousand people filed past her daughter's open casket, but for the most part they remained orderly. Emma had dressed Bonnie in a pretty blue negligee. A white veil covered her face in an attempt to disguise the mutilation caused by the posse's bullets.

Clyde was buried on Friday afternoon at Dallas's Western Heights Cemetery. He shared a grave with his brother Buck. During the interment, flowers were dropped from a plane flying overhead. The minister delivering the eulogy pleased Cumie by mentioning how Clyde had prayed regularly for his entire life. The crowd in the cemetery was so tightly packed that pallbearers had trouble carrying Clyde's casket to the graveside. Former Barrow Gang member Joe Palmer risked his life by coming into Dallas to attend the service. He mingled with the crowd and wasn't noticed by the police observing the proceedings.

Bonnie's funeral was on Saturday. Her sister, Billie Jean, still in custody for allegedly shooting the highway patrolmen in Grapevine on April 1, was allowed to attend in chains. Though Emma Parker boycotted Clyde's services on Friday, all the surviving Barrows attended Bonnie's funeral on Saturday. In an odd, uncharacteristically conciliatory gesture, Emma allowed Clyde's brother L.C. to be one of Bonnie's pallbearers. Bonnie was laid to rest in Fish Trap Cemetery beside the graves of her niece and nephew who died the previous fall. Police provided more crowd control than they had for Clyde's service the previous day. A large floral arrangement was collectively sent and paid for by Dallas newspaper vendors. In two days they'd sold almost a half-million copies of extra editions featuring stories about the ambush and funerals.

As Bonnie had predicted in her poem, she and Clyde did go down together. But she could never have anticipated the extent of the mythology that would continue to grow about them, or the misery that their families would still have to endure. Clyde's and Bonnie's lives were over, but not their legacy.

AFTERWARD

"People only live happily ever after in fairy tales."

—Blanche Barrow

CHAPTER 41

Consequences

Nineteen thirty-four was a fatal year for prominent criminals in America. Clyde's and Bonnie's deaths in the Gibsland ambush were just the first in a series. During May and June of 1934, Congress passed several national crime bills designed to give J. Edgar Hoover and his Division of Investigation agents more authority to pursue criminals. Bank robbery became a federal rather than a state crime—thieves could no longer elude pursuit by traveling from one state to another. Tough new federal gun laws decreed harsher penalties for using machine guns while committing criminal acts. With expanded authority to pursue the criminals Hoover had begun calling "America's most wanted"—who all robbed banks and used machine guns—his agents dogged the interstate steps of the most famous lawbreakers and began picking them off. John Dillinger was shot and killed on July 22, two months after Clyde and Bonnie died. Pretty Boy Floyd was gunned down by federal agents on October 22, and Baby Face Nelson suffered the same fate on November 27. Ma Barker and her son Fred were killed by agents in a gun battle on January 16, 1935. The most prominent outlaw celebrities had been eliminated.

Texas also acted to curtail crime. Ma Ferguson lost the fall 1934 gubernatorial race to James V. Allred, who pledged to make the state safer for its citizens. In 1935 the Texas legislature established a new headquarters division in Austin for state law enforcement agencies. Its new Bureau of Identification and Records finally provided all Texas lawmen access to fingerprints, mug shots, and other key data as well as staff to carry out ballistics tests. For the first time, there was even a statewide police radio network. As with the tougher federal laws, Clyde and Bonnie's crimes weren't the sole impetus for radically upgrading law enforcement in Texas. But they were certainly key contributing factors.

Clyde and Bonnie also continued to impact the lives of their families and others who'd been involved in some way with them. Just two weeks after their deaths, there was positive news: Bonnie's younger sister, Billie Jean, and Raymond Hamilton's brother Floyd were cleared in the Easter Sunday murder of highway patrolmen Wheeler and Murphy. Ballistics tests proved that the bullets that killed the officers were fired by BARs found in Clyde's car following the Gibsland ambush. The news wasn't as happy for the lawmen who'd gunned down Clyde and Bonnie on May 23. About the same time Billie Jean and Floyd were set free, the six Gibsland posse members received their share of the pooled reward money. In Arcadia on the afternoon of the ambush, Smoot Schmid had promised his deputy Ted Hinton that they'd divide $26,000 between them, but most of the state, county, and business organizations that had pledged sums reneged on their promises. Frank Hamer, Manny Gault, Henderson Jordan, Prentiss Oakley, Bob Alcorn, and Hinton each got checks for $200.23. For Hamer, at least, it didn't matter as much. He had all of Clyde and Bonnie's guns, which he and his family gradually sold off to memorabilia collectors. When Cumie Barrow and Emma Parker learned that Hamer possessed their late children's arsenal, they wrote and asked him to return the guns. The Barrows and Parkers were still impoverished and badly needed the money they would have realized from selling the guns themselves. Hamer refused.

Bienville Parish sheriff Henderson Jordan, who the Barrow family subsequently believed had Clyde's cash-crammed suitcase, also had a plan for additional ambush-related income. The bullet-pocked Ford V-8 sedan Clyde had driven into the ambush was still locked in Arcadia's city impound lot. Despite all the bullet damage to its sides, windows, windshield, and trunk, the car's powerful engine still ran smoothly. To Jordan's way of thinking, the car was ambush booty that belonged to the six lawmen, too. He declared that "five other men and myself risked our lives to make that car what it is today. What we did to it is what makes it valuable. We deserve any profit to be made from it."

But Ruth Warren of Topeka, Kansas, disagreed. Ever since post-ambush news reports identified the now famous "Death Car" as the vehicle stolen from her home on April 29, Warren had been asking Jordan to return it to her. Jordan's lawyer notified Warren that she could have her car back for $15,000. Warren hired a lawyer of her own, and a federal judge in Shreveport ruled that Jordan had to return the car to her. She drove it home to Topeka, and in August rented the Ford for $150 a week to Charles W. Stanley, who referred to himself as "the Crime Doctor." Stanley loaded the car onto a flatbed truck and toured the country with it, using the chance to see the sievelike vehicle as an enticement for people to listen to his anticrime lectures. Admission was free, but Stanley suggested audience members each donate a dime toward his expenses.

Losing the Death Car was a setback for Henderson Jordan, but his disappointment was nothing compared to the consternation of Henry Methvin. Henry and his parents had expected Hamer to deliver the Texas pardon just as soon as Clyde and Bonnie were dead, but months passed without further word from the former Texas Ranger. Finally on August 14, Governor Ferguson announced the pardon, which noted that "[Henry Methvin] gave to the authorities in Louisiana valuable information that led to the apprehension and capture of one Clyde Barrow and one Bonnie Parker." The Methvins assumed their son's problems with the law were over so long as he avoided future crimes. Henderson Jordan suggested to Henry that he stay inside Bienville Parish limits, and Henry went to work at a local lumber mill. Then on September 12 an Oklahoma court issued a warrant for Henry's arrest for the murder of Commerce constable Cal Campbell. Texas might have pardoned Henry for his crimes in that state, but Oklahoma never promised to pardon him for anything. Henry was arrested in Shreveport, extradicted to Oklahoma, and promptly tried, convicted of murder, and sentenced to death. His mother, Ava, and family friend John Joyner went to Oklahoma to testify during Henry's appeal, and in their testimony they explained in detail how the family had cooperated with Hamer and Jordan in arranging the Gibsland ambush. Hamer supported their statements, and Henry's sentence was commuted from death to life imprisonment. He was paroled after serving eight years.

Back in Dallas, the Barrows and Parkers were trying to get on with their lives during the summer of 1934 when they were approached by writer Jan Fortune. She explained she wanted to work with the families and write the true story of Clyde's and Bonnie's lives. Emma Parker agreed to cooperate, and so did Clyde's sister Nell. Fortune interviewed both women at length, and in the fall published *Fugitives*. The completed book outraged both families. Clyde's sister Marie called *Fugitives* "romanticized, sentimentalized claptrap," and Nell Barrow protested that she "never told the writer any of that stuff." But the families never sued the author—probably because by the time *Fugitives* was published they had much more serious legal concerns.

New, tougher federal laws called for punishment not only of bank robbers but also of those who in any way aided or abetted them. By fall 1934, rumors began to swirl in Dallas that the government planned to prosecute everyone who "harbored" Clyde and Bonnie during their two-year crime spree. It turned out to be true: beginning late in the year, members of the Barrow and Parker families as well as friends and former partners of Clyde and Bonnie began to be arrested. They were held in the Dallas County jail to await trial in the spring. Cumie Barrow was locked up along with her sixteen-year-old daughter, Marie. Emma and Billie Jean Parker were also incarcerated. For reasons never made clear, the government was selective regarding who was prosecuted. Clyde's father, Henry, brother Jack, and sisters Artie and Nell and Bonnie's brother, Buster, weren't charged. But Marie's husband, Joe Bill Francis, was, and so were Raymond Hamilton's mother and stepfather. In all, there were twenty defendants, including Henry Methvin, W. D. Jones, and Blanche Barrow, who were transferred to the Dallas County jail from their respective prisons.

The trial began on February 22, 1935. The men and women were tried separately. Cumie Barrow had to be carried into the courtroom on a chair. Clyde's brother L.C. was disgusted to find that he was shackled to Henry Methvin during court proceedings. The Barrows had long since decided Henry was the squealer who betrayed Clyde and Bonnie. When Cumie testified, she made no apologies about seeing Clyde whenever she could—he was her son, she said, and she loved him no matter what crimes he might have committed.

The trial lasted four days, and in the end all twenty defendants either pleaded or were found guilty. The maximum sentence for harboring was two years in prison, and sentences ranged from the full two years for Raymond Hamilton's brother Floyd to one hour in police custody assessed to teenager Marie. Cumie Barrow and Emma Parker each were sentenced to a month in jail. Prosecutor Clyde Eastus told the press that "the United States Attorney's office and the Department of Justice Division of Investigation are very pleased with the conviction of these persons. We feel that the result will have a wholesome effect on others who are harboring or concealing persons wanted by the government."

When Cumie Barrow and Emma Parker were released from jail in late March, they were offered employment: Charles Stanley, the Crime Doctor, wanted them to tour the country with him and the Death Car. The Depression was still in full force, and the Barrows and Parkers needed any income they could get. Cumie and Emma signed on. Henry Barrow was hired by Stanley, too, along with the father of recently slain celebrity criminal John Dillinger. Marie Barrow and her husband, Joe Bill Francis, were brought along to handle ticket sales. During the programs, which were often held at county fairs, Stanley would present a slide show and then make a speech about the horrors of crime. Emma Parker, the Barrows, and John Dillinger Sr. would answer questions about their infamous children. The programs drew packed houses, but after a few weeks the combined toll of strenuous travel and reliving painful memories proved too much for Cumie and Emma. Along with Henry, Marie, and Joe Bill they dropped off the Crime Doctor's tour and went home to Dallas. Cumie began writing her own memoir to counter Jan Fortune's *Fugitives*, but the few dozen pages she managed were never published.

Crime Doctor Charles Stanley's show was a smash everywhere but in Frank Hamer's hometown of Austin. Stanley was confronted there by Hamer and Manny Gault. It had been made public during Henry Methvin's Oklahoma trial that the Methvin family set up Clyde and Bonnie to be ambushed, but that made little difference to Hamer. He stubbornly stuck to his version of events—the public had no right to know the identity of his informant. As Stanley performed his regular program onstage in Austin, discussing as usual how retired Texas Ranger captain Frank Hamer orchestrated the ambush with the help of the Methvin family, Hamer and Gault vaulted up beside him. The towering lawman roared, "I'm Frank Hamer," and slapped Stanley across the face. Then he and Gault confiscated Stanley's slides and warned him never to put on his show again.

Stanley didn't sue Hamer—in Texas, no jury would have found against the legendary lawman. But he didn't obey Hamer and stop performing his program, either. He had a duplicate set of slides, which were mostly mug shots of Clyde and John Dillinger. When Stanley returned to Texas in the fall of 1939 for a performance at the State Fair in Dallas, he was concerned enough that Hamer might show up to hire two guards—Bob Alcorn and Ted Hinton. There was no love lost between Hamer and the two Dallas County deputies. Alcorn and Hinton were ready for a confrontation, but Hamer never appeared.

Stanley finally shut down the Death Car tour during the early 1940s. He had eventually purchased the Ford V-8 sedan from Ruth Warren, and in 1952 Stanley sold the car to a film producer who planned to make a movie about Depression-era criminals. The film was never produced, and after changing hands several more times the Ford ended up on display at Whiskey Pete's Casino in Primm, Nevada.

Many of the people associated with Clyde and Bonnie didn't have obvious scars like the bullet holes in the doors of the Death Car, but they were damaged all the same. One way or the other, their interaction with the criminal couple affected all of them for the rest of their lives.

Frank Hamer never returned to active duty with the Texas Rangers. Instead he would occasionally sign on with oil companies as a special investigator to prevent illegal strikes and root out industrial sabotage. His reputation suffered somewhat after the Gibsland ambush—many people believed Clyde and Bonnie had not been given a genuine opportunity to surrender. But Hamer was still considered the ultimate gun-toting lawman. When Hamer visited Hollywood in 1940, Western film star Roy Rogers asked for his autograph. During the last few years of Hamer's life he was debilitated following a case of heat stroke. He died in 1955 at the age of seventy-one.

In 1937, Manny Gault was allowed to rejoin the Texas Rangers. He was promoted to captain, the same high rank his former boss Frank Hamer had once held, and died in 1947.

A year after the Gibsland ambush, Henderson Jordan supplemented his salary as Bienville Parish sheriff by buying a half-interest in an Arcadia auction barn. His daughter claimed that her father's hair turned white because of the trauma involved in killing Clyde and Bonnie. Jordan died in an automobile accident in 1958. He had been succeeded as Bienville Parish sheriff by Prentiss Oakley, who often admitted to friends that he fired prematurely on May 23, 1934. Oakley died unexpectedly in 1957.

Bob Alcorn eventually left the Dallas County sheriff's department and tried his hand at selling cars. When he tired of that, he became a Dallas County court bailiff. Alcorn died on May 23, 1964, the thirtieth anniversary of the ambush outside Gibsland.

Ted Hinton resigned as a Dallas County deputy to run a trucking company and manage a motel in the Dallas suburb of Irving. The surviving members of the Barrow family came to consider him a trusted friend. Hinton acted as an intermediary between the Barrows and the press, passing along requests for interviews and usually reporting refusals. When Clyde's younger brother, L.C., fell on hard times, Hinton helped out by hiring him as a truck driver. Both Hinton and Bob Alcorn made unsuccessful attempts to run for sheriff of Dallas County. They blamed their defeats in part on voters remembering, and resenting, that they'd shot Bonnie Parker. When Hinton died in 1977, he had been the last surviving ambush participant.

Smoot Schmid never realized his dream of being elected governor of Texas. But he was reelected Dallas County sheriff until 1946. Then Schmid retired to take a seat on the state prison Board of Pardons and Parole. He died in 1963.

Lee Simmons fared much worse. In September 1935 he resigned as prison general manager after a series of investigations revealed widespread corruption and mistreatment of inmates in the Texas prison system. Simmons entered private business and died in 1957.

Several Barrow Gang partners didn't outlive Clyde and Bonnie by very long. Joe Palmer was recaptured on June 15, 1934; he and Raymond Hamilton, who was already in custody, were both sentenced to die on "Old Sparky," Texas's infamous electric chair. On July 22 they managed a spectacular escape from the prison death house in Huntsville. Palmer was apprehended in August and Raymond was caught in April. They went to the electric chair on May 10, 1935. Palmer died first. With his last words, Raymond Hamilton denied killing John Bucher in Hillsboro on April 30, 1932. Then, as he was strapped into the chair, Raymond said "Well, goodbye, all."

W. D. Jones completed his prison term and moved to Houston. He developed addictions to drugs and alcohol. On the night of August 20, 1974, Jones went home with a woman he'd just met in a bar and was shot to death by her jealous boyfriend.

Ralph Fults and Floyd Hamilton did much better. Both committed more crimes and served multiple prison terms in and out of Texas—Hamilton spent several years in an Alcatraz cell next to the legendary "Bird Man"—before finally finding religion and reinventing themselves as public service speakers and youth leaders. Floyd Hamilton died in 1984 and Ralph Fults in 1993.

Henry Methvin was paroled from the Oklahoma state prison in McAlester on March 18, 1942. He returned home to Bienville Parish and worked there until the night of April 19, 1948, when, apparently drunk, he fell asleep on a railroad track and was cut in half by a Southern Pacific passenger train. Henry's father, Ivy, died two years earlier in 1946 when he was struck by a car.

The surviving Parkers and Barrows mostly found their post–Clyde and Bonnie lives blighted, too. Following her thirty-day prison term and short stint touring with Crime Doctor Charles Stanley, Emma Parker returned home to Dallas. She died in 1944 at age fifty-seven—physically and spiritually broken, friends were certain, by the tension and tragedy brought into her life by her beloved daughter Bonnie.

Bonnie's older brother, Buster, was also debilitated. Though he was never accused of having anything directly to do with the Barrow Gang's crimes, the stigma still seemed to haunt him. Buster drank heavily and died in 1964. He was fifty-six.

Billie Jean Parker, Bonnie's little sister, served the year-and-a-day prison term she was assessed in the harboring trial and returned to Dallas. She remarried and raised her brother Buster's daughter—the child was named Bonnie after her infamous aunt. Billie Jean died in 1993.

Henry and Cumie Barrow continued living in the family service station in West Dallas. Their daughter Marie and son-in-law Joe Bill Francis lived with them. On the night of September 4, 1938, Marie and her older brother L.C. got into a bar fight with former harboring trial codefendant Baldy Whatley, who trailed the Barrow siblings to the service station afterward and fired a shotgun into the house. The pellets struck Cumie in the face, permanently affecting her vision.

In 1940, Henry sold the service station and used the proceeds to purchase a small house on Lawrence Street in Dallas. It was the first time the elder Barrows experienced the luxury of indoor plumbing. Cumie didn't have long to enjoy a flush toilet. She died two years later in 1942 at age sixty-seven. Henry lived another fifteen years, dying at eighty-three in 1957. The Barrows are buried together beside the grave shared by their sons Buck and Clyde.

The Barrows' eldest son, Jack, survived his mother but not his father. Jack Barrow had always kept a distance from his outlaw younger brothers. He was determined to raise his four daughters free of the slightest criminal taint. But on October 14, 1939, Jack Barrow killed Otis Jenkins in a bar fight. The other Barrows swore that Jack was only defending himself, but he was sentenced to a short prison term. After his release, Jack came home to his family in Dallas. He died in 1947. Jack was fifty-two.

Artie and Nell Barrow both escaped prosecution at the 1935 harboring trial and were the only surviving Barrow children to avoid future brushes with the law. Nell died in 1968 at age sixty-three, and Artie lived to age eighty-one before passing away in 1981.

L.C. and Marie Barrow never escaped the influence of Clyde and Buck. L.C. served several prison terms for robbery and forgery. Records at the Texas Prison Museum in Huntsville indicate that L.C. claimed addictions to drugs and alcohol. But he eventually got his life in order and worked for several companies as a truck driver. L.C. mourned Clyde for the rest of his life. Sometimes, mention of his brother reduced him to tears. L.C. was sixty-six when he died in 1979.

Marie divorced Joe Bill Francis and fell in with a series of criminal gangs. She spent time in prison, missing Cumie's funeral in 1942 because she was incarcerated, but eventually moved back to Dallas and married ex-con Luke Scoma. The marriage lasted, and even thrived, though Scoma made his late-life living stealing lawn mowers from discount chain stores. In the 1990s, Marie met Dallas memorabilia collector-dealer Charles Heard, and arranged through him to sell Clyde's remaining possessions. These included the shirt and pants he was wearing during the Gibsland ambush, his pocket watch, and the lever-action .22 rifle Clyde owned as a child. Heard bought the shirt from Marie for $35,000 and resold it for $75,000 to the same Nevada casino that owns the Death Car. Marie got $27,000 for Clyde's rifle and $20,000 for the pocket watch. She and Heard then cut Clyde's "death pants" into small swatches, mounted the bits of cloth on certificates attesting to their authenticity, and sold the swatches for $200 at museums and up to $500 at memorabilia auctions. When Marie gave the blue wool trousers to her new partner to cut into squares, Heard protested, "These couldn't have been Clyde's pants. They're way too small, and the legs are too short." Marie replied, "We were poor as church mice, so Mamma cut them down to fit one of the [grand]kids." Heard looked closely at the garment. Despite its alterations and many washings, bloodstains were still clearly visible.

In 1998 Marie began working with Dallas historian Jonathan Davis on a memoir she intended to contradict everything in *Fugitives*, but refused to allow the finished book to be published after deciding it didn't portray the Barrow family in a sufficiently positive light. Marie began working on a new memoir with Arkansas writer Phillip Steele, but she died in February 1999 after they'd just begun collaborating. Steele went ahead with a book anyway, publishing *The Family Story of Bonnie and Clyde* in 2000. In accordance with Marie's wishes, this second memoir left out many details about Clyde and the rest of the Barrows that had been included in her original project with Jonathan Davis.

But before Marie died, she and Billie Jean Parker rekindled their friendship—and welcomed the company of a third woman who'd survived all the Barrow Gang tribulations.

On March 24, 1939, Blanche Caldwell Barrow was released from prison in Missouri. Blanche moved back to Texas, and in 1940 married a Dallas construction supervisor named Eddie Frasure. She never lost touch with the surviving Barrows, and after Frasure died in 1969, Blanche began visiting Marie Barrow on a regular basis. Marie in turn reintroduced Blanche to Billie Jean Parker, who was now married to Arthur Moon and preferred to be called simply "Jean." Blanche and Jean Moon became such fast friends that Marie was jealous. The three women spent a great deal of time together in various combinations fishing, drinking beer, and reminiscing. A few years before her death from cancer in 1988, Blanche said that "I talk of these incidents [with Clyde and Bonnie] as if I were not a part of any of it, like a character in a book I once read." By then, the terrifying misadventures that Blanche remembered—and wrote about in her posthumously published prison diary—had little in common with the image of Clyde and Bonnie that grew even more glamorous and glittering following their deaths.

CHAPTER 42

The Legend of Bonnie and Clyde

Clyde and Bonnie were barely in their graves when Jan Fortune's *Fugitives* reached bookstore shelves in the fall of 1934. Through the device of embellishing many of Nell Barrow's and Emma Parker's original comments, Fortune essentially presented Clyde as a hot-tempered, soliloquy-spouting philosopher and Bonnie as a high-spirited Southern belle. These caricatures reinforced the public's perception of the couple as glamorous celebrity bandits who, though dead, remained reliable sources of entertainment.

Hollywood thought so. In January 1937 Fritz Lang released *You Only Live Once*, with Henry Fonda and Sylvia Sidney featured as a husband and wife engaging in increasingly violent crime after Fonda's character is wrongly accused of murder during a bank robbery. The characters and plot were clearly based on Clyde and Bonnie, and the overall effect was to suggest they were well-meaning young people forced into killing by callous and/or incompetent lawmen. From the late 1930s through the 1950s, several other films—*Persons in Hiding*, *Gun Crazy*, *They Live by Night*—also presented one-dimensional interpretations of Clyde and Bonnie, focusing on overly dramatized gunplay or romance as dictated by the whims of the directors. The worst, by far, was 1958's *The Bonnie Parker Story*, which depicts Bonnie as a sleazy femme fatale who seduces a series of lovers into committing criminal acts. In the film, Bonnie's main love interest is Guy Darrow rather than Clyde Barrow. Identifying Bonnie by her real name and altering Clyde's was indicative of a gradual reversal of their supposed roles in the mind of the public. By the 1950s, it had become fashionable to think of Bonnie rather than Clyde as the actual leader of the Barrow Gang—she was the kill-crazy criminal mastermind, and he was the love-struck minion.

The impetus for this wildly inaccurate reappraisal came more from print than film. Inspired by Dashiell Hammett's brilliant private eye fiction of the 1920s and early 1930s, a new generation of American writers including Raymond Chandler and Ross Macdonald wrote a flood of thriller novels in the 1940s and 1950s featuring dogged protagonists who cracked cases after refusing to succumb to the lethal charms of evil, law-breaking women. This fresh theme was welcomed by the true crime magazines whose supply of front-cover material had waned after the deaths of Clyde, Bonnie, John Dillinger, Pretty Boy Floyd, and Ma Barker. The concept of a sexy, calculating gun moll clearly captivated the public, and given the best-known alternative real-life option—no matter how malign the magazines might try to make her appear, Ma Barker was still a dumpy, middle-aged woman—Bonnie Parker was inevitably remolded into a sultry schemer. A typical story appeared in the March 1956 edition of *Argosy* magazine. "Killer in Skirts" included the subheading of "She was blonde and stacked and ninety pounds straight out of hell—tommy-gunning, stogy-smoking Bonnie Parker, America's deadliest sweetheart." Writer Marvin H. Albert described Bonnie as a "pretty blonde in [an] over-tight sweater" with the butt of an unlit cigar clenched between her teeth while "her arms lovingly cradled a submachine gun." Bonnie, Albert wrote, "would shoot a man for no reason. That's how she got her kicks." The blitz of Bonnie-as-Clyde's-manipulator stories was so ubiquitous and persuasive that even retired Dallas County deputies Bob Alcorn and Ted Hinton began telling friends that perhaps Bonnie had goaded Clyde into all that violence after all.

And there public perception of Clyde and Bonnie stalled for another decade. They were conscienceless killers, she was probably the boss, and they wreaked a few years of colorful havoc before dying together in a final climactic gun battle. As the readership of true crime magazines declined, so did interest in Clyde and Bonnie. Like Charles Lindbergh and Jack Dempsey, they were icons from an American era that was no longer relevant to a public whose entertainment needs now were met with TV sitcoms and rock 'n' roll. Fascination with them was mostly over.

Blanche Caldwell Barrow Frasure certainly thought so. She enjoyed her new life with husband Eddie. They traveled a lot and were able to build a pleasant country home in the Dallas suburb of Seagoville after Eddie received a promotion at the architect's business where he worked. Blanche's reputation for running with the Barrow Gang seemed permanently in her past until 1965 when she was contacted by actor Warren Beatty. Beatty told Blanche that he had purchased the rights to a new screenplay about Clyde and Bonnie. This film, he said, would use their real names. Because they had been recognized celebrities, anyone could use them as characters in a movie. But Beatty wanted to pay Blanche for the right to use her name and character, too. Beatty met with Blanche and her lawyer and showed them the prospective script. It seemed fairly truthful to Blanche. She allowed the use of her name in the film, and was pleased to be paid enough to build a new fence around her property in Seagoville. Beatty said he'd play Clyde, an actress named Faye Dunaway would portray Bonnie, Buck would be played by Gene Hackman, and Estelle Parsons would take the role of Blanche. During 1966, some scenes in the movie were filmed around Dallas. L.C. Barrow visited the set, walked up to Beatty and Hackman and piped, "Howdy there, brothers!"

Bonnie and Clyde premiered at a film festival in Montreal on August 4, 1967. The order of the names in the title was the first departure from the Barrow Gang legend. Until Beatty's movie, Clyde's name always came before Bonnie's. But the film's immense, ongoing popularity changed that. Bonnie now had top billing.

The surviving Barrows resented that and much more. Blanche said later that the final version of *Bonnie and Clyde* was much different from the script she'd originally been shown by Beatty. In the movie, Clyde suffers from a low libido and erectile dysfunction. W. D. Jones and Henry Methvin are melded into a single character. Blanche Barrow is saddled with the scheming personality of Mary O'Dare, and shrieks more often than she speaks. After viewing the film Blanche said truthfully, "That movie made me look like a screaming horse's ass." She had signed an agreement with Beatty, so she didn't sue Warner Brothers, the studio that produced the movie. But Clyde's sisters Artie and Nell and brother L.C. did, claiming that because the film contained so many untruths it "maliciously and deliberately vilified [Clyde and Bonnie] and those connected with them." Billie Jean Parker Moon and W. D. Jones filed similar suits. All their claims were dismissed. The judges ruled that Clyde and Bonnie were public figures, and that neither Nell, Artie, L.C., Billie Jean, or W.D. had been specifically referred to or identified in the movie.

But one lawsuit hit paydirt. *Bonnie and Clyde* depicted Frank Hamer as a bumbling lawman who'd been kidnapped by the Barrow Gang and pursued them for revenge. That clearly was false—Ted Hinton was still around to swear that Hamer had never seen, let alone met, Clyde and Bonnie until the morning of the Gibsland ambush. Hamer's widow settled for an undisclosed amount from Warner studios—enough, great-nephew Harrison Hamer said forty years later, to see her through "the rest of her days."

Audiences loved the film just as much as the Barrows, Parkers, and Hamers hated it. Thanks to taut storytelling and memorable performances by the featured cast, *Bonnie and Clyde* rekindled fascination with the real-life couple. The public now imagined Clyde and Bonnie to be as tall and physically attractive as the stars who portrayed them in the movie. Beatty got their undying love for each other right, as well as Clyde's cocky attitude and Bonnie's poetic bent. But there was nothing of West Dallas in the film—Clyde and Bonnie's impoverished childhoods and social frustrations were never established. *Bonnie and Clyde* emphasized fancy clothes and gory gunplay, but didn't touch on the mundane, routine Barrow Gang misery of camping in cars and dining on cans of cold beans. In the movie, Clyde didn't limp from the self-amputation of two toes, and Bonnie wasn't crippled in a car crash. Thanks to *Bonnie and Clyde,* they were once again glamorous without too many distractingly gritty details.

The interest in Clyde and Bonnie renewed by Beatty and his film never abated. Gibsland, a dying town after the interstate replaced the railroad, has experienced a limited renaissance with two Bonnie and Clyde museums and a Bonnie and Clyde Festival each May on the anniversary of the ambush. A Bonnie and Clyde symposium in Kansas City based on the shootout in Platte City has become an annual event. A fortieth anniversary DVD edition of *Bonnie and Clyde* was a best-seller.

In Dallas, both the city historical society and entrepreneur Ken Holmes offer "Bonnie and Clyde" tours that last several hours. The Barrow family service station still stands on old Eagle Ford Road, which has been renamed Singleton Boulevard. West Dallas has been incorporated into the main city, but it is still full of shacks, pothole-pocked roads, and suspicious-looking characters loitering on corners. Few people would live there if they had other options. The tours take in the service station, the house a few blocks away where Clyde shot down Fort Worth deputy Malcolm Davis on January 6, 1933, one of Bonnie's old schools, and a few places where she and Clyde worked. They also include visits to Clyde's and Bonnie's graves.

Bonnie rests beside her mother, Emma, nephew Buddy, and niece Jackie in upscale Crown Hill Memorial Park. All four were moved there in the 1940s when visitors overran the smaller Fish Trap Cemetery where they were initially interred. A receptionist in the Crown Hill office says cheerfully, "Oh, we have lots of people coming to see Bonnie."

Bonnie's grave is easy to find. It's about a hundred yards to the left of the main Crown Hill entrance. On any given day, tokens are left there by fans—plastic flowers, small cheap crosses, business cards, and scraps of paper with scribbled poems or lines from the Bible ("Yea, though I walk through the Valley of the Shadow of Death" seems to be a favorite). Bonnie's headstone is larger than many in the cemetery, and necessarily so because of its lengthy inscription:

As the flowers are all made sweeter by the sunshine
and the dew, so this old world is made brighter
by the lives of folks like you.

About three miles away, Clyde is buried in Western Heights Cemetery with his brother Buck. Cumie, Henry, and Jack Barrow lie in adjacent plots. It's much harder to get to Clyde's grave than Bonnie's. Western Heights is cramped and surrounded by a chain-link fence whose gates are usually padlocked. That doesn't keep Clyde seekers away. Part of the fence by the gates is perpetually yanked down to provide a convenient foothold. The grave they want to see is tucked in a far back corner of the property. Emma Parker had taken out a small life insurance policy on Bonnie, so she could pay for a large headstone. Henry and Cumie Barrow had no extra money, so after Buck died they told Clyde they would wait until his death, then bury him with his brother and buy one headstone for both.

Clyde understood. He even told Henry and Cumie the message he wanted carved on the headstone. Seventy-five years after he and Bonnie died outside Gibsland, the four-word motto Clyde asked his parents to inscribe remains true in ways he could never have imagined:

Gone but not forgotten.

Note on Sources

There is a great deal of disagreement about many dates and events in the lives of Clyde Barrow and Bonnie Parker, including the year in which Clyde was born and whether Bonnie really smoked cigars (1910, probably; and she didn't, definitely). Some of this stems from the lack of public records kept in the small towns where they were born and in the slum where they grew up. Media accounts of their crime spree include all sorts of exaggerated or downright false claims about what they did and when. The problem is exacerbated by many books about them that rely too heavily on these inaccurate news reports, or else on interviews with people who claimed far more intimate relationships with the Barrow Gang than they actually possessed.

Fugitives: The Inside Story of Clyde Barrow and Bonnie Parker was published just months after their deaths in 1934. "Editor" Jan Fortune interviewed Nell Barrow, Clyde's sister, and Emma Parker, Bonnie's mother, for the book, and presented them as addressing readers in the first person. Both the Barrow and Parker families were appalled by the result; they claimed Fortune made up much of the text, mostly in the sections devoted to Clyde's and Bonnie's criminal careers. But because it was the first, and because it claimed to come right from the lips of family members, *Fugitives* was accepted as gospel by much of the general public.

In 1979, former Dallas County deputy Ted Hinton's memoir *Ambush* was published some time after his death. He had been the last surviving member of the six-man posse that ambushed Clyde and Bonnie on a back highway outside Gibsland, Louisiana, in 1934, and swore his book told the only true, complete story. That does not seem to be the case; one friend of Hinton's said Ted never told the story the same way twice. Few Barrow-storians—except Hinton's loyal son Boots—accept Ted's version of the ambush, which has the posse squatting on a mosquito-infested hill for two nights rather than part of one.

The only other "relatives" book ever published came in 2003, when Clyde's youngest sister, Marie Barrow Scoma, coauthored *The Family Story of Bonnie and Clyde* with Arkansas historian Phillip Steele. Marie died soon after the pair began work on the book, and afterward Steele relied heavily on information from Shawn Scoma, Marie's adopted son, who was subsequently caught trying to sell forged Bonnie and Clyde memorabilia and is currently in prison for second-degree murder. A new generation of professional and amateur Bonnie and Clyde scholars found the book to be rife with errors, mostly caused by Marie completely overlooking or drastically altering instances in Clyde's life that might make her beloved older brother look bad.

Since then, there have been a few works of solid Barrow Gang scholarship published, all of which are helpful in putting together an objective, plausible delineation of what really happened during the short, violent lives of Clyde and Bonnie. These include James R. Knight and Jonathan Davis's *Bonnie and Clyde: A Twenty-first Century Update*, published in 2000 by Eakin Press; *On the Trail of Bonnie and Clyde Then and Now*, Winston G. Ramsey's exhaustive travelogue along every back road the outlaw couple traveled, published by After the Battle Press in 2003; John Neal Phillips's well-researched *Running with Bonnie and Clyde: The Ten Fast Years of Ralph Fults*, published by the University of Oklahoma Press in 1996 and offering readers for the first time a glimpse of Clyde and Bonnie through the eyes of one of their criminal cohorts; and in 2004 the posthumous *My Life with Bonnie and Clyde* by Blanche Caldwell Barrow (also from the University of Oklahoma Press), a diary discovered and edited by John Neal Phillips after Buck Barrow's widow died in 1988. Blanche's apparent purpose was to present herself as a martyr, but she was present during crucial events and her eyewitness accounts are invaluable. In working on these books, Phillips and Davis variously had the inestimable advantage of friendships with Marie Barrow Scoma, Buddy Barrow Williams (L. C. Barrow's stepson), Rhea Leen Linder (Bonnie Parker's niece), and Blanche Caldwell Barrow, as well as Ralph Fults and several other Barrow Gang intimates. (Buddy and Rhea Leen are still living, and have cooperated completely on this book.) In all my own lengthy research, I never found any of these four books to have exaggerated or misrepresented the smallest detail, though in some cases those interviewed and the authors themselves honestly disagree about where, how, and when some things happened. I have particularly relied on those books—and on interviews with Davis, Phillips, Linder, and Buddy Barrow Williams—in compiling *Go Down Together*.

But throughout my own book, particularly in early chapters dealing with the Barrow family's unsuccessful struggle to survive on country farms and subsequent move to West Dallas, I had the additional advantage of working from two other revealing, unpublished manuscripts. After the publication of *Fugitives*, which she had declined to work on with Jan Fortune, Cumie Barrow, Clyde's mother, attempted to write her own memoir. She never finished after making several false starts, and the resulting pages jump erratically from one time frame to the next. There are, essentially, three versions, one in which Cumie names names, a second in which she protects some identities, and another written in the third rather than first person. There are few even remotely sequential page numbers, making it impossible in my prologue and chapter notes to cite specific pages. I could number them myself, but there is no way of knowing what Cumie wrote first, or in what order she intended her memoir sections to be read. But throughout, hers is unmistakably the voice of a mother who loved her children, regretted their mistakes and deaths, and endured her sorrow through a profound, fundamentalist Christian faith. The manuscript was furnished to me for use in this project by Buddy Barrow Williams.

Then Jonathan Davis offered an additional prize. Before he coauthored his book with historian James Knight, and before Marie Barrow Scoma had her brief collaboration with Phillip Steele, Jonathan and Marie had spent two years working on a memoir by Marie that, when completed, she angrily rejected as having too many negative stories about her family. Jonathan painstakingly researched everything Marie claimed, and felt the two had produced an accurate portrait of a family that made more than its share of mistakes but never stopped being loyal to one another. Compared to the later *Family Story of Bonnie and Clyde*, the unpublished manuscript is 100 proof whiskey rather than watered-down beer. Here we have Clyde Barrow and Bonnie Parker describing in detail to their families some of the most notorious incidents in their careers—the Easter Sunday murders of two Texas highway patrolmen; the Dexfield Park shootout where Buck and Blanche Barrow had to be left behind; the Eastham Prison Farm raid that was reportedly masterminded by Clyde, but wasn't. It's simply amazing material, and some of it has never been made public before. Jonathan later supplied the leads—Barrow Gang enthusiast-historian Terry Whitehead of Blackwell, Oklahoma, also made invaluable contributions—to information that may untangle the most persistent mystery remaining in the saga of Bonnie and Clyde: How, exactly, could Texas Ranger Frank Hamer be so certain they would drive by the ambush spot at or around 9 A.M. on Wednesday, May 23, in 1934?

For this book, besides extensive interviews with expert historians, reliable authors, most of the few surviving men and women who had actual contact with the Barrow Gang, and Buddy Barrow Williams and Rhea Leen Linder, the two surviving members of the Barrow and Parker families still willing to talk to authors, I've based many of my conclusions on the four books cited here, plus the two unpublished manuscripts. In most other cases, including but far from limited to *Fugitives*, *Ambush*, and *The Family Story of Bonnie and Clyde*, I've tried to sift through the inaccuracies and utilize some specific passages that appear to reflect honest memory and not self-aggrandizing or ghostwritten exaggeration. And in virtually every instance, I give precedence to testimony from those who were there when something happened.

The hit 1967 film *Bonnie and Clyde* starring Warren Beatty and Faye Dunaway is inaccurate in any number of ways. It's wisest to consider it entertainment, not actual history.

Notes

Prologue

PAGE

1 *If it had been raining twenty miles west of Dallas:* Cissy Stewart Lale interview. She noted specifically that "motorcycle patrols could not occur during inclement weather because so many roads were still dirt, and the motorcycles would become stuck in the mud."

2 *Bonnie also spent some time sitting on the grass:* Jan I. Fortune ed., with Nell Barrow and Emma Parker, *Fugitives* (Ranger Press, 1934), pp. 160–61.

2 *Thanks to newsreels at movie theaters:* Jim Wright interview.

3 *But Henry, an escaped con who'd joined the gang ten weeks earlier:* Marie Barrow Scoma with Jonathan Davis unpublished manuscript, pp. 176–80.

4 *Clyde and Bonnie came to epitomize the edgy daydreams:* Orville Hancock interview.

Chapter 1: Henry and Cumie

Much of the information in this chapter is taken from the unpublished memoir of Cumie Barrow, and from the unpublished collaborative manuscript of Marie Barrow Scoma and Jonathan Davis that Marie rejected as making her family look bad. Specific pages in the Marie-Davis manuscript can be cited, but most of Cumie's pages aren't numbered.

All quotes by Cumie Barrow are taken directly from her manuscript.

A great deal of weight is also given to material from interviews with Davis, Charles Heard, John Neal Phillips, and Sandy Jones, all of whom spent many hours with Marie Barrow Scoma; Buddy Williams Barrow, who was told of the early Barrow family farming years by his stepfather, L.C. Barrow, and stepgrandfather, Henry Barrow; Cissy Stewart Lale, former president of the Texas State Historical Association; and Archie McDonald, professor of history and also a former president of the Texas State Historical Association, as well as the East Texas Historical Association.

Worth Wren Jr. provided background for my general descriptions of tenant farming in general and cotton farming in particular.

PAGE

9 Henry Barrow's background: Cumie Barrow unpublished manuscript; Marie Barrow Scoma with Davis unpublished manuscript, pp. 2–4. A census of Nacogdoches County residents taken in 1900 indicates Henry was born in Alabama, perhaps in 1876 rather than 1873.

9 *Tenant farming, in those years, had several attractions:* Cissy Stewart Lale interview.

10 *Jim apparently remarried in Texas:* James R. Knight with Jonathan Davis, *Bonnie and Clyde: A Twenty-first Century Update* (Eakin, 2005), p. 4.

10 *Horse racing was a popular recreation:* Cumie Barrow unpublished manuscript.

10 *Henry would say later:* Ibid.

11 *he moved to nearby Nacogdoches:* Ibid.

11 Cumie Barrow's background: Ibid.

11 *She had a knack for playing instruments:* Ibid.; Jonathan Davis interview.

12 *The bride was sixteen:* Cumie Barrow unpublished manuscript. Cumie claimed she was ten months younger than her husband, which would make 1873 the year of Henry's birth. Some census records indicate he was born in 1876. But that would make him fifteen at the time of his wedding, very young for a groom even in that era of early marriage. Cumie would have had no reason to misrepresent Henry's age in her memoir. Of course, it's possible he lied about it, either to his wife or to county officials conducting the census.

12 *Forty percent of all Americans lived on farms:* U.S. Department of Commerce, *Historical Statistics of the United States, Colonial Times to 1970*, pp. 457, 465.

12 *During good years, even a smallish tenant farm:* Richard D. White, *Kingfish: The Reign of Huey P. Long* (Random House, 2006), pp. 126–27; Worth Wren Jr. interview.

12 *the first half-decade of her marriage:* Cumie Barrow unpublished manuscript.

12 *The fortunes of Nacogdoches farmers:* Marie Barrow Scoma with Davis unpublished manuscript, pp. 6–8.

12 *Later there would be considerable dispute:* Ibid., p. 2.

13 *but still he wouldn't give up the dream:* Cumie Barrow unpublished manuscript.

13 *The first was Clyde in 1910, and his date of birth:* Marie Barrow Scoma with Davis unpublished manuscript, p. 2; once more, there's contradiction in a census—the only one in which Clyde appears, compiled in Ellis County in 1910, lists the boy's age as one. But it might have been taken late in that year, when he was *almost* one. Again, Cumie's Bible seems the most reliable source for an actual date of birth.

13 *L.C. (the initials were his full name):* Marie Barrow Scoma insisted this was true, and in her memoir Cumie Barrow identifies the boy only as L.C. One well-connected Barrow family source believes L.C. stood for Lee Carl.

13 *All four Barrow sons were addressed:* Buddy Barrow Williams interview.

13 *"I suppose we weren't a very happy family":* Fortune, ed., *Fugitives*, p. 24; Cissy Stewart Lale, Jonathan Davis, John Neal Phillips, and Archie McDonald interviews.

13 *Henry came home to their three-room shack:* John Neal Phillips, *Running with Bonnie and Clyde: The Ten Fast Years of Ralph Fults* (University of Oklahoma Press, 1996), pp. 42–43; John Neal Phillips, Jonathan Davis, and Buddy Barrow Williams interviews. A 1910 Ellis County census places the Barrows on a tenant farm in Trumbull rather than Telico. Essentially, those communities are interchangeable. The Barrows always said they farmed three miles outside Telico.

14 *"We had no time, then, for day dreaming":* Cumie Barrow unpublished manuscript.

14 *Cumie divided that struggle:* Jonathan Davis interview.

14 *Although they had to go to country school:* Buddy Barrow Williams interview.

14 *The Jesus worshipped by Cumie Barrow:* Cissy Stewart Lale and Archie McDonald interviews.

14 *Youngest child Marie would later recall:* Jonathan Davis interview. In *Fugitives* (page 25), Nell Barrow is quoted as saying, "I don't remember ever getting any spankings," and goes on to say that none of the Barrow children were ever punished. Just two paragraphs earlier, though, she's in fear of receiving "the spanking of a lifetime" from Cumie. This is one of many instances in *Fugitives* where Jan Fortune apparently wrote what she wanted rather than what she was told. Anyone who knew Marie Barrow Scoma—or Cumie, for that matter—never doubted the Barrow kids all knew the business end of a switch.

14 *Cumie was the Barrow parent who did the hitting:* Jonathan Davis interview.

15 *none of the Barrow children grew up hating:* Jonathan Davis, Sandy Jones, and Charles Heard interviews.

15 *Most of the Barrow kids didn't give Cumie cause for concern:* Buddy Barrow Williams interview.

15 *the theater in Telico was a three-mile walk:* Fortune, ed., *Fugitives*, p. 26. On something this basic, we can assume Fortune didn't do any embellishing.

15 *Buck started out attending school:* Cumie Barrow unpublished manuscript; Marie Barrow Scoma with Davis unpublished manuscript, p. 8.

16 *her brother, she said, wasn't above "lifting" a bird:* Fortune, ed., *Fugitives*, p. 28.

16 *And Buck developed a personal philosophy:* Buddy Barrow Williams interview.

16 *He didn't like school any more than Buck did:* Cumie Barrow unpublished manuscript; Marie Barrow Scoma with Davis unpublished manuscript, p. 8; Buddy Barrow Williams and Jonathan Davis interviews.

16 *Bud had to be the one in charge:* Fortune, ed., *Fugitives*, p. 27; Jonathan Davis interview.

16 *Cumie recalled that Bud "could shoot good":* Cumie Barrow unpublished manuscript.

16 *Bud's temper was different, too, from his older brother's:* Jonathan Davis interview.

17 *when Bud believed he had no other option:* Buddy Barrow Williams interview.

17 *Perhaps Bud's greatest pleasure was music:* Cumie Barrow unpublished manuscript.

17 *"We have both learned since":* Ibid.

18 *When World War I ended:* Robert A. Caro, *The Path to Power: The Years of Lyndon Johnson* (Alfred A. Knopf, 1982), p. 89; Cissy Stewart Lale, Worth Wren Jr., and Archie McDonald interviews.

18 *Cotton had been selling:* Knight with Davis, *Bonnie and Clyde*, p. 9; *Historical Statistics of the United States*, p. 517.

18 *Between 1910 and 1918, the average value:* Ibid., p. 463.

19 *Henry wouldn't quit:* Marie Barrow Scoma with Davis unpublished manuscript, p. 12.

20 *hitch up the old white horse:* Jonathan Davis interview. Some believe it was a mule, not a horse.

Chapter 2: The Devil's Back Porch

Once again, much of the material in this chapter comes from the unpublished manuscripts of Cumie Barrow and Marie Barrow Scoma. Background on the city of Dallas is derived from Patricia Evridge Hill's excellent *Dallas: The Making of a Modern City; The WPA Dallas Guide and History* edited by Gerald Saxon; *Ambush* by Ted Hinton; *Texas: A Compact History* by Archie McDonald; and *The Portable Handbook of Texas* published by the Texas State Historical Association. In the Dallas section, interviews with Archie McDonald and Cissy Stewart Lale were also invaluable, particularly regarding the city's effort to keep out the riffraff.

Details on the Barrow family's life in the West Dallas campground were also provided by Buddy Barrow Williams, Jonathan Davis, Sandy Jones, and John Neal Phillips, all of whom discussed in detail with Marie this part of her life. Buddy also heard stories from his stepfather, L.C., and stepgrandfather "Poppa Henry."

Newspaper accounts comprise the bulk of the background on how Dallas leaders tried desperately to discourage farm refugees from coming to the city.

John Slate, curator of the Dallas Municipal Archives, was generous with his time and assistance in scouring voluminous untitled records for key passages, several of which are quoted in this chapter.

PAGE

21 *Dallas was a fine place to live in 1922:* Patricia Evridge Hill, *Dallas: The Making of a Modern City* (University of Texas Press, 1996), p. 129; Roy R. Barkley and Mark F. Odintz, eds., *The Portable Handbook of Texas* (Texas State Historical Association, 2000), pp. 261–65; Dallas city archives, general information; Archie McDonald and Cissy Stewart Lale interviews.

22 *Dallas leaders' vision encompassed more than economic prosperity:* Cissy Stewart Lale interview; http://www.bigtex.com/aboutus/history/, the official Web site of the State Fair of Texas.

22 *The goal of its leaders, many believed:* Cissy Stewart Lale interview.

22 *In 1905, businessmen formed the 150,000 Club:* Barkley and Odintz, eds., *The Portable Handbook of Texas*, p. 261.

22 *One chamber publication claimed:* Hill, *Dallas*, p. 129.

23 *And, gradually, it worked:* Barkley and Odintz, eds., *The Portable Handbook of Texas*, pp. 262–63.

23 *There was opportunity for young arrivals:* Cissy Stewart Lale and Archie McDonald interviews.

23 *It was understood that Dallas:* Ibid.

23 *It took Dallas eighty years to reach its population goal:* Dallas Municipal Archives, population totals by decade.

24 *At first, civic leaders tried to stem the tide:* "Life on the Farm Depicted by Woman," *Dallas Morning News*, March 15, 1920; "Railroad Will Help to Make Farms Attractive," *Dallas Morning News*, July 15, 1920; "Farmers Discuss Spirit of Unrest," *Dallas Morning News*, August 2, 1920; "Population in Greater Dallas Up to 308,000," *Dallas Morning News*, May 5, 1930.

24 *And there Dallas differed again:* Cissy Stewart Lale interview.

24 *The bridges and levees of Dallas:* Jonathan Davis interview; Phillips, *Running with Bonnie and Clyde*, pp. 43–44.

24 *Its fetid air and swarming bugs:* Hill, *Dallas*, p. 129; *General Survey of Housing Conditions*, Dallas Municipal Archives.

24 *In 1948, when a social service agency: Inside West Dallas: A Report by the Council of Social Agencies of Dallas*, Dallas Municipal Archives.

25 *So they went to West Dallas:* Marie Barrow Scoma with Davis unpublished manuscript, pp. 13–15; Jonathan Davis, Buddy Barrow Williams, Sandy Jones, and Cissy Stewart Lale interviews.

25 *mostly the Barrows had to depend on the Salvation Army:* Jonathan Davis and Charles Heard interviews; Marie Barrow Scoma with Davis unpublished manuscript, pp. 15–16.

25 *So each morning he hitched up the horse:* Cumie Barrow unpublished manuscript; Jonathan Davis, Buddy Barrow Williams, and John Neal Phillips interviews.

26 *Other people's trash had become:* Buddy Barrow Williams interview.

26 *He was building a house:* Buddy Barrow Williams and Jonathan Davis interviews; Cumie Barrow unpublished manuscript; Knight with Davis, *Bonnie and Clyde*, p. 10.

26 *Bud was splitting time:* Marie Barrow Scoma with Davis unpublished manuscript, p. 13; Jonathan Davis interview.

26 *Cumie even made a new best friend named Tookie Jones:* Jonathan Davis interview.

26 *West Dallas was essentially a lawless place:* Archie McDonald, Cissy Stewart Lale, Pat Ziegler, and Jim Wright interviews.

26 *Victims on the east side of the Trinity:* Buddy Barrow Williams interview.

27 *"Suspicion," in those days:* Mitchel Roth interview.

27 *When he arrived in the city:* Cumie Barrow unpublished manuscript; Marie Barrow Scoma with Davis unpublished manuscript, pp. 16–17.

27 *The pit bull hated everyone:* Marie Barrow Scoma with Davis unpublished manuscript, pp. 16–17.

28 *Then Henry had another of his spells:* Jonathan Davis interview.

28 *But Cumie insisted that the invalids:* Sandy Jones interview.

Chapter 3: Clyde

Bill Sloan, a longtime staffer at the *Dallas Times-Herald*, knew and interviewed both Bob Alcorn and Ted Hinton. Pat Ziegler, a professor at Sam Houston State University in Huntsville, Texas, is the niece of Louise Barrett, who grew up in West Dallas with Clyde Barrow. Their insights were especially helpful in describing daily life for the kids growing up in that slum.

Sections of the flawed *Fugitives* and *The Family Story of Bonnie and Clyde* were useful for this chapter. Marie Barrow, who was highly critical of almost everything in *Fugitives*, did not disagree with passages from that book where Nell Barrow described her little brother's early criminal exploits. Anything cited from Marie's early childhood reminiscences in her book with Phillip Steele has been corroborated by at least one additional source.

The unpublished manuscripts of Cumie Barrow and Marie Barrow Scoma with Jonathan Davis continued to provide key information.

PAGE

29 *if you wanted to go to the picture show:* "Eugene O'Brien Is Star of Film at the Jefferson," *Dallas Morning News*, January 15, 1924; "Talking Movies Have Reached Practical Stage and Will Be on Exhibition Here This Week," *Dallas Morning News*, February 14, 1926.

29 *He spent hours gazing:* Phillip W. Steele with Marie Barrow Scoma, *The Family Story of Bonnie and Clyde* (Pelican, 2000), p. 29.

29 *Some nights, Clyde would go over:* Ibid. pp. 34–35.

30 *Two of the closest:* Jonathan Davis interview.

30 *Clyde went over to see them:* Steele with Marie Barrow Scoma, *The Family Story of Bonnie and Clyde*, p. 29.

30 *Artie was telling everyone:* Buddy Barrow Williams interview.

30 *he attended Sidney Lanier High:* Phillips, *Running with Bonnie and Clyde*, p. 44. In *Fugitives*, Nell Barrow states Clyde attended "Cedar Valley School" in Dallas, but that was for elementary grades. Marie and L.C. were the Barrow kids who went to Cedar Valley.

30 *Often Clyde and L.C. never made it to school:* Knight with Davis, *Bonnie and Clyde*, pp. 13–14; Marie Barrow Scoma with Davis unpublished manuscript, pp. 18–19; Jonathan Davis and Buddy Barrow interviews.

30 *Cumie warned him:* Cumie Barrow unpublished manuscript; Marie Barrow Scoma with Davis unpublished manuscript, p. 24.

30 *That desire wasn't unique to Clyde:* Archie McDonald, Cissy Stewart Lale, and Pat Ziegler interviews.

31 *His new teachers:* Cissy Stewart Lale interview.

31 *For West Dallas kids, the object of going to school:* Archie McDonald and Jonathan Davis interviews.

31 *Across the country, only about 40 percent:* Richard Polenberg. *One Nation Divisible: Class, Race, and Ethnicity in the United States Since 1938* (Viking, 1980), p. 20.

31 *So Clyde took a job:* Marie Barrow Scoma with Davis unpublished manuscript, p. 22; Phillips, *Running with Bonnie and Clyde,* pp. 44–45; interview with Sandy Jones.

32 *In Dallas and all across America:* Cissy Stewart Lale interview.

32 *Would-be union organizers claimed:* Hill, *Dallas,* p. 130.

32 *When Clyde went to the movies:* Jim Wright, Archie McDonald, Buddy Barrow, and Cissy Stewart Lale interviews.

32 *It was bad enough on the east side of the Trinity:* Pat Ziegler, Buddy Barrow Williams, and Jim Wright interviews.

33 *But the main attraction, when they could afford it:* Pat Ziegler and Archie McDonald interviews.

33 *He tried the most traditional means:* Jonathan Davis and Buddy Barrow Williams interviews; Knight with Davis, *Bonnie and Clyde,* pp. 15–16. In *The Family Story of Bonnie and Clyde,* Marie Barrow Scoma says Clyde also earned money as a part-time West Dallas pimp. Buddy Barrow Williams says that isn't true, and there is no corroboration to be found. Cumie Barrow overlooked many of the crimes committed by her sons, but she would have been outraged by Clyde sharing money earned through prostitution.

33 *he even tried to enlist in the navy:* Buddy Barrow Williams interview.

34 *Clyde looked at his father:* Archie McDonald interview.

34 *Many West Dallas teenagers engaged in petty theft:* Ibid.

34 *He started dipping his toe in the criminal waters:* Bill Sloan interview. In *Fugitives*, Nell Barrow denies Clyde stealing even a single chicken, and points out there's no record of it in Dallas police files. But Bob Alcorn told Sloan that juvenile chicken thieves were warned and released into their parents' custody rather than being formally charged.

34 *Eleanor Bee Williams was a pretty high school student:* Phillips, *Running with Bonnie and Clyde*, pp. 45–46; Knight with Davis, *Bonnie and Clyde*, p. 16; John Neal Phillips and Jonathan Davis interviews. In *Fugitives*, Nell Barrow identifies Clyde's first serious girlfriend as "Anne B." Clyde did have a later girlfriend named Anne. It's possible Nell was simply trying to conceal Eleanor's identity.

35 *Then Eleanor and Clyde quarreled:* Marie Barrow Scoma with Davis unpublished manuscript, p. 22; John Neal Phillips and Jonathan Davis interviews.

35 *Despite the Broaddus debacle:* Cumie Barrow unpublished manuscript.

36 *Decades later, asked about long-standing rumors:* John Neal Phillips interview. He was able to track down Eleanor and record her memories of dating Clyde Barrow.

36 *Clyde had been out of jail for only about three weeks:* Fortune, ed., *Fugitives*, p. 36; Marie Barrow Scoma with Jonathan Davis unpublished manuscript, p. 23; Jonathan Davis and Buddy Barrow Williams interviews.

36 *the police began referring to Buck and Clyde:* Ted Hinton, as told to Larry Grove, *Ambush: The Real Story of Bonnie and Clyde* (Shoal Creek, 1967), p. 9.

36 *Clyde would frequently be picked up at work:* Cumie Barrow unpublished manuscript; Marie Barrow Scoma with Davis unpublished manuscript, pp. 26–27; interview with Buddy Barrow Williams.

36 *Cumie wrote that her son:* Cumie Barrow unpublished manuscript.

36 *Henry made a rare attempt at parental counseling:* Hinton, *Ambush*, p. 9.

37 *One girl named Gladys made a particular impression:* Fortune, ed., *Fugitives*, p. 37.

37 *The postcard became one of Marie's favorite mementos:* John Neal Phillips interview. Marie showed the postcard to Phillips.

37 *There had been automobiles on America's roads since the mid-1890s:* David E. Kyvig, *Daily Life in the United States* (Greenwood, 2002).

37 *But by 1912, inventors had perfected electric starting engines: Science of Automotive Engineering*, Franklin Institute, 1936.

37 *Many car owners fell into the habit:* Cissy Stewart Lale interview.

38 *Nell caught Clyde:* Fortune, ed., *Fugitives*, p. 38.

38 *There was considerable profit:* Bill Palmer interview.

38 *he was held for "investigation":* Knight with Davis, *Bonnie and Clyde*, p. 19.

38 *He was arrested on August 13:* Marie Barrow Scoma with Davis unpublished manuscript, pp. 29–31; Jonathan Davis, John Neal Phillips, and Buddy Barrow Williams interviews.

39 *Clyde had a new, clearly undesirable friend:* Fortune, ed., *Fugitives*, p. 38; Phillips, *Running with Bonnie and Clyde*, p. 46; Marie Barrow Scoma with Davis unpublished manuscript, pp. 31–33.

39 *Sometime in the fall of 1929:* Fortune, ed., *Fugitives*, pp. 39–40. Though Marie Barrow was critical of *Fugitives*, according to Jonathan Davis she agreed with Nell's description of the policemen's accusations regarding Clyde.

40 *There was at least one happy day for Henry Barrow:* Jonathan Davis and Buddy Barrow Williams interviews.
40 *Many Texas families never even realized:* Archie McDonald interview.
41 *Buck had a new girlfriend:* Marie Barrow Scoma with Davis unpublished manuscript, p. 33.
41 *Cumie was ecstatic:* Jonathan Davis, Sandy Jones, and John Neal Phillips interviews.
41 *Marie wrote that Blanche struck the Barrows:* Cumie Barrow unpublished manuscript.
41 *The cocky Barrow brothers had bragged:* Buddy Barrow Williams interview.
41 *In the small town of Henrietta:* Knight with Davis, *Bonnie and Clyde*, pp. 22–23.
42 *Buck sent a letter to his parents:* Cumie Barrow unpublished manuscript.
43 *They hoped that close call:* Marie Barrow Scoma with Davis unpublished manuscript, p. 34; Sandy Jones, Charles Heard, Buddy Barrow Williams, and Jonathan Davis interviews.

Chapter 4: Bonnie

There's much less information about Bonnie Parker's early life than there is about Clyde Barrow's. *Fugitives* includes commentary from her mother, Emma, and cousin Bess. It seems obvious much of *Fugitives* is contrived by author-interviewer Jan I. Fortune to appeal to a scandal-obsessed public, but Emma Parker's memories of Bonnie's childhood appear valid if not objective. Emma always portrayed her children as pure-hearted and, if they made mistakes, she believed they did so only because they were lured into error by others. This regularly voiced opinion did not endear her to the Barrows.

In 1968, not long after the historically inaccurate Warren Beatty movie was released to critical acclaim and boffo box office ticket sales, Bonnie's younger sister, Billie Jean, participated in a lengthy interview that was released by RCA as a long-playing record album. Again allowing for a family member's desire to paint Bonnie in the best light possible, there is some very good, insightful material there. In her later years, Billie became close friends with Blanche Caldwell Barrow and Marie Barrow Scoma. Blanche and Marie recounted some of Billie's reminiscences about Bonnie to John Neal Phillips, Sandy Jones, and Jonathan Davis.

Dallas County deputy Ted Alcorn was clearly infatuated with Bonnie. An early chapter of *Ambush* describes the friendship they struck up when he patronized a café where Bonnie worked as a waitress. Like *Fugitives*, much of *Ambush* seems factually skewed, but Alcorn's near-worshipful account of how he and Bonnie met and became friends offers a helpful glimpse into how she went about charming men.

Cissy Stewart Lale, Archie McDonald, and Pat Ziegler have valuable insights into the harsh, hopeless lives of poor young women from the Dallas slums during the Depression. Census rolls from that period as well as the 1910s and 1930s helped flesh out where Emma Parker lived and worked and who lived in the Parker household at different times.

Bonnie's diary excerpts have been reprinted in several articles and books with no variation. Quotes here are taken from the diary material in *Fugitives*, but were verified through checking the same material in other places.

PAGE

44 *The worse her circumstances were in life:* Jonathan Davis interview.

44 *It began in the little West Texas town of Rowena:* Francis Edward Abernathy, ed., *Legendary Ladies of Texas* (Texas Folklore Society, 1994), p. 166; Phillips, *Running with Bonnie and Clyde*, p. 81; Jonathan Davis interview.

45 *As far as her mother, Emma, was concerned:* Buddy Barrow Williams and Jonathan Davis interviews.

45 *Emma approvingly described Buster as "sober":* Fortune, ed., *Fugitives*, p. 43.

45 *Rowena's community life:* Ibid.

45 *One of Charles Parker's brothers came to Rowena:* Ibid., p. 44.

45 *Charles Parker died:* 1900 McLennan County census; 1910 Runnels County census; Fortune, ed., *Fugitives*, p. 44. Rumors persist that Charles actually deserted his family, and Emma just claimed he'd died. Given her obsession with appearances, this is possible.

46 *So Emma looked for work:* 1930 Dallas County census; Hill, *Dallas*, p. 130.

46 *Like West Dallas:* Phillips, *Running with Bonnie and Clyde*, pp. 81–82.

46 *Every Sunday morning: The Truth About Bonnie and Clyde as Told by Billie Jean Parker, Bonnie's Sister,* RCA LPM-3967.

46 *While Emma was at work:* Fortune, ed., *Fugitives*, pp. 44–48.

47 *One of the most memorable moments:* Abernathy, ed., *Legendary Ladies of Texas*, p. 166; Fortune, ed., *Fugitives*, p. 45; Jonathan Davis interview.

47 *Bonnie had a hot temper:* Jonathan Davis interview; Fortune, ed., *Fugitives*, pp. 44–45.

47 *She expected special consideration from her family, too: The Truth About Bonnie and Clyde as Told by Billie Jean Parker.*

47 *Puberty brought with it an obsession:* Pat Ziegler, Archie McDonald, and John Neal Phillips interviews.

48 *There wasn't even a realistic chance:* Archie McDonald, Cissy Stewart Lale, Bill Sloan, and Pat Ziegler interviews.

48 *But there was another kind of option: The Truth About Bonnie and Clyde as Told by Billie Jean Parker;* Cissy Stewart Lale, Sandy Jones, and Archie McDonald interviews.

49 *Bonnie met Roy Thornton in high school:* Fortune, ed., *Fugitives*, pp. 49–51; Steele with Marie Barrow Scoma, *The Family Story of Bonnie and Clyde*, pp. 37–38.

49 *Bonnie loved children and wanted a baby:* Jonathan Davis, Buddy Barrow Williams, Sandy Jones, and Charles Heard interviews.

50 *In August 1927, Roy disappeared:* Knight with Davis, *Bonnie and Clyde*, p. 25; Phillips, *Running with Bonnie and Clyde*, p. 82; Jonathan Davis interview.

50 *In her first entry:* All diary excerpts are found in Fortune, ed., *Fugitives*, pp. 51–54.

51 *she found a job waitressing at Hargrave's Café:* Phillips, *Running with Bonnie and Clyde*, p. 83; Jonathan Davis and John Neal Phillips interviews. There is some disagreement about which cafés Bonnie worked at, and when. In *Fugitives*, Emma Parker states Bonnie worked at Marco's first. Ted Hinton in *Ambush* says the café by the courthouse was called the American Café. The consensus seems to be Hargrave's, then Marco's.

51 *Most of those tips were meager:* Archie McDonald and Cissy Stewart Lale interviews.
51 *She became special friends:* Jonathan Davis, John Neal Phillips, and Ken Holmes interviews.
51 *Her wardrobe might have reflected income:* Cissy Stewart Lale and Jonathan Davis interviews.
51 *Roy finally came back:* Steele with Marie Barrow Scoma, *The Family Story of Bonnie and Clyde*, p. 38; Fortune, ed., *Fugitives*, pp. 55–56.
52 *She told Hinton she wanted to be "a singer":* Hinton, *Ambush*, pp. 7–10; Abernathy, ed., *Legendary Ladies of Texas*, p. 163.
52 *Emma, ever alert for evidence:* Fortune, ed., *Fugitives*, pp. 50–51.
52 *convents throughout the state:* Cissy Stewart Lale interview.
53 *The Depression was taken as just one more sign:* Archie McDonald interview.
53 *Bonnie's brother, Buster, married Clarence Clay's sister:* Jonathan Davis and Buddy Barrow Williams interviews. There are conflicting opinions of why Bonnie was at the party, or even if there was a party at all. Some accounts have her hiring out there as a temporary housekeeper because Clay's sister had broken her arm. The important thing is, in early January, she and Clyde met at that house and fell instantly in love.
53 *just like Ronald Colman:* Bonnie mentioned in her diary that she had seen and loved these two films.
53 *Being with him promised some fun:* Cissy Stewart Lale interview.
53 *a short man so sensitive about his height:* John Neal Phillips interview.
53 *Clyde didn't take Bonnie over to the campground right away:* Marie Barrow Scoma with Davis unpublished manuscript, p. 36.
53 *Emma's first impression:* Fortune, ed., *Fugitives*, p. 58.
54 *Emma finally suggested he just go ahead and spend the night:* Ibid., p 59.
54 *Clyde had to sleep on the living room couch:* Steele with Marie Barrow Scoma, *The Family Story of Bonnie and Clyde*, p. 38.

Chapter 5: Dumbbells

"The Waco Jailbreak of Bonnie and Clyde," a lengthy article by Richard J. Veit in the December 1990 issue of *Waco Heritage and History*, provides many details of Clyde Barrow's conviction in a McLennan County court, his spectacularly incompetent escape attempt, and his subsequent harsh sentencing by an outraged Judge Richard Munroe. The article was provided to me by the Baylor University library in Waco.

The unpublished manuscripts of Cumie and Marie Barrow offered illuminating counterpoint to the descriptions by Emma Parker in *Fugitives* of how Bonnie reacted after Clyde's initial arrest, and her early relationship with the Barrow family.

For the first time, there are newspaper articles about Clyde's criminal activities. The *Waco Times-Herald* covered the adventures of the "baby dumbbells" at great length, if in subjective, uncomplimentary fashion.

Winston Ramsey's exhaustive *On the Trail of Bonnie and Clyde Then and Now* has excellent descriptions of Middletown and the geographic aspects of the escapee's bungled robberies and subsequent recapture by Ohio police. Archives at the Texas Prison Museum and the Texas Ranger Hall of Fame yielded court records and graphic, horrifying information about the Texas prison system circa 1930 and infamous Eastham Prison Farm.

The descriptions of Buck Barrow's prison break come directly from the unpublished memoirs of Cumie and Marie Barrow.

In this chapter and the next, much of the material regarding Eastham Prison Farm and the history of the Texas prison system comes from interviews with James Willett. He is the former Huntsville warden and currently serves as director of the Texas Prison Museum.

Letters from Bonnie to Clyde in prison, and Clyde's letters to her in West Dallas, are reproduced in several books. Here, they are all cited by the pages upon which they appear in *Fugitives*.

PAGE

55 *Clyde went quietly:* Fortune, ed., *Fugitives*, pp. 58–59.

55 *There was nothing calm about Bonnie's reaction:* Ibid.

56 *When she wasn't visiting Clyde:* Steele with Marie Barrow Scoma, *The Family Story of Bonnie and Clyde*, pp. 38–39; Fortune, ed., *Fugitives*, p. 59; Claire Bond Potter, *War on Crime: Bandits, G-Men, and the Politics of Mass Culture* (Rutgers University Press, 1998), p. 82.

56 *Cumie took in Bonnie's heavily mascaraed eyes:* Cumie Barrow unpublished manuscript.

57 *Eleven-year-old Marie, grown enough to be tantalized:* Bryan Woolley, *Mythic Texas: Essays on the State and Its People* (Republic of Texas Press, 2000), p. 141; Marie Barrow Scoma with Davis unpublished manuscript, pp. 37–38.

57 *Ever the opportunist:* Fortune, ed., *Fugitives*, pp. 59–60.

57 *"I was so blue and mad and discouraged":* Ibid., pp. 61–62. In *War on Crime*, author Claire Bond Potter claims this occurred in Waco rather than Dallas, but Bonnie was not taken by surprise when Clyde was transferred from Denton to the McLennan County jail.

57 *"They only think you are mean":* Fortune, ed., *Fugitives*, p. 63.

58 *Unlike Denton, the Waco jurists:* Richard J. Veit, "The Waco Jailbreak of Bonnie and Clyde," *Waco Heritage and History*, December 1990.

58 *On the same day Clyde was indicted:* Phillips, *Running with Bonnie and Clyde*, pp. 47–48.

58 *Perhaps encouraged by a note from Bonnie:* Veit, "The Waco Jailbreak of Bonnie and Clyde."

58 *Clyde joined Turner before Judge Richard Munroe:* Ibid.

58 *Cumie returned to West Dallas:* Cumie Barrow unpublished manuscript; Marie Barrow Scoma with Davis unpublished manuscript, pp. 38–39.

59 *In the main prison at Huntsville:* James Willett interview.

59 *he whispered details of a getaway plan:* Cumie Barrow unpublished manuscript; Fortune, ed., *Fugitives*, pp. 68–69; Marie Barrow Scoma with Davis unpublished manuscript, p. 40; Jonathan Davis interview.

60 *Clyde passed her a note:* Cumie Barrow unpublished manuscript.

60 *She finally buckled an extra belt:* Fortune, ed., *Fugitives*, p. 69; Marie Barrow Scoma with Davis unpublished manuscript, p. 41.

61 *When she returned to the jail that evening:* Veit, "The Waco Jailbreak of Bonnie and Clyde."

61 *About 7:30 in the evening:* Ibid.; Winston G. Ramsey, *On the Trail of Bonnie and Clyde Then and Now* (After the Battle Press, 2003) pp. 28–30.

62 *Clyde's auto-stealing skills worked to their advantage:* Veit, "The Waco Jailbreak

of Bonnie and Clyde"; Ramsey, *On the Trail of Bonnie and Clyde Then and Now*, pp. 28–30.

62 *She fretted at her cousin's house:* Fortune, ed., *Fugitives*, pp. 68–69.

62 *The newspaper made it clear:* "Trio Leaves Trail of Stolen Cars," *Waco Times-Herald*, March 13, 1930.

62 *Bonnie may have been offended:* Veit, "The Waco Jailbreak of Bonnie and Clyde."

63 *two strange men came up the sidewalk:* Fortune, ed., *Fugitives*, p. 70. There are several versions of this event. Some sources claim Bonnie was approached by the two men after she returned to Dallas. Others state that Clyde himself returned to West Dallas to find her. But Clyde was preoccupied with escape, and the trail of stolen cars indicates that he, Turner, and Abernathy were nowhere near West Dallas in the days immediately after the Waco jailbreak. Clyde would not have known Bonnie had decided to go home. Evidence overwhelmingly indicates that the mysterious duo were Waco friends of Clyde who'd been asked by him to tell Bonnie he was fine and would send for her soon.

63 *Bonnie hitchhiked back home:* Ibid.

63 *When she got there:* Ibid.

63 *On the afternoon of March 17:* Ramsey, *On the Trail of Bonnie and Clyde Then and Now* pp. 31–37; Veit, "The Waco Jailbreak of Bonnie and Clyde"; Marie Barrow Scoma with Davis unpublished manuscript, p. 41.

64 *Clyde told the Middletown police his name was Robert Thomas:* Some sources indicate he gave the alias "Robert Thorn." Either is certainly possible.

64 *McLennan County sheriff Leslie Stegall arrived in Middletown:* Veit, "The Waco Jailbreak of Bonnie and Clyde."

64 The Waco Times-Herald *was jubilant:* "Baby Thugs Captured," *Waco Times-Herald*, March 18, 1930.

65 *A Waco reporter even made the trip:* Marie Barrow Scoma with Davis unpublished manuscript, p. 41.

65 *When Clyde, Turner, and Abernathy arrived back in Waco:* Veit, "The Waco Jailbreak of Bonnie and Clyde."

65 *Criticism in the local paper:* Ibid.; Phillips, *Running with Bonnie and Clyde*, p. 48; Marie Barrow Scoma with Davis unpublished manuscript, p. 41–42.

66 *Clyde stayed in the county jail:* Phillips, *Running with Bonnie and Clyde*, pp. 48–49, Veit, "The Waco Jailbreak of Bonnie and Clyde."

66 *They apparently argued during the visit:* Fortune, ed., *Fugitives*, pp. 72–73.

66 *During the rest of the spring and all of the summer of 1930:* Phillips, *Running with Bonnie and Clyde*, pp. 48–49, Veit, "The Waco Jailbreak of Bonnie and Clyde"; Knight with Davis, *Bonnie and Clyde*, p. 34.

67 *Youthful, first-time offenders were often kept inside the Walls:* James Willett interview.

67 *Here, on 13,000 acres:* Phillips, *Running with Bonnie and Clyde*, p. 23.

67 *It was almost certainly a capricious decision:* James Willett interview.

Chapter 6: The Bloody 'Ham

James Willett, former Huntsville warden and current director of the Texas Prison Museum in Huntsville, was both generous and amazingly objective in his descriptions of the Texas prison system and Eastham Prison Farm during the time of Clyde Barrow's incarceration. Besides his own testimony, he urged me to read *Texas Gulag*, a history of Texas laws and prisons written by former prison counselor Gary Brown. Brown's book focuses on "the Chain Gang Years" of 1875–1925, but most of the appalling conditions and rules he describes were still in place from 1930 to 1932 when Clyde was an Eastham inmate.

Beyond my own observations, most physical descriptions of the main Huntsville prison facility and Eastham Prison Farm come from interviews with historian John Neal Phillips. Phillips's *Running with Bonnie and Clyde*, written with the help of Ralph Fults, is the basis for sections detailing Clyde's earliest experiences on Eastham farm. Though they were separated by prison administrators, Clyde told Fults in detail about what happened to him later in Camp 1, including his rape by and subsequent murder of building tender Ed Crowder.

As always, unpublished manuscripts by Cumie Barrow and Marie Barrow Scoma proved invaluable.

PAGE

68 *On the night of September 17, 1930:* Phillips, *Running with Bonnie and Clyde*, pp. 6–8.

68 *In Russell's thirty years of service:* Gary Brown, *Texas Gulag: The Chain Gang Years* (Republic of Texas Press, 2002), pp. 90–91.

68 *The One Way Wagon was as intimidating:* Phillips *Running with Bonnie and Clyde*, pp. 21–22; John Neal Phillips and James Willett interviews.

69 *The philosophy of the Texas prison system in 1930:* James Willett interview; Brown, *Texas Gulag*, pp. vii–viii.

70 *Just nine months before:* "New Questions Come to Fore on Prison Tour," *Dallas Morning News*, January 27, 1930.

70 *His concept of reform:* Paul M. Lucko, "Counteracting Reform: Lee Simmons and the Texas Prison System, 1930–1935," *East Texas Historical Journal* 30, no. 2 (1992), pp. 19–27.

70 *He especially endorsed frequent use of "the bat":* Ibid.; Brown, *Texas Gulag*, pp. 34–38.

71 *they were ordered to lick it:* Brown, *Texas Gulag*, p. 37.

71 *Simmons welcomed Fults back:* Phillips, *Running with Bonnie and Clyde*, p. 37.

71 *Together, the two camps usually had:* James Willett interview; Phillips, *Running with Bonnie and Clyde*, pp. 37–40.

72 *there had been 302 escape attempts:* Texas Department of Criminal Justice records.

72 *The farm's manager, B. B. Monzingo:* Lucko, "Counteracting Reform," p. 23.

72 *Clyde learned this as soon as he arrived:* Phillips, *Running with Bonnie and Clyde*, pp. 38–41.

72 *Field work at Eastham was exhausting:* James Willett interview; Brown, *Texas Gulag*, pp. 187–89.

72 *they talked as they chopped:* Phillips, *Running with Bonnie and Clyde*, p. 39.

73 *Food on the prison farms:* Brown, *Texas Gulag*, p. 137.

73 *At night they were marched:* John Neal Phillips and James Willett interviews.

73 *Building tenders received:* Brown, *Texas Gulag*, pp. 186–87; John Neal Phillips and James Willett interviews.

73 *On Clyde's first night:* Phillips, *Running with Bonnie and Clyde*, pp. 39–41.

74 *Clyde did the opposite:* John Neal Phillips interview.

74 *And, years later, Fults admitted that they had:* Phillips, *Running with Bonnie and Clyde*, p. 52.

75 *A new enemy was waiting for him there:* Marie Barrow Scoma claimed Ed Crowder bought her brother for three packs of cigarettes as soon as Clyde arrived in Huntsville. That would mean Clyde was abused by Crowder for almost two years instead of one. But that simply isn't possible. Crowder lived in the dormitory of Camp 1, and Clyde was initially placed in Camp 2. Prisoners from both camps sometimes worked alongside each other, but there wouldn't have been an opportunity for Crowder to attack Clyde until the younger man moved into the Camp 1 dormitory.

75 *Ed Crowder was a monster:* Jonathan Davis, James Willett, and John Neal Phillips interviews; "Convict Flees Solitary Cell," *Dallas Morning News*, May 7, 1929; "Ed Crowder Is Taken," *Dallas Morning News*, June 25, 1927; Texas state prison records.

75 *When Ed Crowder got his huge hands on Clyde Barrow:* John Neal Phillips, Jonathan Davis, Sandy Jones, and James Willett interviews; Marie Barrow Scoma with Davis unpublished manuscript, p. 42; Phillips, *Running with Bonnie and Clyde*, pp. 53–54.

76 *Scalley encouraged Clyde:* John Neal Phillips and Jonathan Davis interviews; Phillips, *Running with Bonnie and Clyde*, pp. 53–54; Texas Department of Criminal Justice records; "Convict Killed in Knife Battle on State Farm," *Dallas Morning News*, October 31, 1931; "Scalley Is No-Billed," *Dallas Morning News*, November 21, 1931.

77 *During the last few months of 1930:* Steele with Marie Barrow Scoma, *The Family Story of Bonnie and Clyde*, p. 46; Fortune, ed., *Fugitives*, pp. 74–76.

78 *In 1931, Jack, Artie, and Nell Barrow helped their father:* Buddy Barrow Williams interview; Marie Barrow Scoma with Davis unpublished manuscript, p. 15; Steele with Marie Barrow Scoma, *The Family Story of Bonnie and Clyde*, pp. 33–34.

79 *Bootleg hooch was another product for sale:* Marie Barrow Scoma always denied this, but Buddy Barrow Williams heard the story directly from his stepfather, L.C. Barrow, and from "Poppa Henry" Barrow himself. It's certainly odd that Marie thought bootlegging was too awful to admit to.

79 *Clyde thought he might persuade his father:* Jonathan Davis interview; Cumie Barrow unpublished manuscript.

79 *Blanche had divorced her first husband:* Blanche Caldwell Barrow, edited by John Neal Phillips, *My Life with Bonnie and Clyde* (University of Oklahoma Press, 2004), pp. 5–9; Cumie Barrow unpublished manuscript; Steele with Marie Barrow Scoma, *The Family Story of Bonnie and Clyde*, pp. 46–47.

80 *Eastham Prison Farm was nicknamed:* James Willett and John Neal Phillips interviews; "Prisoners Maim Selves to Get Away from Farm," *Dallas Morning News*, December 17, 1933.

81 *cutting off his entire left big toe and part of a second toe:* W. D. Jones, "Riding with Bonnie and Clyde," *Playboy*, November 1968. There is considerable debate over which toes on which foot were chopped off. I base my own belief on testimony from Barrow Gang member W. D. Jones, who saw Clyde's bare feet often enough to know.

81 *On February 2, he was still learning to walk:* Phillips, *Running with Bonnie and Clyde*, p. 58; Cumie Barrow unpublished manuscript. A few books claim

Clyde was pardoned on February 8, but Cumie had been working for two years to arrange her son's release. She would have known the correct date of his pardon.

81 *The twenty-one-year-old told his family:* Cumie Barrow unpublished manuscript.

Chapter 7: Decision

The Worst Hard Time, Timothy Egan's superb book about the Dust Bowl, was seminal to this chapter, as were Cissy Stewart Lale's personal reflections on living during that awful, traumatic time. The unpublished manuscripts of Cumie Barrow and Marie Barrow Scoma offered firsthand accounts of Clyde's unhappy return to West Dallas from Eastham Prison Farm. Ralph Fults shared his memories of reuniting with Clyde with John Neal Phillips in *Running with Bonnie and Clyde*. The best perspective of Emma Parker's deviousness regarding Bonnie's ongoing romance with Clyde comes from Billie Jean Parker's interview on the RCA record issued in 1968.

PAGE

82 *So when Clyde limped up to her front door:* Fortune, ed., *Fugitives*, pp. 79–80.

82 *Clyde and Bonnie fell into a passionate embrace:* Ibid.

83 *Emma tried to talk her daughter out of rekindling the romance: The Truth About Bonnie and Clyde as Told by Billie Jean Parker.*

83 *Bonnie began staying every possible minute with Clyde:* Cumie Barrow unpublished manuscript; Marie Barrow Scoma with Davis unpublished manuscript, p. 48.

83 *he insisted that all his new shirts be made of silk:* Hinton, *Ambush*, p. 13; Fortune, ed., *Fugitives*, p. 78.

83 *he wanted to open an automotive parts and repair shop:* Cumie Barrow unpublished manuscript; Jonathan Davis and Buddy Barrow Williams interviews.

83 *Cotton prices dropped to four cents a pound:* White, *Kingfish*, pp. 127–28.

83 *An average of twenty thousand farms across America failed:* Caro, *The Path to Power*, p. 241.

83 *All "negro unemployed" in Dallas were strongly advised:* "Back-to-Farm Move Advised for Negroes," *Dallas Morning News*, February 16, 1932.

84 *For more than a year:* Timothy Egan, *The Worst Hard Time: The Untold Story of Those Who Survived the Great American Dust Bowl* (Houghton Mifflin, 2006), pp. 88, 101.

84 *The first resulting massive dust storm:* Ibid., p. 88.

84 *In West Dallas, the effects of the dust storms:* Cissy Stewart Lale interview.

85 *During the last few weeks of February 1932:* Cumie Barrow unpublished manuscript; Fortune, ed., *Fugitives*, p. 80.

85 *In late February, Nell Barrow had a suggestion:* Jonathan Davis interview; Fortune, ed., *Fugitives*, p. 80; Cumie Barrow unpublished manuscript.

86 *Right after he arrived in Massachusetts:* Cumie Barrow unpublished manuscript; Hinton, *Ambush*, p. 14; Sandy Jones and Buddy Barrow Williams interviews.

86 *As soon as Clyde found work: The Truth About Bonnie and Clyde as Told by Billie Jean Parker;* Cumie Barrow unpublished manuscript.

86 *Fults had been released from the prison farm:* Marie Barrow Scoma with Davis unpublished manuscript, pp. 48–49; Phillips, *Running with Bonnie and Clyde*, pp. 60–64.

87 *But it was enough for Fults to smuggle in some hacksaw blades:* In *Running with Bonnie and Clyde*, Fults is adamant that he smuggled in the blades so Raymond Hamilton could break out of the McKinney jail. In *Depression Desperado*, Sid Underwood's biography of Raymond Hamilton, Underwood writes that Hamilton bribed a jail trusty to get him the blades. But there is no record of Fults and Hamilton meeting under any other circumstances, and Hamilton was later willing to join the gang that Clyde Barrow and Fults had formed. It seems logical that Fults had made a good first impression by helping Hamilton cut his way out of the McKinney jail cell.

87 *One of his first acts, Fults expected:* John Neal Phillips interview. Jonathan Davis feels Fults always exaggerated Clyde's determination to raid Eastham Prison Farm in retaliation for his mistreatment there. But Clyde's initial crimes after turning to full-time lawbreaking were intended to raise the money necessary to fund an Eastham prison break attempt.

87 *A few days later, Bonnie told her mother, Emma:* Steele with Marie Barrow Scoma, *The Family Story of Bonnie and Clyde*, p. 50. There is some uncertainty about the exact date when Bonnie left home to travel with Clyde. In *Fugitives* on page 80, Emma specifies it was March 20, 1932, but that may be incorrect by several days. She may have kept living at least part-time with her mother until her April 1932 misadventures in Kaufman.

88 *The world, in his opinion:* John Neal Phillips and Buddy Barrow Williams interviews.

88 *Bonnie wanted adventures in her life:* Jonathan Davis and Cissy Stewart Lale interviews.

88 *They had no long-term plan:* Buddy Barrow Williams and John Neal Phillips interviews.

89 *They realized there would be inevitable consequences:* Buddy Barrow Williams and Jonathan Davis interviews.

Chapter 8: A Stumbling Start

Much of the material in this chapter is based on *Running with Bonnie and Clyde*, the memoir written by Ralph Fults with the help of John Neal Phillips. Along with the memoir by Blanche Barrow, this is the only extended reminiscence about crimes committed by Bonnie and Clyde from someone who was right there with them. Phillips painstakingly fact-checked everything Fults told him, and with one notable exception (which will be discussed later in this chapter's notes) found that everything could be corroborated.

Also seminal to this chapter are *Bonnie and Clyde: A Twenty-first Century Update* by James R. Knight with Jonathan Davis and *On the Trail of Bonnie and Clyde Then and Now* by Winston G. Ramsey. Interviews with John Neal Phillips, Jonathan Davis, Rick Mattix, Buddy Barrow Williams, Sandy Jones, Cissy Stewart Lale, Archie McDonald, James Willett, Ken Holmes, and, especially, Bill Palmer were also helpful.

PAGE

93 *After dark on March 25, 1932:* Phillips, *Running with Bonnie and Clyde*, pp. 59–60; Knight with Davis, *Bonnie and Clyde*, p. 43; Ken Holmes interview.

94 *Raymond Hamilton let him know it:* Sid Underwood, *Depression Desperado:*

The Chronicle of Raymond Hamilton (Eakin, 1995), p. 5; Jonathan Davis interview.

94 *Fults and Clyde had a different plan:* John Neal Phillips interview.

94 *In the 1930s, almost every Texas family had a gun or two:* Archie McDonald and Cissy Stewart Lale interviews.

94 *Even Thompson submachine guns:* Rick Mattix interview.

94 *Fults preferred banks to small businesses:* John Neal Phillips interview.

95 *In 1924, Rand McNally published:* Potter, *War on Crime*, p. 84.

95 *Clyde loved the newfangled maps:* Jonathan Davis interview.

95 *Clyde, Fults, and Hamilton drove through Oklahoma, Kansas, and Iowa:* Phillips, *Running with Bonnie and Clyde*, pp. 67–70; John Neal Phillips interview. There is absolutely no existing record of the First National Bank in Lawrence being robbed of $33,000 by Clyde Barrow, Ralph Fults, and Raymond Hamilton in late March or early April of 1932. That doesn't mean it didn't happen as Fults described it; many public records have been lost or misplaced over the years. The amount claimed by Fults strikes several Bonnie and Clyde scholars, especially Rick Mattix, as ludicrous. But John Neal Phillips, who is meticulous in all his research, says he chose to believe and publish Fults's claim because everything else Fults told him checked out. The most important, and inarguable, fact is this—the gang pulled a robbery somewhere during that time that netted them enough money to buy an arsenal of high-caliber weapons soon afterward, which meant the Eastham raid could be attempted.

96 *Raymond Hamilton wanted nothing further to do with them:* Ibid., p. 70.

96 *Clyde and Fults drove back to Texas:* Ibid., p. 71.

97 *Her mother was less friendly:* Ibid., p. 72.

97 *they met with four local crooks:* Ibid., pp. 73–75; John Neal Phillips interview.

97 *nobody had ever attempted to orchestrate a break from the outside:* James Willett interview.

97 *But Clyde was especially concerned:* Jonathan Davis interview.

97 *In preparation for the raid:* Phillips, *Running with Bonnie and Clyde*, pp. 74–75.

97 *They were joined by another recruit:* Ibid.

97 *the gang members planned a simultaneous April 11 stickup:* Ibid., p. 73

98 *Clyde and Fults knew two brothers in Amarillo:* Knight with Davis, *Bonnie and Clyde*, p. 44.

98 *their car broke down:* Phillips, *Running with Bonnie and Clyde*, pp. 76–78; Jonathan Davis interview.

99 *But whatever mayhem Clyde and Fults were hoping to commit:* Buddy Barrow Williams interview.

99 *car gas gauges in the early 1930s:* Sandy Jones interview.

99 *Rural mail carrier Bill Owens:* Bill Palmer interview.

100 *Jack Hammett offered to hit a hardware store:* Phillips, *Running with Bonnie and Clyde*, pp. 78–79.

100 *On April 17, Clyde and Fults drove Bonnie:* Knight with Davis, *Bonnie and Clyde*, p. 45. It's suggested in several books and articles that Bonnie also met with and forewarned Joe Palmer and Henry Methvin, who were both also on Eastham farm at the time, and who broke out when Clyde and Bonnie were involved the raid of January 16, 1934. Palmer and Methvin were prisoners on the

farm when Clyde Barrow was incarcerated there. He certainly might have been friends with them. But it is only certain that Bonnie talked to Aubrey Scalley on this occasion, and it's never going to be certain whether Clyde met Palmer and Methvin for the first time during the January 1934 raid.

100 *As a building tender, Scalley was able:* James Willett interview.

101 *Fults didn't mind her tagging along:* Phillips, *Running with Bonnie and Clyde*, p. 80.

101 *Before leaving for Tyler:* Fortune, ed., *Fugitives*, p. 80. Emma says in *Fugitives* that Bonnie took part in the Tyler car theft trip "a few days" after Clyde returned from Massachusetts. This is one of the first major errors and/or omissions in the book. Many more follow.

101 *Still, Fults asked to stop on the way:* Phillips, *Running with Bonnie and Clyde*, p. 86.

101 *Things went as planned in Tyler:* Knight with Davis, *Bonnie and Clyde*, p. 45.

101 *Unfortunately for the would-be gun thieves:* Phillips, *Running with Bonnie and Clyde*, pp. 87–92; John Neal Phillips interview. In *On the Trail of Bonnie and Clyde Then and Now*, Winston Ramsey claims the aborted Clyde-Fults raid happened in Mabank rather than Kaufman.

102 *In spring 1932, almost all the back farm roads:* Archie McDonald, Cissy Stewart Lale, and Jim Wright interviews.

102 *When they came upon a farmhouse:* Knight with Davis, *Bonnie and Clyde*, p. 46; John Neal Phillips interview.

103 *Now they were really in trouble:* Phillips, *Running with Bonnie and Clyde*, pp. 90–92.

103 *Clyde made a quick decision:* Knight with Davis, *Bonnie and Clyde*, pp. 46–47.

104 *Back on the banks of Cedar Creek:* Phillips, *Running with Bonnie and Clyde*, pp. 95–97; John Neal Phillips interview.

Chapter 9: Bonnie in Jail

The unpublished manuscripts of Cumie Barrow and Marie Barrow Scoma are specific about Bonnie's positive attitude while incarcerated in Kaufman. Emma Parker in *Fugitives* is just as definite that Bonnie was distraught and completely antagonistic toward Clyde. Probably the best proof that Bonnie couldn't decide how she really felt comes from *Poetry from the Other Side*, the collection of ten poems she wrote while in the Kaufman jail. One of these, "Suicide Sal," has long provided fodder for historians and armchair psychologists, but most of them have made an inadvertent error.

"Suicide Sal" became public in April 1933, when police in Joplin found a copy of it among the possessions Bonnie left behind when she fled during a shootout. That version has been quoted and analyzed ever since—but it isn't the original that Bonnie wrote in Kaufman. In the ten months after her release from jail, she had continued to tweak the poem, making constant changes in the ongoing editing process. The original version, along with the nine additional *Other Side* poems, was given by Bonnie as a keepsake to Mrs. Adams, the wife of the Kaufman jailor. These handwritten manuscripts were eventually auctioned off to David Gainsborough Roberts of England, a private collector of various crime- and entertainment-related memorabilia. Through the good offices of Jonathan Davis, Mr. Roberts made Bonnie's original work available for this book.

PAGE

105 *Clyde meant what he had promised Bonnie:* Marie Barrow Scoma with Davis unpublished manuscript, p. 52; Jonathan Davis and Buddy Barrow Williams interviews.

105 *Clyde learned Hammett hadn't followed through:* Knight with Davis, *Bonnie and Clyde*, pp. 46–47; John Neal Phillips interview.

106 *The next afternoon, Clyde, Russell, and Rogers:* Knight with Davis, *Bonnie and Clyde*, p. 47; Jonathan Davis interview.

106 *immediate communication was always a problem:* Mitchel Roth interview.

107 *The crimes in Electra, Kaufman, and Celina were now linked:* Phillips, *Running with Bonnie and Clyde*, p. 97.

107 *He soon learned that Fults had been moved:* Ibid., p. 98.

107 *Bonnie was in less danger:* Cumie Barrow unpublished manuscript; John Neal Phillips interview.

108 *Texas juries were notorious for leniency toward women:* Archie McDonald and Cissy Stewart Lale interviews.

108 *So Clyde decided that acquiring a new bankroll:* Jonathan Davis interview.

108 *Marie, Clyde's little sister, recalled:* Marie Barrow Scoma with Davis unpublished manuscript, p. 51.

109 *Bonnie swore she was through with Clyde forever:* Fortune, ed., *Fugitives*, p. 89.

109 *Emma considered bailing her out:* Ibid., pp. 81–82.

109 *Bonnie whiled away the hours writing poetry:* Jonathan Davis interview.

109 *All ten poems reflect:* The original *Poems from the Other Side* manuscript, made available from the collection of David Gainsborough Roberts. All excerpts cited in this chapter are directly quoted from this source.

110 *Emma Parker read the poem:* Fortune, ed., *Fugitives*, pp. 82–83.

110 *Emma could be forgiven for near-hysteria:* Knight with Davis, *Bonnie and Clyde*, p. 187.

110 *it would have been worse had Emma seen:* Jonathan Davis interview. There is no evidence Bonnie let her mother read all the poetry she had written in jail.

111 *Emma Parker believed her sweet daughter was corrupted by Clyde:* Jonathan Davis and Ken Holmes interviews.

111 *He thought of a likely target:* Marie Barrow Scoma with Davis unpublished manuscript, p. 52. Marie Barrow believed it was possible that J. N. Bucher's son was in on the robbery with Clyde, setting up the robbery of his parents' store in return for a cut of the proceeds. There is no way to be certain.

112 *Clyde noticed Bucher's wife, Madora, staring at him:* Marie Barrow Scoma with Davis unpublished manuscript, p. 52; John Neal Phillips interview.

112 *Rogers and Russell wouldn't pass up:* Jonathan Davis interview.

112 *Proprietors of small-town Texas general stores:* Cissy Stewart Lale interview.

112 *Clyde "felt the job was jinxed":* Marie Barrow Scoma with Davis unpublished manuscript, p. 52.

112 *Russell and Rogers banged on the door:* The description of this crime is mostly taken from Knight with Davis, *Bonnie and Clyde*, pp. 50–51, and the unpublished memoirs of Cumie Barrow and Marie Barrow Scoma (pp. 52–54), since both relied on Clyde's description of the events. Alternate theories on how J. N. Bucher died include Mrs. Bucher diving for the gun in the safe, with her hus-

band dying in the resulting shootout, and the fatal bullet accidentally ricocheting into Bucher's body when Ted Rogers tried to shoot open the store safe. As with why Bucher's store was chosen for the holdup in the first place, there's no way to really know.

112 *under Texas law:* Cissy Stewart Lale interviews.

113 *she immediately picked him out:* Knight with Davis, *Bonnie and Clyde*, p. 52.

113 *Because of their frequent arrests together:* Jonathan Davis interview.

113 *Texas governor Ross Sterling . . . authorized a $250 reward:* Marie Barrow Scoma with Davis unpublished manuscript, p. 57.

113 *astronomical at the time:* Mitchel Roth interview.

Chapter 10: Murder in Stringtown

The killing of Atoka County undersheriff Eugene Moore may be the best documented of any incident in the short, violent criminal career of Clyde Barrow. It occurred in front of dozens of eyewitnesses who told their stories to police and newspaper reporters. Clyde Barrow talked about the shootout at length with his family, though he tried to put most of the blame on Raymond Hamilton. Marie Barrow Scoma and Cumie Barrow wrote extensively about Stringtown, and what Clyde said happened there, in their respective unpublished memoirs.

But the best, most detailed account comes directly from someone who was there. In June 2000 I met in Stringtown with Duke Ellis, who as a teenager was playing guitar at the dance when all the shooting started. He still had vivid memories of Sheriff Charley Maxwell telling him during a band break that he was about to arrest three well-dressed strangers for drinking before "the boys" punched them out for flirting with local girls. Duke very objectively described everything that subsequently happened, including his part in carrying the gravely wounded sheriff to a nearby house and watching while the local bootlegger poured raw whiskey down his throat in a successful effort to keep him alive.

Almost every book about Bonnie and Clyde has a slightly different version of how, when, and why Sheriff Maxwell approached Clyde and Raymond Hamilton. Several accounts have Maxwell as well as Eugene Moore dying in the battle. In fact, Maxwell survived and was an honored guest at Raymond Hamilton's execution on May 10, 1935. Time can affect any memory, and since Duke Ellis died in 2004 I wasn't able to conduct a follow-up interview with him just to see if he'd tell the same story twice. But he was there, so I have given credence to his version of events.

Several books and newspaper accounts claim there were four rather than three interlopers at the Stringtown dance. This is extremely unlikely. Clyde, Raymond, and Ross Dyer pulled the Neuhoff heist in Dallas without a fourth partner. Dyer often used the name Everett Milligan (Knight with Davis, *Bonnie and Clyde: A Twenty-first Century Update*, p. 54) and that may have caused some confusion. Duke Ellis saw only three men on the night of August 5.

PAGE

114 *Though the local newspapers didn't identify the leading suspects:* Buddy Barrow Williams and Jonathan Davis interviews.

114 *the Dallas police came by the Barrow place:* Cumie Barrow unpublished manuscript.

114 *It wasn't a matter of the local cops losing interest:* Cissy Stewart Lale interview.

115 *Fults got word to Clyde:* The entire description of the failed escape attempt by

Ralph Fults and Hilton Bybee is taken from Phillips, *Running with Bonnie and Clyde*, pp. 98–99; John Neal Phillips interview.

115 *For the rest of May 1932 and the first few weeks of June:* Marie Barrow Scoma with Davis unpublished manuscript, p. 56.

115 *On June 17, Bonnie was called before the grand jury:* Steele with Marie Barrow Scoma, *The Family Story of Bonnie and Clyde*, p. 56; Phillips, *Running with Bonnie and Clyde*, p. 101.

115 *Bonnie gave her collection:* Jonathan Davis interview.

116 *Emma felt her daughter:* Fortune, ed., *Fugitives*, p. 89.

116 *The Barrow family knew better:* Marie Barrow Scoma with Davis unpublished manuscript, p. 56.

116 *But logic held little attraction for Bonnie Parker:* Cissy Stewart Lale, Archie McDonald, Sandy Jones, and Jonathan Davis interviews.

116 *She wasn't the only one:* Phillips, *Running with Bonnie and Clyde*, p. 102; Underwood, *Depression Desperado*, pp. 10–11.

117 *Marie Barrow had became best friends:* Marie Barrow Scoma with Davis unpublished manuscript, p. 58; Jonathan Davis interview.

117 *Bonnie lived there with them:* Steele with Marie Barrow Scoma, *The Family Story of Bonnie and Clyde*, pp. 56–57; Fortune, ed., *Fugitives*, p. 89.

117 *The re-formed Barrow-Hamilton team:* Marie Barrow Scoma with Davis unpublished manuscript, p. 59.

117 *While Bonnie nervously listened to the radio:* Cumie Barrow unpublished manuscript.

117 *That night the gang celebrated:* Marie Barrow Scoma with Davis unpublished manuscript, p. 59.

118 *Clyde realized he was persona non grata:* Charles Heard and Ken Holmes interviews.

118 *Clyde was in a party mood:* Jonathan Davis interview.

118 *It was a small-scale event:* Duke Ellis interview.

119 *During the Depression, many small-town men:* Mitchel Roth and Ben Procter interviews.

119 *Moore, thirty-one, had been making a comfortable living:* Mike Royko, "They Haven't Seen the Movie," *Chicago Daily News*, March 17, 1968.

119 *Fifteen dollars a week was about the norm:* Cissy Stewart Lale interview.

119 *So long as things remained peaceful:* Duke Ellis interview.

119 *Later, Clyde swore to his family:* Marie Barrow Scoma with Davis unpublished manuscript, p. 63.

120 *Maxwell leaned forward:* The entire account of the shooting, including Clyde's escape attempt when he overturned the Ford V-8, is based on my interview with Duke Ellis.

120 *Within hours, a massive manhunt was underway:* Duke Ellis interview; Ramsey, *On the Trail of Bonnie and Clyde Then and Now*, pp. 62–65.

121 *At 7 A.M. on August 6:* Cumie Barrow unpublished manuscript.

121 *It was clear to Clyde and his family:* Buddy Barrow Williams interview.

121 *he might have been able to wangle a life sentence:* Cissy Stewart Lale and Ben Procter interviews.

122 *The rest of the Barrows didn't minimize the consequences:* Marie Barrow Scoma with Davis unpublished manuscript, pp. 65–66; Cumie Barrow unpublished manuscript.

122 *As soon as he'd had his meeting with Cumie:* Cumie Barrow unpublished manuscript; Buddy Barrow Williams interview.
122 *Bonnie had spent the previous evening:* Fortune, ed., *Fugitives*, pp. 90–91.
123 *She constantly told family and friends:* Phillips, *Running with Bonnie and Clyde*, pp. 80–81.

Chapter 11: Clyde and Bonnie on the Run

Much of the information about Clyde and Bonnie's adventures in New Mexico and their frantic flight from there back to Texas comes from two sources: Marie Barrow Scoma's unpublished memoir and *On the Trail of Bonnie and Clyde Then and Now* by Winston Ramsey, which utilizes stories that ran in local newspapers. Nell Barrow discussed the family meeting with Clyde and Bonnie in *Fugitives*. While parts of that book are clearly made up or at least wildly exaggerated, this passage relating how Clyde found out he was wanted for yet another murder rings true.

Marie's memoir is specific about Clyde and Bonnie's "Midwest tour," citing the unsigned postcards they sent back to the Barrows along the way.

Cissy Stewart Lale and Archie McDonald had firsthand knowledge of "country hospitality" during the Depression. A report published in 2003 by the Texas Historical Commission includes an excellent account of the history of motels in America.

For a story on the twenty-fifth anniversary of the 1934 ambush outside Gibsland, Arkansas, reporter Orville Hancock tracked down men and women whose families had accepted Bonnie and Clyde as guests while they were on the run from the law. Many remembered being offered rides on the running boards of Clyde's cars, and how Bonnie was always charming even though Clyde was sometimes prone to sulky silence.

Historian Ben Procter's lifelong study of the Texas Rangers and law enforcement in Texas allowed him to offer invaluable insights about the strengths and weaknesses of the officers pursuing Clyde and Bonnie, including how cops in Texas and New Mexico were notorious for ineffective communication with each other.

PAGE

124 *Bonnie announced she'd come for a visit with her new husband:* Ramsey, *On the Trail of Bonnie and Clyde Then and Now*, p. 66.
124 *Raymond had a separate hiding place:* Underwood, Depression Desperado, p. 15.
125 *Clyde's hair had been dyed a bright, unnatural shade of red:* Fortune, ed., *Fugitives*, pp. 95–96. In several other accounts, Clyde is wearing a bright red wig. But Nell was there, so her account is given credence.
125 *Clyde liked the idea:* Buddy Barrow Williams and Jonathan Davis interviews.
125 *communications between police in Texas and its neighboring state to the west:* Ben Procter interview.
125 *In Texas, the speed limit was 45 miles per hour:* Cissy Stewart Lale interview.
125 *He drove, as always, in his stocking feet:* Sandy Jones interview.
125 *He never liked to let anyone else drive:* Jones, "Riding with Bonnie and Clyde."
125 *Soon after her guests settled in, Aunt Millie became suspicious:* Marie Barrow Scoma with Davis unpublished manuscript, p. 68; Jonathan Davis interview. Deputy Johns did not confirm Millie Stamps had contacted him about her guests' suspicious behavior until after Clyde and Bonnie died in the Gibsland ambush.

126 *Johns thought Millie Stamps's niece:* Knight with Davis, *Bonnie and Clyde*, p. 57.
126 *In the early 1930s, three hundred miles even on paved highways:* Cissy Stewart Lale interview.
127 *A frenzied search was underway:* Knight with Davis, *Bonnie and Clyde*, p. 58.
127 *In San Antonio, Clyde drove endlessly:* The day after his release, Deputy Johns made a lengthy statement to the media about his ordeal. Several years later, the *Carlsbad Current-Argus* ran an even lengthier first-person account. This was where Johns admitted he'd been tipped off by Bonnie's aunt.
128 *he and Raymond found a suitable Ford V-8 to steal in Victoria:* Ramsey, *On the Trail of Bonnie and Clyde Then and Now*, pp. 70–73. The entire description of the attempted ambush in Wharton and the gang's escape comes from this source.
129 *That's how Emma Parker learned that Bonnie wasn't working:* Fortune, ed., *Fugitives*, p. 94.
129 *they broke into the state guard armory:* Jonathan Davis interview.
130 *He didn't like Clyde to begin with:* John Neal Phillips and Jonathan Davis interviews.
130 *"they lived off of small robberies that Clyde committed":* Marie Barrow Scoma with Davis unpublished manuscript, p. 70.
130 *they found a medicine bottle in it:* United States Department of Justice/Federal Bureau of Investigation document I.C. #26-31672, December 14, 1934 (revised October 1983), *Clyde Champion Barrow–Bonnie Parker.*
130 *This car theft was the first federal crime charged to Clyde:* Knight with Davis, *Bonnie and Clyde*, p. 59; Ben Procter interview.
130 *Clyde was still a tiny criminal fish:* Rick Mattix interview.
130 *A series of postcards:* Jonathan Davis interview.
131 *They didn't consider robbing a bank to be a good option:* Ben Procter interview.
131 *Clyde and Bonnie liked to stay at motor courts:* Jonathan Davis interview; the history of motels comes from *Statement of Historic Context for Route 66 Through Texas* published in February 2003 by the Texas Historical Commission.
132 *Particularly in rural areas during the Depression:* Archie McDonald and Cissy Stewart Lale interviews.
132 *Clyde and Bonnie always paid:* Orville Hancock interview.
132 *Most of these families were so poor themselves:* Cissy Stewart Lale interview.
132 *one out of every eight farms in the United States:* Caro, *The Path to Power*, p. 241.
132 *She was always sociable:* Orville Hancock interview.
133 *Whenever possible, Clyde tried to park by a creek:* Jonathan Davis interview.
133 *Bonnie hated the primitiveness of it:* John Neal Phillips interview.
133 *Clyde liked to drink himself:* In both her published and unpublished memoirs, Marie Barrow Scoma claimed her brother didn't drink at all. But many other witnesses, including Duke Ellis in Stringtown and Clyde's sister-in-law Blanche, said they'd seen Clyde drinking and/or drunk. Bonnie, according to historian Jonathan Davis in an interview, "may not have been an alcoholic, but based on what I've been told by witnesses she was at least the next closest thing to one."
133 *They had arguments that occasionally escalated:* Jonathan Davis and John Neal Phillips interviews.
133 *Clyde even stole a typewriter for Bonnie:* Sandy Jones interview.

133 *Whenever their wardrobes needed replacing:* Buddy Barrow Williams and Jonathan Davis interviews.
134 *As Clyde drove past the Barrow service station:* Fortune, ed., *Fugitives*, p. 101.

Chapter 12: The Price of Fame

As a longtime Texas journalist, Cissy Stewart Lale was an excellent source regarding the problems caused for Texas newspapers by the Depression, and why so many reporters wrote stories embellishing or even inventing crimes committed by Clyde Barrow. Marie Barrow Scoma's unpublished memoir had the best insights regarding the brief partnership between Clyde and Hollis Hale and Frank Hardy.

PAGE
135 *In 1932, most Texas journalists were not about to let facts:* Cissy Stewart Lale interview.
136 *But that wasn't the story told:* August 30, 1932, letter from Sheriff J. C. Willis, Dallas Municipal Archives.
137 *It wasn't because the cops didn't know who she was:* Archie McDonald interview.
137 *Clyde and Raymond and Bonnie were often what people talked about:* Jim Wright and Cissy Stewart Lale interviews.
137 *Nobody realized Raymond had split off:* Jonathan Davis interview.
138 *a young man entered Little's Grocery:* Knight with Davis, *Bonnie and Clyde*, pp. 61–62; Ramsey, *On the Trail of Bonnie and Clyde Then and Now*, pp. 76–77.
138 *Walter Enloe, a Grayson County deputy sheriff:* Knight with Davis, *Bonnie and Clyde*, pp. 62–63; Jonathan Davis interview.
139 *Nell Barrow wrote that her brother was philosophic:* Fortune, ed., *Fugitives*, p. 101.
139 *He and Bonnie began saving:* Jonathan Davis, Sandy Jones, John Neal Phillips, and Buddy Barrow Williams interviews.
140 *He and Bonnie wouldn't camp any longer:* Buddy Barrow Williams interview; Jones, "Riding with Bonnie and Clyde."
140 *Being the leader of a gang would give even more heft:* Archie McDonald and Cissy Stewart Lale interviews.
141 *Clyde recruited two new partners:* Knight with Davis, *Bonnie and Clyde*, p. 63.
141 *Uncharacteristically, Clyde now took his time:* Marie Barrow Scoma with Davis unpublished manuscript, p. 74.
141 *Very few women went into banks:* Cissy Stewart Lale interview.
141 *it didn't go as they'd anticipated:* Knight with Davis, *Bonnie and Clyde*, pp. 63–64; Ramsey, *On the Trail of Bonnie and Clyde Then and Now*, pp. 79–80.
142 *Frank Hardy and Hollis Hale reacted differently:* Marie Barrow Scoma with Davis unpublished manuscript, p. 74.
143 *On December 19, while Fults and Rogers were waiting:* Phillips, *Running with Bonnie and Clyde*, pp. 109–10; John Neal Phillips interview.

Chapter 13: Raymond and W.D.

When W. D. Jones was captured in Houston in November 1933, he provided a supposedly complete confession about all the crimes committed during his months on the road with Bonnie and Clyde. As the Barrow family liked to point out, W.D. claimed he was unconscious much of the time, either knocked out or drunk or passed out from fear. Thirty-five years later, Jones gave a far different version of many events in an interview with *Playboy* magazine. His testimony is valuable because he was a first- rather than secondhand observer. It's necessary to sift through both the confession and the magazine interview, picking out statements that appear to be best supported by other interviews and whatever facts about the Barrow Gang that are indisputable. In several cases, all pointed out in appropriate notes, it's guesswork based on what Clyde, Bonnie, and/or W.D. seem most likely to have said and done under the circumstances in which they found themselves.

PAGE

144 *Raymond made his return to crime:* Phillips, *Running with Bonnie and Clyde*, p. 117.

144 *he teamed up with small-time hood Gene O'Dare:* Ibid.

145 *they began pursuing local girls:* Marie Barrow Scoma with Davis unpublished manuscript, p. 76. There are several versions of how Raymond was captured, including one where he was betrayed by a man he'd worked with on construction jobs in Bay City.

145 *he had ice skates strapped to his feet:* Phillips, *Running with Bonnie and Clyde*, p. 119.

145 *The first time she saw Raymond:* Underwood, *Depression Desperado*, p. 23.

146 *Throughout Clyde's life he demonstrated:* John Neal Phillips interview.

146 *Clyde's sister Marie recalled many years later:* Jonathan Davis and Charles Heard interviews.

147 *had a request for Clyde and Bonnie:* Jonathan Davis interview; Marie Barrow Scoma with Davis unpublished manuscript, pp. 77–78; W. D. Jones confession transcript, November 18, 1933, Dallas Municipal Archives; Jones, "Riding with Bonnie and Clyde." W.D. said later Clyde asked him to come. That seems unlikely, but Clyde undoubtedly did see some advantage in having an extra person along as a lookout.

147 *Late Christmas morning:* Ramsey, *On the Trail of Bonnie and Clyde Then and Now*, pp. 80–85; Knight with Davis, *Bonnie and Clyde*, pp. 65–67. In his confession, W.D. said he backed out of robbing the store with Clyde. In *Playboy* he claimed that he stood guard outside while Clyde pulled the job. His first version is probably true since Clyde was so angry at him afterward.

148 *Then Clyde spotted a Ford Model A roadster:* Marie Barrow Scoma with Davis unpublished manuscript, pp. 79–80; Phillips, *Running with Bonnie and Clyde*, pp. 112–13: Ramsey, *On the Trail of Bonnie and Clyde Then and Now*, p. 82. W. D. Jones always claimed Clyde fired the shot that killed Doyle Johnson. All other versions of the event have both Clyde and W.D. shooting at him.

149 *Clyde told W.D. that whether he liked it or not:* Jones, "Riding with Bonnie and Clyde."

149 *West Dallas crooks Les Stewart and Odell Chambless robbed:* Marie Barrow Scoma with Davis unpublished manuscript, pp. 80–82.

150 *Richard "Smoot" Schmid took office:* Hinton, *Ambush*, pp. 1–5.

150 *Raymond Hamilton later swore:* Underwood, *Depression Desperado*, p. 22.

150 *Clyde suggested that Lillian bring a radio to Raymond:* Phillips, *Running with Bonnie and Clyde*, pp. 119–20.

151 *He, Bonnie, and W.D. spent the next several hours:* Jones confession.

151 *Bonnie had been drinking:* Fortune, ed., *Fugitives*, p. 106.

151 *They set up the ambush for Odell Chambless anyway:* The description of the failed ambush has been gleaned from several sources: Phillips, *Running with Bonnie and Clyde*, pp. 115–20; Marie Barrow Scoma with Davis unpublished manuscript, pp. 82–85; Jones confession; Jones, "Riding with Bonnie and Clyde"; Hinton, *Ambush*, pp. 30–34.

152 *"four other guns began going off right in my face":* Fortune, ed., *Fugitives*, p. 107.

152 *W. D. Jones began firing wildly from the car:* W.D. claimed in his confession that Bonnie did the shooting. In his interview with *Playboy*, he admitted that the whole time he was with Bonnie and Clyde, "she never fired a gun. But I'll say she was a hell of a loader."

152 *He passed his fourteen-year-old sister, Marie:* Marie Barrow Scoma with Davis unpublished manuscript, p. 84.

152 *Rain began pouring down:* Jones confession.

153 *On January 8, Raymond was caught trying:* Knight with Davis, *Bonnie and Clyde*, p. 70.

154 *Schmid did have a new deputy:* Hinton, *Ambush*, p. 33.

Chapter 14: "It Gets Mixed Up"

In his November 1968 interview with *Playboy* magazine, W. D. Jones went into great detail about life on the run with Bonnie and Clyde. Though most of Jones's descriptions of shootouts and robberies in his November 1933 "confession" to Smoot Schmid and the Dallas County police are highly suspect, there is no reason to think he's exaggerating when he tells about what the Barrow Gang liked to eat and where they slept from January 6 through the end of March in 1933.

In her unpublished memoir and in late-life conversations with Jonathan Davis, Charles Heard, Sandy Jones, and John Neal Phillips, among others, Marie Barrow Scoma reflected on how her brother and Bonnie lived during those months. Marie was occasionally permitted to ride with them for a day or two, so she spoke from firsthand experience.

So did Billie Jean Parker, Bonnie's younger sister. In 1968, just after Warren Beatty's brilliant but historically inaccurate film *Bonnie and Clyde* reestablished the outlaw couple's grip on the public imagination, Billie Jean was interviewed for what became a spoken-word album from RCA. The LP *The Truth About Bonnie and Clyde as Told by Billie Jean Parker* is long out of print even in this era of CD reissues and downloads, but for anyone with a turntable and sense of history it's well worth tracking down in flea markets. Billie Jean spent weeks at a time on the road with Clyde, Bonnie, L.C., and later Buck and Blanche Barrow. The stories she has to tell about her big sister and Clyde are exceptionally insightful.

This chapter also contains the first few annotations from *My Life with Bonnie and Clyde*, the memoir written by Blanche Barrow and edited for publication after her death by John Neal Phillips. Though it's self-serving in the extreme, Blanche's book still offers one more invaluable, firsthand look at Clyde and Bonnie during both action-packed and leisure times.

PAGE

155 *The car veered off the road into a muddy field:* Marie Barrow Scoma with Davis unpublished manuscript, p. 84. In W. D. Jones's November 1933 confession to Dallas County police, he claimed Clyde awakened three different farmers who teamed up to pull the car free.

156 *during these months they wielded a screwdriver:* Steele with Marie Barrow Scoma, *The Family Story of Bonnie and Clyde*, pp. 69–71.

156 *They'd keep going until Clyde announced:* Jones, "Riding with Bonnie and Clyde."

156 *W.D. snapped a photo of Bonnie posing:* Ibid.

156 *W. D. Jones was afraid of the dark:* Sandy Jones interview; Blanche Caldwell Barrow, *My Life with Bonnie and Clyde*, p. 42.

156 *Later, lawmen in Texas would spread rumors:* Ben Procter interview.

157 *bologna-and-cheese sandwiches:* Jones, "Riding with Bonnie and Clyde."

157 *the kind of personal grooming that remained important to Bonnie:* Ibid.

157 *Twenty-four-year-old Thomas Persell had eked out a living:* Knight with Davis, *Bonnie and Clyde*, p. 71.

158 *Persell said later that Clyde was "quite profane":* Ramsey, *On the Trail of Bonnie and Clyde Then and Now*, pp. 92–95.

158 *W.D. and Persell pried a battery out of a car:* Knight with Davis, *Bonnie and Clyde*, pp. 72–73.

159 *Clyde and Bonnie sent a steady stream of postcards:* Marie Barrow Scoma with Davis unpublished manuscript, p. 86.

159 *Clyde and Bonnie would simply drive past:* Buddy Barrow Williams interview.

159 *Jack and Artie, rarely saw their brother:* Jonathan Davis interview.

160 *Clyde and Bonnie gave their families money:* Buddy Barrow Williams interview.

160 *Nell had a question for her brother Clyde:* Fortune, ed., *Fugitives*, pp. 107–9.

160 *A few times, he even allowed Billie Jean Parker: The Truth About Bonnie and Clyde as Told by Billie Jean Parker.*

Chapter 15: The Shootout in Joplin

Firefights can't help but be confusing to everyone involved, so it's no surprise that several conflicting accounts exist concerning what happened on the afternoon of April 13, 1933, in Joplin. Blanche Barrow's memoir, W. D. Jones's confession to Dallas County police, Jones's interview thirty-five years later in *Playboy*, the unpublished memoirs of Cumie and Marie Barrow (providing Clyde's and Bonnie's accounts), and statements by Joplin police officers to the media all offer different perspectives and scenarios that just don't reconcile. Many of the discrepancies are minor—was Bonnie rewriting "Suicide Sal" when the shooting started, or was she cooking red beans and rice?—but others are more substantial. If he was as severely wounded as he later claimed, how did W. D. Jones get up and down the apartment stairs so quickly and often during the gun battle? Did Blanche Barrow really help pull dying Harry McGinnis out of the driveway? How many shots were fired by the police, and why didn't the cops keep shooting at the Barrow Gang as they drove away in their stolen Ford V-8 sedan?

There's no way to be certain. The description of the gun battle in this chapter represents a best guess based on what we know about the participants and why they might deliberately or subconsciously alter their version of events. All descriptions of the apartment and its surrounding neighborhood are exact, though, the result of a lengthy visit to Joplin and over an hour spent inside the apartment and garage.

But the biggest question regarding the Joplin gunfight on April 13, 1933, is this: Did Bonnie Parker pick up a rifle and start shooting at the police from a window in the apartment? In her unpublished memoir Marie Barrow Scoma unequivocally stated she did: "Bonnie grabbed a gun and looked out the window down at the area immediately in front of the garage. She saw the police car parked there and saw one of the officers behind it firing into the garage. Bonnie fired at this man, but missed him."

In *Fugitives*, Clyde's sister Nell says Bonnie told her she fired shots in Joplin, but that admission is part of another long, flowery monologue that sounds suspiciously like something editor Jan I. Fortune might have embellished or invented for dramatic effect.

Yet W. D. Jones in his 1968 interview with *Playboy* was also definite: "During the five big gun battles I was with them [which included Joplin], she never fired a gun." Bonnie's mother, Emma, and sister, Billie Jean, were adamant that Bonnie didn't fire even one bullet from the time she met Clyde until her death.

Later, months after Joplin, Bonnie probably did fire a gun during a robbery attempt that went awry. But it is also likely she didn't pick up a gun and shoot at a policeman in Joplin. Things were happening fast there. Afterward, none of the apartment windows were reported broken, so Bonnie would have had to open one of them to fire through. That would have taken a few more seconds, and if she'd shot at one of the policemen, probably Tom DeGraff, he certainly would have fired back. No damage to the apartment interior or exterior from bullets was ever mentioned—all the shots from Wes Harryman, McGinnis, and DeGraff were aimed at Clyde, W.D., and Buck in the garage.

W.D. was there, and Clyde's sisters weren't. In 1968, W.D. had no reason to lie in an effort to protect Bonnie's memory. It's also possible Bonnie might have exaggerated her actions that day when telling the story to Marie and Nell later on. Weighing all the evidence, to me the most likely conclusion is that Bonnie didn't fire a gun in Joplin.

Much of the general information about the Barrow Gang in this chapter is gleaned from Blanche Barrow's memoir. Blanche had a knack for capturing small details of the gang's daily life. The section on American media in 1933 and its creation of a glamorized legend regarding Bonnie and Clyde is mostly based on interviews with Cissy Stewart Lale, Jim Wright, Jonathan Davis, Sandy Jones, Archie McDonald, Buddy Barrow Williams, and John Neal Phillips.

PAGE

162 *Whenever Blanche, Cumie, and Buck's sisters Nell and Marie came to visit him:* Cumie Barrow unpublished manuscript; Marie Barrow Scoma with Davis unpublished manuscript, pp. 57, 70.

163 *Cumie never liked having women other than her daughters:* Buddy Barrow Williams and Jonathan Davis interviews; Blanche Caldwell Barrow, *My Life with Bonnie and Clyde*, p. 22.

163 *The day after Buck returned:* Ibid., pp. 24–31.

164 *Clyde talked about a new plan he had to raid Eastham prison:* In her memoir, Blanche says Clyde was planning this raid to free Raymond Hamilton, but that can't be right. In late March 1933, Raymond still hadn't been sentenced for the murder of John Bucher; he wasn't back in Huntsville yet, and Clyde had no way of knowing if he would be assigned to Eastham once he got there.

165 *they paid a hefty $50:* Blanche Caldwell Barrow, *My Life with Bonnie and Clyde*, p. 49. The gang rented the apartment for one month, and decided to give notice and vacate after two weeks. Clyde told Buck and Blanche they could have the leftover deposit money, "about twenty-five dollars."

165 *Harold Hill, who lived in an adjacent house:* Brad Belk interview.

165 *Playing house was a new experience:* Blanche Caldwell Barrow, *My Life with Bonnie and Clyde*, pp. 44–45.

166 *Clyde preferred death to prison:* Buddy Barrow Williams interview.

166 *all five of them continued to live:* Jones confession; Blanche Caldwell Barrow, *My Life with Bonnie and Clyde*, pp. 44–48.

167 *Clyde wanted a new car:* Jones confession.

167 *a little girl named Beth:* Marie Barrow Scoma with Davis unpublished manuscript, p. 90.

167 *Joplin had been a hotbed for bootleggers:* Rick Mattix interview.

167 *Clyde and Bonnie had a terrible fight:* Blanche Caldwell Barrow, *My Life with Bonnie and Clyde*, pp. 48–49.

168 *He finally convinced his big brother:* Marie Barrow Scoma with Davis unpublished manuscript, p. 91.

168 *April 13 was a Thursday:* The description of the day, and the gun battle, comes from a variety of sources—Brad Belk interview; Phillips, *Running with Bonnie and Clyde*, pp. 125–29; Blanche Caldwell Barrow, *My Life with Bonnie and Clyde*, pp. 51–57; Marie Barrow Scoma with Davis unpublished manuscript, pp. 91–94; Jones confession; Steele with Marie Barrow Scoma, *The Family Story of Bonnie and Clyde*, pp. 78–79; Cumie Barrow unpublished manuscript; Knight with Davis, *Bonnie and Clyde*, pp. 77–80; Ramsey, *On the Trail of Bonnie and Clyde Then and Now*, pp. 100–13; Fortune, ed., *Fugitives*, p. 114.

170 *So Clyde trimmed a thin tree branch:* Jones, "Riding with Bonnie and Clyde."

171 *at dawn the fugitives found themselves in Shamrock:* Blanche Caldwell Barrow, *My Life with Bonnie and Clyde*, pp. 58–59.

172 *Smoot Schmid ordered deputies Bob Alcorn and Ted Hinton:* Hinton, *Ambush*, pp. 39–47.

172 *Several glittering rings and sets of earrings:* Knight with Davis, *Bonnie and Clyde*, p. 79. Blanche Barrow believed the cops mistook the glass baubles she and Bonnie bought at Kress's for real diamonds.

173 *That made it easy to trace the car:* Although Clyde was in the habit of frequently switching license plates so the cars he stole couldn't be traced back to their owners, he apparently didn't bother this one time.

173 *Decent women puffed decorously on cigarettes:* Cissy Stewart Lale interview. One widespread legend is that in the original photo, Bonnie held a rose rather than a cigar between her teeth, and someone in the photo lab superimposed the cigar instead to make the photo more shocking. But that would certainly have tested the era's photo processing technology and besides, in his *Playboy* interview, W. D. Jones said Bonnie borrowed one of his cigars for the gag photo.

174 *Many Depression-era newspapers subscribed:* William J. Helmer and Rick Mattix, *The Complete Public Enemy Almanac* (Cumberland, 2007), p. 303; Potter, *War on Crime*, p. 93.

174 *publishers in Texas weren't the only ones:* Cissy Stewart Lale interview.

174 *editors of the crime magazines didn't hesitate:* Rick Mattix, Cissy Stewart Lale, Jonathan Davis, and Jim Wright interviews.

175 *in the minds of many Americans they elevated Clyde and Bonnie:* Jim Wright and Archie McDonald interviews.
175 *With their celebrity came controversy:* Rick Mattix and Jim Wright interviews.
176 *over the course of the next several months:* Jonathan Davis, Bill Sloan, John Neal Phillips, and Rick Mattix interviews.
176 *Their whole image was one of glamour:* Jim Wright interview.

Chapter 16: Shooting Stars

Harold Caldwell, a board member of the small but excellent Collingsworth County Museum, is well versed in the events there on June 9–10 involving the Barrow Gang. Museum director Doris Stallings also has considerable insights, many of these based on interviews with now deceased observers (and two participants!) and access to several key items left behind, and now on permanent display at the museum. Between them, Caldwell and Stallings offer a new, more illuminating explanation of what happened to Clyde and Bonnie in and around the small West Texas town of Wellington just before 10 P.M. on June 10, 1933.

Blanche Caldwell Barrow's *My Life with Bonnie and Clyde* continues to be a valuable source of information, though it is always necessary to filter from Blanche's testimony her frequent descents into self-righteousness and equally infinite self-pity. As historian John Neal Phillips, who knew Blanche well, likes to emphasize, she was a woman who "liked to get people going at each other." But she was also there with the gang during some particularly critical moments.

The unpublished manuscripts by Cumie Barrow and Marie Barrow Scoma with Jonathan Davis inform us of how the rest of the Barrow family reacted during this first phase of Clyde and Bonnie's national fame. *Bonnie and Clyde: A Twenty-first Century Update* and *On the Trail of Bonnie and Clyde Then and Now* do an admirable job of reporting specific events. This chapter does contain one significant disagreement about a date, which will be included in the notes that follow.

PAGE
177 *In 1933, Miss Sophia Stone of Ruston, Louisiana:* Knight with Davis, *Bonnie and Clyde*, p. 83; Marie Barrow Scoma with Davis unpublished manuscript, p. 96; Ramsey, *On the Trail of Bonnie and Clyde Then and Now*, pp. 115–17.
178 *She said later they were dressed shabbily:* Jonathan Davis interview.
179 *Clyde informed the two exactly who their captors were:* Blanche Caldwell Barrow, *My Life with Bonnie and Clyde*, p. 61.
179 *Even in a bad mood, Bonnie was too social:* Knight with Davis, *Bonnie and Clyde*, p. 84.
179 *Clyde ordered Stone and Darby to get out:* Blanche Caldwell Barrow, *My Life with Bonnie and Clyde*, p. 62.
179 *On their way through Hope:* Ibid., p. 63.
180 *Stone was eager to supply reporters:* Ramsey, *On the Trail of Bonnie and Clyde Then and Now*, p. 117.
180 *it seemed likely W.D. would make his way back to West Dallas:* Knight with Davis, *Bonnie and Clyde*, p. 84. In their unpublished memoirs, both Clyde's mother, Cumie, and sister Marie insist Clyde brought W.D. back to West Dallas immediately after the Joplin shootout with the goal of removing the impressionable teenager from a life of crime. After that, Marie writes, an unnamed man joined the Barrow Gang for a short time and participated in the Ruston car theft

and kidnapping. After Clyde brought W.D. home, they write, the teenager moped around West Dallas, getting into trouble—Cumie says he was picked up by the cops for some minor transgression and sentenced to a few weeks on a county work farm—and spending much of his free time at the Barrow service station trying to see Clyde again and talk his way back into the Barrow Gang. This hardly meshes with what we know about Clyde and W.D.'s relationship. Clyde found him to be a handy member of the gang, always subservient and available for the smallest errands. Blanche, who was involved in the Ruston events, writes in her memoir that W.D. became separated from the rest of the gang. This seems to be one instance when Clyde's mother and sister either subconsciously or deliberately "misremembered" to make Clyde look good. Far from being unwilling to corrupt a younger boy, he was glad to make use of W.D.

180 *Their visit was kept short:* Cumie Barrow unpublished manuscript; Marie Barrow Scoma with Davis unpublished manuscript, p. 97.

181 *They weren't staging these robberies:* Blanche Caldwell Barrow *My Life with Bonnie and Clyde*, p. 65.

181 *there is no record of them sneaking into a department store:* Archie McDonald interview.

181 *they'd hand money over to L.C. and Marie:* Marie Barrow Scoma with Davis unpublished manuscript, p. 98.

181 *L.C. purchased many of Clyde's snappy suits and hats:* Ibid.

182 *Other famous criminals like Dillinger and Pretty Boy:* Sandy Jones and Jonathan Davis interviews.

182 *Now such families might very well recognize the gang:* Orville Hancock interview.

183 *Bonnie chewed on pieces of lemon peel:* Bill Sloan interview.

183 *They'd seen her posed pictures:* Orville Hancock interview.

183 *he and Buck cased the place:* Blanche Caldwell Barrow, *My Life with Bonnie and Clyde*, p. 66; Ramsey, *On the Trail of Bonnie and Clyde Then and Now*, pp. 119–21; Knight with Davis, *Bonnie and Clyde*, pp. 84–85.

184 *She later told her family that she'd missed deliberately:* Fortune, ed., *Fugitives*, p. 121.

185 *She could have gone back to her father:* John Neal Phillips interview.

185 *They snatched up all the money they could:* Ramsey, *On the Trail of Bonnie and Clyde Then and Now*, pp. 122–29; Knight with Davis, *Bonnie and Clyde*, p. 85. Blanche wrote in her memoir that the take was only $100, clearly because she wanted to give the impression that every moment of her time with Bonnie and Clyde was spent in a state of near-starvation-level poverty. Much of it was, but not all, and certainly not after the robbery in Okabena.

185 *Clyde and Buck lost their tempers:* John Neal Phillips interview; Blanche Caldwell Barrow, *My Life with Bonnie and Clyde*, p. 71.

186 *Blanche, sitting between them, recalled later:* Blanche Caldwell Barrow, *My Life with Bonnie and Clyde*, pp. 72–77.

186 *Nell Barrow remembered that she and Artie:* Fortune, ed., *Fugitives*, p. 117. Nell also wrote that Blanche took the cab to the family service station, not Jack's house.

187 *Blanche thought those three had taken advantage of her absence:* Blanche Caldwell Barrow, *My Life with Bonnie and Clyde*, pp. 78–80.

187 *Cumie brought red beans, corn bread, and fried chicken:* Woolley, *Mythic Texas*, p. 137.
187 *Photos were snapped:* Jonathan Davis interview.
187 *Clyde and Buck gave the other Barrows:* Blanche Caldwell Barrow, *My Life with Bonnie and Clyde*, p. 80.
187 *As a birthday gift:* Marie Barrow Scoma with Davis unpublished manuscript, pp. 99–100.
187 *Everyone teased Blanche about her tight new pants:* Fortune, ed., *Fugitives*, p. 117.
187 *A teacher at her high school:* Marie Barrow Scoma with Davis unpublished manuscript, p. 100.
187 *Then he asked his mother to contact the Joplin police:* Ibid., p. 99.
188 *Then Emma Parker asked Bonnie to walk down the road:* Fortune, ed., *Fugitives*, pp. 122–23.
188 *Cumie had no better luck with Buck:* Cumie Barrow unpublished manuscript; Fortune, ed., *Fugitives*, p. 122.
188 *Bonnie's younger sister, Billie Jean, apparently came along: The Truth About Bonnie and Clyde as Told by Billie Jean Parker.*
188 *On June 2, a jury finally passed sentence:* Phillips, *Running with Bonnie and Clyde*, p. 134.
189 *Clyde and Buck apparently had only one disagreement:* Blanche Caldwell Barrow, *My Life with Bonnie and Clyde*, p. 87.
189 *Then late on the night of June 10:* In her memoir, Blanche recounts two different rendezvous, one immediately after she had her reunion with her father and then a second set for the night of June 10. Nobody else mentions two rather than one—this is an instance where it might have happened, or else Blanche could be mistaken. Either way, Bonnie, Clyde, and W.D. set out from West Dallas, probably on June 8, to meet with Buck and Blanche on the bridge between Erick and Sayre on June 10.
189 *They probably spent the night of June 8:* Other books cite June 9 as the night Clyde, Bonnie, and W.D. spent in Vernon. But interviews with Doris Stallings and Harold Caldwell seem to establish that on June 9 the trio was already in Wellington. They probably left West Dallas a day earlier than has been previously realized.
190 *the arrival of three well-dressed strangers:* Harold Caldwell and Doris Stallings interviews.

Chapter 17: Disaster in Wellington, Murder in Arkansas

In 1980, Jack Pritchard gave an extended interview to members of the Collingsworth County Museum board about the events of June 10. These are amazing in that they're in no way self-laudatory. Forty-seven years after the events, Pritchard told a plain story without embellishments in "Eyewitness Account of Bonnie & Clyde Escapade." Wellington city marshal Paul Hardy also offered his account of what happened, and Winston Ramsey reprinted almost all of it in *On the Trail of Bonnie and Clyde Then and Now*. Cumie and Marie Barrow Scoma's unpublished manuscripts provide Clyde's version of what happened.

In 1997, James R. Knight, coauthor with Jonathan Davis of *Bonnie and Clyde: A Twenty-first Century Update*, published a well-researched article, "Incident at Alma: The Barrow Gang in Northwest Arkansas," in the *Arkansas Historical Quarterly*, that includes much of the detail about the flight of the Barrow Gang to Fort Smith and the murder of Marshal Henry Humphrey in Alma.

The physical description of Wellington and its surrounding countryside come from personal observation. It is desolate out there.

PAGE

191 *Sam and Sallie Pritchard had their extended family over:* "The Rounds of One Old Country Boy," by Jack Pritchard as told to the Covington County Museum, 1980. Almost the entire description of the event from the perspectives of the Pritchards and the Cartwrights comes from this article.

192 *Her right leg was coated with acid:* Rhea Leen Linder interview.

192 *the hide on right her leg was gone:* Jones, "Riding with Bonnie and Clyde."

193 *Gladys began swabbing her wounds with baking soda:* Knight with Davis, *Bonnie and Clyde*, p. 87.

193 *He told W.D. to stay at the house:* Marie Barrow Scoma with Davis unpublished manuscript, p. 104.

193 *Based on Alonzo Cartwright's description:* Ramsey, *On the Trail of Bonnie and Clyde Then and Now*, pp. 134–40.

194 *Gladys Pritchard Cartwright worried that her baby:* Pritchard, "The Rounds of One Old Country Boy." In her unpublished memoir, Marie Barrow Scoma said the shooting occurred while Clyde was still down in the riverbed retrieving guns. But Jack Pritchard was there and Marie wasn't.

195 *When Bonnie was carried over to Buck's car:* Blanche Caldwell Barrow, *My Life with Bonnie and Clyde*, p. 95.

195 *But he was touched by how gentle they had been with Bonnie:* Marie Barrow Scoma with Davis unpublished manuscript, pp. 106–7.

195 *Wellington residents trooped out to the crash site:* Harold Caldwell and Doris Stallings interviews.

196 *Each day when they stopped, Blanche was dispatched:* Blanche Caldwell Barrow, *My Life with Bonnie and Clyde*, p. 97.

196 *They rented two cabins:* Knight with Davis, *Bonnie and Clyde*, p. 90.

196 *he went to the office of Dr. Walter Eberle:* Blanche Caldwell Barrow, *My Life with Bonnie and Clyde*, p. 98; Knight with Davis, *Bonnie and Clyde*, p. 90.

197 *Ted Hinton even visited the Barrows and Emma Parker:* Hinton, *Ambush*, pp. 53–54.

197 *But Clyde wanted Billie Jean:* Marie Barrow Scoma with Davis unpublished manuscript, p. 107; *The Truth About Bonnie and Clyde as Told by Billie Jean Parker.*

197 *Around midnight Ted Hinton drove into West Dallas:* Hinton, *Ambush*, pp. 54–55.

198 *Things hadn't gone well in Fort Smith:* Blanche Caldwell Barrow, *My Life with Bonnie and Clyde*, pp. 98–101.

199 *Clyde insisted that his brother and W.D.:* Marie Barrow Scoma with Davis unpublished manuscript, p. 109.

199 *Buck and W.D. left the Twin Cities Tourist Camp:* James R. Knight, "Incident at Alma: The Barrow Gang in Northwest Arkansas," *Arkansas Historical Quarterly* 56, no. 4 (Winter 1997), pp. 404–7.

199 *he did relieve Ewell of thirty-five cents:* Ramsey, *On the Trail of Bonnie and Clyde Then and Now*, p. 145.

200 *As it happened, the fifty-one-year-old Humphrey:* Knight, "Incident at Alma," pp. 402–3, 404–7.

202 *Another clipped off two of W.D.'s fingertips:* Jones, "Riding with Bonnie and Clyde."

203 *By then, Crawford County sheriff Albert Maxey had another charge besides murder:* Knight, "Incident at Alma," pp. 407–20; Marie Barrow Scoma with Davis unpublished manuscript, p. 113.

204 *Clyde quickly organized the gang's escape:* Marie Barrow Scoma with Davis unpublished manuscript, p. 112; Blanche Caldwell Barrow, *My Life with Bonnie and Clyde,* pp. 101–4.

204 *he didn't want to steal their property: The Truth About Bonnie and Clyde as Told by Billie Jean Parker.*

Chapter 18: The Last Interlude

Blanche Caldwell Barrow's *My Life with Bonnie and Clyde* continues to be a valuable resource, but as the tragic events of Platte City/Dexter begin to play out, Blanche's recollection of them becomes increasingly colored by self-pity and an ongoing obsession with blaming everything that happened there on Clyde. I don't accept some of her more outrageous claims, including that just before the Platte City shootout Buck accused Clyde of a willingness to sacrifice everyone else to save himself. But her account can't be completely dismissed—Blanche was *there*.

PAGE

205 *Dr. Julian Fields of Enid, Oklahoma:* Knight with Davis, *Bonnie and Clyde,* p. 97.

206 *he took Billie Jean just over the Texas state line:* Marie Barrow Scoma with Davis unpublished manuscript, pp. 113–14; Blanche Caldwell Barrow, *My Life with Bonnie and Clyde,* pp. 106–7. Blanche writes that Clyde didn't send Billie Jean home until after July 4, but Marie makes it clear she was back in West Dallas at least a week earlier. Marie is more reliable on dates than Blanche.

206 *The Barrow brothers returned about 4 A.M.:* Blanche Caldwell Barrow, *My Life with Bonnie and Clyde,* pp. 107–8; Ramsey, *On the Trail of Bonnie and Clyde Then and Now,* pp. 153–55.

207 *In a series of postcards to West Dallas:* Marie Barrow Scoma with Davis unpublished manuscript, p. 116.

207 *Bonnie "never walked any more straight": The Truth About Bonnie and Clyde as Told by Billie Jean Parker;* Cumie Barrow unpublished manuscript.

207 *W. D. Jones said later:* Jones, "Riding with Bonnie and Clyde."

208 *the five of them showed up in Fort Dodge, Iowa:* Ramsey, *On the Trail of Bonnie and Clyde Then and Now,* pp. 156–57; Knight with Davis, *Bonnie and Clyde,* pp. 99–100.

208 *Buck didn't want to stop for the night:* Blanche Caldwell Barrow, *My Life with Bonnie and Clyde,* pp. 109–10.

208 *That was when a gang of mobsters:* Helmer and Mattix, *The Complete Public Enemy Almanac,* pp. 352–54; Rick Mattix interview.

209 *He pulled up at Slim's Castle:* Knight with Davis, *Bonnie and Clyde,* p. 100.

209 *Buck and W.D. curled up on the floor of the Ford:* Blanche Caldwell Barrow, *My Life with Bonnie and Clyde,* p. 110.

210 *they had never been the target of any organized pursuit:* Knight with Davis, *Bonnie and Clyde*, p. 101.

210 *Joplin chief of detectives Ed Portley sent a letter:* Joplin Archives, July 18, 1933. Copy obtained from Texas Rangers Hall of Fame in Waco, Texas.

210 *Though coordinated pursuit of criminals was practically unheard of on an interstate basis:* Ben Procter and Mitchel Roth interviews.

Chapter 19: The Platte City Shootout

Blanche Barrow's *My Life with Bonnie and Clyde* offers her detailed perspective on the horrific gunfight in Platte City, plus events leading up to and following the battle. Clyde Barrow gave his version of events to his family, and they are included in his sister Marie's unpublished memoir.

There are two additional sources of fresh, insightful material. Crime historian Rick Mattix privately published *The "Bloody Barrows" Come to Iowa*, a fourteen-page, meticulously researched article about Platte City and Dexfield Park that includes material gleaned from interviews with several now deceased witnesses. Retired Missouri highway patrolman Thomas Whitecotton, a member of the posse that shot it out with the Barrow Gang in Platte City, recorded his reminiscences for the highway patrol archives in 2006.

PAGE

211 *N. D. Houser . . . was suspicious:* Knight with Davis, *Bonnie and Clyde*, p. 100.

211 *undoubtedly looted earlier in the day from the cash registers and gum machines:* This is speculation, but still informed. A witness to subsequent Barrow Gang gas station robberies in Oklahoma said they routinely broke into gum machines as part of their holdups.

211 *He gave her more loose change:* Blanche Caldwell Barrow, *My Life with Bonnie and Clyde*, p. 111.

212 *He told his family later:* Marie Barrow Scoma with Davis unpublished manuscript, p. 117.

212 *When Buck woke up:* Blanche Caldwell Barrow, *My Life with Bonnie and Clyde*, p. 112.

212 *The Barrow Gang had no idea:* Thomas Whitecotton, *To Serve and Protect: A Collection of Memories* (Missouri State Highway Patrol archives, 2006).

213 *he didn't get the hoped-for offer of cooperation:* Francis Williams, "The Day Bonnie and Clyde Shot It Out with the Law in Ferrelview," *Discover North*, March 1974, p. 4.

214 *At some point, either Clyde or Blanche walked:* This is a point of considerable dispute. According to newspaper accounts, witnesses remember Blanche going to the drugstore for medical supplies. Her jodhpurs made a distinct impression. But in her unpublished memoir, Marie Barrow Scoma says her brother Clyde not only ran the errand, he realized lawmen were gathering near the cabins, sneaked back, and told the others to pack and get ready to run. The attack occurred before they could get away. That doesn't seem likely. Clyde had avoided going outside at all, and as leader of the gang he always told Blanche or W.D. to run errands. I suspect Clyde didn't want his family to know that his poor decision to stay an extra night at the Red Crown cabins resulted in Buck being fatally wounded. By spinning a tale of how he alertly noticed the law preparing to strike and almost foiled the attack, he attempted to mitigate his guilt. The only reason

not to completely discount Clyde's version is that in her memoir, Blanche herself says Clyde went to get the medicine, taking W.D. with him. She may have been confused. What is certain is that Clyde did not sneak back to the cabins and tell everyone they had to go before the law descended on them. Patrolman Thomas Whitecotton's testimony notes the attack was launched at 1 A.M., at least six or seven hours after Clyde would have gone to the drugstore. Clyde told his family the assault on the cabins occurred about 10 P.M.

214 *Buck and Blanche talked about what they wanted to do next:* Blanche Caldwell Barrow, *My Life with Bonnie and Clyde*, pp. 112–13. Blanche adds that they also talked about dying and being buried together, but that is probably embellishment.

215 *Around 1 A.M. on July 20, Baxter and Coffey gathered their men together:* The description of the gun battle and the gang's subsequent escape blends information from these sources: Whitecotton, *To Serve and Protect*; Mattix, *The "Bloody Barrows" Come to Iowa*, pp. 2–4; Blanche Caldwell Barrow, *My Life with Bonnie and Clyde* pp. 115–24; Jones confession; Marie Barrow Scoma with Davis unpublished manuscript, pp. 119–20; Rick Mattix interview.

215 *Coffey's nineteen-year-old son, Clarence, was one of the highway patrolmen:* Most historians, writing about the Platte City shootout, indicate Clarence Coffey was a civilian witness. But his May 23, 1979, obituary in the *Kansas City Star* states he was a member of the highway patrol and participated in the gun battle.

Chapter 20: The Battle of Dexfield Park

Blanche Barrow's *My Life with Bonnie and Clyde*, Marie Barrow Scoma's unpublished memoir, and Rick Mattix's *The "Bloody Barrows" Come to Iowa* are essential in describing the events in Dexfield Park on July 24, 1933. But there's a third source of critical, insightful information. In July 2007, I interviewed ninety-three-year-old Marvelle Feller at an assisted living facility just outside Dexter. A charming man whose memory remained pristine, he enjoyed spending an hour recalling his meeting with Clyde, Bonnie, and W.D. in the aftermath of the park attack. Afterward, Feller's daughter-in-law Doris, who currently heads the town's historical society, took me on a tour of the former Dexfield Park as well as the farm once owned by her father-in-law's family. Artifacts in the town museum were also instructive.

Based on reminiscences of her father-in-law and other longtime Dexter residents, Doris Feller has written an article titled *The Beginning of the End for Bonnie and Clyde*. Information from that article is also included in this chapter.

PAGE

220 *Clyde and W.D. dug a grave for Buck:* Marvelle Feller interview.

220 *She kept telling him she wanted to go with him:* Blanche Caldwell Barrow, *My Life with Bonnie and Clyde*, p. 126.

220 *He made a clumsy attempt to disguise:* Marvelle Feller interview.

221 *W.D. confessed he was ready to give up:* Blanche Caldwell Barrow, *My Life with Bonnie and Clyde*, pp. 126–27.

221 *Later it would become town lore:* Doris Feller interview.

221 *Clyde bought several shirts:* Mattix, *The "Bloody Barrows" Come to Iowa*, p. 4; Marvelle Feller interview.

222 *he might be able to fulfill a promise:* Knight with Davis *Bonnie and Clyde*, pp. 105–6.

222 *they'd tried to pluck it out with tweezers but failed:* Blanche Caldwell Barrow, *My Life with Bonnie and Clyde*, p. 128.
222 *Henry Nye, a hired hand for one of the local farmers:* Marvelle Feller and Doris Feller interviews.
223 *he told store clerk and night marshal John Love about what he'd found:* Mattix, *The "Bloody Barrows" Come to Iowa*, p. 5.
223 *Bonnie, wracked with pain herself, generously offered:* Blanche Caldwell Barrow, *My Life with Bonnie and Clyde*, p. 128.
223 *Back in Dexter, the lawmen convened to plan:* Marvelle Feller interview; Mattix, *The "Bloody Barrows" Come to Iowa*, p. 5.
224 *Then someone in the posse stepped on brittle brush:* Mattix, *The "Bloody Barrows" Come to Iowa*, pp. 5–7; Marvelle Feller interview; Blanche Caldwell Barrow, *My Life with Bonnie and Clyde*, pp. 129–35; Marie Barrow Scoma with Davis unpublished manuscript, pp. 122–24.
226 *Bonnie told W.D. she wished she had a gun:* Fortune, ed., *Fugitives*, p. 140.
226 *nineteen-year-old Marvelle Feller wondered:* Marvelle Feller and Doris Feller interviews.
227 *that car was found abandoned in Broken Bow:* Mattix, *The "Bloody Barrows" Come to Iowa*, pp. 7–8; Marie Barrow Scoma with Davis unpublished manuscript, p. 125.

Chapter 21: Buck and Blanche

Marie Barrow Scoma's unpublished memoir offers the Barrow family take on what happened to Buck and Blanche. Blanche, of course, offers a firsthand account in *My Life with Bonnie and Clyde*. Billie Jean Parker described the scene at Buck's deathbed in a 1968 interview. In Platte City a lovely woman named Lu Durham, the daughter of the doctor who treated Blanche in the Platte County Jail, was especially helpful in recounting her father's description of how his famous patient looked and acted.

PAGE
228 *Doctors Keith Chapler and Robert Osborn were performing an early-morning tonsillectomy:* Knight with Davis, *Bonnie and Clyde*, pp. 108–10.
228 *At first the lawmen tried to keep them separated:* Blanche Caldwell Barrow, *My Life with Bonnie and Clyde*, pp. 135–36.
229 *Schmid or one of his officers provided money: The Truth About Bonnie and Clyde as Told by Billie Jean Parker.*
229 *two Arkansas lawmen came to Perry:* Knight with Davis, *Bonnie and Clyde*, pp. 113–14.
230 *Buck was delirious whenever he was conscious: The Truth About Bonnie and Clyde as Told by Billie Jean Parker.*
230 *Emma tried to lend moral support to Cumie:* Marie Barrow Scoma with Davis unpublished manuscript, p. 125.
230 *Marie Barrow told friends later:* Jonathan Davis interview.
231 *A Des Moines doctor extracted glass from her eyes:* Blanche Caldwell Barrow, *My Life with Bonnie and Clyde*, pp. 138–39.
231 *Blanche was interrogated:* Ibid., pp. 139–40; Knight with Davis, *Bonnie and Clyde*, pp. 113–14.
231 *she had to face another, and far more terrifying, interrogator:* Blanche Caldwell Barrow, *My Life with Bonnie and Clyde*, p. 289 (editor's note); Knight with

Davis, *Bonnie and Clyde*, p. 114; Ann Hagedorn, *Savage Peace: Hope and Fear in America* (Simon & Schuster), pp. 327–33, 370–71, 413.

232 *On Tuesday afternoon, July 25, Blanche was handed over:* Blanche Caldwell Barrow, *My Life with Bonnie and Clyde*, pp. 140–41.

232 *Dr. Durham liked Blanche:* Lu Durham interview.

232 *On Saturday, July 29, Blanche woke up in her Platte City cell:* Blanche Caldwell Barrow, *My Life with Bonnie and Clyde*, pp. 142–43.

233 *they found a poem titled "Sometime":* Ibid., pp. 197–98.

Chapter 22: Struggling to Survive

Because they lay low to heal from the injuries suffered at Dexfield Park, very little specific is known about Clyde and Bonnie's movements during August 1933. There is also considerable confusion about what criminal acts they committed once they were back in Texas. In *Ambush,* Ted Hinton insists the duo reintroduced themselves in their home state by robbing an East Texas oil company office. Marie Barrow Scoma is just as certain they weren't involved. Newspapers credited them with dozens of Dallas-area robberies, but again there's no definitive proof of anything.

Details on the Sowers ambush are mostly gleaned from Marie Barrow Scoma's unpublished memoir and Ted Hinton's *Ambush*. Neither is entirely objective, but both of them were there.

Oklahoma historian Terry Whitehead interviewed Bessie Floyd, Pretty Boy's sister-in-law, in December 1990. She recalled quite well her encounter with Clyde and Bonnie following the ambush in Sowers.

PAGE

234 *they were all wrapped in sheet:* Jones, "Riding with Bonnie and Clyde."

234 *Clyde decided to throw off potential pursuit:* Marie Barrow Scoma with Davis unpublished manuscript, p. 128.

235 *But W.D. told Clyde and Bonnie the same thing:* Ibid., pp. 128–29.

235 *The Barrows and Parkers were shocked at Bonnie's appearance:* Fortune, ed., *Fugitives*, pp. 145–46.

236 *They planned to bury him alongside Buck:* Marie Barrow Scoma with Davis unpublished manuscript, p. 140.

236 *He volunteered to drive his mother and sisters:* Ibid., pp. 133–34.

236 *Small-time Texas hoodlums Henry Massingale and Dock Potter:* Ibid., pp. 129–33.

237 *In mid-October, tragedy struck the Parker family:* Fortune, ed., *Fugitives*, p. 149.

237 *she began drinking heavily again:* Jonathan Davis interview.

237 *Emma intensified her efforts to talk Bonnie into leaving Clyde:* Marie Barrow Scoma with Davis unpublished manuscript, p. 141.

238 *the Barrows and Parkers wondered why Smoot Schmid and his deputies:* Fortune, ed., *Fugitives*, p. 148.

238 *the Barrows and Parkers referred to Clyde and Bonnie as "Mr. and Mrs. Howard":* Buddy Barrow Williams interview.

238 *he confided to deputies Bob Alcorn and Ted Hinton:* Hinton, *Ambush*, p. 104.

238 *Clyde convened a family gathering to celebrate:* Cumie Barrow unpublished manuscript. In that memoir, Cumie said they were celebrating her sixty-first birthday. But she was born in 1874, so in 1933 she turned fifty-nine.

239 *Their car was driven by Joe Bill Francis:* Marie Barrow Scoma with Davis unpublished manuscript, pp. 141–44.
239 *Years later, the Barrow family decided:* Buddy Barrow Williams interview.
239 *The lawmen were well armed:* Hinton, *Ambush*, p. 104.
240 *he suddenly felt something was wrong:* Woolley, *Mythic Texas*, pp. 137–38.
240 *Cumie, curled under the dashboard:* Cumie Barrow unpublished manuscript.
240 *Driving west of downtown Dallas:* Hinton, *Ambush*, pp. 107–8.
241 *They contacted a doctor:* Knight with Davis, *Bonnie and Clyde*, p. 120.
241 *"too careless with the lives of civilians":* Rick Mattix interview.
241 *Clyde and Bonnie went to Sallisaw:* Terry Whitehead interview.
241 *"a couple of kids stealing grocery money":* Sandy Jones interview.
242 *Paperboys hawked extra editions:* Phillips, *Running with Bonnie and Clyde*, p. 165.
242 *He and his men had found bloodstains:* Hinton, *Ambush*, p. 107.
243 *he fell back on the alibi suggested by Clyde:* Jonathan Davis interview; Marie Barrow Scoma with Davis unpublished manuscript, p. 148; Jones confession.
243 *The one Clyde immediately wanted to hunt down and kill:* Phillips, *Running with Bonnie and Clyde*, p. 167; Fortune, ed., *Fugitives*, pp. 151–52; Marie Barrow Scoma with Davis unpublished manuscript, pp. 146–47.
244 *now, he confided where and when only to Cumie:* Marie Barrow Scoma with Davis unpublished manuscript, p. 150.
244 *Cumie even recorded the dates of Clyde's visits:* Cumie Barrow unpublished manuscript.
244 *they brought baskets full of fruit:* Fortune, ed., *Fugitives*, p. 153.

Chapter 23: The Eastham Breakout

James Willett, former Huntsville prison warden and current director of the Texas Prison Museum, was especially insightful about the January 1934 raid on Eastham Prison Farm. John Neal Phillips, who collaborated with Ralph Fults on *Running with Bonnie and Clyde*, also had a great deal of information to contribute. His own painstaking research, including "walking the ground" at the escape site, contributed to this chapter.

PAGE
245 *As soon as he arrived at Eastham Prison Farm:* Phillips, *Running with Bonnie and Clyde*, pp. 159–160.
245 *Prison officials didn't take it seriously:* James Willett interview.
245 *Palmer suffered from various respiratory diseases:* Patrick M. McConal, *Over the Wall: The Men Behind the 1934 Death House Escape* (Eakin, 2000), pp. 66–69.
246 *Mullen claimed Raymond had promised him $1,000:* Knight with Davis, *Bonnie and Clyde*, p. 124.
246 *Fred Yost, an old acquaintance of Raymond's:* Underwood, *Depression Desperado*, p. 41; Hinton, *Ambush*, p. 118.
246 *Clyde hated the plan:* John Neal Phillips interview; Marie Barrow Scoma with Davis unpublished manuscript, p. 148; Jonathan Davis interview; Floyd Hamilton, *Public Enemy Number One* (Acclaimed Books, 1978), pp. 30–31. Floyd Hamilton claimed in his memoir that he was close friends with Clyde. Marie

Barrow Scoma insisted the two barely knew each other. The truth probably lies somewhere in between.

246 *Around 1:30 or 2:00 A.M.:* James Mullen, "I Framed Ray Hamilton's Prison Break: Confessions of an Ex-Convict, *Startling Detective Adventures*, November 1934.

247 *Palmer pretended to suffer an asthma attack:* Knight with Davis, *Bonnie and Clyde*, p. 126.

247 *Clyde's current ride was another black Ford V-8 coupé:* Phillips, *Running with Bonnie and Clyde*, p. 169.

247 *He hurriedly switched places with another prisoner:* Several books state that Raymond stabbed a Squad One prisoner in the back and took his place, but that seems unlikely. The guards would have noticed a body falling to the ground. Probably Raymond simply asked a Squad One member to trade places with him.

247 *Joe Palmer walked up to them with a .45 in his hand:* McConal, *Over the Wall*, pp. 96–97. Bill Palmer says his cousin ordered Crowson to raise his hands and only shot him when the high rider went for his gun. It's possible.

248 *Hilton Bybee fled with them, and so did two other prisoners:* There is considerable disagreement about which Eastham Farm inmates were originally included in the breakout plot. Raymond Hamilton, Palmer, and Fults certainly were, and Fults said in *Running with Bonnie and Clyde* that he asked Raymond to let Hilton Bybee go in his place. But there is no real evidence that Henry Methvin was ever part of the original group. Floyd Hamilton noted in *Public Enemy Number One* that Methvin "joined in the escape" during all the confusion after Joe Palmer shot Major Crowson and Raymond Hamilton wounded Olin Bozeman.

248 *Though French kept on running:* Some versions of the breakout story have French riding out with Clyde and the others, then splitting off from them later on January 16. But eight passengers would not have fit in the V-8 coupé, so French must never have been in the car.

248 *By the time he stopped for gas in Hillsboro:* McConal, *Over the Wall*, p. 103.

248 *Clyde called the Barrow service station:* Marie Barrow Scoma with Davis unpublished manuscript, p. 157.

249 *Major Crowson lingered until January 27:* McConal, *Over the Wall*, pp. 99–101.

250 *she and former Texas Ranger Frank Hamer loathed each other:* Harrison Hamer and Ben Procter interviews.

250 *Lee Simmons wanted the only lawman in Texas who was as famous:* Publicly, Simmons stated Hamer was always his first choice, but it is possible he may have asked two other Texas Ranger captains to head the Barrow Gang hunt before approaching Hamer. Both Tom Hickman and Manuel "Lone Wolf" Gonzaullas later said they turned down the assignment because they did not want to kill Bonnie Parker. Ben Procter interview; Phillips, *Running with Bonnie and Clyde*, p. 354.

Chapter 24: Hamer

Interviews with Harrison Hamer, great-nephew of Frank Hamer, and with historian Ben Procter, widely acknowledged as the foremost living expert on all things related to the Texas Rangers, provided much of the information included in this chapter. Also of great help was *"I'm Frank Hamer,"* a biography published in 1968 that is based to a large extent on a series of interviews granted by Frank Hamer to historian Walter Prescott Webb.

PAGE

251 *Frank Hamer almost became an outlaw himself:* Harrison Hamer interview; John H. Jenkins and H. Gordon Frost, *"I'm Frank Hamer": The Life of a Texas Peace Officer* (Pemberton, 1968), pp. 16–17.

251 *Three years earlier, Hamer and one of his brothers:* Jenkins and Frost, *"I'm Frank Hamer,"* pp. 12–15; Harrison Hamer and Ben Procter interviews.

252 *Founded in 1835 as a small, elite force:* Barkley and Odintz, eds., *The Portable Handbook of Texas*, pp. 861–63.

252 *Hamer, rising quickly to a captaincy, told his troops:* Ben Procter interview.

252 *By the end of his Ranger career he was credited:* Robert Caro, *Means of Ascent: The Years of Lyndon Johnson* (Alfred A. Knopf, 1990), p. 326.

252 *He established his reputation:* Barkley and Odintz, eds., *The Portable Handbook of Texas*, p. 405.

252 *An early legend had him arriving alone:* Ben Procter interview.

252 *Even celebrities were starstruck:* Jenkins and Frost, *"I'm Frank Hamer,"* p. 74.

253 *he wasn't shy about claiming near-superpowers:* Ben Procter, *Just One Riot: Episodes of Texas Rangers in the 20th Century* (Eakin, 1991), pp. 8–9; Ben Procter interview.

253 *Several times, Hamer resigned and took other employment:* Barkley and Odintz, eds., *The Portable Handbook of Texas*, p. 405.

253 *He despised the politics of Ma Ferguson:* Harrison Hamer interview; Phillips, *Running with Bonnie and Clyde*, p. 201; Jenkins and Frost, *"I'm Frank Hamer,"* pp. 174–77.

254 *So he resigned his commission on February 1, 1933:* In *Texas Rangers and the Mexican Revolution*, authors Charles H. Harris III and Louis R. Sadler state that Hamer resigned outright with no "inactive status" involved. Since he never rejoined the Rangers, it's immaterial.

254 *just over three times the monthly $150:* Procter, *Just One Riot*, p. 7.

254 *Hamer wasn't immediately interested:* Harrison Hamer interview; Jenkins and Frost, *"I'm Frank Hamer,"* pp. 207–8; Phillips, *Running with Bonnie and Clyde*, p. 4.

254 *Ferguson, he promised, would even grant Hamer the authority:* Knight with Davis, *Bonnie and Clyde*, p. 140.

254 *Hamer was concerned about providing:* Harrison Hamer interview.

254 *Hamer would be authorized to take:* Marie Barrow Scoma with Davis unpublished manuscript, p. 164; Jonathan Davis interview.

254 *Simmons assured him that wouldn't be a problem:* Phillips, *Running with Bonnie and Clyde*, p. 4; Ben Procter interview.

Chapter 25: The New Barrow Gang

Marie Barrow Scoma's unpublished memoir helps illuminate what Clyde and Bonnie said and did directly following the Eastham Prison Farm break. Bill Palmer's interview filled in certain details about Joe Palmer.

Dr. Glenn Jordan's interview with Bienville Parish sheriff Henderson Jordan and transcripts of testimony by Ava Methvin and her son Henry during his murder trial in

Oklahoma were helpful in discerning the dates that Clyde and Bonnie first visited the Methvin family in Louisiana.

PAGE

259 *Shortly after 1 P.M. on Tuesday, January 23:* Knight with Davis, *Bonnie and Clyde*, pp. 131–33.

260 *Mullen was the type who'd cause trouble:* Mullen later claimed Raymond Hamilton paid him only $75 of the amount owed.

260 *Hilton Bybee didn't care one way or the other:* John Neal Phillips interview; Phillips, *Running with Bonnie and Clyde*, pp. 172–73.

260 *just three days after their successful robbery in Iowa:* Ramsey, *On the Trail of Bonnie and Clyde Then and Now*, pp. 208–9.

260 *there was trouble between Palmer and Raymond:* Bill Palmer interview; Marie Barrow Scoma with Davis unpublished manuscript, p. 164; Knight with Davis, *Bonnie and Clyde*, p. 133.

261 *Now Palmer wanted to see her:* Bill Palmer interview.

261 *Then Palmer wanted to go to Houston:* Knight with Davis, *Bonnie and Clyde*, p. 133.

262 *Things didn't go quite as smoothly:* Ramsey, *On the Trail of Bonnie and Clyde Then and Now*, pp. 210–11.

262 *Afterward the gang traveled to Bienville Parish:* Dr. Glenn Jordan interview on October 12, 1958, with Henderson Jordan (they were not related—Dr. Jordan was head archivist for Northeastern University in Monroe, Louisiana); trial testimony of Ava Methvin and Henry Methvin, September 1934.

262 *Clyde got lost:* Ramsey, *On the Trail of Bonnie and Clyde Then and Now*, pp. 212–13.

263 *Clyde and Bonnie had some of their sparkle back:* Marie Barrow Scoma with Davis unpublished manuscript, pp. 165–66.

263 *Nicknamed "Tush Hog" by other inmates:* Knight with Davis, *Bonnie and Clyde*, p. 125.

263 *Nobody besides Raymond found anything to like:* Marie Barrow Scoma with Davis unpublished manuscript, pp. 158–59; Hamilton, *Public Enemy Number One*, p. 33.

264 *they broke into the state armory:* Ramsey, *On the Trail of Bonnie and Clyde Then and Now*, pp. 214–15.

264 *Laborer Ollie Worley, who'd just cashed his $27 paycheck:* Knight with Davis, *Bonnie and Clyde*, pp. 136–37.

265 *Raymond suggested that they divide the loot:* Cumie Barrow unpublished manuscript: Knight with Davis, *Bonnie and Clyde*, p. 137.

265 *During the week that the gang spent in Terre Haute:* Jonathan Davis interview; Marrie Barrow Scoma with Davis unpublished manuscript, p. 170.

265 *Clyde and Bonnie still had fights:* Marie Barrow Scoma with Davis unpublished manuscript, p. 171.

Chapter 26: Hamer on the Trail

Frank Hamer, Lee Simmons, Bienville Parish sheriff Henderson Jordan, and Dallas County deputy Ted Hinton all offered conflicting versions of when and how Clyde and Bonnie were first betrayed in March and then ambushed in May. Their various testimonies combine into one of the most dazzling displays of deliberate obfuscation in modern history. Such widely varied accounts can't be dismissed as different people honestly recalling the same events in different ways. Motive becomes an issue, and they all had reason to lie. Hamer was fanatical about protecting sources. Simmons was interested in resurrecting his own public image, which was damaged after the January 16, 1934, breakout from Eastham Prison Farm. Jordan wanted to present himself as the critical dealmaker. Nobody can account for Ted Hinton's highly improbable reminiscences, especially concerning how he and Bob Alcorn joined Hamer's posse, and the events of the May 23 ambush itself. Some people who knew him suspect he became delusional late in life.

If all written history by nonparticipants is "best guess," then my descriptions in this and subsequent chapters are based mostly on testimony by Ava and Henry Methvin at Henry's murder trial in Oklahoma five months after the May 23 ambush. At this point, neither Methvin had any reason to lie. Frank Hamer provided the Oklahoma court with documentation that Henry and his family betrayed Clyde and Bonnie. Both Methvins were reasonably specific about how they initially contacted Henderson Jordan and the deals they tried to put together through him with Hamer and FBI agent Lester Kindell.

No two writers are likely to look at the convoluted material available and draw the same conclusions. My reasoning regarding presentation of each disputed date and incident is explained in the appropriate chapter notes.

PAGE

267 *On February 11 he drove to Dallas in a Ford V-8:* Jenkins and Frost, *"I'm Frank Hamer,"* p. 210; Phillips, *Running with Bonnie and Clyde*, p. 210.

267 *West Dallas denizens always kept a sharp eye out for the cops:* Jonathan Davis interview.

268 *The Dallas County sheriff and his deputies had plenty of stories to tell Hamer:* Hinton, *Ambush*, pp. 128–32. Though he seems to wildly exaggerate subsequent events, Ted Hinton had no reason to embellish his office's frequent failures to catch Clyde and Bonnie.

268 *Hamer wanted to hear those stories and more:* Jenkins and Frost, *"I'm Frank Hamer,"* pp. 210–11. Hamer's methodical approach to tracking criminals was well known to his peers and the public.

268 *At a recently abandoned Barrow Gang camp outside Wichita Falls:* Jenkins and Frost, *"I'm Frank Hamer,"* p. 211. There's no reason to doubt Hamer went to these places and found these clues.

269 *He soon believed he'd discerned a pattern:* Rick Mattix interview.

269 *Sometimes when he camped in his V-8 at night:* Harrison Hamer interview.

269 *Hamer had no respect for Bonnie Parker:* Ben Procter interview.

270 *So Hamer decided he would try to trap the couple:* Jenkins and Frost, *"I'm Frank Hamer,"* p. 212.

271 *During the first four weeks of his pursuit:* Hamer claimed afterward that he discovered a Barrow Gang hideout in Louisiana on February 17, but because he didn't trust the sheriff with jurisdiction there he "arranged to have Barrow's hideout moved into a parish where the officers were more reliable. In a comparatively short time the hideout was established in Bienville Parish at a place well known to me" (*"I'm Frank Hamer,"* pp. 211–12). This is palpably false. Not even Frank Hamer could have "arranged" for the gang's hideout to be moved—Clyde wouldn't have cooperated. Clearly, this was one way Hamer tried to dis-

guise the Methvin family's betrayal of Clyde and Bonnie. Bienville Parish sheriff Henderson Jordan and Ava and Henry Methvin all testified later that the Methvins first approached Jordan early in March, and Hamer was only summoned to Bienville Parish several days after that. But when Hamer talked about discovering the gang's Louisiana hideout by himself in February, no contemporary journalists checked to verify his story. Hamer's reputation was so fearsome that few reporters would have dared contradict him, and there is no evidence that any of them tried.

In *Running with Bonnie and Clyde*, Ralph Fults said that Frank Hamer and Bob Alcorn met in Bienville Parish with Henderson Jordan and Ivy Methvin on February 19; in his interview with Dr. Glenn Jordan, Sheriff Jordan vaguely refers to the date of this first meeting as "in the early Spring of 1934." Ava Methvin testified in Oklahoma that her son Henry, Clyde, and Bonnie visited them in Louisiana around the 1st of March, and that during the visit Henry called her aside to say he wanted to betray Clyde and Bonnie in exchange for a pardon from the state of Texas.

271 *he was contacted by Henderson Jordan:* Henderson Jordan interview with Dr. Glenn Jordan, October 12, 1958; Ava Methvin, *Methvin* v. *Oklahoma A-9060*.

Chapter 27: The Methvins Make a Deal

Much of the material in this chapter is based on Henderson Jordan's 1958 interview with Dr. Glenn Jordan, and on testimony in Henry Methvin's Oklahoma trial by Henry and Ava Methvin and John Joyner, erroneously identified in court transcripts as "Joiner." There is additional information from the unpublished manuscript by Marie Barrow Scoma with Jonathan Davis. A great deal of information about the Methvin family comes from transcriptions of video interviews conducted by Oklahoma historian Terry Whitehead with Clemmie Methvin, daughter-in-law of Ivy and Ava Methvin, and with Percy and Willie Methvin, Henry Methvin's cousins and contemporaries. Whitehead generously provided me with DVD copies of the interviews for use in this book. To my knowledge, they have not been previously made available to other authors.

Almost all dates of meetings involving Henderson Jordan, Ivy Methvin, John Joyner, L. A. Kindell, Prentiss Oakley, and/or Frank Hamer are approximate. When meeting with law enforcement officials, there is no record of Ivy Methvin mentioning that Raymond Hamilton and Mary O'Dare were with the gang during their early March visit. Raymond and Mary left the gang in Terre Haute on March 6. We know from Cumie Barrow's and Marie Barrow Scoma's unpublished manuscripts that Clyde, Bonnie, and Henry were back in West Dallas for a visit on March 12, so it would follow that Clyde and Bonnie brought Raymond home between those days, not on March 1 as Ava Methvin testified later in an Oklahoma court.

PAGE

272 *Many of the people in Bienville Parish, Louisiana:* All the details in this chapter about Ivy and Ava Methvin's background and personalities, and the family's version of Henry's arrest and imprisonment, are taken from Terry Whitehead's video interviews with Clemmie, Percy, and Willie Methvin.

273 *In 1934, TB was considered a mysterious, monstrous affliction:* Archie McDonald, Wayne Carter, and Boots Hinton interviews.

274 *Clyde's reservation about the Cole place:* Jonathan Davis and Sandy Jones inter-

views. In her unpublished memoir, Marie Barrow Scoma writes that Clyde and Bonnie didn't begin using the Cole house as a daytime resting place until May. But Bienville County sheriff Henderson Jordan told an interviewer that he hoped to trap Clyde and Bonnie there as early as March.

274 *The parish itself was in the heart:* Boots Hinton, Virginia Becker, and Olen Walter Jackson interviews.

274 *John Joyner requested a top-secret meeting:* Henderson Jordan interview with Dr. Glenn Jordan, October 12, 1958; Ava Methvin, *Methvin v. Oklahoma A-9060.*

275 *the Barrow Gang had twice come to Bienville Parish for visits:* Ava Methvin, *Methvin v. Oklahoma* A-9060.

275 *Jordan, a country cop who had no background in the law:* Henderson Jordan interview with Dr. Glenn Jordan, October 12, 1958.

276 *Hamer said later that Jordan "agreed":* Jenkins and Frost, *"I'm Frank Hamer,"* p. 222.

276 *On March 24, Kindell met with Jordan again:* Marie Barrow Scoma with Davis unpublished manuscript, pp. 182–83.

Chapter 28: Bloody Easter

Dallas journalist Bill Sloan generously shared details from his interview with now deceased Dallas County deputy Bob Alcorn about the Grapevine murder site. Marie Barrow Scoma's unpublished memoir provided Clyde's perspective of what happened on April 1, 1934.

There is some disagreement whether Joe Palmer came to Dallas that day with Clyde, Bonnie, and Henry Methvin. In her memoir, Marie Barrow Scoma insists Palmer wasn't with her brother at all that day, but in *Fugitives* Bonnie's mother, Emma, is equally adamant that it was Joe Palmer who hitchhiked into Dallas to tell the Barrows and Parkers that Clyde and Bonnie were waiting for them in Grapevine. Somebody's lying, and in this case I believe it is Marie. Because the premeditated murder of Wade McNabb undoubtedly didn't jibe with Marie's constant portrayal of her brother as someone who killed only when he felt he was cornered, I think she simply tried to mention Joe Palmer in her memoir as seldom as possible, and, when she did, to declare that Clyde really had very little to do with him.

PAGE

279 *Henry yanked wire from a fence:* Fortune, ed., *Fugitives*, p. 159.

279 *This time, it was Clyde who made the suggestion:* Knight with Davis, *Bonnie and Clyde*, p. 142.

279 *Local authorities decided it was a Barrow Gang job:* Marie Barrow Scoma with Davis unpublished manuscript, p. 172.

279 *Clyde, Bonnie, and Henry met with the Barrows and Parkers:* Cumie Barrow unpublished manuscript.

280 *Since leaving the Barrow Gang on March 6:* Underwood, *Depression Desperado*, pp. 50–55.

281 *Joe Palmer hitchhiked back into West Dallas:* Knight with Davis, *Bonnie and Clyde*, p. 145; Fortune, ed., *Fugitives*, p. 159.

282 *Bonnie got out of the car to play for a while:* Fortune, ed., *Fugitives*, pp. 160–61.

282 *Bonnie chewed on bits of lemon peel:* Bill Sloan interview.

283 *Clyde swore to his family later:* Marie Barrow Scoma with Davis unpublished manuscript, pp. 176–80.
284 *when Dallas County deputy Bob Alcorn arrived on the scene:* Bill Sloan interview.
285 *That news alarmed Floyd Hamilton:* Underwood, *Depression Desperado*, p. 55.
285 *Clyde drove away from the murder site:* Marie Barrow Scoma with Davis unpublished manuscript, p. 177.
286 *These stories devastated Clyde's mother, Cumie:* Jonathan Davis interview.

Chapter 29: Hamer Forms a Posse

Two long interviews with Oklahoma historian Terry Whitehead at his home in Blackwell helped me capture the Barrow Gang–induced nervousness of residents all around the state on April 5 and 6, 1934. Terry, whose taped interviews with surviving members of Henry Methvin's families have already contributed to previous chapters, also gave me access to his lengthy video session with Lee Phelps of Commerce, Oklahoma. Phelps's reminiscences are the basis for my description of the terrible weather there on the night of April 5 and the mud that subsequently clogged roadsides.

Jonathan Davis lent me his copy of the April 1934 *Texas Bankers Record*.

PAGE
287 *But the outcry against Clyde and Bonnie after Grapevine:* Phillips, *Running with Bonnie and Clyde*, pp. 183–84; Knight with Davis, *Bonnie and Clyde*, p. 147.
288 *Then Hamer approached Smoot Schmid:* Like many historians, I'm ambivalent about the veracity of *Ambush*, the memoir of Dallas County deputy Ted Hinton. The book contains many descriptions that seem either impossible or else wildly exaggerated. According to Hinton, Lee Simmons approached Smoot Schmid and begged him to let Frank Hamer join Hinton and Deputy Bob Alcorn in *their* pursuit of Clyde and Bonnie. Hinton then writes that he and Alcorn had to bring Hamer up to date after the Dallas County sheriff reluctantly agreed. Yet we know from other documentation that Schmid had been cooperating with Hamer all along, and even sent Alcorn—not Hinton—to Louisiana prior to April 1934 to meet with John Joyner and Henderson Jordan to discuss a possible pardon for Henry Methvin. So I'm discounting Hinton's version of how he and Alcorn joined Hamer's posse. But I'm accepting his account of how the four posse members used two cars and tracked the Barrow Gang into Oklahoma. It's well documented that the posse went there in pursuit of Clyde and Bonnie right after the shootings in Grapevine on April 1. Hinton didn't *always* stretch the truth or completely alter the facts.

But there is also a discrepancy about when and where the four-man posse formed in *"I'm Frank Hamer."* Authors John H. Jenkins and H. Gordon Frost based their descriptions of Hamer's pursuit of Clyde and Bonnie on interviews granted by Hamer to journalists and historians after the ambush in Gibsland. Hamer deliberately misled them about dates and locations to conceal the role played by the Methvin family. Jenkins and Frost quoted Hamer as stating he "traveled alone" hunting the Barrow Gang until April 10, when he met with L. G. Phares and agreed to let Manny Gault join him. Shortly after that, Hamer added, he met for the first time with Henderson Jordan in Bienville Parish, Louisiana. But Jordan and several members of the extended Methvin family agreed that Hamer made his deal with the Methvins in Louisiana in March, and on April 8, the *Daily News Record* in Miami, Oklahoma, reported that Hamer and his posse were in the state pursuing the Barrow Gang.

289 *Almost immediately, the Texans discovered:* Hinton, *Ambush*, pp. 138–39. The entire scene in Durant is taken from this source.

289 *On Thursday afternoon, April 5, rumors spread:* Ibid., pp. 139–40.

290 *Some kept their children home from school:* Terry Whitehead interview.

290 *It wasn't easy traveling by car anywhere in Oklahoma on April 5:* Terry Whitehead interview of Lee Phelps.

Chapter 30: Another Murder

Terry Whitehead's video interview with Lee Phelps provides an exceptional eyewitness account of the shooting of Commerce town constable Cal Campbell on April 6, 1934. Following his release after being held about fifteen hours as a hostage by the Barrow Gang, Commerce chief of police Percy Boyd twice described the not altogether unpleasant ordeal—first to reporters immediately afterward, and later in testimony at the spring 1935 harboring trial in Dallas of many members of the extended Barrow and Parker families. This is one of the best-documented events in the twenty-six-month history of the Barrow Gang. Marie Barrow Scoma, writing many years later and always ready to blame everything on the man she called "Henry the Rat," claimed in her unpublished memoir that Boyd and Campbell drove to State Road after hearing someone in a parked car—Henry Methvin—was threatening passersby with a rifle. But Boyd's testimony was clear—he and Campbell were responding to a report of possible drunks parked along the road.

PAGE

291 *Just after 9 A.M. on Friday, April 6:* Terry Whitehead interview; Knight with Davis, *Bonnie and Clyde*, pp. 148–49.

292 *Boyd said later that Cal Campbell apparently thought he saw a gun:* Knight with Davis, *Bonnie and Clyde*, p. 148.

292 *Sixteen-year-old Lee Phelps, working in the tower:* Terry Whitehead interview of Lee Phelps.

292 *After Grapevine, Clyde was taking no chances with Henry:* Marie Barrow Scoma with Davis unpublished manuscript, p. 185.

292 *Clyde noticed several onlookers:* Terry Whitehead interview of Lee Phelps; Knight with Davis, *Bonnie and Clyde*, p. 149.

293 *He had a length of chain:* Percy Boyd said a chain was used to haul Clyde's Ford out of the ditch. Lee Phelps thought it might have been a rope.

293 *It had been almost forty minutes:* Terry Whitehead interview.

293 *Clyde exaggerated slightly as he screamed:* Knight with Davis, *Bonnie and Clyde*, p. 149.

293 *Percy Boyd expected to die:* Ramsey, *On the Trail of Bonnie and Clyde Then and Now*, pp. 224–26; Terry Whitehead interview; Terry Whitehead interview of Lee Phelps.

294 *So Clyde could break into a gum machine:* Terry Whitehead interview.

294 *Clyde and Bonnie were concerned that Boyd's shirt was stained with blood:* Ramsey, *On the Trail of Bonnie and Clyde Then and Now*, p. 226.

294 *Bonnie had even asked Boyd for a favor:* Knight with Davis, *Bonnie and Clyde*, p. 150.

295 *It was a tremendous opportunity:* Terry Whitehead interview; Knight with Davis, *Bonnie and Clyde*, p. 150.

Chapter 31: The Letters of April

In print and in conversation, Marie Barrow Scoma vehemently denied the letters to Amon Carter and Henry Ford were written by her brother. While it's fun to think they were, Marie was almost undoubtedly right. Clyde wouldn't have signed a bogus middle name to the Ford letter, and the Carter letter was mailed from the small North Texas hamlet of Decatur on a date when the Barrow Gang had fled the state for Oklahoma following the Grapevine murders. Still, many historians have accepted them as Clyde's handiwork. No one will ever know for certain.

Much of the information about Raymond Hamilton's activities and arrest in April 1934 comes from *Public Enemy Number One*, the memoir of his brother Floyd. Floyd Hamilton's book exaggerates his relationship with Clyde Barrow, but the Hamilton brothers were close and it seems logical that Floyd would have known how Raymond felt after being wrongly associated with the Grapevine killings.

PAGE

296 *he wasn't going to let the same thing happen again:* Hamilton, *Public Enemy Number One*, pp. 37–38.

297 *Even Percy Boyd had assumed:* Ramsey, *On the Trail of Bonnie and Clyde Then and Now*, p. 226.

297 *they holed up in a small house:* Marie Barrow Scoma with Davis unpublished manuscript, pp. 185–86.

299 *Clyde's family swore it wasn't authentic:* Jonathan Davis interview.

299 *Henry Methvin was sent ahead by train:* Fortune, ed., *Fugitives*, p. 163.

299 *As soon as the fugitives reunited:* Ibid., pp. 164–65.

300 *he and Bonnie were finally aware:* Marie Barrow Scoma with Davis unpublished manuscript, pp. 191–92; Jonathan Davis interview.

300 *Lee Simmons told reporters later:* Jenkins and Frost, *"I'm Frank Hamer,"* p. 245.

301 *the couple didn't still sleep in the Cole house:* Wayne Carter, Sandy Jones, and Robert Brunson interviews.

301 *Raymond was broke again:* Underwood, *Depression Desperado*, pp. 73–74.

302 *Bonnie bought Palmer a new suit:* Knight with Davis, *Bonnie and Clyde*, p. 156.

302 *The Ford was Cordoba gray:* Sandy Jones interview.

Chapter 32: The Noose Tightens

In August 1934 *American Detective* magazine published a lengthy interview with Lee Simmons in which the Texas prison general manager discussed in detail Frank Hamer's pursuit of Bonnie and Clyde. Simmons wasn't completely open—he refused to be specific about how the Methvin family was involved.

On October 12, 1958, Henderson Jordan granted a rare interview to Dr. Glenn Jordan. In it, he was candid about Ivy Methvin's reluctant cooperation after Hamer decided to ambush Clyde and Bonnie in Bienville Parish.

Copies of the log kept during the April 18–30 tap of the Barrow family phone are available through both the Dallas public library system and the city of Dallas archives. They are fascinating. Clyde's nephew Buddy Barrow Williams explained the family code words and names to me.

PAGE

303 *Schmid stepped up harassment of the Barrows:* Hinton, *Ambush*, pp. 146–47; Fortune, ed., *Fugitives*, p. 165.

304 *the Barrows and Parkers had long assumed:* Buddy Barrow Williams interview.

306 *Ted Hinton wrote later:* Hinton, *Ambush*, p. 145.

307 *Jordan invited Kindell instead of Hamer to come to Arcadia:* Marie Barrow Scoma with Davis unpublished manuscript, p. 189.

307 *Dowis didn't make it easy for the lawmen:* Steele with Marie Barrow Scoma, *The Family Story of Bonnie and Clyde*, p. 117.

307 *Dowis reluctantly issued a pair of BARs:* In *Ambush*, Ted Hinton wrote that Dowis handed over a single BAR. But in an interview with me in July 2000, Dowis insisted he lent two BARs to the posse, and that he was subsequently informed both were used in the May 23 ambush outside Gibsland.

Chapter 33: Final Meetings

The description of Clyde's May 7 meeting with his father, Henry, comes from two sources: the unpublished manuscripts of Cumie Barrow and Marie Barrow Scoma. The accounts in each are practically identical.

PAGE

309 *Joe Palmer didn't go with them:* Knight with Davis, *Bonnie and Clyde*, p. 158.

309 *They offered local kids rides:* Orville Hancock interview.

310 *Bonnie was in a contemplative mood:* Fortune, ed., *Fugitives*, pp. 165–69.

310 *Bonnie was probably referring to the National Recovery Administration:* It is also possible she meant the National Rifle Association, which was in existence in 1934. But the line "We're not working nights" makes it far more likely that the reference was to the government office established by Franklin Roosevelt to create better working conditions and job compensation for working-class Americans.

313 *On Monday night, May 7:* Cumie Barrow unpublished manuscript; Marie Barrow Scoma with Davis unpublished manuscript, pp. 203–5. Some books about Bonnie and Clyde state the meeting between Clyde and Henry occurred on May 9, but Cumie and Marie agree in their memoirs that it was May 7.

Chapter 34: A New Line of Work

On Friday, May 25, 1934, two days after Clyde and Bonnie died in the Gibsland ambush, the front page of the *Dallas Dispatch* included a story with the headline "Barrow Planned Jail Break: U.S. Marshal Reveals Plot for Delivery of Stevens Gang." According to the article, Marshal J. R. (Red) Wright had learned O. D. Stevens agreed to pay Clyde Barrow $18,000 for breaking himself and partners W. D. May and M. T. Howard out of the Tarrant County jail. Wright told the *Dispatch* reporter (no specific byline appeared on the story) that "Barrow was to appear at night under guise of an officer seeking lodging for a prisoner . . . Once inside the jail, they were to take charge of [the] guards and free the prisoners." The fact that Marshal Wright publicly acknowledged the Clyde-Stevens deal is significant. No lawman in the Dallas–Fort Worth area during that era was more esteemed by his peers. In *Ambush,* Dallas County deputy Ted Hinton described Wright as "one of the giants of Southwest law enforcement," and in his memoir Hinton was not given to praising too many others besides himself.

The article was only two columns long, and it was dwarfed by the main headline and story of the day: Emma Parker had sat up all Thursday night by the coffin of her daughter Bonnie, who was to be buried on Friday morning. The purported Stevens-Barrow deal was immediately forgotten. There were no follow-up stories in the *Dallas Dispatch,* the *Morning News,* or any other area newspapers. It appears that once Clyde and Bonnie were dead, the fact that Clyde had cut a deal to free a Fort Worth criminal kingpin was considered of no further interest.

On May 7, 1934, Henry Barrow saw that his son Clyde had a suitcase full of money, too much to be the $700 stolen by the Barrow Gang in Everly, Iowa, on May 3. Between the Everly robbery and the May 23 ambush outside Gibsland, Louisiana, where Clyde and Bonnie died, there is no record of the gang committing any other holdups. I believe it's because they had the money from Stevens, and Clyde spent the interim planning the Tarrant County jail breakout attempt.

We know that in mid-April, Clyde told a gathering of Barrows and Parkers outside West Dallas that he and Bonnie wanted to buy land in Louisiana that they could use for family visits. Bonnie's mother, Emma, ridiculed the idea in *Fugitives,* saying everyone knew the couple would never have that kind of money, but let them talk about it because it was good to see them so excited about something. On May 7 in West Dallas, Henry Barrow, who was illiterate, got the impression that the two papers Clyde wanted to sign had something to do with property or money. Since Clyde couldn't be involved in any public land transaction, my best guess is that he wanted to sign and give to his parents a last will and testament leaving them all his possessions, including the money from Stevens. The $18,000 could not have been traced back to any robbery committed by Clyde.

PAGE

315 *The remote, well-guarded farm property:* James Willett interview.

315 *a month later when someone organized:* Jonathan Davis interview.

316 *Everybody in the Dallas–Fort Worth criminal underground:* Buddy Barrow Williams and Jonathan Davis interviews.

317 *There's evidence Clyde tried to hire:* Division of Investigation/U.S. Department of Justice Document No. 62-619, memorandum dated July 23, 1934, regarding possible April 1934 meeting of Arthur "Pretty Boy" Floyd and the Barrow Gang.

319 *On May 9, Hamer and his posse:* Marie Barrow Scoma with Davis unpublished manuscript, p. 207.

Chapter 35: Haven

Video interviews by Oklahoma historian Terry Whitehead with Percy, Willie, and Clemmie Methvin are integral to this chapter. All three provided colorful descriptions of Methvin family interactions with Clyde and Bonnie during May 1934. Clemmie and Willie are now deceased and at nearly one hundred years of age Percy Methvin no longer receives visitors, so the Whitehead videos are the best possible record available. I also relied on testimony from Ava and Henry Methvin during Henry's September 1934 murder trial in Oklahoma.

Robert Brunson took me to the campsite outside Mangham where, as a fifteen-year-old, he encountered Clyde and Bonnie.

PAGE

320 *During the first three weeks in May 1934:* Terry Whitehead interviews with Clemmie and Willie Methvin.

321 *Clyde's sister Marie and other Barrow family members said later:* Jonathan Davis and Buddy Barrow Williams interviews.

321 *The only member of the extended Methvin clan:* Terry Whitehead interview with Clemmie Methvin.

322 *Hamer and his posse could still have jumped the couple:* Ivy Methvin and Henry Methvin, *Methvin v. Oklahoma A-9060.*

323 *Ralph Fults received an unsigned postcard:* Phillips, *Running with Bonnie and Clyde,* p. 5.

323 *Around mid-May, he did set up:* Robert Brunson interview.

324 *Now Floyd was informed he was also being detained:* Hamilton, *Public Enemy Number One,* p. 48.

324 *On Saturday, May 19, she was arrested there and extradited: The Truth About Bonnie and Clyde as Told by Billie Jean Parker.*

324 *Marie was an impulsive girl:* Jonathan Davis interview.

324 *on this same fateful weekend:* Hinton, *Ambush,* p. 157; Jonathan Davis and Boots Hinton interviews.

Chapter 36: The Beginning of the End

Beginning with the last weekend of their lives, there are several convoluted, conflicting versions of what Clyde, Bonnie, the Hamer posse, the Methvin family, and Bienville Parish sheriff Henderson Jordan did, and when. With the exception of Percy Methvin, none of the participants is still living. It's necessary to read through their memoirs and interviews and try to piece together the most logical sequence of events. Each had strong motivation to represent the final days of the Barrow Gang in a misleading way.

Frank Hamer routinely lied about details of cases to protect his sources. In this case, he did not want to reveal his agreement with Ivy Methvin, so he concocted a simple story about setting an ambush for Clyde and Bonnie in the woods outside Gibsland where they maintained a "mail drop" or spot where friends could leave them messages. According to Hamer, he and his posse drove into Louisiana on May 22, set up across the road from where Clyde and Bonnie were bound to come to check for messages, and shot them when they did on the morning of May 23.

In *Ambush*, Ted Hinton claimed the Hamer posse arrived in Shreveport on Saturday, May 19, discovered on Monday that over the weekend Henry Methvin had split off from Clyde and Bonnie at the Majestic Café, drove into Arcadia where they met Henderson Jordan for the first time, set up the ambush on Sailes–Jamestown road on Monday night, and waited there until Wednesday morning, when Clyde and Bonnie finally drove by. Hinton also wrote that Ivy Methvin never cooperated with the posse in advance. Instead, when he drove along the road on the morning of May 23, the posse captured him and handcuffed him to a tree to prevent him from warning Clyde and Bonnie. After the ambush, Methvin threatened to sue the officers unless they granted his son a pardon from the Texas state government. Possibly Hinton was trying to protect Ivy Methvin, too. His scenario is demonstrably wrong—testimony in Henry Methvin's subsequent trial for murder in Oklahoma clearly established how Frank Hamer made his deal with the Methvin family, and that the posse was only in place beside the Sailes–Jamestown road for a single night.

When Henderson Jordan broke his silence on the subject of the ambush in a single interview in October 1958, his version was even stranger than Hinton's. According to Jordan, the Texas posse had moved its operations to Shreveport and was waiting there when he contacted them on Tuesday, May 22, to say it was time to spring the trap on Clyde and Bonnie. They met that night and Jordan led the Texans to the spot on the Sailes–Jamestown road that he had chosen for the ambush. Jordan clearly did not want to admit Hamer came to him in Gibsland on Monday and demanded that the plan move forward. And, by claiming he only learned from Ivy Methvin on Tuesday that an ambush was possible, Jordan didn't have to explain why he dithered all day on Monday, trying to delay until he could contact Division of Investigation Special Agent L. A. Kindell in New Orleans.

We're now privy to enough information to piece together some of Clyde and Bonnie's movements on Monday and Tuesday independent from what Hamer, Hinton, and Jordan said and wrote. In their interviews with Terry Whitehead, Percy and Willie Methvin confirmed that Clyde and Bonnie met Henry Methvin at Black Lake on the night of either Monday, May 21, or Tuesday, May 22. FBI file I.C. #26-31672, obtained under the Freedom of Information Act, also notes that "it was learned Bonnie and Clyde, with some of the Methvins, had staged a party at Black Lake, Louisiana on the night of May 21, 1934." Ava and Henry Methvin's testimony in Henry's Oklahoma murder trial reveals that on the afternoon of May 22, Clyde and Bonnie arrived at the Methvin home looking for Henry. They were told by Ivy Methvin that they should come back around nine the next morning, and Henry would be there. This accounts for the original plan—Bonnie and Clyde would be ambushed on their way to the Methvins' on Tuesday afternoon—and the final scenario—they were ambushed going back to the Methvins' on Wednesday morning.

This is independently corroborated by Robert Brunson. On the morning of May 22, he met Clyde and Bonnie in the palmetto outside Mangham, Louisiana. They told him they were leaving in the afternoon to go "up around Arcadia." Clearly, they left Black Lake on the night of the 21st, camped out near Mangham, and planned to return to Bienville Parish the next day to meet Henry at his parents' home. When they arrived, Henry wasn't there. As requested by Henderson Jordan, Ivy Methvin told them to come back for Henry in the morning around 9 A.M. That allowed Jordan and the Texas lawmen to set up their ambush on the Sailes–Jamestown road, the only route south from Gibsland and Highway 80 that Clyde and Bonnie could take to get there. They knew when the couple would be coming—around 9 A.M.—and the road they would be taking.

In a few instances, details from *Ambush* and Henderson Jordan's 1958 interview still ring true, and I have incorporated them where indicated. Mostly, I rely on Terry Whitehead's interviews with Percy, Willie, and Clemmie Methvin, the testimony by Ava and Henry Methvin about their deal with Frank Hamer, and the fresh, fascinating reminiscences of Robert Brunson, which provide the basis for much of the next chapter.

PAGE

325 *On Sunday night, May 20:* Henry Methvin testified in Oklahoma that he alerted Ava and Ivy to his pending escape from Clyde and Bonnie on the night before they went to Shreveport. Neither Ava nor Henry were certain of the exact date. *Methvin v. Oklahoma A-9060.*

325 *They had laundry to drop off:* Willie and Percy Methvin both thought Henry

might have eluded Clyde and Bonnie at a dry cleaner's instead of the Majestic Café. Terry Whitehead interviews with Willie and Percy Methvin.

326 *On Monday Hamer telephoned:* In *Ambush*, p. 158, Ted Hinton writes that Hamer called Shreveport chief of police Bryant, with no first name given. On May 21, 1934, the Shreveport chief of police was named Dennis Bazer.

326 *the man in the photo had the same eyes and pimply face:* Hinton, *Ambush*, p. 159.

327 *When the Texas lawmen were gone:* Jonathan Davis interview; Marie Barrow Scoma with Davis unpublished manuscript, pp. 208–10.

327 *he and some of his relations met Clyde and Bonnie out at Black Lake:* Terry Whitehead interview with Percy Methvin; FBI document I.C. #26-31672.

328 *They drove to their camp in Mangham instead:* Robert Brunson interview.

Chapter 37: "Do You Know Any Bank Robbers?"

When I interviewed him in his home in Mangham on July 28, 2007, eighty-nine-year-old Robert Brunson wasn't completely certain whether he met Clyde and Bonnie on Monday, May 21, or Tuesday, May 22, though he thought it was probably Tuesday. Based on what can be ascertained about their movements, it was on Tuesday. That means Brunson was one of the last people to have a long conversation with them before they died.

All the details of this morning meeting out in the palmetto come directly from my interview with Brunson. He didn't just tell me what happened—he and his daughter put me in their truck and drove me out to the spot. Seventy-four years later, Brunson led me through the brush and showed me where his dog Black Boy "bayed" Clyde and Bonnie. The narrow dirt wagon track remains intact.

Harrison Hamer, the great-nephew of Frank Hamer, granted me a lengthy interview and discussed what "Captain Frank" told family members afterward about the Gibsland ambush. Jonathan Davis elaborated on the Barrow family's opinions of what happened, and Henderson Jordan's 1958 interview provided a few details. Key information was gleaned from the Oklahoma murder trial testimony of Ava and Henry Methvin. Ava told the jury how she and Ivy "set up" Bonnie and Clyde for an ambush on Wednesday morning, May 23.

In *Ambush*, Ted Hinton insisted that the Sailes–Jamestown road ambush stakeout lasted two nights instead of one, beginning on Monday instead of Tuesday. Beyond Hinton's own word, there is absolutely no other evidence of this. Hinton's two-day description is particularly contradicted by Frank Hamer's phone call to his family on Tuesday night, made just before the posse left for the ambush site. According to Hinton, they were already crouched in the backcountry brush at that time, and there weren't any telephones out on the berm. Ted Hinton would later prove himself to be a good man and loyal friend to the surviving Barrows—why he would invent a story about being at the ambush site two nights instead of one is a question I'm not able to answer.

PAGE

329 *On the morning of Tuesday, May 22:* Robert Brunson interview.

330 *After Clyde took a picture of the boy with Bonnie:* Brunson told me that "thirty years later or more I got a letter . . . and the negatives of those two pictures were in the letter. I did away with them and the letter. I didn't want to be involved with the Barrow Gang no way. I figure after the ambush, [Bonnie's] family was

given all her personal things and they was stuck in a box in an attic or something for years. Then somebody looked in the box, saw the camera had film in it, and got that film developed. They saw my address and sent the negatives. I guess I should have kept them."

331 *whether Clyde and Bonnie would drive to Ivy and Ava Methvin's place:* Ava Methvin, *Methvin v. Oklahoma A-9060.*

331 *This unpaved backcountry byway was what locals termed "a three-rut":* Boots Hinton interview.

332 *He was staying with his cousin Willie:* Terry Whitehead interview with Willie Methvin.

332 *Ivy Methvin came outside:* Ava Methvin trial testimony, *Methvin v. Oklahoma A-9060.*

332 *Sheriff Jordan finally gave up trying to contact L. A. Kindell:* Marie Barrow Scoma with Davis unpublished manuscript, pp. 208–10.

332 *Jordan called Frank Hamer at the Inn Hotel:* Henderson Jordan interview with Dr. Glenn Jordan, October 12, 1958; Hinton, *Ambush*, p. 157.

332 *Hamer didn't believe Clyde would ever give up:* Harrison Hamer interview.

333 *Jordan insisted that the elder Methvin be there:* Henderson Jordan interview with Dr. Glenn Jordan, October 12, 1958.

333 *on Tuesday night he called his family back in Texas:* Harrison Hamer interview.

Chapter 38: The Setup

Frank Hamer, Ted Hinton, and Henderson Jordan all gave wildly varying accounts of the ambush. The six-man posse was essentially split into three camps—Hamer and former Ranger Manny Gault, Dallas County deputies Hinton and Bob Alcorn, and Bienville Parrish lawmen Jordan and Prentiss Oakley. They did not like or trust each other. In describing the hours before the bullets started flying, I've picked through all three conflicting versions, but have also relied heavily on the research of Sandy Jones of Fort Collins, Colorado. Several years ago, Jones received permission to conduct a hands-on study of the so-called Death Car, the 1934 Ford V-8 in which Clyde and Bonnie died on the morning of May 23, 1934. Jones then commissioned an exact replica of the car, took it to the ambush site outside Gibsland, and conducted exhaustive tests to estimate as exactly as possible what happened there. He established, to his satisfaction and mine, who stood where on the hill that morning, what shots were fired from which angles, and how long the ambush lasted from the first shot to the last.

Hinton claimed only one Browning Automatic Rifle was used that morning—by him—but my interview with Colonel Henry Dowis established that the posse had two BARs, and Jones now believes there probably was a second BAR in use.

Jones also provided information about the other guns used in the ambush, including Prentiss Oakley's choice of weapon.

PAGE

334 *The six-man posse reached the hilltop:* Henderson Jordan interview with Dr. Glenn Jordan, October 12, 1958.

334 *The two BARs from the Dallas state guard armory:* Sandy Jones interview.

335 *there were physical discomforts on the hilltop, too:* Hinton, *Ambush*, pp. 163–64.

335 *The six men squatted about ten feet apart:* The order in which the members of

the posse sat and waited on the hilltop is based on Sandy Jones's research at the ambush site. According to Ted Hinton in *Ambush*, the order was Hinton, Alcorn, Oakley, Jordan, Gault, and Hamer. Everyone agreed later that Hamer anchored the line.

335 *They each hefted weapons selected especially for the ambush:* Sandy Jones and Bob Fischer, "It's Death to Bonnie and Clyde," *OklahombreS*, Winter 1999. Jones originally believed the posse used only one BAR during the ambush. After reviewing the testimony of Colonel Weldon Dowis, he now believes there may have been two.

336 *it's likely that Jordan temporarily deputized:* Ted Hinton wrote in *Ambush* that Jordan failed to do this, rendering illegal the actions of the Texas lawmen that morning. It seems extremely unlikely that a man as meticulous as Frank Hamer would have ignored something so obvious.

336 *Hamer liked and trusted him more than he did Hinton:* Harrison Hamer interview. Hamer's disdain for Hinton is clear from the stories about the ambush that he told his family. It seems clear from Boots Hinton's version of events that day that the feeling was mutual.

336 *According to subsequent Oklahoma court testimony by his wife, Ava: Methvin v. Oklahoma, A-9060.*

336 *the posse helped Ivy position his truck:* Jones and Fischer, "It's Death to Bonnie and Clyde."

337 *Finally Jordan snarled:* Henderson Jordan interview with Dr. Glenn Jordan, October 12, 1958.

337 *Each time, Methvin had to stumble down the hill:* Ibid.

337 *Hamer had no doubt he was coming:* In *Ambush*, Hinton wrote that the posse was ready to give up when Clyde hadn't arrived by 9 A.M., and decided to wait no longer than thirty more minutes. To put it mildly, this seems unlikely.

337 *"This is him," Hinton whispered to Alcorn:* Hinton, *Ambush*, p. 168.

337 *Ivy Methvin hustled down the hill:* Where Ivy Methvin spent the ambush is a source of ongoing contention. Hinton insists in *Ambush* that Ivy spent the entire time handcuffed to a tree on the hilltop. Buddy Barrow Williams is certain Ivy never was near Clyde and Bonnie during all the shooting. But Willie and Percy Methvin both told Terry Whitehead years later that it was miraculous their uncle didn't suffer a single scratch from the posse's barrage while he was down on the road near Clyde and Bonnie in their car.

Chapter 39: The Ambush

Because Frank Hamer, Henderson Jordan, and Ted Hinton gave such varying descriptions of the ambush, I rely here for the most part on the investigation conducted in 1998 by Sandy Jones, who examined the Death Car and subsequently staged his own ambush reenactment using a car identical to the Ford V-8 sedan driven by Clyde on May 23, 1934. Almost all the specific details come from Jones—which ambush participant stood where on the hill, why Clyde must have come to a complete stop beside Ivy Methvin's truck, how Hamer leaned over the Ford and fired several final shots into Bonnie's body. Jones reenacted the ambush six different times, and on each occasion sixteen seconds elapsed between the first and final shots.

Other details come from interviews with Jonathan Davis, Buddy Barrow Williams, and Walter Olen Jackson, Ted Johnson, Robert Pitts Thomas, and Janice Thomas. Jackson, Johnson, and the Thomases all lived in and around Gibsland in May

1934. Their collective comments are the basis for my statement that "propinquity never entirely erased trepidation."

PAGE

338 *The locals eating breakfast at Ma Canfield's:* Ted Johnson, Robert Pitts Thomas, and Janice Thomas interviews.

338 *Afterward, the people in the café would disagree:* Jonathan Davis interview.

338 *Ivy Methvin, who got an uncomfortably close look:* Terry Whitehead interview with Willie Methvin.

338 *Bonnie was wearing a red dress:* Sandy Jones believes the dress might have been blue, since Bonnie's tam was that color. Jones believes Bonnie's massive blood loss fooled witnesses into thinking her dress was red. That might be a stretch.

339 *the young deputy couldn't control himself:* Though everything else about their versions of what happened during the ambush might differ, all the posse members recalled that Prentiss Oakley fired the first shots. Henderson Jordan said later that he was just calling out to Clyde and Bonnie to surrender when Oakley stood and fired. Bob Alcorn said that Oakley killed Clyde just as Frank Hamer shouted for Clyde and Bonnie to give themselves up. Probably, no such offer was made. The lawmen didn't want it to seem that they began shooting without giving the couple the opportunity to surrender.

340 *In those few seconds, Bonnie screamed:* This was something else all six lawmen agreed about afterward.

341 *A mile away in the pine forest:* Olen Walter Jackson interview.

341 *Ted Hinton told people that:* Buddy Barrow Williams interview.

Chapter 40: "Well, We Got Them"

Though *Running with Bonnie and Clyde* is based on the recollections and career of Ralph Fults, author John Neal Phillips also wrote at length and impressively about events in Arcadia following the ambush of Clyde and Bonnie. Much of the material gathered by Phillips is included here. Interviews with Virginia Becker, Jonathan Davis, Bill Palmer, and Boots Hinton were also helpful. Despite the many questionable passages in their books, Jan Fortune's *Fugitives* and Ted Hinton's *Ambush* do contain small, telling details about the afternoon of May 23 and the confusion surrounding Clyde's and Bonnie's funerals. Material from Marie Barrow Scoma's unpublished memoir is also critical to this chapter.

PAGE

342 *Now he wanted someone to help him:* Phillips, *Running with Bonnie and Clyde*, p. 207.

342 *Ted Hinton produced his 16-millimeter movie camera:* Boots Hinton interview.

343 *The gunfire temporarily deafened them:* Hinton, *Ambush*, p. 182.

343 *Hamer took the guns and the tackle box:* Harrison Hamer and Jonathan Davis interviews.

343 *Bob Alcorn grabbed Clyde's saxophone:* Bill Sloan interview; Marie Barrow Scoma with Davis unpublished manuscript, p. 217.

343 *The Barrows always believed it was taken by Henderson Jordan:* Buddy Barrow Williams, Jonathan Davis, and Virginia Becker interviews.

343 *Hamer telephoned Lee Simmons:* Lee Simmons, "Barrow-Parker Death Ambush," *American Detective*, August 1934.

343 *Word spread quickly in Gibsland:* John Paul Field interview.
344 *Observing the carnage wasn't enough for many of them:* Boots Hinton interview.
344 *With the two corpses still in its front seat:* Hinton, *Ambush*, pp. 173–82.
344 *screeching children swarmed around the car:* Virginia Becker, Ted Johnson, Robert Pitts Thomas, and John Paul Field interviews; Phillips, *Running with Bonnie and Clyde*, p. 209.
345 *Grasping hands snatched at the corpses:* Phillips, *Running with Bonnie and Clyde*, p. 210.
345 *The journalists wanted a statement from Hamer:* Hinton, *Ambush*, p. 186.
346 *he liked the idea of giving the crowd outside a good look:* Ben Procter interview.
346 *one of the funeral parlor staff sprayed the gawkers:* Phillips, *Running with Bonnie and Clyde*, p. 213.
346 *He pulled Alcorn and Hinton aside and told his two deputies:* Hinton, *Ambush*, p. 186.
346 *He'd gotten lost on the way:* Marie Barrow Scoma with Davis unpublished manuscript, p. 218.
346 *Ted Hinton noticed that the Barrows and Parkers:* Hinton, *Ambush*, p. 190.
347 *Emma Parker told family and friends:* Jonathan Davis interview; Marie Barrow Scoma with Davis unpublished manuscript, p. 218.
347 *Ten thousand people overran:* Phillips, *Running with Bonnie and Clyde*, pp. 215–16.
347 *Emma Parker guessed later:* Fortune, ed., *Fugitives*, p. 174.
347 *During the interment:* Phillips, *Running with Bonnie and Clyde*, pp. 216–17; Marie Barrow Scoma with Davis unpublished manuscript, pp. 219–20.
348 *Though Emma Parker boycotted Clyde's services on Friday:* Marie Barrow Scoma with Davis unpublished manuscript, pp. 220–21; Fortune, ed., *Fugitives*, pp. 174–75; Phillips, *Running with Bonnie and Clyde*, p. 219; Bill Palmer interview.

Chapter 41: Consequences

Interviews with Charles Heard, Mitchel Roth, Rick Mattix, John Neal Phillips, Bill Sloan, Boots Hinton, Ken Holmes, Sandy Jones, Buddy Barrow Williams, Harrison Hamer, Virginia Becker, and Jonathan Davis all helped shape much of this chapter. In 2000, I also conducted an extensive interview with now deceased Phillip Steele, who collaborated with Marie Barrow Scoma on *The Family Story of Bonnie and Clyde*.

Most of the basic information about the post-1934 lives and deaths of people related to or associated with Clyde and Bonnie comes from *Bonnie and Clyde: A Twenty-first Century Update*, pp. 182–94. Sources of additional information are noted separately.

PAGE
351 *Nineteen thirty-four was a fatal year:* Mitchel Roth and Jonathan Davis interviews; Mitchel Roth, "Bonnie and Clyde: The End of the Texas Outlaw Tradition," *East Texas Historical Journal* 2 (1997); Helmer and Mattix, *The Complete Public Enemy Almanac*, pp. 27–28, 44, 52–53, 67.
352 *the six Gibsland posse members received their share:* Hinton, *Ambush*, p. 192.

352 *He had all of Clyde and Bonnie's guns:* Harrison Hamer interview.
353 *To Jordan's way of thinking:* Ramsey, *On the Trail of Bonnie and Clyde Then and Now*, pp. 270–71.
353 *Stanley loaded the car onto a flatbed truck:* Ibid., p. 272; Charles Heard and Sandy Jones interviews.
354 *Back in Dallas, the Barrows and Parkers were trying:* Marie Barrow Scoma with Davis unpublished manuscript, pp. 223–24; Jonathan Davis interview.
354 *Clyde's brother L.C. was disgusted to find:* Marie Barrow Scoma with Davis unpublished manuscript, pp. 225–26.
354 *The trial lasted four days:* Here is a complete list of the harboring trial defendants and their sentences: Cumie Barrow, thirty days; L.C. Barrow, one year and one day; Audrey Barrow (L.C.'s wife), fifteen days; Marie Barrow, one hour; Joe Bill Francis, sixty days; Emma Parker, thirty days; Billie Jean Parker Mace, a year and a day; Henry Methvin, fifteen months; W. D. Jones, two years; Blanche Caldwell Barrow, a year and a day; Hilton Bybee (Eastham escapee on January 16, 1934), ninety days; Alice Hamilton Davis (Raymond's mother), thirty days; Steve Davis (Raymond's stepfather), ninety days; Mary O'Dare, a year and a day; Joe Chambliss (Mary's father), sixty days; Floyd Hamilton (Raymond's brother), two years; Mildred Hamilton (Floyd's wife), one hour; James Mullen (helped plan the Eastham farm break), four months; Baldy Whatley (West Dallas thug who knew Clyde), a year and a day; John Basden (robbed a bank with Raymond and admitted to two meetings with Clyde and Bonnie), a year and a day. All those defendants who were already in jail had the new terms added to their previous sentences. All details of the sentencing in this chapter are gleaned from Knight with Davis, *Bonnie and Clyde*, pp. 180–81.
355 *Charles Stanley, the Crime Doctor, wanted them to tour the country:* Jonathan Davis and Charles Heard interviews; Marie Barrow Scoma with Davis unpublished manuscript, pp. 226–28.
355 *Stanley was confronted there by Hamer:* Jenkins and Frost, *"I'm Frank Hamer,"* pp. 258–59; Marie Barrow Scoma with Davis unpublished manuscript, pp. 227–28; Charles Heard and Ben Procter interviews.
356 *Stanley finally shut down the Death Car tour:* Ramsey, *On the Trail of Bonnie and Clyde Then and Now*, pp. 272–73.
356 *His reputation suffered:* Harrison Hamer interview.
356 *His daughter claimed that her father's hair turned white:* Virginia Becker interview.
357 *The surviving members of the Barrow family:* Buddy Barrow Williams, Boots Hinton, and Bill Sloan interviews.
359 *It was the first time the elder Barrows experienced:* Marie Barrow Scoma with Davis unpublished manuscript, p. 230.
359 *The other Barrows swore that Jack:* Buddy Barrow Williams interview.
359 *Sometimes, mention of his brother reduced him to tears:* Ibid.
359 *Marie met Dallas memorabilia collector-dealer Charles Heard:* Charles Heard interview.
360 *In 1998 Marie began working with Dallas historian Jonathan Davis:* Jonathan Davis and Charles Heard interviews.
360 *Blanche began visiting Marie Barrow:* Blanche Caldwell Barrow, *My Life with Bonnie and Clyde*, pp. 183–191.
360 *"I talk of these incidents":* Ibid., p. 196.

Chapter 42: The Legend of Bonnie and Clyde

Winston G. Ramsey, John Neal Phillips, James Knight, and Jonathan Davis have conducted valuable research into books and films based on the criminal careers of Clyde and Bonnie. *On the Trail of Bonnie and Clyde Then and Now; My Life with Bonnie and Clyde*; and *Bonnie and Clyde: A Twenty-first Century Update* all contain extensive information on this subject. For an excellent summation of how Dashiell Hammett's private eye fiction affected themes in suspense thrillers of the 1940s and 1950s, I recommend William F. Nolan's introduction to *Nightmare Town*, a collection of Hammett short stories published by Alfred A. Knopf in 1999.

I have taken Ken Holmes Jr.'s "Bonnie and Clyde" tour in Dallas and recommend it to anyone interested in the lives and times of the couple. John Neal Phillips also conducts occasional "Bonnie and Clyde" tours for the Dallas Historical Society, and with his grasp of the subject and storytelling talent they must certainly be worthwhile. The opinions expressed about current conditions in the neighborhoods formerly known as West Dallas are entirely my own.

PAGE

362 *A typical story appeared:* "Killer in Skirts" by Marvin H. Albert, *Argosy*, March 1956.

362 *Bob Alcorn and Ted Hinton began telling friends:* Bill Sloan interview.

363 *Blanche Barrow Caldwell Frasure certainly thought so:* Blanche Caldwell Barrow, *My Life with Bonnie and Clyde*, pp. 178–83.

363 *Until Beatty's movie, Clyde's name always came before Bonnie's:* Buddy Barrow Williams interview.

364 *Hamer's widow settled for an undisclosed amount:* Harrison Hamer interview.

366 *Emma Parker had taken out a small life insurance policy on Bonnie:* Fortune, ed., *Fugitives*, p. 174.

Bibliography

CITED INTERVIEWS. Dates of interviews appear in parentheses; except where noted, all interviews were conducted in person by the author.

Virginia Becker (March 3, 2007) is a lifelong resident of Arcadia, Louisiana, and manager of the Arcadia–Bienville Parish Depot Museum, which includes a wing devoted to Bonnie and Clyde. Her father became business partners with Henderson Jordan after Jordan retired as parish sheriff.

Brad Belk (September 26, 2007) is director of the Joplin Museum Complex. As part of the effort to have the apartment at 3347½ 34th Street recognized as a historic site by the National Register of Historic Places, he made an exhaustive study of the April 13, 1933, shootout there. He also arranged a private tour of the apartment for me. It is still maintained almost exactly as it was when the Barrow Gang occupied it for two weeks.

Robert Brunson (July 28, 2007) was fifteen on May 22, 1934, when he stumbled upon Clyde and Bonnie in their camp outside Mangham, Louisiana. His is the last recorded conversation with the outlaw couple.

Harold Caldwell (August 22, 2007) lives in Wellington, Texas, and is board chairman of the Collingsworth County Museum. His father interacted with Clyde and Bonnie on the day before the terrible crash that left Bonnie burned and permanently crippled.

Ron Calhoun (February 13, 2008) is the former political reporter of the *Dallas Times-Herald.* He knew and often talked to retired Dallas County deputy Ted Hinton.

Wayne Carter (May 26, 2007) of Gibsland, Louisiana, is the descendant of the owner of "the Old Cole Place," which Clyde and Bonnie used as a hideout.

Jonathan Davis (August 8, August 18, September 24, 2007, plus numerous e-mail communications) of Plano, Texas, is coauthor of *Bonnie and Clyde:*

A Twenty-first Century Update. He was close friends with Marie Barrow Scoma and served as coauthor of her unpublished memoir, which he generously made available for this project.

Lieutenant Colonel Weldon Dowis (June 2000) was a captain in the 144th Infantry of the Texas National Guard in 1934, with jurisdiction over the weapons in the state's Dallas armory. He checked out two Browning Automatic Rifles to Frank Hamer for use in the pursuit and ambush of Bonnie and Clyde.

Lu Durham (July 20, 2007) is the daughter of Dr. Silas Durham, who treated Blanche Barrow's eye injury while she was a prisoner in the Platte City jail. Lu was a teenager when the Platte City shootout occurred and her father met Blanche.

Duke Ellis (June 2000) was playing guitar at a country dance in Stringtown, Oklahoma, where Clyde Barrow and Raymond Hamilton shot and killed Atoka County undersheriff Eugene Moore and seriously wounded Sheriff Charley Maxwell. Ellis died in 2004.

Marvelle Feller (July 19, 2007) was nineteen on July 24, 1933, when Clyde, Bonnie, and W. D. Jones fled from the shootout in Dexfield Park, Iowa, and stole the Feller family car at gunpoint. He helped carry the wounded Bonnie from the nearby woods to the car. He was joined in his interview by **Harold** and **Doris Feller,** his son and daughter-in-law, local historians who successfully raised money to place a monument commemorating the Dexfield Park incident.

John Paul Field (May 26, 2007), a lifelong Gibsland resident, was nine years old on May 23, 1934. He was one of the children who ran to the road to peek into the bullet-riddled car and gawk at Bonnie's and Clyde's bodies after the wrecker towing the Death Car broke down in front of the Gibsland public school.

Harrison Hamer (April 9, 2007) is the great-nephew of Texas Ranger captain Frank Hamer. He retains the Hamer family records at his home outside San Saba, Texas.

Orville Hancock (March 13, 2007, and several phone conversations) enjoyed a long career as a journalist in Arkansas and Texas. In May 1954, for research on a story commemorating the twentieth anniversary of the Gibsland ambush, Hancock traveled through Arkansas and Louisiana inteviewing men and women who had met Bonnie and Clyde.

Charles Heard (May 5, 2007) befriended Marie Barrow in 1997 when he helped auction her older brother Clyde's remaining possessions. He later became co-owner of the Bonnie and Clyde Ambush Museum in Gibsland, Louisiana.

Boots Hinton (March 10, 2007, and January 4, 2008) is the son of Dallas deputy Ted Hinton; he is currently the only daily staff member at the

Bonnie and Clyde Ambush Museum in Gibsland. Boots remains adamant that Hamer's posse waited two days for Bonnie and Clyde to appear at the ambush site.

Ken Holmes (December 5, 2007) owns and operates the Bonnie and Clyde Ambush Museum in Gibsland. He organizes the annual Bonnie and Clyde Festival held in the town on the anniversary weekend of the May 1934 ambush. Ken, who lives in Dallas, also conducts a "Bonnie and Clyde" tour there, taking visitors to various points of interest. He has served as a consultant to several film documentaries about the outlaw couple.

Olen Walter Jackson (March 10, 2007) lived in Gibsland at the time of the Hamer posse ambush. He was working for a logging company near the ambush site, and heard all the shooting.

Sandy Jones (August 24, 2007, plus several e-mail communications) is president of the John Dillinger Historical Society and owner of one of the most extensive collections of Bonnie and Clyde memorabilia. In 1998 he was allowed to conduct an extensive hands-on study of the Death Car, and afterward built an exact replica. He then exhaustively reenacted the ambush, including how Clyde Barrow must have manipulated the foot pedals during the attack for the original car to coast as far and in the direction it did following the first shots fired.

Henderson Jordan, retired Bienville Parish sheriff, gave an extensive interview about the Gibsland ambush to Dr. Glenn Jordan on October 12, 1958. He otherwise routinely refused interview requests after leaving law enforcement.

Cissy Stewart Lale (April 25, July 12, and August 4, 2007, plus numerous phone interviews) is past president of the Texas State Historical Association. Her areas of particular expertise include women's history in Texas, the history of the Dallas–Fort Worth metroplex, and the Dust Bowl. She has contributed articles to innumerable magazines and scholarly journals.

Rhea Leen Linder (September 15 and September 29, 2007) was originally named Bonnie Ray Parker by her father, Bonnie Parker's older brother, Buster. She changed her name in part because she did not want her friends in school to know she was related to her infamous aunt. In recent years, she has embraced Bonnie's controversial legacy, and she cooperated enthusiastically with this book.

Billie Jean Parker Mace (1968) was four years younger than her sister Bonnie. In 1968, soon after the release of the popular Warren Beatty film that the surviving Barrow and Parker families insisted was a gross misinterpretation of the Barrow Gang's real story, Billie recorded an interview that was released by RCA as a long-playing record album.

Rick Mattix (July 19 and September 28, 2007, plus numerous e-mail communications) is the author or coauthor of several articles and books concerning the 1930s gangster era, including *The Complete Public Enemy Almanac*.

Archie McDonald (May 18, 2007, plus several e-mail communications) is a past president of the Texas State Historical Association, a past president of the East Texas Historical Association, a history professor at Stephen F. Austin University in Nacogdoches, and the author of many articles and several books dealing with Texas history.

Bill Palmer (July 2, 2007) is the great-nephew of Joe Palmer, who was broken out of Eastham Prison Farm on January 16, 1934, and became a temporary member of the Barrow Gang. Much of Bill Palmer's information about his great-uncle and the Barrow Gang comes from his late aunt Faye, who was her brother Joe's lifelong confidante.

Lee Phelps, a native of Commerce, Oklahoma, was the last surviving witness to the April 6, 1934, shootout that left Deputy Sheriff Cal Campbell dead. He was interviewed on video on May 10, 1997, by Oklahoma historian and Bonnie and Clyde enthusiast Terry Whitehead, and his comments are taken directly from that video after a viewing on July 17, 2007, at Whitehead's residence.

John Neal Phillips (August 18 and September 11, 2007, plus several e-mail communications) is the author of *Running with Bonnie and Clyde: The Ten Fast Years of Ralph Fults* and the editor of Blanche Barrow's posthumous memoir, *My Life with Bonnie and Clyde*. He has written extensively about the Barrow Gang for magazines and historical journals, and leads an annual "Bonnie and Clyde" tour for the Dallas Historical Society.

Ben Procter (June 1, 2007), a past president of the Texas State Historical Association, is the author of several books, including *Just One Riot: Episodes of Texas Rangers in the 20th Century,* and is professor emeritus of history at Texas Christian University in Fort Worth.

Mitchel Roth (June 24, 2007) is an author-historian whose area of specialization is Texas law enforcement. He is a professor of Criminal Justice at Sam Houston State University in Huntsville.

Bill Sloan (May 9, 2007) is the author of several works of nonfiction and a former writer for the *Dallas Times-Herald.* While still in college he conducted several interviews with former Dallas County deputy and Gibsland ambush participant Bob Alcorn, who was a friend of the Sloan family's.

Doris Stallings (August 22, 2007) is the director of the Collingsworth County Museum in Wellington, Texas.

Terry Whitehead (July 17 and September 30, 2007) of Blackwell, Oklahoma, is a Bonnie and Clyde scholar who, in the 1980s and 1990s, traveled the country conducting videotaped interviews with survivors who had interacted with the Barrow Gang. He generously allowed viewings and made copies of critical tapes for reference purposes for this book.

James Willett (June 26, 2007) is a former warden at Huntsville State Prison. He is now director of the Texas Prison Museum in Huntsville.

Buddy Barrow Williams (May 25, June 3, and September 9, 2007, plus numerous phone calls and e-mail exchanges) is the stepson of L.C. Barrow, Clyde Barrow's youngest brother. He bases much of his testimony on what he was told by his stepfather, by Marie Barrow Scoma (in her later years Buddy would drive her everywhere), and by his stepgrandfather Henry Barrow. Buddy also made stepgrandmother Cumie Barrow's unpublished memoir available for this book.

Worth Wren Jr. (October 7, 2007) has spent most of his long career in journalism reporting on agribusiness, and his annual *Farm and Ranch Report* in the *Fort Worth Star-Telegram* was a Texas staple for several decades.

Jim Wright (September 9, 2007, and several phone interviews) is former speaker of the U.S. House of Representatives. During the Barrow Gang's crime spree, he was a teenager living first in Oklahoma and later in Dallas, Texas.

Pat Ziegler (April 18, 2007) is on the faculty of Sam Houston State University in Huntsville. Her mother and aunt grew up in West Dallas with Clyde Barrow.

Books

Abernathy, Francis Edward, ed. *Legendary Ladies of Texas*. Texas Folklore Society, 1994 (chapter written by John Neal Phillips and Andre L. Gorzell).

Baker, Olivia. *The Justice from Beacon Hill: The Life and Times of Oliver Wendell Holmes*. HarperCollins, 1991.

Barkley, Roy R., and Mark F. Odintz, eds. *The Portable Handbook of Texas*. Texas State Historical Association, 2000.

Barrow, Blanche Caldwell, edited by John Neal Phillips. *My Life with Bonnie and Clyde*. University of Oklahoma Press, 2004.

Barrow, Cumie. Unpublished manuscript. (Copy courtesy of Buddy Barrow Williams.)

Boyle, David. *The Troubadour's Song*. Walker, 2005.

Brown, Gary. *Texas Gulag: The Chain Gang Years, 1875–1925*. Republic of Texas Press, 2002.

Brown, Norman. *Hood, Bonnet, and Little Brown Jug: Texas Politics, 1921–1928.* Texas A&M University Press, 1984.

Calvert, Robert A., and Arnoldo De Leon. *The History of Texas.* Harlan Davidson, 1990.

Caro, Robert A. *Means of Ascent: The Years of Lyndon Johnson.* Alfred A. Knopf, 1990.

———. *The Path to Power: The Years of Lyndon Johnson.* Alfred A. Knopf, 1982.

Casad, Dede W. *My Fellow Texans: Governors of Texas in the 20th Century.* Eakin, 1995.

Cawelti, John G., ed. *Focus on Bonnie and Clyde.* Prentice Hall, 1973.

DeFord, Miriam Allen. *The Real Bonnie and Clyde.* Ace, 1968.

Douglas, C. L. *The Gentlemen in White Hats: Dramatic Episodes in the History of the Texas Rangers.* State House Press, 1992.

Egan, Timothy. *The Worst Hard Time: The Untold Story of Those Who Survived the Great American Dust Bowl.* Houghton Mifflin, 2006.

Fleming, Thomas. *The Illusion of Victory: America in World War I.* Basic Books, 2003.

Fortune, Jan I., ed., with Nell Barrow and Emma Parker. *Fugitives: The Inside Story of Clyde Barrow and Bonnie Parker.* Ranger Press, 1934. Reissued as *The True Story of Bonnie and Clyde.* Signet, 1968.

Goodwin, Doris Kearns. *No Ordinary Time: Franklin and Eleanor Roosevelt: The Home Front in World War II.* Simon & Schuster, 1994.

Hagedorn, Ann. *Savage Peace: Hope and Fear in America, 1919.* Simon & Schuster, 2007.

Hammett, Dashiell. *Nightmare Town.* Alfred A. Knopf, 1999.

Hamilton, Floyd. *Public Enemy Number One.* Acclaimed Books, 1978.

Harris III, Charles H., and Louis R. Sadler. *Texas Rangers and the Mexican Revolution: The Bloodiest Decade, 1910–1920.* University of New Mexico Press, 2007.

Helmer, William J., and Rick Mattix. *The Complete Public Enemy Almanac.* Cumberland House Publishing, 2007.

Hendrickson, Kenneth E., Jr. *The Chief Executives of Texas.* Texas A&M University Press, 1995.

Hill, Patricia Evridge. *Dallas: The Making of a Modern City.* University of Texas Press, 1996.

Hinton, Ted, as told to Larry Grove. *Ambush: The Real Story of Bonnie and Clyde.* Shoal Creek, 1979.

Jenkins, John H., and Gordon H. Frost. *"I'm Frank Hamer": The Life of a Texas Peace Officer.* Pemberton, 1968.

Johnson, Paul. *A History of the American People.* HarperCollins, 1997.

Johnson, Robert L. *Hunger for the Wild: America's Obsession with the Untamed West.* University Press of Kansas, 2007.

Kilgore, D. E. *A Ranger Legacy: 150 Years of Service to Texas.* Madrona, 1973.

Knight, James R., with Jonathan Davis. *Bonnie and Clyde: A Twenty-first Century Update.* Eakin, 2003.

Kyvig, David E. *Daily Life in the United States, 1920–1939.* Greenwood, 2002.

McConal, Patrick M. *Over the Wall: The Men Behind the 1934 Death House Escape.* Eakin, 2000.

McCullough, David. *Truman.* Simon & Schuster, 1992.

McDonald, Archie P. *Texas: A Compact History.* State House Press, 2007.

Milner, E. R. *The Lives and Times of Bonnie and Clyde.* Southern Illinois University Press, 1996.

O'Neal, Bill. *The Bloody Legacy of Pink Higgins: A Half-Century of Violence in Texas.* Eakin, 1999.

Phillips, John Neal. *Running with Bonnie and Clyde: The Ten Fast Years of Ralph Fults.* University of Oklahoma Press, 1996.

Polenberg, Richard. *One Nation Divisible: Class, Race and Ethnicity in the United States Since 1938.* Viking, 1980.

Potter, Claire Bond. *War on Crime: Bandits, G-Men and the Politics of Mass Culture.* Rutgers University Press, 1998.

Procter, Ben. *Just One Riot: Episodes of Texas Rangers in the 20th Century.* Eakin, 1991.

Ramsey, Winston G. *On the Trail of Bonnie and Clyde: Then and Now.* After the Battle Press, 2003.

Roth, Mitchel P. *Crime and Punishment: A History of the Criminal Justice System.* Thomson Wadsworth, 2005.

Saxon Gerald, ed. *The WPA Dallas Guide and History.* University of North Texas Press, 1992.

Scoma, Marie Barrow, with Jonathan Davis. Unpublished manuscript. (Copy courtesy of Jonathan Davis.)

Shelton, Gene. *Manhunter: The Life and Times of Frank Hamer.* Berkley, 1997.

Shotwell, John. *A Victim of Revenge, or Fourteen Years in Hell.* E. J. Jackson Co., 1909.

Steele, Phillip W., with Marie Barrow Scoma. *The Family Story of Bonnie and Clyde.* Pelican Publishing Co., 2000.

Toland, John. *The Dillinger Days.* Random House, 1963.

Treherne, John. *The Strange History of Bonnie and Clyde.* Cooper Square, 2000.

Tydings, Millard E. *Before and After Prohibition.* Macmillan, 1930.

Underwood, Sid. *Depression Desperado: The Chronicle of Raymond Hamilton.* Eakin, 1995.

Utley, Robert M. *Lone Star Lawmen: The Second Century Texas Rangers.* Oxford, 2007.

Walker, Donald R. *Penology for Profit: A History of the Texas Prison System, 1867–1912.* Texas A&M University Press, 1988.

Watson, William P. *Union, Justice, and Bonnie & Clyde.* Everett, 1989.

White, Richard D., Jr. *Kingfish: The Reign of Huey P. Long.* Random House, 2006.

Woolley, Bryan. *Mythic Texas: Essays on the State and Its People.* Republic of Texas Press, 2000.

Wright, Jim. *Weatherford Days.* Madison, 1996.

Newspapers and Wire Services

Associated Press

"Doctor Is Sought by Clyde Barrow for Wounded Girl," July 27, 1933.
"Prison Warden in Admission Some Truth in Reports," May 24, 1934.
"Sheriff of Parish Tells How Barrow Drove into Trap," May 24, 1934.
" 'Easiest Way,' Says Blanche Barrow," May 24, 1934.
"Aunt Not Sorry," May 24, 1934.

Chicago Daily News

Mike Royko, "They Haven't Seen the Movie," March 17, 1968.

Daily News Record (Miami, Oklahoma)

———, April 8, 1934.

Dallas Dispatch

"Think Bandit and Girl in Hideout Critically Hurt," November 24, 1933.
"Barrow Planned Jail Break; U.S. Marshal Reveals Plot for Delivery of Stevens Gang," May 25, 1934.
"Methvin Pardoned for Putting Clyde and Bonnie on Spot," August 14, 1934.

Dallas Morning News

"Life on the Farm Depicted by Woman," March 15, 1920.
"Where Can 'Greater Dallas' Be Built," April 4, 1920.
"United States Population Estimated at 105,000,000," June 26, 1920.
"Railroad Will Help to Make Farms Attractive," July 15, 1920.
"Farmers Discuss Spirit of Unrest," August 2, 1920.
"County of Dallas Tops Census List," September 21, 1920.
"Population of Precincts and Towns in County," September 24, 1920.

"Expect to Complete City Directory in Ten Days," November 10, 1920.
"5,379 Farms in Dallas County," September 10, 1921.
"Texas a Tenant State," November 2, 1921.
"Farm Tenantry in Texas Increasing," March 5, 1922.
"Auto Stealing is now an industry," April 9, 1922.
"Motorists' Own Carelessness Cause of Many Robberies," April 30, 1922.
"Eugene O'Brien is Star in Film at Jefferson," June 11, 1922.
"Eugene O'Brien Is Star of Film at the Jefferson," January 15, 1924.
"Ever Had Your Automobile Stolen?" January 11, 1925.
"Automobiles Make New Problems for Police Departments to Solve," March 8, 1925.
"Talking Movies Have Reached Practical Stage and Will Be on Exhibition Here This Week," February 14, 1926.
"Two Face Charges of Robbing Houston Bank," March 19, 1926.
"Gets 15-year Sentence for Robbery of Bank," June 7, 1926.
"35 Convicts Escape from Prison Farm," June 23, 1927.
"Ed Crowder Is Taken," June 25, 1927.
"Seventieth of Cars Licensed with Third of Legal Time Gone," December 9, 1928.
"Break Out of 'Solitary' Two Still in Prison," May 8, 1929.
"Convict Flees Solitary Cell," May 7, 1929.
"Texas Led Road Building in 1928," September 16, 1929.
"New Questions Come to Fore on Prison Tour," January 27, 1930.
"Jail Breaker to Lose His Concurrent Terms," March 13, 1930.
"Three Waco Fugitives Are Captured in Ohio," March 19, 1930.
"Three Who Escaped Jail at Waco are Returned," March 23, 1930.
"Two Deny Part in Slaying of Gouge," March 26, 1930.
"Cities' Growth Main Interest Census Gives," April 6, 1930.
"Eight Convicts Tear Up Floor and Flee Farm," April 10, 1930.
"Population in Greater Dallas Up to 308,000," May 7, 1930.
"Road Building Progress for State Notable," May 17, 1930.
"Prison Lands Flooded," June 1, 1930.
"Census Shows Roads' Traffic in Texas Heavy," September 4, 1930.
"Citizens Slow Securing Seals," January 4, 1931.
"Decline Shown in Employment in Texas," March 8, 1931.
"Convict Killed in Knife Battle on State Farm," October 31, 1931.
"Blowing Soap Bubbles Is Aid in Trying for Rosebud Mouth," November 7, 1931.
"No Idle Hands Seen in State's Prison System," November 12, 1931.
"Scalley Is No-Billed," November 21, 1931.
"Back-to-Farm Move Advised for Negroes," February 16, 1932.
"Victim in Holdup Killed by Bandits," May 1, 1932.

"Police Hold Two For Questioning in Bucher Death," May 2, 1932.
"Affray at Rural Dance Kills One, Another Wounded," August 7, 1932.
"Three Suspects, Wharton Police Stage Gun Fight," August 16, 1932.
"Clerk in Grocery, Protesting Holdup, Is Slain by Bandit," October 12, 1932.
"Identity of Hijacker Who Shot Sherman Man Believed to Be Known," October 13, 1932.
"Women Relatives of Outlaws Grilled as Slayers of Deputy Sheriff Escape," January 8, 1933.
"Crime Trail of Youthful Band Reaches Across All Southwest," January 8, 1933.
"Throng of Friends Attend Funeral of Deputy Slain Here," January 9, 1933.
"Revive Temple Murder Inquiry," January 9, 1933.
"Third Woman Arrested as Outlaw Accomplice in Search for Killers," January 9, 1933.
"Tip-offs Many in Killer Hunt," January 10, 1933.
"Tough Two-Gun Girl with Desperadoes Who Killed Davis," January 13, 1933.
"2nd Week's Chase Pursuing Slayers with Few Results," January 15, 1933.
"Killer Suspect Gives Up with Iron-Clad Alibi," January 19, 1933.
"Pretty Boy Is New Suspect in Killing; Jesse James Next?" January 20, 1933.
"Bad Boy Hamilton Sure of His Neck in Trials in Dallas," January 22, 1933.
"Sheriff Dies in Gun Fight With Bandits," January 24, 1933.
"Convicted of Two Hijackings, Hamilton Assessed 55 Years," January 26, 1933.
"Slayers at Rhome Kill Third Officer Inside of Month," January 28, 1933.
"Registered Mail Pouches Stolen in Fort Worth Holdup," February 22, 1933.
"Mail Holdup Loss Remains Mystery to Outside World," February 23, 1933.
"Postal Inspectors Follow Clues That Get Them Nowhere," February 24, 1933.
"Postal Bandits Thought Hiding Near Fort Worth," February 25, 1933.
"Jury Fails to Agree on Hamilton Verdict," March 18, 1933.
"Automobile Driver License Is Favored," March 18, 1933.
"Raymond Hamilton Jury Still Unable to Agree," March 19, 1933.
"Hamilton Jury Fails to Agree; Discharged," March 21, 1933.
"Five Get Pardons and One Paroled," March 24, 1933.
"Mother Hugs Belief Her Boys Not Killers as Older Sons Hunted," April 15, 1933.
"Former Owner of Killers' Car Says Sold It to Buck Barrow Week After Received Pardon," April 16, 1933.
"Searchers for Barrow Brothers Meet with Keen Disappointment," April 18, 1933.
"Notorious Pair Reported Seen in Local Haunts," April 29, 1933.

"Hillsboro Witness Kidnapped and Tied with Barbed Wire," May 31, 1933.
"Raymond Hamilton Convicted," June 3, 1933.
"Waco Man Charged with Temple Murder in 1932," June 11, 1933.
"Barrow Boys Take Two Officers Captive After Car Crashes," June 12, 1933.
"Alleged Slayers of Missing Men Held as Robbers," July 11, 1933.
"Cache of Drugs Found in Search for Missing Men," July 12, 1933.
"Wire-Bound Bodies of Missing Trio Found," July 13, 1933.
"Stains on Murder Car Human Blood, Chemist Declares," July 15, 1933.
"Triple Murder Case Comes Up Tomorrow," July 19, 1933.
"Barrow Brothers Both Set Free by Texas Executives," July 23, 1933.
"Buck Barrow Dying After Battle but Clyde and Companions Flee," July 25, 1933.
"He's My Boy, Sobs Barrow's Mother; I Want to See Him," July 25, 1933.
"Wounded Barrow Admits Shooting Arkansas Officer," July 26, 1933.
"Mother at Bedside as Buck Barrow's Death Seems Near," July 27, 1933.
"Buck Barrow Dies of Bullet Wounds in Iowa Hospital," July 30, 1933.
"Buck Barrow Burial to Be Held Monday," July 31, 1933.
"Quiet Funeral Marks Finish to Barrow's Career of Crime," August 1, 1933.
"Barrow's Bond Set at $1,500," August 30, 1933.
"Barrow Reported with Companions Coming to Dallas," September 4, 1933.
"First Triple Murder Case to Open Monday," October 16, 1933.
"Clyde Barrow and His Wife, Wounded, Evade Trap, Flee in Hail of Bullets and Hold Up and Injure Two Autoists," November 23, 1933.
"Shaking with Fear, Prisoner Tells of More Barrow Killings," November 26, 1933.
"Barrow Again on Move, Say Three Reports," November 27, 1933.
"Barrow's Career of Past Is Told, Not Whereabouts," November 28, 1933.
"O. D. Stevens Admits Guilt in Narcotics Case," December 13, 1933.
"Prisoners Maim Selves to Get Away from Farm," December 17, 1933.
"Barrow's Companion Indicted in Slaying," December 19, 1933.
"Police Get Thrill Chasing Barrow Back into Texas," December 21, 1933.
"Effort to Free Leader of Gang Is Frustrated," January 14, 1934.
"Clyde Barrow, in Desperate Raid, Frees 5 from Prison Farm," January 17, 1934.
"Bonnie There, Also; Desperado's Light of Love Keeps Horn Blowing During Fusillade," January 17, 1934.
"Prison Officials, Warned of Hamilton's Escape Plot, Ridiculed It, Dallas Men Say," January 18, 1934.
"The Eastham Raid," January 18, 1934 (editorial).
"Barrow's Bandit Gang Accused in Hugo Hijacking," January 19, 1934.
"Simmons Fires Three Guards at Eastham Prison," January 22, 1934.
"State Will Offer $1,000 for Barrow," February 10, 1934.

"First of Triple Murder Suspects Is Given Death," February 25, 1934.
"Bank Bandits, Thought to Be Barrow and Hamilton, Get $4,138 and Escape," February 28, 1934.
"Deputies to Quiz Arrested Pair on Lancaster Holdup," March, 1, 1934.
"Not Guilty Pleas Offered in T&P Mail Robbery," March 4, 1934.
"Freed by Barrow, Recaptured Lifer Again Breaks Jail," March 24, 1934.
"Fort Worth Mail Robbery Case Set for Trial Monday," March 25, 1934.
"Stevens Denies He Participated in Mail Robbery," April 1, 1934.
"Robber Locks Seven in Vault, Gets $1,865 Then Kidnaps Woman," April 1, 1934.
"Witness Tells of Seeing State Highway Police Killed in Cold Blood," April 2, 1934.
"Shoot First, Cops Told in Killer Hunt," April 2, 1934.
"Highway Patrol Is Mobilized in Hunt for Barrow," April 4, 1934.
"Convict Killed for Vengeance; Rat, Says Note," April 4, 1934.
"Highways Combed; Radio Stations Repeatedly Broadcast Number of Clyde's Car," April 7, 1934.
"Mail Robber Trio Gets 27 Years Each Plus Heavy Fines," April 8, 1934.
" 'Never Killed,' Says Hamilton to Governor," April 9, 1934.
"Hamilton Parts Ways with Barrow, He Writes Lawyer, Remitting $100," April 9, 1934.
"Mail Robber, Escape Foiled, Now in Chains," April 27, 1934.
"Ray Hamilton's Girl Brought to Dallas; Does Not See Him," April 27, 1934.
"Through with Hamilton, Mary O'Dare Says," April 27, 1934.
"They Can't Win," April 29, 1934.
"Floyd Hamilton to Get Hearing in Court Today," May 16, 1934.
"Mary O'Dare Gets Privilege of Talk with Bank Bandit," May 18, 1934.
"Floyd Hamilton Held with Bonnie's Sister for Patrol Murders," May 22, 1934.
"Bonnie Parker's Sister Unworried at Murder Charge," May 23, 1934.
"Clyde Barrow and Bonnie Parker Trapped and Killed," May 24, 1934.
"Twelve Murders in Two Years Is Clyde Barrow's Bloody Record, and More than Hundred Thefts," May 24, 1934.
"Little Louisiana Town Is Thronged by Curious Crowd," May 24, 1934.
"Glad She Died like She Did, Roy Thornton, Bonnie's Spouse, Says," May 24, 1934.
"Funerals to Inscribe Finis on Bloody Saga of Outlaws," May 24, 1934.
"Wages of Sin," May 24, 1934 (editorial).
"Burial Plans for Bandits Are Unknown," May 25, 1934.
"Bonnie Parker's Sister Presents Alibi Testimony," May 25, 1934.
"Court May Refuse Billie Mace Bail to Go to Funeral," May 26, 1934.
"Bandit buried with only 100 at last rites," May 26, 1934.

"Hearing Recessed and Billie Mace Taken to Funeral," May 27, 1934.
"Missing Methvin, Billie Mace Seeks Another Witness," May 29, 1934.
"Sheriff Believes Barrow, Parker Killed Patrolmen," May 29, 1934.
"Expert is making Ballistics Test," May 29, 1934.
"Ballistics Tests May Win Freedom for Billie Mace," May 31, 1934.
"Mrs. Mace Freed When Expert Puts Blame on Barrow," June 1, 1934.
"Billie Parker Mace Plans to Go on Stage," June 7, 1934.
"Guard to Go on Trial," August 13, 1934.
"Floyd Hamilton Is Indicted in Prison Break at Eastham," August 18, 1934.
"Clyde Barrow Shelterers to Be Prosecuted," January 13, 1935.
"Eighteen Arrested for Aiding Clyde, Bonnie," January 29, 1935.
"Barrow-Parker Gang Workings to Be Revealed," January 30, 1935.
"Floyd Hamilton Caught; Ray's Car Found," February 6, 1935.
"Barrow's Guilt to Be Aired in Federal Court," February 17, 1935.
"Barrow Gang Fight Case on Technicality," February 22, 1935.
"Will Plead Mothers' Love as Defense in Harboring Murderers," February 22, 1935.
"Convict Tells How He Aided Hamilton Flee from Prison," February 23, 1935.
"Murder of Hamilton Planned by Former Pal, Clyde Barrow," February 24, 1935.
"Bandit Case Expected to Go to Jury Monday," February 25, 1935.
"Fate of Group in Harboring Case to Jury," February 26, 1935.
"Barrow Aiders Given 1 Hour to Two Years," February 27, 1935.
"Mothers Finish Terms in Conspiracy Cases," March 28, 1935.
"Hamilton, Cornered in Fort Worth Railroad Yards, Surrenders Meekly When Guns Trained on His Head," April 6, 1935.
"Morbidly Curious Attend Burial of Raymond Hamilton," May 12, 1935.
"Everyman's Idea of Texas Sheriff, That Was Schmid," July 1, 1963.
"Barrow Sidekick Notes Then, Now," April 13, 1968.
"B&C Driver (Real One) Files Suit," April 25, 1968.
"Hamer Kin Sue 'B&C' Film Firm," October 8, 1968.
"Barrow Kin Sue Makers of Movie," November 5, 1969.
"Barrow Kin Lose Suit in Tyler Court," May 29, 1971.
"Confusion robs tales of pair's whereabouts," Aug. 24, 1988.

Dallas Times-Herald

"Here Is Story of Bonnie and Clyde, Penned by Gungirl Before She Died, Asking for Burial—Side by Side," May 24, 1934.

Des Moines Tribune

"3 of Barrow Gang Escape Posse; Reported Fleeing in Kossuth County," July 24, 1933.
"Marvin Barrow, Captured Outlaw, Not Expected to Live," July 24, 1933.

Fort Worth Star-Telegram

"Bandits Slay Two Officers Near Grapevine," April 2, 1934.
"Bandit Couple Pierced by 50 Bullets," May 24, 1934.
"On the Trail of Bonnie and Clyde," June 25, 2000.

Joplin Globe

"Desperadoes Kill Two Officers Here," April 14, 1933.
"Desperadoes Sought in Killings of Two Peace Officers," April 15, 1933.

Kansas City Star

"The Cabin Fortress," July 20, 1933.
"Dr. Coffey, Known for Shootout with Bonnie and Clyde, Dies," May 23, 1979.
"Outlaws' Violent History Included Area Chapter," December 1, 1999.
"Firsthand Tales about Bonnie and Clyde," July 25, 2007.

McAllen Monitor

"Texas Crime and Violence Rife in the 1930s," September 14, 1986.

New York Herald

"Young Girls Are Using Much Paint," December 3, 1920.

Platte Press Dispatch

"Machine Gun-Blazing Fight with Bonnie, Clyde in Platte's Past," July 13, 1994.

Platte Shopper-News

"Red Crown Recalls Legend of Barrow Gang," February 11, 1987.

Waco Times-Herald

"Trio Leaves Trail of Stolen Cars," March 12, 1930.
"Baby Thugs Captured," March 18, 1930.

Wellington Leader

"Kidnappers of Local Officers Still at Large," June 15, 1933.
"Believe Woman with Barrows, Hurt in Wreck Here, Given Treatment," June 29, 1933.

Magazines, Periodicals, and Privately Published Material

Albert, Marvin H. "Killer in Skirts." *Argosy,* March 1956.
Bond, Jack. "Raymond Hamilton's Daring Death Cell Escape." *Startling Detective Adventures*, October 1934.
Cartwright, Gary. "The Whole Shootin' Match." *Texas Monthly*, February 2001.
Cartwright, Gladys Pritchard. "Bonnie and Clyde." *Collingsworth County History*, 1984.
Crumbaker, Marge. "Bonnie, Clyde and 2 Who Remember Them." *Texas Tempo,* November 1968.
Feller, Doris. *The Beginning of the End for Bonnie and Clyde—Dexfield Park, Dexter, Iowa, July 20–24, 1933.* Dexter Historical Society, 2007.
Johns, Joe. "Kidnapped by Bandits." *True West*, September 1981.
Jones, Sandy, and Bob Fischer. "It's Death to Bonnie and Clyde." Several publications courtesy of Outlaw Archives Press.
Jones, W. D. "Riding with Bonnie and Clyde." *Playboy*, November 1968.
Jones, W. D., as told to Clarke Newlon. "I Saw Clyde Barrow Kill Five Men." *Startling Detective Adventures*, May 1934.
Knight, James R. "Incident at Alma: The Barrow Gang in Northwest Arkansas." *Arkansas Historical Quarterly* 56, no. 4 (Winter 1997).
"The Line-up." *True Detective Mysteries*, May 1933 and September 1933.
Lucko, Paul M. "Counteracting Reform: Lee Simmons and the Texas Prison System, 1930–1935." *East Texas Historical Journal* 30 no. 2 (1992).
Mattix, Rick. *The "Bloody Barrows" Come to Iowa.* Privately published.
Mullen, James. "I Framed Ray Hamilton's Prison Break: Confessions of an Ex-Convict." *Startling Detective Adventures*, November 1934.
Newlon, Clarke. "Clyde Barrow on the Spot." *Startling Detective Adventures*, July 1934.
Portley, Ed, Joplin Chief of Detectives, as told to C. F. Waers. "The Inside Story of Bonnie Parker and the Bloody Barrows." *True Detective Mysteries*, June, July, August, September, and October 1934.
Pritchard, Jack. "Eyewitness Account of Bonnie & Clyde Escapade." Collingsworth County Museum Archives, 1980.
Roth, Mitchel. "Bonnie and Clyde: The End of the Texas Outlaw Tradition." *East Texas Historical Journal* 2 (1997).
Science of Automotive Engineering. The Franklin Institute, 1936.

Simmons, Lee. "Barrow-Parker Death Ambush." *American Detective*, August 1934.

Texas Bankers Record. April 1934.

Veit, Richard J. "The Waco Jailbreak of Bonnie and Clyde." *Waco Heritage and History*, December 1990.

Whitecotton, Thomas. *To Serve and Protect: A Collection of Memories.* Missouri State Highway Patrol Archives, 2006.

Williams, Francis. "The Day Bonnie and Clyde Shot It Out with the Law in Ferrelview." *Discover North*, March 1974.

Young, Robert. "The Guns of Frank Hamer." *Quarterly of the National Association for Outlaw and Lawman History*, Summer 1982.

Government Publications and Records

Barrow phone tap transcripts, Dallas Municipal Archives.

Bienville Parish Coroner's Inquest, May 23, 1934—Coroner, Dr. J. L. Wade.

Division of Investigation/United States Department of Justice Document 62–619, memorandum dated July 23, 1934, regarding possible April 1934 meeting of Arthur "Pretty Boy" Floyd and the Barrow Gang.

General Survey of Housing Conditions, City of Dallas, August 1938.

General Survey of Housing Conditions, Dallas Municipal Archives.

Historical Statistics of the United States, Colonial Times to 1970, U.S. Department of Commerce.

Inside West Dallas: A Report by the Council of Social Agencies of Dallas, Dallas Municipal Archives.

Jones, W. D., confession transcript, November 18, 1933, Dallas Municipal Archives.

Joplin Museum Complex application to the National Register of Historic Places, September 20, 2007.

Population totals, Dallas Municipal Archives.

Portley, Ed, Chief of Detectives, July 18, 1933, letter, Joplin Archives.

Statement of Historic Context for Route 66 Through Texas, Texas Historical Commission, February 2003 (principal authors Monica Penick and Gregory Smith).

Texas Department of Criminal Justice Prison records.

Texas Department of Transportation records (originally Texas Highway Department), 1917–1930.

Texas Prison System Annual Report, 1928.

Uniform Crime Reports for the United States and Its Possessions, Fourth Quarterly Bulletin, Division of Investigation, United States Department of Justice.

United States Bureau of the Census records.

United States Department of Justice/Federal Bureau of Investigation Document I.C. #26-31672, December 14, 1954 (revised October 1983), *Clyde Champion Barrow–Bonnie Parker*.

Willis, Sheriff J. C., August 30, 1932, letter, Dallas Municipal Archives.

Recording

The Truth About Bonnie and Clyde as Told by Billie Jean Parker, Bonnie's Sister, RCA LPM-3967, 1968. Produced by Felton Jarvis. Billie Jean Parker interviewed by Jud Collins.

Web Sites

http://www.bigtex.com/aboutus/history, the official Web site of the State Fair of Texas.

http://www.dallashistory.org/history/dallas/dallashistory.htm

http://www.fbi.gov/libref/historic/history/text.htm

http://www.kettering.edu/visitors/about/charles_kettering.jsp

http://modelt.org

Acknowledgments

I could not have written *Go Down Together* without the input of Andrea Ahles Koos, my longtime research assistant–sounding board who always says exactly what she thinks whether I want to hear it or not. Marcia Melton is a dogged researcher who can find practically any article or legal document, no matter how obscure or supposedly unavailable it may be. It was a pleasure to work with Roger Labrie; his thorough editing reflected constant respect for the subject matter, and I learned a lot in the process. It's a privilege to be edited by him, and to be published by Simon & Schuster. I'm fortunate that Jim Donovan, now a best-selling historian in his own right, remains willing to serve as my literary agent.

Mike Blackman, Christopher Radko, Carlton Stowers, Cissy Stewart Lale, Archie McDonald, Sandy Jones, and Doug Perry all read along as I wrote. Their constructive criticisms continually helped shape the book.

Several author-historians were generous with their time and Barrow Gang knowledge. They include John Neal Phillips, Rick Mattix, Bill Sloan, Ben Procter, and Sandy Jones. Terry Whitehead's videotaped interviews with members of the Methvin family and Commerce shootout witness Lee Phelps provided invaluable information. Jonathan Davis shared key material, and was always willing to have one more meeting to answer my questions.

Buddy Barrow Williams and Rhea Leen Linder are credits to their Uncle Clyde and Aunt Bonnie, respectively.

Thanks to everyone who granted me interviews: Virginia Becker, Robert Brunson, Harold Caldwell, Wayne Carter, Jonathan Davis, Lu Durham, Doris Feller, Harold Feller, Marvelle Feller, John Paul Field, Harrison Hamer,

Orville Hancock, Charles Heard, Boots Hinton, Ken Holmes, Olen Walter Jackson, Ted Johnson, Sandy Jones, Cissy Stewart Lale, Rhea Leen Linder, Rick Mattix, Archie McDonald, Bill Palmer, John Neal Phillips, Ben Procter, Mitchel Roth, Bill Sloan, Doris Stallings, Janice Thomas, Robert Pitts Thomas, Terry Whitehead, James Willett, Buddy Barrow Williams, Jim Wright, and Pat Ziegler.

I'm certain that for the past two years Charles Caple, Mary and Charles Rogers, Robert Fernandez and Larry Wilson, Felix Higgins, Melinda Mason, Zeke Wahl, Diana Andro, Broc Sears, Zonk Lanzillo, Rich Billings, Wilson McMillion, Phyllis Stone, and Scott Nishimura have all heard much more than they wanted to about Clyde Barrow and Bonnie Parker.

And special thanks are due to Victoria Meyer, Kelly Walsh, and all the other talented people working in the Simon & Schuster publicity department.

Everything I write is always for Nora, Adam, and Grant.

Index

Photography Credits

Courtesy of Sandy Jones. Photo owned by the National Museum of Crime and Punishment: 1, 5

Courtesy of Buddy Barrow Williams: 2, 19, 27

From the collections of the Texas/Dallas History and Archives Division, Dallas Public Library: 3, 6, 8, 9, 10, 26, 29

Courtesy of Jonathan Davis: 4

From the Collection of David Gainsborough Roberts: 7

Huntsville Arts Commission, archived photograph from walkercountytreasures .com*: 11

Texas Prison Museum, Texas Department of Criminal Justice: 12

Courtesy of the *Joplin Globe* and Joplin Museum Complex: 13

Courtesy of the Library of Congress: 14

CORBIS: 15

Dallas Municipal Archives, City Secretary's Office, City of Dallas (Collection 91–019, Dallas Police Department Historic Case Files): 16, 17

Copyright 2009, The Des Moines Register and Tribune Company. Reprinted with permission: 18

Courtesy of Bill Sloan: 20, 24

Courtesy of the Texas Ranger Hall of Fame and Museum, Waco, TX: 21, 23, 25

Courtesy of Rick Mattix: 22, 28

* Reproduced with permission of the City of Huntsville, Texas, this photo is from a digitization project done in consultation with John Stokes under a TexTreasures grant from the Texas State Library and Archives Commission. Project partners are the Walker County Genealogical Society, the Walker County Historical Commission, Sam Houston State University, and Sam Houston Memorial Museum.

About the Author

Jeff Guinn is the best-selling author of numerous books of fiction and nonfiction. An award-winning investigative journalist and former books editor, he is a frequent guest on national radio and television programs. Guinn lives in Fort Worth, Texas.

1

Bonnie Parker and Clyde Barrow in spring 1933. This photo was taken from unprocessed film discovered by police following an April 13 gun battle in Joplin, Missouri. The Barrow Gang had yet to learn that exposed car license plates like the one in this picture made it easier for their pursuers to track them.

2

In a rare formal family photograph taken sometime in 1911, Cumie Barrow poses with four of her children. From the left they are Buck, Artie, Nell, and one-year-old Clyde on his mother's lap. Cumie was a stern Christian fundamentalist who never spared the rod where her children were concerned. All the Barrow offspring but open-mouthed baby Clyde seem to have already adopted their mother's habitual tight-lipped expression.

3

The slums of West Dallas. When the Barrow family arrived there from farm country in 1922, they were too poor even to live in a hovel similar to these. For several years, they slept under their wagon in a nearby campground.

4

A period postcard features downtown Dallas seen from the west, the same view available to the Barrows after they relocated to the West Dallas slum. As a teenager, Clyde would stand in the campgrounds and stare across the Trinity River at the towering skyscrapers and other elegant buildings.

5

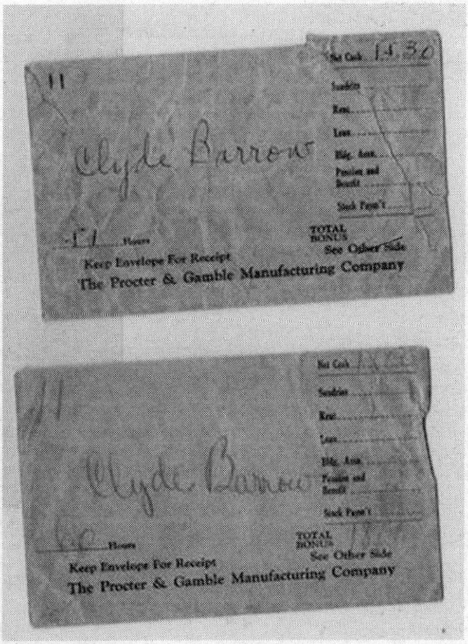

Clyde initially tried to earn an honest living after quitting high school in 1926. His first job paid one dollar a day, so he moved on to Procter & Gamble for the princely salary of thirty cents an hour. It wasn't enough to bankroll the glamorous lifestyle Clyde wanted, so he turned to crime.

6

Other teenage girls from the Dallas slums settled for snapshots taken at Fair Park booths, but that wasn't good enough for Bonnie Parker. Around 1925 when she was about fifteen, Bonnie scraped together enough money to pay for this studio glamour portrait.

7

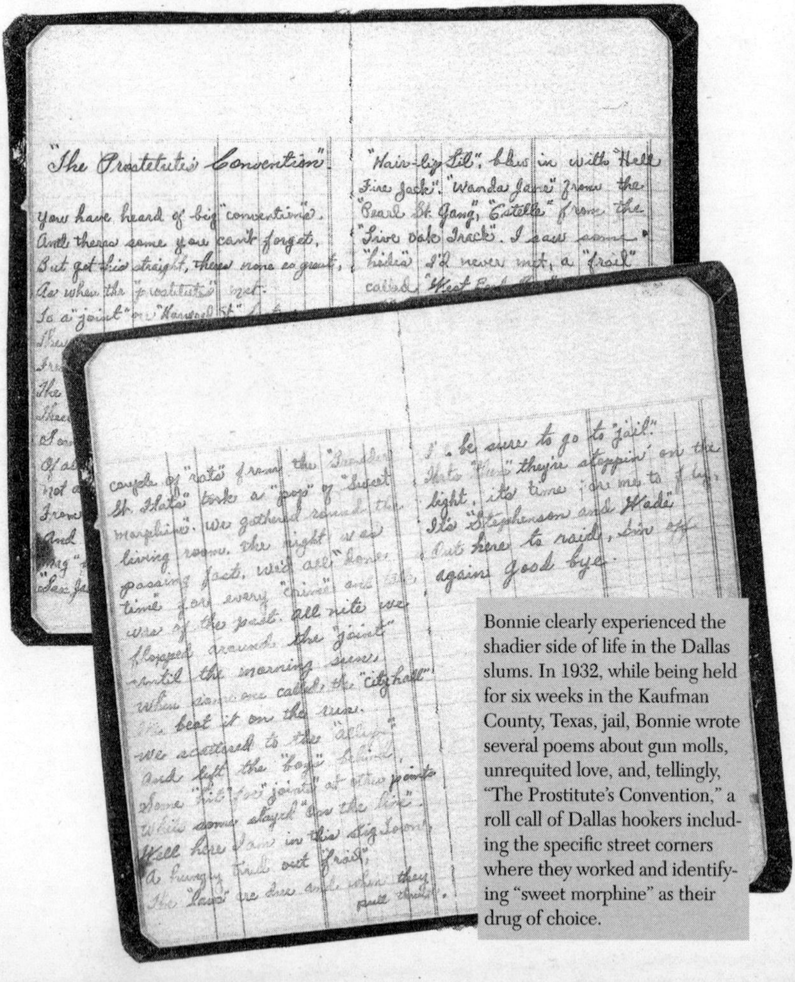

"The Prostitute's Convention"

You have heard of big "conventions".
And there's some you can't forget,
But get this straight, there's none so great,
As when the "prostitutes" met.

"Hair-lip Lil", blew in with "Hell Fire Jack", "Wanda Jane" from the "Pearl St. Gang", "Estelle" from the "Live Oak Track". I saw some "hides" I'd never met, a "frail" called [illegible]

[illegible] took a "pop" of "Sweet morphine". We gathered round the living room. the night was passing fast. we'd all "done time" for every "crime" [illegible] of the past. all nite we flopped around the "joint" until the morning sun, when someone called, the "city hall" [illegible] beat it on the run.
We scattered to the "alley"
And left the "boys" behind,
[illegible]
While some stayed "on the line".
[illegible]

[illegible] be sure to go to "jail". [illegible] they're steppin' on the light, its time for me to fly. Its "Stephenson and Wade" out here to raid, [illegible] again good bye.

Bonnie clearly experienced the shadier side of life in the Dallas slums. In 1932, while being held for six weeks in the Kaufman County, Texas, jail, Bonnie wrote several poems about gun molls, unrequited love, and, tellingly, "The Prostitute's Convention," a roll call of Dallas hookers including the specific street corners where they worked and identifying "sweet morphine" as their drug of choice.

Bonnie married West Dallas thug Roy Thornton in September 1926, just before her sixteenth birthday. This picture of the newlyweds was taken sometime before Roy deserted her for good three years later.

9 Henry, Clyde's father, eventually built a flimsy shack for the Barrows on the West Dallas campgrounds. Later, it was moved a few blocks by wagon to Eagle Ford Road, where Henry turned the structure into this Star Service Station. He also brewed and sold illegal bootleg whiskey there.

10

Mug shots taken by the Dallas police of sixteen-year-old Clyde Barrow after his arrest in December 1926 for car theft. Charges were never filed, but over the next few years Clyde and the Dallas cops had many more opportunities to renew their acquaintance.

11

Mounted "long riders" with rifles herd inmates to the fields at Eastham Prison Farm in central Texas. Prisoners were often required to run rather than walk, and the work picking cotton or tending other crops was brutal. Sentenced to seven consecutive two-year terms in 1930, scrawny Clyde Barrow cut off two of his own toes to avoid the field labor he felt certain would kill him before his fourteen years at the farm were completed.

12

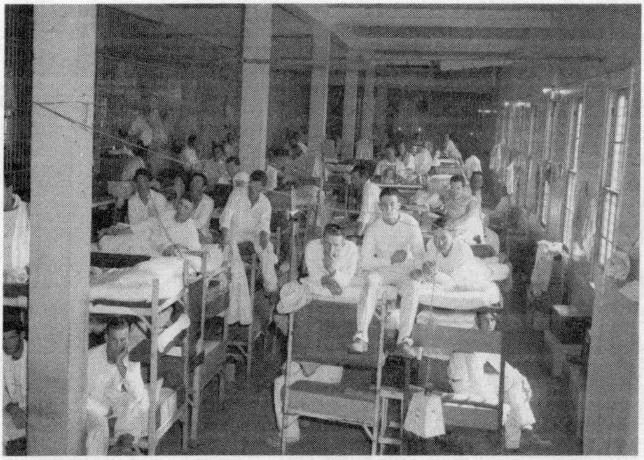

Inmates slept on two- or three-tiered bunk beds in the prison dormitories. There was little room and absolutely no privacy. Whenever there were disturbances, guards would fire rounds into the ceiling, then aim progressively lower until order was restored. Shower areas were behind the rows of bunks—this was where Clyde murdered Ed Crowder in 1931 after the hulking fellow prisoner had been raping him for months.

13

JOPLIN GLOBE, SATURDAY, APRIL 15, 1933.

House Where Bandits Killed Two Officers and Open Country Which Afforded Escape

This scene, photographed by a Joplin Globe staff photographer, shows the house and premises on Thirty-fourth and Oak Ridge Drive, where two Texas bandits opened fire on a squad of officers late Thursday, instantly killing a Newton county constable and fatally wounding a Joplin detective.

The house is located on the north side of the street and faces south. The bandits and two women occupied the upper floor, the first floor being a garage. Thirty-fourth street runs east and west, and the picture shows the open country extending more than a block east to Main street, and also to the south and southeast of the house. Location of the house, affording this open space, apparently was selected by the bandits because it afforded a wide view of persons approaching and also provided open county, with a good roadway, for a hurried get-away.

The officers approached from the east. A car containing State Highway Patrolmen G. B. Kahler and W. E. Grammer stopped at the west corner of the house and the car with Constable G. W. Harryman, City Detective Tom DeGraff and Motor Car Detective Harry McGinnis stopped in the driveway a few feet from a door of the double-door garage.

When Harryman and McGinnis got out of their car, one of the bandits was standing in a door of the garage. He immediately opened fire, slaying Harryman and mortally wounding McGinnis. Harryman fell dead inside the garage door. McGinnis fell at the side of the driveway.

One of the desperadoes released the brakes of the police car, and with their own car pushed it off the road. With the two women with whom they had occupied the house, the bandits then fled in their car east to Main street and south on that highway. It was believed at first that one of the bandits was shot before he entered his car, but that fact has not been established.

Doors of the garage and trees in the vicinity were sprayed with bullets. Bullet holes are shown in the panes of glass and in the garage door on the left.

Shortly after Clyde was paroled from Eastham Prison Farm in early 1932, he and Bonnie embarked on a life of crime. They proved to be bumbling rather than masterful criminals—Bonnie even spent several months locked in a small-town Texas jail—but Depression-era newspapers, desperate to attract readers, exaggerated their exploits. In 1933, Clyde, Bonnie, and their companions made headlines when they had to shoot their way past police while fleeing a rented apartment in Joplin, Missouri.

14

When the gang fled Joplin, they left behind most of their belongings, including a roll of undeveloped film. When the police processed it, many of the photos showed Clyde and Bonnie in gag poses, including some where they playfully brandished guns at each other.

15

When this photo of Bonnie Parker appeared in newspapers and magazines around the country, the Barrow Gang immediately became a national sensation. The cigar dangling from Bonnie's mouth caused even more frenzied comment than the pistol in her hand. In 1933, decent American women discreetly puffed cigarettes and never inhaled. After the photo appeared, Bonnie tried in vain to convince the public that she didn't smoke cigars.

16

Clyde, on the left, poses with his hero-worshipping henchman W. D. Jones, who was only sixteen when he joined the Barrow Gang just before Christmas 1932. W.D. eventually became disenchanted with the criminal lifestyle and left the gang, but not before having several fingertips blasted off during a gunfight in Arkansas.

Cumie Barrow rejoiced when her son Buck married Blanche Caldwell, a preacher's daughter. This photo was taken in 1931. Blanche begged Buck not to join his younger brother's gang, predicting it would end badly for him and for her. Blanche was right on both counts.

17

18

On July 24, 1933, a posse of lawmen and civilians surrounded the Barrow Gang in Dexfield Park, Iowa. Clyde, Bonnie, and W. D. Jones escaped. Buck, gravely wounded a few days earlier in a spectacular gun battle in Platte City, Missouri, and Blanche, nearly blinded by glass splinters in the same gunfight, were captured. Blanche, on the left, screamed as a photographer from the Des Moines newspaper snapped her photo. Hardly able to see, she thought he wielded a gun rather than a camera. On the lower right, a man in overalls bends over Buck's fallen body. Buck died five days later.

19

After Buck's death, Clyde and Bonnie made even more visits to Texas to meet with their families. Standing from left to right are Bonnie's sister Billie Jean, Clyde, Cumie, and Clyde's younger brother, L.C. Kneeling are Clyde's sister Marie, Bonnie's mother Emma, and Bonnie. Note the coat obscuring the car license plate—Clyde had learned a lesson from the film left behind in Joplin.

20

While the public believed the Barrow Gang spent its spare time in luxurious hotel hideouts, Clyde and Bonnie actually spent most nights in primitive backcountry camps, sleeping in their car, bathing in streams, and frequently eating their meals out of cans. They often spread a blanket on the ground and laid out their arsenal of guns for cleaning. Clyde didn't mind roughing it, but Bonnie was afraid of bugs, snakes, and thunderstorms.

21

Clyde, Henry Methvin, and Raymond Hamilton sometime between January 16, 1934, when Clyde helped break Henry and Raymond out of Eastham Prison Farm, and March 6, when Raymond left the Barrow Gang. Clyde always insisted that, in public or posing for pictures, his subordinates dress in suits—the Barrow Gang had an image to uphold.

22

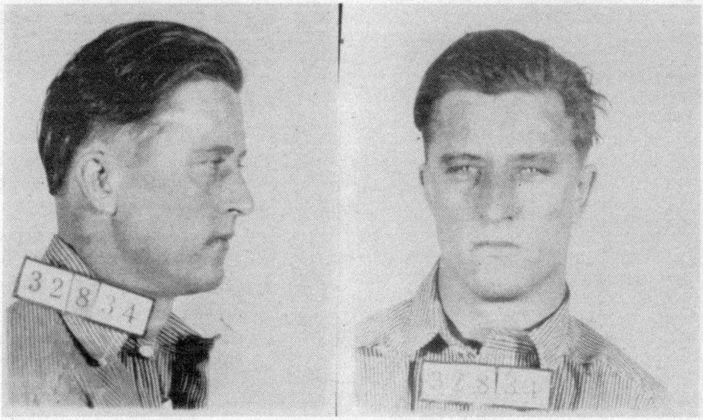

Henry Methvin was a bad-tempered small-time hood from Louisiana who was serving a ten-year sentence for attempted murder in Texas when Clyde broke him out of Eastham Prison Farm. Though Henry pretended to be a loyal Barrow Gang member and enthusiastically participated in two separate killings of lawmen, the Methvin family was anxious to betray Clyde and Bonnie in return for a pardon for Henry from Texas authorities.

23

The six-man posse that pursued Clyde and Bonnie in northeast Louisiana was led by legendary Frank Hamer, who had left the Texas Rangers but was recruited by state officials to end the Barrow Gang's two-year reign of terror. Hamer was joined by Dallas deputies Ted Hinton and Bob Alcorn, Manny Gault of the Texas Highway Patrol, and Sheriff Henderson Jordan and his deputy, Prentiss Oakley, of Bienville Parish, Louisiana. Standing left to right are Oakley, Hinton, Alcorn, and Gault. Squatting in front are Hamer and Jordan.

24

Following the May 23, 1934, ambush outside Gibsland, Louisiana, the bullet-riddled Ford V-8 with Clyde's and Bonnie's bodies still sprawled inside was towed to the parish county seat of Arcadia. Thousands of spectators gawked along the way, and some were disappointed that in death the two seemed so small and harmless. On man said of Clyde, "He was nothing but a little bitty fart."

25

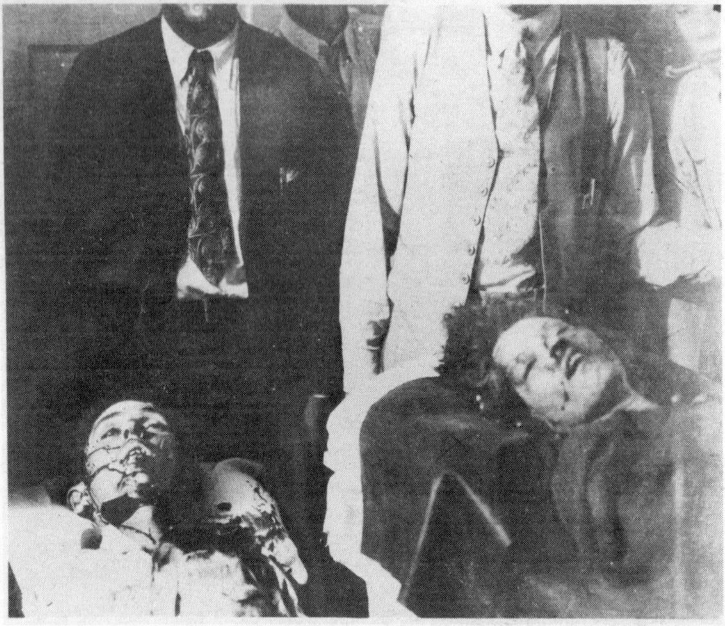

The bodies of Clyde and Bonnie were displayed on tables in the back room of Arcadia's Conger's Furniture Store, which doubled as the parish coroner's laboratory. Photographers were allowed to snap pictures before Dr. J. L. Wade conducted a cursory examination that concluded the cause of death was gunshot wounds.

26

More than ten thousand spectators shoved their way into a Dallas funeral home on May 24 when Clyde's body was made available for visitation. Emma Parker claimed twenty thousand people attended Bonnie's visitation at a different funeral home, but that was probably an exaggeration.

27

In death as in life, Clyde and Bonnie provided entertainment for Depression-weary Americans. The so-called Death Car was on display at state fairs all over America for much of the next decade.

28

Newsreels depicting the scenes of Barrow Gang crimes and garish footage from the coroner's laboratory in Arcadia were popular attractions at movie theaters. As this poster indicates, the Barrow Gang "shorts" routinely received top billing over full-length feature films.

29

Bonnie and Clyde shortly before their deaths. Bonnie could no longer stand by herself—Clyde had to hold her up. For the last year of her life, Bonnie mostly hopped rather than walked because of the terrible leg burns she'd suffered in a car wreck caused by Clyde's reckless driving outside Wellington, Texas. Despite everything, they remained inseparable until the end.